PENGUIN BOOKS

THE PENGUIN COMPANIO

C000121249

Timothy Bainbridge was born i
at Uppingham School and Gonvill
1969, PhD 1973). In 1972 he joine
ment where he was responsible for education and Home Office issues.
Since 1974 he has worked in the European Parliament in Luxembourg,
Brussels and London. His principal interests are music and art history.
Married with one son, he lives in Hennuyères (Belgium) and London.

Anthony Teasdale was born in 1957 and educated at Slough Grammar
School and Balliol and Nuffield Colleges, Oxford, where he took BA
and M.Phil degrees. He has worked for the European Parliament and the
EU Council of Ministers in Brussels, and as Special Adviser to the
Foreign and Commonwealth Office in London. A former Research
Fellow of Nuffield College, Oxford, he writes and lectures widely on
EU institutional issues.

... Cheshire in 1947 and was educated
... and Caius College, Cambridge (BA
... the Conservative Research Depart-
... worked ... Home Office ...

TIMOTHY BAINBRIDGE
with ANTHONY TEASDALE

The Penguin Companion
to European Union

PENGUIN BOOKS

PENGUIN BOOKS

Published by the Penguin Group
Penguin Books Ltd, 27 Wrights Lane, London w8 5tz, England
Penguin Books USA Inc., 375 Hudson Street, New York, New York 10014, USA
Penguin Books Australia Ltd, Ringwood, Victoria, Australia
Penguin Books Canada Ltd, 10 Alcorn Avenue, Toronto, Ontario, Canada m4v 3b2
Penguin Books (NZ) Ltd, 182–190 Wairau Road, Auckland 10, New Zealand

Penguin Books Ltd, Registered Offices: Harmondsworth, Middlesex, England

First published 1995
Reprinted with corrections 1996
10 9 8 7 6 5 4 3 2

Set in 9.5/11 pt Bembo Monophoto
Filmset by Datix International Limited, Bungay, Suffolk
Printed in England by Clays Ltd, St Ives plc

À Colombo ou à Nagasaki je lis les Baedekers
De l'Espagne et du Portugal ou de l'Autriche-Hongrie;
Et je contemple les plans de certaines villes de second rang,
Et leur description succincte, je la médite.
Les rues où j'ai habité sont marquées là,
Les hôtels où j'allais dîner, et les petits théâtres.

Ce sont des villes où ne vont jamais les touristes,
Et les choses n'y changent de place pas plus
Que les mots dans les pages d'un livre.

Valéry Larbaud, *Europe* (1913)

Contents

Preface

This book is a Companion rather than a dictionary in that it aims to present not only facts, but also arguments. This is especially true of the longer entries dealing with matters of current controversy (in respect of which it could be said that the arguments are themselves political facts). In some of these entries I have also included a few sentences of speculation: the purpose of these is primarily to point the reader in the direction of what seem to me to be interesting lines of inquiry. To this limited extent the material in this book is projected forward into an uncertain future. I hope that in those entries in which facts, arguments and speculation are combined the distinction between the three elements is sufficiently clear for there to be no confusion between them.

As its title implies, the principal focus of this book is on the institutions, policies and procedures of the European Union. However, to a greater extent than is usually the case, full account has been taken of the large number of other European institutions, many of which predate the Union and overlap with the Union's activities to a confusing extent. Some readers may feel that the book merely mirrors the confusion, but I take the confusion to be part of the picture. There would be something essentially misleading about a book that reduced the European Union to a number of neatly interlocking institutions.

The fact remains that one of the characteristic features of Europe today is the extraordinarily large number of institutions, formal and informal, national, international and supranational, set up for many different purposes at different times on a variety of legal bases, operating in different fields to varying degrees of effectiveness. This Companion deals only with the main ones, and seeks to clarify the differences as well as the relations between them without suggesting an orderliness where in fact none exists (indeed, the trend is in the opposite direction). To take a simple example, a comprehensive picture of measures being taken internationally against the drug problem in Europe today would have to take account of the Pompidou Group (the responsibility of the Council of Europe), Interpol, Europol (an aspect of the Justice and Home Affairs 'pillar' of the Maastricht Treaty, in this field the successor of the Trevi Group), the Schengen Group of countries, the European Parliament's committees of inquiry, the inclusion by the Commission of anti-drug clauses in draft agreements with certain countries, and the European Monitoring Centre for Drugs and Drug Addiction in Lisbon.

Evident in the book as a whole is a historical bias, founded upon the belief that an essential part of understanding the European Union is a knowledge of the course of postwar integration, its failures as well as its successes. The successes are fully dealt with, in the sense that all the steps in the direction of where the Union now finds itself are described. The failures – the wrong turnings along the way – are in some cases as revealing as the successes (for an example, see Fouchet Plan), but considerations of space did not allow them all to be described in detail.

Considerations of space have also made it impossible for entries on individual countries systematically to include basic information on size, population, GNP, form of government, and so on. Instead, these entries concentrate on each country's relations, current and historic, with what is now the European Union, special mention being made of high and low points in the relationship and of characteristic negotiating attitudes and policy priorities considered over time. All countries in the European Economic Area have separate entries (the Benelux countries are considered together; see also **micro-states**), as do Cyprus, Malta and Turkey. It is a matter for real regret that within the space available the countries of central and eastern Europe could be dealt with only very cursorily under such headings as Visegrad states, Baltic states and Europe Agreements.

Included amongst the entries are biographies of people who have made notable contributions to European integration. Many of them, of course, had or still have distinguished careers in national politics, but in conformity with the underlying purpose of the book it is primarily their European activities that are described here. Overall, the choice of whom to include may seem somewhat idiosyncratic, but I have given preference to people (such as Aristide Briand and Altiero Spinelli) about whom material is not readily and generally available, at least in English.

With reference to particular areas of policy touched on in this book, my aim has been not so much to give an up-to-the-minute account (almost impossible in any case) of the state of affairs, but to provide the essential historical, political and legal underpinnings of progress to date and currently in prospect. In these entries the focus is almost exclusively upon the actions of the European Union and its institutions, since however valuable the work done by other bodies may be (for example, by the Council of Europe in respect of the protection of the environment), it is the power of the Union to make binding laws that matters in the end. One reason why I have quoted so extensively from the Treaty of Rome and other Treaties (see Note to the Reader) is that few aspects of the

Union are so prone to misunderstanding, wilful or otherwise, as the scope and purpose of legislative and other action on the part of its institutions.

Of these institutions, the one described at the greatest length is the European Parliament. There are two reasons for this: it is the most complex of the institutions, and the one that has changed most over the past four decades in terms of its composition and its powers. Even its location is far from straightforward. It also happens to be the most controversial of the institutions.

Another category of entry deals with the technical expressions that constitute so important and characteristic a part of what is sometimes termed 'Eurospeak'. Many of the older expressions date back to the time when French was by far the dominant language in the Six, and, in any case, the institutions and procedures drew heavily on French politico-constitutional models. Some of them have remained French (*acquis communautaire*), some have been at least partially assimilated into English (rapporteur), and some – perhaps the most confusing – have acquired a spurious Englishness in translation in spite of few people being entirely sure of their meaning (comitology, subsidiarity). Irritating though such expressions may be, it must be said that many of them genuinely lack an English equivalent: they are perhaps best regarded as a compact and convenient mental shorthand which, once learnt, is undeniably useful.

The wider problems posed by the multiplicity of official languages in the European Union are well known. Not the least of them is that a controversial idea may become still more controversial in translation, and in unforeseen ways. For example, what is normally referred to in English as the 'hard core' of countries was *feste Kern* in the German original. The word *fest* means 'solid, firm': to translate it as 'hard' introduces associations of exclusiveness and of an unsympathetic attitude to outsiders not present in the original, and it was these associations at least as much as the idea itself that occasioned resentment. In French it was translated as *noyau dur*, the primary meaning of *noyau* being the stone of a fruit, bringing with it associations of durability and germination.

To the outsider, the European Union may be thought to move with glacier-like slowness. This observation will very quickly be found to be false by anyone who seeks to write a book about it that is not already out of date on publication. More than ever, with an enlargement just accomplished and another to the East in prospect, the integration of Europe is, in the familiar phrase, 'a journey to an unknown destination'; and the journey is proceeding with what is on any historical scale quite astonishing speed. When the pace was more leisurely, in the 1960s and 1970s, questions about the ultimate destination were not posed with any great urgency, but now the pace has quickened, the passengers are being thrown about with greater violence, and the demands for clear answers have become more pressing. Is the train still on the main line? Or is it in a long, cunningly contrived siding? Has it jumped the points somewhere, with the result that no one knows where it is going? And when might the passengers next have an opportunity to get off?

It is often remarked that the European Union is *sui generis* in the sense that it fits neatly into no established constitutional model and, moreover, shows no sign of doing so in the future. In the Union's affairs there will continue to be a three-way tension between the supranational, the intergovernmental and the bureaucratic. Some readers will be familiar with the executive toy that consists of a metal ball freely suspended over a triangular base, at each angle of which a magnet is concealed. The ball is set in motion: it wobbles at random, under the influence of each magnet in turn, and finally settles in the magnetic field of one of them. The time taken depends on the vigour with which the initial impulse is given. Something of the same fascination may be felt in observing what happens when a radical new idea is tossed into the Union's institutional system.

So much can be said with some certainty: the European Union will not move into major new areas of policy, with the probable exception of defence and security (the groundwork for which has already been partially laid in the Common Foreign and Security Policy 'pillar' of the Maastricht Treaty). In this sense the move towards a superstate governing every aspect of our lives has been halted. Underpinned by subsidiarity, there will continue to be an uneasy equilibrium between the powers of the Union's own institutions and those of national or regional authorities. Neither the Scandinavians, whose level of contentment with their own institutions is quite high, nor the East Europeans, who have only recently regained control over their own affairs, seem to me at all likely to be willing to countenance new powers for supranational institutions based in Brussels. At the same time there is a clear majority against the renationalization of areas currently covered by action under the Treaties: hence the equilibrium.

The apogee of legislative action seems to me to have been passed. In opting for enlargement, the European Union and its predecessors have moved from a small, relatively homogeneous group of countries to a very much larger, more disparate group. The next wave of enlargement (Cyprus, Malta, central and eastern Europe) will confirm this trend. Against this background, it is unrealistic to imagine that legislation can play the role it has played so far as the cement of integration. Indeed, the difficulties of drawing up legislation for so disparate a group of countries (unless it is so permeated with opt-outs, derogations and special conditions as to be meaningless) are immense. The future coherence of the Union is likely to depend not on new legislative action but on the enforcement of legislation already in place, and, as things stand at present, enforcement is largely in the hands of member states.

Not only is a Union of 15 states qualitatively different from a Community of 6, the geographical context has changed, and nowhere is this more true than in the European countries adjoining the Union's eastern frontier. The threat of armed conflict has receded with the end of the Cold War, but other less tangible threats have taken its place: rapid economic growth in the Far East, Islamic fundamentalism and poverty on the southern shore of the Mediterranean, and the political uncertainty engendered in the former Soviet Union by the painful transition to a market economy. It remains to be seen whether or not these challenges can act as a motivating force in European integration, and whether or not the Union will show itself capable of rising to them.

Amongst the few things the Union has in common with other international or supranational bodies is great difficulty in attracting public interest. The debates conducted at Union level, however fascinating to insiders, tend to impinge upon the public consciousness only if they become mixed up with national politics – and the mixture normally results in the arguments themselves becoming distorted or confused by virtue of having been articulated in a national context. One day the distinction between European politics and national politics may become clearer, but until then, the curiously hybrid nature of what currently passes for European political debate will continue to stand in the way of a clear understanding of the issues.

Although it is no part of my purpose to attack or defend the European Union in this book, a word about my own position might be useful to readers wanting to make allowances for possible bias. Professionally, I have worked in one of the Union's institutions (the European Parliament) for more than 20 years. As far as Euro-fanaticism is concerned, I can only say, as President Clinton once replied in a different context, that I 'never inhaled'. However, I regard European integration as without doubt one of the most worthwhile as well as one of the boldest experiments in the civilized conduct of human affairs ever undertaken, with many remarkable and permanent successes to its credit and with many valuable lessons to be learnt from its less frequent failures. The record deserves to be better known.

Timothy Bainbridge
June 1995

Acknowledgements

In writing this book I have made extensive and I hope accurate use of advice from many friends and colleagues in the European Parliament and elsewhere. In particular, I am grateful to Casilda Grigg for her help when the book was at the formative stage: her confident grasp of the material allied to an unfailing sense of style were invaluable. On the production side, I must express my thanks to Janet Berry, Alison Biesmans, Patricia Halligan, Elspeth Senior, Pat Walsh and Deborah Warren, all of whom devoted their time and technical skills with great good humour to what must have seemed a confusing and disjointed manuscript. At the crucial final stage the work of typing and retyping fell to Lindsay Kirkby: I am especially grateful to her for her patience and help.

Anthony Teasdale has made a special contribution to this book, by providing a number of entries on areas where he has a particular interest or expertise. These include entries on various aspects of the Council of Ministers and on certain important episodes in the European Union's history, such as the Fouchet Plan, the Stuttgart Declaration, and the Werner and Delors reports. The book as a whole has benefited greatly from his understanding of the political and economic forces which have shaped the Union.

Dr Paul Beaumont, one of the co-authors of *EC Law*, very kindly read the manuscript in its not-quite-final stage. The book owes much to his vigilance, as it does to the copy-editing of Barbara Horn.

Note to the First Reprint

The first edition of this *Companion* went to press in June 1995. A reprint has given me an opportunity to make some corrections, to bring some facts up to date, to modify some of the cross-references and to make a few additions both to the text and to the bibliography. I would be very glad to receive, via the publishers, suggestions for further improvement.

Timothy Bainbridge
December 1995

Note to the Reader

References to the Treaties

Throughout this *Companion* references are made to the Treaties on which the European Union is founded. This has been done for two reasons: first, because there is no substitute for knowing what the Treaties actually say; and second, because the relevant Treaty references allow the reader to go into various issues at greater depth with the aid of other books or documents. The great majority of references are to the 1957 Treaty of Rome establishing the European Economic Community (EEC) or to the 1992 Maastricht Treaty, formally the Treaty on European Union (TEU). Specialists will be aware that many of the references to these Treaties could be supplemented by parallel references to other Treaties, such as the 1951 Treaty of Paris establishing the European Coal and Steel Community (ECSC), but in order to prevent the text from becoming overburdened these supplementary references have mostly been omitted.

In conformity with normal academic usage, the different Treaties are referred to by their initials. In addition to the Treaties mentioned above, reference is also made to the Treaty establishing the European Atomic Energy Community (EAEC) and to the Single European Act (SEA). In the absence of any indication to the contrary, the year is the year in which the Treaty was signed, not the year of entry into force.

European Community or European Union?

Strictly speaking, the European Community (as the European Economic Community became generally known) now embraces all three communities, that is, the EEC, the ECSC, and the EAEC (see above). Since the entry into force of the Maastricht Treaty in November 1993, the European Community has become a component part of the European Union, and legally there remains a difference between the two. In certain contexts the difference is an important one, and wherever necessary the distinction is made clear in this *Companion*. However, for general purposes – and in conformity with the usage adopted by the media – 'the European Union' or 'the Union' is used to refer to what used to be known as the European Community (or earlier still as the Common Market). The only major exceptions to this rule are where reference is being made to the past (it would clearly be nonsensical, for example, to say that the United Kingdom joined the European Union in 1973), in quotations and in compound expressions such as Community law or Community preference.

The ECU

The ECU (European Currency Unit) is used in all areas of the Union's finances, including grants to member states under the structural funds, loans from the European Investment Bank, and of course the Budget itself. All sums in ECUs have been converted into their approximate sterling equivalents, the great majority of them at a rate between 75p and 80p to the ECU.

The Penguin Companion
to European Union

Abatement

Under the **Fontainebleau Agreement** the United Kingdom is refunded part of its contribution to the **Budget** of the European Union. The sum, which is calculated annually, is technically known as the abatement, but more commonly as the British Budget rebate or refund (see **British Budget problem**, **contributions and receipts**).

Accession

The act of joining the European Union is known as 'accession' and the treaties that embody the conclusions of the negotiations between applicant states and the member states of the Union are known as 'Treaties of Accession' (see **enlargement**). Such treaties include 'Acts of Accession' in which the precise conditions of accession and the adjustments to the founding **Treaties** are specified. The procedures governing accession are set out in Article O of the **Maastricht Treaty**. New member states are normally allowed periods of adjustment (known as **transitional periods**) in sectors in which too rapid an adoption of Union rules might cause difficulty; for example, Spain and Portugal had to wait seven years (until 1 January 1993) before **free movement of persons** as provided for under Article 48 of the **Treaty of Rome** came into effect.

ACP states

The ACP (African, Caribbean and Pacific) states are the countries associated with the member states of the European Union under the **Lomé Convention**. When the Convention was first signed in 1975 there were 46 ACP states, but the number has since increased to 70. Of the present total, about half are members of the Commonwealth. The total population of the ACP states is about 450 million people. ACP states may benefit from **European Investment Bank** (EIB) lending as well as from the **European Development Fund**. For further details, see **development policy**. The ACP states are:

Angola	Barbados	Botswana
Antigua and Barbuda	Belize	Burkina Faso
Bahamas	Benin	Burundi

Cameroon	Haiti	Sao Tomé and
Cape Verde	Jamaica	Principe
Central African	Kenya	Senegal
Republic	Kiribati	Seychelles
Chad	Lesotho	Sierra Leone
Comoros	Liberia	Solomon Islands
Congo	Madagascar	Somalia
Côte d'Ivoire	Malawi	Sudan
Djibouti	Mali	Surinam
Dominica	Mauritania	Swaziland
Dominican Republic	Mauritius	Tanzania
Equatorial Guinea	Mozambique	Togo
Eritrea	Namibia	Tonga
Ethiopia	Niger	Trinidad and Tobago
Fiji	Nigeria	Tuvalu
Gabon	Papua New Guinea	Uganda
Gambia	Rwanda	Western Samoa
Ghana	St Kitts and Nevis	Vanuatu
Grenada	St Lucia	Zaire
Guinea	St Vincent and the	Zambia
Guinea Bissau	Grenadines	Zimbabwe
Guyana		

Acquis communautaire

The phrase *acquis communautaire*, sometimes translated as 'the Community patrimony', denotes the whole range of principles, policies, laws, practices, obligations and objectives that have been agreed or that have developed within the European Union. The *acquis communautaire* includes most notably the **Treaties** in their entirety, all legislation enacted to date, and the judgments of the **Court of Justice** (see also *finalités politiques*).

The significance of the *acquis* is most obvious when new member states join the Union (see **enlargement**). They are legally obliged to accept not only the Treaties, but all previous legal decisions taken by the various Union institutions, all agreements within and between those institutions about their operation, and all international agreements concluded by the Union. Moreover, new member states 'are in the same situation as the present Member States in respect of declarations or resolutions of, or other positions taken up by, the Council ... [or] adopted by common agreement of the Member States'. Accordingly, they are required to 'observe the principles and guidelines deriving from those declarations, resolutions or other positions' and to 'take such measures as may be necessary to ensure their implementation' (Article 3.3 of Acts of Accession).

A good example of this process in practice was the acceptance on accession of the objective of **Economic and Monetary Union** (EMU) by Greece, Spain and Portugal even though they had played no part in shaping that objective, and even though at the time it was embodied only in Declarations of the European Council rather than in specific Treaty Articles or other legally binding texts.

Although the principle of the *acquis communautaire* is recognized in successive Acts of Accession, it is not referred to explicitly by name, nor does it appear in the Treaties establishing the **European Communities**, the **Merger Treaty** or the **Single European Act** (SEA). However, under the **Maastricht Treaty**, one of the objectives of the new European Union is 'to maintain in full the *acquis communautaire* and build on it' in a fashion consistent with 'ensuring the effectiveness of the mechanisms and the institutions of the Community' (Article B TEU).

The fact that the *acquis communautaire* includes judgments of the Court of Justice is of cardinal importance, since it entails recognition by the member states of the **primacy** of Community law and the principle of **direct effect**.

Action Committee for Europe

See **Action Committee for the United States of Europe**.

Action Committee for the United States of Europe (ACUSE)

ACUSE was founded by **Jean Monnet** in October 1955, following his resignation as President of the High Authority of the **European Coal and Steel Community** (ECSC) the previous year. Its purpose was to act as a pressure group for closer European integration by bringing together leading personalities of all parties from **the Six**, plus, in later years, the United Kingdom. It played an important part in building momentum towards the **European Economic Community** (EEC) in the mid-1950s, and during the 1960s it acted as an international focus for political opposition to the anti-federalist European policies of President **Charles de Gaulle** of France. ACUSE was dissolved by Monnet himself in 1975. Ten years later a successor body, the Action Committee for Europe, was formed with a similar purpose, but it was far less prominent than Monnet's organization, mainly because it lacked a dominant personality of driving European ambition as its head.

In a famous phrase ACUSE was described by Jean-Jacques Servan-Schreiber as a 'kind of federal authority of the mind'. ACUSE's statements and declarations over its period of greatest influence (1955–67) were published by the Royal Institute of International Affairs (Chatham House) in no. 9 of the European series of booklets, March 1969. An account of ACUSE by Pascal Fontaine may be found in the proceedings of the symposium organized by the Commission to mark the centenary of Monnet's birth (10 November 1988).

Additionality

'Additionality' is a jargon word denoting the principle whereby sums received from the **Budget** of the Union in support of particular projects (most commonly from the **structural funds**) are supposed to be additional to those received from national sources. The great temptation – and few member states have been able always to resist it – is to allow receipts from Brussels to take the place of national aid. There is a revealing case-study of this in Paul McAleavey, 'The politics of European regional development policy: additionality in the Scottish coalfields' (*Regional Politics and Policy*, Vol. 3, no. 2, Summer 1993).

Adenauer, Konrad (1876–1967)

Chancellor of the Federal Republic of Germany from 1949 to 1963, Konrad Adenauer was a key figure in the postwar reconstruction of West Germany and in its reintegration into western Europe and the Atlantic Alliance.

Adenauer entered politics at an early age and by 1917 had been elected Mayor of Cologne. Dismissed by the Nazis in 1933, he went into retirement, but in 1945 re-emerged as Mayor and as a co-founder of the Christian Democratic Union (CDU) in the Rhineland. In October 1945 he was dismissed from the office of mayor by the British Military Governor of the North Rhine province, who accused him of having 'failed in his duty to the people of Cologne', placed restrictions on his movements, and banned him from all political activity. In spite of this the following year he became Chairman of the CDU in the British zone of occupation, and played a central role in the negotiations with the Allies on the Constitution of the new Federal Republic. In 1949, at the age of 73, he was elected to the Bundestag and on 15 September 1949 he was elected (by a one vote margin) as Federal Chancellor.

Adenauer's chancellorship spanned the admission of West Germany into the **Council of Europe** (1950) and the **North Atlantic Treaty Organization** (NATO) (1955). Acting as his own foreign minister from 1951 until 1955, Adenauer ensured West Germany's position as a founder member of the three **European Communities** and resolved the dispute with France over the **Saarland**. At a meeting in Moscow in 1955 he secured the agreement of the Soviet government to the return of German prisonersof-war still held in the USSR. In 1963 a Franco-German friendship treaty was signed (see **Franco-German cooperation**), an initiative to which Adenauer attached great importance.

In the 1961 Bundestag elections the Christian Democrats lost their overall majority. The coalition with the Free Democrats (Liberals) proved difficult, and in October 1963 Adenauer announced his retirement as Chancellor. He remained a member of the Bundestag and until 1966 continued as chairman of the CDU.

Adenauer took a close and active interest in European unification. In two interviews in an American newspaper in March 1950 he suggested a complete union between France and Germany, but in spite of support from **Charles de Gaulle** this plan came to nothing. In his *Memoirs 1945–1953* (English edition, 1966) he wrote of the **Schuman Plan** of May 1950: 'I was in full agreement with the French Government that the significance of the Schuman proposal was first and foremost political and not economic. This Plan was to be the beginning of a federal structure of Europe.'

By virtue of his dignity, experience, authority and integrity, Adenauer was the ideal embodiment of the 'new Germany' that emerged from the ruins of 1945. Although an enthusiastic supporter of European integration, he was at the same time anxious to establish good relations with the United States. He was on friendly terms both with de Gaulle and with the British. Stephen Spender met him in 1945 when he was again Mayor of Cologne: 'He has an energetic, though somewhat insignificant appearance: a long lean oval face, almost no hair, small blue active eyes, a little button nose and a reddish complexion. He looks remarkably young and he has the quietly confident manner of a successful and attentive young man' (*European Witness*, 1946). He was an extremely astute and determined politician with a European and international reputation that few of his successors as Chancellor have matched.

Advocate-General

The **Court of Justice** of the European Union is composed of 15 judges and 9 advocates-general. The role of the advocate-general, which has no equivalent in English law, is to present, on the basis of the facts and arguments submitted by all the parties, a 'reasoned submission' in open court. This submission, known as the **Opinion**, seeks to identify the points of law at issue, to remind the Court of precedents with a bearing on the case, and to recommend what judgment the Court should reach. The judges then retire to deliberate in camera without the advocate-general being present. The Court usually, but not always, follows the advocate-general's recommendation, which has no legal force but is printed together with the final judgment in *European Court Reports*.

African, Caribbean and Pacific states

See **ACP states**.

Airbus

Amongst the best-known European collaborative projects, Airbus is also amongst the most successful. Airbus began in 1965 as an Anglo-French proposal. The West German government expressed a strong interest and a Memorandum of Understanding was signed by the three governments in 1967. Two years later, the British government withdrew, although Hawker Siddeley (later British Aerospace) remained a partner in its own right. Airbus Industrie was founded as a **European economic interest grouping** in 1970. The first Airbus flew in 1972. Six years later the British government bought its way back into the consortium, taking a 20 per cent share. The British, French and German aircraft industries remain the most important participants in the Airbus project, which now also involves smaller-scale participation by Belgian, Dutch and Spanish firms. The main assembly plant is in Toulouse; British Aerospace is chiefly concerned with the design and manufacture of the wings. The Airbus consortium is now engaged in the development of the Future Large Aircraft (FLA), a military transport aeroplane.

The Airbus project has given rise to difficulties with the American aircraft industry, especially Boeing, which suspects European governments of subsidizing Airbus in a fashion inconsistent with the rules laid down in the **General Agreement on Tariffs and Trade** (GATT). The counter to this charge is that Boeing and the rest of the American aircraft industry benefit from enormous *de facto* subsidies by virtue of their close involvement in defence-related research and procurement.

Albert–Ball Report

Commissioned by the European Parliament (see **Kangaroo Group**), the Albert–Ball Report was published in July 1983 under the title *Towards European Economic Recovery in the 1980s*. The authors were a French and a British economist, Michel Albert and James Ball. The report drew attention to the Community's failure to establish a true **Single Market**, to the absence of a programme for research and development that would enable the Community to compete more effectively with Japan and the United States, and in general to the failure to allow industry and commerce to take full advantage of the economies of scale that were part of the economic logic of the Treaties. The authors claimed that the restrictions placed by national regulations on the free flow of goods, services and capital within the Community cost each worker the equivalent of a week's wages every year. The report contributed to the mood of enthusiasm for the completion of the single market, a process set in train by the publication in June 1985 of the **Cockfield White Paper** (see also **non-Europe**).

Allied Rapid Reaction Corps (ARRC)

The ARRC was one of many ideas put forward as part of the overall review of the role and structure of the **North Atlantic Treaty Organization** (NATO). With the virtual disappearance of the threat of massive armed attack against any of the NATO states, the Alliance's New Strategic Concept (agreed at the November 1991 NATO summit in Rome) lays emphasis on the need for smaller forces with 'enhanced flexibility, and mobility', amongst them, in a 'limited but militarily significant proportion, ground, air and sea immediate and rapid reaction elements able to respond to a wide range of eventualities' (point 47). When fully operational, the ARRC will have a full complement of 80,000 troops capable of being mobilized in seven days.

Annual legislative programme (ALP)

Towards the end of every year the **European Commission** publishes its ALP for the following year. The ALP is discussed in particular with the **European Parliament**, with a view to reaching agreement as early as possible in the year to which the ALP refers. This procedure was introduced as a means of expediting the large number of legislative proposals brought forward in the late 1980s under the **Single Market** programme and as a contribution to greater openness (see **transparency**).

The ALP establishes priorities amongst the various items of forthcoming draft legislation. Special symbols are used to denote items likely to require an environmental impact assessment (see **environment policy**), those that need to be considered in the light of their impact on business in general and small businesses in particular, and those that 'should be preceded by broad discussions'. Overall, account is taken of the need to apply **subsidiarity**. The **Council of Ministers** draws up its own list of priorities in the form of a declaration in response to the ALP agreed between the Commission and the Parliament.

Anti-dumping

Dumping, as defined by the **General Agreement on Tariffs and Trade** (GATT), is the placing of goods on an export market at a price that does not reflect the cost of production in the country of origin. A charge of dumping must show evidence of material injury to the domestic industry in the country of importation. Under the European Union's **Common Commercial Policy** (CCP), the **Commission**, rather than individual member states, is responsible for investigating allegations of dumping and for imposing duties on goods shown to have been dumped (confirmed by the **Council of Ministers** in the form of a Regulation). Anti-dumping decisions may be appealed against in the **Court of Justice** or the **Court of First Instance**. Overzealous use of the Commission's powers in this field may lead to accusations of a **Fortress Europe**.

Approximation

This is the word used in **Articles 100 and 100a** of the **Treaty of Rome** to denote what is more commonly known as **harmonization**.

Articles 100 and 100a

These two Articles of the **Treaty of Rome** provide the legal basis for what is commonly known as **harmonization**, i.e., the elimination, by means of the creation of common standards, of barriers to trade that spring from member states' different requirements in respect of health, safety, technical specifications, consumer protection, and product standards generally. The two Articles are accordingly of fundamental importance in the creation of the **Single Market**.

Until the **Single European Act** (SEA) in 1986 progress towards the Single Market had been slow because Article 100 requires the **Council of Ministers** to act by **unanimity**. Although Article 100 remains in force, its place as the legal basis for most Single Market measures has been taken by Article 100a, which was added to the Treaty by Article 18 of the SEA.

Referring back to Article 7a EEC (also added by the SEA), which underlined the importance of and defined the Single Market, Article 100a allows the Council to act by **qualified majority** on most Single Market measures. Key exceptions, listed in Article 100a.2, are 'fiscal provisions, . . . the free movement of persons, . . . [and] the rights and interests of employed persons', which continue to be dealt with under Article 100.

Under Articles 100 and 100a, consultation with the **European Parliament** and the **Economic and Social Committee** is mandatory. In the case of draft legislation brought forward under Article 100a, the Parliament plays an influential role under the **co-decision procedure**.

Article 113 Committee

The Article 113 Committee is a committee of national officials meeting regularly in Brussels to prepare the decisions of the **Council of Ministers** in the field of external trade policy. The existence of the Committee is specifically sanctioned by Article 113 of the **Treaty of Rome**. This obliges the **Commission** to secure a negotiating mandate from the Council before opening negotiations with third countries and organizations and to consult the Council continuously during the negotiating process. The Article 113 Committee acts on the Council's behalf and meets at the level of national trade directors or their deputies. Some tasks are delegated to working groups (dealing with such matters as textiles, dumping and steel) or to negotiating groups that convene in international fora, such as the World Trade Organization (WTO). The **Maastricht Treaty** extends the Article 113 model to all other international economic agreements with third countries, creating a similar committee or committees for negotiations conducted under Article 228.

Article 235

All three of the founding **Treaties** of the **European Communities** provide a legal basis for action to be taken in furtherance of objectives not covered by specific treaty Articles. In the **Treaty of Rome** such a basis is to be found in Article 235, which reads:

> If action by the Community should prove necessary to attain, in the course of the operation of the common market, one of the objectives of the Community and this Treaty has not provided the necessary powers, the Council shall, acting unanimously on a proposal from the Commission and after consulting the European Parliament, take the appropriate measures.

In a 1971 judgment the **Court of Justice** took a broad view of what 'in the course of the operation of the common market' means, so allowing the **Commission** to use Article 235 EEC as the basis for its right to negotiate the European Road Transport Agreement (the **ERTA case**, Case 22/70). This was a fundamental decision in defining the Commission's role in external relations.

In general the Commission has been careful not to overuse Article 235, but has not always succeeded in avoiding a challenge in the Court. In 1989 the Court ruled in favour of the United Kingdom, which had challenged the enactment on the basis of Article 235 of a vocational training programme for young people (Case 56/88). In spite of occasional controversy, Article 235 has proved its usefulness: for example, it is the legal basis for **Cooperation Agreements**, since these are not provided for in the Treaties.

Arusha Convention

The Arusha Convention was a trade and aid agreement between **the Six** and the East African countries of Kenya, Tanzania and Uganda, signed in Arusha, Tanzania, in 1969. It entered into force in January 1971, but was soon superseded by the **Lomé Convention** of 1975.

Assent procedure

The assent procedure was a mechanism introduced by the **Single European Act** (SEA) to give the **European Parliament** the right of **veto** over certain important decisions, of a non-routine legislative character, taken by the **Council of Ministers**. The procedure required the Parliament to give its assent by an absolute majority in favour of the act in question before it could be adopted by the Council, and applied to two areas: the conclusion of **Association Agreements** with third states (Article 238 of the **Treaty of Rome**) and the **accession** of new member states to the Community (Article 237 EEC). The **Maastricht Treaty** recasts both provisions: membership of the Union is subject to approval by an absolute majority in the Parliament (Article O TEU), but only a simple majority is now needed for Association Agreements. The Parliament's assent must now be given to almost all international agreements. The assent procedure has also been extended to certain legislative matters (see Weatherill and Beaumont, *EC Law*).

Assizes

In November 1990, just as the **Intergovernmental Conferences** (IGCs) that led a year later to the **Maastricht Treaty** were getting under way, an all-party conference of about 250 members of the 12 **national parliaments** in the European Community and of the **European Parliament** (MEPs) was held in Rome to discuss **European Union**. This meeting, known as the *assises* (sittings) in French, became known as the 'assizes' in English. The proportion of MEPs was fixed at one-third of the whole, and the conference was conducted largely on the basis of European Parliament procedures (although there was some argument over whether participants should sit in national delegations, as national parliamentarians preferred, or in **political groups**). A final resolution was adopted that broadly reflected the more 'European' views of the MEPs, as a result of which many national parliamentarians felt that they had been outmanoeuvred; the suggestion that such assizes should be held regularly or even turned into a new Community body (the 'Congress') was rejected.

A 'Declaration on the Conference of the Parliaments' (as the assizes are sometimes known) was appended to the Maastricht Treaty. This simply invites the national parliaments and the European Parliament 'to meet as necessary', and commits the governments to consult such a conference 'on the main features of the European Union'. This **Declaration** was preceded by a general 'Declaration on the role of national parliaments in the European Union', which speaks of the importance of encouraging 'greater involvement' of national parliaments, in the context of which the assizes experiment should be viewed.

In spite of some enthusiasm for the idea within the British **presidency** of the **Council of Ministers** (July to December 1992), no assizes have been held since November 1990. At a meeting of presidents of parliaments in Dublin in May 1993, it became clear that no assizes would be held before the June 1994 European elections. It was agreed (against the wishes of the President of the European Parliament) that at future assizes participants would sit in national delegations and that no final declaration would be drawn up. This decision is likely to stifle the idea that better contacts between the national parliaments and the European Parliament could be established through regular assizes.

Association Agreement

Association Agreements are provided for in the **Treaty of Rome**: 'The Community may conclude with one or more States or international organizations agreements establishing an association involving reciprocal rights and obligations, common action and special procedures' (Article 238 EEC). Agreements drawn up under this Article, negotiated by the **Commission** on a mandate from the **Council of Ministers**, require the assent of a simple majority of the Members of the European Parliament (MEPs; see **assent procedure**).

The Treaty description of Association Agreements is very loose, and such agreements are now conventionally subdivided into three distinct types:

1 **Europe Agreements**, with the states of central and eastern Europe: these make explicit provision for eventual full membership of the European Union, but do not guarantee it;
2 Development Association Agreements, such as those with the **Maghreb** and **Mashreq** states; the **Lomé Convention** is also an agreement of this type;
3 The **European Economic Area** (EEA) Agreement, with the states of the **European Free Trade Association** (EFTA). Like the Europe Agreements, the EEA Agreement is designed to facilitate full membership of the Union for those states that wish to join.

Although the expression 'Europe Agreements' was not in use at the time they were concluded, the Association Agreements with Turkey (1963), Malta (1970) and Cyprus (1972) are also of this type, since in each case explicit reference is made to full membership.

It should be noted that association is with the European Community, not with the European Union. This means, for example, that associated states are involved neither in the **Common Foreign and Security Policy** (CFSP) nor in the cooperation in matters of **Justice and Home Affairs** (JHA), which are activities of the European Union under the **Maastricht Treaty**.

Association for the Monetary Union of Europe (AMUE)

The AMUE was founded in 1987 as a business pressure group for the adoption of a single currency in Europe. It is supported by a number of leading European multinationals – including Philips, British Petroleum, Volkswagen, Fiat, Alcatel, and Rhône-Poulenc – as well as most major European banks. AMUE organizes regular conferences on monetary integration, publishes pamphlets and studies, and adopts policy positions on **Economic and Monetary Union** (EMU). It has national chapters and a small central secretariat based in Paris. Membership is 'open to any business ... provided it shares [AMUE's] vision of Europe as a single currency zone'.

Austria

Like Germany, Austria was occupied by the Allies after the Second World War. The last Soviet troops left Austria in 1955, and the country's present republican constitution dates from that year. A condition of Soviet withdrawal was a constitutional commitment to **neutrality**. For this and for other reasons, Austria has never been a member of the **North Atlantic Treaty Organization** (NATO). However, Austria did participate in the **Marshall Plan**, was a founder member of the **Organization for European Economic Cooperation** (OEEC), and in 1956 joined the **Council of Europe**. In 1960 Austria became a founder member of the **European Free Trade Association** (EFTA).

Unlike certain other EFTA states, Austria was from the very beginning attracted by the idea of close ties with the European Community. Negotiations (1965–7) for an **Association Agreement** with the Community under Article 238 of the **Treaty of Rome** were unsuccessful, but by 1973 Austria, in common with the other EFTA states, had a free trade agreement with the Nine (see **the Six**). By 1977, under the terms of this agreement, most industrial goods were subject to free trade arrangements, and by 1984 these had been extended to all industrial goods. However, the Community's decision the following year to complete the **Single Market** led Austria, once again, to review the question of accession to the Community. By the end of the 1980s the reduction in East–West tension made it possible for neutral Austria to make explicit its commitment to the West, and on 17 July 1989 a formal application to join the three **European Communities** was submitted.

The application laid emphasis on Austria's commitment to neutrality, and this was dealt with at length in the Commission's generally favourable Opinion delivered in August 1991 (*Bulletin of the European Communities*, supplement 4/92). As the Opinion noted, not only did Austria already have free trade with the Twelve, it was, already (along with other parties to the **European Economic Area** Agreement) bound to apply most of the Single Market legislation that is a substantial part of the *acquis communautaire*. The problem of neutrality arose primarily because of the **Common Foreign and Security Policy** (CFSP) provisions of the **Maastricht Treaty**. It would clearly be unacceptable if a member state were constitutionally prevented from participating in or carrying out a decision, say, to apply economic sanctions against a third country or to undertake some other action in the foreign policy field agreed by the Union partners. The Commission noted that although Article 224 EEC allows member states a **derogation** from Treaty rules in the event of war or where they conflict with 'obligations . . . accepted for the purpose of maintaining peace and international security', the application of the latter condition is confined to action agreed by the Security Council of the United Nations.

Negotiations with Austria presented few difficulties and were concluded in March 1994. The most substantial point of difference was over the Transit Agreement for goods vehicles passing through Austrian territory. This Agreement, concluded in 1992 for 12 years, was replaced by a transitional period of 3 years beginning in 1995, during which the system of 'ecopoints' provided for in the Agreement to limit pollution will apply while a permanent solution is being sought. If a solution is not found, a further three-year transitional period (to 2000) will come into effect. If the original aim of a 60 per cent reduction in pollution has still not been achieved by the end of this period, a further three-year extension is automatically granted.

Austrian accession was approved by the European Parliament in May 1994 and by popular referendum on 12 June 1994 (the turnout was 81.3 per cent; 66.4 per cent in favour). Austria became the thirteenth member of the European Union on 1 January 1995.

Baltic states

The three Baltic states – Estonia, Latvia and Lithuania – concluded free trade agreements with the European Union in July 1994. All three states now have **Europe Agreements** and are members of the **Council of Europe**. Contacts between the Baltic states and Scandinavian countries have also been established within the framework of the **Nordic Council**. See also **Pact on Stability in Europe**.

Bank for International Settlements (BIS)

Known as the 'central banks' bank', the BIS was founded in 1930 to promote cooperation between central banks and to facilitate international financial operations. Most European countries' central banks, East and West, participate in the activities of the BIS, together with the United States, Canada, Japan, Australia and South Africa. Its headquarters are in Basle, Switzerland. About 85 per cent of its total share capital is in the hands of the participating central banks.

Worldwide, about 80 central banks have deposits with the BIS, which manages about 10 per cent of foreign exchange reserves. The BIS cooperates closely with the International Monetary Fund and provides a forum for the coordination of international monetary policy.

Until the establishment of the **European Monetary Institute** (EMI), the BIS acted as the secretariat for the Committee of Governors of European Community Central Banks and for the Board of Governors of the **European Monetary Cooperation Fund**. The former General Manager of the BIS, Baron Alexandre Lamfalussy of Belgium, was appointed President of the EMI with effect from 1 January 1994.

Basic Research in Industrial Technologies

See BRITE-EURAM.

Belgium

See **Belgo-Luxembourg Economic Union, Benelux**.

Belgo-Luxembourg Economic Union (BLEU)

BLEU was set up under a convention signed in 1921, initially for a period of 50 years, Luxembourg having failed to establish a similar arrangement with France. Frontier controls between the two countries were effectively removed on 1 May 1922. Since 1971 the Union, which was dissolved in 1940 and reactivated in 1945, has been renewed by tacit agreement for 10-year periods. BLEU still exists within **Benelux**. The two countries hold their gold and foreign exchange reserves in common, the Belgian and Luxembourg francs are maintained at parity, and each country's currency is legal tender in the other. Although in recent years there has been talk of the Luxembourg franc breaking its ties with the (less reliable) Belgian franc, on the whole the relationship has been a successful one.

Benelux

The name Benelux is formed from the first syllables of Belgium, the Netherlands and Luxembourg, and came into general use in the immediate postwar years. The governments-in-exile of the three countries adopted a **customs union** treaty in London in 1944 that led to the establishment of the Benelux Customs Union on 1 January 1948. Ten years later in The Hague a Treaty of Union was signed, which came into force in 1960, by which date the three countries were already linked as members of the three **European Communities**. Article 233 of the **Treaty of Rome** refers to the 'regional unions' between Belgium and Luxembourg (i.e., the **Belgo-Luxembourg Economic Union**, BLEU) and between Belgium, Luxembourg and the Netherlands (i.e., Benelux), and explicitly allows such unions to exist and flourish within the broader Treaty framework. The Benelux arrangement – providing for the free movement of goods, services, capital and labour between the participating countries – was very much seen as a model for the wider economic integration of Western Europe. As the **European Economic Community** (EEC) developed, the rationale for Benelux declined, although throughout the integration process it remained significantly in advance of the Community in its chosen fields of activity. The vanguard role once played by Benelux is today performed by the **Schengen Agreement** for complete free movement amongst its participating states.

The Benelux arrangement is more ambitious than BLEU, with a broader range of goals: common employment and social security policies, close coordination of macro-economic and budgetary policies, and the eventual adoption of a full monetary and fiscal union, with a single currency and harmonized taxes. Although the latter objectives have not been realized, the Benelux countries did succeed in abolishing internal restrictions on trade and adopting a common external tariff some years ahead of the Community as a whole, and in pioneering a passport-free area with common treatment of third-country nationals, something that remains to be achieved throughout the Union several decades later.

Benelux is governed by the Committee of Ministers, assisted by various institutions, including an interparliamentary council, an economic and social council, a court of justice and a secretariat based in Brussels. The secretary-general is always of Dutch nationality. This institutional structure bears a distinct resemblance to that adopted for **the Six** in the 1950s. It reflects the common perceptions of the architects of both systems about the political importance of supranational structures, representational bodies and legal adjudication in economic integration. The costs of Benelux are met by direct contributions from the three countries, Belgium and the Netherlands paying 48.5 per cent each and Luxembourg the remainder.

The word 'Benelux' was invented in 1947 by F. M. Aspelagh, the Belgian correspondent of *The Economist*, to describe the proposed customs union between the three countries. In search of an original and amusing way of popularizing the concept, the author initially lighted on the word 'Nebelux'. 'After some hesitation I changed it to "Benelux". That sounded much better, but I was still not completely satisfied. It sounded more like a brand of vacuum cleaner than a concept of economic geography. Nonetheless I decided to give it a chance, and used it for the first time in *The Economist* on 6 August 1947. The rest is history.'

Benelux is the only survivor of a number of comparable customs unions proposed in the late 1940s and 1950s. France and Italy discussed such a union in 1949, and later considered joining the Benelux arrangement. This was opposed by the Netherlands, on the grounds that it might disrupt the progress then beginning to be made on a broader front (i.e., the **Council of Europe** and the **Organization for European Economic Cooperation**). With exotic names like Fritalux and Finebel (to which must be added the land of Bizonia, an amalgamation of the British and American sectors of occupied Germany), these projects now survive only as fossils in the bedrock of European integration.

The Benelux countries have always been in favour of European integration, which enjoys strong cross-party support. Many Benelux politicians have held high and influential office in European institutions, including **Paul-Henri Spaak** and Sicco Mansholt (see **Mansholt Plan**); Gaston Thorn, **Jacques Santer** (both from Luxembourg), and Jean Rey, who were presidents of the **Commission**; and Joseph Luns and Willy Claes, who served as secretaries-general of the **North Atlantic Treaty Organization** (NATO). The policy of Benelux governments within the European

Union has been as far as possible to support the Commission as the guardian of the European interest and as a counterbalance to the dominant role inevitably played by the larger states. The fact that **Brussels** and Luxembourg are the headquarters of so many European institutions plays a part in creating a favourable climate of official opinion towards European integration (see **seat of the institutions**). Such integration allows the Benelux countries to play a more influential role as partners than would be allowed them within a conventional power system.

Berlaymont

The 13-storey building in the form of an irregular four-pointed star has become widely known as the headquarters of the **European Commission** in Brussels, and, like 'Whitehall', is used as a symbol of officialdom. Built in the 1960s on the site of a former monastery of the same name, the Berlaymont building was rented by the Commission from the Belgian government. In 1990 it was discovered that the internal walls had a high asbestos content which was potentially injurious to health, and since 1992 the building has been left empty while refurbishment is carried out. It is thought unlikely that the Commission will return to the Berlaymont building before the end of the decade. Meanwhile, the Commissioners and the Secretariat-General are housed in the Breydel building.

Brezhnev Doctrine

In 1968, the year of the 'Prague Spring' uprising in Czechoslovakia, Leonid Brezhnev, General Secretary of the Soviet Communist Party, announced that the Soviet Union had the right to interfere in the internal affairs of its satellite states in central and eastern Europe if it appeared that Communism or the hegemony of Moscow (the two were identified) was under threat. This became known as the Brezhnev Doctrine, although it was merely the formal expression of what had been the case *de facto* since Stalin's time. Under the terms of the **Warsaw Pact** the Soviet Union was entitled to keep military forces in the satellite states. The Brezhnev Doctrine was challenged by the principles laid down in Basket I of the Helsinki Final Act (see **Conference on Security and Cooperation in Europe**), amongst which were respect for sovereignty, non-interference in internal affairs, and the inviolability of frontiers. Although all Warsaw Pact states were signatories to the Final Act, the Brezhnev Doctrine remained a feature of Soviet foreign policy until it was abrogated by Mikhail Gorbachev in 1988.

Briand, Aristide (1862–1932)

Aristide Briand was a leading Socialist politician of the French Third Republic, several times prime minister and foreign minister from 1925 until his death. He was one of the first advocates of what he called 'a system of European Federal Union', which, as the representative of the French government in Geneva, Briand proposed to the **League of Nations** on 5 September 1929. The 27 European members of the League agreed to discuss the proposal, and on 17 May 1930 the French government circulated a memorandum setting out the proposal in more detail.

The memorandum spoke of the need for 'a permanent regime of solidarity based on international agreements for the rational organization of Europe'. Interestingly, Briand cited 'the possibilities of enlarging the economic market' as one of the reasons why such an organization was imperative, and referred to the 20,000 kilometres of new national frontiers within Europe created by the Treaty of Versailles. Throughout the memorandum he stressed that the Federal Union was in no way intended to supplant the League, but instead to work within it as one of the regional organizations specifically sanctioned by the League Covenant. The proposal fell well short of a 'federal' arrangement in the conventional sense: 'It is on the plane of absolute sovereignty and of entire political independence that the understanding between European nations must be brought about ... under a system of federal union fully compatible with respect for traditions and for the characteristics peculiar to each people.'

The memorandum was considered in detail by a special study group chaired by Sir Eric Drummond, Secretary-General of the League. There the proposals 'died a lingering death, killed by increasing international friction and mistrust' (H. W. V. Temperley, *The Whispering Gallery of Europe*, 1938). Jointly with Gustav Stresemann and Austen Chamberlain, Briand was awarded the Nobel Peace Prize in 1926 in recognition of his achievement in negotiating the Locarno Pacts, and is frequently cited, especially by French writers, as one of the founding fathers of the European Community.

BRITE–EURAM

BRITE (Basic Research in Industrial Technologies for Europe) is a **research** programme, operational since 1985, which has been merged with EURAM (European Advanced Materials), concerned with advanced materials and their industrial applications. The BRITE–EURAM programme is particularly designed to help small and medium-sized enterprises (SMEs), individually or jointly, undertake or commission research into new design and manufacturing processes, many including new, improved or recycled materials, particularly in the aeronautics industry.

British Budget problem

Reduced to its essentials, the British Budget problem – which overshadowed the United Kingdom's relations with the rest of the European Community from 1979 to 1984 – was that although amongst the poorer member states in terms of per capita gross national product (GNP), the United Kingdom was the second largest net contributor to the **Budget**. Both the pre-1979 Labour Government and the post-1979 Conservative Government of **Margaret Thatcher** believed this to be inequitable. Various temporary solutions were agreed, but a longer-term settlement was not reached until the Fontainebleau meeting of the European Council in June 1984.

It was realized at the time of the entry negotiations that because of the way the Community's system of **own resources** worked, the United Kingdom, with its relatively high revenue from tariffs and levies, would be a substantial contributor to the Budget. On the receipts side, the efficiency of British agriculture meant that payments to the United Kingdom under the **Common Agricultural Policy** (CAP) were relatively small. The problem was solved (or rather sidestepped) in three ways: the British were given a seven-year **transitional period**, they were told that new spending policies from which they could expect to benefit were soon to be established and, most importantly, they were assured that if an 'unacceptable situation' were to arise, the Community would find equitable solutions. (See also **contributions and receipts.**)

Although the **European Regional Development Fund** was established with strong British support in 1973, it was clearly on too small a scale to make a real difference to the overall pattern of the United Kingdom's contributions and receipts. Accordingly, the Budget issue featured in the Labour Government's **renegotiation** demands of 1974/5. At the Dublin meeting of the **European Council** in March 1975 a 'corrective mechanism', with which the Government expressed itself satisfied, was agreed. However, the mechanism had one fatal flaw: it was triggered only if the member state concerned had an overall deficit on its balance of trade. Thanks to North Sea oil, this was not the case, and nothing was ever paid to the United Kingdom under the Dublin arrangement.

When the Conservatives took office in 1979, the transitional period was over, and the forecasts of British net contributions to the Budget showed all too clearly that the problem was getting worse: from 1980 onwards, Community membership seemed likely to cost the United Kingdom almost £1 billion a year. This was the moment at which, in the view of

Christopher Tugendhat, the Commissioner then responsible for the Budget, 'an act of statesmanship' on the part of the French and German leaders, **Valéry Giscard d'Estaing** and Helmut Schmidt, 'could have solved the British budget problem before it got out of hand'. Instead, they chose to turn the issue into 'a trial of strength' (*Making Sense of Europe*). At the European Council meeting in Dublin in November 1979 Mrs Thatcher was provoked into demanding 'our money back', a phrase that called into question the whole idea of own resources belonging to the Community as of right. It also suggested that the British stance was prompted by the idea of a *juste retour* rather than by a broader notion of equity.

Certainly the fact that the problem had already been addressed in Labour's renegotiation made Mrs Thatcher's task more difficult. There was great reluctance in the Community to countenance a permanent solution based on objective criteria, and for 1980 and 1981 a temporary solution was found. However, the Commission was invited, under the so-called 'Mandate of 30 May [1980]', to draw up a general study of budgetary imbalances for consideration by the European Council. This was done a year later and broadly supported the British case, but even by the end of 1981 no further progress had been made.

The following year, in May 1982, a more radical tactic was tried. The British Minister of Agriculture, Peter Walker, invoked the **Luxembourg Compromise** in an attempt to veto the annual agricultural prices settlement, on the grounds that its budgetary consequences entitled the United Kingdom to regard it as a 'very important national interest'. Of the other member states, only Denmark and Greece agreed with this reasoning, and the prices settlement was voted through against the British veto. A further temporary arrangement was made for the British budgetary contribution in 1982.

By the following year circumstances had changed in the United Kingdom's favour. The Community was running out of money, and the ceiling on **value-added tax** (VAT) could be raised only with the unanimous agreement of all member states (including ratification by **national parliaments**). At the European Council meeting in Stuttgart in June 1983 Mrs Thatcher made it very clear that her consent was conditional upon a permanent solution to the British Budget problem and upon new measures to enforce budgetary discipline in the Community. A change in French attitudes was perhaps prompted by the realization that in the wake of enlargement to include Portugal and Spain France was also likely to become a net contributor to the Community Budget. A further *ad hoc* arrangement was made for the British net contribution for 1983.

Twelve months of negotiations followed, from which emerged an agreement to calculate the disparity in the British Budget contribution on the basis of the difference between the British share of Community expenditure and the proportion of the Community's VAT-based revenue contributed by the United Kingdom. The **abatement**, as it was known, was to be paid for each year in the form of a reduced VAT-based contribution in the following year, a method that had the advantage (as the Council saw it) of keeping the **European Parliament** out of the picture, the Parliament's budgetary powers being limited to the expenditure side of the Budget. At the Fontainebleau European Council in June 1984 agreement was finally reached, to the effect that the revision of the own resources system, under which the VAT ceiling was finally raised from 1 to 1.4 per cent, would allow the United Kingdom a further *ad hoc* abatement of 1 billion ECUs for 1984 and thereafter a two-thirds reduction in the difference between the British contribution to VAT-based revenue and the amount of Community expenditure in the United Kingdom. As had been the case since 1982, a special arrangement was made that allowed West Germany – by far the biggest net contributor to the Budget – to pay a reduced share of what would otherwise have been a substantial proportion of the British rebate. In its first full year of operation (1985) the rebate amounted to about £1 billion. Since 1984, the rebate has amounted to about £16 billion (pre-1984 refunds to about £3 billion).

Since the **Fontainebleau Agreement** the rebate has occasionally been called into question, but the arrangement is now certain to last at least until the end of the century under an agreement reached at the Edinburgh meeting of the European Council in December 1992.

In proportion to British GNP or British public sector expenditure the sums at stake were never large. Throughout the negotiations the United Kingdom emphasized that it was prepared to be a modest net contributor to the Budget and that its case rested not on the idea of a *juste retour* but on the assurance given about the resolution of 'unacceptable situations' in the course of the negotiations on British accession to the Community. Although it may be true that the pugnacity of Mrs Thatcher's negotiating style offended and alienated some other member states, it is doubtful if anything less than her tenacity allied to a mastery of complex detail could have yielded, in the end, so satisfactory a result. Nor was it to be expected that a British government firmly committed to constraints on public expenditure could possibly let the issue lie. In retrospect, it reflects little credit on the Community that the problem should have taken so long to resolve and used up so much of the creative energies of ministers, officials and Community institutions. The impact of this long-running dispute on British public attitudes towards the Community was, not surprisingly, very damaging, whatever benefits there may have been for Mrs Thatcher's personal standing as a resolute defender of British interests. Whether the whole episode sprang from a desire on the part (principally) of the French to 'punish' the United Kingdom for joining the Community so late may never be wholly clear. The conclusion reached by Sir Michael Butler, who as British Permanent Representative in Brussels from 1979 until 1985 was deeply involved in the Budget issue, was that 'you can only get your way in the Community by sustained will-power, careful planning and skilled negotiation; but also that, if you have these things and a good case, the Community has in the end to take account of it. The British had a good case' (*Europe: More than a Continent*).

Bruges speech

On 20 September 1988 **Margaret Thatcher**, then Prime Minister of the United Kingdom, made a speech at the **College of Europe** in Bruges, Belgium, on the future of the European Community. The speech was widely interpreted as a counterblast to the federalist vision of **Jacques Delors**, the President of the **Commission**, since it reasserted the primacy of the member states within the integration process. The political background, national and European, to the speech is fully described in Hugo Young's biography of Mrs Thatcher, *One of Us*.

The speech did not call into question the United Kingdom's membership of the Community: 'Britain does not dream of some cosy, isolated existence on the fringes of the Community. Britain's destiny is in Europe, as part of the Community.' Nor was Mrs Thatcher opposed to the member states working 'more closely together on the things we can do better together than alone . . . whether it be in trade, in defence, or in our relations with the rest of the world'. However, the essence of the speech was the need to maintain the pre-eminence of the member states and to do nothing that might impair that national diversity which was a source of Europe's strength: 'Europe will be stronger precisely because it has France in as France, Spain in as Spain, Britain in as Britain, each with its own customs, traditions and identity.' The speech gave rise to concern not only because of the hostility it showed towards agreed objectives (the abolition of frontier controls, for example) but also because of its essentially intergovernmental vision of the Community's future (see **intergovernmentalism**).

For many commentators the speech was the first unequivocal expression of that distaste for Community institutions which served the Conservatives so badly in the **European elections** held nine months later. Within weeks of its delivery the so-called 'Bruges Group' was founded, formally on a cross-party basis, but in reality mainly composed of Conservatives who shared Mrs Thatcher's (largely illusory) fears of a European superstate in which national identity would be submerged and national **sovereignty** overridden (see **'identikit Europe'**).

Brussels

The national capital of Belgium with a population of almost 1 million people, Brussels is also the self-styled 'capital of Europe'. Many European Union institutions and bodies are located there: the **Council of Ministers**, the **European Commission** (see **Berlaymont**), the **Economic and Social Committee**, and the **Committee of the Regions**. The **European Parliament** has many of its staff in Brussels, and most meetings of its committees are held there and, since 1993, a small number of short plenary sessions (see **seat of the institutions**). The **national representations** of the member states are also in Brussels, together with many diplomatic missions accredited to the Union. Most European-wide lobbying organizations have their headquarters in Brussels. Brussels is also the home of the **North Atlantic Treaty Organization** (NATO) (since 1967), the **North Atlantic Assembly** and, since 1990, the **Western European Union** (WEU). The annual value to Brussels of the rents paid by European Union institutions and of salaries paid to officials has been estimated at over 20 billion Belgian francs (about £400 million); this figure could be doubled if the expenses of others, such as journalists, lobbyists and permanent representations, are also taken into account.

Brussels, Treaty of

Signed in March 1948, the Treaty of Brussels was an agreement on mutual military assistance and economic, social and cultural cooperation between the United Kingdom, France and the **Benelux** countries. It provided for intergovernmental consultations through a ministerial Council (Article 7) and was intended to protect the signatory states against a renewal of German aggression and the increasingly explicit threat from the USSR. The Treaty contained an automatic military assistance provision (Article 4) and called for signatory states to set up a permanent Military Committee. The Treaty was concluded for 50 years and provided the basis both for the **North Atlantic Treaty Organization** (NATO) and for the **Western European Union** (WEU; established by the modified Brussels Treaty of 1954).

Warmly welcomed by President Truman, the Brussels Treaty was largely the initiative of Ernest Bevin, the Foreign Secretary in Britain's postwar Labour Government. It built upon the Franco-British **Dunkirk Treaty** signed the previous year, and was a key element in Bevin's policy of what he called 'Western Union'. Introducing the policy in the House of Commons on 22 January 1948, Bevin said: 'The time for consolidation of Western Europe is ripe ... The old-fashioned concept of the balance of power should be discontinued.' Britain, he said, was now 'thinking of Western Europe as a unity'. The Brussels Treaty gave rise to great hopes that the United Kingdom was prepared to take the lead in the unification of Western Europe. In the event these hopes were disappointed: the economic, social and cultural provisions of the Treaty came to nothing; the defence component was soon rendered more or less irrelevant by the establishment of NATO; and it became clear that the United Kingdom was extremely reluctant to take part in the setting up of supranational institutions. The Treaty was, however, of some psychological importance in that it gave encouragement to those in the United States who wanted to see European countries coming together to resolve their postwar problems.

Budget of the European Union

The Budget of the European Union embraces revenue (see **own resources**), expenditure upon common policies, and the running costs of the institutions. The annual procedure for the adoption of the Budget centres upon proposals for expenditure (unlike the budget in the United Kingdom, which is concerned with the raising of revenue). Although the Union engages in borrowing and lending (see below), under Article 199 of the **Treaty of Rome** expenditure must be matched by revenue in each budgetary year. Responsibility for drawing up and implementing the Budget rests with the **Commission**; the **Council of Ministers** and the **European Parliament** constitute the joint budgetary authority; and the annual audit is carried out by the **Court of Auditors** (see also **discharge procedure**).

The procedure for the adoption of the Budget is an area in which the European Parliament's powers have increased very substantially since 1970. It is set out in Article 203 EEC, and each of the main stages has to be completed by a specific deadline in the course of the year preceding that to which the Budget relates.

The first stage is the drawing up of estimates by each institution and the consolidation of these by the Commission into the preliminary draft Budget (PDB). This is forwarded to the Council and to the European Parliament, normally in late May, examined by the Council, and adopted as the draft Budget (DB) before 31 July. The Parliament's first reading of the DB is in October, and at this stage it may propose modifications to items of **compulsory expenditure** or amendments to non-compulsory expenditure: the latter are subject to a 'maximum rate of increase', which is calculated by the Commission in the light of growth projections and rates of inflation and which can be changed only by agreement between the Council and the Parliament. Thus amended by the Parliament, the DB is returned to the Council. The Council's second reading takes place in November with advice from a delegation of the Parliament, and at this stage the amounts of compulsory expenditure – upon which the Council has the last word – are normally fixed. The remaining stage, the Parliament's second reading in December, concentrates upon non-compulsory expenditure (still within the maximum rate). If the Parliament is broadly satisfied with the DB overall, it may adopt the Budget by a majority of its total membership and three-fifths of the votes cast; if there are 'important reasons' why it is not satisfied, it may reject the DB as a whole by a majority of its total membership and two-thirds of the votes cast, as it did for the first time in 1979.

If adopted, the Budget can then be implemented. If it is not adopted, a system known as 'provisional twelfths' comes into effect, which requires expenditure in each month to be no more than one-twelfth of the total expenditure in the previous year. This system continues until a new Budget is adopted. The Treaty allows the Commission to submit draft supplementary or amending budgets to take account of unforeseen circumstances.

Although the budgetary procedure and the Budget itself are on an annual basis, multiannual spending programmes involve commitments spread over longer periods. This is done by means of 'differentiated appropriations', in respect of which a distinction is drawn between commitments and payments. Nor is each annual Budget worked out in isolation: all calculations are made within multiannual 'financial perspectives', of which the most recent, covering the period 1993–9, was agreed by the **European Council** in Edinburgh in December 1992.

There is one major item of expenditure that remains outside the Budget: the **European Development Fund** (EDF). The EDF is financed by direct contributions from member states and is managed by a steering committee.

Most of the borrowing and lending by the Union is done through the **European Investment Bank** (EIB) in Luxembourg, which is required to operate in conjunction with the **structural funds** and which has its own statute in a **protocol** to the Treaty of Rome (see also **New Community Instrument**).

With successive **enlargements** and the gradual broadening of Community activities, overall expenditure through the Budget has increased very markedly since the 1960s. In 1960, at 1993 prices, expenditure was just under £300 million and was 0.03 per cent of Community gross domestic product (GDP). By the time of the first enlargement in 1973 it had risen

European Union expenditure 1970, 1980 and 1988–94 (General Budget,[1] EDF[2] and ECSC[3])

	1970	1980	1988	1989	1990	1991	1992	1993	1994
Total Union expenditure (million ECUs)	3 576	16 455	42 495	42 284	45 608	55 156	60 501	69 233	72 304
Per capita expenditure (ECUs)	19	63	131	130	139	160	174	199	207
Union expenditure as % of public-sector expenditure in member states	1.90	1.70	2.30	2.10	2.00	2.20	2.20	2.40	2.40
Annual rate of growth of Union expenditure (%)			16.90	– 0.50	7.90	20.90	9.70	14.40	4.40
Annual rate of growth of member states' expenditure (%)			6.00	7.50	10.10	14.10	6.80	4.60	4.00
Union expenditure as % of member states' GDP	0.74	0.80	1.05	0.96	0.96	1.07	1.12	1.19	1.24

The final line (expenditure as % of GDP) gives the best indication of the growth of Union expenditure. Inflation tends to 'swell' figures in ECUs and annual growth rates. But Union expenditure is none the less growing faster than member states' national expenditure, the volume of which is much larger. However, Union expenditure tends to replace rather than supplement national expenditure as new powers are transferred to the Union.

[1] 1970, 1980, 1988–92: actual payments; 1993 and 1994: appropriations for payments in the Budget.
[2] European Development Fund.
[3] European Coal and Steel Community.

Source: European Commission, *The Budget of the European Union* (February 1994) to just over £12 billion (0.53 per cent of GDP) and by 1995 to about £60 billion (1.2 per cent of GDP), which is about equal to the amount spent on social security annually in the United Kingdom. This is also equivalent to about £176 per capita for every inhabitant in the Union, but – as the **MacDougall Report** showed long ago – it is well short of the amounts that would be necessary to have a perceptible macro-economic effect on growth patterns, regional development or average levels of prosperity. Nor can it increase much between 1995 and 1999, member states having agreed not to let the Budget exceed 1.27 per cent of GDP. The Budget agreed between the Council of Ministers and the European Parliament for 1995 amounted to 80.9 billion ECUs.

As is well known, by far the biggest element in the Budget is price support under the **Common Agricultural Policy** (CAP), i.e. under the 'guarantee' section of the **European Agricultural Guidance and Guarantee Fund** (EAGGF). In 1994 this represented almost 50 per cent of total commitments. The structural funds took a further 31.5 per cent. The third largest element, at 5.8 per cent of the total, was development assistance and expenditure arising from other agreements with third countries ('external actions'). All other items were below 5 per cent; the Commission's own administrative costs were 3 per cent.

The provisions in the **Maastricht Treaty** on how operational costs arising from the **Common Foreign and Security Policy** (CFSP) or cooperation in the field of **Justice and Home Affairs** (JHA) will be met allow member states the choice of charging them to the Budget (in which case the normal procedures apply) or paying for them directly; in both cases administrative costs are borne by the Budget.

Even this summary account of the budgetary procedure is suggestive of the many arguments and finely balanced compromises that have gone into the making of the procedure in its present form. In addition to the Treaty, the procedure is governed by various **interinstitutional agreements**, but these have not always been effective in forestalling or resolving arguments between the Parliament and the Council. For example, in December 1985 the President of the Parliament declared the 1986 Budget adopted, but the Parliament's amendments had exceeded the maximum rate and the Council challenged the Parliament's decision in the **Court of Justice**. The Parliament lost the case, but the 1986 Budget as finally agreed took account of the Parliament's concerns.

The Budget was always intended to be an instrument of policy. However, it is essentially too small to make much difference except in limited areas. This has not prevented the Budget from being a major cause of dispute both between member states (see **British Budget problem**) and between the institutions. The European Parliament – in common with most parliaments at some time in their history – has used its budgetary powers to wrest concessions from the Council and the Commission. The Parliament's powers over non-compulsory expenditure are not limited merely to adjusting (normally increasing) the sums for each item of expenditure. The Parliament may decide to shift a particular sum allocated by the Commission for a particular purpose into the 'reserve' (known as Chapter 100), and the sum in question can be released from the reserve only when the Parliament is satisfied that the purpose is soundly based or is modified in some way consistent with the Parliament's views.

The next major development as far as the budgetary procedure is concerned is the review in the course of the 1996 **Intergovernmental Conference** (IGC) of the relevant provisions of the Treaty, 'including the arrangements relating to compulsory and non-compulsory expenditure . . . in order to achieve interinstitutional cooperation on a partnership basis' (statement annexed to the Interinstitutional Agreement of 29 October 1993 on budgetary discipline and improvement of the budgetary procedure: *Official Journal*, 7 December 1993). This review may result in the abandonment of the compulsory/non-compulsory distinction, with a corresponding extension of the Parliament's powers. The Parliament has already gained two small but not insignificant victories by securing agreement to the effect that financial protocols to agreements with non-member countries will henceforth be classified as non-compulsory and that the Council will examine the possibility of incorporating the European Development Fund (see above) into the Budget.

In the longer term the Budget can develop only if at least a proportion of the Union's revenue is raised directly from the taxpayer, with the European Parliament having a say in how this is done. At present the Parliament has virtually no responsibility for revenue-raising and this has resulted, understandably, in the Parliament being broadly on the side of increased expenditure. It would be wholly consistent with the practice in other federal or quasi-federal systems if a proportion of an individual taxpayer's taxes went to the central authority directly rather than indirectly through national authorities. Such a system would reflect the extent to which the Budget of the Union bears costs that would otherwise be borne by national budgets, such as agricultural support. If taxation without representation is tyranny, representation without taxation may encourage irresponsibility.

Budgetary discipline

The phrase 'budgetary discipline' denotes the constraints within which the **Budget** of the European Union is drawn up, especially the 'financial perspective' and the limits agreed by member states on **own resources**.

Measures to ensure sound financial management are described under **discharge procedure** and **Court of Auditors** (see also **fraud**).

In addition to the requirement in Article 199 of the **Treaty of Rome** that 'revenue and expenditure . . . shall be in balance', Article 201a EEC (resulting from the **Maastricht Treaty**) says that 'with a view to maintaining budgetary discipline, the **Commission** shall not make any proposal for a Community act . . . without providing the assurance that [it] is capable of being financed within the limit of the Community's own resources'. This requirement relates only to such costs as may fall upon the Budget; it does not oblige the Commission to assess overall compliance costs. However, under a **Declaration** annexed to the Treaty of Rome, the Commission is required 'to take account in its legislative proposals of costs and benefits to the Member States' public authorities and all the parties concerned'.

The agreement reached by the **European Parliament**, the **Council of Ministers**, and the European Commission on 29 October 1993 (*Official Journal*, 7 December 1993) specifies that the 1993–9 financial framework annexed to the agreement is the 'reference framework for interinstitutional budgetary discipline'. The three institutions undertake to regard the amounts set out in the perspective as the 'annual ceiling on Community expenditure'; own resources are allowed to rise to a maximum of 1.27 per cent of overall gross national product (GNP) by 1999. Within these overall ceilings, price support under the **European Agricultural Guidance and Guarantee Fund** (EAGGF) is subject to a particularly tight limit, agreed in 1988, and may not rise by more than 74 per cent of the rise in GNP. Over the period 1993–9, price support is due to fall from 53.5 per cent of the Budget to 48 per cent.

Budgetary discipline became linked in the early 1980s with the **British Budget problem** by virtue of **Mrs Thatcher**'s insistence that no new own resources would be forthcoming unless expenditure were made subject to stricter controls than had so far been applied. Two meetings of the **European Council** in Brussels (June 1987 and February 1988) laid the foundations for the present system of budgetary discipline, set out in the October 1993 **interinstitutional agreement** referred to above. This agreement also embodies guidelines for the annual procedure for drawing up the Budget.

Cabinet

The French word *cabinet* is used to denote the small group of officials who make up the private offices of senior ministers in France and other countries, of members of the **European Commission**, and of other very senior figures in the European Union, such as the president of the **European Parliament**. By virtue of their closeness to persons of political influence, members of *cabinets* can and do play an influential role, which normally extends well beyond the specific responsibilities of the person to whom they are attached.

Capital movements

Article 3a of the **Treaty of Rome** defines the **Single Market** as one in which all obstacles to the free movement of goods, persons, services and capital have been removed. Article 67 EEC required member states to 'abolish between themselves all restrictions on the movement of capital belonging to persons resident in the member states and any discrimination based on the nationality or on the place of residence of the parties or on the place where such capital is invested'. Articles 68–73 EEC set out the means whereby this general principle was to be applied and the exceptions to it. Gradual progress was made in the 1960s and 1970s, leading up to the adoption in 1988 of a general Directive (see **legal instruments**) requiring capital movements to be entirely freed by July 1990 (Spain, Portugal, Greece and Ireland were allowed to apply restrictions for a little longer). The matter was placed under the general supervisory control of the **Monetary Committee** and the Committee of **Central Bank Governors**. Member states were allowed to take 'protective measures' in the event of 'short-term capital movements of exceptional magnitude' (Article 2 of the Directive).

The **Maastricht Treaty** repealed Articles 67–73 EEC with effect from 1 January 1994 and substituted Articles 73a–g EEC, placing capital movements legislation within the framework of **Economic and Monetary Union** (EMU). Free movement of capital has been assured since that date (except in relation to Greece, which was granted an extension until 1 January 1995), and the **European Monetary Institute** (EMI) is now the supervisory authority. The legislation applies throughout the **European**

Economic Area (EEA). In principle, free movement of capital now extends to transactions involving non-member states.

Cassis de Dijon case

The 1979 judgment of the **Court of Justice** in the case known as 'Cassis de Dijon' (*Rewe-Zentrale AG* v *Bundesmonopolverwaltung für Branntwein*, Case 120/78) established that a product lawfully manufactured and on sale in one member state may be imported into another without restriction. This principle, sometimes known as mutual recognition of product standards, is of the greatest importance in facilitating the free circulation of goods within the **Single Market** and obviates the need for detailed **harmonization** of product standards to guarantee such circulation.

Cassis de Dijon is a blackcurrant-based liqueur manufactured in France. The West German spirits monopoly sought to ban its import into the German market on the grounds that its alcoholic content was below the minimum (25 per cent by volume) laid down by German law for liqueurs. The Court did not accept this argument. The case illustrates the role that the Court has not infrequently played in furthering the objects of the Community, in this case the removal of **non-tariff barriers** to trade between the member states.

Cecchini Report

In the **Cockfield White Paper** of June 1985 the **Commission** identified the legislative measures that would be needed if the **Single Market** were to be created. In 1988 a second report by a committee of experts, chaired by a senior Commission official, Paolo Cecchini, was published under the title *1992: The European Challenge*. This report identified the impediments – such as different national practices, testing standards, and bureaucratic obstruction – that stood in the way of the free flow of goods, services, persons and capital within the Community. The report's calculation that such impediments cost the Community some 5 per cent of its gross domestic product (GDP) annually was widely quoted, as was the assertion that their removal would result in a one-off gain variously calculated at between 4.3 and 6.4 per cent of GDP and deliver non-inflationary growth of 7 per cent in the medium term and 5 million new jobs. The report was based in part on the findings of a survey amongst 11,000 businessmen, who identified frontier formalities and the failure to agree on Community-wide product standards as the key elements in the problem.

CEN

See *Comité Européen de Normalisation*.

CENELEC

See *Comité Européen de Normalisation*.

Censure motion

Under Article 144 of the **Treaty of Rome**, the **European Parliament** may dismiss the **European Commission** on the basis of a motion of censure passed by a two-thirds majority of votes cast representing a majority of the Members of Parliament (MEPs). The Commission is required to resign 'as a body': motions of censure may not be directed against individual Commissioners. The reasons why so few motions of censure have ever been put to the vote and why none has ever been adopted are discussed under **European Parliament**.

Central bank governors

The governors of the central banks of the member states of the European Union are closely involved in the operation of the **European Monetary System** (EMS), play an important role in the coordination of monetary policy and are set to acquire substantial new powers in the move towards **Economic and Monetary Union** (EMU). Collectively they have become an economic power-centre in their own right since 1980, reflecting the growing importance of coordinated exchange-rate management and monetary discipline.

There is no reference to the central bank governors in the original **Treaty of Rome**. They were first given institutional standing in May 1964, when the Council of Economic and Finance Ministers (**Ecofin Council**) decided to complement the existing **Monetary Committee** by establishing a parallel body to coordinate the activities of the various national central banks at Community level. The resulting organ, known as the Committee of Central Bank Governors, brought together the governors and their senior staff to discuss developments of mutual concern.

The remit of the Committee was to 'hold consultations concerning the general principles and the broad lines of policy of the central banks' and to 'exchange information at regular intervals about the most important measures that fall within the competence of the central banks, and to examine those measures'. In practice, the Committee's work was given real substance only once the promotion of exchange-rate stability had become a major Community objective.

The first attempt to develop EMU, following the **Werner Report** of 1970, led to a major enhancement of the Committee's role. In March 1971 it was entrusted with coordinating intervention on the currency markets to sustain the so-called '**Snake**'. A decision of the Ecofin Council of the same month strengthened cooperation between central banks in respect of interest rates and money supply. Two years later, in April 1973, the Committee was appointed in its entirety to serve as the board of governors of the new **European Monetary Cooperation Fund** (EMCF).

Although the Werner-inspired EMU project failed, the subsequent development of the EMS in 1978–9 strengthened the position of the central bank governors, and their Committee became the routine management agency for intervention within the EMS. All governors now regard their respective national jobs as having a very important European component. It was a striking reflection of this growing stature that when it was decided to relaunch the EMU process at the European Council meeting in Hanover in June 1988 by commissioning the **Delors Report**, the membership of the committee for the new study was composed almost exclusively of the central bank governors.

The organization and remit of the Committee of Central Bank Governors were redefined at the beginning of stage 1 of EMU in July 1990. An 'economic unit' was added to the existing secretariat to provide analytical support to the work of the Committee. The Committee's responsibilities were revised and the right of the Committee's chairman to attend meetings of the Ecofin Council, whenever it dealt with matters 'involving the tasks of the Committee', was formalized.

Under the provisions of the **Maastricht Treaty** the central bank governors will play a crucial part in the new monetary union. The Committee of Central Bank Governors and the EMCF merged in January 1994 to form the **European Monetary Institute** (EMI). At the end of stage 2 the EMI will be transformed into the **European Central Bank** (ECB), which will itself control the operations of a European System of Central Banks.

Central Commission for the Navigation of the Rhine

With its headquarters in Strasbourg, the Commission has a strong claim to be the oldest European organization, having been established by the Congress of Vienna in 1815. It is responsible for all aspects of navigation on the Rhine. The four riparian states (France, Germany, the Netherlands and Switzerland) together with Belgium and the United Kingdom take part in the work of the Commission.

CEPT

See **European Conference of Postal and Telecommunications Administrations**.

CERN

See **European Organization for Nuclear Research**.

Chamber of States

In a federal state (see **federation**) with a two-chamber parliamentary system, the upper chamber may be composed of representatives of the provinces or regions that make up that state. The lower chamber, by contrast, is composed of directly elected representatives of the people. For example, in Germany the upper chamber (the Bundesrat) is composed of representatives of the *Länder* that make up the Federal Republic. It is sometimes suggested that within the European Union the **Council of Ministers** might develop one day into a Chamber of States, the clear implication being that the real decision-making power would shift to the lower chamber, i.e., the **European Parliament**.

Channel Islands

The Channel Islands and the Isle of Man are not part of the European Union and although free movement of agricultural produce and industrial goods between them and the Union was assured under the United Kingdom's 1972 Accession Treaty, they are not part of the Union's customs territory. They are accordingly exempt from Union rules on the free movement of labour, competition, right of establishment, value-added tax (VAT), and so on, and are not represented in the **European Parliament**.

Channel Tunnel

The idea of a 'fixed link' between England and France was first seriously put forward in the nineteenth century and trial lengths of tunnel were bored on both sides of the Channel in 1882. However, there was opposition to a tunnel as a potential threat to national security, and – in spite of French support – this opposition was still strong enough to lead the House of Commons to reject a tunnel scheme by 179 votes to 172 in June 1930. The steady postwar growth in cross-Channel passenger and freight traffic led to a tunnel scheme being approved by the British and French governments in 1966. Nine years later the project was abandoned. In 1982 the Eurotunnel consortium was formed, and their proposal for a rail-only tunnel was accepted. The Anglo-French Channel Tunnel Treaty was signed on 12 February 1986 and ratified the following year. Tunnelling started on the English side in December 1987 and on the French side two months later. The breakthrough was achieved on 1 December 1990, and six months later 150 kilometres of tunnelling (two 50-kilometre railway tunnels and a service tunnel beside them) had been completed. The tunnel was officially opened by the Queen and President Mitterrand in May 1994.

The Eurotunnel scheme is a tunnel extending between Folkestone and Calais, of which approximately 38 kilometres are under the sea bed. Cars, lorries and coaches are transported on special wagons by frequent shuttle services operating day and night. The tunnel may also be used by freight and passenger trains, the latter known as 'Eurostar', on the services between London, Paris and Brussels. In addition to its impact on the ferry services, it is estimated that the Channel Tunnel will save 20,000 aircraft movements a year.

Built at a cost of over £9 billion by a consortium of 10 French and British companies, the Channel Tunnel is the most ambitious of several major European transport infrastructure projects either planned or under construction (see **trans-European networks**). These include a bridge across the Straits of Messina between Sicily and the mainland of Italy, a bridge-and-tunnel scheme across the Great Belt (the sea channel between Sealand and Jutland in Denmark), and a bridge between Denmark and Sweden. The Channel Tunnel is the world's second longest railway tunnel, after the 53.85-kilometre Seikan tunnel between the islands of Honshu and Hokkaido in Japan bored at a depth some five times greater.

Charter of Paris

The signing of the Charter of Paris for a New Europe on 21 November 1990 by the states participating in the **Conference on Security and Cooperation in Europe** (CSCE) was widely regarded as the end of the Cold War. Made possible by the collapse of Soviet hegemony in central and eastern Europe, the Charter reiterated the ideas and principles set out in the **Helsinki Final Act** and marked the transition of the CSCE from a negotiating process to a permanent institution. The signatory states declared that 'henceforth our relations will be founded on respect and cooperation'.

In the section headed 'New structures and institutions of the CSCE process', the Charter noted the need for 'a new quality of political dialogue and cooperation and thus development of the structures of the CSCE'. The structures, set out in detail in a supplementary document, included a Council composed of Foreign Ministers, a Committee of Senior Officials, a small permanent secretariat based in Prague, an Office for Free Elections (since renamed) in Warsaw, a Conflict Prevention Centre in Vienna, and a CSCE parliamentary assembly. The CSCE Assembly met for the first time in Budapest in July 1992 and has a small secretariat in Copenhagen.

Christian Democracy

Christian Democracy, the largest and most successful family of centre and centre-right political parties in postwar Europe, can trace its intellectual antecedents back to the nineteenth century. Today's Christian Democrat (CD) parties are descended from those which sided with the Church in the disputes between Church and State, and which took the lead in opposing the essentially secular Socialist parties based upon universal suffrage.

By far the most influential CD parties are the Christian Democratic Union (CDU) of Germany and its Bavarian sister-party, the Christian Social Union, but CD parties are also well established in the **Benelux** countries. Until its recent collapse, the Italian CD party was the second largest in Europe, and had been in power, alone or in various coalitions, since the war. By contrast, CD parties have always been weak in Scandinavia. In France, the Mouvement Républicain Populaire (of which **Robert Schuman** was a prominent member) was overshadowed by parties made up of followers of **Charles de Gaulle**. In Spain and Portugal the legacy of the Franco and Salazar dictatorships was to secularize politics, thus ruling out explicitly confessional parties, although in both countries the CDs have close allies. In Ireland the CDs are represented by Fine Gael, and in Greece by New Democracy.

In the **European Parliament** the CDs and their allies form the Group of the European People's Party (EPP; see **transnational political parties**), the second largest of the **political groups**. For almost 25 years CDs were by far the largest group in the Parliament, but the arrival of British Labour MEPs in 1975 finally gave the advantage to the Socialists. Many newly emergent parties in central and eastern Europe claim a kinship with Christian Democracy. Europe-wide, the European Union of Christian Democrats (EUCD) has some 45 member parties. The EUCD is part of the Christian Democratic International, which links European CD parties with CD parties in other countries, mainly in Central and South America.

Christian Democrats, including **Konrad Adenauer** and **Alcide de Gasperi** as well as Schuman, were amongst the most active early supporters of European integration. Unlike the Socialists, the CD parties voted solidly in favour of the **Treaty of Paris** and the **Treaty of Rome** when they were submitted to **national parliaments** in the 1950s. The first president of the **European Commission** was a German CD, **Walter Hallstein**. Other prominent CDs include former Italian Foreign Minister, Prime Minister and President of the European Parliament, Emilio Colombo (see **Genscher–Colombo Plan**) and the Belgian Leo Tindemans (see **Tindemans Report**).

All CD parties lay emphasis in their policy pronouncements on the role of people in society, and on the need for the free market to be tempered by social justice. Many have strong links with Christian trade unions and the Roman Catholic Church. On institutional questions CDs are federalists almost without exception. They are supporters of the Atlantic Alliance. Some CD parties take their confessional basis very seriously, and this leads them for example to condemn abortion and to oppose most forms of genetic engineering. The EPP manifesto for the 1994 European elections was entitled *Unity in Diversity*.

The problem for the CDs in recent years has been the fact that although CD parties are well established in most member states of the Union, the Union is set to expand northwards and eastwards into countries lacking any CD tradition – a problem that the Socialists do not have to face. This means either a compromise with orthodox CD principles in the search for new allies or a diminished standing in an enlarged Union. The prospect of an alliance with the British and Danish Conservatives in the European Parliament brought the issue to a head: and with some misgivings the CDs opted for compromise. Within a few years, the EPP will have a majority of parties that are not, strictly speaking, CD parties in terms of their origin, history or source of inspiration. The success in recent years of right-wing parties has allowed the CDs to retain their self-image as the parties of the centre, but once they no longer have opponents on their right they may find it increasingly difficult to find a position to occupy that distinguishes them from moderate Socialists.

Although there is a very small CD party in the United Kingdom, it is not affiliated to the EUCD. Some commentators have suggested that had Christian Democracy ever taken root in the United Kingdom, it would have been amongst moderate members of the Labour Party. It was Labour's postwar Chancellor, Sir Stafford Cripps, who wrote *Towards Christian Democracy* (1945).

R. E. M. Irving, *The Christian Democratic Parties of Western Europe* (Edinburgh, 1979), is useful as background. Michael Burgess, 'Political Catholicism, European unity and the rise of Christian Democracy' is a revealing essay (see Smith and Stirk, *Making the New Europe*, 1990).

Churchill, Winston (1874–1965)

Winston Churchill's reputation as one of the pioneers of postwar European integration rests primarily on his **Zürich speech** of 1946 (see also **United States of Europe**), but, as Michael Charlton and others have shown, Churchill's belief that the future of western Europe was bound up with closer integration was expressed five years earlier in his 'morning thoughts'

(*The Price of Victory*). Churchill was one of the first political figures to express support for Coudenhove-Kalergi's **Pan-Europa**, in an article in the New York *Saturday Evening Post* of 15 February 1930. After the war Churchill devoted several major speeches to the theme of a united Europe, of which one of the best-known was delivered at the 1948 **Congress of Europe** in The Hague and in which he called for a 'European Assembly' as 'the voice of United Europe' (see also **European Army**). However, on being returned to power as Prime Minister in 1951 Churchill did not materially alter the European policies of the previous Labour Government, notably their rejection of the **Schuman Plan**.

This apparent contradiction may be explained by Churchill's ambivalent attitude to British participation in moves towards European unity. In his *Saturday Evening Post* article Churchill said:

> The attitude of Great Britain toward unification or 'federal links' would, in the first instance, be determined by her dominant conception of a United British Empire. Every step that tends to make Europe more prosperous and more peaceful is conducive to British interests ... We have our own dream and our own task. We are with Europe but not of it. We are linked, but not comprised. We are interested and associated, but not absorbed.

In Zürich 16 years later he referred to Great Britain only as 'the friend and sponsor of the new Europe', but in a speech in the Albert Hall on 14 May 1948 (a week after the Congress in The Hague) he said that 'if Europe united is to be a living force, Britain will have to play her full part as a member of the European family'. Earlier that year he had said that 'this European policy of unity can perfectly well be reconciled with and adjusted to our obligations to the Commonwealth and Empire of which we are the heart and centre' (House of Commons, 23 January 1948). However, as presented in Martin Gilbert's biography, the balance of the evidence seems to be that Churchill (by now well into his 80s) did not favour British membership of the **European Economic Community** (EEC) when the question arose in the 1960s.

Churchill's view of the United Kingdom's world role was at the point of overlap between three interlocking circles: the Commonwealth, the Atlantic Alliance and Europe. What he would have thought of the supranational institutions on which the European Union is founded must remain a matter for speculation (although some idea may be gained from his view of the Schuman Plan; see **European Coal and Steel Community**). With regard to **sovereignty**, he admitted in The Hague that European unity required 'some sacrifice or merger of national sovereignty', but he added that 'it is also possible ... to regard it as the gradual assumption by all the nations concerned of that larger sovereignty which can also protect their diverse and distinctive customs and characteristics and their national traditions'.

Churchill's active career was exceptionally long and eventful. His views certainly changed over time (as indeed did the United Kingdom's circumstances) and perhaps at no point were fully thought through, but the fact that he lent his enormous prestige to the cause of European unity in the decade after the war was of cardinal importance.

Citizens' Europe
See **People's Europe**.

Citizenship

The **Maastricht Treaty** amended the **Treaty of Rome** to create citizenship of the European Union. Under Article 8 EEC, 'every person holding the nationality of a Member State shall be a citizen of the Union'. Succeeding Articles set out the rights appertaining to citizenship: 'to move and reside freely within the territory of the Member States' (Article 8a); to vote and stand for election in municipal and European elections in the member state in which he or she resides (Article 8b); to receive protection from diplomatic and consular authorities of any member state in any country in which the member state of which he or she is a national is not represented (Article 8c); to petition the **European Parliament** and refer matters to the **Ombudsman** (Article 8d). Under Article 8e these rights may be strengthened or supplemented by the **Council of Ministers**, acting unanimously on a proposal from the **Commission** and after consulting the European Parliament.

In a **Declaration** annexed to the Treaty it is specified that 'the question whether an individual possesses the nationality of a Member State shall be settled solely by reference to the national law of the Member State concerned'. States may forward to the Council **presidency** details of those who are to be considered their nationals for the purpose of establishing their claim to citizenship of the Union. This is particularly important for the United Kingdom, which in the British Nationality Act 1981 has defined several distinct categories of British national; of these, only British citizens, British subjects with the right of abode and those who are British Dependent Territories citizens by virtue of a connection with Gibraltar are entitled to citizenship of the Union.

Many opponents of the Maastricht Treaty suggested that the creation of Union citizenship, an initiative of the Spanish government, was one more move in the direction of a European superstate. Although it is true that the idea of citizenship is normally associated with a state (but not exclusively:

we may speak of 'Commonwealth citizens'), the Declaration noted above specifically leaves entitlement to citizenship in the hands of member states. In fact, citizenship of the Union is no more than a very modest enhancement of the rights nationals of member states already enjoy, and the most important of them, the right to move and reside freely anywhere in the Union, is quite significantly restricted by various provisions designed to prevent people of inadequate means becoming a 'burden' on the social security system of the member state where they choose to reside. It will be noted too that voting in national elections anywhere in the Union is not a generalized right. All proposals to this effect meet with objections from member states with large numbers of potential voters possessing the nationality of another member state (for example, Luxembourg has many Portuguese).

Citizenship is to be distinguished from the measures taken in connection with a **People's Europe**, although several of these, such as the **European passport**, are intended to give citizens of the member states a livelier sense of their new status as citizens of the Union. There is a useful politico-legal study of citizenship in Elizabeth Meehan, *Citizenship and the European Community* (1990). The politico-legal issues raised by citizenship are discussed in Rey Koslowski, 'Intra-EU migration, citizenship and political union', *Journal of Common Market Studies*, Vol. 32, no. 3, September 1994.

Cockfield White Paper

In March 1985 the **European Council** decided to give priority to the creation of 'a single large market by 1992', and called upon the **Commission** to draw up 'a detailed programme with a specific timetable before its next meeting'. The task fell to Lord Cockfield, the newly appointed Commissioner responsible for trade matters within the Community (the so-called '**internal market**'). The White Paper he produced for the June 1985 meeting of the European Council in Milan identified some 300 legislative measures that would be needed to establish the **Single Market**. These measures were concerned with three kinds of barrier to trade: physical barriers (frontier controls), technical barriers (such as different product standards), and fiscal barriers (different rates of excise duty and value-added tax). The list of measures was accompanied by a timetable specifying deadlines both for Commission draft proposals and for the Council's final decisions. The Milan meeting of the European Council endorsed the White Paper, the ambitiousness of which was a powerful influence on the negotiations that led to the **Single European Act** (SEA; see also **Cecchini Report, non-Europe**).

Lord Cockfield was never in any doubt about the political importance of the Single Market. In the conclusion of his White Paper he wrote:

Europe stands at the crossroads. We either go ahead – with resolution and determination – or we drop back into mediocrity. We can now either resolve to complete the integration of the economies of Europe; or, through a lack of political will to face the immense problems involved, we can simply allow Europe to develop into no more than a free trade area.

His own account of the Single Market programme is to be found in his essay 'The real significance of 1992' in Crouch and Marquand (eds), *The Politics of 1992* (1990) and in Cockfield, *The European Union: creating the Single Market* (Oxford, 1994).

Co-decision procedure

'Co-decision' is a procedure introduced by the **Maastricht Treaty** to reinforce the role of the **European Parliament** in the legislative process. It is set out in Article 189b of the **Treaty of Rome**. The main difference between the co-decision procedure and the **cooperation procedure** is that the former allows the Parliament at the final stage to veto by an absolute majority a legislative measure upon which agreement cannot be reached with the **Council of Ministers**.

The co-decision procedure was modelled on a procedure that already existed in relation to the **Budget** of the European Union, under which the Parliament and the Council, as the 'joint budgetary authority', endeavour to reach agreement in a **conciliation** committee. In the absence of such an agreement the Parliament can, as a last resort and by an absolute majority, reject the Budget.

One important side-effect of the co-decision procedure is that it weakens the power of the **Commission**. By negotiating in the conciliation committee, the Council and the European Parliament can largely exclude the Commission. Equally, the procedure allows the Council to side-step the requirement that it can adopt only by unanimity amendments rejected by the Commission, since failure to agree in conciliation allows the Council to return to the **common position**.

The key areas to which the co-decision procedure applies are the free movement of workers (Article 49 EEC), **freedom of establishment** (Article 54 EEC), the services sector (Article 66 EEC), **Single Market** measures (Articles 100a–b EEC), education (Article 126 EEC), culture (Article 128 EEC), health and consumer protection (Articles 129 and 129a EEC), **trans-European networks** (Article 129b EEC), and the environmental action programmes (Article 130s.3 EEC). The Parliament has pressed for co-decision to be extended into most other areas.

Cohesion

The word 'cohesion' was introduced into the **Treaty of Rome** by the 1986 **Single European Act** (SEA), which added a new Title V on 'economic and social cohesion' (now Articles 130a–e EEC). This was done on the insistence of the poorer member states, which feared that the completion of the **Single Market** would further strengthen the position of the more prosperous states. 'Cohesion' was the term used to encompass the notions of solidarity and harmonious economic development. The basic text was agreed at a meeting of the European Council in Luxembourg in December 1985.

Cohesion Fund

The original text on **cohesion** in the **Treaty of Rome** did little more than reiterate the role of the **structural funds** and provide for better coordination between them. This did not satisfy the poorer states, because although by 1986 several of them were benefiting from the **Integrated Mediterranean Programmes** (IMPs), these programmes were due to end in 1992. In Maastricht in December 1991 agreement was reached on a further change to the Treaty requiring the **Council of Ministers** to establish a Cohesion Fund by December 1993 (Article 130d EEC). The purpose of the Fund is 'to provide a financial contribution to projects in the fields of environment and **trans-European networks** in the area of transport infrastructure'. A protocol on economic and social cohesion annexed to the **Maastricht Treaty** restricted access to the Cohesion Fund to member states with a per capita gross domestic product (GDP) of less than 90 per cent of the Union average (i.e., to Greece, Ireland, Portugal and Spain) and obliged them to pursue economic policies tending towards **convergence**. These conditions were further refined at the Edinburgh meeting of the European Council in December 1992 (see **Edinburgh Growth Initiative**). Appropriations from the **Budget** for the Cohesion Fund amounted to £1.7 billion (2.15 billion ECUs) in 1993, rising to £2.1 billion (2.6 billion ECUs) in 1999.

College of Europe

Founded in 1949 in Bruges, Belgium, on the basis of a resolution adopted by the European Cultural Conference (see **European Cultural Centre**), the College of Europe offers postgraduate courses in various disciplines relevant to European integration. It has about 200 students of about 20 different nationalities; the languages of instruction are English and French. The lecture to mark the opening of the College's academic year is normally delivered by a well-known European figure, the most celebrated recent example being Margaret Thatcher's **Bruges speech** of September 1988. Although the College is in part financed by a contribution from the **Budget** of the European Union, it is not a Union body (see also **European Institute of Public Administration, European University Institute**).

COMECON

COMECON, or CMEA (the Council for Mutual Economic Assistance), was established in January 1949 to promote and facilitate all forms of economic cooperation between the Communist states of central and eastern Europe. Founder members were the USSR, Bulgaria, Czechoslovakia, Hungary, Poland and Romania, countries that had been prevented by Stalin from taking part in the **Marshall Plan** and from joining the **Organization for European Economic Cooperation** (OEEC). Membership was later extended to Albania (1949–61) and the German Democratic Republic (1950), and to non-European Communist states: Mongolia (1962), Cuba (1972) and Vietnam (1978). Under Article 4 of the COMECON Charter adopted in 1959, all decisions had to be unanimous, but in fact the organization was overwhelmingly dominated by the USSR. The headquarters of COMECON were in Moscow.

The first formal contacts between COMECON and the European Community took place in 1976, at a time when the USSR was still barely prepared to recognize the Community and when the Community disputed COMECON's right to negotiate on behalf of its member states. Unsurprisingly, these contacts led to no concrete result and were broken off after the USSR's invasion of Afghanistan in 1980. Resumed six years later, the negotiations resulted in a mutual recognition agreement in 1988, by which time the Community had concluded commercial agreements (in most cases limited to specific sectors) with Bulgaria, Czechoslovakia, Hungary, Poland and Romania. Within a year or so of the 1988 agreements the Community had wide-ranging commercial agreements with all European COMECON states except the German Democratic Republic (whose trade with the Community was covered by special arrangements: see **German reunification**), including the USSR.

The collapse of the Soviet empire in central and eastern Europe in 1989–90 completely transformed trading patterns between COMECON states and led to the strongest of the COMECON economies, that of the German Democratic Republic, becoming part of the European Community. In June 1991 the remaining members of COMECON resolved to wind up the organization; this was formally accomplished in September 1991. Since then, several former members of COMECON have expressed interest in joining the European Union and **Europe Agreements** have been concluded with Hungary, Poland, the Czech Republic, Slovakia, Bulgaria, Romania and the Baltic states.

COMETT

The Community Action Programme in Education and Training for Technology, operational since 1987, promoted cooperation between industry and universities, with the help of training partnerships and exchanges, and databanks, conferences and seminars on COMETT projects. Since 1995 COMETT has been absorbed into the **Leonardo** programme.

Comité Européen de Normalisation (CEN)

Set up in 1961, CEN is a body concerned with laying down standard technical specifications for manufactured goods in all fields except electrical goods (for which the equivalent body is CENELEC, set up in 1973). Eighteen countries take part in CEN and CENELEC, which are financed by grants from the **Commission** and contributions from industry. CEN and CENELEC have taken over much of the detailed work of **harmonization** since the adoption in 1985 of the 'new approach'.

Comitology

The word 'comitology' is used to denote the complex of issues that centre upon the various types of committee which oversee the implementation of **Community law**. The role of these committees has given rise to disputes with direct bearing on the balance of power between national authorities and institutions of the European Union, notably the **European Commission** and the **European Parliament**. Not yet fully assimilated into English, 'comitology' is a translation of the French *comitologie*. It was first used in C. Northcote Parkinson's *Parkinson's Law* (1958) and defined in his *In-laws and Outlaws* (1962) as the study of committees and how they operate ('the latest of the biological sciences').

Article 155 of the **Treaty of Rome** states that, in addition to the powers of decision it enjoys as of right, the European Commission exercises 'the powers conferred on it by the **Council** [of Ministers] for the implementation of the rules laid down by the latter' (i.e., Community law). Both types of Commission power are subject to the supervision of various committees (see below), all of them composed of national experts with a Commission official in the chair. Their subject matter is for the most part highly technical: for example, seed types, food additives, the thickness of safety glass. However, many committees deliberate on matters of very great concern to the interested parties as well as to national governments, and their essentially secretive mode of operation has prompted fears about the extent to which they are subject to adequate democratic control.

It was recognized at the time of the negotiations that led to the **Single European Act** (sea) that the abundance of technical legislation made necessary by the **Single Market** programme would in turn lead to a further proliferation of committees. Accordingly, the opportunity was taken to clear the undergrowth by classifying the various types of committee and codifying their powers. The Commission produced a proposal that the Council adopted in 1987 in a radically modified form, against the wishes of the Commission and the European Parliament, in a fashion inconsistent (so it was alleged) with member states' undertakings at the time of the sea. The Parliament sought to have the Council's decision annulled by the **Court of Justice**, but the action was rejected as inadmissible.

In the 1987 decision the three basic types of committee were laid down as follows:

1 An advisory committee, which is empowered to deliver **Opinions** on Commission proposals; the Commission is required only to 'take utmost account' of such Opinions (Procedure I).
2 A management committee, which similarly delivers Opinions on Commission proposals; in this case the Commission can be forced to incorporate the committee's Opinion by the Council acting by **qualified majority**. If the Committee fails to deliver an Opinion, the Commission proposal takes immediate effect (Procedure II). Management committees are most commonly used in connection with the detailed implementation of the **Common Agricultural Policy** (cap).
3 A regulatory committee is similar to a management committee, except that in the event of the rejection of a Commission proposal or the failure to deliver an Opinion the matter is referred to the Council. Under this procedure (III), the Council may reject the proposal by simple majority within three months.

The choice of which type of committee is responsible for overseeing the implementation of a piece of legislation is specified in the legislation itself, to which the Parliament may propose amendments. In a report to the European Parliament in 1989 the Commission professed itself to be content with the system, on the grounds that it was normally able to enlist the support of the national experts who sit on the various committees and in the light of the fact that reference to Council (with the possibility of a veto) under Procedure III above was very rare indeed.

The European Parliament is less content, regarding the committee system as part of the **democratic deficit**. Without necessarily challenging the need for such committees or altering the basic typology, the Parliament has tended to favour opening up committee proceedings or laying upon committees the obligation to keep the Parliament's own committees in touch with their deliberations and decisions. The Commission is understandably ambivalent about these ideas, since it could not necessarily count upon the Parliament as an ally.

Commission

See **European Commission**.

Committee of the Regions

The **Maastricht Treaty** established a new European Union body, the Committee of the Regions (Article 198a EEC). This was done at the instigation of Germany and Spain, both countries with a strong regional element in their constitutional arrangements. The Committee, composed of 222 'representatives of regional and local bodies', has 'advisory status' and shares a joint secretariat in Brussels with the **Economic and Social Committee**. Since July 1994 it has had its own secretary-general. Members of the Committee of the Regions and their substitutes are appointed for a four-year term by the **Council of Ministers** on proposals from the member states. Although this is not required by the Treaty, nearly all members of the Committee hold elective office at regional or local level in their countries of origin (see also **regionalism**).

Consultation of the Committee of the Regions is specifically required by the Treaty only in a very small number of areas. However, under Article 198c EEC either the Council or the **European Commission** may consult the Committee if it thinks fit, and the Committee itself may on its own initiative submit **Opinions** on matters affecting regional interests.

Common Agricultural Policy (CAP)

The CAP has been for many years the most important European policy in terms of the number of people directly affected, its share of the **Budget** and the extent of the powers transferred from national to European level. Its origins may be traced back to the original compact between France and West Germany when the **Treaty of Rome** was first being drafted by **the Six**: guaranteed markets for French agricultural products in exchange for wider markets for German manufactured goods.

The objectives of the CAP are set out in Article 39 EEC: an increase in agricultural productivity by means of 'technical progress and ... the rational development of agricultural production', 'a fair standard of living for the agricultural community', stable markets, the 'availability of supplies', and 'reasonable prices' for consumers. Underpinning these objectives are three essential principles: the free movement of agricultural products within the member states, **Community preference** and financial solidarity in the sense that all member states must share in the costs arising from the CAP.

That agriculture should be subsidized was not in doubt, since in common with all other European countries the Six already supported their agricultural sectors in various ways. In seeking to establish the basis for a common system, the Six opted for support by means of price mechanisms rather than direct income support (a decision taken at the **Stresa Conference**), operated with the aid of European market organizations (usually known as regimes) for the various products (Article 40 EEC). The first of such organizations, for cereals, pork, eggs and poultry meat, came into effect in 1962, several others following over the next four years.

Initially, the **Commission** sought only to coordinate national agricultural policies. The first attempt at reform came with the **Mansholt Plan**, first published in 1968. The Plan sought to reduce the number of people employed in agriculture and to encourage the formation of larger, more efficient units of agricultural production. These reforms were to be effected through the 'guidance' section of the **European Agricultural Guidance and Guarantee Fund** (EAGGF, more commonly known by its French acronym, FEOGA) set up in 1962 and divided into two sections in 1964. Although eventually adopted in a less ambitious form, the Mansholt Plan set the pattern for the development of the CAP.

It is easy to understand why in the Treaty objectives of the CAP, drawn up at a time when food shortages in Western Europe were still a vivid memory, such emphasis was laid on increases in agricultural productivity. However, by the early 1980s greater efficiency, backed by technical progress, was resulting in huge, unsaleable surpluses of certain products, at an enormous cost to the Budget. The taxpayer, it was said, was paying twice over, first through higher prices and second through subsidized storage or disposal of unwanted produce. Subsidized exports were doing damage to other countries' export markets, and notorious episodes like the sale of cut-price butter to the USSR further damaged the credibility of the CAP with the public.

In 1983 the Commission published proposals for fundamental reform, which were followed up two years later by a Green Paper. Basically, the Commission sought to bring supply and demand into balance, cut back on open-ended price support, compensate farmers for loss of income and introduce new ways ('stabilizers') of reducing production still further in certain problem sectors. However, it was not until February 1988 that the **European Council** was able to agree on a comprehensive package of reform measures, including an 'agricultural guideline' limiting the growth of CAP expenditure to 74 per cent of the growth in the Budget overall (see **future financing**).

The 1988 decisions were followed up by further measures affecting the CAP, such as the reform of the **structural funds**, the extension of **quotas**, the introduction of **set-aside**, measures to encourage early retirement from agriculture, and schemes to encourage farmers to use less intensive production techniques and to diversify away from products already in surplus.

The reform process was taken a stage further with the publication of additional Commission papers in February 1991 and July 1991. These papers, put forward by Ray MacSharry, the Irish Commissioner responsible for the CAP, were the basis for another reform package agreed by the **Council of Ministers** at a 50-hour meeting in May 1992. The centrepiece was a move away from near-total reliance on price support towards direct income aids, to take place over the period 1993–6 and initially affecting only the main product sectors. This was accompanied by substantial reductions in guaranteed prices and the introduction of extremely complicated schemes to compensate farmers in the short term for loss of income. It is these schemes that in recent years have involved farmers in so much detailed paperwork. At least initially, the cost to the Budget has been greater, but in the long run the reforms should reduce the pressure on the Budget, make the CAP more consistent with the protection of the environment, and answer the criticisms made in the **General Agreement on Tariffs and Trade** (GATT) and elsewhere that the Union is failing to heed the worldwide trend towards a reduction of subsidies in agriculture.

The reforms have not altered the procedures under which the CAP is managed. The special Committee on Agriculture, an offshoot of **COREPER** (see also **national representations**), prepares meetings of the Council of Agriculture Ministers, with the aid of several other specialized committees. Each product covered by the CAP has its own **management committee**. The system of price support has many variations, but basically it requires the Commission to present annually a set of price proposals for the following marketing year. These proposals are discussed with the **European Parliament** (although expenditure in this sector is classified as **compulsory expenditure** under Article 203 EEC) and eventually agreed by the Council of Ministers. If the price that can be obtained for a product within the Union falls below the agreed price, unsold produce may be purchased and taken into **intervention** and stored for future sale or disposal. If the produce can be sold outside the Union but only at a price below the agreed price, then the producer becomes entitled to an export refund to cover the difference. Intervention buying is by far the largest single item in the whole Budget. A further measure of protection is provided by levies on imported produce so that it enjoys no price advantage over what is produced within the Union. Alternatively, domestic producers may receive some form of production subsidy. Not all the products covered by CAP regimes benefit from both intervention and external protection. Overall, such regimes cover some 90 per cent of total agricultural production within the Union.

Within this very broad overall picture, all kinds of special schemes – for particular products, for particular types of farming, for particular regions, for small farms, etc. – have been introduced, some only of short duration, many of them prompted less by strictly agricultural considerations than by the requirements of social, regional or environmental policy or by those emanating from international pressure.

The CAP is further complicated by the agri-monetary system, the so-called 'green currencies'. The breakdown in 1969 of the Bretton Woods international monetary system resulted in a degree of price instability that was in conflict with the requirement in Article 39 EEC for stable markets (see above). Accordingly, a method for converting CAP prices into the national currencies in which farmers are actually paid ('green rates') was introduced, together with monetary compensatory amounts (MCAs) to be paid or levied on member states' trade in agricultural products to prevent any exploitation of the difference between market rates and green rates. Initially introduced on a temporary basis, the agrimonetary system was a central feature of the CAP for over 20 years, and was eventually radically modified as part of the 1992 reforms. The new system, which applies to the bulk of CAP expenditure (including the **Common Fisheries Policy**), eliminated MCAs as incompatible with the **Single Market** and brought green rates and market rates more closely into line pending the accomplishment of **Economic and Monetary Union** (EMU), when farmers can be paid in ECUs. Further refinements to the system in the form of conversion factors, reference periods and compensatory aids were added to take account of fluctuations in the value of national currencies and falls in farm incomes. The system was agreed with great difficulty by the Council of Ministers in December 1992.

This outline of the mechanisms that govern the CAP illustrates the extent to which, since its inception, it has allowed ample scope for **fraud**. The system is so complex that fair and equal enforcement of the rules governing payments from the CAP – a matter largely in the hands of member states' authorities – is extremely difficult. Efforts to make the system simpler have met with only limited success.

The CAP has long been an irritant in international trade relations. First, Commonwealth countries such as Australia and New Zealand resented the loss of British markets as a consequence of the United Kingdom's accession to the Community in 1973, a loss only partially compensated for by special arrangements for butter and lamb. More recently, Australia and New Zealand became leading members of the Cairns Group of countries fiercely critical of the Community's stance on agricultural matters in GATT. The United States too had some well-publicized arguments with the Community over such matters as subsidies for oilseed production, and these were not resolved until the so-called 'Washington Accord' of November 1992 (almost two years after the Uruguay Round of GATT negotiations had been due to end). More generally, the CAP and the possibility that its principles and mechanisms might be extended to other sectors have contributed to the fear of a **Fortress Europe**. The fact remains that in spite of the protection afforded under the CAP and the degree of self-sufficiency, the Union is by far the world's largest importer of agricultural products.

Throughout its 30-year history the CAP has attracted criticism not only as the cuckoo in the budgetary nest but also as a uniquely wasteful, bureaucratic way of supporting agriculture, managed on the basis of marathon negotiating sessions in Brussels amongst ministers over whom agricultural lobbies exercise an unhealthy sway. The CAP, it is said, shields farmers from market disciplines, prevents food from being bought on the 'world market' and cuts across other policies. This is particularly true in the United Kingdom, with its small and relatively efficient agricultural sector (the result of an agricultural revolution two centuries ago) and a public used to 'cheap food' for several generations by virtue of the Empire and Commonwealth connection. The United Kingdom has a particular grievance in that low receipts from agricultural spending were one of the causes of the **British Budget problem**. The CAP's defenders point to it as the 'cornerstone' of European integration and as the policy by which the member states have achieved self-sufficiency in most temperate products, relatively stable prices and a growth in farm incomes at a time when expenditure on food (as a percentage of consumer expenditure overall) is steadily falling throughout the industrialized world. Food prices have risen more slowly than prices generally and, in any case, decisions on prices taken under the CAP directly affect only the price paid to the producer: prices in the shops reflect other costs, such as processing, packaging, transport and retail margins. Some of the most dramatic rises have been in relation to products not covered by the CAP, such as coffee and tea. Moreover, the CAP has promoted and facilitated a shift away from employment on the land, which at any other period of European history would have been accompanied by extreme hardship and possibly violent revolution. In 1958 employment in agriculture within the Six was some 20 per cent of total employment. By 1990 it had fallen to 5.5 per cent (the 1992 average for the European Union overall was 5.8 per cent).

Together with agriculture itself, the CAP is going through a time of great uncertainty. Budgetary pressures will remain acute; there are new member states to accommodate, with heavily subsidized agricultural sectors and many mountainous or sub-arctic regions to consider; and there is the need to open up the Union to agricultural exports from central and eastern Europe. In several member states agricultural lobbies remain powerful, backed by a significant rural vote, and in the European Parliament the Committee on Agriculture has often shown itself to be ambivalent about reform proposals involving hardship for farmers. And there are obvious injustices in a system that tends to reward large, efficient farmers in prosperous countries with relatively small agricultural sectors such as Denmark and the Netherlands. For these and for other reasons, the CAP will remain a sensitive area (proof of this is the fact that the agricultural portfolio in the Commission is never given to someone from one of the large member states). The resolution of the problems affecting the CAP is made no easier by the fact that the definition of 'efficiency' in agriculture is no longer clear-cut and the Treaty objectives no longer self-evidently right.

Common Commercial Policy (CCP)

The CCP was named in Article 3 of the **Treaty of Rome** as one of the activities of the **European Economic Community**, and its main elements were set out in Articles 110 to 116 EEC. Linked as they were in a **customs union**, it was obviously essential for the member states to draw up common policies with respect to their trading relations with the rest of the world. Article 112 EEC required them to harmonize their systems of export aids, and Article 113 EEC identified the need for 'uniform principles' to underpin the CCP with regard to tariff rates (see **Common External Tariff**), the conclusion of trade agreements, liberalization measures, the promotion of exports, and instruments of commercial defence against dumping and subsidies (see **anti-dumping**). The role of the **Commission** as negotiator on behalf of the member states (see also **Article 113 Committee**) is laid down in this Article, under which the **Council of Ministers** is empowered to act by **qualified majority**. The powers of the European Parliament in this field are described under **assent procedure**.

The European Union is by far the biggest trading bloc in the world. Excluding trade between member states, the Union's exports are approximately 15 per cent of the world's total, comfortably outstripping those of the United States and Japan. The Union's position is still stronger if the exports of the countries linked to it in the **European Economic Area** (EEA) are also included. The Union has an even larger share of total imports, and is the world's biggest importer of agricultural products. Overall, the Union has had a steadily growing trade deficit with the rest of the world since 1986, but is an important net exporter in the services sector. Member states have substantial investments in very many countries. The Union itself has trade or **Cooperation Agreements** with some 115 countries worldwide (see also **Association Agreements**, **Europe Agreements**).

Historically, the European Union has been in favour of free trade, calling for the 'progressive abolition of restrictions on international trade and the lowering of customs barriers' (Article 110 EEC). The Commission represents the member states in the trade talks conducted under the auspices of the **General Agreement on Tariffs and Trade** (GATT) – since 1995 the World Trade Organization (WTO) – and in other bodies such as the **Organization for Economic Cooperation and Development** (OECD) and the United Nations Conference on Trade and Development (UNCTAD). Once the effects of the **Generalized System of Preferences** (GSP) are taken into account, the Union has one of the lowest average levels of industrial tariff in the world (although this low average conceals high tariffs in certain 'sensitive' sectors such as textiles and consumer electronics).

The sectoral breakdown of the Union's visible trade has changed little in the past few years. Surpluses in chemicals, machinery and transport equipment do not quite make up for deficits in raw materials and energy. Other sectors are broadly in balance. Geographically, the outstanding change has been the steady growth since 1980 in the proportion of overall trade taken up by industrialized countries at the expense of developing countries (although the latter still represent about a third of the total). The United States is by far the Union's most important trading partner, followed by Japan (for imports) and Switzerland (for exports). The states of South-east Asia (Hong Kong, Singapore, South Korea and Taiwan) are amongst the fastest-growing markets. However, partly as a consequence of the **Single Market** programme, trade between member states is growing more quickly than trade between the Union and the rest of the world (see **intra-Community trade**).

In spite of substantial national and political differences between member states in trade policy, the Union has, on the whole, achieved a high degree of coherence and consistency in trade matters. This is not to say that it has always acted wisely or even in good time (such are the difficulties in arriving at common positions), but in most areas member states have accepted the need to act as one. Notorious exceptions to this include the French and Italian restrictions on imports of Japanese cars, the unilateral embargo introduced by Greece on trade with the former Yugoslav republic of Macedonia, and the last-minute bargaining instigated by France over the GATT agreement. The Union has also largely succeeded in dispelling the fears of a **Fortress Europe** prompted by the Single Market programme, in spite of the recession still affecting the economies of many member states.

Of great importance to the overall pattern of the Union's trade in the longer term will be the opening up of new markets in central and eastern Europe. The Europe Agreements provide these countries with asymmetric (i.e., non-reciprocal) access to the Union's market, but problems remain in some of the sectors (steel, for example) in which they might have a hope of competing.

In the institutional field, problems may arise over the relation between the CCP and the **Common Foreign and Security Policy** (CFSP) since a trade embargo may be used as a political weapon. A new Article 228a was added to the Treaty of Rome by the **Maastricht Treaty**, empowering the Council in the event of a CFSP decision 'to interrupt or to reduce, in part or completely, economic relations with one or more third countries', to take 'the necessary urgent measures . . . by a qualified majority on a proposal from the Commission'. In such circumstances it is probable that the trade of some member states will be worse affected than that of others, and the use of the qualified majority could hardly fail to be controversial.

Common Customs Tariff

See **Common External Tariff**.

Common External Tariff (CET)

The Common External Tariff (CET), also known as the Common Customs Tariff (CCT), is the means whereby duties are imposed on goods entering the Union. A necessary feature of a **customs union**, the CET is managed by the **Commission** under the **Common Commercial Policy** (CCP). Revenues from the imposition of the CET form part of the Union's **own resources**.

Common Fisheries Policy (CFP)

Article 38 of the **Treaty of Rome** makes it clear that fish and fish products are to be considered as agricultural products, and in consequence the CFP is based on the same principles as the **Common Agricultural Policy** (CAP). The first CFP was drawn up by **the Six** in the early 1970s with a view to presenting the applicant states – Denmark, Ireland, Norway and the United Kingdom, all of them with important fishing interests – with a *fait accompli*. It was partly the unacceptability of this CFP that caused Norway to vote against membership in the 1972 referendum. The major concession secured by the three new member states was an extension of coastal fishing rights from 6 to 12 miles (9.6 to 19.3 kilometres), a significant move away from the principle of free access enshrined in the Treaty.

The situation was radically transformed in 1975 by the unilateral declaration by several Atlantic states of 200-mile (322-kilometre) exclusive economic zones (EEZs). These EEZs, confirmed in 1982 in the Convention on the Law of the Sea, had the effect of denying access to many fishing grounds traditionally fished by fleets from the member states. The following year a revised CFP was agreed for a 10-year period, to be followed by a review and an extension for a further 10 years. This review was completed by the **Council of Ministers** in December 1992 and a new Regulation adopted. Spain and Portugal have been fully incorporated into the CFP since 1 January 1996, in line with the 10-year **transitional period** provided for in their Treaties of Accession.

In its present form the CFP recognizes the 12-mile coastal exclusion zones (see above) as long as 'traditional rights' are respected and maintains the system of total allowable catches (TACs) and quotas. The most controversial aspect of the CFP is the decommissioning of vessels and the payment of compensation to owners and fishermen. Technological advances, which make fishing more efficient, together with the need to conserve fish stocks have resulted in the total fleet (some 80,000 vessels) being greatly in excess of actual requirements. The **Commission** proposed very drastic cuts and the creation of a new Objective 6 under the **structural funds** regulation, which would have allowed fishing communities affected by the cuts to receive assistance. In the event the cuts were made less drastic and the Objective 6 proposal was turned down, but the need for a licensing system for fishing boats was accepted.

Fishing is an important industry in many peripheral regions where there are few alternative forms of employment. Overall, fisheries (including both at sea and on-shore activities) employ more than 600,000 people in the member states, all of which (with the exception of Ireland) are net importers of fish and fish products, for which demand continues to rise. At the same time, the scientific evidence points to the need to conserve fish stocks more prudently, such stocks having been badly affected by overfishing and marine pollution.

Some of the pressure on the fish stocks in the European Union's waters is relieved by agreements that allow access to the EEZs of other countries. There are now about 30 agreements on fisheries, some of them allowing reciprocal access, and approximately a quarter of the total catch of the Union's fleet is in the waters of non-member countries. Many of these agreements, such as those with developing countries in the Indian Ocean and the South Atlantic, involve the payment of financial compensation.

Enforcing CFP rules remains a problem. Quotas and TACs, allocated amongst member states, are drawn up annually with reference to particular species. In some fishing grounds this may require fishermen to discard by-catches of species for which the quota has already been met. Enforcement is still largely the responsibility of member states' own inspectorates, although there is also a small inspectorate attached to the Commission whose job it is to ensure that enforcement is even-handed. Measures have been agreed to regulate mesh sizes and to deal with the problem of 'quota-hopping' (i.e., a vessel switching its country of registration from one member state to another to secure a more lucrative catch: see **Factortame case**). The British government's conservation measure limiting the number of days fishing vessels may spend at sea has not been adopted as part of the CFP.

Common Foreign and Security Policy (CFSP)

One of the two intergovernmental '**pillars**' (see **intergovernmentalism**) of the **Maastricht Treaty**, the CFSP embraces all those means by which the **European Union** seeks to exercise influence in foreign affairs (setting aside exclusively economic or commercial aspects of external relations). Title V of the Maastricht Treaty, composed of a single Article J subdivided into 11 sections, is concerned not so much with the substance of the policy (although a set of broad and uncontroversial objectives is laid down in Article J1) but with the machinery for consultation between member states and Union institutions on CFSP matters and for 'concerted and convergent action'.

The CFSP has developed out of and replaced the system known as European Political Cooperation (EPC). From the 1960s onwards it was evident, most notably in the foreign affairs field, that there were areas in which, although they were not formally within the competence of the European Economic Community, governments of member states could usefully act in consultation and in concert with one another. At a **summit** meeting in The Hague in December 1969 **the Six** invited their foreign ministers to make proposals for political unification. This was done in a report drafted by a committee of senior officials chaired by Vicomte Etienne Davignon of the Belgian foreign ministry (and later a long-serving member of the **European Commission**) and known as the first Davignon Report. The Report was submitted to the governments of the Six and to those of the four applicant states (Denmark, Ireland, Norway and the United Kingdom), debated in the **European Parliament** and adopted in its final form by the foreign ministers on 27 October 1970.

The Report made four basic recommendations. Foreign ministers should meet every six months in what was known as the Conference of Foreign Ministers meeting in Political Cooperation, to distinguish it from the

Foreign Affairs Council; the heads of foreign ministries of member states should form a 'Political Committee'; six-monthly meetings known as 'colloquies' should be held with the Political Affairs Committee of the European Parliament; and the president-in-office of the **Council of Ministers** should submit an annual report on political cooperation to the European Parliament. In addition, a regular exchange of telegrams, coordinated by the **presidency**, would ensure a copious flow of information between foreign ministries (see COREUR). These proposals were described in the Report as 'the first practical endeavours to demonstrate to all that Europe has a political vocation'. A second Davignon Report, requested at the Paris summit in October 1972, increased the frequency of ministers' meetings to four times a year and strengthened the involvement of embassies of member states, including those accredited to international organizations.

The main feature of EPC was its intergovernmental character. It took place largely outside the Community framework: the Commission had no right of initiative, the foreign ministers were not subject to the procedures laid down in the Treaty for decision-making in the Council, recourse could not be had to the **Court of Justice**, and not until 1976 was the Conference of Foreign Ministers meeting in Political Cooperation prepared to answer questions from the European Parliament. The range of subjects included 'all important foreign policy questions [which] concern European interests whether in Europe itself or elsewhere where the adoption of a common position is necessary or desirable' (second Davignon Report, paragraph 11), but, although part of the *acquis communautaire*, EPC remained outside the Treaty.

The so-called London Report on EPC, adopted in October 1981, made some important improvements to the procedures, including a swifter response to crises, fuller involvement on the part of the Commission, the creation of the **troika** and the addition of a small EPC secretariat based in Brussels. More importantly, the London Report mentioned 'security' for the first time in the context of EPC, in line with an agreement reached at an informal meeting of foreign ministers in Venlo, the Netherlands, earlier in the year.

When EPC was finally given Treaty status in Title III of the 1986 **Single European Act** (SEA), the provisions did little more than codify the procedures already established. The drafting made it clear that EPC remained outside the normal ambit of the Community institutions (although the Commission was to be 'fully associated' and the European Parliament 'closely associated' with it). The signatory states expressed their readiness 'to coordinate their positions more closely on the political and economic aspects of security' (Article 30.6 SEA).

The Maastricht Treaty signalled the end of EPC and the beginning of the CFSP. Procedurally, it introduced a distinction between 'cooperation' (or 'coordination') and 'joint action'. The Council is empowered to decide by unanimity which shall be the areas for joint action and to define the scope, duration, objective and nature of such action. Within each area so defined the Council must also decide which matters may be subject to decision by **qualified majority**. The **European Council** is empowered to 'define the principles and general guidelines for the common foreign and security policy', which, as with all its decisions, it will do on the basis of consensus. The cost of any CFSP actions is borne either by the **Budget** or by the member states 'in accordance with a scale to be decided'. The Political Committee (see above) is instructed to work alongside **COREPER** (see **national representations**) in monitoring the international situation, contributing to Council meetings and following up CFSP decisions. In a **Declaration** annexed to the Treaty the signatory states agreed to examine the Political Committee–COREPER relationship at a later stage, together with the 'practical arrangements' for merging the EPC secretariat with the secretariat of the Council.

Article J5 makes particular reference to the obligation laid upon member states belonging to the Security Council of the **United Nations** to 'concert and keep the other Member States fully informed'. Permanent members (i.e., France and the United Kingdom) are required to 'ensure the defence of the positions and the interests of the Union'.

All the above provisions bear equally upon foreign policy and security. The latter is dealt with in more detail in Article J4: the CFSP 'shall include all questions related to the security of the Union, including the eventual framing of a common defence policy, which might in time lead to a common defence'. The **Western European Union** (WEU), described as 'an integral part of the development of the Union' (i.e., the European Union created by the Maastricht Treaty), is requested 'to elaborate and implement decisions and actions of the Union which have defence implications'. By this provision, WEU is integrated with the European Union as an executive arm of the CFSP. However, the **Treaty of Brussels**, upon which WEU is founded, is due to be re-examined in 1998, and Article J4 will be revised to take account of whatever takes its place. The role of WEU within the CFSP and its relations with the **North Atlantic Treaty Organization** (NATO) were dealt with in more detail in a declaration annexed to the Treaty by those member states (all except Denmark, Ireland and Greece) that at the time of the agreement also belonged to WEU. Under this Declaration it was decided *inter alia* to transfer the headquarters of the WEU from London to Brussels and to allow representatives of member states in the WEU Council to be the same as those in

NATO, an arrangement known as 'double-hatting'. Since the Maastricht Treaty was agreed, the WEU Council at a meeting in Rome in November 1992 decided to extend WEU membership to Greece, observer membership to Denmark and Ireland, and associate membership to the other European members of NATO not belonging to the European Union (Iceland, Norway and Turkey).

Although the CFSP provisions in the Maastricht Treaty were a substantial advance on EPC, they did not significantly enhance the role of the European Parliament. Under Article J7 the presidency is invited merely to 'consult the European Parliament on the main aspects and the basic choices' of the CFSP and to ensure that the Parliament's views 'are duly taken into consideration'. The presidency and the Commission are instructed to keep the Parliament informed of CFSP developments, and, because CFSP matters are now dealt with by the Foreign Affairs Council, the Parliament's normal rights with respect to oral and written questions and the submission of recommendations apply in full to the CFSP.

The alleged inadequacy of democratic control, at the national or European level, is an argument that was raised when EPC was first established and is still being raised in respect of the CFSP. The counter-arguments are based on the self-evident need for speed and confidentiality in this field, and on the fact that whether or not the procedures are strictly within the ambit of the Community institutions, ministers in any case remain responsible to their **national parliaments**. This is of particular importance when CFSP decisions have to be taken by unanimity (see above), including the CFSP 'guidelines' set by the European Council. The arguments as far as national parliaments are concerned are very fully set out in a House of Lords report entitled *Scrutiny of the Intergovernmental Pillars of the European Union* (November 1993).

The European Parliament is less well placed to exert influence on the CFSP, but it should be noted that under the Single European Act revision of Article 238 of the **Treaty of Rome** the Parliament's **assent** must be given to all agreements with third countries, including revisions to existing agreements or financial protocols. Its new power under Article 138b EEC to request the Commission to submit draft proposals is of limited value in this context since the Commission has no exclusive right of initiative in the CFSP field.

Another argument heard since the origins of EPC is that the procedures allow only for a 'lowest common denominator' approach. The brakes – to which all member states have ready access – are more powerful than the engine as a whole, with the result that the Community has all too often failed to exercise an influence commensurate with its political and economic weight. While admitting that EPC procedures allowed individual member states to hold the others to ransom (as Greece attempted to do over Macedonia), the fact is that there is always a balance to be struck between national sovereignty – of which foreign policy is a key expression – and the common interest. Whether the same happens under CFSP procedures remains to be seen. What might be for some critics a lack of cohesion is for others a welcome flexibility. Within international institutions like the United Nations or multilateral negotiating fora like the **Conference on Security and Cooperation in Europe** the member states have held together reasonably well. The CFSP procedures allow individual member states to continue to deal with essentially bilateral foreign policy problems (Hong Kong, for example, in the British case) with only minimum reference to other member states, but if there exists a general political will to deal with an issue on a cooperative basis, the CFSP procedures will enable this to be done. However, as in other areas, procedures can of themselves neither engender such a will nor substitute for it.

It is probably the ending of the distinction between the Conference of Foreign Ministers meeting in EPC and the Foreign Affairs Council and the introduction of qualified majority voting that will prove to be the most important features of the CFSP. At the Maastricht meeting the European Council issued the first set of 'guidelines' for the CFSP, identifying the CSCE, disarmament and arms control, nuclear non-proliferation, and the transfer of military technology (including arms exports) to third countries as areas upon which the foreign ministers should concentrate (see also **Pact on Stability in Europe**). To this not unambitious agenda should, of course, be added the crisis in the former Yugoslavia and the security situation of central and eastern Europe: if the CFSP can address these issues it will have proved its worth.

There is a useful collection of essays in Walter Carlsnaes and Steve Smith (eds), *European Foreign Policy* (1994), including an excellent one by Frank Pfetsch on the European Union as a 'foreign policy actor'. There is also a thoughtful essay by Douglas Hurd, 'Developing the Common Foreign and Security Policy', *International Affairs*, Vol. 70, no. 3, July 1994.

Common Market

The 'Common Market' was the name by which what later became the European Community was generally known, although, strictly speaking, it referred only to the **European Economic Community** established under the **Treaty of Rome**. As a technical expression to denote the commercial relations between member states of the European Union, its place has been taken by **Single Market**.

Common position

The end of the first stage of the two-reading **cooperation procedure** and **co-decision procedure** is reached when the **Council of Ministers** agrees on a 'common position'. This common position will often take account of amendments put forward by the **European Parliament** at first reading (see below) and may also be influenced by the opinions of the **Economic and Social Committee** and the **Committee of the Regions**. The common position is sent back to the European Parliament for the second reading.

The two-reading procedure was introduced by the 1986 **Single European Act** (SEA) which came into effect in July 1987. Studies have shown that more than 40 per cent of the Parliament's first-reading amendments are accepted in the Council's common position. This estimate should be treated with some caution, since no distinction is drawn between technical or linguistic amendments and those that substantially alter the proposal.

The expression 'common position' is also found in the **Maastricht Treaty** provisions on the **Common Foreign and Security Policy** (CFSP) to denote the stance adopted by the member states on foreign policy and security issues. Article J2.2 TEU enjoins the Council of Ministers 'whenever it deems it necessary ... [to] define a common position', and member states are instructed to 'ensure that their national policies conform to the common positions'. A similar provision may be found in Article K5 TEU, with reference to **Justice and Home Affairs** (JHA).

Common transport policy

Although Article 3 of the **Treaty of Rome** called for 'a common policy in the sphere of transport' (see also Article 74 EEC), few specific requirements were laid down. Article 75 EEC referred only to the need for 'common rules applicable to international transport', rules governing the provision of transport services by non-residents in each member state, 'measures to improve transport safety' and 'any other appropriate provisions'. In its original form Article 84 EEC specified that the common transport policy applied only to rail, road and inland waterways, but this was amended by a provision in the 1986 **Single European Act** (SEA) that allowed the **Council of Ministers** to decide whether and how to extend it to sea and air transport.

In spite of the experience gained from the removal of subsidies and discriminatory price-fixing under the earlier **European Coal and Steel Community** (ECSC) Treaty, progress towards even the basic aims of a common transport policy was extremely slow. In 1982 the **European Parliament** brought a case under Article 175 EEC against the Council of Ministers for **failure to act**: in 1985 the **Court of Justice** ruled partially in the Parliament's favour and since then progress has been a little faster.

The central problem has been to combine liberalization with **harmonization** of the conditions of competition. Substantial state involvement in transport is at least as old as the building of the railways, and vested interests, public and private, are numerous, powerful and well entrenched in the transport sector. At the same time transport costs have a significant impact on economic activity and competitiveness, especially in the peripheral regions, and on individual travellers and taxpayers. Finally, the interaction between transport, energy use and the environment is now widely accepted, as is the contribution that an efficient transport system can make to the success of the **Single Market**. In terms both of its contribution to the Union's gross national product (GNP) and the number of people directly or indirectly employed, the transport sector has a claim to be amongst the very largest industries in Europe.

In May 1965 the Council of Ministers adopted a framework decision on the harmonization of provisions affecting competition in rail, road and inland waterway transport. However, it was not until 1968 that the normal Treaty rules on **competition policy** were applied to this sector (although in a way that allowed many exemptions and **derogations** to be granted). The following year agreement was reached in the form of two Regulations (see **legal instruments**) governing drivers' hours and the installation of recording equipment (the tachograph) in certain vehicles in commercial use. Both Regulations have since been revised.

Another difficult area was that of technical specifications for road vehicles. Most controversial of all were those for heavy lorries. Maximum width, height, total weight and weight per axle were laid down in 1984 (revised 1986), but at first only for international traffic between member states. Further work was done in connection with the need to facilitate the free flow of goods under the Single Market programme.

Article 77 EEC allows state aids to be maintained 'if they represent reimbursement for the discharge of certain obligations inherent in the concept of a public service'. This provision, of great importance to the railways, obviously required a common definition of a 'public service' and accounting systems that would allow revenues from state aids to be clearly identified. Both these aims were achieved in a series of Regulations over the period 1969 to 1991.

With respect to roads, the most significant recent achievement has been the introduction, with effect from 1 January 1993, of a system of Community licences governing access to the market for commercial road transport. This system replaced the restrictive and protectionist system of quotas in force until that date. Progress has also been made on the liberalization of cabotage regulations for goods and passenger transport. Of the various cost factors affecting road transport, the ones that have proved most difficult to deal with are taxes: on fuel, on heavy goods vehicles and the issue of road tolls.

Notwithstanding the provisions of Article 84 EEC (see above), the **Court of Justice** ruled in 1974 that Treaty rules on competition applied to air transport (see also **Nouvelles Frontières case**). The first substantial package of measures was agreed in December 1987 in the form of two Regulations (since revised) covering air transport between member states and the nature of the exemptions from competition rules that the Council was able to grant. The Commission was given supervisory and investigative powers similar to those it already possessed in other areas of competition policy. As a result of these Regulations and the subsequent revisions competition rules now broadly apply to the air transport sector, domestic and international, within the member states. Restrictions, however, remain on the access of new airlines to established routes, on the development of new routes, and on cabotage. Some of these problems were partially resolved in a second package of measures adopted in June 1992. Included in this package was a new Regulation on air fares, under which an airline may be granted approval for a new fare between two member states as long as neither government raises an objection (previously, both governments had to give their consent). The Commission has a right of final decision in the event of a dispute. This is intended to facilitate and encourage competition between airlines. The Commission's decision to approve further subsidies for Air France in 1994 (see **state aids**) cast doubt on its commitment to this objective (see also **Eurocontrol**).

The main aim of policy in the sea transport sector has been to open up competition within the member states and to allow European fleets to meet competition from low-cost third countries. Two packages of measures have been adopted, the first in December 1986 on the application of competition rules and the second in June 1992 on cabotage. The Commission has proposed the creation of a European shipping register (EUROS) and more stringent rules on the carriage of dangerous goods, including those capable of causing serious pollution.

Progress towards a common transport policy is being carried forward under a Commission study entitled *Sustainable Mobility*, which sets out longer-term transport objectives in relation to other policy areas such as energy and the environment. The Commission has identified 58,000 kilometres of roads, 23,000 kilometres of high-speed railway lines, and 250 airports as the essential basis of the Union's transport infrastructure. Also of relevance to transport policy is the programme of **trans-European**

networks (TENs) introduced into the Treaty of Rome (Articles 129b–d) by the **Maastricht Treaty**. TENs are intended to help create a cost-effective transport system, planned on a European basis, with special attention to the development of the high-speed rail network. Transport also features prominently in the fourth framework programme (1994–8) of **research** undertaken by the European Union.

Transport is widely believed to be an area of growing importance for the Union. This is due not only to the impact of the Single Market but also to the prospect of **enlargement** and the need to establish better links with central and eastern Europe. This is in marked contrast to the very slow progress made in the 1960s and 1970s. A European Transport Community was an idea considered by **the Six** in the 1950s, based on the model of the ECSC, and eventually rejected in favour of the **European Economic Community** and the **European Atomic Energy Community** (Euratom). Experience to date with the common transport policy suggests that the decision was a judicious one.

Communism

The Communist parties of Western Europe were at the apogee of their influence during the immediate postwar years, helped by their links with resistance movements in continental Europe and by the fact that the Soviet Union had been an ally of the West. Since then they have been (with some exceptions) in long and probably terminal decline, a process accelerated by the Soviet interventions in Hungary (1956) and Czechoslovakia (1968) and the break-up of the Soviet empire in central and eastern Europe. The rise of so-called 'Eurocommunism' (that is, Communist policies tempered by a willingness to work through democratic institutions and without subservience to Moscow) may be seen in retrospect to have slowed but not halted this progressive decline.

Communist parties were unremittingly hostile to the first moves towards European integration. Taking their cue from Moscow, they interpreted the **Marshall Plan** as American imperialism backed by military–industrial interests and the **North Atlantic Treaty Organization** (NATO) as an instrument of American domination. Communist parties voted against the **Treaty of Paris** and the **Treaty of Rome** in the **national parliaments** of **the Six**. Until the Eurocommunism of the 1970s Communists remained almost wholly uninvolved in European integration, the only notable exception being **Altiero Spinelli** (who later left the party).

Eurocommunism was mainly an Italian phenomenon, and the fact of its being pro-European was one of its principal distinguishing features. However, the other well-established Western European Communist party, the French, remained loyal to Moscow. The division ran through other

Communist parties, such as the Greek Communists (who developed both pro- and anti-European wings) and through the Communist group in the **European Parliament** (see **political groups**), although it was not until 1989 that it finally split apart. In policy terms Eurocommunism was indistinguishable from moderate Socialism, and in the 1984 European elections in Italy the Communists secured a larger share of the votes than the Christian Democrats. The triumph was short-lived, and by 1990 the party was split, the majority of its MEPs joining the Socialists in the European Parliament two years later. The Communists are the fifth largest group in the European Parliament. They have chosen the name United European Left, although, in fact, they remain divided into old-style Communists and Eurocommunists, and can normally be relied upon to vote with the Socialists.

Community law

Community law is of three basic types: the **Treaties** and related instruments such as the Own Resources Decision (see **own resources**); legislation, mainly Regulations, Directives, and Decisions (see below); and the case-law embodied in rulings of the **Court of Justice**. Together these constitute the major part of the *acquis communautaire*, to which may be added international agreements to which the Union is a party.

Sometimes referred to as primary legislation, the Treaties are the basis of the European Union's legal order. As amended by the Acts of Accession consequent upon successive **enlargements**, by the **Single European Act** (SEA) and by the **Maastricht Treaty** they serve as the Union's constitution and as the legal basis for all legislation. They are dynamic in that they not only establish a particular set of relations between signatory states but also set out a programme of action for the future. They lay down a pattern of rights and obligations not so much between the signatory states as between the states and the Communities thereby established. They enjoy **primacy** in that they and the legislation based upon them take precedence over national law. They are self-contained in that they contain provisions (i.e., procedures and institutions) for enforcement, interpretation and the settlement of disputes without recourse to outside bodies. These characteristics combine to make the Treaties profoundly different from other international treaties.

Although the Treaties have the force of law, not all their provisions are of **direct effect**. Some Treaty Articles confer specific rights upon individuals (direct effect), while others confer rights only by virtue of the obligations they impose upon member states. In both cases such rights are enforceable at law. However, there are also Articles that embody general principles that must first be translated into specific legislation before they can have legal effect. Many cases before the Court of Justice have centred upon the distinction that must be drawn between these different types of Treaty commitment.

The Treaties apply throughout the territory of the member states, with the exception of the Faeroes, the **Channel Islands** and the Isle of Man, and the British Sovereign Base Areas in Cyprus, and the partial exception of the French overseas departments and the Finnish Åland Islands. Special arrangements, differing from case to case, apply to all these territories and to **Gibraltar**. **Greenland** is now listed amongst the **overseas countries and territories** (OCTs). The Treaties also apply extra-territorially in the case of firms operating inside the member states but whose headquarters are outside (a principle established in Case 48/69, *ICI* v *Commission*, and of great importance in **competition policy**).

The power conferred by treaty upon the Union institutions to make laws distinguishes the Union from essentially intergovernmental organizations such as the **Council of Europe**. Founded upon the doctrine of the separation of powers, the legislative procedures set out in the Treaties give each of the four main institutions a specific role: the **Commission** proposes new laws; the **European Parliament** examines and may amend them; the **Council of Ministers** adopts the legislation in its final form, sometimes jointly with the Parliament; and the Court of Justice adjudicates on disputes arising from the interpretation and application of Community law. This basic model is subject to many variants: the **Budget** procedure is significantly different, and both the SEA and the Maastricht Treaty introduced new procedures that affect the balance and distribution of powers between the institutions.

Secondary legislation (sometimes referred to as derived legislation) is made up of the legislative acts of the Union institutions, primarily Regulations, Directives, and Decisions. Article 189 EEC defines these three types of legal instrument. A Regulation 'shall have general application. It shall be binding in its entirety and directly applicable in all Member States' (i.e., without the need for national implementing legislation: see below). Regulations are published in the *Official Journal* and enter into force either on the date specified in the text or on the twentieth day after publication (Article 191 EEC). Much of the day-to-day management of the **Common Agricultural Policy** (CAP) is carried out by means of Regulations, with the Commission acting on the basis of powers granted to it by the Council of Ministers. The Commission may also make Regulations in its capacity as the institution responsible for implementing Council Decisions (Article 145 EEC), and the Council too may make Regulations in order to discharge its responsibilities under the Treaties. A Regulation can be used only in cases provided for by treaty and must be based on a specific Article or Articles of one or more of the Treaties. A general reference to a Treaty or to **Article 235** EEC is not sufficient.

A Directive is 'binding, as to the result to be achieved, upon each Member State to which it is addressed, but shall leave to the national authorities the choice of form and methods'. Directives, which must be based on a specific treaty Article, have to be implemented in national law by governments of member states acting in accordance with their normal constitutional procedures, and most Directives are sufficiently loosely worded to allow member states a degree of flexibility in the details.

A Decision, which may be issued either by the Council or the Commission, is 'binding in its entirety upon those to whom it is addressed'. Like a Regulation, it must be based on a specific treaty Article and needs no national implementing legislation. It may be addressed to a member state, a corporation or an individual. 'Administrative Decisions' are for the most part either internal acts of the institutions (e.g., on staff matters) or Decisions by the Commission on the allocation of funds or the execution of policies such as those concerned with dumping or **state aids**.

Article 189 EEC also allows the Council and the Commission to deliver Recommendations and **Opinions**, but since these have 'no binding force' they are not regarded by all authorities as part of Community law in the strict sense. Their purpose is primarily to persuade or to assist in the interpretation or application of other legal acts.

The deliberations of the Union institutions may also be published in the form of **Resolutions**, Communications, Action Programmes, Guidelines, and so on. As a general rule, these are not of binding effect and many fall into the category of 'framework legislation'; that is, a comprehensive statement of aims and principles in a particular policy area, which is then followed up by detailed legislative proposals. For such acts to have juridical force, they must be consistent with procedural requirements, confer rights or impose obligations on persons, Union institutions or member states, and be subject to judicial review in the Court of Justice.

Some idea of the volume of legislation currently in force may be gained from the fact that the 1992 Agreement on the **European Economic Area** (EEA) lists some 1,700 items of legislation in 22 annexes. Community legislation is stored in the CELEX database within 17 subject areas. An annual directory is published, giving the reference numbers of all Community legislative acts currently in force (the earliest dates from 1952), with the exception of acts of very limited scope and duration relevant to the day-to-day management of the CAP or the **customs union**.

If a member state has difficulty in applying a Regulation or implementing a Directive, it may seek a temporary waiver, known as a **derogation**. The Regulation or Directive may make specific provision for such derogations, which are normally granted only with the unanimous consent of the Council and only for a limited period. If a derogation is granted, national law (if any) continues to apply to the matter covered by the Regulation or Directive in question. Exceptionally, a member state may apply national legislation that is stricter than the relevant Community legislation, in order, for example, to protect the environment (this was the subject of a Court ruling in 1988 in the case of *Commission v Denmark, Re Disposable Beer Cans*, Case 302/86: see **environment policy**).

Article 5 EEC enjoins the member states to 'take all appropriate measures, whether general or particular, to ensure fulfilment of the obligations arising out of this Treaty or resulting from action taken by the institutions of the Community'. The responsibility for ensuring that member states do this falls to the Commission under Article 169 EEC:

> If the Commission considers that a Member State has failed to fulfil an obligation under this Treaty, it shall deliver a reasoned opinion on the matter after giving the State concerned the opportunity to submit its observations. If the State concerned does not comply with the opinion within the period laid down by the Commission, the latter may bring the matter before the Court of Justice.

As noted above, one of the criteria for establishing whether or not a legislative act has juridical force is the extent to which it confers rights or imposes obligations on persons, institutions or member states. The situation with regard to Regulations and Decisions is relatively straightforward, but several cases have been brought in the Court of Justice to establish whether or not a Directive, adopted but not yet implemented in national law, confers rights. Broadly speaking, if the wording of a Directive is sufficiently precise and unambiguous and the time limit for its implementation in national law has expired, that Directive may be said to confer rights on individuals in their dealings with the state and to take precedence over national law (see **Francovich case**).

The Treaties and the legislation based upon them are neither sufficiently precise nor sufficiently comprehensive to cover all legal eventualities. This fact has provided scope for the Court of Justice, as the interpreter of Community law and as the arbiter of disputes, to contribute very fundamentally to the corpus of Community law.

The Court's prime function is to 'ensure that in the interpretation and application [of the Treaties] the law is observed' (Article 164 EEC). The Court's position is an exceptionally powerful one, in that there is no appeal from its rulings, it can strike down as illegal the legislative acts of member states or Union institutions, and it is a source of law in its own right. Nevertheless, springing as it does from a variety of legal traditions, it has had to bring about a synthesis of these traditions with respect both to its mode of operation and the substance of its judgments. Its power to interpret Community law is exercised in the light of the fundamental purposes of the Treaties and the internal logic of particular policies, and this has led the Court (as is the case with the United States Supreme Court) to play an important 'integrationist' role. Interpretations may be incidental to a judgment or embodied in a **preliminary ruling**.

As a supreme court, the Court of Justice is not formally bound by precedent. However, the self-evident need for consistency, coherence and equality of treatment ensures that precedents are taken into account, although no point of law is ever settled by reference to precedent alone. The precedents that have guided the Court in a given judgment are cited in the reasoning (see below).

Judgments of the Court are published periodically in *European Court Reports*. The only authentic text of a judgment is the one in the language of the case. A judgment is composed of two parts: the reasoning (which will normally draw upon the submission of the **advocate-general**); and the judgment itself. Underpinning the Court's judgments and Community law as a whole are certain fundamental doctrines, some of them familiar in national law and others arising from the unique nature of the Union. Amongst them are the autonomy of Community law – its separateness from national law and the independence of the law-making and law-enforcing Union institutions – and the functional and programmatic unity of the **European Economic Community**, the **European Coal and Steel Community** (ECSC) and the **European Atomic Energy Community** (Euratom) as participants in a joint endeavour within the framework of the Union. These two doctrines are complemented by a third, that of the primacy of Community law. This was expressed in the Court judgment in the Van Gend en Loos case in 1963 (Case 26/62): 'The Community constitutes a new legal order of international law, in favour of which the States within certain areas have limited their sovereign rights.' The duties of national courts to apply Community law were spelt out the following year in *Costa* v ENEL (Case 6/64). In its judgment the Court emphasized that Community law cannot be overridden by 'domestic legal provisions . . . without being deprived of its character as Community law and without the legal basis of the Community itself being called into question'.

In a famous 1974 judgment Lord Denning, then Master of the Rolls, described the impact of Community law upon English law as a 'rising tide', which, inexorably, makes its way up the broad estuaries into the very smallest creeks and inlets of national life. Based upon a continental tradition of civil law, Community law is indeed substantially different from English law, but this should not obscure the fact that it is also different from any other comparable body of law. It has some of the characteristics of international law, but of municipal law too; it is both public and private; and it relies on both enactment and precedent. It draws, however, upon a common heritage of principles – due process, equality before the law, *non bis in idem*, the right to be heard – which serve to mitigate the unfamiliarity of its procedures. Community law has served both to advance the process of integration along the paths set out in the Treaties and to consolidate such progress as has been made. Whether or not the law can continue to play so central a role in a more heterogeneous Union in which attitudes to law widely differ is open to question.

Community preference

'Community preference' is a well-established feature of the **Common Agricultural Policy** (CAP) under which, by a system of import levies and export refunds, member states are expected and encouraged to give preference to agricultural goods from within the Union over those from outside. Such practices run obviously counter to the doctrine of free trade and tend to maintain prices of products covered by CAP rules at relatively high levels.

Community preference gave rise to difficulties at the time of British accession to the European Community, since the British government did not want to place imports from Commonwealth countries (such as butter from New Zealand) at a disadvantage. More recently, Community preference created problems in the negotiations on the **General Agreement on Tariffs and Trade** (GATT) and in respect of agricultural imports from central and eastern Europe. Community preference also imposes constraints on imports of agricultural products from developing countries that compete with those covered by the CAP.

Community preference is vigorously supported by member states (such as France, Denmark and Ireland) with large agricultural sectors and substantial exporting capacity. This support can claim only very slender justification in the **Treaty of Rome**: Article 44.2 EEC refers to the system of minimum prices under the CAP and adds that they 'shall not be applied so as to form an obstacle to the development of a natural preference between Member States'.

Community trade mark

Under a Regulation agreed in the **Council of Ministers** on 20 December 1993, businesses may secure trade mark protection throughout the whole **European Economic Area** (EEA) by registering the trade mark with the Office for Harmonization in the Internal Market in Alicante, Spain.

Previously, full protection could be guaranteed only under separate procedures in each member state. National trade mark protection continues to be available. A similar regulation applies to designs and models.

Competition policy

The operation of 'a system ensuring that competition in the internal market is not distorted' is one of the activities of the European Community under Article 3g of the **Treaty of Rome**. Article 85 EEC prohibits undertakings from entering into 'agreements . . . and concerted practices which may affect trade between Member States and which have as their object or effect the prevention, restriction, or distortion of competition within the Common Market'. Included under this heading are price-fixing and market-sharing arrangements, production controls, and discriminatory contracts intended to place particular trading parties at a disadvantage. However, exempted from this general prohibition are agreements or practices that contribute to 'improving the production or distribution of goods or to promoting technical or economic progress, while allowing consumers a fair share of the resulting benefit' (Article 85.2 EEC).

Article 86 EEC prohibits 'any abuse by one or more undertakings of a dominant position within the common market or in a substantial part of it . . . in so far as it may affect trade between Member States'. Articles 85 and 86 EEC apply to all economic sectors except the **Common Agricultural Policy** (CAP) and the **common transport policy**, which have their own competition rules. The coal and steel industries are covered by Articles 65 and 66 of the **Treaty of Paris**.

Under Article 90 EEC publicly owned undertakings (including monopolies of a commercial character) are bound by the rules of competition 'in so far as the application of such rules does not obstruct the performance . . . of the particular task assigned to them. The development of trade must not be affected to such an extent as would be contrary to the interests of the Community.'

Article 89 EEC gives the **Commission** a general responsibility to enforce Articles 85 and 86 in cooperation with the authorities of member states and the right to conduct investigations either at their request or on its own initiative. The means whereby the Commission may discharge this responsibility were defined in Council Regulation 17/62. Under this Regulation the Commission is empowered to request information from undertakings suspected of practices prohibited under Articles 85 and 86 EEC. The Commission may carry out 'all necessary investigations', including examination and copying of business records, 'ask for oral explanations on the spot', and 'enter any premises, land and means of transport' owned by the undertakings under investigation. The Commission may impose fines on undertakings found to have supplied 'incorrect or misleading information' or to have failed to supply information on request. The Commission may also 'by decision' impose fines ranging from 1,000 to 1 million ECUs 'or a sum in excess thereof but not exceeding 10% of turnover in the preceding business year' on undertakings found to have infringed Articles 85 and 86 EEC, assessed with regard 'to the gravity and to the duration of the infringement' (for example, in July 1994 the Commission announced fines totalling over £100 million on 19 companies found to have fixed prices over several years in the market for cardboard packaging). Failure to supply information, submit to an investigation or abandon a prohibited practice may incur a 'periodic penalty payment' imposed by the Commission at rates ranging between 50 and 1,000 ECUs a day. The Commission is under an obligation to keep the relevant national authorities informed of an investigation and its decisions may be reviewed in the **Court of First Instance** in the event of a fine being imposed. Subject to these provisos, its powers in respect of suspected infringements of competition rules are absolute.

The Commission is required to draw up an annual report on its activities in respect of competition policy. This report is debated by the **European Parliament**. The competition rules apply to any enterprise doing business within the Union even if it has neither branches nor subsidiaries on Union territory (this was established by the Court of Justice in a 1988 ruling concerned with woodpulp).

Competition policy (which also covers **state aids** and **merger controls**) is one of the areas in which the Commission is most powerful, and the decisions that the Commission is required to take are sometimes very sensitive politically. In recent years three very active Commissioners, Peter Sutherland, Sir Leon Brittan and Karel Van Miert, have been instrumental in making competition policy much more effective. It was obvious that if the **Single Market** programme was to bring benefits to consumers, the removal of trade barriers would have to be accompanied by a vigorous competition policy. Amongst the most controversial issues are the block exemptions from competition rules granted, for example, to exclusive distribution agreements – such as those in the motor industry – and franchise agreements. Some of the more bureaucratic requirements have been eased: there is no longer any obligation to inform the Commission of an agreement between undertakings that together have less than a 5 per cent share of the market within the Union for the products affected by the agreement.

Doubts remain as to whether the Commission has adequate resources, in staff numbers and expertise, to enforce the competition policy. Even with the cooperation of national authorities (whose own standards of enforcement are uneven), Commission investigations continue to give rise to complaints about delays and unnecessary secrecy. Complaints against the Commission in this field may be brought in the Court of First Instance. It has also been suggested that a new European agency, independent of the Commission, should be set up to enforce competition rules, but this has been resisted by the Commission on the grounds that essentially political judgements are often involved in competition cases. This and other related issues are very fully discussed in a report by the House of Lords Select Committee on the European Communities, *Enforcement of Community Competition Rules* (December 1993). See also Sir Leon Brittan, *European Competition Policy* (1992).

Compulsory expenditure

Compulsory expenditure (sometimes known as obligatory expenditure) is a technical term used in relation to the **Budget**. The definition, which is not set out very clearly in the Treaties, was laid down in a joint Council–Parliament–Commission **Declaration** in 1982 as being expenditure that must be entered into the Budget if the Community is to meet its internal and external obligations. The difference between compulsory and non-compulsory expenditure is essentially political, since it has a bearing on which arm of the joint budgetary authority, the **Council of Ministers** or the **European Parliament**, has the last word on the various items in the Budget: the Parliament has the last word only on non-compulsory expenditure. Easily the most important element within compulsory expenditure is price support under the **Common Agricultural Policy** (CAP). Arguments over the classification of expenditure have occasionally arisen between the Council and the Parliament. In 1995 just over 50 per cent of the total Budget was compulsory expenditure: in 1980 it was over 80 per cent.

Concentric circles

The idea of concentric circles is used most commonly as a model of how Europe as a whole might develop. Typically, the member states of the European Union occupy the central core; members of the **European Economic Area** occupy a second circle; European states with **Association Agreements** make up a third circle; and in some models a fourth circle is composed of other former Eastern bloc countries. All versions of this model allow for movement from one circle to another, the assumption being that countries will gravitate towards the central core.

The model is also sometimes used to describe how the Union itself should operate. A central core is composed of activities in which all member states participate, surrounded by a second circle of activities in which member states may choose to be involved. In some models a third circle of activities offers a further choice of options, in which non-member states may also become engaged. Decision-making in the second and third circles is carried out not under **Treaty of Rome** procedures – the scope of which is limited to activities in the central core – but by means of intergovernmental procedures. This model, of which there are many variants, is sometimes referred to as the **variable geometry** Europe.

There are several examples of a Europe of concentric circles, although there is no authority for such a model in the founding Treaties. The **Exchange-Rate Mechanism** (ERM) of the **European Monetary System** (EMS), as set up in 1979, was outside the central core by virtue of the fact that sterling was not involved and the Italian lira was in a broader band. Similarly, only 12 of the 15 member states participate in the **European Space Agency**, plus Norway and Switzerland. And the development model set out in the **Maastricht Treaty** – a 'Union' based upon three **'pillars'** – could also be expressed as an inner and an outer circle, since the provisions for cooperation in justice, home affairs, security and foreign policy lie outside the central core by virtue of their essentially intergovernmental character and the possibility that non-member states may become involved.

Conciliation

'Conciliation' is the word used to describe the procedure whereby the **European Parliament** and the **Council of Ministers** seek to resolve their differences over the substance or wording of a legislative text. Introduced in 1975 as part of the procedure for reaching agreement on the **Budget**, conciliation has since become an important feature of the **co-decision procedure**. Conciliation takes place in a conciliation committee composed of representatives of the European Parliament and the Council.

Confederation

The main difference between a confederation and a **federation** is that the former lays more emphasis on the independence of the constituent parts, the corollary of which is a weaker central authority. The longest-established confederation in Europe is Switzerland, with its unique mixture of central institutions and a vigorous tradition of local decision-making at the level of the cantons. The distinction is neatly caught in two German expressions: *Staatenbund* (a confederation of states) and *Bundesstaat* (a federal state).

Conference on Security and Cooperation in Europe (CSCE)

The CSCE, the first stage of which was concluded by the signing of a 'Final Act' in Helsinki on 1 August 1975, was an attempt to reconcile the conflicting interests of the Atlantic Alliance and the countries of the **Warsaw Pact**. All European countries (except Albania, which did not join the CSCE until June 1991) took part in the negotiations that resulted in the Final Act together with the United States and Canada, a total of 35 states. Broadly, the countries of the Eastern bloc were interested in military security and in extending economic and technological cooperation with the West, while the countries of the West were interested in promoting human rights in the East.

These different priorities were reflected in the four 'baskets' into which the Final Act was divided. Basket I was concerned with security and disarmament. It laid down certain principles for the conduct of relations between states: respect for sovereignty, non-interference in internal affairs, inviolability of frontiers, renunciation of force as a means of settling disputes, and respect for human rights. Basket II dealt with economic, scientific and technological cooperation and the protection of the environment. Basket III was entitled 'Cooperation in Humanitarian and Other Fields'. The fourth Basket was concerned with following up the commitments entered into by the signatory states. The Helsinki Final Act prompted the formation of many human rights monitoring groups in the countries of the Eastern bloc.

The Helsinki meeting was succeeded by CSCE follow-up meetings in Belgrade (1977–8), Madrid (1980–83), Vienna (1986–9) and Helsinki (1992). In between such meetings, expert groups discussed particular aspects of the subjects covered by the Final Act, such as human rights, cultural and human conflicts, and the peaceful settlement of disputes. Linked to the CSCE were the conferences on confidence and security-building measures (CSBMs: Stockholm, 1984–6) and on conventional forces in Europe (CFE, 1989–92). Of the follow-up meetings, the one that yielded the most substantial results was the meeting concluded in Vienna in January 1989. For the first time a permanent mechanism for monitoring human rights was agreed by all 35 countries.

The following year, heads of government met in Paris for the first time since the 1975 meeting in Helsinki. The first CFE Treaty was signed on 19 November 1990 and the **Charter of Paris** for a New Europe two days later. The Paris summit, originally proposed by Mikhail Gorbachev, was a forum for reviewing the changes taking place in central and eastern Europe and for finding ways of overcoming the remaining divisions. Also signed in Paris was the so-called 'Vienna Document', a new package of CSBMs agreed in Vienna just before the summit. The CSCE Paris summit marked the end of the Cold War.

The importance of the Charter of Paris for the future of the CSCE was that it created a number of new institutions. Decision-making is now the responsibility of a Council, made up of foreign ministers, assisted by a Committee of Senior Officials, who prepare meetings of the Council and implement its decisions. The CSCE has its own secretariat, operating in Vienna since 1993, the Conflict Prevention Centre, also based in Vienna, the Office for Democratic Institutions and Human Rights (formerly the Office for Free Elections) in Warsaw and a High Commissioner on National Minorities in The Hague. It should be noted that all these bodies are very small: the CSCE secretariat, for example, has a staff of 75 people. The CSCE also has its own Parliamentary Assembly, which met for the first time in Budapest in July 1992. These new institutions underline the shift that took place in Paris from securing new commitments in respect of human rights, open markets, democratic institutions and disarmament to ensuring that commitments already entered into are honoured. They also illustrate the extent to which the CSCE has become a permanent process: formally, it is now the Organization for Security and Cooperation in Europe (OSCE). Since the dissolution of Yugoslavia and the USSR and the division of Czechoslovakia there are 54 states participating in the CSCE, and the territory covered by the CSCE extends from Vancouver to Vladivostok.

The European Union is not represented as such in the CSCE. However, the Helsinki Final Act of 1975 was signed by Aldo Moro in his capacity as President-in-Office of the **Council of Ministers**, and the Paris Charter was signed by **Jacques Delors** as President of the Commission. The position taken by the member states of the Union in the CSCE is now discussed as part of the **Common Foreign and Security Policy** (CFSP) and in meetings of the **European Council**.

All parties to the Charter of Paris are agreed on the need to make the conflict-prevention and dispute-settlement machinery more effective. The crisis in Yugoslavia has underlined the weakness of machinery that is backed neither by military force nor by the threat of economic sanctions, and the difficulty of maintaining the credibility of an intergovernmental organization required to operate on the basis of consensus. A first step – as several participating states have proposed – might be to transform the commitments so far embodied in the Paris Charter and other declarations into a formal CSCE Treaty (see also **Pact on Stability in Europe**).

Congress of Europe

Held in The Hague in May 1948, the Congress of Europe was attended by more than 800 politicians, lawyers, academics, economists, etc., from almost every country in Europe. Its President-of-Honour was **Winston Churchill**. It was organized by the International Committee of the

Movements for European Unity and led directly to the foundation in October 1948 of the **European Movement**.

The Congress adopted a 'Message to Europeans', which called for 'a united Europe, throughout whose area the free movement of persons, ideas and goods is restored'. This would be underpinned by a 'Charter of Human Rights', a Court of Justice to guarantee those rights, and a 'European Assembly where the live forces of all our nations shall be represented'. These ideas were worked out in more detail in a political report considered by the Congress, which prompted a number of specific resolutions adopted by unanimity.

The Congress, the name of which was a deliberate echo of the 1815 Congress of Vienna attended by the victorious powers at the end of the Napoleonic wars, represents the high-water mark of enthusiasm for European integration in the immediate postwar period. It sought, on an all-party basis, to bring pressure to bear upon governments and to enlist popular support for integrationist ideas. Although it had substantial impact at the time, the Congress may be seen in retrospect to have been not wholly successful. The main ideas put forward were embodied the following year in the statute of the **Council of Europe**.

Conservatism

Although the Conservatives have a claim to be the longest-established political family in Europe, there were no Conservative parties of any importance in **the Six**. Consequently, it was not until the **accession** of Denmark and the United Kingdom to the European Community in 1973 that a Conservative Group was formed as one of the **political groups** in the **European Parliament** and Conservatives participated in both the **Commission** and the **Council of Ministers**. However, the Christian Democrats (see **Christian Democracy**) retained their position as by far the strongest political force amongst the parties of the centre and the centre-right. In May 1992 the British and Danish Conservative Members of the European Parliament (MEPs) joined the Christian Democrats as allied members in the Group of the European People's Party (the Conservatives do not sit with the Christian Democrats in the Parliamentary Assembly of the **Council of Europe**).

Although in recent years the Labour Party has become identified as 'the party of Europe' in the British political context, it was in fact the Conservative Government of Harold Macmillan that in 1961 first sought British membership of the European Community, thereby abandoning the reservations of **Winston Churchill** and Anthony Eden; the party has maintained its pro-European stance (with varying degrees of enthusiasm) ever since. The Danish Conservative Party (founded as the Party of the ever since. The Danish Conservative Party (founded as the Party of the Right, Høyre, in the nineteenth century, and refounded as the Conservative Party in 1915) has also been consistently pro-European, as has its Norwegian counterpart (which retains the name Høyre).

In most European languages 'conservative' means 'reactionary', and only in Denmark, Poland and the United Kingdom are there parties with the word 'Conservative' in their name. The Conservatives' image as a party lacking a confessional basis, hostile to federalism (see **federation**), strongly committed to free market economics and uninterested in social questions (an image powerfully reinforced by **Margaret Thatcher**) makes them an object of suspicion to Christian Democrats, who pride themselves on their position as parties of the centre. One of the aims of the **European Democrat Union**, founded in 1978, was to overcome this Conservative–Christian Democrat divide, but it has been only partially successful.

Some of the newly formed parties in central and eastern Europe have drawn inspiration from, for example, the privatization programme carried out by Conservative governments in the United Kingdom, but in the longer term they are not likely to develop into authentic Conservative parties. In the European Union, Conservatism will probably remain an Anglo-Scandinavian phenomenon, while maintaining good bilateral relations with parties such as the Christian Democrats in Germany, the Moderates in Sweden, the Partido Popular in Spain, and elements within the centre-right in France.

Constituent assembly

Historically, a constituent assembly is a body of elected parliamentarians that is set (or sets itself) the task of drawing up and enacting a constitution, often against a background of revolution. Within the first directly elected **European Parliament** (1979–84) there were many Members (MEPs) who saw this as the Parliament's historic role. Before the elections of June 1979 a poll was taken amongst 742 candidates (62 per cent of whom were elected) to establish what proportion of them saw the Parliament as a constituent assembly. The results showed very wide variations between the nationalities: over 88 per cent of Belgian, German, Italian and Luxemburgish candidates supported the idea, by comparison with 29 per cent of British candidates, 11 per cent of Danish candidates, and only 3 per cent of French candidates.

In the Parliament **Altiero Spinelli** soon established himself as the leader of those demanding a new constitution for the Community. He was responsible for the creation of the **Crocodile Club** and later (January 1982) for the setting up of the Committee on Institutional Affairs. Briefly, his aim was for the Parliament to adopt a constitution and then, with the aid of **national parliaments** and national governments, to set in train the process of **ratification**. The draft constitution would be the main issue in the second European elections of 1984: public debate would centre upon its provisions and (if all went well) the parties supporting the constitution would be swept to power. Soon after, the constitution would enter into force.

For a number of reasons, this did not happen. The **Draft Treaty establishing the European Union** (DTEU), as the constitution was called, was not adopted in its final form until February 1984, too late for it to be included in party manifestos, and by a majority, which, although comfortable, was hardly overwhelming (237 votes to 31 with 43 abstentions, in a Parliament of 434 members).

Since 1984 the European Parliament has on several occasions returned to the idea of being a constituent assembly. Simultaneous with the 1989 European elections, a referendum was held in Italy inviting the electorate to endorse (which they did) the proposal that the 1989–94 European Parliament should be a constituent assembly. The Parliament's most recent attempt to draw up a new constitution (the Herman Report, adopted in February 1994 with 154 votes in favour, 84 against and 46 abstentions) called for a 'constitutional convention' to be held bringing together MEPs and members of national parliaments. Working on the basis of the Herman Report, this convention would prepare 'guidelines for the constitution of the European Union, and . . . assign to the European Parliament the task of preparing a final draft'.

Consultation procedure

The **Treaty of Rome** provides for consultation with many different institutions and bodies under various decision-making procedures, but the expression 'consultation procedure' is normally reserved for the simplest form of one-stage consultation between the **Council of Ministers** and the **European Parliament**. This is to distinguish it from other procedures under which the Parliament has more power to enforce its views (see **assent procedure, cooperation procedure, co-decision procedure**; see also **reconsultation**).

Originally, virtually all the Parliament's powers were exercised under a simple consultation procedure, and neither the Council nor the **Commission** was obliged to take much account of the Parliament's views. In the 1970s the Parliament acquired additional powers over the **Budget**. The indispensability of consultation with respect to legislation was first underlined in the 1979 **isoglucose case**, and the other procedures have been developed since that date. However, there are several important areas of decision-making – such as the **Common Foreign and Security Policy**

(CFSP) and **Economic and Monetary Union** (EMU) – in which the European Parliament's involvement remains limited to simple consultation.

Consumer policy

The original **Treaty of Rome** made no provision for consumer policy. The new **Article 100a** EEC, added by the **Single European Act** (SEA), referred to the need for 'a high level of protection' for consumers in the **Single Market**. Not until the **Maastricht Treaty** added a new Article 129a EEC was there a legal base for 'specific action which supports and supplements the policy pursued by the Member States to protect the health, safety and economic interests of consumers and to provide adequate information to consumers'. Article 129a.3 allows member states to maintain or introduce 'more stringent protective measures', in line with a principle laid down by the **Court of Justice** in the 1986 Danish beer-can case (*Commission* v *Denmark*, Case 302/86: see **environment policy**).

In spite of the frailty of the legal base in the original Treaty, an action programme for consumer policy was adopted by the European Council in 1972. However, except for the setting up of the Consumers' Consultative Committee the following year, little was achieved. As in other areas, the drive to complete the Single Market led to more rapid progress, since it was evident that opening markets would meet with fierce consumer resistance unless high standards of consumer protection were maintained. Broadly, the aim was to enable consumers to make informed choices between competing products, to make use of goods or services safely and to be in a position to claim redress in the event of not being satisfied.

The first of these aims led to measures on unit pricing, on standard quantities for prepackaged products, on labelling and on misleading advertising. The second aim has resulted in legislation on the use of additives in foodstuffs, on dangerous substances and on general product safety. The third aim gave rise to the controversial Product Liability Directive of 1985, which entitles the consumer to bring proceedings against the producer of a product that has caused damage without having to prove negligence on the part of the producer. Other related measures include legislation on door-to-door sales, on common rules for all forms of credit, on package holidays and timeshare sales, on toy safety, on unfair terms in contracts and on cosmetic products.

In 1990 the Consumers' Consultative Committee became the Consumers' Consultative Council, and at about the same time the Consumer Policy Service was set up in the **Commission**. In order to monitor the application of consumer policy measures the Commission has sought to assist national consumer bodies (virtually non-existent in many member states) and in particular to promote more cooperation between them. The main Brussels-based consumers' lobby is the European Bureau of Consumers' Unions, known by its French acronym BEUC.

In the light of the limited legal base for consumer policy and the application of **subsidiarity** it is clear that there is little scope for a substantial extension of consumer protection measures. It is more likely to be a question of refining existing measures, for example, in the light of new scientific evidence.

Contributions and receipts

The overall pattern of member states' contributions to and receipts from the Union's **Budget** is difficult to calculate, since the **Commission**, the only institution in possession of all the figures, is wary of providing information that in its view tends to encourage a narrow 'profit and loss' approach to membership of the Union. The economic costs of membership, it may be argued, can be expressed in cash terms, whereas many of the economic benefits, some of them long-term, cannot be so expressed. The Union's revenue under the system of **own resources**, although it is broken down into 'contributions' from each member state, is in fact composed of monies to which the Union is entitled as of right, not of subscriptions analogous to those paid to other international organizations. Agricultural levies and customs duties under the **Common External Tariff**, which form part of the Union's own resources, are collected by member states on the Union's behalf and paid over, the member states retaining one-tenth of the proceeds to cover their collection costs. One side-effect of this system is that tariffs and levies payable on goods imported through Rotterdam will appear as part of the Netherlands' 'contribution', whatever the final destination of the goods.

Detailed calculations of contributions and receipts were first made in the late 1970s when the argument over the British contribution (see **British Budget problem**) first arose. More recently, they have entered into the discussions on **future financing**, the prospect of a fifth own resource, and **enlargement**, since, inevitably, applicant states want to know how much membership will cost.

The fullest and clearest official tables showing contributions and receipts may be found in the reports by the **Court of Auditors**. The following table shows which member states were net beneficiaries, overall and per capita, from the Budget in 1993. It should be noted that almost 10 per cent of expenditure (administration, overseas aid, etc.) cannot be attributed to particular member states. A minus sign denotes a positive balance.

Net contributions, 1993

Member state	Net contributions (£m)	Per capita (£)
Belgium	−46	−5
Denmark	−293	−57
France	794	14
Germany	9,210	113
Greece	−3,220	−311
Ireland	−1,847	−519
Italy	1,188	21
Luxembourg	−148	−375
Netherlands	1,033	68
Portugal	−1,953	−209
Spain	−2,406	−62
United Kingdom	2,433	42

Source: House of Commons Research Paper, November 1994

The table shows that by far the biggest contributor, both overall and per capita, is Germany, and that the biggest overall beneficiaries are Greece and Spain. However, there are some anomalies: Denmark and Luxembourg, both amongst the most prosperous member states, are per capita beneficiaries too.

Calculations of future contributions and receipts are very hazardous. Some member states, notably France, receive substantial sums in agricultural price support from the **European Agricultural Guidance and Guarantee Fund** (EAGGF), but the actual level of such receipts is dependent upon movements in world prices and other factors. Similarly, projections of member states' contributions to the VAT-based and GNP-related own resources contain assumptions about economic performance. The three newest member states – Finland, Sweden and Austria – are expected to be net contributors, although in the short term Finland may be a net beneficiary.

Convergence criteria

The timetable for **Economic and Monetary Union** (EMU) laid down in the **Maastricht Treaty** as an addition to Article 109 of the **Treaty of Rome** (Articles 109a–m) makes EMU conditional upon the 'sustainable convergence' of the economies of member states (Article 109j). The first of the four convergence criteria is 'a high degree of price stability ... apparent from a rate of inflation which is close to that of, at most, the three best performing Member States'. The second is the elimination of public sector deficits defined as 'excessive' in accordance with criteria laid down in Article 104c EEC and in a protocol on the **excessive deficit**

procedure. The third is observance of the 'normal fluctuation margins' provided for in the **Exchange–Rate Mechanism** (ERM) for at least two years, with no devaluation against the currency of any other member state. The fourth criterion, which relates to the sustainability of the convergence, is the level of long-term interest rates, which must not exceed by more than 2 per cent the average of interest rates in the three best-performing member states, assessed in terms of price stability.

Under the same Article the **European Commission** and the **European Monetary Institute** (EMI) are required to make regular reports to the **Ecofin Council** on the economic performance of member states with reference to these four criteria. Together with other economic indicators, these reports will enable the Council (meeting as the **European Council**) to decide whether 'a majority of the Member States fulfil the necessary conditions for the adoption of a single currency' and on whether or not to proceed to the third stage of EMU. This decision, by **qualified majority**, must be taken no later than 31 December 1996 (for further details, see **Economic and Monetary Union**).

Cooperation Agreement

Article 113 of the **Treaty of Rome** specifies that the **Common Commercial Policy** (CCP) should be based on 'uniform principles', one of which is the conclusion of tariff and trade agreements. These are negotiated by the **Commission** on the basis of a mandate laid down by the **Council of Ministers** and under the general oversight of the **Article 113 Committee**. Consultation of the **European Parliament** is not required for agreements concluded under Article 113 (see Article 228.3 EEC).

The simplest form of trade agreement, normally concluded for a period of five years and often restricted to a particular product, is now known as a 'first generation' agreement. This is because in the 1980s it was found necessary to conclude more elaborate and ambitious agreements providing for economic and other forms of cooperation over a wider field. Article 113 EEC was not thought to be an adequate legal base for such 'second generation' Cooperation Agreements, and so **Article 235** EEC was used in addition. Cooperation Agreements of this type, which are each managed by a joint committee, normally allow for financial assistance from the Union and are open-ended in the sense that they contain a *clause évolutive*, which provides for cooperation to be extended into new fields. Agreements of this type have been concluded with India, China, Pakistan and several countries in Latin America.

A still more ambitious 'third generation' of Cooperation Agreements has since been developed. These are similar to the 'second generation' agreements, but contain extra elements such as human rights clauses, joint undertakings in the fight against drug-trafficking, and regular political contacts. Such agreements have been concluded with certain countries in Latin America and are a model for future relations with many countries in South-east Asia. The human rights clauses in particular have proved controversial, since some countries regard them as a form of interference in their internal affairs.

Cooperation procedure

The cooperation procedure, which is set out in Article 189c of the **Treaty of Rome**, was introduced by the 1986 **Single European Act** (SEA) as a means of strengthening the role of the **European Parliament** in the legislative process, thus going some way towards correcting the **democratic deficit**. This, it was feared, had been opened still wider by the extension under the SEA of **qualified majority voting** (QMV) in the **Council of Ministers**. It allows for the Parliament to be consulted twice before a legislative measure is enacted (see below). The cooperation procedure was further developed by the **Maastricht Treaty** as the **co-decision procedure** (Article 189b EEC).

Under the cooperation procedure the Commission forwards a draft proposal to the Council of Ministers. At the same time the European Parliament (and frequently the **Economic and Social Committee** and the **Committee of the Regions**) begins its examination of the proposal; when completed, this is forwarded to the Council as the Parliament's **Opinion**. The Council's conclusion, adopted by QMV, is reached in the form of a **common position**, and this is sent back to the Parliament accompanied by an explanation of the views of the Council and the Commission. The Parliament may then, by simple majority, adopt the common position or fail to take action: in either case, the Council may then proceed to formal enactment of the proposal as embodied in its common position. However, by absolute majority, the Parliament may seek to amend the common position or reject it altogether.

If the Parliament votes to reject a common position, the Council must act unanimously to have it reinstated. If (as is more usual) the Parliament has adopted amendments to the common position, the Commission then has an opportunity to re-examine its original proposal in the light of these amendments, and to forward the results of the re-examination to the Council with all the Parliament's amendments. The Council may adopt by unanimity amendments that the Commission has not incorporated in its revised proposal. Also by unanimity, it may amend the revised proposal. It may adopt and enact the revised proposal by QMV. If it fails to take a decision within a deadline, the proposal falls.

Amongst the areas to which the cooperation procedure applies are: measures to prohibit discrimination on grounds of nationality (Article 6 EEC), rules governing international transport and transport safety (Article 75 EEC), the **European Social Fund** (Article 125 EEC), specific actions in relation to the environment (Article 130s EEC), development policy (Article 130w EEC), and social policy (Article 2 of the Social Protocol: see **Social Chapter**).

The introduction of the cooperation procedure (the SEA came into force in July 1987) not only gave the Parliament a second opportunity to influence the substance of legislation but also changed the balance of power between the institutions of the Union to the Parliament's advantage. By using the threat of outright rejection, the Parliament is in a stronger position to enforce its views upon the Commission and the Council. The procedure also requires the Parliament to exercise greater discipline as a consequence of the need to muster an absolute majority to reject or amend the Council's common position (this in turn has had an effect on relations between the **political groups** in the Parliament).

The cooperation procedure has been criticized for being too complicated. At one stage in the negotiations that led to the SEA a much simpler solution was proposed: the Council of Ministers should deliberate on a legislative proposal as amended by the Parliament. This was not acceptable to certain member states, which took the view that this procedure would make the Parliament too powerful, nor to the Commission, which feared the virtual elimination of the 'brokerage' role from which much of its power derives. The procedure that finally emerged was a compromise.

COREPER

'COREPER' is derived from *Comité des représentants permanents* (Committee of Permanent Representatives), a body provided for in Article 151 of the **Treaty of Rome**. The Permanent Representatives are the Brussels-based ambassadors of the member states of the European Union (see **national representations**). COREPER's most important task is the preparation of meetings of the **Council of Ministers** (see also **political directors, UKREP**).

COREUR

COREUR is the system by which the foreign offices of the member states of the European Union exchange information in the form of circulated telegrams, telex messages and faxes, under the overall supervision of the **political directors** and their assistants (the 'European correspondents'). First devised as an essential tool of **European Political Cooperation**, the COREUR network, involving many thousands of communications every year, has been maintained as part of the **Common Foreign and Security Policy** (CFSP).

COST

The scheme known as COST (European Coordination of Scientific and Technical Research) was set up in 1971 to promote cross-frontier collaboration between about 20 European countries in such fields as information technology, environmental protection, meteorology, health care and transport.

Coudenhove-Kalergi, Count Richard (1894–1972)

Born in Tokyo, the son of a diplomat in the Austro-Hungarian Embassy and a Japanese mother, Coudenhove-Kalergi was the best-known pioneer of the idea of a united Europe throughout the second quarter of this century. In Berlin and Vienna in the 1920s Coudenhove-Kalergi began his campaign for what he called **Pan-Europa** in a long series of books and articles. In 1922 he founded his 'Pan-European Union' and in October 1920 he convened a 'European Congress' in Vienna. This was followed by further congresses in Berlin (1930), Basle (1932), Vienna (1935) and New York (1943). He received the support and sympathy of many of the leading statesmen of the day (such as Walter Rathenau, **Aristide Briand**, **Winston Churchill**, and Thomas Masaryk) and of other figures in public life (such as the violinist Bronislaw Hubermann). In 1943 he drew up a constitution for a **United States of Europe** and submitted it for approval to all the foreign ministers of European states opposed to the Axis powers. After the war, at a meeting in Gstaad on 5 July 1947, he founded a 'European Parliamentary Union' with himself as Secretary-General. In 1952 he refounded his Pan-European Union, which became a member organization of the **European Movement** (although it later broke away). Coudenhove-Kalergi's approach to European integration was essentially political, as opposed to the more technocratic, economically oriented approach of **Jean Monnet** and his supporters. This led him to sympathize very strongly with **Charles de Gaulle**, who, from a different standpoint, also viewed European integration in political terms and whose principled opposition to the division of Europe brought about by the Yalta Agreement Coudenhove-Kalergi much admired. Although Coudenhove-Kalergi's ideas met with a sympathetic response amongst many politicians and intellectuals of all parties and nationalities, he was never successful in attracting mass support. An account of his activities and ideas may be found in his *An Idea Conquers the World* (1953).

Council for Mutual Economic Assistance

See COMECON.

Council of Economic and Finance Ministers

See **Ecofin Council**.

Council of Europe

Founded in 1949, the Council of Europe is an intergovernmental consultative organization with a current membership of 38 countries and 6 with 'special guest status'. It was set up in response to a resolution adopted by the 1948 **Congress of Europe**, with its seat (at the suggestion of Ernest Bevin) in **Strasbourg**, and is not an institution of the European Union. Much of its work is concerned with human rights, education, culture and cooperation in such fields as the protection of the environment, medical ethics and the fight against drugs. More recently, the Council of Europe has been very active in respect of constitutional and legislative reform in the countries of central and eastern Europe.

The founder members of the Council of Europe were Denmark, Sweden, the United Kingdom, Norway, Ireland, Italy, Luxembourg, France, the Netherlands, Belgium and Greece. In 1950 they were joined by Iceland, Turkey and (in an act of reconciliation first suggested by **Winston Churchill**) the Federal Republic of Germany. Austria joined in 1956 once Russian forces had withdrawn from Austrian territory. Cyprus, Switzerland and Malta joined in the 1960s, Portugal, Spain and Liechtenstein in the 1970s, San Marino and Finland in the 1980s. The first of the former Communist countries to join were Hungary (1990) and Czechoslovakia (1991). They have since been followed in rapid succession by Albania, Andorra, Bulgaria, Estonia, Latvia, Lithuania, Macedonia, Moldova, Poland, Romania and Slovenia. In 1995 Ukraine became the thirty-eighth member state. 'Special guest' members are Belarus, Bosnia-Herzegovina, Croatia and (likely to join in 1996) Russia.

The three main institutions of the Council of Europe are the Committee of Ministers (foreign ministers or their deputies), the Parliamentary Assembly (formerly the Consultative Assembly, composed of 263 members and 263 substitutes appointed from and by **national parliaments** and divided into five **political groups**), and the Congress of Local and Regional Authorities of Europe. The Council of Europe has its own secretariat of approximately 1,200 officials, headed by a secretary-general elected by the Assembly. Meeting in plenary session four times a year, the Parliamentary Assembly adopts **Resolutions** addressed to the Committee of Ministers, which takes decisions by consensus, addressed to member states in the form of Recommendations. The Congress (which is bicameral, with one chamber for local authorities and another for regional authorities) may also adopt Resolutions. The official languages of the Council of Europe are French and English, but interpretation from and into other languages may be provided at the expense of individual national delegations at meetings of the Parliamentary Assembly and the Congress.

The European Commission of Human Rights and the Court of Human Rights are organs of the Council of Europe (see **human rights**; it is proposed to merge the two into a single court).

Unlike the institutions of the European Union, the institutions of the Council of Europe have no power to make laws. Instead, a consensus reached at the level of the Committee of Ministers may be embodied in a convention, which is then open for signature by individual states. Less formally, the consensus may be drawn up as a charter or code. There are now some 150 conventions, charters or codes: amongst the best known are the 1950 European Convention on Human Rights, the 1954 European Cultural Convention, the 1979 Berne Convention on the protection of rare and endangered animals and plants, the 1981 Convention on data protection and the 1990 Convention on measures to locate, freeze and confiscate assets associated with organized crime.

The Council of Europe has an annual budget of approximately £132 million (1994), made up largely of contributions from member states. It operates certain specialized loan facilities: for example, under its 'Eurimages' programme, European film companies can borrow against estimated revenues from co-productions.

In its historical context the Council of Europe was a compromise between those who advocated European integration along supranational lines and those who, although in favour of a wide measure of cooperation, wanted national governments to retain firm control over the process. In its very early years the Council of Europe was indeed the main forum for debate over the future of Europe: it was where, for example, Churchill first called for the creation of a **European Army**. However, like many compromises, it satisfied nobody. Governments largely ignored the Council's recommendations and by 1951 **the Six** had with the signing of the **European Coal and Steel Community** (ECSC) Treaty embarked upon a more ambitious project. The first blow to the Council of Europe's prestige came in 1952 when the ECSC Common Assembly, not the Council of Europe Assembly, was chosen to draw up the treaty for a **European Political Community** (although a compromise solution was later found in the form of an *ad hoc* assembly). By the end of the 1950s the focus of attention had shifted decisively away from the Council of Europe and towards what was to become the European Community and, later, the European Union.

Until the end of the 1980s the importance of the Council of Europe was limited to three main areas. First, it was a forum in which countries not belonging to the European Community could remain in touch with the integration process. Second, membership of the Council of Europe was an indispensable proof of democratic credentials for countries (like Portugal and Spain in the mid-1970s) wanting to regain their international respectability after periods of dictatorship. This aspect of the Council's role was reinforced by the decision to suspend the membership of Greece and Turkey during periods of military rule, and played an important part in the Council's re-emergence after the collapse of Communism. Third, the Council made steady and substantial progress in the field of human rights, an area largely excluded from the European Community Treaties.

Since 1989 the Council of Europe has acted as an antechamber for countries of central and eastern Europe, the majority of which are, in the longer term, interested in membership of the European Union. In response to their demands the Council has set up a European Commission for Democracy through Law, based in Venice, to advise on questions of legal and constitutional reform and the operation of democratic institutions. The Council has also inaugurated a series of summit meetings for heads of government, the first of which was held in Vienna in October 1993.

Council of Ministers

The Council of Ministers is the principal decision-making body within the European Union. It has both executive and legislative powers, the former devolved in many areas to the **Commission** and the latter in some cases exercised jointly with the **European Parliament** (see **co-decision procedure**). The Parliament and the Council form the joint budgetary authority (see **Budget**). The Council is responsible for authorizing, overseeing and concluding negotiations with non-member countries. Under the **Common Foreign and Security Policy** (CFSP) and **Justice and Home Affairs** (JHA) provisions of the **Maastricht Treaty**, the Council may adopt **common positions** or take **joint actions**. Overall, the Council acts within guidelines laid down by the **European Council** of heads of state or of government. The **presidency** of the Council changes every six months.

Articles 145 to 154 of the **Treaty of Rome** set out the powers, composition and procedures of the Council. Article 145 EEC gives the Council the power to coordinate the economic policies of member states, to take decisions and to confer implementing powers on the Commission. Article 146 EEC requires the Council to be composed 'of a representative of each

Member State at ministerial level, authorized to commit the government of that Member State' (this wording, introduced by the Maastricht Treaty, allows federal states such as Belgium or Germany to be represented if necessary by a minister from a provincial or *Land* government). Article 148 EEC specifies that decisions should normally be taken by majority and lists the weightings for the vote of each member state under the **qualified majority voting** (QMV) system (see below). The same Article says that abstentions do not count in decisions requiring unanimity. The Council's Rules of Procedure were published in the *Official Journal* on 10 December 1993 (L304).

The Council of Ministers may convene in any configuration it chooses. In practice, it divides its work into several distinct subject-based councils that operate in parallel. The senior council within this structure is the Council of Foreign Ministers (officially called the General Affairs Council), and the Foreign Minister of each member state is its lead representative on the Council. Exceptionally, the European Council may meet as the Council of Ministers, for example when the decision is taken when and whether to proceed to stage 3 of **Economic and Monetary Union** (EMU; Article 109j EEC).

The Foreign Affairs Council normally meets monthly, as do the Councils of Agriculture Ministers, and of Economics and Finance Ministers (see **Ecofin Council**). There are regular, but less frequent, meetings of the Industry, Environment, Research, Transport, Social Affairs, Fisheries and Budget Councils. Less frequent still are meetings of ministers of development, energy, justice, consumer affairs, regional affairs, culture, education and health. From time to time joint or 'jumbo' Councils may be arranged to discuss issues that cross the boundaries of any one Council's responsibilities. Examples include the joint Ecofin and Agriculture Council of June 1987 on agricultural spending, and the joint Foreign Affairs and Agriculture Council of January 1992 to discuss the Uruguay Round. In all, the Council has in recent years met on average about 80 times a year.

Although the Council of Ministers is the chief forum for the representation of national interests in the decision-making process, the Council's acts are those of a fully-fledged Union institution, made on behalf of and in the name of the Union as a whole. In its capacity as the legislature, the Council can adopt any of the types of **legal instrument** provided for in the Treaties. It can also issue non-binding recommendations to member states or adopt **Resolutions**. Its non-legislative activities usually take the form of 'conclusions' – issued by the presidency, with or without the unanimous approval of the whole Council – which represent the emerging lines of an agreement that may subsequently be converted into legislative action.

The Councils established for each of the three original European Communities were amalgamated in 1967 by the **Merger Treaty**. The powers of today's Council are based on those in the originating Treaties, as elaborated by subsequent amendments.

The Council can take decisions by **unanimity**, QMV or simple majority voting. The Treaties provide that, except where otherwise prescribed, simple majority voting will be the norm. However, in nearly all areas the Treaties require either QMV or unanimity. For the greater part of the Community's history, unanimity was the operating principle of the Council, even where theoretically a decision could be taken by qualified or simple majority. The extension of majority voting in 1966, when the third stage of the 'transitional' phase of the Community's development came into effect, was overshadowed by an informal agreement, concluded in January of that year, known as the **Luxembourg Compromise**. This in practice gave any member state a right of **veto** on a matter that it considered to touch on a 'very important' national interest. This meant that votes were rarely, if ever, taken, except sometimes on detailed agricultural or budgetary issues, and an objection from any member state – whether or not a 'very important' interest was really at stake – was enough to kill a proposal.

The member state holding the presidency is responsible for organizing the business of the Council. The presidency is assisted by a permanent general secretariat of 2,300 officials based entirely in Brussels and grouped into six policy-related directorates-general which service the respective Councils. They draw up the minutes of the Council, suggest compromise texts to the presidency and ensure that the acts of the Council are properly transposed into legal form and duly published in the *Official Journal*. The Council secretariat also contains a legal service, whose impartial advice on the form and Treaty basis of any proposal carries considerable authority with the member states. However, the Council secretariat's capacity to influence the content of decision-making is often inversely proportional to the size of the member state holding the presidency. The five largest member states tend to find that their own **national representations** in Brussels are so large that they can free themselves of reliance on the technical expertise and institutional memory of the Council secretariat. Smaller member states are much more reliant.

Officials from the national representations meet together regularly to prepare the various decisions to be taken by ministers in full Council. There are two tiers, COREPER (see also **national representations**) and working groups. COREPER – an acronym for the French rendering of 'Committee of Permanent Representatives' – brings together the ambassadors of member states, their deputies and relevant colleagues, to discuss the agenda of forthcoming meetings of the Council of Ministers. COREPER's influence is often greater than that of the formal meetings of the Council which it prepares. In the foreign policy field a political committee (see **political directors**) performs many of the same functions as COREPER and in the **justice and home affairs** field a coordinating committee does the same.

Working groups, made up of mid-rank civil servants from the national representations and (where necessary) domestic ministries, prepare the ground before items are taken to COREPER and then the full Council. The purpose of discussion in both tiers is to identify in precise detail the points of agreement and discord on any proposal, and to try to resolve remaining disagreements so that the higher body (COREPER or the full Council) can focus on major points of dispute. Once a point has been settled at a lower level, the presidency will try to avoid its being reopened at a higher level. The power of mid-rank civil servants in this system is thus significant. Council agendas are divided into A and B points, the former being issues that have already been satisfactorily concluded at an official level.

COREPER and the working groups are also serviced by the Council secretariat and chaired by the country holding the presidency. As in the full Council, the Commission is normally present at, and participates in, all their meetings.

The Council normally meets in Brussels, but three times a year (April, June and October) it meets in Luxembourg, as part of the 1965 arrangement on the provisional location of various institutions (see **seat of the institutions**). In addition, the presidency normally convenes one 'informal' weekend meeting of each Council in its own country (see **Gymnich meetings**). These are, by definition, not formal or official meetings of the Council, and have no legal status. Usually they are devoted to open-ended discussion of large and difficult problems on the Council's agenda, in the hope of finding new common ground. Informals do not reach conclusions as such, and normally issue no communiqués. They can, however, be the scene for important political breakthroughs, although their rather cloudy and often unverifiable outcomes can render them easy prey to sensationalist media reporting.

Similar to full Council meetings but distinct from them in law are the gatherings of 'Representatives of the Governments of Member States meeting in Council'. These take certain decisions which the Treaties specify as being for the member states acting collectively by 'common accord' rather than for the Council as an institution of the Union. Sometimes these decisions are taken in practice by the European Council and then formalized as having been taken by representatives 'meeting in Council' later, and include matters such as appointments to the Commission or the **Court of Justice** and the location of the institutions. The right of Members of the European Parliament (MEPs) to put questions to the Council does not extend to matters decided on the basis of agreement between the governments of member states.

In spite of hesitant moves in the direction of greater openness (see **transparency**), the Council remains the most secretive as well as the most powerful of the institutions of the Union. Together with a review of the threshold for agreement under QMV (see above), opening up the Council – the only legislature in the democratic world that takes decisions largely in secret – is likely to feature prominently on the agenda of the 1996 **Intergovernmental Conference** (IGC) on institutional reform. So too will the possibility of the Council sharing legislative power with the European Parliament over a wider field and of **national parliaments** individually or collectively asserting much more influence over the Council.

What is unlikely to happen even in the longer term is that the Council will become a **Chamber of States** in a bicameral system, in which the Commission is the real European government. This, in simple terms, is what some of the enthusiasts for European integration in the 1950s thought would happen. One of the central features of the institutional development of the Union is the permanence and vitality of national interests as represented in the Council.

Court of Auditors

Expenditure by institutions of the European Union is subject to both internal and external controls. Internal controls are the responsibility of the Directorate-General for Financial Control (DG XX) in the **European Commission** and of similar bodies in other institutions. External controls have since 1977 been the responsibility of the Court of Auditors, a separate institution composed of one appointee (or 'Member') from each member state and a staff of about 400 people. It is based in Luxembourg.

External financial controls, of which the Court is the principal symbol, have been very substantially strengthened since the establishment of the European Communities. Initially, responsibility for financial control was vested with a small Audit Board composed for the most part of officials from the national audit offices or Ministries of Finance of the member states. Under a Council Decision of 15 May 1959 the Audit Board – the members of which were appointed for a five-year period by the Council of Ministers – was required 'to exercise its functions in the general interest of the Communities'. Its main task was to draw up a report on the Communities' annual income and expenditure, a report that was forwarded to the Council and (from 1970) the **European Parliament** with the annual accounts prepared by the Commission as part of the **discharge procedure**.

The first **enlargement** of the Community (1973), several well-publi-cized instances of fraud in the **Common Agricultural Policy** (CAP), and the growth in the size of the **Budget** reinforced a feeling, especially amongst Members of the European Parliament (MEPs), that the Audit Board lacked the resources, independence and authority to do its job effectively. The Parliament was also interested in strengthening its own powers of democratic control over Community expenditure, and the new Audit Office for which the Parliament pressed was expected to work very closely with the Parliament's Budgets Committee. A report entitled *The Case for a European Audit Office* was published in September 1973.

In July 1975 the representatives of the member states signed a treaty on budgetary and financial provisions, which, *inter alia*, enhanced the budget-ary powers of the European Parliament. Under this treaty, which came into effect in 1977, important changes were made to external financial controls. The Audit Board was replaced by a Court of Auditors. The term of office of the members of the Court was extended from five to six years, and they were given the right to elect from amongst their own number a president for a renewable three-year term. The Council is required to consult the European Parliament on appointments to the Court.

The Court's remit covers not only all the Union institutions but all national, regional and local bodies that receive or handle Union funds both in the member states and elsewhere (for example, in developing countries). Since the definition of Union funds includes not only those entered in the annual Budget but also borrowing and lending through the **European Investment Bank** (EIB), the total volume of expenditure for which the Court is responsible is very large.

The Court's findings are contained in a report adopted by simple majority of its members in November every year. The Court is required to verify that all revenue and expenditure is consistent with the relevant legal provisions, that good accounting practice has been followed, that financial management has been sound and that financial objectives have been met. This is done on the basis of documentary or on-the-spot audits. The Court also produces special reports on particular subjects, and is required to give its opinion on any changes proposed by the Commission to the financial regulations or to the system of **own resources**.

The title 'Court' is a misnomer. It was chosen because several member states have similar bodies known as 'courts', but in fact the Court has no power to pass sentence, insist on repayment of misappropriated funds or impose any kind of sanction. The Court's powers are confined to drawing irregularities and shortcomings to the attention of the responsible authorities in the institution concerned, which may or may not act upon the Court's advice. If no action is taken, all the Court can do is to draw attention to the fact in a subsequent report and withhold its approval of the institution's accounts for the financial year in question. The Court has persistently drawn attention to the Council's failure adequately to consider the Court's reports, a criticism endorsed by the House of Lords Select Committee on the European Communities (*Fraud against the Community*, February 1989; *Financial Control and Fraud in the Community*, July 1994). The **Maastricht Treaty** gave the Court the full status of an institution, and this will allow the Court for the first time to bring actions in its own right in the **Court of Justice**.

There is some evidence that the effectiveness of the Court of Auditors has been diminished by the fact that there is no consensus within the Community or even amongst the members of the Court on the proper role of an auditor. The narrow definition of auditing is concerned solely with the correspondence between the allocation of funds, the disbursement of those funds and the propriety of the accounting procedures. A broader definition would give the Court autonomous investigative powers and allow it to undertake 'value for money' auditing, but so far there has been great reluctance to allow the Court a more political role, and the Court has not pressed for it.

Court of First Instance (CFI)

Article 11 of the **Single European Act** (SEA) authorized the **Council of Ministers** to 'attach to the **Court of Justice** a court with jurisdiction to hear and determine at first instance . . . certain classes of action or proceeding brought by natural or legal persons'. This provision was added to the **Treaty of Rome** as Article 168a. Briefly, its purpose was to relieve the overburdened Court of Justice of certain categories of action (see below) that were already taking up a disproportionate amount of the Court's time. The CFI, composed of a judge from each member state appointed for six years (the judges elect their own president for a three-year term), became operational on 1 November 1989. Cases are normally heard by a panel of three or five judges.

The jurisdiction of the CFI at first extended to disputes between the Community institutions and their employees (staff cases); actions brought against the **Commission** under the **Treaty of Paris** in respect of levies, production quotas, prices, restrictive agreements and concentrations; and actions brought against the Commission for wrongful application or failure to apply the competition provisions of the Treaty of Rome. In 1993 the CFI's jurisdiction was extended to include actions (other than those brought by Community institutions or member states) to annul

Community legislation, for failure to enact such legislation and certain other types of action. Actions relating to anti-dumping measures and to intellectual property, except those brought by the Community or member states, were transferred from the Court of Justice to the CFI in 1994. Decisions of the CFI may be appealed against in the Court of Justice within a two-month deadline, but only with respect to points of law. The CFI is not empowered to give **preliminary rulings**.

Court of Justice

The Court of Justice, which is based in Luxembourg, is the final arbiter in disputes arising from the Community **Treaties** or the legislation based upon them. It was one of the four Community institutions established in 1951 under Article 7 of the **European Coal and Steel Community** (ECSC) Treaty. It has a general responsibility under Article 31 of the ECSC Treaty, Article 164 of the **Treaty of Rome** establishing the **European Economic Community** (EEC), and Article 136 of the Euratom Treaty (see **European Atomic Energy Community**) 'to ensure that in the interpretation and application [of these Treaties], the law is observed'.

The structure, jurisdiction and powers of the Court are laid down in the Treaties; the references that follow are to the Treaty of Rome. The organization and procedures of the Court are set out in the Statute of the Court, annexed as a protocol to each of the three Treaties. The Court consists of 15 judges (Article 165), one from each member state. The judges are assisted by nine **advocates-general** (Article 166). The task of the advocates-general is to make 'reasoned submissions' in open court on the cases upon which the Court is required to adjudicate. Both the judges and the advocates-general are appointed by the governments of the member states for a six-year term (Article 167), but to ensure continuity, a system of partial replacement is applied every three years, with the possibility of reappointment. The president of the Court is elected by the judges from amongst their number for a three-year term, and may be re-elected. The judges and advocates-general are required to be 'persons whose independence is beyond doubt and who possess the qualifications required for appointment to the highest judicial offices in their respective countries or who are jurisconsults of recognized competence'. The Court normally sits as a panel of three or five judges, and less frequently in plenary session, for which a quorum of seven is sufficient. The senior official of the Court is the Registrar.

The Court's main areas of jurisdiction are as follows:

1 Failure on the part of a member state to fulfil a Treaty obligation (Articles 169 to 171)

Such an action may be brought either by the **Commission** or by another member state. In both cases the Commission is required to deliver a 'reasoned opinion', having given the state or states concerned an opportunity to submit their observations. If the Court finds that a member state has failed to fulfil a treaty obligation, the state is required 'to take the necessary measures'.

2 Judicial review (Articles 173, 174 and 176)

The Court is empowered to 'review the legality' of **legal instruments** adopted by the **Council of Ministers** or the Commission, and certain acts of the **European Parliament**. Actions under this provision may be brought by the Council, the Commission, or by a member state, or by the European Parliament (but only to protect its own prerogatives). Individuals or entities possessing legal personality may also bring such actions in respect of Regulations or Decisions directly concerning them, but these actions are heard in the **Court of First Instance** (CFI). The Court may declare void the legal act which is the subject of the complaint, and require the offending institution to take the 'necessary measures'. The most common grounds for bringing an Article 173 action is the inadequacy of the legal base.

3 Failure to act (Articles 175 and 176)

If the Council, the Commission or (since the **Maastricht Treaty**) the European Parliament fails to act and in so doing infringes a requirement laid down in the Treaties, a member state or any Community institution (Commission, Council or Parliament, and, since the Maastricht Treaty, the **Court of Auditors**) may bring an action before the Court 'to have the infringement established'. Individuals may bring such actions on the same basis as in 2 above. Once again, the Court may require the offending institution to take the 'necessary measures'.

4 Preliminary rulings (Article 177)

In the event of a question of Treaty interpretation or the validity or interpretation of acts of the Community institutions being raised before a national court, that court may request the Court of Justice to give a **preliminary ruling**. The Court's ruling *must* be sought when such a question is raised before a national court against whose decisions there is no final appeal. The Article 177 procedure is used to resolve any question of incompatibility between Community law and national law.

The Court also has jurisdiction in cases brought by Community officials against the Community institutions and disputes involving the Community's **competition** rules, but in such cases the Court's jurisdiction is now exercised by the CFI, introduced under the **Single European Act** (SEA) and established under a Council Decision of 24 October 1988.

The number of cases brought before the Court has increased spectacularly since 1970. In that year 79 cases were brought, but by 1985 the number had increased to 433 and is now running at an annual average of about 400. Even though many cases are disposed of in groups, and although some do not result in the Court having to give a final judgment, the backlog of cases pending has inexorably increased (and it was this that led to the decision to establish a Court of First Instance). A preliminary ruling usually takes more than 18 months to be delivered, and a direct action is rarely resolved in less than two years.

The Maastricht Treaty incorporates several changes to the Treaty of Rome provisions concerning the Court of Justice. The Court is given the power to impose 'a lump sum or penalty payment' on a member state found to have failed to fulfil a treaty obligation (new Article 171). Legal acts of the European Parliament may be challenged under the judicial review procedure, and failure to act on the part of the Parliament may also be subject to an action before the Court if the Treaty is thereby infringed. The **European Central Bank** is also brought within the Court's jurisdiction.

The Court's procedures are based almost wholly on written submissions from the contending parties. One of the Union's official **languages** is chosen as the procedural language, but otherwise the normal Community rules on the use of official languages apply. French and English are the working languages. The governments of member states and Union institutions may choose to intervene in actions in which they are not directly involved. There is no appeal against the Court's judgments, which are published periodically in *European Court Reports*. They are binding with effect from the date of delivery. Judgments are delivered in the name of the Court as a whole, i.e., dissenting opinions (if any) are not recorded.

Under Articles 105 to 107 of the 1992 agreement establishing the **European Economic Area** (EEA), the Court (together with the CFI, the **European Free Trade Area** (EFTA) Court and the courts of final appeal in the EFTA countries) is required to transmit its judgments on matters covered by the EEA Agreement to the EEA Joint Committee, which is responsible for the 'homogeneous interpretation of the Agreement'.

The Court has played a discreet but substantial role in furthering the objectives laid down in the Treaties, a role similar to that played by the United States Supreme Court with respect to the US Constitution. The Court has done this by working within a tradition of interpretation that allows the 'ultimate purpose' of a piece of legislation to be taken into consideration. This means that it is entirely legitimate, with respect to a particular text, to take not only the exact purport of the words into account, but also anything that may usefully and convincingly be adduced about the intention behind the words. This has resulted in the Court tending to give a 'dynamic' rather than a strictly literal interpretation of treaty provisions, and this has proved a key element in some of the Court's most noteworthy judgments (see also **Community law**). The classic account of this aspect of the Court's work is Hjerte Rasmussen, *On Law and Policy in the European Court of Justice* (The Hague, 1986).

Crocodile Club

Founded in Strasbourg in 1980 and named after the restaurant in which its members met, the all-party Crocodile Club was the creation of **Altiero Spinelli** and other Members of the **European Parliament** (MEPs) who shared his enthusiasm for institutional reform. The Club acquired more official status as the Federalist Intergroup for European Union and continues to produce a bilingual newsletter (*Crocodile*) on institutional matters.

Cultural policy

Cultural policy is primarily the responsibility of the **Council of Europe**. Since the early 1950s the Council of Europe has been very active in respect of the documenting and conservation of historic buildings, the mounting of major exhibitions, the safeguarding of minority cultures, the role of culture in education and the promotion of cross-frontier cooperation in various fields of creative activity (for example, through the 'Eurimages' programme). To this end, as in other areas of the Council of Europe's work, various conventions have been drawn up. At the level of symbolism, the Council of Europe was also responsible for the **European anthem** and the **European flag**.

A new Article 128 was added to the **Treaty of Rome** by the **Maastricht Treaty**. This Article refers to the contribution to be made 'to the flowering of the cultures of the Member States, while respecting their national and regional diversity and at the same time bringing the common cultural heritage to the fore', but does not allow 'any harmonization of the laws and regulations of the Member States'. (See also **European Cultural Centre.**)

Earlier references to cultural policy may be found in such documents as the 1973 declaration on **European identity**, the 1975 **Tindemans Report** on European Union, the 1983 **Stuttgart Declaration**, and the 1985 report of the **People's Europe** Committee. From the mid-1980s a series of agreements was reached, although because there was no legal base many of them lacked legislative force. They included measures to combat audio-visual piracy, the introduction of a **European City of Culture** scheme, the encouragement of commercial sponsorship for cultural activities, the provision of money in the **Budget** to contribute towards the translation and publication of 'important works of European culture', various measures on copyright and a common system of export licences for goods of cultural value. Certain **Single Market** measures also have a cultural dimension: for example, the tax treatment of secondhand goods and of auction houses. The European Community Youth Orchestra was founded in 1985 to mark European Music Year.

The November 1992 Council conclusions on guidelines for Community cultural action emphasized that such action 'should not supplant or compete with activities organized at national or regional level, but provide added value and promote interchange between them'. The Commission has brought forward proposals on measures to safeguard and promote public awareness of the cultural heritage (see also **Socrates**, **European University Institute**, **Kaleidoscope 2000**).

Customs union

A customs union is a territory within which there are no internal barriers to the free movement of goods and in respect of which a single set of rules, tariffs, quotas, etc., is applied to goods entering the territory from outside. The expression is normally used to denote a territory within which two or more contiguous states have agreed to form such a union. A customs union is a 'regional trading arrangement' within the meaning of Article XXIV of the **General Agreement on Tariffs and Trade** (GATT), and the members of a customs union are exempt from the requirement to accord 'most favoured nation' treatment to non-members.

A customs union may be either an end in itself or a means towards a political end. In the last century the best-known examples of customs unions were the Prussian-dominated *Zollverein* and the abolition of the restrictions on trade applied by the city-states of pre-unification Italy: before 1848, for example, there were no fewer than eight tolls payable at frontiers on goods being transported over the 240 kilometres from Milan to Florence. Both these examples are customs unions that were quite clearly an economic means to a political end, but in the present century the **Belgo-Luxembourg Economic Union** (BLEU) and the Switzerland–Liechtenstein customs union are examples of arrangements with an exclusively economic purpose.

The **League of Nations**, through its Committee for European Union, attempted to foster the establishment of customs unions. But in 1933 G. D. H. and Margaret Cole, in a section headed 'The strangling of European trade' in *The Intelligent Man's Review of Europe Today*, commented: 'The moral is that if Europe is to be lifted out of the present depression . . . this cannot possibly be accomplished by a direct attack on tariffs, embargoes, exchange restrictions and the other secondary phenomena

of national distress, but only by a courageous attempt to remove the underlying economic causes of the trouble.' Six years later such very modest
progress as had been made was halted by the outbreak of war. However,
the period immediately after the war gave rise to several proposals for new
customs unions in Western Europe. The French expressed an interest –
partly as a means of containing Germany – in a customs union with Italy
and the **Benelux** countries. Other combinations, with ingenious names
like Fritalux or Finebel, were suggested. The Scandinavian countries too
were discussing a customs union amongst themselves, although both
Sweden and Denmark were more interested in establishing themselves in
continental markets. The Americans, both bilaterally and through the
Organization for European Economic Cooperation (see **Organization
for Economic Cooperation and Development**), did their best to
encourage the removal of barriers to trade within Western Europe. The
British, on the other hand, adopted a more cautious attitude, because
they were suspicious of the federalist ambitions held all too clearly by
many of the advocates of closer integration and because they believed
British involvement in a European customs union to be incompatible with
the system of Commonwealth preference and the sterling area upon which
their trading arrangements were still largely based. The political and
economic background to those discussions is set out in Chapter VII of
Milward, *The Reconstruction of Western Europe 1945–1951*.

The failure of the **European Defence Community** in 1954 prompted
the pioneers of European integration to try economic means to secure
their objective. With the success of the **European Coal and Steel
Community** (ECSC) behind them, it was obviously the time to attempt
something similar on a more ambitious scale. The **Treaty of Rome** lays
down as one of the foundations of the **European Economic Community**
'a customs union which shall cover all trade in goods and which shall
involve the prohibition between Member States of customs duties on
imports and exports and of all charges having equivalent effect, and the
adoption of a common customs tariff in their relations with third countries'
(Article 9 EEC). Ambitious deadlines were set for the progressive elimination of customs duties and quantitative restrictions (i.e., quotas) on trade
between member states. A general exemption (Article 36) was granted to
allow restrictions to be maintained 'on grounds of public morality, public
policy or public security; the protection of health and life of humans,
animals or plants; the protection of national treasures . . . [and] of industrial
and commercial property'.

Eighteen months ahead of schedule, the customs union amongst **the Six**
was completed. In a declaration to mark the occasion on 1 July 1968 the
Commission announced: 'By beginning the unification of the European

territory in this first form, the Six are taking a decisive step in the economic history of the continent.' But, the Commission said, the customs union must lead on to economic union, which in turn would lead on to 'a political Europe . . . [with] genuine federal institutions'.

As with all customs unions, economists are divided in their assessment of what impact the removal of tariffs and quotas had on trade amongst the Six, and on the balance between 'trade creation' and 'trade diversion' effects (see Swann, *The Economics of the Common Market*). What is undeniable is that over the first 10 years of the European Economic Community's existence (1958–68) trade between the member states grew by an annual average of 28.4 per cent.

In spite of this, progress towards economic union proved much more difficult. The removal of tariffs and quotas left **non-tariff barriers** intact. The service sector was assuming greater importance in the economy as a whole, and **freedom of establishment** and the harmonization of national legislation regulating, for example, banking and insurance were far from being achieved. Fiscal harmonization was proving a sensitive subject for certain member states. And by the early 1970s, with the first of the oil crises, it was clear that the years of postwar growth in the 1950s and 1960s were at least temporarily at an end. The Community's political energies were directed towards other areas, such as **enlargement** and institutional reform. Nevertheless, the customs union achieved on 1 July 1968 was an essential first step and was recognized internationally as a substantial triumph for the Community. Not until 1 January 1993, with the establishment of the **Single Market**, was a step of such significance taken towards one of the key objectives of the Treaty.

Cyprus

Cyprus became a British protectorate in 1878, but by the 1920s there was a strong campaign amongst Greek Cypriots for union (*enosis*) with Greece. The island became independent in 1960. In 1974, the last year of military rule in Greece, Turkish forces invaded Cyprus to protect the Turkish minority population, and since that date the northern third of the island has been under Turkish control. In 1983 the 'Turkish Republic of Northern Cyprus' (TRNC) proclaimed its independence. The TRNC is not recognized internationally, and successive United Nations (UN) Resolutions have condemned the partition of the island.

The year before the Turkish invasion Cyprus concluded an **Association Agreement** with the Community. The Agreement was intended to lead in two stages to a **customs union**. The first stage was not completed until 1987, and the second stage is due for completion in 1997. In line with UN Resolutions, the Community recognizes the government of the Republic

of Cyprus as the only duly constituted authority entitled to speak on
behalf of the island's population (some 720,000 people, of whom about 18
per cent are Turkish Cypriots living in the TRNC). Accordingly, protests
from the TRNC side were ignored when on 3 July 1990 the Cypriot
government applied for full membership of the Community on behalf of
the whole island.

The **Opinion** of the **Commission** was generally favourable (*Bulletin of
the European Communities*, supplement 5/93). Cyprus was shown to have
adapted very well to Community policies under the Association Agreement.
It now has a per capita gross domestic product (GDP) substantially higher
than that of Greece or Portugal. The Commission noted that both the
communities on the island supported Cypriot membership of the Union in
the belief that it would help to resolve internal tensions. However, the
Commission also drew attention to the problem that would arise if there
were no internal constitutional settlement before accession negotiations
began, and in general terms to the need to address the issue of **micro-
states** being admitted to the Union. The member states broadly endorsed
the Commission's conclusions, and at the Corfu meeting of the **European
Council** in June 1994 they agreed that in the next round of **enlargement**
negotiations Cyprus and Malta would be given priority. It was subsequently agreed that such negotiations would begin in 1997/8. Since February 1994 there has been an official European Union observer at talks
between the Cypriot government and the TRNC.

Cyprus is a member of the UN, the **Council of Europe**, and the
Conference on Security and Cooperation in Europe. The Cyprus
dispute was referred to amongst the Commission's reservations in its 1989
Opinion on possible Turkish accession to the Community (see **Turkey**).

Declaration

The results of discussions at meetings of the **European Council** are expressed in the form of 'conclusions of the Presidency'. Latterly, these have been supplemented by Declarations embodying more detailed agreements on points of substance. These Declarations have no legal force, but can be of great political importance as pointers to future legislative action. For example, the Dublin meeting of the European Council in June 1990 agreed a long Declaration on the environment. For the Declarations annexed to the Treaties, see **protocol**.

de Gasperi, Alcide (1881–1954)

Born in the Trentino (north-east Italy, then belonging to Austro-Hungary), de Gasperi's political career began as a member of the Imperial Parliament in Vienna. In 1918 he took Italian citizenship and became active as a journalist. A devout Catholic, he was one of the founders of the Partito Popolare Italiano (a forerunner of **Christian Democracy**). He was arrested and imprisoned in 1927 for his opposition to Fascism, but was released as a result of the intercession of Pope Pius IX, who secured for him a minor post in the Vatican library. De Gasperi continued his political work both as a Christian Democrat and as a member of the Resistance. During the Second World War he drew up the political programme of a new, specifically Catholic, political party and in 1943 outlined in *Idee recostruttive della Democrazia Cristiana* the structure of the post-Fascist Italian state. He guided Democrazia Cristiana during the delicate period between the armistice and the constitution of the new state. In December 1944 he became Foreign Minister, and Prime Minister a year later. His position was confirmed when Democrazia Cristiana emerged as the largest party, with 35 per cent of the vote, in the elections for the constituent assembly, held in June 1946. He was Prime Minister in the eight coalition governments that ruled Italy in the period up to 1953. He was active both in the postwar reconstruction of Italy (he was a strong advocate of regional autonomy) and in ensuring that Italy played a full part in the Atlantic Alliance and in the movement towards European integration led by **Robert Schuman** and **Jean Monnet**. In 1954 he was elected President of the Common Assembly of the **European Coal and Steel Community**

(ECSC), the forerunner of the **European Parliament**. He died in August 1954, a few days before the collapse of the **European Defence Community**. Alcide de Gasperi is regarded, particularly by Italian Christian Democrats, as one of the founding fathers of the European Community.

De Gaulle, Charles (1890–1970)

The wartime leader of the Free French, Charles de Gaulle withdrew from politics in 1946. He returned to power in 1958 (the year in which the **European Economic Community** came into operation), and was elected President the following year.

The Constitution of the Fifth Republic, largely designed by de Gaulle, gave the president substantial powers and (in its revised form, adopted by referendum in 1962) an independent political mandate of seven years. Amongst de Gaulle's highest priorities were the re-establishment of French pre-eminence in world affairs, most especially in Europe, and reconciliation with Germany (see **Franco-German cooperation**). De Gaulle's concern with French prestige and with national **sovereignty** led him to take a largely unsympathetic view of a Community built upon and administered by supranational institutions. However, he remained a strong supporter of European integration as a counterpoise to American dominance. That such integration should be along French lines became very clear in the abortive negotiations on the **Fouchet Plan** in 1961.

In 1963 and again in 1967 de Gaulle vetoed the United Kingdom's applications to join the European Community. De Gaulle saw the United Kingdom as a rival to French influence in Europe, and mistrusted the British attachment to free trade and the close British association with the Americans. His decision in 1966 to withdraw from the integrated military command structure of the **North Atlantic Treaty Organization** (NATO) was also prompted by a mistrust of American involvement (see also **Soames affair**).

In the early 1960s de Gaulle quarrelled with the **European Commission**, then led by its first president, **Walter Hallstein**. This quarrel was one of the causes of the 'empty chair crisis' of 1965 and the so-called **Luxembourg Compromise** reached the following year. Underlying these disputes was de Gaulle's vision of a *Europe des patries* in which the nation-states should remain pre-eminent.

De Gaulle was largely successful in restoring French self-esteem in the wake of the conflicts in Indo-China and Algeria and the chronic political instability that characterized the Fourth Republic. The political party that he founded (originally the Union pour la Nouvelle République) is still a powerful force in French politics as the Rassemblement pour la République (RPR). Many of de Gaulle's ideas about the way in which Europe should be integrated were taken up by his successors: for example, the creation of the **European Council** by **Valéry Giscard d'Estaing** was intended to strengthen the role of the states in Community decision-making.

De Gaulle retired in 1969 and died the following year. His autobiography remained unfinished. The standard biography of de Gaulle is by Jean Lacouture, *De Gaulle* (3 vols, Paris, 1984–6).

Delors, Jacques (b. 1925)

Jacques Delors entered politics through the civil service and the trade union movement. A Socialist, he was elected to the **European Parliament** in 1979, and returned to national politics in 1981 on his appointment as Economics and Finance Minister. Four years later, in 1985, he became President of the **European Commission**, serving until January 1995.

Delors was by far the most influential President of the Commission since **Walter Hallstein**. His presidency was marked by the **Single Market** programme, the accession of Portugal, Spain, Austria, Finland and Sweden (see **enlargement**), **German reunification**, the **Single European Act** (SEA) and the **Maastricht Treaty** (the latter containing the timetable for **Economic and Monetary Union** (EMU); see also **Delors Report**), the agreement on **future financing**, and the **European Economic Area** (EEA). In all these developments Delors was personally and deeply involved.

On the debit side of his presidency was the mood of crisis and uncertainty in 1992–3, triggered by the rejection of the Maastricht Treaty in the first Danish referendum of June 1992 and its near-rejection in the French referendum three months later. This was accompanied by the shocks to the **Exchange-Rate Mechanism** (ERM) in September 1992 and August 1993. Delors brought to the presidency a broad strategic vision, a clear model of the society and of the Union he wanted to create, and an inexhaustible appetite for detail. At the same time his management style within the Commission itself was criticized for a certain aloofness. He established good working relations with the principal European leaders of his day (with the partial exception of **Margaret Thatcher**) and with the European Parliament. There is an astute, comprehensive, and sympathetic portrait of Delors in Charles Grant's *Delors: The House that Jacques Built* (1994).

Delors Report

The Delors Report of April 1989 made recommendations on **Economic and Monetary Union** (EMU) that led directly to the **Intergovernmental Conference** (IGC) on EMU and to the EMU provisions of the **Maastricht Treaty**. The Hanover meeting of the **European Council** in June 1988 invited a committee composed of the governors of the central banks of the member states and three independent economists under the chairmanship of **Jacques Delors** to study and bring forward proposals for 'concrete stages' leading to EMU. The Committee's unanimously agreed report was discussed by the European Council in Madrid in June 1989.

The first chapter of the report made the case for EMU as an essential complement to the **Single Market**. The second chapter set out the key components of EMU, including a **European Monetary Institute** (EMI) and a **European Central Bank** (ECB), and the need for 'irrevocably fixed exchange rates between national currencies and, finally, a single currency'. National economic policies, it was proposed, would have to be 'placed in an agreed macro-economic framework and be subject to binding procedures and rules'. The report recognized that a greater degree of **convergence** in respect of the economic performance of member states would have to be achieved if EMU were to work successfully. The third and final chapter set out the three stages ('discrete but evolutionary steps') in which EMU would be created. Crucially, the report observed that for the whole enterprise to secure the necessary credibility 'the decision to enter upon the first stage should be a decision to embark on the entire process'. The report reached the inevitable conclusion that proposals of this importance would, if agreed, have to be embodied in changes to the **Treaty of Rome**, and so it recommended the convening of an IGC under Article 236 EEC (since replaced by Article N TEU).

In Madrid the main obstacle was the position of the British government of **Margaret Thatcher**. Most other countries were prepared to accept the report's proposals, but Mrs Thatcher was unwilling to let sterling enter the **Exchange-Rate Mechanism** (ERM) under Stage 1 of EMU, very unwilling to allow embarking upon Stage 1 to be construed as a commitment to the whole EMU process and very unenthusiastic about the idea of an IGC on EMU. Under strong pressure from her Chancellor of the Exchequer, Nigel Lawson, and her Foreign Secretary, Sir Geoffrey Howe – both of whom had threatened to resign – Mrs Thatcher announced her acceptance of Stage 1 on condition that Stages 2 and 3 be left open and no IGC convened. The Delors Report, the European Council concluded, was 'a good basis for further work'. This compromise, unsatisfactory to most member states, lasted throughout the autumn, but at the Strasbourg meeting of the European Council in December 1989 it was agreed, on a proposal from President Mitterrand and against a lone British objection, to convene an IGC on EMU the following year.

Democratic deficit

The phrase 'democratic deficit' is loosely used to characterize decision-making procedures in which insufficient provision is made for democratic control. In fact, the expression refers specifically to powers transferred under the Treaties from the national level to the Community or Union level, and to the extent to which powers formerly subject to a satisfactory degree of democratic control at the national level cease to be subject to the same degree of control once so transferred. The expression is most commonly used to support arguments for increasing the powers of the **European Parliament**, but those opposed to such an increase point to the greater role that **national parliaments** might also play in ensuring that decisions are arrived at in a democratic fashion. This latter argument was given new force by the fact that since the **Single European Act** (SEA) decisions in the **Council of Ministers** have normally been taken on the basis of **qualified majority voting** (QMV), thus depriving national parliaments of the power of veto they enjoyed by virtue of the *de facto* unanimity required by the **Luxembourg Compromise**. The **Maastricht Treaty** sought to reduce the democratic deficit by granting the European Parliament a right of co-decision (see **co-decision procedure**) in certain areas. However, it also established important new areas of Union activity – the **Common Foreign and Security Policy** (CFSP) and **Justice and Home Affairs** (JHA) – with only very modest provision for parliamentary involvement, national or European.

Demography

Of a world population of approximately 5.5 billion people (1993), about 10 per cent live in the member states of the **Council of Europe**. With an average annual growth rate of 1.75 per cent, the population of the world is on course to double in 40 years. In the Council of Europe member states the 'natural' increase (i.e., not including immigration) is falling: it was only 0.39 per cent in 1991.

Not only are Europeans declining as a percentage of the total world population, they are also significantly older on average. This has resulted in unusually high dependency ratios: the number of people not of working age expressed as a percentage of the number of people of working age. In most member states of the European Union, this percentage is between 45 and 50 per cent, but in Ireland, with its significantly higher proportion of young people in the population as a whole, the figure is 59.5 per cent.

These broad averages conceal wide variations. In northern Europe (Scandinavia and the British Isles) life expectancy is longer and the proportion of the population over 65 correspondingly higher. In southern and eastern Europe the proportion of the population under 15 tends to be well above the European average, but this is as much a consequence of lower life expectancy as of higher birth rates.

Population density also varies widely within Europe. With more than

1,100 people per square kilometre, Malta is one of the most densely populated countries in the world; with only 3 people per square kilometre, Iceland is one of the emptiest. Within the European Union the extremes are the Netherlands (376 people per square kilometre) and Finland (15 people per square kilometre).

The Council of Europe publishes a comprehensive annual report entitled *Recent demographic developments in Europe*, from which the above information is taken (1993 and 1994 editions). See also Daniel Noin and Robert Woods (eds), *The Changing Population of Europe* (Oxford, 1993).

Denmark

In the 1960s Denmark followed the United Kingdom, a fellow member of the **European Free Trade Association** (EFTA), in applying to join **the Six**. The vetoes twice exercised by **Charles de Gaulle** on British entry had as a side-effect the blocking of Danish entry too. Like the United Kingdom, Denmark joined the Community on 1 January 1973, after an October 1972 **referendum** in which 63.3 per cent of the votes were cast in favour of membership. The key argument was economic: a substantial proportion of Danish trade was with the United Kingdom, and it was felt that Denmark could not afford to see the British market disappear behind the **Common External Tariff** (CET).

For the remainder of the 1970s and the first half of the 1980s Denmark played its full part as a responsible, law-abiding, but not especially enthusiastic member of the Community. The relationship was neatly symbolized by the Market Committee, the Danish parliament's instrument for controlling Danish ministers in the **Council of Ministers** (see **national parliaments**), which served to reassure public opinion that moves towards closer integration could not be made without national parliamentary authority.

In 1988 Denmark gained an important victory in the so-called 'Danish beer-can case' (*Commission* v *Denmark*, Case 302/86; see **environment policy**), which established the principle that member states were free to impose more stringent requirements in pursuit of Treaty objectives than those agreed at Community level. As one of the richest member states with an efficient and profitable agricultural sector, Denmark was reticent about attempts to reform the Community's finances and the **Common Agricultural Policy** (CAP), and took only a negative interest in institutional reform.

From the mid-1980s a mood of growing hostility to European Union and the threat it allegedly posed to traditional Danish liberties coincided with a period of unstable minority government. In February 1986 a referendum was needed to ratify the **Single European Act** (SEA) – 56.2

per cent voted in favour – since the previous month the Danish parliament had voted to reject it on the grounds that it gave more powers to the **European Parliament**. Matters were finally brought to a head by a referendum on 2 June 1992, when by a majority of less than 2 per cent (45,000 votes) the Danish people voted against the **Maastricht Treaty** in spite of the fact that the Danish parliament had approved it.

In October of that year the Danish government published a paper entitled *Denmark in Europe*. In essence, this laid down conditions – mainly in the form of exemptions and **opt-outs** from what had been agreed at Maastricht – for the holding of a second referendum. The Edinburgh meeting of the **European Council** in December 1992 reached agreement on the Danish demands, which reflected the preoccupations that had led to the 'No' vote in June. The Maastricht Treaty provisions on **citizenship** were clarified; Denmark's decision not to participate in stage 3 of **Economic and Monetary Union** (EMU) was recognized, as was its refusal to become involved in 'decisions and actions of the Union which have defence implications' (which would include ceding the **presidency** of the Council as necessary); and the right of a member state to introduce or maintain more stringent provisions was reiterated with respect to working conditions, social policy, consumer protection and the environment. A second referendum was held on this basis in May 1993 and, with 56.8 per cent of the vote in favour, the Danish electorate approved the Maastricht Treaty. In the June 1994 European elections anti-Maastricht candidates secured 4 of the 16 Danish seats in the **European Parliament**.

As the United Kingdom has the Commonwealth and the 'special relationship' with the United States, so Denmark has Nordic cooperation (see **Nordic Council**) as an alternative focus of loyalty to the European Community. For 21 years Denmark was the only Scandinavian member of the Community, and thought of itself as a bridge between the two while enjoying a unique status in each. As a small country with an economy closely linked to Germany's, Denmark's future role within the Union is now uncertain with the prospect of EMU by the end of the decade. Meanwhile, Denmark can be relied upon to resist any large-scale moves towards closer integration. There is an analysis of the politico-legal consequences of the special arrangements made for Denmark in relation to the Maastricht Treaty in David Howarth, 'The compromise on Denmark and the Treaty on European Union', *Common Market Law Review*, Vol. 31, no. 4, August 1994.

Derogation

A derogation is a temporary waiver from a Regulation or a Directive. Derogations are normally granted only by unanimous agreement of the

Council of Ministers (see **Community law**). Under Article 109k of the **Treaty of Rome** member states that do not meet the **convergence criteria** are automatically entitled to a derogation from the arrangements to adopt a single currency as part of the third stage of **Economic and Monetary Union** (EMU).

Development policy

Development policy was at first limited, in the words of Article 131 of the **Treaty of Rome**, to the 'non-European countries and territories' that had 'special relations' with one or other of the member states and which were listed in Annex IV of the Treaty. The purpose of associating these **overseas countries and territories** (OCTs) with the Community was 'to promote [their] economic and social development . . . and to establish close economic relations between them and the Community as a whole'. As a first step, member states undertook to apply the same rules to trade with the OCTs as they applied to trade with each other, and each OCT would in return accord to all member states and to other OCTs the same treatment in matters of trade as was applied to the member state with which it had 'special relations'. At the time of **the Six** the OCTs were all Dutch or French overseas possessions, but as the process of decolonization got under way in the 1960s it became obvious that something more ambitious was called for. This led to the conclusion of the **Yaoundé** and **Arusha Conventions** in 1963 and 1969 with 21 newly independent African states. British accession to the Community in 1973 meant that similar arrangements had to be made with a large number of former British possessions. The European Union now has **Association Agreements** with some 115 developing countries worldwide.

The centrepiece of this policy is the **Lomé Convention**, first signed in Lomé, the capital of Togo, in 1975 and since renewed three times. The Convention governs trade and aid arrangements with 70 **ACP states**, allowing all ACP industrial products and most ACP agricultural products free access to the Community market. The current Convention (Lomé IV, 1990–2000) made available 12 billion ECUs (approximately £9.5 billion) under the **European Development Fund** over the period 1990–95 and a further 14.7 billion ECUs for the period 1996–2000.

The European Union and its member states are by far the biggest donors of development assistance worldwide, their contribution representing almost half of total official development aid, and more than that of the United States and Japan combined. In particular, they are the biggest aid donors in sub-Saharan Africa, South America and southern Asia (India, Pakistan, Nepal, Bangladesh and Sri Lanka). Aid represents about 0.55 per cent of total gross national product (GNP): short of the United Nations target of 0.7 per cent, but steadily growing.

The Union's development policy has certain special characteristics that set it apart from the policies of other major aid donors. First, aid is distributed more evenly across the range of recipient countries. The six largest beneficiaries of aid receive only about 20 per cent of total Union aid, by comparison with 44 per cent of US aid and 50 per cent of Japanese aid. This underlines the fact that aid from the Union is disbursed with less regard for strategic or commercial factors. However, particularly under Article 5 of the Lomé IV Convention, more emphasis is now being laid on observance of human rights and 'good government' in recipient countries. Another distinctive feature is the fact that the Union gives more aid than other donors to agricultural and rural development projects, which represent some 50 per cent of total expenditure.

The Union and its member states are also the most important trading partners of the developing countries, taking over 20 per cent of Third World exports. Under the Union's **Generalized System of Preferences** (GSP) many Third World products enjoy privileged access, and a substantial proportion of the European Development Fund under the Lomé Convention is allocated to the STABEX and SYSMIN schemes, which guarantee ACP countries against the loss of foreign currency earnings arising from fluctuations in world commodity prices. The concerns of developing countries that the European Union was becoming protectionist as a consequence of the **Single Market** programme (see **Fortress Europe**) and was turning its attention to central and eastern Europe have not been borne out by the Union's current policies.

Only a small proportion of the total aid budgets of member states is spent through the Union. The overall figure is about 15 per cent, but this conceals wide differences: barely 7 per cent of Denmark's aid budget is disbursed through the Union, while the equivalent figure for Greece is 87 per cent. Both the Union and the individual member states make contributions to the various United Nations specialized aid agencies (such as the High Commission for Refugees and the World Food Programme), and the member states also make independent contributions to other multilateral aid agencies, most notably the International Bank for Reconstruction and Development and the International Development Agency. Another important feature of the Union's aid policy is that the main instrument, the European Development Fund, is made up of direct contributions from member states and is not part of the **Budget** (and is for this reason not subject to the **European Parliament**'s powers of decision and control over budgetary matters). Other forms of development expenditure are, however, 'budgetized'. European Development Fund expenditure is about 45 per cent of total development expenditure.

Development policy with respect to non-Lomé countries outside Europe and the Mediterranean basin is best considered area by area.

Africa

All African states south of the Sahara are signatories to the Lomé Convention, except South Africa, which applied for membership in November 1994. Until recently, assistance to South Africa was limited to a special fund for the victims of apartheid and contributions to various humanitarian causes, but an interim **Cooperation Agreement** has now been concluded. For North Africa, see **Maghreb** and **Mashreq**.

Central America and the Caribbean

All the independent states in the Caribbean except Cuba and Belize are signatories to the Lomé Convention. Aid is also given to the countries of the Central American Common Market: Costa Rica, El Salvador, Guatemala, Honduras and Nicaragua.

South America

Development policy in South America is founded upon relations with regional groupings:

- the Andean Pact, established in May 1969 (Bolivia, Ecuador, Colombia, Peru and Venezuela);
- the Latin American Integration Association, established in 1980, replacing the Latin American Free Trade Association (Argentina, Bolivia, Brazil, Chile, Colombia, Ecuador, Mexico, Paraguay, Peru, Uruguay and Venezuela);
- the Mercosur Council, which manages the **customs union** established in 1991 between Argentina, Brazil, Paraguay and Uruguay.

These bodies form part of the Latin American Economic System, set up in 1975, which also includes the countries of the Central American Common Market (see above) and a number of countries in the Caribbean.

The Middle East

The oil-rich Arab countries and the United States are the largest aid donors in this region (a very high proportion of US aid is concentrated upon Israel). Aid of various types has been given to all countries in the region: Israel, Jordan, the Lebanon, Syria, the Yemen Arab Republic. Iran and Iraq have received only food or emergency aid (see also **Mashreq**).

Southern Asia

The European Union is the largest (and Japan the next largest) aid donor in the region, which includes India, Pakistan, Sri Lanka, Bangladesh, Afghanistan and a number of small states bordering on northern India.

Although it is outside the Lomé Convention, India receives more Union aid than any other country in the world.

Far East

Japan is the largest aid donor in the region, but aid from the European Union – especially to China – has shown a marked increase over the past decade. Other major beneficiaries include Thailand, Indonesia and the Philippines.

There is a very full and critical account of the neo-colonial character of the European Union's development policy in Enzo R. Grilli, *The European Community and the Developing Countries* (Cambridge, 1993).

D'Hondt system

Named after a Belgian political scientist (see below), the d'Hondt system is widely used in continental Europe as a feature of various forms of proportional representation. It is also used within the institutions of the European Union (especially the **European Parliament**) as a formula for distributing a fixed number of positions (such as committee chairs) amongst groups of different numerical strengths or amongst various nationalities.

The following example illustrates how the d'Hondt system works. Seven posts have to be distributed amongst five political parties as follows:

	A	B	C	D	E
Number of members	110	80	42	30	16

The d'Hondt system requires these numbers to be divided first by 1, then by 2, then by 3, and so on as necessary. The resulting quotients are then ranked by size, the seven highest establishing the entitlement to the seven posts available:

	A	B	C	D	E
÷ 1	**110.0**	**80.0**	**42.0**	**30.0**	16.0
÷ 2	**55.0**	**40.0**	21.0	15.0	8.0
÷ 3	**36.7**	26.7	14.0	10.0	5.3
÷ 4	27.5	20.0	10.5	7.5	4.0

The d'Hondt system favours large parties but also protects the position of other parties. If the allocation were simply put to the vote, Party A could combine with Party B, C or D to deny posts to other parties. Several variants exist that correct the bias in favour of large parties. For the purpose of the calculation parties can choose temporarily to pool their numbers. From the example given above it will be seen that the d'Hondt system can be used to establish not only entitlement to posts but also the order of bids: Party A has first, third and sixth choice, Party B second and fifth, and so on. A fuller description of the d'Hondt system may be found in any handbook of electoral systems.

Victor d'Hondt published his *Système pratique et raisonné de la représentation proportionnelle* in 1882. The system was originally devised to ensure an equitable distribution of parliamentary seats amongst Catholics and Liberals and between the different language communities in Belgium (see A. M. Carstairs, *A Short History of Electoral Systems in Western Europe*, 1980).

Direct effect

Together with **primacy**, direct effect is one of the fundamental principles of **Community law**. In its judgment in the Van Gend en Loos case (Case 26/62), the **Court of Justice** said:

> Independently of the legislation of Member States, Community law . . . not only imposes obligations on individuals but is also intended to confer upon them rights which become part of their legal heritage. These rights arise not only where they are expressly granted by the Treaty but also by reason of obligations which the Treaty imposes in a clearly defined way upon individuals as well as upon the Member States and upon the institutions of the Community.

In other words, the **Treaties** are not merely a compact between states entailing rights and obligations for those states and for the institutions established by those Treaties, but are the foundations of a distinct legal order entailing rights and obligations for individuals (see Weatherill and Beaumont, *EC Law*, and Rudden, *Basic Community Cases*; see also **Van Duyn case, Francovich case).**

Directorate-general (DG)

A DG is the main administrative unit within the **European Commission**. Each Commissioner is responsible for one or more DGs, of which there are at present about 20. The DGs, which vary in size, are each headed by a director-general and are dedicated to particular areas of policy. Most are located in Brussels. In addition to the DGs, there are a number of other services, such as the Legal Service, the Translation Service, and the Statistical Office (see **Eurostat**).

Discharge procedure

Under Article 205a of the **Treaty of Rome** the **European Commission** is required to submit annually to the **European Parliament** and the

Council of Ministers 'the accounts of the preceding financial year relating to the implementation of the budget . . . [and] a financial statement of the assets and liabilities of the Community'. The responsibility for approving these accounts (known as 'granting the discharge') rests with the Parliament under Article 206 EEC, acting with the aid of a recommendation from the Council and the annual report of the **Court of Auditors**. The discharge procedure is an important element both in **budgetary discipline** and in the Parliament's powers with respect to the **Budget**. The granting of discharge has not infrequently been delayed but has only once been refused (in 1984, in respect of the 1982 accounts). The consequences of a refusal are not set out in the **Treaties**; some authorities believe that if it were backed up by a **censure motion** the Commission would have to resign.

Discrimination on grounds of nationality

Discrimination on grounds of nationality between nationals of the member states is prohibited under Article 6 of the **Treaty of Rome** in all areas covered by the Treaty. Article 48.2 EEC prohibits discrimination specifically in respect of employment, pay and working conditions.

'Employment in the public service' is an important exception to this provision, under Article 48.4 EEC. Different countries have different definitions of what constitutes 'public service', and in response to a case involving Belgian railways the **Court of Justice** laid down its own definition: employment 'connected with the specific activities of the public service in so far as it is entrusted with the exercise of powers conferred by public law and with responsibility for safeguarding the general interests of the State, to which the specific interests of local authorities . . . must be assimilated' (*Commission* v *Belgium*, Case 149/79). This definition would clearly include national and local civil servants, the armed forces and the police as part of the public service, but exclude many public-sector employees. For example, in recent years the **Commission**, prompted by questions in the **European Parliament**, has taken action against rules requiring tour guides attached to tourist offices in Italian cities to be Italian. The Commission has also brought pressure to bear upon educational establishments to allow all nationals of the member states to enjoy the same treatment with regard to tuition fees as nationals of the home state.

The Treaty provisions prohibiting discrimination on grounds of nationality are of great importance in relation to **free movement of persons** and **freedom of establishment**, especially in frontier areas, and in connection with travel and tourism. Also of interest is the case of Mr Cowan, a British tourist mugged on the Paris Metro, who was denied the compensation for victims of criminal violence to which he would have been entitled had he been French. The Court of Justice ruled that as a tourist he was a recipient of services, a sector covered by the Treaty, and was therefore entitled to the same protection and compensation as a French citizen (Case 186/87).

Dooge Committee

Otherwise known as the Ad Hoc Committee for Institutional Affairs, the Dooge Committee (chaired by James Dooge, an Irish Senator) was set up at the **European Council** meeting in Fontainebleau in June 1984. Its task was 'to make suggestions for the improvement of the operation of European cooperation in both the Community field and that of political, or any other, cooperation'. The Committee was deliberately modelled on the **Spaak Committee** in the sense that its members were personal representatives of the members of the European Council and of the President of the **Commission**. The Committee presented an interim report in November 1984 and a final report in March 1985.

The Committee called for a 'qualitative leap ... demonstrating the common political will of the Member States', and the eventual formulation of 'a genuine political entity ... i.e. a European Union'. Foreshadowing the **Maastricht Treaty**, this Union would act 'according to procedures which could vary depending whether the framework is that of intergovernmental cooperation, the Community Treaties, or new instruments yet to be agreed'. Amongst the 'priority objectives' the Committee endorsed the idea of a **single market** created 'on the basis of a precise timetable' (an idea then being worked out in what was published three months later as the **Cockfield White Paper**) and a strengthening of the **European Monetary System** (EMS). Under 'Promotion of the common values of civilization' the Committee supported measures to protect the environment, the introduction of a 'European social area, as the logical follow-on from an economically integrated, dynamic and competitive Community', and the promotion of common cultural values.

The section on 'the search for an external identity' was more cautious. The recommendations amounted to a few practical measures for improving **European Political Cooperation** (EPC), including the creation of an EPC secretariat, the gradual incorporation of security issues into EPC and greater efforts 'to draw up and adopt common standards for weapons systems and equipment'.

The final section on changes to the institutions and procedures was the most radical. A majority of the Committee supported more frequent use of **majority voting** in the **Council of Ministers**, with the requirement for unanimity being applied only 'in certain exceptional cases'. The **presidency** would be obliged to put a matter to the vote within 30 days at the request of three member states or the Commission. The British, Danish and Greek representatives also accepted that more use would have to be made of majority voting, but wanted to grant the presidency more discretion and to retain the practice laid down in the **Luxembourg Compromise** of allowing discussion to continue until unanimity was reached whenever a member state considered that 'very important interests' were at stake.

The Committee proposed to reduce the number of Commissioners to one for each member state. The president should be appointed by the European Council, and he or she should then propose to the governments the names of the other Commissioners. At the beginning of its term of office, the Commission 'should receive a vote of investiture on the basis of its programme' from the **European Parliament**.

The Committee proposed that the Parliament should enjoy a right of co-decision with the Council, although in a way different from that eventually adopted in the Maastricht Treaty (see **co-decision procedure**). The Parliament should also have the right to give its approval to all accession and **Association Agreements** (see **assent procedure**) and should have 'responsibility in decisions on revenue' as part of the **Budget** procedure. The Committee pointed to the 'increased representativeness' that would flow from the 'standardization of voting procedures' for European elections (see **uniform electoral procedure**).

In conclusion, the Committee recommended the calling of an **Intergovernmental Conference** (IGC) 'to negotiate a draft European Union Treaty'. When their report was considered at the Milan meeting of the European Council in June 1985, the proposal to convene an IGC was carried by majority vote, the British, Danish, and Greek representatives voting against. This was the IGC that negotiated the **Single European Act** (SEA).

The vote in the European Council was the final proof of what had become evident in the Dooge Committee's discussions and in their final report: a fundamental division between a minority who favoured only a minimalist approach to institutional reform and a majority prepared to go much further. Almost every page of the report contained footnotes and reservations, and the Danish and Greek representatives entered general reservations at the end. As an exercise in moving the Community forward, the Dooge Committee was only partially successful and cannot compare with the Spaak Committee. Nevertheless, many of its proposals were taken up either in the SEA or later in the Maastricht Treaty.

Draft Treaty establishing the European Union (DTEU)

The DTEU, adopted by the **European Parliament** in February 1984 by 237 votes to 31 with 43 abstentions, was largely the work of **Altiero**

Spinelli. It was the Parliament's principal contribution to the negotiations that led to the 1986 **Single European Act** (SEA).

Spinelli believed that the 1979–84 Parliament, the first to be directly elected, had a historic right and moral duty to act as a **constituent assembly**. Working initially with friends and associates in the **Crocodile Club**, Spinelli was instrumental in setting up the Institutional Affairs Committee of the Parliament in January 1982. As the Committee's principal **rapporteur**, Spinelli drew up a draft treaty, which was approved in outline on 14 September 1983. This was then submitted to constitutional experts and presented to the Parliament for final adoption the following February.

Article 1 DTEU proclaimed the establishment of a European Union. The institutions of the Union followed the familiar pattern of Parliament, **Council of Ministers**, **Commission**, **Court of Justice** and **European Council**, but with some differences. For example, the Council of the Union (Article 20 DTEU) was to be made up of 'representations' of the member states 'led by a minister who is permanently and specifically responsible for Union affairs'. More original was the distinction in Article 10 DTEU between 'common action' and 'cooperation', the latter being essentially intergovernmental in character (in this area the DTEU anticipated the '**pillar**' structure of the **Maastricht Treaty**). Provision was made for activities to be transferred from the sphere of cooperation to common action, but not vice versa. In parallel with this was a distinction between exclusive competence for the Union and concurrent competence – that is, competence exercised jointly with member states (Article 12 DTEU). The same Article contains a definition of **subsidiarity**, referred to in general terms in the Preamble: 'The Union shall only act to carry out those tasks which may be undertaken more effectively in common than by the Member States acting separately.'

The most controversial of the 87 Articles was Article 82 DTEU. This allowed for the Treaty to enter into force once it had been ratified 'by a majority of the Member States of the Communities whose population represents two-thirds of the total population of the Communities'. By this provision Spinelli sought to circumvent the procedure for treaty revision then contained in Article 236 of the **Treaty of Rome**, which required unanimous agreement (Spinelli in any case always underlined the fact that the DTEU was an entirely new treaty, not an amendment to an existing one). However, the way Article 82 DTEU was worded prompted opposition from those who feared it would lead to a **two-speed Europe**.

In the event, only the Belgian and Italian parliaments adopted resolutions calling for the DTEU to be ratified. More cautious expressions of support were received from other parliaments. However, in June 1984 at the

Fontainebleau European Council the heads of government set up what became known as the **Dooge Committee** to prepare proposals on institutional reform. The Committee endorsed the idea of a new treaty, and proposed that it be guided, amongst other suggestions, 'by the spirit and method of the draft treaty voted by the European Parliament'.

When the DTEU was adopted in outline by the Parliament in a form some way removed from his original intentions, Spinelli had the perfect simile. He compared himself to the fisherman in Hemingway's *The Old Man and the Sea*, who catches his huge fish after a long struggle, only to find, on reaching the shore, that, lashed to the side of his boat, his catch has been largely eaten away during the voyage home.

Dual mandate

In the European Union someone who is a member both of a national parliament and of the **European Parliament** is said to hold a 'dual mandate'. Although the dual mandate is not prohibited under the **European Elections Act** of 1976, it is contrary to national electoral law in several member states. It is also prohibited by many political parties under their own internal rules.

Until the first European elections in 1979 all Members of the European Parliament (MEPs) held a dual mandate since all were appointed by and from **national parliaments**. By the 1970s the growth in the Parliament's activities was already making the dual mandate very demanding, and although there were still many dual mandate MEPs in the 1979–84 Parliament, within a few years the number was negligible.

Dual mandate MEPs do not draw two full salaries. In the United Kingdom they are entitled to one-third of their House of Commons salary (as in other member states, the two salaries are the same).

There are those who advocate the dual mandate on the grounds that it promotes and facilitates contact between the European Parliament and national parliaments, and so helps to keep any sense of rivalry to a minimum. It also allows prominent figures in national politics to become involved (however superficially) in European politics, which may, in turn, raise the level of public interest in the European Parliament. On the other hand the steady increase in the degree of expertise and commitment required to be an effective MEP makes the dual mandate practically impossible in all but exceptional cases.

Dublin Asylum Convention

The Convention, signed in 1990 but still not yet in force, provides for applications for asylum to be examined by whichever member state first receives the asylum seeker, unless there are good reasons why the case should be handled by another member state. It is designed to forestall the possibility of asylum-seekers trying one member state after another (or several member states simultaneously) in order to gain entry into the Union, and is a logical extension of the commitment under Article 7a of the **Treaty of Rome** to create 'an area without internal frontiers in which the free movement of . . . persons . . . is ensured'. The Convention also allows the authorities of member states to exchange information on asylum-seekers. It does not affect the eligibility for asylum or the procedures for examining applications for asylum, both of which are laid down in the 1951 United Nations Convention on Refugees. Under the **Maastricht Treaty** asylum questions are now handled within the framework of cooperation in the fields of **Justice and Home Affairs** (JHA; see also **External Frontiers Convention**).

Dunkirk, Treaty of

Signed in March 1947, the Treaty of Dunkirk between the United Kingdom and France was the first postwar European security pact. Composed of only six Articles, of which the second required the signatory states to provide each other with 'military and other support and assistance' in the event of an attack, the Treaty was concluded for an initial period of 50 years, after which it was to remain in force unless either party gave a year's notice of withdrawal.

The Treaty was a 'regional arrangement' of the type encouraged by Article 52 of the United Nations Charter. As the preamble makes clear, it was directed against the possibility of 'a renewal of German aggression', and was prompted by the French government's sense of France's vulnerability (the only other security pact France had at the time was with the USSR). The Treaty led directly to the more ambitious **Treaty of Brussels** of 1948.

Ecofin Council

The Council of Economics and Finance Ministers of the European Union, widely known as Ecofin, is the second most important division of the **Council of Ministers** after the Foreign Affairs Council. It meets on average once a month, usually on a Monday, to discuss the macro-economic situation in the member states, coordinate the Union's position in international financial institutions (such as the International Monetary Fund), and adopt legislation in respect of tax harmonization, financial liberalization and the financing of the Union. The Ecofin Council is also responsible for the application of **budgetary discipline** and the coordination of export credit policy among the member states. (The annual **Budget** is discussed in the Budget Council – often the same ministers – rather than by Ecofin.) The finance ministers meet informally at least once every six months in the country holding the **presidency** of the Council. In preparing major decisions the Ecofin Council is assisted by the **Monetary Committee**, a high-level group of national officials. The Ecofin Council's responsibilities were formally extended by the **Maastricht Treaty** to include overall supervision, in collaboration with the **European Monetary Institute** (EMI), of the progress of member states towards **Economic and Monetary Union** (EMU) with particular reference to **convergence** and the **excessive deficit procedure**.

Economic and Monetary Union (EMU)

The provisions governing EMU were added to the **Treaty of Rome** by the **Maastricht Treaty**. They set up a number of new institutions and specify the stages by which EMU is to be achieved, by 1999 at the latest (see below).

Although amongst the most ambitious of the European Union's objectives, EMU was not mentioned in any of the **Treaties** until the 1986 **Single European Act** (SEA). The goal of EMU was first set at a meeting of the heads of government of **the Six** in The Hague in 1969, with 1980 as the target date. This decision led to the 1970 **Werner Report** and was repeated at the Paris **summit** of October 1972, but the adverse economic circumstances of the early 1970s resulted in little being achieved. The idea of EMU was relaunched by **Roy Jenkins** as President of the **Commission** in 1977, and with strong support from Helmut Schmidt and **Valéry Giscard d'Estaing** this led to the **European Monetary System** (EMS). EMU was taken up again by **Jacques Delors** in 1985, and was mentioned both in the Preamble and in an amendment to the Treaty of Rome contained in the SEA. In 1988 work began on what became known as the **Delors Report**, which in turn led to the decision to convene an **Intergovernmental Conference** (IGC) on EMU. The conclusions of this IGC were a key component of the Maastricht Treaty.

The Maastricht Treaty mentions EMU in the Preamble, and refers to it together with the **Single Market** in Article B TEU as one of the means by which the Union will 'promote economic and social progress which is balanced and sustainable'. A reference to EMU was added to Article 2 EEC by the Maastricht Treaty, and Article 3a EEC refers to 'the irrevocable fixing of exchange rates leading to the introduction of a single currency, the ECU, and ... a single monetary policy and exchange-rate policy', but the main elements of the institutions managing EMU and the stages by which it is to be achieved are set out in Articles 102a–109m EEC.

The first stage, by a decision of the Madrid European Council in June 1989, began on 1 July 1990, with the removal of exchange controls in 8 of the 12 member states (with the others to follow), the inclusion in principle of all currencies in the narrow band of the **Exchange-Rate Mechanism** (ERM), and measures to encourage **convergence**. No new institutions were required. The second stage began on 1 January 1994, with the newly created **European Monetary Institute** (EMI), based in Frankfurt, gradually assuming a coordinating role. During this stage member states except Denmark and the United Kingdom are expected to take steps, if necessary, to make their central banks independent of government. Before the end of 1996 the **Council** at the level of heads of government must decide, by qualified majority, whether a majority of countries (not including Denmark: see below) satisfy the convergence criteria, so that the transition may be made to the third stage by those that qualify. The Council must also decide whether it is 'appropriate' to begin the third stage and, if so, when (the **European Parliament** must be consulted). If by the end of 1997 no date has been set, the third stage begins automatically on 1 January 1999, with the European Council having decided at least six months before which states 'fulfil the necessary conditions for the adoption of a single currency'.

The single currency is specified as the ECU (see above). At the beginning of stage 3 the participating states must adopt the 'irrevocably fixed' rates at which the ECU will be substituted for national currencies and 'take the other measures for the rapid introduction of the ECU as the single currency' (Article 109l EEC). The **European Central Bank** (ECB) will be the sole issuing authority for ECU banknotes.

As well as a single currency the third stage entails the creation of a **European System of Central Banks** (ESCB), composed of the ECB (replacing the EMI) and representatives of the national central banks. Member states that do not meet the criteria for entry into the third stage are in effect excluded from these institutions (see **derogation**) but at least every two years or at the request of a member state its qualifications for entry are re-examined by the Council after consultation with the European Parliament and with advice from the **Commission** and the ECB.

Protocols annexed to the Treaty of Rome contain the statutes of the EMI, the ESCB and the ECB. Another commits all signatory states, 'whether they fulfil the necessary conditions for the adoption of a single currency or not, [to] respect the will for the Community to enter swiftly into the third stage'. The protocol on the British **opt-out** recognizes that 'the United Kingdom shall not be obliged or committed to move to the third stage . . . without a separate decision to do so by its government and parliament'. Denmark was granted a similar opt-out, but a year later at the Edinburgh European Council in December 1992 Denmark's definitive decision not to participate in the third stage was recognized. In the course of ratifying the Maastricht Treaty both the German Bundestag and the parliament of the Netherlands secured a say in the decision to move to stage 3 (for the German position, see **Karlsruhe judgment**).

Since the Maastricht Treaty was signed, economic recession and instability in the currency markets (arising partly from Germany's high interest rates, maintained as a consequence of **German reunification**) have cast doubt on whether or not EMU is attainable and on which member states might be in a position to participate in the third stage in 1997 or 1999. The issue is further complicated by the **accession** of new member states during the intervening period, although all have accepted the goal of EMU as part of the *acquis communautaire*. EMU raises, in the most acute form, the question of a **two-speed Europe** (see also **variable geometry**), since it prefigures the emergence of a **hard core** of member states, including France and Germany, sharing a common currency. It also raises, in the perspective of longer-term **enlargement**, the question of **wider versus deeper**, since EMU, if attained, would constitute a deepening well beyond anything the applicant states from central and eastern Europe could hope to take part in for at least a generation.

Most important of all, EMU raises issues of **sovereignty**. EMU entails the transfer of powers hitherto exercised exclusively by governments to an independent ECB, including the right to authorize issues of currency, which, together with the associated right of seigniorage, has been the exclusive prerogative of monarchs for literally thousands of years. But it also invites governments to reflect on the limitations of sovereignty, since without EMU the Union's economic future will be dominated by the Deutsche Mark, with the German economy further strengthened by its privileged access to the new markets of central and eastern Europe. EMU is seen by many as the only means of containing German economic hegemony in the longer term.

The Maastricht Treaty and the Treaty of Rome do not describe EMU as an end in itself but as one contributing to 'economic and social progress' (Article B TEU) and 'price stability' (Article 3a EEC). The underlying contention is that the efficiency and therefore the benefits of the Single Market can be maximized only if consumers, manufacturers, traders and investors are spared the costs and risks involved in currency exchanges. Competition will be made keener if prices can be compared more clearly across borders. It is also argued that the Union will be better able to advance its interests in international economic fora with a common currency and be less vulnerable to large-scale currency speculation.

EMU places monetary powers in the hands of the ECB, but leaves fiscal powers with member states. The **Budget** of the European Union is too small to be an effective instrument of macro-economic policy, and likely to remain so. In any case, the Treaty provisions make no mention of any role the ESCB and ECB might play in decisions on the Budget. The German government insisted that the ECB, modelled on the Bundesbank, should be wholly independent of national governments and Union institutions; it remains to be seen whether a controversial new body that is not allowed to take instructions itself will have the authority and the political acumen to play an effective role in the continuous negotiations that underpin Union decision-making.

Europe has experimented with monetary union once before, establishing a 'Latin Monetary Union' which lasted from 1865 to 1925. In 1793 the revolutionary government in France reformed the currency on a decimal basis and two years later substituted the franc for the livre. The value of the franc was fixed at 4.5g of pure silver. In 1803 gold coins were introduced, and the value of gold was fixed at 15.5 times that of silver. This 'bimetallic' system was extended throughout Napoleon's empire and by 1850 had also been adopted in Belgium, Lombardy, the Veneto and Switzerland.

In the 1850s the relative value of the two metals began to shift, silver becoming relatively more expensive. The different states took different measures to correct this, making the confusion worse. In 1865, on the initiative of the Belgian government, a conference took place in Paris at which order was restored. Basically, the silver content of the smaller coins was reduced, but each country's five-franc coins and all gold coins were made legal tender throughout the territory of France, Italy, Belgium and Switzerland. Greece also joined the Union. The system worked so well that other countries followed suit, and within a few years it had been extended to Spain, Serbia, Romania and several smaller states. More importantly, the Austro-Hungarian Empire adopted a similar system, involving coins minted with the national denomination on one side and the value in francs on the other.

The last quarter of the nineteenth century saw a steady rise in the value of gold, the pace of which was slackened but not halted by the discovery of gold in South Africa. This gave rise to further instability within the Latin Union, but other countries (Finland, Bulgaria, Russia) continued to adopt similar systems. The system was also of course extended to the colonies of participating states. Not until the First World War shifted the balance decisively in favour of paper money did the Union break down. It was formally dissolved in 1925.

Economic and Social Committee (ESC)

The ESC of the European Union is an unelected tripartite representative body, established by the **Treaty of Rome** (Articles 193–8 EEC), which advises the **Council of Ministers** on draft legislation in certain subject areas. The ESC – frequently known as 'EcoSoc' – is not one of the five institutions of the Union: the Council, the **Commission**, the **European Parliament**, the **Court of Justice** and the **Court of Auditors**. Instead, it 'assists' the Council and Commission. It has few formal powers, no budget of its own, and a failure on its part to deliver an Opinion can only delay the Council from adopting the legislative act in question for one month.

The ESC consists of 222 members and an equal number of substitutes nominated by member states for a renewable four-year term. Those chosen are 'representatives of the various categories of economic and social activity, in particular, representatives of producers, farmers, carriers, workers, dealers, craftsmen, professional occupations and representatives of the general public' (Article 193 EEC). In practice each member state, whose delegations range in size from 6 to 24, nominates individuals drawn from three categories: employers, trade unionists and 'other interests'. Three groups corresponding to these categories are established through the ESC's rules of procedure. Most governments nominate equal numbers to each category even though it is not strictly necessary for them to do so. Members of the ESC are paid no salary, but receive travel and accommodation expenses.

The ESC's two-year presidency rotates between the three groups, and the Committee is managed by a bureau also composed on a tripartite basis.

The ESC conducts its advisory work by means of nine 'sections' covering different areas of Union activity. When a legislative proposal is received, the relevant section will nominate a small 'working group' from among its members to prepare a draft report, including suggested amendments to the Commission's text. The report of the working group, which acts by consensus and does not vote, is normally accepted by the section meeting more or less intact. The section then communicates the opinion so agreed to the monthly plenary session of the ESC. Amendments to the draft report are admissible from any member at either section or plenary stage.

Members vote in a personal capacity, and sit alphabetically rather than by group. In practice, however, the employers (Group One) and trade unionists (Group Two) each tend to vote as a bloc, giving the representatives of 'other interests' (Group Three) the decisive votes. Members from the latter category, who are often self-employed, tend to represent the prevailing ideological assumptions of the ruling parties in the countries that nominate them. Members from Groups One and Two, by contrast, are often appointed by national governments on the basis of recommendations by employers' organizations and trade unions.

The ESC has frequently been criticized as a throw-back to the corporatist assumptions of the 1950s and 1960s in continental Europe with their emphasis on the role of the **'social partners'**. Its conception owes much to the French Conseil Economique et Social, which featured in the constitutional design of both the Fourth and Fifth Republics. There has been frequent talk of abolishing the ESC. For a long time after the first direct elections in 1979 the European Parliament was particularly critical of the ESC's continued existence, especially after the latter started to publicize itself, rather maladroitly, as 'the other European Assembly'.

However, in the **Maastricht Treaty**, the ESC is in effect strengthened by making it the home of a new advisory body, the **Committee of the Regions**, which is serviced by the 500-strong secretariat of the ESC and shares the ESC's meeting rooms in Brussels.

Economic Commission for Europe (ECE)

A regional commission of the United Nations, the ECE was established in 1947 with its headquarters in Geneva. The governments of every European country together with Israel, Canada and the United States participate in the ECE, which is intended to promote cooperation between participating states over a wide range of technical, industrial and economic issues. The ECE holds an annual plenary session but most of the work is done in working parties and meetings of experts. The working languages are English, French and Russian. The 1975 Final Act of the **Conference on**

Security and Cooperation in Europe sought to encourage signatory states to use the ECE to implement the Act's provisions in the economic, technical and environmental fields. The ECE cooperates as necessary with many intergovernmental and non-governmental organizations of a very specialized character (such as the European Flexible Bulk Container Association or the International Federation of Pedestrians) and has done useful work on technical specifications and statistical information.

ECU

See **European Currency Unit**.

Edinburgh Growth Initiative

Agreed at the Edinburgh meeting of the **European Council** in December 1992, the Edinburgh Growth Initiative was a multiannual programme of coordinated measures undertaken at both Community and national level to counteract recession. The emphasis was on capital investment and investment in a more highly skilled, more flexible workforce.

At the Community level the Edinburgh Growth Initiative included a temporary loan facility of about £4 billion within the **European Investment Bank** (EIB) to help finance infrastructure projects (especially **trans-European networks**) and a new **European Investment Fund** with a capital of about £1.6 billion intended in particular to benefit small and medium-sized enterprises (SMEs). The **structural funds** were to be doubled over the six-year period 1994–9 and a **Cohesion Fund** worth almost £11 billion was set up over the same period. The EIB loan facility was increased in 1993. The **Commission** estimated that the Edinburgh Growth Initiative was responsible for an extra 0.6 per cent of real gross domestic product (GDP) in 1994.

Education policy

Article 126 of the **Treaty of Rome** added by the **Maastricht Treaty** allows the Community to 'contribute to the development of quality education by encouraging cooperation between Member States and, if necessary, by supporting and supplementing their action, while fully respecting the responsibility of the Member States for the content of teaching and the organization of education systems and their cultural and linguistic diversity'. The Article specifies that action is to be aimed at 'developing the European dimension in education', especially the teaching of languages (see **Lingua**), encouraging student and teacher exchanges (see **ERASMUS**) and fostering cooperation with non-member countries and international organizations such as the **Council of Europe**. The **Council of Ministers** is empowered to adopt 'incentive measures' or Recommendations (see **legal instruments**); 'harmonization of the laws and regulations of the Member States' is specifically excluded, as it is in **cultural policy**.

This new legal base for education policy reflected but did not extend the scope of measures already taken in this field, many of them based on a first action programme of 1976 (see **mutual recognition of qualifications**, COMETT, **European University Institute, European Centre for the Development of Vocational Training, European Training Foundation, Socrates, Leonardo**).

Empty chair crisis

The 'empty chair' (or *chaise vide*) crisis took place in the period July–December 1965, when French ministers, on the instructions of President **Charles de Gaulle**, refused to take part in meetings of the **Council of Ministers** and the French permanent representative (see **national representations**) was withdrawn from Brussels. On 18 October 1965 this manoeuvre was reflected in the **European Parliament** by a refusal on the part of Gaullist members to take part in votes on matters with a bearing on the Community's future. The empty chair crisis was and remains the most serious breakdown in the Community's operation.

The empty chair crisis was part of President de Gaulle's long dispute with the Community and its institutions (particularly the **Commission** under the presidency of **Walter Hallstein**), which resulted eventually in the **Luxembourg Compromise** of January 1966. France was opposed to the Commission's proposals for financing the **Common Agricultural Policy** (CAP), to the introduction of **own resources**, to the granting of more extensive budgetary powers to the European Parliament and, in particular, to the prospect of **majority voting** being introduced into the deliberations of the Council of Ministers. In more general terms France was also opposed to what it saw as the supranational pretensions of the Community institutions.

None of France's partners among **the Six** shared these objections to developments in the Community, many of which had been specifically provided for in the **Treaty of Rome**. The empty chair crisis resulted in a victory for France in the sense that the practice followed in the Council after the Luxembourg Compromise embodied the French view of how the Council should operate. The introduction of own resources was postponed until 1970. Whether or not it was a tactic intended primarily to secure de Gaulle's re-election to the presidency of France in December 1965 is open to dispute.

Energy policy

Since the coal industry was covered by the **European Coal and Steel Community** (ECSC) Treaty and nuclear energy by the **European Atomic Energy Community** (EAEC or Euratom) Treaty, the **Treaty of Rome** in its original form contained no reference to energy policy. A new energy chapter was proposed in the negotiations that led up to the **Maastricht Treaty**, but it was decided to come back to this question in the 1996 **Intergovernmental Conference** (IGC). However, three incidental references were added to the Treaty of Rome: Article 31 EEC, which lists 'measures in the spheres of energy, civil protection and tourism', amongst the 'activities' of the Community, Article 129b EEC on **trans-European networks** (TENs) and Article 130s.2 EEC on environmental measures 'significantly affecting' the energy options of a member state. The energy industries are covered by the normal Treaty rules on **competition**, state aids, etc., and indigenous energy supplies are treated as 'natural resources' within the meaning of Article 130r EEC, which requires their 'prudent and rational utilization'.

The first attempt at a comprehensive energy policy was made in a Decision (see **legal instruments**) of the **Council of Ministers** in April 1974, prompted by the unedifying and ill-coordinated scramble for energy supplies that followed the first oil crisis. A more considered statement on long-term (to 1995) energy objectives was drawn up in September 1986. It was decided that the Community should seek to reduce its dependence on imported energy, that member states should encourage energy-saving schemes, that minimum stocks should be maintained against emergencies and that encouragement should be given to research into alternative sources of energy. In line with the first objective, coal was to be made more competitive.

In fact, progress has been made in respect of most of these objectives. Energy consumption per capita has fallen by about 30 per cent since 1975, and energy dependence from 60 to 50 per cent. However, formidable obstacles remain in the way of an energy policy, of which the most striking is the continuing controversy over nuclear energy. Although nuclear energy represents about a quarter of the Union's total energy production, this figure conceals very wide disparities between member states, many of which produce no nuclear energy at all. Amongst the remainder, production of nuclear energy as a percentage of total production ranges from over 90 per cent (Belgium) and 80 per cent (France) to 1 per cent (the Netherlands). These figures underline the enormous differences between the overall pattern of energy production in member states, differences that may also be found in respect of coal and natural gas.

The main difficulty in the way of ensuring that in the European Union hard coal retains its present share (about 20 per cent) of the energy market is that imported coal is now cheaper than coal mined in the member states. Only the United Kingdom, Germany, Spain and France are coal producers, and understandably the idea that coal production in these countries should be subsidized meets with resistance from other member states and other energy suppliers.

At present the emphasis is on opening up the energy market by encouraging cross-border trade in energy and more competitive pricing policies. Commitments entered into at the United Nations Conference on Environment and Development (Rio de Janeiro, 1992) and elsewhere on the environmental aspects of energy policy are also being reflected in proposals for new legislation. Energy-related projects (including the **Joint European Torus**) are the second largest element in the current framework programme for **research**. Finally, the **European Energy Charter** is designed to promote cooperation and reciprocal market access with the countries of central and eastern Europe and the former Soviet Union.

Engrenage

Literally 'meshing in' (as of cog-wheels), *engrenage* is a term used to describe the practice of involving national civil servants with the work of the Union institutions, notably the **Commission**. This involvement was of particular importance in the early development of the Community, not only because the Commission was then much smaller and less influential but also because it furnished a means whereby national bureaucracies could be encouraged to approach problems (especially those of a technical nature) from a European standpoint and acquire the habit of working together, which was essential to the functionalist theory of integration (see **functionalism**). For this reason, *engrenage* became and remains an established feature of Brussels decision-making. The present scale of *engrenage* is best demonstrated by the large number of Brussels-based committees staffed jointly by Commission officials and national civil servants (see **comitology**) and of 'national experts' working in Brussels on short-term contracts.

Enlargement

Enlargement is the process by which countries join the European Union. Article O of the **Maastricht Treaty** specifies that 'any European State may apply to become a member of the Union. It shall address its application to the Council, which shall act unanimously after consulting the Commission and after receiving the assent of the European Parliament, which shall act by an absolute majority of its component members' (see also **Association Agreements**).

In practice, the procedure is as follows:

1 application by the candidate state to the **Council of Ministers**;
2 delivery of formal **Opinion** by the **Commission** (this can take up to three years) and consultation with the **European Parliament**;
3 if the Council, acting unanimously, decides to go ahead, negotiations then begin between the applicant state and the **presidency** of the Council (representing the member states) and the Commission;
4 a draft **accession** treaty is initialled by the applicant state and by representatives of the member states;
5 approval by an absolute majority in the European Parliament;
6 ratification by all signatory states 'in accordance with their respective constitutional requirements' (Article O TEU; this may involve a referendum, especially if amendments to the applicant country's constitution are involved);
7 formal signature of accession treaty;
8 entry into force on an agreed date (although there will normally be **transitional periods** in certain sectors, e.g., **free movement of persons**).

The basic qualifications for full membership of the Union are that the applicant is a European state (see **Morocco**), that it is able and willing to assume the political and economic obligations of membership, that it is ready to accept the *acquis communautaire* (including the *finalités politiques*), and that it is a democracy in which **human rights** are respected and guaranteed.

Five enlargements involving 10 countries have taken place since 1957.

Country	Applied	Joined
Ireland	July 1961	January 1973
United Kingdom	August 1961	January 1973
Denmark	August 1961	January 1973
Greece	June 1975	January 1981
Portugal	March 1977	January 1986
Spain	July 1977	January 1986
East Germany	–	October 1990, as a consequence of **German reunification**
Austria	July 1989	January 1995
Sweden	July 1991	January 1995
Finland	March 1992	January 1995

Other applications for membership have been made as follows:

Country	Applied	Background
Norway	April 1962	Draft accession treaty rejected by referendum, September 1972
Turkey	April 1987	Unfavourable Commission Opinion, December 1989
Morocco	July 1987	Rejected by the Council as a non-European state
Cyprus	July 1990	Favourable Commission Opinions, June
Malta	July 1990	1993. In Corfu (June 1994), the European Council undertook to include Malta and Cyprus in the next round of enlargement negotiations
Switzerland	June 1992	
Norway	December 1992 (second application)	Draft accession treaty rejected by referendum, November 1994
Hungary	March 1994	In June 1993 the European Council
Poland	April 1994	recognized membership as a long-term
Romania	June 1995	goal for all former Eastern bloc countries
Slovakia	June 1995	willing and able to join the European
Latvia	October 1995	Union
Estonia	December 1995	
Bulgaria	December 1995	
Lithuania	December 1995	
Czech Rep.	January 1996	

Of the current applicants three have long-standing Association Agreements: Turkey (1963), Malta (1970) and Cyprus (1973), and many have **Europe Agreements**. In all cases a very substantial proportion of that country's trade is already with the Union.

The end of the Cold War removed the inhibition that neutral countries such as Austria, Finland, Malta, Sweden and Switzerland felt about becoming too explicitly aligned with the West (see **neutrality**). It also led to applications for membership from Hungary, Poland and other former Communist countries. Although negotiations will not begin until the 1996 **Intergovernmental Conference** (IGC) is concluded, the European Council meeting in Copenhagen in June 1993 committed the Union to working towards membership for all the **Visegrad states**, plus Bulgaria and Romania.

Inevitably, enlargement has become entangled with other priorities. The European Council meeting in Maastricht in December 1991 agreed that negotiations with applicant states could begin 'as soon as the Community has terminated its negotiations on **own resources** and related issues in 1992', and invited the Commission to submit a paper on enlargement to the next meeting of the European Council in Lisbon (published as *Europe and the Challenge of Enlargement*). However, by the time of the Lisbon meeting the Danish referendum result on the Maastricht Treaty had introduced a further element of uncertainty with respect to the future shape and character of the Community, and the discussion on enlargement was necessarily only tentative. The heads of government were able merely to reaffirm their determination that the Community should remain open to duly qualified applicants and that negotiations should proceed from the beginning of 1993. Allowing time for ratification, this meant that no enlargement could take place before 1995 at the earliest.

No official definition exists of what is meant in the Treaty by a 'European State'. Membership of the **Council of Europe** extends to countries, such as Turkey and Cyprus, whose claims to being European on geographic grounds are slight, although Turkey has long also been accepted as a European member of the **North Atlantic Treaty Organization** (NATO). To require applicant countries to be Christian would exclude Turkey, but it would also exclude the Muslim republics emerging from the break-up of Yugoslavia as well as those once part of the USSR (although not Armenia). Neither geographically nor culturally has there ever been a clearly defined eastern frontier of Europe.

The requirement that applicant states be democratic and respect human rights is more clear-cut. The Preamble to the Maastricht Treaty refers to the member states' 'attachment to the principles of liberty, democracy and respect for human rights and fundamental freedoms and of the rule of law', and Article F2 TEU commits the Union to respect fundamental rights. By virtue of accepting the *acquis communautaire* applicant states become party to the tripartite Council–Commission–European Parliament declaration of 1977 on human rights. Applicant states are in effect required to be parties to the Council of Europe's European Convention on Human Rights and to accept the right of individual petition under the Convention. It was on the issues of democracy and human rights that the Community refused to conclude Association Agreements with the Spain of General Franco and the Portugal of Salazar (both countries applied as long ago as 1962) and 'froze' the Association Agreement with Greece during the seven-year dictatorship of the Colonels (1967–74). Doubts persist about Turkey's human rights record, and these have often been raised as arguments against Turkish accession.

The problems presented by continuing enlargement are primarily institutional, political and economic. Although there has recently been a move in the direction of more decisions being taken in the Council by **qualified**

majority voting (QMV), many of the most important can still be taken only by unanimity (changes to the **Treaties**, for example, or to the system of own resources). Similarly, the kind of consensus that is the foundation of the Union's **Common Foreign and Security Policy** (CFSP) is already difficult to attain, and can only become more difficult as the number of member states increases and their interests become more diverse. It will clearly be impossible to allow each member state one Commissioner, and if it is assumed to be impractical for the European Parliament to have more than 650 or 700 Members (MEPs), some hard decisions may have to be taken to reduce the number of MEPs currently allocated to each member state in order to allow room for growth.

Small states present a particular problem: it would clearly not be reasonable to allow Malta, for example, to block a decision acceptable to all the other member states. The system for rotating the **presidency** may have to be reviewed again, since the task of occupying the presidency is an increasingly complex one likely to impose intolerable strains on smaller states. Even larger states, which could expect to hold the presidency every 10 years or so, would find it more difficult by virtue of having fewer officials with experience of previous presidencies. **Languages** also present a problem. The 11 official languages currently in use give rise to 110 language combinations, but with only 3 new languages the number of combinations would rise to 182, with enormous consequences in cost and potential inefficiency.

The central political problem springs from the inevitably more heterogeneous nature of an enlarged Union. Across the whole range of issues agreement becomes more difficult to reach, unless it is achieved with the aid of so many derogations and special protocols as to render it more or less meaningless. Equal implementation and enforcement of Union legislation at the national level also become much more difficult, especially for countries in central and eastern Europe; the example of the concessions that had to be made to the former East Germany is instructive. Acceptance of the *acquis communautaire* (some 12,000 pages of rules and regulations) poses great difficulties both for countries that have been suffering from gross over-regulation for almost two generations and for those that have not yet allowed regulation so broad a scope within national (especially economic) life.

The differences in prosperity between the Union and several of the applicants are very striking. The poorest member state is Portugal, with a per capita gross domestic product (GDP) of about $7,500, whereas that of Poland is under $2,000. Disparities on this scale suggest that the countries of central and eastern Europe will require enormous transfers of resources from the **structural funds** and that it will be a long time before they are ready for the full range of **Single Market** disciplines and those implicit in a common currency.

Behind these arguments lies the question of **wider versus deeper**. Widening, once the Union moves beyond the members of EEA, will make deepening more difficult; deepening, in turn, makes widening more difficult, since it makes the criteria for entry into the Union more demanding. Even if it can be shown that successive enlargements have on the whole quickened the pace of integration, the Union is now faced with enlargement on an unprecedented scale: an additional six countries, with more to follow. This fact alone is a token of the Union's success and at the same time the greatest single challenge it has to face. The hard fact remains that the Treaties are so framed and the *acquis communautaire* so developed that only advanced, industrialized democracies with stable institutions can meet the obligations they entail without difficulty. This is especially true of several of the Union's key objectives, such as **Economic and Monetary Union** (EMU), even if the political issues are set aside. However, if the Union were to ease the requirements implicit in the Treaties and in the *acquis communautaire* and to lose sight, however temporarily, of its objectives, it could lose a momentum that it might never recover. It is commonly said that enlargement is a 'political imperative', but if this is so it will radically transform the negotiation process. Until now, negotiation has involved applicant states adapting to Community disciplines, and already there are signs that the two roles may be reversed.

Environment policy

Not referred to in the original **Treaty of Rome**, environment policy became an area for Community action on the basis of a decision at the October 1972 meeting of the **European Council**. Articles dealing with the environment (Articles 130r–t EEC) were added to the Treaty by the 1986 **Single European Act** (SEA); in their original form, they contained the first Treaty reference to **subsidiarity**. Environmental protection is referred to in the preamble to the **Maastricht Treaty**, which added 'a policy in the sphere of the environment' to the list of Community activities contained in Article 3 EEC. Most environmental legislation, together with decisions on which areas are to be the subject of legislative action, is covered by the **cooperation procedure**.

Article 130t EEC allows member states to maintain or introduce 'more stringent protective measures'. This provision arose from a judgment of the **Court of Justice** in the Danish beer-can case (*Commission v Denmark*, Case 302/86). The Court ruled that a Danish law to the effect that beer and soft drinks could be marketed only in reusable containers was justified in terms of the protection of the environment, which was to be regarded as taking precedence over the obligation on member states under Article 30 EEC not to enact measures restricting imports from other member states. The incorporation of this ruling into the Treaty is of great importance to other member states with high standards of environmental protection.

Environment policy has always been based on successive 'action programmes': the current programme, the fifth, was agreed in December 1992. These programmes are underpinned by a series of principles set out in Article 130r.2, those of preventive action, of rectification at source wherever possible and of polluter responsibility (the 'polluter pays principle'). Emphasis is also laid on the importance of other policies being assessed in terms of their impact on the environment. In 1990 it was decided to establish a **European Environment Agency** to help monitor the state of the environment and in 1992 an eco-labelling scheme was agreed for products recognized as 'environmentally friendly' in accordance with Union-wide criteria.

The principle of preventive action was reinforced by the requirement laid down in a 1985 Directive that all projects, public or private, above a certain cost should be the subject of an Environmental Impact Assessment. The extent to which this was controversial with member states may be illustrated by the fact that it was the twenty-third draft that was eventually agreed; the Directive came into force in 1988.

Legislation at Union level applies to air pollution (pollutants from motor vehicles, greenhouse gases, sulphur dioxide), water pollution (both bathing water and drinking water), waste disposal, the transport of dangerous substances and noise. Much of this legislation sprang from the need to prevent member states' different standards in these matters acting as a barrier to the **free movement of goods** or to fair and equal competition within the **Single Market**.

For the protection of the natural environment, the Union works very closely with international bodies and within guidelines laid down by international conventions. It has used its position as a major trading power to stamp out the trade in products derived from seal pups and is being pressed to take similar action with respect to exotic birds and tropical hardwoods. The Union is a party to many international conventions on areas particularly at risk, such as the Mediterranean (Barcelona Convention, 1976) and the Antarctic (Canberra Convention, 1980), and was represented at the 1992 United Nations Conference on Environment and Development in Rio de Janeiro.

Environmental protection has been identified through opinion polls as an area in which there is a consistently high level of public support for action at Union level. This is reflected in the many resolutions on environmental matters adopted by the **European Parliament**. It is also an area in which various collaborative projects are being undertaken with the countries of central and eastern Europe, such as those under the **PHARE** programme. The **enlargement** of the Union has increased the number of member states with a strong interest in environment policy. For these reasons, it is an area in which Union involvement is certain to increase.

A specialist survey may be found in Ludwig Kramer, *European Environmental Law Casebook* (1993).

Equal treatment

Equal pay for men and women is guaranteed under Article 119 of the **Treaty of Rome**. 'Pay' is defined as 'the ordinary basic or minimum wage or salary and any other consideration . . . which the worker receives . . . in respect of his employment from his employer'. This principle was enshrined in a **Directive** adopted by the **Council of Ministers** on 10 February 1975 and further enforced by a ruling from the **Court of Justice** (*Gabrielle Defrenne* v *Sabena*, Case 43/75) stating that Article 119 EEC was of **direct effect** in cases of 'direct and overt discrimination'.

In a 1990 judgment of the Court the phrase 'and any other consideration' in Article 119 EEC (see above) was held to include redundancy payments and payments under an occupational pension scheme (*Barber* v *Guardian Royal Exchange Assurance Group*, commonly referred to as 'the Barber judgment', Case C262/88). As with the Defrenne case, the Court ruled that its judgment was not of retroactive effect (except in respect of claims already submitted), but in view of the enormous implications of the ruling for employers and pension schemes throughout the member states, the governments added a **protocol** to the **Maastricht Treaty** stating that claims could not be made under the Barber judgment for periods of employment prior to 17 May 1990. (See also judgments of September 1994, especially the 'Coloroll' case, Case C200/91.)

Since equal pay was the only aspect of equal treatment specifically covered by the Treaty, a Council Directive of 1976 on access to employment, training, promotion and working conditions was enacted under **Article 235** EEC. Article 5.1 made it clear that 'working conditions' included dismissal, and in a 1986 judgment the Court ruled that compulsory retirement was a form of dismissal and thus covered by the requirements of equal treatment (*Marshall* v *Southampton and South-West Hampshire Area Health Authority*, Case 152/84). In Case C177/88 the Court ruled that refusal to employ someone on grounds of pregnancy constituted discrimination and in a second case, *Webb* v *EMO Air Cargo* (Case C32/93, judgment 14 July 1994), that pregnancy was inadequate as grounds for dismissal.

Finally, in 1978 the Council adopted a Directive on equal treatment in respect of social security schemes, including those for the self-employed.

However, it was not possible to reach agreement on the equalization of pensionable ages for men and women, and Article 7 allows member states to continue applying their own rules to this and other sensitive matters.

Equal treatment is also addressed in the Social Protocol (see **Social Chapter**) annexed to the Maastricht Treaty, and basically the key legislation is now in place. As an area of European Union activity, equal treatment is a good example of how over a 20-year period legislation may be underpinned, reinforced and occasionally advanced by rulings of the Court of Justice. However, as a **Commission** memorandum of June 1994 on equal pay for work of equal value makes clear, there are still serious discrepancies: for example, in respect of manual work, women's average wages are only 54.2 per cent of men's in the United Kingdom. Even in Denmark, the member state that has the best record on equal pay, the figure is 84.5 per cent.

There is a helpful study of equal treatment in Evelyn Ellis, 'Recent case law of the Court of Justice on the equal treatment of women and men', *Common Market Law Review*, Vol. 31, no. 1, February 1994.

ERASMUS

The European Community Action Scheme for the Mobility of University Students, which came into effect in July 1987, promoted exchanges between universities and institutes of higher education in different member states, at both student and teacher level. By 1994 it was helping over 40,000 students and 8,000 teachers annually. A similar scheme known as TEMPUS (Trans-European Mobility Programme for University Studies) fosters cooperation with central and eastern Europe, including the former Soviet Union. With effect from 1995, ERASMUS was merged into the **Socrates** programme.

ERTA case

On 20 March 1970 the **Council of Ministers** discussed the position to be taken by the member states of the European Community in relation to the European Road Traffic Agreement, then being negotiated under the auspices of the United Nations **Economic Commission for Europe**. The **European Commission** challenged the Council's conclusions in the **Court of Justice** (Case 22/70) on the grounds that since this was a Community matter the **Treaty of Rome** (Article 228 EEC) gave the Commission an **implied competence** in the negotiating procedure that the Council had ignored. The Court decided in the Commission's favour with respect to the admissibility of the Commission's complaint, thus confirming the principle that one Community institution may challenge an act of another, but rejected the substance. The ERTA case was of great importance in that it served to establish the role of the Commission in external relations.

Espace judiciaire européen

Variously translated as 'European legal area' and 'European judicial area', the *espace judiciaire européen* was a proposal put forward by **Valéry Giscard d'Estaing** as President of France in 1977. The idea behind the proposal was to establish a common framework in respect of all those legal matters with a Community dimension (for example, member states' policies on extradition, visas, asylum, police procedures), since the absence of such a framework might impede cooperation between police forces, immigration officers and judicial authorities. At a more abstract level the *espace judiciaire européen* was regarded as a contribution to a sense of **European identity** by virtue of its guaranteeing citizens of the member states a common corpus of basic legal rights. As might have been expected, progress towards such an *espace* has been slow in the face of legal, constitutional, political and practical difficulties, but the easing of frontier controls under the **Single Market** programme has made the need for cooperation in the field of law and order more urgent. Concrete results have been achieved at the practical level (see **Europol, Schengen Agreement, Trevi Group**), much of it outside the framework of the Community institutions. The **Council of Europe**, for example, has long been active in this field: the European conventions on extradition (1957), mutual assistance in criminal matters (1959), and the suppression of terrorism (1977) were all drawn up by the Council. The intergovernmental character (see **intergovernmentalism**) of work in this area was further underlined by the procedures laid down in the **Justice and Home Affairs** (JHA) '**pillar**' of the **Maastricht Treaty**.

ESPRIT

The European Strategic Programme of Research and Development in Information Technology is a **research** programme that became operational in 1984. It gives help from the **Budget** to firms, universities and research institutes for projects concerned with advanced information technology.

EUREKA

The European Research Cooperation Agency was established in 1985 to encourage cross-border research projects in advanced technology. A French initiative, it was intended to reduce the fragmentation from which European high-technology industries suffered by comparison with their American and Japanese competitors. EUREKA participants include all the countries of the **European Economic Area** (EEA) together with Switzerland and Turkey.

Euro

The name given by the Madrid European Council (December 1995) to the single currency due to be introduced as part of **Economic and Monetary Union**.

Eurobarometer

Eurobarometer is the name given to the twice-yearly surveys of public opinion in the member states of the European Union carried out by polling organizations on behalf of the **European Commission**. Such surveys have been conducted and published regularly since 1973, and are composed of both 'tracking' questions, used to establish overall trends, and questions that relate to current issues. A standard sample of 1,000 people is used in each member state, except for Luxembourg (500 people), the United Kingdom (1,000 in Great Britain, 300 in Northern Ireland), and Germany (1,000 in the former West Germany, 1,000 in the former East Germany). The regular surveys are supplemented by *ad hoc* surveys on particular issues, such as drug abuse, German reunification, biotechnology, or amongst particular sectors of society, such as the young or the self-employed. Of particular interest is the twentieth anniversary edition of *Eurobarometer* (May 1994), which summarizes trends over the period since 1973.

Eurocontrol

The European Organization for the Safety of Air Navigation was founded in 1960 to promote and facilitate cooperation amongst participating states in all aspects of air safety. Its headquarters are in Brussels, and it also operates the Upper Area Control Centre at Maastricht in the Netherlands.

All member states of the European Union except Spain, Italy, Finland and Sweden participate in Eurocontrol, together with Cyprus, Malta, Turkey, Norway, Hungary, Switzerland and Slovenia. Eurocontrol has not developed as intended into an international agency responsible for air traffic control in western Europe as a consequence of the reluctance of countries, for political and sometimes military reasons, to surrender national control of their airspace or even to press ahead with the technical coordination of different systems. However, attempts to wind up Eurocontrol altogether have so far been resisted, although western European airspace remains subject to several autonomous administrations operating from various centres. The report published in January 1994 by the Comité des Sages for Air Transport and entitled *Expanding Horizons* called for a renewed effort to harmonize and integrate air traffic control systems in Europe and for Eurocontrol procedures to be reformed to allow decisions to be taken by majority vote.

Eurocorps

On 14 October 1991 President **François Mitterrand** of France and Chancellor **Helmut Kohl** of Germany informed the President-in-Office of the **European Council** that they proposed to form a Franco-German corps in which the armed forces of other **Western European Union** (WEU) states could participate. At a meeting in La Rochelle on 22 May 1992 a timetable for the setting up of a corps of 35,000 troops was agreed. The headquarters would be in Strasbourg, France, and the corps, initially under the command of a German general, would be fully operational by October 1995. A joint committee would oversee relations between participating countries and other organizations concerned with security. Since the La Rochelle agreement Belgium, the Netherlands, Luxembourg, Spain, Italy and Poland have all formally expressed an interest in participating, Belgium having committed almost half its land forces to the corps (whose *de facto* working language is English).

The idea of a Eurocorps is consistent with the provisions in Article J of the **Maastricht Treaty** on the **Common Foreign and Security Policy** (CFSP) and with the decision to strengthen WEU as the European element within the **North Atlantic Treaty Organization** (NATO). Coordination of the Eurocorps with NATO was the subject of an agreement reached on 21 January 1993 by the North Atlantic Council, SACEUR (Supreme Allied Commander Europe) and the Chiefs-of-Staff of the states participating in the Eurocorps. Under this agreement Eurocorps forces are 'double-hatted'; that is, they may be assigned either to NATO or to national authorities within the WEU framework. For the foreseeable future the Eurocorps is likely to be dependent upon the United States in respect of satellite intelligence and rapid deployment by air or by sea.

The Eurocorps, which builds upon the experience gained from the Franco-German brigade (see **Franco-German cooperation**), is still some way short of the **'European army'** envisaged as a key component of the **European Defence Community**. Its role, reflecting the new security situation in Europe brought about by the ending of the Cold War, will be centred upon crisis management, peace-keeping and humanitarian action rather than straightforward deterrence. The crisis in Yugoslavia and the general sense of European helplessness that it engendered created the climate of opinion from which grew the idea of the Eurocorps, together with the realization that the United States was neither willing nor able to go on playing the role of global policeman (see 'The European Corps', Document 1400, WEU Assembly, 23 November 1993). In July 1994 Eurocorps units were invited for the first time to take part in the Bastille Day parade in Paris.

Eurocrats

'Eurocrat' is a mildly pejorative term, modelled on the word 'bureaucrat', to denote an official of one of the institutions or bodies of the European Union. The total number of such officials is about 27,000, of whom about 19,000 work for the largest of the institutions, the **European Commission**. Between a quarter and a third of these officials are employed in connection with interpretation and translation.

With a few exceptions at very senior level, recruitment is done on the basis of publicly advertised competitions organized by language, on the basis of which 'reserve lists' are drawn up of eligible people who may subsequently (sometimes months or years later) be offered specific posts as they become available. The age limit for recruitment is normally 35.

Posts within each institution are divided into four grades: A-grade posts (LA for translators and interpreters), for which a university degree is necessary; B-grade posts, e.g., archivists, senior secretaries and office managers; C-grade posts, most of them secretaries; and D-grade posts, e.g., ushers, drivers and security staff. Proficiency in at least two official **languages** is required for all grades. Within each grade are numerical rankings, from 1 (the most senior) down to 8 in the case of A grades, to 3 (B grades), to 5 (C grades), and to 4 (D grades). A director-general, for example, is an A1, a director an A2, a head of division an A3, and so on. Each of these numerical rankings contains a number of 'steps', which are largely indicative of length of service in a particular post. Only nationals of the member states may be employed in the institutions, and informal quotas are established to ensure an appropriate distribution of A-grade posts amongst the various nationalities.

Promotion within the institutions is based upon internal competitions judged by 'juries' upon which the staff unions are represented. However, senior posts (A3 and above) are not infrequently filled by *parachutage*; that is, by someone brought in from outside (usually from a national civil service) or someone who has entered the institution by some unorthodox means, for example, via the *cabinet* of a Commissioner or one of the political groups in the **European Parliament**.

Under a **protocol** to the **Treaty of Rome** employees of the institutions of the European Union – as is normally the case with employees of international organizations – are exempt from national income tax on their salary and expenses wherever they work, but not from most other forms of tax. Instead, they pay income tax to the Union itself at rates of up to 40 per cent.

The compulsory retirement age is 65, but officials can retire earlier with a reduced pension. When a new member state joins the Union, posts have to be found at every level within the institutions for nationals of that member state. For long-serving officials, their retirement may be brought forward by 'golden handshakes' or occasionally by means of what is known as *pantouflage* (from *pantoufles*, French for slippers), the creation of agreeable sinecures.

In general, the institutions of the Union are not overstaffed, as the House of Lords Select Committee on the European Communities confirmed in a 1988 report entitled *Staffing of the Community Institutions*. Many posts in the Commission remain unfilled because of budgetary constraints, and there is more recourse than in the past to short-term contracts. The number of posts has not kept pace with the widening of the Union's responsibilities, although this problem could be partially solved by more flexible procedures for transfers from one field of activity to another within the same institution.

There are very few general studies of Eurocracy. **Altiero Spinelli**'s *The Eurocrats*, David Coombes's *Politics and Bureaucracy in the European Community: A Portrait of the Commission of the EEC* and Anthony Sampson's *The New Europeans* are all more than 20 years old. Slightly more recent is the 1979 *Spierenburg Report*, which contains an analysis as true now as it was then of certain structural shortcomings in the Commission. Some entertaining glimpses of the upper reaches of the Commission may be found in **Roy Jenkins**'s 1989 *European Diary* covering his period as President (1977–81) and in Charles Grant's biography of **Jacques Delors**, *Delors: The House that Jacques Built* (1994). The most recent study is by Geoffrey Edwards and David Spence, *The European Commission* (Harlow, 1995).

Eurogroup

In 1968 the defence ministers of the European countries belonging to the **North Atlantic Treaty Organization** (NATO), with the exception of France and Iceland, decided to set up an informal twice-yearly meeting in order to coordinate their positions more closely on security issues and thus to strengthen Europe's contribution to the Atlantic Alliance. Known as the 'Eurogroup', these meetings provided a forum in which member states of the European Community could discuss specifically European security questions without infringing Ireland's neutrality or compromising France's status as a member of the Alliance outside NATO's integrated military command. In 1986 the **Single European Act** (SEA) made it possible for member states of the Community to discuss 'political and economic aspects of security' (Article 30.6 SEA) and five years later this provision was further developed in the **Maastricht Treaty** (see **Common Foreign and Security Policy**). The **Western European Union** (WEU) has now taken the place of the Eurogroup as the main European component of the Atlantic Alliance (see also **Independent European Programme Group**).

Euromyths

'Euromyths' is the general term given to the stories about the 'barmy Brussels bureaucrats' that regularly feature in the British press. The great majority of them have no basis in fact. Most take the form of some threat to the British way of life. In November 1992 the Foreign Office attempted to refute some of the most frequently repeated Euromyths. Three distinct types of story were identified: 'Euromyths', which have no basis in fact; 'Euroscares', largely founded upon misapprehensions as to the impact or purpose of some agreed measure; and 'Eurolunacies', defined as 'genuine examples of unnecessary or intrusive Community rules'. This typology was repeated in *Facts and Fairytales*, a 1993 booklet, and in two brochures published by the London office of the **Commission**. The Commission identified a very important fourth category of story, those in which the outrage or absurdity springs from the overzealous implementation or enforcement by national authorities of a measure agreed in Brussels or which may be traced back to regulations of purely national origin.

As a form of subversive, anti-bureaucratic humour, Euromyths have extraordinary resilience and vitality. Unfortunately, the refutation is almost always less arresting than the original story. Although not exclusively a British phenomenon, Euromyths in the United Kingdom, in terms of abundance and variety, exceed those to be found in other member states. They are both a symptom and a cause of the low esteem in which the institutions of the European Union, especially the Commission, are generally held.

Europa

In ancient times 'Europa' was both a person and a geographical expression. The myth of Europa is well known: the daughter of Agenor, King of Tyre, she attracted the attentions of Zeus. In order to seduce her, he transformed himself into a bull and, having enticed her on to his back, carried her away to Crete. There she eventually married the King of Crete and bore several sons, one of whom was King Minos, the builder of the labyrinth.

Geographically, Europa originally denoted the mainland of Greece, as opposed to the islands. As Greek colonization extended north and west, so the territory known as Europa was similarly extended, in contradistinction to Asia and Libya (North Africa). This tripartite division of the known world was the one adopted by Herodotus and later by the Romans. The growth of the Roman Empire brought with it a further extension of Europa as far as the Rhine to the north, the Straits of Gibraltar to the south and the British Isles to the west.

Europe's eastern frontier was always more problematic, as indeed it has remained. In the absence of an obvious geophysical feature most ancient geographers settled on the River Don as the frontier. Only centuries later did the Ural Mountains become the accepted eastward limit of Europe.

Neither myth nor geography can shed much light on the origin of the word 'Europa'. Some etymologists have traced it back to a Semitic word, *Erib*, meaning darkness (i.e., the direction in which the sun set). But if the word is of Greek origin, it means 'broad-faced' (possibly an attribute of the moon goddess), and there the trail goes cold.

The origin of the 'idea of Europe', the growth of a sense of European identity and the connection between Europe and Christendom are discussed in Denys Hay, *Europe: The Emergence of an Idea* (1957; rev. edn 1968). See also Chapter 1, 'The problem of definition', in Max Beloff, *Europe and the Europeans* (1957); and Chapter 1, 'The discovery of Europe', in J. R. Hale, *The Civilization of Europe in the Renaissance* (1993).

Europartenariat

Europartenariat is a business cooperation scheme, operational since 1987, run by the **Commission** to encourage small and medium-sized enterprises (SMEs) to establish cross-frontier links. Extended to include non-member states in central and eastern Europe, Europartenariat's twice-yearly meetings, each held in a different European city, allow business-men from a particular region to meet their counterparts in other countries.

Europe *à la carte*

Similar to **variable geometry** and open to the same objections, 'Europe *à la carte*' is a model of European integration in which individual member states decide whether or not to participate in a particular activity on a case-by-case basis. It is the opposite to the holistic approach to integration, and if widely adopted would result in the undermining of the notion of an *acquis communautaire*. The British **opt-out** from the **Social Chapter** is an example of an *à la carte* approach to Europe.

Europe Agreements

A new type of **Association Agreement** under Article 238 of the **Treaty of Rome**, Europe Agreements were devised to allow central and eastern European countries to strengthen their commercial and political ties with the European Union. The first Europe Agreements were signed in 1991 with Czechoslovakia, Hungary and Poland. An important feature of Europe Agreements is the emphasis laid on institutions and procedures allowing for political dialogue (see below). All the Agreements provide for the progressive removal of barriers to free trade, for economic and technical cooperation and for financial assistance.

Article 1 of each of the Europe Agreements says that the aim of the Agreement is 'to provide an appropriate framework for [the associated state's] gradual integration into the Community'. No deadline is set. The associated state is required to ensure that future legislation is compatible with Community legislation as the major condition for integration into the Community. Complete free trade is to be established over a 10-year period.

Political dialogue is conducted at several levels, including that of heads of state with the **presidency** of the Council and the president of the **Commission**, an Association Council at ministerial level, parliamentary contacts with the **European Parliament**, and regular consultation between foreign offices and embassies.

The Europe Agreements with Hungary and Poland came into force in February 1994, and those with Bulgaria and Romania in February 1995. The dissolution of Czechoslovakia on 1 January 1993 made it necessary to modify the 1991 Agreement in negotiations with the two successor states, the Czech Republic and Slovakia, and for temporary Agreements to remain in force. Europe Agreements have since been extended to the Baltic states and Slovenia. The overall condition is that these countries operate a market economy based upon free elections, the rule of law and respect for human rights.

By way of complement to the Europe Agreements, provision has been made for 'structured dialogue' between the European Union and the countries of central and eastern Europe. This dialogue is based upon their participation three times a year in meetings of the **Council of Ministers**.

There is a great deal of useful background material on Western Europe's postwar relations with central and eastern Europe in Peter van Ham, *The EC, Eastern Europe and European Unity* (1993).

Europe 2000

Europe 2000: the development of the Community's territory was the name of a study published by the **Commission** in 1991. It sought to combine data on economic activity, land use, population movements, telecommunications and transport links to give a composite picture of the member states as a basis for action in particular sectors (such as **trans-European networks**). Amongst the study's findings was the emergence of a southern 'arc of prosperity' stretching from Catalonia through Mediterranean France into northern Italy, to which Austria and Bavaria may now be added, complementing the well-established London–Amsterdam–Ruhr–Paris quadrilateral in the north. The study drew attention to the problems likely to arise as a result of rapid population growth on the Community's southern frontier (the population of the **Maghreb** countries is likely almost to double by the year 2025) and the difficulties still faced by peripheral regions in seeking to attract investment, a much higher proportion of which is now flexible with respect to the choice of location.

European Agency for Safety and Health at Work

An advisory committee on safety, hygiene and health protection at work was set up in 1974 to assist the **Commission** with the drafting of legislation in these areas. In 1990 the Commission proposed the establishment of an agency, and in October 1993 it was agreed that the Agency should be located in Spain (see **seat of the institutions**). Bilbao was the city chosen by the Spanish government. The role of the Agency is to gather and disseminate information on health and safety at work, coordinate national actions and research programmes, and provide technical support for the Commission in these areas.

European Agricultural Guidance and Guarantee Fund (EAGGF)

As its name implies, EAGGF (sometimes known by its more pronounceable French acronym FEOGA) is concerned with two quite distinct purposes. The 'guidance' part of the Fund is one of the four **structural funds** and gives assistance to help reform farm structures and to develop rural areas. The 'guarantee' section, much the larger, is responsible for the price support that is a key feature of the **Common Agricultural Policy** (CAP; see **intervention**). The EAGGF was set up under Article 40.4 of the **Treaty of Rome** and came into operation in 1962.

The Guidance section of the EAGGF is directed towards objectives laid down in the 1988 reforms of the structural funds. Objective 5a is to support structural reforms in agriculture, and projects anywhere in the Union may qualify for assistance under this heading. Objective 5b is to promote the development of rural areas, including, of course, diversification away from agriculture; to qualify for assistance projects must be in one of the areas designated by the **European Commission** as eligible for Objective 5b support. However, unlike the other structural funds, action under Objective 5a is governed directly by Regulations (see **legal instruments**) laid down by the **Council of Ministers**. These provide *inter alia* for incentives for early retirement, special aids for agriculture in mountainous regions, and for the definition of environmentally-sensitive areas (ESAs).

Action under Objective 5b, to which the other structural funds and the **European Investment Bank** (EIB) may also contribute, is taken in conformity with development plans drawn up by member states and agreed with the Commission as Community Support Frameworks. All EAGGF support is given in the form of grants. With the **accession** of Finland and Sweden, Objective 6 was added to allow assistance to be given to agriculture in sparsely populated Arctic regions.

The Guarantee section of the EAGGF pays for the intervention buying of produce when prices fall below the minimum guaranteed prices fixed annually for each product. Only certain products are covered by a common organization of the market (sometimes known as a 'regime') involving intervention; those that are represent about 70 per cent of total agricultural production. Such products also benefit from export refunds, paid from the Guarantee section of the EAGGF, when prices on world markets fall below those within the member states. A further 25 per cent of agricultural production is covered only by external protection and not by intervention. The remaining 5 per cent of agricultural production may also be a charge upon the EAGGF in the form of other types of price support or direct aids to producers.

Over 95 per cent of EAGGF expenditure is in the Guarantee section, which is classified as **compulsory expenditure** within the **Budget**. The EAGGF overall is almost half of the Budget.

European anthem

An orchestral arrangement by Herbert von Karajan of the main theme of the last movement of Beethoven's *Ninth Symphony* (his setting of Schiller's 'Ode to Joy' for choir, soloists and orchestra) was adopted in 1962 by the **Council of Europe** as the European anthem.

European Armaments Agency

A European Armaments Agency is identified in paragraph 5 of the first of the two **Declarations** on **Western European Union** (WEU) annexed to the **Maastricht Treaty** as a 'proposal [to] be examined further'. The Franco–German summit of May 1994 called for the creation of such an agency, open to all WEU states, as a further development of the already extensive bilateral cooperation between the two countries on arms-related issues. For the background to this proposal, see **Independent European Programme Group**.

European Army

On 11 August 1950 **Winston Churchill** moved a resolution in the Consultative Assembly of the **Council of Europe** that called for 'the immediate creation of a unified European Army subject to proper European democratic control and acting in full cooperation with the United

States and Canada'. Although the resolution was passed, it was not acted upon by the Committee of Ministers, but Churchill's speech made a great impact and was part of the current of ideas that flowed into the **Pleven Plan** of September 1950, which, in turn, provided the basis for the 1952 agreement on a **European Defence Community** amongst **the Six**.

The background to Churchill's proposal was the outbreak of the Korean War on 25 July 1950 and the worsening situation in central and eastern Europe as the Communist parties strengthened their hold. The proposal was controversial not least because it implied that the Germans should be allowed to rearm. The following month the United States suggested that German divisions should be allowed to serve within the **North Atlantic Treaty Organization** (NATO), which had been founded the previous year; however, West Germany did not become a member until 1955. Churchill's reference to 'proper European democratic control' clearly meant that he saw this as a task for the Council of Europe, but in fact the Council has never become involved in security matters. More than 40 years later, the proposal for a European Army was partially realized in the 1991 decision to establish the **Eurocorps**.

European Atomic Energy Community

Commonly known as Euratom, the European Atomic Energy Community (EAEC) was established by **the Six** under a treaty signed in Rome on 25 March 1957, the same day as the better-known **Treaty of Rome** establishing the **European Economic Community**. The object of Euratom, in the words of Article 1 EAEC, was to create 'the conditions necessary for the speedy establishment and growth of nuclear industries'.

After the failure of the **European Defence Community** it was clear that if the impetus of European integration was to be maintained, progress would have to be made on some less controversial front. The **Spaak Committee** had been invited to consider the areas of agreement identified by the 1955 **Messina Conference** and these, it was thought, could be subdivided into a proposal for a **customs union** and another for an atomic energy community along the lines of the **European Coal and Steel Community** (ECSC). Accordingly, two treaties were drafted (see **Pierre Uri**), of which the one on atomic energy was thought at the time to be the more important.

The enormous potential of atomic energy was fully realized in the early 1950s, as was the damage that could be done if fissile materials were to fall into the wrong hands. It was also realized that, like coal and steel in an earlier generation, the possession of nuclear weapons could be decisive in the event of war and, then as now, the French were nervous about the possibility of nuclear weapons being in German hands. Western Europe's reliance on the Middle East for its energy needs was underlined in the most dramatic way possible when as a result of President Gamal Abdel Nasser of the United Arab Republic seizing control of the Suez Canal on 26 July 1956 petrol rationing had to be introduced. All these factors pointed in the direction of a common effort on the part of the Six to develop atomic energy.

The institutions of Euratom were set up on the same quadripartite model that had served for the ECSC: an Assembly, a Council of Ministers, a Commission, and a Court of Justice, advised by an Economic and Social Committee (Article 2 EAEC). The Assembly, the Court, and the Economic and Social Committee were, from the beginning, institutions common to all three Communities, but until the 1965 **Merger Treaty** came into force in July 1967 Euratom had its own Brussels-based Commission and its own Council of Ministers. As was the case with the Commission provided for under the Treaty of Rome, the powers of the Euratom Commission were more limited than those of the ECSC's High Authority. The first President of the five-member Euratom Commission was a Frenchman, Louis Armand. A Scientific and Technical Committee of national experts was attached to the Commission in an advisory capacity.

The procedures and the **legal instruments** used by Euratom are the same as those used by the European Economic Community. The chapter headings of the Euratom Treaty indicate the range of activities pursued under the Treaty: promotion of research; dissemination of information; health and safety; investment; supplies of 'ores, source materials and special fissile materials' (the responsibility of the Euratom Supply Agency); safeguards; and external relations.

Of particular interest is the **Joint Research Centre** (JRC) established under Article 8 EAEC. Managed by the Commission, the JRC is in fact composed of nine separate institutes spread over four sites: Ispra (Italy), Petten (the Netherlands), Karlsruhe (Germany) and Geel (Belgium). The **European University Institute** was also founded under the Euratom Treaty.

From 1957 until 1967 Euratom had its own budget, divided into two parts, one for administration and another for research and investment. In 1967 the administrative budget was incorporated into the European Economic Community's general **Budget** and three years later the research and investment budget was also merged with the general Budget.

European Bank for Reconstruction and Development (EBRD)

The EBRD, based in London, is devoted to promoting structural reform and the transition to a market economy in the countries of central and eastern Europe and the former Soviet Union. It is not to be confused with the **European Investment Bank** (EIB) or the **European Central Bank** (ECB). The EBRD has a membership of 59 lender and borrower countries, the latter known as 'countries of operation' (see below).

The EBRD was created as a response to the collapse of Communism in central and eastern Europe. In 1989 President **François Mitterrand** of France proposed the creation of a specialized development bank to promote economic restructuring and the liberalization of markets in the region, which would in turn help to underpin the transition to democracy. Less explicitly, the French government perhaps hoped to create a 'European' body that would counterbalance German economic and political influence. Many Western governments were initially sceptical, arguing that assistance could as effectively be directed to the region through bilateral channels or through established international agencies such as the International Monetary Fund (IMF), the World Bank or the EIB. However, with strong German support the proposal was endorsed by the **European Council** at Strasbourg in December 1989. It was agreed that membership of the EBRD would be open to non-European countries, but the member states of the Community, the Community itself and the EIB would together have a majority shareholding (51 per cent). The United States is the largest single shareholder (10 per cent), followed by Japan (8.5 per cent).

The Strasbourg decision resulted in the EBRD being given a mandate 'to promote, in consultation with the IMF and the World Bank, productive and competitive investment in the States of Central and Eastern Europe, to reduce, where appropriate, any risks related to the financing of their economies, to assist the transition towards a more market-oriented economy and to speed up the necessary structural adjustments'. In April 1990 Jacques Attali, special adviser to President Mitterrand, and widely credited as the originator of the idea, was appointed as President of the EBRD (against opposition from Japan and the United States, but with British support in exchange for French support for London as the EBRD's headquarters).

The EBRD began operations a year later. The 'countries of operation' are Albania, Bulgaria, the Czech Republic, Hungary, Poland, Romania, Slovakia, the former Soviet Union (including the Baltic states) and the former Yugoslavia. The Bank's political purpose is evident from the fact that it can lend only to countries 'committed to and applying the principles of multiparty democracy, pluralism and market economics', and when these principles are clearly at risk (as they were during the abortive coup in Moscow in August 1991) the EBRD's operations in that country are subject to review.

The EBRD's subscribed capital amounts to 10 billion ECUs (almost £8 billion), and it may borrow on international capital markets. At least

60 per cent of its lending in each country must be to private-sector projects, although this gives rise to problems of definition in respect of projects in countries in which the boundaries of the public and private sectors are difficult to draw. The EBRD deals directly with project sponsors as well as with governments, and offers loans at near-market rates. It may also take an equity stake or offer loan guarantees. It is both a merchant bank, dealing with commercially competitive borrowers, and a development bank, promoting the development of infrastructure in recipient countries, with a commitment to respect the environment. The EBRD has supported 251 projects in 24 countries since 1991.

The collapse of the Soviet Union and of Yugoslavia not only greatly increased the number of countries of operation but also made the problem of reconstruction more complex, and on a scale well beyond what the EBRD's founders originally envisaged. The allegations of waste, extravagance and mismanagement that brought about the resignation of Jacques Attali in June 1993 damaged, at least temporarily, the EBRD's credibility, and it remains to be seen whether under his successor as president, Jacques de Larosière, the EBRD can make a significant and lasting contribution to the economic development of central and eastern Europe and the former Soviet Union.

European Broadcasting Union (EBU)

Founded in Torquay in 1950 and based in Geneva, the EBU enables broadcasting companies in almost every European country, plus Algeria, Egypt, Libya, Morocco and Tunisia, to consult each other on legal, technical, legislative and commercial aspects of cross-frontier broadcasting. Through Eurovision and Euroradio the EBU also promotes international collaboration in programme production and transmission. EBU, which works in English and French, is involved with the European Union's MEDIA programme, has official relations with the **Council of Europe** and collaborates with similar regional broadcasting unions worldwide.

European Central Bank (ECB)

Article 4a of the **Treaty of Rome**, added by the **Maastricht Treaty**, establishes both a European System of Central Banks (ESCB) and a European Central Bank (ECB), to be set up as soon as the decision is taken to proceed to stage 3 of **Economic and Monetary Union** (EMU). The precursor of both bodies is the **European Monetary Institute** (EMI) in Frankfurt, which came into operation in January 1994. A statute covering the ESCB and the ECB is annexed as a **protocol** to the Treaty of Rome. Only those member states that participate in stage 3 will be represented in the ESCB and the ECB.

The ESCB is the means whereby the governors of the participating states' central banks (which, under Articles 107 and 108 EEC, must be independent of national governments by the beginning of stage 3) play a role alongside the ECB in the overall direction of EMU. In line with Article 3a EEC, its 'primary objective [is] to maintain price stability' and its basic tasks are to 'define and implement' monetary policy, to conduct foreign exchange operations, 'to hold and manage the official foreign reserves of the [participating] Member States', and 'to promote the smooth operation of payment systems'. The ESCB is also responsible for 'the smooth conduct of policies pursued by the competent authorities relating to the prudential supervision of credit institutions and the stability of the financial systems' (Article 105 EEC).

The ECB, which is part of the ESCB, will, like its precursor the EMI, be managed by a Governing Council composed of central bank governors and a president, who will be appointed by the participating member states after consultation with the **European Parliament** and the Governing Council. The president-in-office of the **Ecofin Council** and a member of the **Commission** will be able to participate in meetings of the Governing Council, but without the right to vote. The ECB will be required to draw up an annual report on the activities of the ECSB and on monetary policy, for presentation to the **European Council**, the **Council of Ministers**, the European Parliament and the Commission (Article 109b EEC). It will have a general right of consultation on all legislation, European or national, in its areas of competence (Article 105 EEC).

The ECB will have the 'exclusive right' to authorize the issue of ECU banknotes, and may issue such notes itself together with national central banks. The ECB also has the power to authorize member states' issues of coins, the specifications of which may be laid down by the Ecofin Council under the **cooperation procedure**.

The decision-making bodies of the ECB will be the Governing Council and the Executive Board. The Council, composed of the Board and the governors of national central banks, will take decisions by simple majority, each member having one vote, the quorum being two-thirds. Certain decisions allow votes to be weighted in accordance with participating states' share of the ECB's capital. In such cases a majority is at least half the shareholders and two-thirds of the subscribed capital. The Council is required to meet at least 10 times a year (Statute, Article 10).

The Board is composed of the president, the vice-president and four other members. All are full-time employees with a non-renewable term of office of eight years. Each has one vote, and decisions will be taken by simple majority (Statute, Article 11).

The ECB's decisions will be in the form of Regulations and Decisions (see **legal instruments**). Both must be published in the *Official Journal*. The ECB may also make recommendations and deliver **Opinions**. In certain circumstances it may impose fines on undertakings that do not comply with its Regulations and Decisions.

European Centre for the Development of Vocational Training

Sometimes known by its French acronym CEDEFOP, the Centre was established in 1975 as a body to advise the **Commission** on various aspects of **social policy** concerned with training: vocational training, comparability of training qualifications, the retraining of women wishing to go back to work, etc. Initially based in Berlin, the Centre has since been moved to Thessaloniki. Persons appointed by national governments, employers' organizations and trade unions as well as the Commission participate in the work of the Centre. Under a Regulation of 1990, a new body, the European Training Foundation, was set up to encourage and assist vocational training schemes in the countries of central and eastern Europe.

European City of Culture

Since 1985 the Council of Ministers of Culture in the European Union has chosen a 'Cultural Capital of Europe'. The city so designated benefits from support from the **Budget**. To date, the title has been bestowed on the following cities:

1985	Athens	1990	Glasgow	1995	Luxembourg
1986	Florence	1991	Dublin	1996	Copenhagen
1987	Amsterdam	1992	Madrid	1997	Thessaloniki
1988	Berlin	1993	Antwerp	1998	Stockholm
1989	Paris	1994	Lisbon	1999	Weimar

With effect from 1994, a parallel scheme for a 'European Cultural Month' has been introduced, involving cities outside the Union. Budapest, Nicosia, Ljubljana, and St Petersburg have been named as participants in this new project, which, like the 'Cultural Capital' scheme, entails a very full programme of concerts, exhibitions, film festivals and other cultural events.

European Coal and Steel Community (ECSC)

The ECSC was established by the Treaty of Paris in 1951. The first of the three European Communities (the others being the **European Economic Community** and the **European Atomic Energy Community**), the ECSC was based upon the **Schuman Plan** of 1950. On 9 May 1950

Robert Schuman, the French Foreign Minister, proposed that French and German coal and steel production should be 'pooled' and placed under a common supranational authority, an initiative that owed its origin to **Jean Monnet**. In the event not only France and West Germany but also Belgium, Italy, Luxembourg and the Netherlands decided to take part, thus forming **the Six**. The ECSC Treaty was concluded for a period of 50 years (Article 97), whereas the EEC Treaty (the **Treaty of Rome**) and the Euratom Treaty are of indefinite duration.

The coal and steel industries were chosen as the two industries essential to the waging of war. If they were placed under a common supranational authority, war between the signatory states would be, in Schuman's words, 'not only unthinkable, but materially impossible'. Coal and steel were also essential to economic recovery, and the experience already gained from the economic cooperation that was a condition of the economic aid received under the **Marshall Plan** suggested that recovery would be more rapid if European countries abandoned the elaborate prewar system of tariffs and quotas. The elimination of such restrictions on trade in coal and steel products amongst the Six was a prime objective of the ECSC Treaty, together with common prices, a common policy on imports, measures to enforce competition and the harmonization of state aids.

The ECSC Treaty, which after ratification came into effect in July 1952, provided for four main institutions: a Special Council of Ministers; a High Authority (of which Monnet was the first president); a Common Assembly composed of 78 members nominated from amongst Members of Parliament in the signatory states; and a Court of Justice for the settlement of disputes. The Treaty thus established the institutional framework that was later used for the more ambitious European Economic Community: the ECSC's High Authority was the prototype of the **Commission**, and the Common Assembly developed into the **European Parliament**. Although by 1958 the two other Communities (see above) had been created, the institutions of the ECSC remained legally separate until the **Merger Treaty** of 1965. All were based in Luxembourg, a 'provisional' arrangement that was to have lasting consequences for the **seat of the institutions**. A **protocol** on relations with the **Council of Europe** was annexed to the ECSC Treaty. It called upon governments to recommend to **national parliaments** that the members appointed to sit in the ECSC Common Assembly 'should preferably be chosen from among the representatives to the Consultative Assembly of the Council of Europe' (Article 1). Both the Common Assembly and the High Authority of the ECSC were required to forward annual reports on their activities to the Council of Europe (Articles 2–3). The motive behind these provisions seems to have been to answer the criticism that the ECSC and the Council of Europe, in spite of

their very different structures and areas of responsibility, might develop on
the basis of mutual jealousy. The protocol makes it clear that at the time
the Council of Europe was regarded as the senior partner.

The ECSC remains the best example of **functionalism**: that is, integration centred upon a strictly limited field with common institutions possessing only the powers required to discharge their responsibilities effectively.
Trade in coal and steel products between the Six rose very rapidly
throughout the 1950s, while the extensive use of the High Authority's
powers to break up cartels and monopolies kept price rises to a minimum.

However, both the structure of the ECSC and the range of powers
exercised by its institutions embodied many compromises and ambiguities.
Monnet's original preference was for a sovereign 'High Authority', but the
Benelux countries – drawing on their experience of a **customs union** –
insisted that the High Authority should be overseen by governments
acting through a Council of Ministers. The Common Assembly's powers
of control were to be exercised over the High Authority, not over the
Council. While the objectives of the ECSC were consistent with free
market philosophy (price transparency, competition, limits on state aids),
the institutions were also given powers of a more *dirigiste* character: to
control imports, for example, or to set prices and place limits on production
in the event of a crisis in the coal or steel industries. The hybrid nature of
the ECSC's institutions and the tension between the different economic
philosophies underpinning the ECSC's powers set a pattern for the European
Economic Community.

The British attitude to the Schuman Plan and to the establishment of the
ECSC was ambivalent. On the one hand, there was enthusiasm for the
prospect of a lasting reconciliation between France and Germany; on the
other, there was opposition to the idea of a 'High Authority' and to the
loss of sovereignty that the existence of such an authority might entail.
The discussion exposed the fault-lines running through the political parties,
which, more than a generation later, are still evident. The first point to be
settled was whether to take part in the negotiations on the Schuman Plan.
Winston Churchill's speech in the House of Commons on 27 June 1950
neatly expressed the dilemma:

> If he [Sir Stafford Cripps, the Labour Chancellor] asked me, 'Would
> you agree to a supranational authority which has the power to tell
> Great Britain not to cut any more coal or make any more steel, but
> to grow tomatoes instead?' I should say, without hesitation, the
> answer is 'No'. But why not be there to give the answer?

The French government had (perhaps wisely) made acceptance in principle
of a High Authority a condition of taking part in the discussions on the

plan. In the Consultative Assembly of the Council of Europe, Conservatives, led by Harold Macmillan, put forward an alternative proposal that would have brought the institutions of what became the ECSC under the auspices of the Council and greatly reduced their supranational character. This proposal attracted little support, and the Six signed the Treaty of Paris on 18 April 1951. Although the Treaty made no provision for associate membership of the ECSC, the United Kingdom concluded an **Association Agreement** with the Six in December 1954.

The supranational institutions provided for, however modestly, under the ECSC Treaty marked a decisive break with the intergovernmental model of integration (see **intergovernmentalism**) typified by such bodies as the Council of Europe and the **Organization for Economic Cooperation and Development** (OECD). The significance of this was not lost upon **Konrad Adenauer**, who in a speech to the Bundestag in 1952 spoke of the 'political meaning' of the ECSC being 'infinitely larger than its economic purpose ... For the first time in history, countries want to renounce part of their sovereignty, voluntarily and without compulsion, in order to transfer it to a supranational structure'. For the United States, John Foster Dulles, the acting Secretary of State, welcomed the Schuman initiative as 'brilliantly creative', adding that it could 'go far to solve the most dangerous problem of our time, namely the relationship of Germany's industrial power to France and the West'. The ECSC and its supranational apparatus were also a decisive step beyond the postwar proposals for the internationalization of the Ruhr and the **Saarland**, although these helped to create the climate of opinion in which the Schuman Plan could find acceptance. The economic and political background to the Schuman Plan and the ECSC is set out in Milward, *The Reconstruction of Western Europe, 1945–51* (1984).

The ECSC was soon overshadowed by the European Economic Community. In March 1959 the High Authority sought to use its emergency powers in the coal industry, but failed to persuade the Council of Ministers to declare the 'state of manifest crisis', which was a necessary preliminary to the use of emergency powers. In the 1970s the Commission (as the successor to the High Authority) used its powers under the ECSC Treaty to restructure the Community's steel industry (the so-called Davignon Plan); these powers are now being used again to effect further restructuring in the wake of the recession and stiffer competition from central and eastern Europe. The ECSC Treaty's provisions for aids to miners' housing and retraining have helped mining communities adjust to the decline of the coal industry. However, there is nothing now done under the ECSC Treaty that could not, with modest adjustments, be brought within the ambit of the Treaty of Rome.

European Commission

Sometimes referred to as the 'civil service' of the European Union, the European Commission is unique amongst international bureaucracies by virtue of its combination of administrative, executive, legislative and judicial activities and responsibilities. In a strict sense the Commission is the 'college' of 20 Commissioners (see below), but the term is also used to denote all the European civil servants (*fonctionnaires*) who work for the institution. Of some 19,000 Commission employees, approximately 14,000 work in Brussels, the official 'seat' of the Commission (see **Berlaymont**, **Eurocrats**).

Under Article 157 of the **Treaty of Rome** the Commissioners are 'chosen on the grounds of their general competence'. The **Maastricht Treaty** extended their term of office from four to five years in order to align it with that of the **European Parliament** (Article 158 EEC), which now plays a decisive role in the appointment of Commissioners. Governments of member states acting 'by common accord' nominate 'after consulting the European Parliament' the president-designate in the year preceding that in which the new Commission is due to take office. They then choose, in consultation with the president-designate, their nominees as the other members of the Commission. Once chosen, the nominees are 'subject as a body to a vote of approval by the European Parliament', and if such approval is granted the governments may then proceed to formal appointment. Vacancies amongst the Commissioners caused by death or retirement are filled by agreement amongst the member states; only in the case of appointing a new president is there an obligation to secure the approval of the European Parliament.

Article 157 EEC specifies that there shall be 20 Commissioners, and that this may be changed only by unanimous agreement. In effect, this means two Commissioners from each of the five largest states, and one from each of the rest. The number of Commissioners has increased with each **enlargement** of the Union, since Article 157 EEC also says that the Commission 'must include at least one national of each of the Member States'. Initially, there were 9 Commissioners. For a brief period after the entry into force of the **Merger Treaty** (see below) in 1967 there were 14, but this was reduced to 9 in 1969 and then raised to 13 in 1973 with the first enlargement. Since then, the total has increased to 20 with the **accession** of Greece, Portugal, Spain (two Commissioners), Austria, Finland and Sweden. After extensive 'hearings' in the European Parliament's committees, the Commission for 1995–2000 was approved by the Parliament on 18 January 1995 by 416 votes to 103, with 59 abstentions. A list of these Commissioners will be found at the end of this entry.

Much stress is laid on the independence of Commissioners. Article 157 EEC requires them to be 'completely independent in the performance of their duties ... [and] neither seek nor take instructions from any government or from any other body'. They are prohibited from engaging 'in any other occupation, whether gainful or not'. On appointment, Commissioners commit themselves to remain independent in an oath sworn before the **Court of Justice** in Luxembourg. Individual Commissioners may be dismissed only by the Court on application from the **Council of Ministers** or the Commission itself. Collectively, the Commissioners may be dismissed by the European Parliament (see **censure motion**).

The Commission may appoint one or two vice-presidents. The allocation of portfolios is also decided (not always entirely amicably) by the Commissioners themselves on a proposal from the president. Each Commissioner takes responsibility for one or more of the 23 **directorates-general** and other ancillary services (such as the Legal Service or **Eurostat**) into which the Commission is divided. The Commissioners meet regularly, normally on Wednesdays, and although Article 163 EEC allows decisions to be taken by simple majority, in practice all major decisions are taken by consensus and the Commission operates on the basis of collective responsibility. Each Commissioner is assisted by a small *cabinet*. The most senior official in the administration is the secretary-general, currently David Williamson (see also **Emile Noël**).

The powers of the Commission are set out in Article 155 EEC. First, the Commission must 'ensure that the provisions of this Treaty and the measures taken by the institutions pursuant thereto are applied'. This function, with reference to which the Commission is sometimes referred to as the 'guardian of the Treaties', empowers the Commission to take action – ultimately, by referring the matter to the Court of Justice – if an institution or, under Article 169 EEC, a member state is in default of its Treaty obligations. Second, the Commission may make Recommendations (see **legal instruments**) or deliver **Opinions** on matters covered by the Treaty. Third, the Commission has 'its own power of decision and [may] participate in the shaping of measures taken by the Council and by the European Parliament in the manner provided for in this Treaty'. This general formulation embodies two quite distinct powers: first, the Commission's autonomous role in such areas as **competition policy**; and, second, its **right of initiative** in the legislative procedure and its involvement at every stage of the legislative process. Finally, the Commission is required 'to exercise the powers conferred on it by the Council for the implementation of the rules laid down by the latter'. Sometimes known as the Commission's 'management role', this is especially important in relation to the day-to-day operation of the **Common Agricultural Policy** (CAP), the **Common Commercial Policy** (CCP) and other areas in which under the **Treaties** action at the Union level has largely replaced that at the national level (but see also **management committee, comitology).**

In addition to the powers laid down in Article 155 EEC the Commission is responsible for negotiating on behalf of member states all bilateral and multilateral agreements to which the Union is a party (Articles 113 and 228 EEC). Under Article 229 EEC the Commission has a general responsibility for 'the maintenance of all appropriate relations' with the United Nations, its specialized agencies, the **General Agreement on Tariffs and Trade** (GATT) – now the World Trade Organization (WTO) – and other international bodies. The Commission has information offices in all member states and delegations in many other countries, including nearly all the countries associated with the Union through the **Lomé Convention**.

The Commission's role in the **Budget** procedure is to draw up the preliminary draft budget with the help of estimates prepared by the other institutions. Under Article 205 EEC the Commission is responsible for implementing the Budget and submitting accounts at the end of each financial year as part of the **discharge procedure**. The Commission is also responsible for the management of the **structural funds**.

Underpinning all these powers is what Article 155 EEC (see above) refers to as the Commission's 'own power of decision', that is, the right to decide for itself on the substance and timing of a particular proposal or other action. For example, throughout the legislative procedure, the Commission has the right to withdraw or amend its proposal; it may decide whether or not to accept amendments put forward by the European Parliament; and it can choose if, when and upon what grounds to bring an action before the Court of Justice. It is the exercise of this power of decision that qualifies the Commission as an autonomous political institution rather than a simple bureaucracy (see also **annual legislative programme**).

In relation to the **Common Foreign and Security Policy** (CFSP) and **Justice and Home Affairs** (JHA) provisions of the Maastricht Treaty the Commission's role is more circumscribed. Although in both areas the Commission is 'fully associated' (Articles J9 and K4 TEU) with developments, it has no exclusive right of initiative and in general terms is less strongly placed to influence the decisions taken by virtue of the essentially intergovernmental nature of the procedures (see **intergovernmentalism**).

Although extensive, the Commission's powers within the decision-making process are less than those of the **High Authority** of the 1951 **European Coal and Steel Community** (ECSC), upon which the Commission is modelled. This is apparent not least in the choice of name: 'Commission' – the ordinary French word for a committee – has none of the grandeur of 'High Authority', and was accordingly chosen by the drafters of the Treaties of Rome establishing the **European Economic Community** (EEC) and the **European Atomic Energy Community** (Euratom) as less provocative. From 1958 until 1967 the ECSC's High Authority and the EEC and Euratom Commissions led separate lives, but from July 1967 they were brought together as the Commission of the European Communities under the 1965 Merger Treaty.

By the time the Merger Treaty was being negotiated, the EEC Commission under its first president, **Walter Hallstein**, had aroused the opposition of French President **Charles de Gaulle**. De Gaulle took exception to what he saw as the Commission's pretensions (such as Hallstein's insistence on receiving the credentials of foreign diplomats accredited to the Communities). De Gaulle used the Commission as the target for his dislike of supranational institutions in general and denounced it in a number of well-publicized press conferences (especially that of 15 May 1962). His dislike of the Commission was partially responsible for the '**empty chair crisis**' of 1965 and so for the **Luxembourg Compromise** of January 1966.

Whatever hostility the Commission may have aroused on the part of the larger member states, the smaller states have always attached great importance to the Commission's role as the guardian of a broader European interest. The involvement of the Commission in all areas and at every level of Union activity is seen as a safeguard against a directorate of large states. This is why, for example, in the **qualified majority voting** (QMV) procedure a distinction is drawn between the majority necessary to adopt a Commission proposal and the majority needed when there is no proposal. It also explains why the smaller states strongly supported **Roy Jenkins** when as Commission President he sought to ensure (against French opposition) that he and his successors had the right to attend international economic summits on behalf of the Community as a whole.

One of the central facts about the Commission is that it has not developed into a European government. The **Council of Ministers** has shown little inclination to become a Chamber of States and the European Parliament has succeeded in exercising greater political authority over the Commission's legislative activities.

On the whole, the Commission has been the loser in the shifting balance of power between the institutions. It has, however, maintained – with some difficulty – its independence of action. What difference the Parliament's recently acquired powers over the appointment of Commissioners (see above) will make remains to be seen.

The fact that the Commission is not elected gives rise to criticism. However, as Sir Leon Brittan has argued, it is precisely the fact of the Commission's *not* being elected that allows the present institutional balance to be maintained, a balance broadly satisfactory to the governments of member states. The procedure under which an incoming Commission must secure the approval of the European Parliament is thought to give the Commission greater democratic legitimacy while falling well short of conferring an independent political mandate.

The 'Brussels bureaucrats' are held in generally low public esteem in the member states, particularly in those with a vigorous popular press. Although in recent years there has been a marked improvement in the quality of publicly available materials on Commission activities and a greater awareness of the need to counter **Euromyths**, the Commission is still very poor at explaining the background to its legislative initiatives. However, the Commission has a good reputation as a relatively open bureaucracy by comparison with most national civil services, and has been active in encouraging greater **transparency** within the Union's institutions.

The Commission has a poor record in respect of its own internal organization. The most wide-ranging report on this, the Spierenburg Report of 1979, identified the main failings: low motivation amongst Commission officials, over-elaborate hierarchies of authority, inflexible responses to changing priorities, all compounded by the usual rivalry and intrigue inevitable in international bureaucracies in relation to appointments and promotions (see **Eurocrats**). Very little action followed from this report, which remains the only large-scale study of its kind.

Amongst the reforms most regularly suggested is a reduction in the number of Commissioners, initially by allowing only one from each state. At present, only the United Kingdom of the five states affected supports this proposal. The others argue that the present system allows for opposition parties or coalition partners to be represented, and that this is important for the overall political balance of the Commission. It is also argued that Commissioners need time to travel, to lobby governments, to attend conferences and in general to maintain a European 'presence' of a kind that would be impossible if all Commissioners were confined to Brussels by pressure of work. The hard fact remains, however, that there are not enough jobs of broadly equivalent weight to provide work for 20 Commissioners.

Of the 80 or so Commissioners (including Members of the High Authority) there have been since 1951, the great majority had experience of middle-ranking or high ministerial office in their country of origin before going to Brussels. A few had non-party backgrounds as senior diplomats or international civil servants. Until 1994 there had been only two women. The trend for at least some members of each Commission to have been Members of the European Parliament (MEPs) is increasing, and will clearly increase more rapidly now that the Parliament has more say in the appointment of Commissioners (see above). There are few examples of Commissioners returning to national political life at a high level. Of the 20

Commissioners who took office in January 1995, 12, including the President, are new. Fourteen have held major political office (seven as prime minister, finance minister or foreign minister), in their country of origin. All but one have been members of their **national parliaments** and seven have also been MEPs.

Commissioners are paid an annual salary (with allowances) of approximately £180,000, vice-presidents and the president slightly more. Their salaries and pensions are paid from the Budget of the European Union; classified as **compulsory expenditure**, they are fixed in relation to the pay of the most senior rank within the Commission's services, that of director-general.

The following table lists the presidents of the Commission (the Commission of the European Economic Community, 1958–67, and the Commission of all three Communities since the Merger Treaty came into force in 1967):

Presidents of the Commission

Period of office	President	Country of origin	Party
1958–67	Walter Hallstein	West Germany	Christian Democrat
1967–70	Jean Rey	Belgium	Liberal
1970–72	Franco Maria Malfatti	Italy	Christian Democrat
1972–3	Sicco Mansholt	Netherlands	Socialist
1973–7	François-Xavier Ortoli	France	UDR (Gaullist)
1977–81	Roy Jenkins	United Kingdom	Labour
1981–5	Gaston Thorn	Luxembourg	Liberal
1985–95	Jacques Delors	France	Socialist
1995–	Jacques Santer	Luxembourg	Christian Democrat

The 1996 **Intergovernmental Conference** (IGC) is likely to give rise to attempts to reduce the Commission's authority and right of independent action. The Commission's critics will argue that as an institution it is an outdated relic of an essentially arrogant, bureaucratic, corporatist view of how the Union should develop, and that it must be downgraded into a secretariat for the Council of Ministers and made subject to democratic control exercised by national parliaments and the European Parliament. Some of its functions (policing the competition policy, for example) should be entrusted to specialist agencies. The majority of senior posts should be held by officials on secondment from national civil services. It should bring forward new legislation only when instructed to do so. Such measures would signal a decisive turn towards an intergovernmental model of integration, and would be opposed very vigorously not only by the Commission itself but by the European Parliament and several governments (especially those of smaller states, for reasons set out above). The case for the Commission – the boldest of all the institutional experiments embodied in the Treaties – must ultimately rest on whether it works, and whether the Union would work better if radical changes were made to the Commission's role. On the whole, the Commission does work. The very rapid progress made since the 1950s could not have been achieved without the Commission acting as motivator, monitor and proposer of compromises, nor without the longer-term view of the integration process that the Commission provides.

Commissioners and their portfolios, 1995–2000

President Jacques Santer
(Luxembourg)

- Secretariat-General, Legal Service, Security Office, Forward Studies Unit, Inspectorate-General, Joint Interpreting and Conference Service
- Spokesman's Service, Monetary matters (with Mr de Silguy), Common Foreign and Security Policy (CFSP; with Mr van den Broek)
- Institutional questions and intergovernmental conference (with Mr Oreja)

Vice-president Sir Leon Brittan
(United Kingdom)

- External relations with North America, Australia, New Zealand, Japan, China, South Korea, Hong Kong, Macao and Taiwan
- Common commercial policy
- Relations with Organization for Economic Cooperation and Development (OECD) and World Trade Organization (WTO)

Vice-president Manuel Marin
(Spain)

- External relations with the Mediterranean (South), Middle and Near East, Latin America and Asia (except Japan, China, South Korea, Hong Kong, Macao and Taiwan)

Martin Bangemann (Germany)

- Industrial affairs
- Information technologies and telecommunications

Karel Van Miert (Belgium)

- Competition

Hans van den Broek (The Netherlands)

- External relations with the countries of central and eastern Europe and of the former Soviet Union, Turkey, Cyprus, Malta and other European countries

	• CFSP (in agreement with the President)
	• External offices
Joao de Deus Pinheiro (Portugal)	• External relations with the ACP states, South Africa and Lomé Convention
Padraig Flynn (Ireland)	• Employment and social affairs
	• Relations with the Economic and Social Committee
Marcelino Oreja (Spain)	• Relations with the European Parliament
	• Relations with the member states on openness, communication and information
	• Culture and audiovisual, and publications office
	• Institutional questions and preparation of the intergovernmental conference of 1996 (in agreement with the President)
Anita Gradin (Sweden)	• Questions linked to immigration and home and judicial affairs
	• Relations with the Ombudsman
	• Financial control, anti-fraud measures
Edith Cresson (France)	• Science, research and development
	• Joint Research Centre
	• Human resources, education, training and youth
Ritt Bjerregaard (Denmark)	• Environment
	• Nuclear security
Monika Wulf-Mathies (Germany)	• Regional policies
	• Relations with the Committee of the Regions
	• Cohesion Fund (in agreement with Mr Kinnock and Mrs Bjerregaard)
Neil Kinnock (United Kingdom)	• Transport (including trans-European networks)
Mario Monti (Italy)	• Internal market, financial service
	• Customs and indirect taxation, direct taxation
Franz Fischler (Austria)	• Agriculture and rural development
Emma Bonino (Italy)	• Consumer policy
	• European Community Humanitarian Office (ECHO)
	• Fisheries
Yves-Thibault de Silguy (France)	• Economic and financial affairs
	• Monetary matters (in agreement with the President)
	• Credit and investments
	• Statistical Office

Erkki Liikanen (Finland)

- Budget
- Personnel and Administration
- Translation and information technology

Christos Papoutsis (Greece)

- Energy and Euratom Supply Agency
- Small and medium enterprises (SMEs)
- Tourism

European Communities

The phrase 'European Communities' is used to denote the **European Coal and Steel Community** (ECSC; **Treaty of Paris**, 1951), the **European Economic Community** (the EEC or 'Common Market'; **Treaty of Rome**, 1957), and the **European Atomic Energy Community** (Treaty of Rome, known as the Euratom or EAEC Treaty, 1957). Since the 1965 **Merger Treaty** the three Communities have shared the same institutions while remaining legally distinct, and have always had the same membership (**the Six**, 1951–72; the Nine, 1973–80; the Ten, 1981–5; the Twelve, 1986–94; the Fifteen, 1995–). In the **Maastricht Treaty** the European Economic Community was officially renamed 'the European Community', and this remains a separate entity within the European Union established by that Treaty.

Since the Maastricht Treaty came into effect, the **Council of Ministers** of the European Communities has called itself the Council of the European Union. The Commission is still formally the Commission of the European Communities or, for most purposes, simply the **European Commission**.

European Community Humanitarian Office (ECHO)

ECHO was set up within the **Commission** in 1991 to make the provision of humanitarian aid more efficient, especially by improving coordination with relief agencies and by enabling the European Union to respond more promptly to calls for emergency aid. ECHO became fully operational in 1993, in which year aid was given to some 50 countries on the basis of over 700 project contracts. Together with the United States, the European Union is the largest donor of humanitarian aid (defined as aid given in response to specific emergencies, as opposed to aid given as part of the Union's **development policy**). In 1994 the European Union gave over £600 million worth of humanitarian aid, much of which went to the former Yugoslavia (this does not include aid given bilaterally by individual member states). Overall, more than 90 per cent of humanitarian aid was given in response to man-made emergencies, such as wars and other regional conflicts. Aid is drawn both from the **Budget** of the European Union and from the **European Development Fund**.

ECHO works very closely with non-governmental organizations (NGOs), such as Oxfam and Children in Need, for the allocation and distribution of humanitarian aid. Overall, NGOs handle some 44 per cent of the aid granted by the Union. The United Nations and its specialized agencies (the High Commission for Refugees, the World Food Programme and the World Health Organization) are also important partners in the aid effort. The United Nations has set up a coordinating body (the Department for Humanitarian Affairs) in collaboration with which ECHO is seeking to improve the international community's preparedness to respond to calls for emergency aid.

The self-evident need for decisions on humanitarian aid to be taken promptly has given rise to special procedures. Within the relevant allocations in the Budget, the Commission can make many of the decisions on its own authority, subject to the overall supervision of the **Council of Ministers** and the **European Parliament**, to which ECHO submits an annual report.

European Company Statute

The original proposal for a European Company Statute dates back to 1975, as an attempt by the **Commission** to facilitate the creation of new multinational companies. The most controversial feature of the proposal was the requirement that workers' rights should be protected by the introduction of a two-tier board, structured along German lines. This met with strong resistance from many employers and several governments, and was eventually dropped. A second proposal was brought forward in 1989 in the form of a statute that companies could choose to adopt (and secure certain tax advantages by so doing). As a **Single Market** measure, it might have benefited from the **qualified majority voting** (QMV) provisions introduced by the **Single European Act** (SEA), but, in fact, since it deals with 'the rights and interests of employed persons' (Article 100a.2 of the **Treaty of Rome**), the requirement that the **Council of Ministers** must be unanimous continues to apply (see also **European Economic Interest Grouping**, **Social Charter**).

European Conference of Ministers of Transport

Set up in 1953 on the initiative of the OEEC (see **Organization for Economic Cooperation and Development**), the European Conference of Ministers of Transport meets twice a year with participants from 23 countries. Concerned primarily with road transport, railways and inland waterways, it is a forum in which governments can discuss technical, administrative and economic aspects of transport policy, on the basis of detailed work at official level. The Conference's main conclusions may be adopted in the form of Conventions, more usually as Resolutions. The Conference is an important source of statistics on transport use, accidents, investment, traffic forecasts and related issues.

European Conference of Postal and Telecommunications Administrations (CEPT)

Known by its French acronym, CEPT was founded in 1959 within the Universal Postal Union (founded 1874). CEPT links the administrations of over 30 countries and has its headquarters in Berne. It provides a forum in which all aspects of posts and telecommunications can be discussed, including tariffs and the standardization of equipment. CEPT is also involved in the technical, legal and commercial aspects of satellite communications.

European Convention on Human Rights

See **human rights**.

European Council

The European Council (not to be confused with the **Council of Ministers** or the **Council of Europe**) is the name given to the regular meetings – sometimes known as 'summits' – of the heads of state or of government of the member states of the European Community and the president of the **European Commission**. This cumbersome formula stems from the fact that the presidents of France and of Finland (the heads of state) attend the European Council together with their prime ministers (the heads of government). Since 1986 the foreign ministers of the member states and one additional Commissioner have also attended meetings of the European Council, which are held either in the country holding the **presidency** of the Council of Ministers or in Brussels.

The **Treaties** establishing the **European Communities** make no mention of the European Council. The first meeting of heads of state or of government was held in Paris in February 1961, and further meetings followed in Bonn (July 1961), Rome (May 1967), The Hague (December 1969), Paris (October 1972) and Copenhagen (December 1973). At a meeting in Paris in December 1974 **Valéry Giscard d'Estaing** suggested that a European Council should be established that would meet three times a year with the possibility of additional special meetings. This was agreed, and the first formal meeting of the new body was held in Dublin in March 1975, the main item for discussion being the conclusion of the British **renegotiation**.

A regular rhythm of three meetings a year was maintained until 1985, by which time the role of the European Council had been more fully set out in the **Stuttgart Declaration**. In 1986 Article 2 of the **Single**

European Act (SEA) gave the European Council official recognition as a Community body. The frequency of its meetings was laid down as 'at least twice a year' and the list of those entitled to attend was extended to include the foreign ministers and the additional Commissioner. Since June 1987 the president of the **European Parliament** has been invited to address the meeting but not to take part in the main proceedings. A Declaration annexed to the **Maastricht Treaty** confirms the practice of inviting economic and finance ministers to meetings of the European Council at which matters relating to **Economic and Monetary Union** (EMU) are discussed. A list of the more important meetings of the European Council since 1969 is to be found at the end of this entry.

The Maastricht Treaty (Article D) described the European Council's role as being to 'provide the Union with the necessary impetus for its development and . . . define the general political guidelines thereof'. The same Article obliged the European Council to submit to the European Parliament a report after each of its meetings and an annual report 'on the progress achieved by the Union'. The role of the European Council is therefore essentially twofold: first, to provide overall political direction to the Union; and second, to resolve problems that have proved intractable at Council of Ministers level. A typical European Council agenda will reflect both elements, encompassing a wide-ranging review of some important issue, domestic or foreign, often on the basis of a Commission paper, and then a more narrowly focused discussion of some internal problem. The Treaty also requires the European Council to 'define the principles of and general guidelines for the **Common Foreign and Security Policy**' (CFSP : Article 18 TEU).

Decisions of the European Council, which are only very rarely put to the vote, are embodied in statements of the president-in-office ('conclusions of the Presidency'; see also **Declaration**). However, to become law they must follow the normal decision-making route, starting with a Commission draft.

European Council meetings afford opportunities for bilateral discussions between leaders. They provide a forum in which political leaders may appear in splendid surroundings, engage in personal diplomacy and take dramatic initiatives; more importantly, these leaders are obliged to invest personal and political capital in the Union's development. They are structured to allow meetings (including lunches and dinners) of varying degrees of intimacy, and because the apparatus of officials, interpreters, security and so on is reduced to a minimum, at least some of the original informal character of European Council meetings is preserved. Inevitably, however, they attract the press and media, representatives of which may easily exceed 1,000 at the average meeting.

Initially opposed by devout Europeans on the grounds that it strengthened the intergovernmental character of the Community (see **intergovernmentalism**), the European Council is now accepted as a necessary part of the Community system (a view shared by **Jean Monnet**, who in a letter to President Giscard d'Estaing described the creation of the European Council as 'the most important decision for Europe since the **Treaty of Rome**'). Recognition came most slowly in the European Parliament, which felt that it lacked any means of influencing or scrutinizing European Council decisions: not until December 1981 were European Council meetings reported to the Parliament by the head of state or of government holding the presidency, a practice begun by **Margaret Thatcher**, continued by all her successors, confirmed in the Stuttgart Declaration and formalized in the Maastricht Treaty (see above).

As some commentators have pointed out, the impulse-giving role of the European Council can very easily be overshadowed by the need to solve problems. If a problem is referred to the European Council, it can only be because neither at official level nor at Council of Ministers level has it been possible to find agreement. Such problems are usually both intrinsically complex and politically sensitive; and by the time they reach the European Council they may well be urgent too. So it can easily happen that a meeting is dominated by a single issue, and less urgent matters (which may well be more important in the longer term) remain unresolved. The problem-solving function places temptation in the way of the Council of Ministers, since a minister in real political difficulty may wish to transfer the risk of domestic odium to his or her prime minister: this is what **François Mitterrand**, in an address to the Royal Institute of International Affairs in January 1987, referred to as the *téléscopage* between the two institutions.

The same problem was touched on in the 1985 report by the **Dooge Committee** on institutional questions: 'The trend towards the European Council's becoming simply another body dealing with the day-to-day business of the Community must be reversed. [It] should play a strategic role and give direction and political impetus to the Community.' In the period since 1985 the trend has been checked if not wholly reversed; and although the European Council is far from being the 'Provisional European Government' that Jean Monnet intended it to be (see Chapter 21 of his *Memoirs*), it is certainly true that all major initiatives in the Union, even if they do not originate in the European Council, must be endorsed by it.

The following is a list of the most important meetings in the period 1969–94.

The Hague, 1–2 December 1969
President Georges Pompidou of France lifts the French veto on British accession to the European Community.

Paris, 19–20 October 1972
[The Prime Ministers of Denmark, Ireland and the United Kingdom attended this summit, although the accession of these three countries did not formally take place until January 1973.] The member states commit themselves to **Economic and Monetary Union** (EMU) and to converting 'their entire relationship into a European Union' by the end of the decade.

Paris, 9–10 December 1974
Decision to establish the European Council. Leo Tindemans, Foreign Minister of Belgium, requested to draw up a report on European Union (see **Tindemans Report**).

Dublin, 10–11 March 1975
Settlement on British **renegotiation**.

Rome, 1–2 December 1975
Agreement on the **European passport** and on **European elections** (planned for 1978).

Brussels, 12–13 July 1976
Agreement on the total number of seats in the European Parliament, and on the allocation of seats to each member state.

Brussels, 5–6 December 1977
Agreement on the introduction of the European Unit of Account (see **European Currency Unit**) from 1 January 1978.

Bremen, 6–7 July 1978
Decision to create the **European Monetary System** (EMS).

Brussels, 4–5 December 1978
Resolution on the EMS. '**Three Wise Men**' commissioned to draw up a report on the Community institutions.

Dublin, 29–30 November 1979
British Budget problem first raised.

Venice, 12–13 June 1980
Venice Declaration on the situation in the Middle East.

London, 26–27 November 1981
Discussion of the **Genscher–Colombo** proposals on European Union. New impulse given to the accession negotiations with Portugal and Spain.

Stuttgart, 17–19 June 1983
Adoption of the Solemn Declaration on European Union (see **Stuttgart Declaration**).

Fontainebleau, 25–26 June 1984
Final settlement of the British Budget problem, accompanied by agreement on new **own resources** and on **budgetary discipline**. Establishment of the **People's Europe** committee and the **Dooge Committee**.

Brussels, 29–30 March 1985
Agreement on **Integrated Mediterranean Programmes**.

Milan, 28–29 June 1985
Agreement (by qualified majority) to convene an **intergovernmental conference** (IGC) under Article 236 EEC to discuss institutional reform. Endorsement of the **Cockfield White Paper** on the **Single Market**.

Luxembourg, 2–3 December 1985
Agreement in principle to extend **qualified majority voting** (QMV) in order to complete the Single Market programme by the end of 1992, to increase the powers of the European Parliament, to give **European Political Cooperation** a sounder legal base, and to extend Community competences (all set out in the SEA, agreed by the Foreign Affairs Council on 16–17 December 1985).

Brussels, 11–13 February 1988
Agreement on the measures to accompany the completion of the Single Market, on various budgetary and agricultural questions (including '**set-aside**') and on the reform of the **structural funds**.

Hanover, 27–28 June 1988
The Delors Committee invited to draw up a report on the achievement of EMU (see **Delors Report**).

Madrid, 26–27 June 1989
Agreement on the various stages leading to EMU.

Strasbourg, 8–9 December 1989
Adoption of the **Social Charter**. Decision to convene an intergovernmental conference (see **Maastricht Treaty**) and to set up the **European Bank for Reconstruction and Development**.

Dublin, 25–26 April 1990
Identification of the main issues for the intergovernmental conferences on political union and EMU.

There were two extraordinary meetings of the European Council in 1990, the first on **German reunification** (Dublin, 28 April) and the second on the Gulf crisis and EMU (Rome, 27–28 October).

Maastricht, 9–10 December 1991
Agreement on the Maastricht Treaty.

Lisbon, 26–27 June 1992
Agreement on guidelines for the **enlargement** of the Community.

Birmingham, 16 October 1992
'Birmingham Declaration' on 'a Community close to its citizens' (includes definition of **subsidiarity**).

Edinburgh, 11–12 December 1992
Agreement on special arrangements for Denmark to allow a second Danish referendum to take place on the Maastricht Treaty. Agreement on **future financing** of the Community. Decision to allow enlargement negotiations to begin with Austria, Finland and Sweden. Adoption of the **Edinburgh Growth Initiative**. Definitive decision on seat of the European Parliament (see **seat of the institutions**).

Copenhagen, 21–22 June 1993
Discussion of Commission White Paper *Growth, Competitiveness and Employment*. Decision that central and eastern European countries with **Europe Agreements** which 'so desire shall become members of the European Union' and that future cooperation 'shall be geared to the objective of membership'. Discussion of openness (see **transparency**) and **fraud**.

Brussels, 29 October 1993
(This extraordinary meeting took place three days before the entry into force of the Maastricht Treaty.) Decision on stage 2 of EMU (to begin 1 January 1994). Establishment of priority topics for the **Common Foreign and Security Policy** (CFSP) and **Justice and Home Affairs** (JHA) cooperation. Decision on sites of various European Union bodies (see **seat of the institutions**).

Brussels, 10–11 November 1993
Adoption of action plan on unemployment on basis of Commission White Paper (see above, June 1993). Agreement on **Pact on Stability in Europe**. Agreement on representation in Commission, European Parliament, etc., of applicant states.

Corfu, 24–25 June 1994
Further discussion of unemployment. Identification of 11 priority projects for **trans-European networks**. Commitment to include Cyprus and Malta in next round of enlargement. Establishment of **Reflection Group** to prepare 1996 IGC.

Essen, 9–10 December 1994
Further discussion of unemployment, financing of trans-European networks, strategy for gradual integration of countries of central and eastern Europe, **Mediterranean policy**, and **fraud**.

European Court

'European Court' may refer either to the **Court of Justice** of the European Communities in Luxembourg or the Court of Human Rights in Strasbourg (see **human rights**). The former, an institution of the European Union, adjudicates on disputes arising from the interpretation or application of the **Treaties** or the legislation based upon them; the latter, an institution of the **Council of Europe**, is concerned solely with cases brought under the European Convention on Human Rights.

European Cultural Centre

Established in Geneva in 1950 on the basis of a resolution adopted at the 1948 **Congress of Europe**, the Centre's main activities are directed towards a better and wider understanding of European culture, which forms the topic of numerous seminars, conferences, publications and research projects. Latterly, the Centre has taken an interest in regionalism. Very active in the 1950s, the Centre was involved in the creation of the **College of Europe**, the **European Centre for Nuclear Research** and the **European Cultural Foundation**.

European Cultural Foundation

Established in Geneva in 1954 as an offshoot of the **European Cultural Centre**, the Foundation moved to Amsterdam in 1960. Active in 22 countries, the Foundation – with the aid of many specialized bodies – works through schools, colleges, universities, the media and cultural organizations to promote cross-frontier cooperation in the social, cultural, educational and environmental fields, linked to European integration. The Foundation was the model for a similar European Foundation proposed in the 1976 **Tindemans Report** (see also **European Union**), but no progress was made with this proposal because of objections from the Dutch government.

European Currency Unit (ECU)

The original European Unit of Account (EUA) was introduced simply as a means of facilitating the European Communities' bookkeeping and as such was used in connection with the **Budget**. When the **European Monetary System** (EMS) was established in 1979, the ECU was brought into service and in 1981 it replaced the EUA.

Like its predecessor, the ECU is a 'basket' of national currencies, each currency's weighting within the basket being fixed as a percentage in line with each country's share of the Union's gross national product (GNP) and of internal trade. The composition of the ECU was frozen on 1 November 1993 in connection with the beginning of stage 2 of **Economic and Monetary Union** (EMU). Currency movements against the dollar are reflected in the central rate of the ECU, which in turn can be used to give cross-rates for or between the national currencies of the member states. The daily value of the ECU is published in the *Official Journal*.

The ECU has established itself in international money markets as a stable alternative to the dollar, the Deutsche Mark and the pound sterling. It is also used as a denomination for bank deposits and travellers' cheques, and for bookkeeping in respect of transactions involving several currencies; for example, European railways use the ECU when each company's share of revenue from the sale of international tickets is being calculated. The ECU is backed by the **European Monetary Institute** (EMI; the successor to the **European Monetary Cooperation Fund**), to which countries participating in the EMS must make available 20 per cent of their gold and dollar reserves. With the exception of some 5 and 50 ECU gold and silver coins minted in Belgium in 1987 to commemorate the thirtieth anniversary of the **Treaty of Rome**, the ECU is not legal tender in any part of the Union.

The proposal for a 'hard ECU' as a common European currency was put forward by the British government in 1990 in the course of the **Intergovernmental Conference** (IGC) on EMU. The idea was that the ECU should circulate alongside national currencies and would float against them in the EMS. It would be 'hard' in the sense that it could not be devalued. If it found sufficient support it might evolve over time into a single currency. The idea was not adopted.

The **Maastricht Treaty** gives the ECU a central role in the third and final stage of the process leading to EMU. Articles 3a.2, 109g, and 109l EEC require the 'irrevocable fixing' of exchange rates between national currencies and the ECU, which is specified as the single currency. At this point the ECU will cease to be a basket currency and will become a currency in its own right, with the **European Central Bank** (ECB) as the issuing authority.

In June 1994 the Commission published a communication on the 'practical problems involved in introducing the ECU as the European Union's single currency'. In fact, the problems range from the practical (conversion of coin-operated machines, implications for government departments responsible for calculating and allocating welfare benefits) to the legal (conversion to ECUs of current contracts) and the psychological. The communication underlines the unprecedented scale of the changeover and identifies three possible approaches: the 'Big Bang', whereby everything is converted within a maximum of two months; the gradual, whereby the ECU would coexist with national currencies for up to two years; and the intermediate. Reference is made to the experience gained from decimalization in the United Kingdom (1961–71) and German monetary unification (1990; see **German reunification**). The four main advantages of the ECU are listed as the elimination of exchange-rate risks and costs for traders within the Union, greater convenience for travellers, a strengthening of 'collective discipline' in the fight against inflation, and 'an affirmation of European identity . . . in international relations'.

By coincidence, the *écu* was a medieval French coin, so called because it bore a shield on one face (the Portuguese escudo is of the same origin). 'ECU' may also be written 'ecu'; some authorities regard it as either singular or plural, others use 'ECUs' or 'ecus' as the plural form. 'Million ECUs' is sometimes written 'MECUs' or 'mecus'. In spite of the Treaty references to the ECU as the single currency, the Madrid meeting of the European Council in December 1995 agreed to rename the single currency the 'Euro'.

European Defence Community (EDC)

With the outbreak of the Korean War in 1950 British and American demands for German rearmament became more insistent. In August 1950 **Winston Churchill** put forward a resolution in the Consultative Assembly of the **Council of Europe** that called for the creation of a **European army** under the authority of a European defence minister and subject to democratic control by the Assembly. The resolution was passed by 89 votes to 5 with 29 abstentions. In this European army, Churchill said in his speech, 'We would all play an honourable and active part.'

On 24 October 1950 the French government put forward a proposal to create amongst **the Six** a European Defence Community (EDC) within which a re-armed West Germany could be contained. The proposal, known as the **Pleven Plan**, was for a European army under a single commander to which member states would second units. The institutional structure was to be the same as that for the **European Coal and Steel Community** (ECSC): a Council of national ministers, a nine-member Commission, a parliamentary assembly and a Court of Justice. Of the 40 divisions, 14 would be French, 12 German, 11 Italian and 3 from the **Benelux** countries, and mixed so that no corps would consist of troops solely of one nationality. There was to be one uniform and one flag, and senior officers would be drawn from all nationalities and be responsible to the institutions of the EDC. The EDC would have its own budget, and make provision both for common procurement and joint training. The EDC Treaty was signed in Paris on 27 May 1952.

At the suggestion of **Alcide de Gasperi**, the Italian Prime Minister, the Treaty also contained provisions in Article 38 for a common external policy and a customs union, but it was left to the newly established ECSC parliamentary assembly (the forerunner of the **European Parliament**) to fill in the details. This they did in the form of an ambitious complementary draft treaty for a **European Political Community** on the grounds that a federal army would need to be made responsible to federal institutions.

In the Benelux countries, West Germany and Italy ratification of the EDC Treaty was accomplished without any serious difficulties. However, in France fear of German domination and loss of national sovereignty gave rise to many misgivings amongst parties of the extreme left and the nationalist right (notably the supporters of **Charles de Gaulle**), and the French government put forward a number of additional **protocols** to the draft treaty to safeguard French interests. These were discussed inconclusively at a conference in Rome in February 1953. Both the United Kingdom and the United States were asked to support the EDC, but this – for different reasons – they declined to do. As Theodore H. White wrote,

'The United States Army wanted German troops, flesh and blood soldiers, quickly, not a long philosophical discussion about the creation of a new super-state' (*Fire in the Ashes*, 1954).

At a conference in Brussels in August 1954 a final attempt was made to salvage the EDC on the basis of a revised treaty, but this failed to resolve the difficulties. On 30 August 1954 the French National Assembly voted by 319 votes to 264, with 43 abstentions, to postpone discussion of the treaty *sine die*, thus effectively killing it. Its victorious opponents sang 'The Marseillaise'.

The failure of the EDC was the first serious setback for the proponents of European unification, but less than a year later, in June 1955, the Six met at the **Messina Conference** to explore whether progress could be made instead on the economic front. And a month after the National Assembly's vote, the British government convened a meeting in London of representatives of the six EDC signatory states, the United Kingdom, the United States, and Canada to discuss defence cooperation, a meeting that led to the establishment of the **Western European Union** (WEU).

European Democrat Union (EDU)

The EDU was founded in Schloss Klessheim near Salzburg in 1978 as an association of Conservative and Christian Democratic political parties, partly in response to the closer links that Socialist parties were then forming in the years immediately preceding the first **European elections** in 1979 (see **transnational political parties**). Replacing an informal system of annual interparty meetings, the EDU aimed to promote the exchange of ideas and the pooling of experience amongst like-minded parties with the aid of standing committees and working groups. Then, as now, its membership was drawn from parties inside and outside the European Community. The EDU was for Scandinavian parties in particular an important means of keeping in touch with Community developments and for many years was virtually the only forum in which Conservatives and French Gaullists cooperated with Christian Democrats. The EDU now has some 37 parties as members or permanent observers, including many from central and eastern Europe. Since its foundation, it has been chaired by the Austrian People's Party. In the 1980s the EDU became a component part of a wider organization along the same lines, the International Democrat Union, which includes amongst others the Republican Party in the United States and centre-right parties in Australia and Japan.

European Development Fund (EDF)

The EDF is the means whereby financial aid is granted to 70 developing countries under the **Lomé Convention**. It is governed by a **protocol** annexed to the Convention: Lomé IV covers the period 1990–2000, and the first financial protocol (1990–95) makes 12 billion ECUs (about £9.6 billion) available over the period, of which 10 per cent is from the **European Investment Bank (**EIB). The second protocol (1996–2000) adds a further 14.7 billion ECUs.

The EDF is not part of the **Budget**, being financed by direct contributions from member states. This has given rise to disagreement with the **European Parliament**.

European Economic Area (EEA)

Established by a treaty signed in Oporto on 2 May 1992, the EEA is a **free trade area** of 18 countries and about 380 million people. It is responsible for about 40 per cent of world trade. The member states are the 15 member states of the **European Union** and Iceland, Liechtenstein and Norway. Switzerland signed the EEA Treaty but rejected it by referendum in December 1992 (a week later Liechtenstein accepted the Treaty by referendum; this decision was reaffirmed in April 1995). A **protocol** making the necessary adjustments to the Treaty was signed on 17 March 1993 and the Treaty came into effect on 1 January 1994.

The EEA Treaty is an **Association Agreement** under Article 238 of the **Treaty of Rome**. It consists of 129 Articles of general provisions, 50 Protocols covering specific issues, and 22 Annexes listing those portions of the *acquis communautaire* that under the Treaty apply throughout the EEA. With very few exceptions, the EEA Treaty takes precedence over other bilateral or multilateral agreements to which the signatory states are party. Article 121 EEA specifies that the Treaty should not affect other regional cooperation arrangements such as the **Nordic Council**, the customs union between Switzerland and Liechtenstein, and the cross-border agreements between Austria and Italy.

The EEA Treaty owed its origin to the mutual desire on the part of the member states of the **European Free Trade Association** (EFTA) and the Community to have closer links. Although each of the EFTA states had a bilateral free trade agreement with the Community (the last barriers to trade in industrial goods were removed on 1 January 1984), all parties agreed in the 1984 Luxembourg Declaration to extend their cooperation still further (the expression *espace économique européen* was used for the first time in this Declaration). This was given greater urgency by the Community's decision to undertake the **Single Market** programme. The first steps were to simplify the formalities governing trade, and in 1986 negotiations began to extend the use of the Single Administrative Document to the EFTA states (see **free movement of goods**). The accession of Spain and Portugal to the Community in the same year was used as a pretext to adjust and extend the free trade agreements into new areas, such as scientific and technological cooperation. In 1987 the Community laid down the so-called 'Interlaken Principles', which made it clear that the Single Market programme enjoyed absolute priority and that the EFTA states could not expect indefinitely to enjoy the economic benefits of free trade with the Community yet choose to stay outside.

In a speech to the **European Parliament** on 17 January 1989 Commission President **Jacques Delors** expressed the Community's willingness to move towards 'a new, more structured partnership with common decision-making and administrative institutions'. Eighteen months later (20 June 1990) negotiations began for the EEA Treaty.

The institutions of the EEA are as follows:

- The EEA Council meets at least twice a year at ministerial level. It is composed of representatives of the governments of the signatory states and of the **European Commission** (Articles 89–91 EEA).
- The EEA Joint Committee meets at least once a month. It is composed of senior officials of the signatory states and takes decisions by consensus, the EFTA states speaking with one voice (Articles 92–94 EEA). The EEA Joint Parliamentary Committee, composed of Members of the European Parliament (MEPs) and parliamentarians from the EFTA states, is required to hold at least two general sessions a year. It has no specific decision-making role but instead may adopt non-binding reports or Resolutions on matters covered by the EEA Treaty (Article 95 EEA).
- The EEA Consultative Committee plays a similar role. It is composed of members of the **Economic and Social Committee** and the EFTA Consultative Committee (Article 96 EEA).

Monitoring the EEA Treaty is carried out by the Commission in the Union and by the EFTA Surveillance Authority in the EFTA states. An EFTA Court is established to work in cooperation with the **Court of Justice** (the original proposal, for a common EEA Court, was ruled unlawful in an **Opinion** of 14 December 1991 by the Court of Justice as inconsistent with the Court's prerogatives as laid down in the EEC Treaty and with the autonomy of the Community's legal order).

The institutions of the EEA have no sovereign authority. It is intended that they and the Union institutions should work in parallel on the basis of consultations and the exchange of information. Legal acts of the Union on matters covered by the EEA Treaty are followed up in an annex to the Treaty agreed in the Joint Committee, with a view to ensuring both legal homogeneity and uniformity of application. Article 107 EEA allows national courts and tribunals in EFTA states to seek rulings in the Court of Justice on the interpretation of EEA rules; such rulings are binding.

The fundamental purpose of the Treaty is to allow the free movement of goods, persons, services and capital throughout the EEA. **Free movement of goods** (Articles 8–27, 53–65 EEA) covers nearly all industrial goods and some agricultural products. Approximately 800 items of Union legislation on the free movement of goods have been integrated into the Treaty. **Free movement of persons** (Articles 28–35 EEA) covers all employed and self-employed persons, with the exception of those in the public service. The entire *acquis communautaire* in this field is integrated into the Treaty. Similarly, **freedom to provide services** (Articles 36–39 EEA) is extended throughout the EEA, as is (with only minor, mostly temporary, exceptions) the free movement of capital (Articles 40–45 EEA).

By way of complement to the four freedoms the EFTA states are enabled under the EEA Treaty to take part in Union **research** programmes. Cooperation in the field of **environment policy** and consumer protection is strengthened. In a Declaration annexed to the Treaty the EFTA states express their support for the 1989 **Social Charter**. The EFTA states also undertake to contribute to social and economic **cohesion**; this will be of direct benefit to the Union's poorer regions. The financial aid will be administered by the **European Investment Bank** (EIB). State monopolies of a commercial character are to be adjusted or progressively eliminated, with some exceptions for those maintained by the Nordic countries on the sale of alcohol. Union rules on competition and state aids will be the model for similar rules applying throughout the EEA.

The EEA Treaty was the most ambitious and comprehensive treaty ever concluded by the Twelve. It remains open to new members (countries acceding to the Union have to join the EEA since the EEA Treaty is part of the *acquis communautaire*; countries joining EFTA may choose whether or not to join the EEA). The major areas of Union policy remaining outside the EEA are relations with third countries (both trading relations and development policy), fiscal policy, the **European Monetary System** (EMS) and **Economic and Monetary Union** (EMU), the **Common Agricultural Policy** (CAP), and the **Common Fisheries Policy** (CFP). Nor does the EEA Treaty cover the **Justice and Home Affairs** (JHA) and **Common Foreign and Security Policy** (CFSP) 'pillars' of the **Maastricht Treaty**. The future of the EEA is uncertain, since three of the original six EFTA signatories (Austria, Finland and Sweden) have joined the European Union, and Switzerland shows no sign of reversing its referendum decision.

For a commentary on the EEA Treaty by three lawyers from the EFTA Surveillance Authority, see Thérèse Blanchet, Risto Piipponen and Maria Clément, *The Agreement on the EEA* (Oxford, 1994).

European Economic Community (EEC)

The EEC was established by **the Six** under the 1957 **Treaty of Rome**. Since the entry into force of the **Maastricht Treaty** in November 1993 it has been officially renamed the European Community (see **European Communities**). The main institutions of the EEC are described under **Council of Ministers, Court of Justice, European Commission** and **European Parliament**; see also especially **Community law, customs union** and **Single Market**. For the origins of the EEC, see **Messina Conference** and **Spaak Committee**.

European Economic Interest Grouping

Substantial differences between member states in the field of company law are thought to inhibit cross-frontier economic activity. The **freedom of establishment** provisions of the **Treaty of Rome** provide for certain basic features of company law to be harmonized under Article 54.3g EEC. In the absence of any progress with the long-projected **European Company Statute** a further measure was taken in 1985: to allow small and medium-sized companies (SMEs) to cooperate within the framework of a European economic interest grouping that would be recognized throughout the member states. To date, few such groupings have been formed.

European Economic Space

The original translation into English of *espace économique européen*, used for the first time in 1984, and since October 1990 officially known in English as the **European Economic Area** (EEA).

European elections

Elections to the **European Parliament**, known as European elections, are held every five years under Article 1 of the 1976 European Elections Act. The first European elections took place in 1979; before that date the Parliament was composed of Members (MEPs) appointed by and from **national parliaments**. Article 7 of the Act contains a commitment to introduce a **uniform electoral procedure** at some unspecified future date, but until that is done, member states use electoral systems of their own choosing.

Because of different national traditions on voting, European elections take place over an agreed four-day period, allowing some member states to vote on a Thursday (as in the United Kingdom) and others on a Sunday. No results are announced until all polling stations are closed.

Electoral systems used in European elections (1994)

Proportional representation, national lists
with preferential voting:
- Denmark
- Luxembourg
- Netherlands

strict party list:
- France
- Germany★
- Greece
- Portugal
- Spain

Proportional representation, regional lists
with preferential voting:
- Belgium (4 regions)
- Italy (5 regions)

Multi-member constituencies, single transferable vote
- Ireland (4 constituencies)
- Northern Ireland (1 constituency)

Plurality ('first past the post') in single-member constituencies
- Great Britain (84 constituencies)

★Parties may choose to present lists on a national or a *Länder* basis, but there is only one national constituency.

Figure 1 shows the results of the four European elections held to date, in terms of the relative strengths of the **political groups** in the European Parliament, together with the overall turnout. More detailed country-by-country results may be found in a number of sources, of which perhaps the most accessible are the successive editions of *The Times Guide to the European Parliament*. The 1979–89 results of national and European elections may also be found in an appendix to Urwin and Paterson, *Politics in Western Europe Today*.

Table 1 shows the results of the June 1994 European elections by country and political group affiliation. Table 2 shows the United Kingdom results for each of the four European elections by seats won and percentage share of the vote. Newly acceding states are not required to hold European elections immediately, but only within a reasonable period of time.

From these tables, it may be seen that overall turnout is slowly declining, although it compares favourably with, for example, turnout in US elections

Figure 1   Percentage of seats held by main political groups, 1979–94

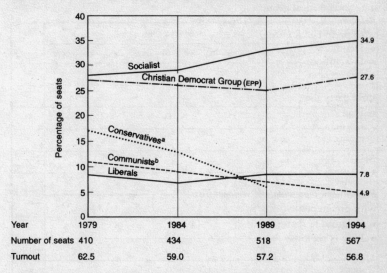

Year	1979	1984	1989	1994
Number of seats	410	434	518	567
Turnout	62.5	59.0	57.2	56.8

ª In May 1992 the British and Danish Conservatives joined the EPP as allied members.
ᵇ After the 1989 European elections, the Communists formed two separate groups, one pro-Europe (28 MEPS) and one anti (14 MEPS). Most of the pro-Europeans joined the Socialist Group in January 1993.

(55 per cent for the Presidential elections of November 1992, 38.7 per cent for the mid-term Congressional and Senate elections of November 1994). The United Kingdom turnout has been consistently well below the average, although it should be noted that voting is notionally compulsory in Belgium, Greece and Luxembourg, and is regarded as a 'civic duty' in Italy. The turnout figures are also affected by the fact that national or local elections are sometimes held at the same time as European elections, making overall comparisons more difficult.

European elections are often described as 'second order' elections, in the sense that voter interest and voter behaviour are closer to those observed in local elections and by-elections than in general elections. Broadly speaking, parties that do well in a national contest may expect to do well in European elections held either at the same time or a few months afterwards. This phenomenon helped the British Conservatives in 1979 and the Forza Italia party in 1994. Governing parties may expect to do badly if European elections fall within the period of mid-term unpopularity. The swings that result from this are particularly marked in Great Britain because of the simple majority voting system in single-member constituencies.

Table 1   Composition of the European Parliament in July 1994 by member state and political group

Member state	Political group										Total
	PES	EPP	ELDR	UEL	FE	EDA	GREEN	ERA	EN	Indeps	
Belgium	6	7	6				2	1		3	25
Denmark	3	3	5			1			4		16
France	15	13	1	7		14		13	13	11	87
Germany	40	47					12				99
Greece	10	9		4			2				25
Ireland	1	4	1			7	2				15
Italy	18	12	7	5	27		4	2		12	87
Luxembourg	2	2	1			1					6
Netherlands	8	10	10				1		2		31
Portugal	10	1	8	3		3					25
Spain	22	30	2	9				1			64
United Kingdom	63	19	2					2		1	87
Total	198	157	43	28	27	26	23	19	19	27	567

Key   PES = Socialists; EPP = European People's Party (Christian Democrats, Conservatives); ELDR = Liberals; UEL = United European Left; FE = Forza Europa; EDA = European Democratic Alliance; ERA = European Radical Alliance; EN = Europe of the Nations (anti-Maastricht).

It cannot be said that European elections are decided on European issues. Most parties make only half-hearted attempts to focus the electorate's attention on such issues, and then (unsurprisingly) only if the polls indicate that this might be advantageous to them. Nor do they get much help from the media, most of which prefer the much more familiar parameters of domestic political debate, such as party splits, clashes of personality and governmental discomfiture. Still less do the campaigns focus upon the European Parliament itself. The hard fact remains that many of the issues in which the average elector is interested – for example, housing, local transport, education, law and order – are never or only very indirectly dealt with in the Parliament, the agenda of which broadly reflects the way in which the Treaties are framed. Summaries of the campaigns may be found in the *Times Guides* (see

Table 2   Results of the European elections in the United Kingdom[a] by seats held and percentage of vote[b]

Party	Seats/% of vote			
	1979	1984	1989	1994
Conservatives	60[c]/50.6	45/40.8	32/34.7	18/27.6
Labour	17/33	32/36.5	45/40.1	62/44
Liberal Democrats/Alliance	–/13.1	–/19.5[d]	–/6.7[e]	2/16.6
Scottish Nationalist Party	1/1.9	1/1.7	1/2.7	2/3.2
Plaid Cymru	–/0.6	–/0.8	–/0.8	–/1
Other	–/0.8	–/0.7	–/15.2[f]	–/7.6[g]
Total number of seats	78	78	78	84

[a] In the three-seat multi-member constituency of Northern Ireland each of the three main parties (Democratic Unionist Party, Ulster Unionist Party, Social Democratic and Labour Party) secured one seat in each of the four elections.

[b] Turnout (UK) was 32.3% in 1979, rose very slightly to 32.6% in 1984, to 36.3% in 1989 and to 36.4% in 1994.

[c] Including 1 in a September 1979 by-election.

[d] Alliance composed of Liberal Democrats and SDP.

[e] 6.2% for Liberal Democrats (SLD), 0.5% for SDP.

[f] Of which 14.9% for the Greens.

[g] Of which 3.2% for the Greens.

above) and in Martin Westlake, *A Modern Guide to the European Parliament* (1994).

The European elections are the world's first and only international elections. In 1994 they involved an electorate of about 265 million people (of whom about 145 million voted), an electorate larger than any except that of India. However, as the results indicate, the campaign was, as before, made up largely of 12 national campaigns with local variants in particular regions. Nor do the results provide much hard evidence of Europe-wide political trends, since losses for one party in one country are often compensated for by gains for a related party in another. The role of **transnational political parties** remains extremely limited and the level of media interest low. In spite of determined efforts in some member states, the number of voters who chose to use their new right to vote in their country of residence within the Union rather than their country of origin (see **citizenship**) was very small. The 1994 European elections were a disappointment to those who believed that the new powers granted to the Parliament in the **Maastricht Treaty** – such as the decisive say in the appointment of the **Commission** – would raise the level of voter interest and mark a stage in the development of transnational democracy (see Brigitte Boyce, 'The June 1994 European elections and the politics of the European Parliament', *Political Affairs*, Vol. 48, no. 1, January 1995).

European Energy Charter

Proposed by Dutch Prime Minister Ruud Lubbers in 1990, the European Energy Charter was agreed in principle by 48 signatory states in December 1991 at a conference in The Hague. The Charter is intended to open up cross-frontier competition in the energy market, particularly between eastern and western Europe, by the creation of a legal framework and guidelines for market access. Such competition will help to stimulate economic recovery in the countries once part of the Soviet bloc. The Charter was followed by a binding European Energy Charter Treaty, signed in December 1994 by all European countries, including the republics of the former Soviet Union. The Treaty recognizes the rights of signatory states over their energy resources.

European Environment Agency

Established on the basis of a Decision (see **Community law**, **legal instruments**) of the **Council of Ministers** on 7 May 1990, the European Environment Agency has as its main task the collection and dissemination of data on the state of the environment. Such data, gathered by means of a 'European environment information and observation network', is an essential adjunct to the Union's **environment policy**, not least in respect of the fair and equal Union-wide enforcement of environmental legislation. The Agency did not come into operation for several years, because agreement could not be reached on where it should be located. By a **European Council** Decision of 29 October 1993 the Agency is sited in Copenhagen (see **seat of the institutions**).

European flag

The European flag – a circle of 12 five-pointed gold stars on a dark blue background – was devised originally by the **Council of Europe** for its own use. Adopted by the Parliamentary Assembly in October 1955 and by the Committee of Ministers two months later, the flag was adopted by the **European Commission** in 1985 for general use by the Community institutions.

Correctly described in heraldic terminology as 'on a field azure, a circle of twelve mullets or, their points not touching', the European flag triumphed over two alternative designs. The first was the very colourful flag of Count Richard Coudenhove-Kalergi's **Pan-Europa**, a golden disc representing the sun on a blue background with a red cross superimposed. The second was the flag of the **European Movement**, a large green E on a white background. A variant of this flag was used by the European Commission until 1985.

The present design was largely the work of Paul Levy, the Council of Europe's Director of Information in the early 1950s. The Turks, then as now members of the Council of Europe, objected on principle to any design incorporating a cross, but did not realize that a circle of 12 gold stars is also a Christian symbol: the Virgin Mary's halo (Revelation 12:1). The fact of there being 12 stars and 12 member states of the European Community in 1985 (accession treaties having been concluded with Spain and Portugal) is coincidental; it is not proposed to follow the example of the Stars and Stripes in the United States and add a star for each new accession.

In line with the recommendations of the Adonnino Committee on a **People's Europe** the European flag is now very widely used. It may be seen on car numberplates, umbrellas and the vehicles of European Union observers and aid workers, as well as on Commission publications. Fliers of the flag and users of the symbol should note that the gold stars must have their single points uppermost.

European Foundation for the Improvement of Living and Working Conditions

The Foundation, a Union body, was set up in 1975 and located in Dublin. Its task is to gather and disseminate information on living and working conditions, promote and coordinate research, and to furnish technical support to the **Commission** in these areas.

European Free Trade Association (EFTA)

EFTA was established by the Stockholm Convention of 1960 in order, in the words of Article 2, 'to promote . . . a sustained expansion of economic activity, full employment, increased productivity and the rational use of resources, financial stability and continuous improvement of living standards' underpinned by 'fair competition' and with a view to contributing to 'the harmonious development and expansion of world trade' (the phrase used in the **General Agreement on Tariffs and Trade** (GATT)). The original signatory states were Austria, Denmark, Norway, Portugal, Sweden, Switzerland and the United Kingdom (known as the Seven, to distinguish them from **the Six**: see below). Iceland acceded to the Convention in March 1970 and Finland in January 1986, having been an Associate member since 1961. Denmark and the United Kingdom withdrew from the Convention on joining the **European Economic Community** in January 1973, as did Portugal in January 1986. A special **protocol** extends the Convention to Liechtenstein, which forms a **customs union** with Switzerland; however, Liechtenstein is not independently represented in EFTA bodies. Of its six remaining members, three – Austria, Finland and Sweden – joined the European Union in January 1995, leaving only Iceland, Norway and Switzerland (plus Liechtenstein) as EFTA states.

EFTA was initiated as a reaction to the setting up of the European Economic Community under the **Treaty of Rome** amongst the Six in 1957 (see **Maudling Committee**). It had not proved possible to establish a **free trade area** amongst all members of the Organization for European Economic Cooperation (see **Organization for Economic Cooperation and Development**) to which both the Six and the Seven belonged, mainly because the Six were anxious to move towards a more ambitious form of association with political goals and supranational institutions. The Six were intent in the first instance upon forming a customs union, and, fearing that this would restrict access to the markets of these countries, the Seven decided to set up a looser free trade area (for industrial products only) of an essentially intergovernmental character (see **intergovernmentalism**). Relations between EFTA and the European Community are described under **European Economic Area**.

The Stockholm Convention formally established only one institution, the EFTA Council. The Council is composed of one representative of each member state and meets twice a month at official level and twice a year at ministerial level. Decisions, each member state having one vote, are normally reached by consensus, but limited scope exists for majority voting too. This structure is reflected in the specialist Standing Committees composed of officials, which advise the Council. Since 1977 there has been a Committee of Parliamentarians from EFTA states (replacing an earlier, less formal pattern of contacts), which discusses matters of common interest to EFTA members and which may be consulted by the EFTA Council. Since 1980 the Committee has had regular contact with the **European Parliament**. The very small EFTA Secretariat in Geneva, headed by a secretary-general, services these bodies, all of which use English as the working language.

European identity

In December 1973 at the Copenhagen **summit** the member states of the European Community adopted a **'Declaration** on the European identity'. The Declaration was in three sections: the first dealt with 'the unity of the nine Member States of the Community' and concluded with the reaffirmation of their intention to transform 'the whole complex of their relations into a **European Union** before the end of the present decade'. This section reviewed progress by the Nine (see **the Six**) towards the establishment of a common market, common institutions and **European Political Cooperation** (then in its infancy), all founded upon 'the cherished values of their legal, political and moral order . . . [and] the rich variety of their national cultures'. The Nine emphasized that 'the construction of a united Europe . . . is open to other European nations who share the same ideals and objectives'. The second section dealt with 'the European identity in relation to the world'. It set out basic guidelines for 'a common policy in relation to third countries', and in its review of the Community's external relations emphasized that 'European unification is not directed against anyone, nor is it inspired by a desire for power'. The very brief concluding section underlined 'the dynamic nature of the construction of a United Europe' and reiterated the commitment to European union.

Coming so soon after the first **enlargement** the Community (which had caused Denmark and the United Kingdom to leave the **European Free Trade Association** (EFTA) and Norway to hold a referendum, which rejected Community membership), the Declaration was an important affirmation of the Community's internal solidarity and openness to the outside world. Both in language and in content it foreshadowed some of the themes and policies that were to preoccupy the Community throughout the 1970s and 1980s, such as 'speaking with one voice' in foreign affairs, development policy and detente. However, subsequent events showed the timetable for European union to be over-optimistic and confidence in the Nine's solidarity exaggerated: within a year of the Declaration the Community's coherence had been seriously damaged by the oil crisis and the British demand for a **renegotiation**.

European Institute of Public Administration

Based in Maastricht in the Netherlands, the Institute was founded in 1981 as a study centre for lawyers, academics and administrators concerned with European integration, especially those aspects with a direct bearing on the quality of management in the public service. The working languages are English and French. Representatives of the governments of the member states of the Union and of the **Commission** make up the Board of Governors, but the Institute is not a Union body (see also **College of Europe**, **European University Institute**).

European Investment Bank (EIB)

Set up under Articles 129–130 of the **Treaty of Rome** (now Articles 198d–e EEC), the EIB has as its main role the financing of capital investment in the member states and in certain non-member countries, especially those in central and eastern Europe, the Mediterranean and developing countries associated with the Union under the **Lomé Convention**. EIB lending outside the Union was 9.6 per cent of total lending in 1993. The Treaty requires the EIB to operate on a non-profit-making basis and 'to contribute . . . to the balanced and steady development of the common market in the interest of the Community'. The EIB's capital is subscribed by member states, and the ministers of finance act as its Board of Governors. The headquarters of the EIB are in Luxembourg. Its management structure is set out in a statute annexed as a **protocol** to the Treaty of Rome.

Working in collaboration with the **structural funds**, the EIB offers loans at rates of interest that reflect market rates to public authorities or private enterprises. The sectors in which the EIB is active are transport, telecommunications, the environment, energy, industry, agriculture and services, with particular emphasis on cross-frontier projects. Loans do not normally exceed 50 per cent of total investment costs, except for projects covered by the **Edinburgh Growth Initiative**. The EIB has its own project appraisal staff. The EIB's lending is now almost 20 billion ECUs (about £16 billion) a year. Further details may be found in the EIB's annual report (see also **New Community Instrument**).

European Investment Fund (EIF)

The **European Council** meeting in Edinburgh in December 1992 agreed on the establishment of an EIF, involving both the **European Investment Bank** (EIB) and privately owned banks in investments in **trans-European networks** and in the encouragement of small and medium-sized enterprises (SMEs). The EIF was set up under Article 30 of the EIB's statute in March 1994: more than 50 banks in the then 12 member states agreed to become founder members of the EIF.

European League for Economic Cooperation

Founded in March 1947 as the *Ligue Indépendante de Coopération Européenne*, the League adopted its present name a year later. In the words of one authority, it was set up as 'an élite group, more particularly of acknowledged economic experts . . . to prepare the way for economic cooperation by international committee work' (Lipgens, *A History of European Integration*, Vol. 1, 1982). Many of its most prominent members had been members of governments-in-exile in London during the Second World War. The League was organized on a national basis, with sections in the United Kingdom, France, Belgium and Luxembourg. Throughout its history the League – which still exists – has laid emphasis on voluntary cooperation as a means to integration, and has thus set itself apart from the common institutions that underpin the European Union.

European Medicines Evaluation Agency

Operational from 1995, the Agency offers a centralized Union-wide registration procedure for new medicinal products, for both human and veterinary use. The Agency also coordinates the work of analogous national agencies, which will continue to certify, on the basis of mutual recognition, products not intended for circulation throughout all member states. To this end the Agency, which is based in London, operates a network linking the 3,000 national officials and experts in the field. Financed from the **Budget** and from fees paid by the pharmaceutical industry, the Agency will, it is hoped, allow registration procedures to be speeded up and minimize duplication of effort amongst national agencies.

European Monetary Cooperation Fund (EMCF)

The EMCF was set up in 1973 as part of the Community's first attempt to achieve **Economic and Monetary Union** (EMU; see **Werner Report**). By the mid-1970s it was clear that the attempt had failed, and the EMCF had fallen into disuse. However, it was revived when the ECU was introduced in 1979 as part of the **European Monetary System** (EMS). Participating member states agreed to deposit 20 per cent of their gold and dollar reserves with the EMCF, which issued ECUs in exchange. Interventions by central banks on the exchange markets as part of the **Exchange-Rate Mechanism** (ERM) were regulated by the EMCF, which was also able to offer short-term credits to help member states' balance of payments. At the beginning of stage 2 of EMU on 1 January 1994 the EMCF was wound up and its functions taken over by the **European Monetary Institute** (EMI).

European Monetary Institute (EMI)

Under Article 109f of the **Treaty of Rome**, as amended by the **Maastricht Treaty**, the EMI was set up at the beginning of stage 2 of **Economic and Monetary Union** (EMU) on 1 January 1994. The EMI is the precursor of the **European Central Bank** (ECB), the central institutional feature of stage 3. Both the EMI and the ECB have their headquarters in Frankfurt. The President is Alexandre Lamfalussy, formerly of the **Bank for International Settlements**. He heads a governing Council, made up of the governors of national central banks.

The EMI's role (Article 109f.2 EEC) is to strengthen both cooperation between central banks and the coordination of the monetary policies of member states, to 'monitor the functioning of the **European Monetary System**' (EMS), take over the tasks of the **European Monetary Cooperation Fund**, and to 'facilitate the use of the ECU and oversee its development'. In addition, the EMI has a general responsibility to make preparations for stage 3 of EMU. The EMI, acting by a two-thirds majority of its Council, is empowered to draw up **Opinions** or Recommendations 'on the overall orientation of monetary policy and exchange-rate policy' and on 'policies which might affect the internal or external monetary situation', in particular the functioning of the EMS. It may also make Recommendations to member states 'concerning the conduct of their monetary policy'. It has a general right of consultation with respect to legislation in its areas of competence. The statute of the EMI is annexed as a **protocol** to the Treaty of Rome.

European Monetary System (EMS)

The EMS, which came into operation in March 1979, was intended to create 'a zone of monetary stability in Europe' and to strengthen cooperation between member states with respect to monetary policy. Its central features are the **European Currency Unit** (ECU) and the **Exchange-Rate Mechanism** (ERM).

The EMS was launched by **Roy Jenkins** in his first year (1977) as President of the **Commission**, after the failure of the first attempt to achieve **Economic and Monetary Union** (EMU; see **Werner Report**). With strong support from Chancellor Helmut Schmidt and President **Valéry Giscard d'Estaing**, the EMS was established in a **Resolution** adopted by the **European Council** in Brussels in December 1978. Described as 'a fundamental component of a more comprehensive strategy aimed at lasting growth with stability, a progressive return to full employment, the harmonization of living standards and the lessening of regional disparities', the EMS was accompanied by measures to help the economic development of less prosperous member states, including a new subsidized loan facility from the **European Investment Bank** (EIB; see also **New Community Instrument**). Technical and administrative improvements to the EMS were made by the **Ecofin Council** in 1987 (the 'Basle–Nyborg Agreements').

Although all member states participate in the EMS, they are not thereby required to join the ERM. The pound sterling did not join the ERM until October 1990 and left in September 1992. The Greek drachma has never been part of the ERM. Membership of the EMS entails being part of the 'basket' of currencies that determines the value of the ECU and depositing 20 per cent of gold and dollar reserves with the European Monetary Institute (EMI).

The EMS has never explicitly and formally been described as a step towards EMU but as a system with merits of its own. However, if EMU is attained in accordance with the current plan, there is little doubt that it will have been built to a substantial extent on the experience gained from the EMS.

European Monitoring Centre for Drugs and Drug Addiction (EMCDDA)

A Union body based in Lisbon, the EMCDDA became operational in 1994. Its main task is to supply member states and European institutions with objective and comparable information on drugs and drug addiction throughout Europe as part of a network covering national drug information centres, specialized agencies and international bodies.

European Movement

Founded in 1948, the European Movement, with national organizations in 18 countries, is the principal all-party pressure-group on behalf of European integration. It brought together a very large number of postwar groups in Western Europe active in the European cause. Its first presidents-of-honour were the French Socialist leader Léon Blum, **Winston Churchill**, **Alcide de Gasperi** and **Paul-Henri Spaak**. The most notable event in the Movement's history was the **Congress of Europe** held in The Hague in 1948. The Movement played an influential part in the establishment of the **Council of Europe**, the **College of Europe**, the **European Cultural Centre**, and in early attempts to design a **European flag**. In some countries the national branch of the European Movement is subsidized from public funds. Its President is **Valéry Giscard d'Estaing**.

European Organization for the Development and Construction of Space Vehicle Launching

See **European Space Agency**.

European Organization for Nuclear Research (CERN)

Normally known by its French acronym, CERN (*Centre Européen pour la Recherche Nucléaire*) dates from a July 1953 convention drawn up under the auspices of the United Nations and is not formally associated with the European Union. CERN has 18 member countries and is a focus for research into peaceful uses of nuclear energy and nuclear physics. Based in Geneva, it has experimental facilities that are amongst the most advanced in the world. CERN is supported financially by direct contributions from participating states. In *The New Europeans* (1968) Anthony Sampson recalls asking a scientist at CERN how many people in Europe really understood the research being carried out there. The answer was 'about 12'; it is doubtful if the situation is very different today.

European Parliament

The European Parliament is composed of 626 Members (MEPs) elected in Union-wide **European elections** held every five years. It has its official 'seat' in Strasbourg (see **seat of the institutions**), but its committees meet in Brussels and its secretariat is divided between Brussels and Luxembourg. Now possessing legislative, supervisory and budgetary powers, the Parliament had only modest beginnings as the Common Assembly of the **European Coal and Steel Community** (ECSC) in 1952.

History, composition and procedure

One of the four main institutions of the European Union, the European Parliament is primarily responsible for exercising democratic scrutiny and control over the Union's decision-making process.

Article 7 of the 1951 Treaty of Paris establishing the **European Coal and Steel Community** (ECSC) made provision for four institutions: a High Authority (later the **European Commission**), a Special **Council of Ministers**, a **Court of Justice** and a Common Assembly. The Assembly, described in more detail in Articles 20–25 of the Treaty, was to 'consist of representatives of the peoples of the States brought together in the Community' and to exercise 'supervisory' powers. Its 78 MEPs were to be nominated by the **national parliaments** of **the Six** from amongst their own members in accordance with procedures laid down by each member state. The seats were allocated as follows:

Belgium	10
France	18
Italy	18
Luxembourg	4
The Netherlands	10
West Germany	18

However, even at this early date it was foreseen that the MEPs would one day be directly elected rather than nominated, and under Article 21.3 of the Treaty the Assembly was empowered to draw up 'proposals for elections by direct universal suffrage in accordance with a uniform procedure in all Member States' (see **uniform electoral procedure**).

In common with the other institutions of the ECSC the Assembly's headquarters and its secretariat (originally 37 people) were established in Luxembourg. Luxembourg could not, however, offer the necessary facilities for plenary sessions of the Assembly, which was required to work in the four official languages used amongst **the Six**: French, German, Italian and Dutch. In July 1952 the ECSC foreign ministers decided that plenary sessions of the Assembly should be held in Strasbourg. **Jean Monnet** relates in his *Memoirs* how the Secretary-General of the **Council of Europe** offered to organize the first session of the Assembly, as part of an attempt, Monnet suspected, to 'take over our parliamentary and ministerial institutions'. In the event, the session was organized by the secretaries-general of the six national parliaments, and opened on 5 September 1952. To underline its separate identity, the Assembly met not on the premises of the Council of Europe but in the Strasbourg Chamber of Commerce. **Paul-Henri Spaak** was elected president by 38 votes to 30, the MEPs voting on party lines although **political groups** had not yet been formed.

The first important change in the status and composition of the Assembly was brought about by the entry into force on 1 January 1958 of the **Treaties** establishing the **European Economic Community** (EEC) and the **European Atomic Energy Community** (Euratom). These two Treaties also provided for each Community to have an Assembly, and – as was done with the Court of Justice and the **Economic and Social Committee** – the remit of the already existing ECSC Assembly was expanded to cover all three Communities under the 'Convention on certain institutions common to the European Communities' signed in Rome at the same time as the EEC and Euratom Treaties. The number of MEPs was almost doubled, to 142, but since no progress had been made with direct elections they were still nominated by their national parliaments:

Belgium	14
France	36
Italy	36
Luxembourg	6
The Netherlands	14
West Germany	36

The first plenary session of the enlarged Common Assembly was held in March 1958. **Robert Schuman** was elected its first president. The powers of the Assembly as set out in the EEC and Euratom Treaties were broadly similar to those laid down in the ECSC Treaty, except that they were now described as 'advisory' as well as 'supervisory' (Article 137 EEC, since revised).

At the first session the new Assembly adopted the name 'European Parliamentary Assembly' in place of the old 'Common Assembly'. Four years later, in March 1962, it changed its name in French and Italian to 'European Parliament' ('Parliament' was already used in the Dutch and German versions of the Treaties). 'Assembly' continued to be used in English for official purposes (often with dismissive intent) until the change to 'Parliament' was formalized in Article 3 of the **Single European Act** (SEA) of 1986.

With the **accession** of Denmark, Ireland and the United Kingdom in 1973, the number of MEPs was further increased from 142 to 198 (Denmark 10, Ireland 10, the United Kingdom 36) and Danish and English were added as official languages. The British and Danish Conservative MEPs formed a new political group, bringing the total to six. In line with the practice followed in other member states, British MEPs were appointed to reflect the strength of the political parties in the lower House, although the MEPs could be drawn from either House of Parliament. This gave the Conservatives 18 of the United Kingdom's entitlement of 36 seats, the Liberals 1 and the Labour Party 17. However, the Labour Party's official policy was in favour of renegotiating the terms of British entry into the Community and, pending the results of such a **renegotiation**, against participating in the Community institutions. Accordingly, the Party did not take up the seats allocated to it. This allowed the Liberals to take an extra seat, and an independent peer took another. The original British delegation to the European Parliament was of 21 rather than 36 MEPs; not until after the **referendum of June 1975** did the Labour Party take up the 18 seats to which they were by then entitled, having secured a 42-seat majority over the Conservatives in the October 1974 General Election. The Scottish Nationalists also won a seat. The Conservatives were reduced to 16 seats, and both the independent and the extra Liberal were squeezed out. However, by convention between the two major parties and to make the whips' calculations easier, the number of MEPs drawn from the House of Commons was kept equal at 12 Conservative, 12 Labour. The balance of MEPs were drawn from the House of Lords.

The shifts within the British delegation served to emphasize the extent to which the European Parliament at this stage in its development was merely an outgrowth of national politics in the member states. The practice of nominating MEPs from national parliaments meant that the composition of all delegations was constantly changing to take account of national election results. During the period of the 'nominated' European Parliament, 1952–79, about 750 MEPs served in the Parliament, some for a few months, others for many years. All were required, by treaty, to exercise a **'dual mandate'**: to be members both of their national parliaments and of the European Parliament. Meanwhile, the powers and responsibilities of the latter were steadily increasing, and it was becoming more and more evident that substance would soon have to be given to the Treaty commitment on direct elections.

In December 1974 the **European Council**, meeting in Paris, decided that direct elections to the European Parliament should be held 'as soon as possible'. The European Council called upon the Council of Ministers to take a decision on the matter in 1976, with a view to direct elections being held 'at any time in or after 1978'. The Paris communiqué added 'the competence of the European Assembly will be extended, in particular by granting it certain powers in the Communities' legislative process'. Both the British and the Danish governments declined to commit themselves on the introduction of direct elections.

In January 1975, after two years of discussions, the European Parliament adopted the Patijn Report on direct elections, the one subject in relation to which the Parliament, rather than the Commission, enjoys a **right of initiative** (Article 138 EEC). The Report proposed that the number of MEPs be increased to 355, that each member state's allocation of seats be strictly related to its population (although Luxembourg, as a special case, was left with the 6 seats it had had ever since 1958) and that the elections should be held on the same day throughout the Community. In the European Elections Act, adopted by the Council of Ministers in September 1976, the Parliament's recommendations on these points were largely ignored: the total number of MEPs was fixed at 410; the four large member states (France, Italy, the United Kingdom and West Germany) would – in spite of population variations amounting to several million people – each have the same number of MEPs (81); and because of different national traditions with regard to the day of the week upon which voting normally takes place, member states were left free to choose any date within a four-day period. The Act laid down the allocation of seats as follows (Article 2):

Belgium	24
Denmark	16
France	81
Ireland	15
Italy	81
Luxembourg	6
The Netherlands	25
United Kingdom	81
West Germany	81
Total	410

Both the total number of seats and the allocation of seats to member states had already been fixed at the Luxembourg meeting of the European Council in July 1976.

The parliamentary term was fixed at five years (Article 3). MEPs could be members of their national parliaments, but could not be government ministers, Commissioners, European civil servants, judges in the Court of Justice, or members of the **Court of Auditors**, of the Economic and Social Committee or of the Board of Directors of the **European Investment Bank** (EIB; Article 6). The right of the Parliament to draw up proposals for a uniform electoral procedure was reiterated (Article 7), but, as in the Patijn Report, the choice of electoral system and the arrangements for by-elections were left to the discretion of individual member states, pending the introduction of a uniform electoral procedure (for which neither the Patijn Report nor the Act set a deadline).

At the Rome meeting of the European Council in December 1975 the date for direct elections was fixed as May or June 1978. However, difficulties with the enabling legislation in the House of Commons (the terms of the Lib-Lab pact required the Labour Government to attempt to introduce a regional list system, which was rejected by the House) meant that the Copenhagen meeting of the European Council in April 1978 decided to postpone the elections for one year until 7–10 June 1979.

The 1979 direct elections, the first international elections in history and involving an electorate of more than 190 million people (exceeded only by that of India), attracted a Community-wide turnout of 62.5 per cent. This overall figure concealed substantial differences: turnout ranged from 91.4 per cent in Belgium, where voting is notionally compulsory, to 32.3 per cent in the United Kingdom. (For detailed results of the 1979, 1984, 1989 and 1994 elections, see **European elections**.) At its first session in July 1979 the European Parliament elected the French Liberal Simone Veil as its President. Five months later, for the first time in its history, the Parliament used its power under Article 203 EEC to reject the Community **Budget** for the following year.

The first directly elected Parliament, 1979 to 1984, set the pattern for subsequent Parliaments in several ways. It showed a real determination not only to use its powers to the full and to increase them wherever possible but also radically to reform the Community's whole institutional structure. This resulted in the Parliament's **Draft Treaty establishing the European Union** (DTEU; the Spinelli Treaty) of February 1984 and a host of resolutions on institutional questions. It sought, with only very partial success, to resolve the practical difficulties arising out of having three places of work, and decided in July 1981 no longer to hold plenary sessions in Luxembourg. Its growing importance internationally was marked by the address given to the Parliament by President Anwar Sadat of Egypt in February 1981, the first of many such addresses by heads of state. It resolved in September 1982 to bring an action in the Court of Justice under Article 175 EEC against the Council of Ministers for the Council's '**failure to act**' in the matter of a **common transport policy**. For the first time, a report at the end of a presidency was given to the Parliament by the president-in-office of the European Council (**Margaret Thatcher** in December 1981). In April 1982 the Parliament tightened its control over Community spending by deferring its grant of **discharge** to the Commission for 1980. The interest and excitement of the directly elected Parliament's first term were not matched in subsequent years.

The accession of Greece in 1981 and of Portugal and Spain in 1986 brought the total number of MEPs to 518. In July 1990 it was decided to admit 18 'observers' from the former East Germany, initially to be appointed by the East German Volkskammer and later by the Bundestag. These observers had speaking rights in committees and political groups but not in plenary sessions, and could neither vote nor hold office. This was obviously only a temporary solution. **German reunification** meant that Germany had a population some 20 million people greater than that of the next largest member state, and clearly this had to be reflected in the number of German MEPs in the Parliament. The suggestion that they be increased by 18 aroused strong opposition from the French, and the matter was not resolved until the Edinburgh meeting of the European Council in December 1992. At the same time, the opportunity was taken to adjust the overall allocation of seats, with effect from the June 1994 European elections. Since the accession of Austria, Finland and Sweden in January 1995 the situation is as follows (pre-1994 numbers in brackets):

Austria	21	
Belgium	25	(24)
Denmark	16	(16)
Finland	16	
France	87	(81)
Germany	99	(81)
Greece	25	(24)
Ireland	15	(15)
Italy	87	(81)
Luxembourg	6	(6)
Netherlands	31	(25)
Portugal	25	(24)
Spain	64	(60)
Sweden	22	
United Kingdom	87	(81)

The organizational structure of the Parliament is laid down in its Rules of Procedure, with respect to which the Parliament is sovereign under Article 142 EEC. A president is elected for two and a half years at the beginning and at the mid-point of every five-year term. Since July 1979 the presidents have been as follows:

1979–82	Simone Veil (France, Liberal)
1982–4	Pieter Dankert (Netherlands, Socialist)
1984–7	Pierre Pflimlin (France, Christian Democrat)
1987–9	Lord Plumb (United Kingdom, Conservative)
1989–92	Enrique Baron (Spain, Socialist)
1992–4	Egon Klepsch (Germany, Christian Democrat)
1994–	Klaus Hänsch (Germany, Socialist)

The president is required under Rule 19 to 'direct all the activities of

Parliament and of its bodies', as well as 'to open, suspend and close sittings
..., maintain order ..., [and] put matters to the vote'. The president
represents the Parliament 'in international relations, on ceremonial occasions and in administrative, legal or financial matters'. The president's
powers may be delegated, normally to one of the vice-presidents (see
below). The president may lead delegations from the Parliament taking
part in the **conciliation** procedure with the Council (Rule 75). It is the
president's responsibility formally to request **reconsultation** of the Parliament in the event of the Council or the Commission failing to abide by
the Parliament's **Opinion** (see below) on a legislative proposal or if the
'nature of the problem with which the proposal is concerned substantially
changes' (Rule 62). The president is also responsible (Annex IV, Rules 4–
5; Article 203.7 EEC) for declaring the Union's Budget adopted. Since June
1987 the president of the Parliament has been able to address meetings of
the European Council.

Vice-presidents of the Parliament are elected every two and a half years
at the same time as the president, but the political groups normally agree
upon the list of candidates. Together with the president and (in an
advisory capacity) the quaestors (see below), the vice-presidents make up
the Bureau of the Parliament. The principal task of the Bureau is to take
'financial, organizational and administrative decisions' (Rule 22). Vice-
presidents share with the president the task of presiding over plenary
sessions of the Parliament. The body known as the Conference of Presidents
(Rules 23–4) is composed of the president and the leaders of the political
groups. It is responsible for 'decisions on the organization of Parliament's
work and ... legislative planning', including the drawing up of the
Parliament's agenda. It is enjoined under the Rules to 'endeavour to reach
a consensus on matters referred to it', but, if necessary, it may take votes
with each leader's vote being weighted to reflect the size of his or her
political group.

The five quaestors are also elected by the Parliament every two and a
half years. Under Rule 25 their responsibility is for 'administrative and
financial matters directly concerning Members', such as allowances, pensions and office accommodation.

The Parliament has 20 standing committees. Each committee has
its own officers elected every two and a half years, but in practice the
candidates for these posts and the number of places in each committee
allocated to each of the political groups are decided by agreement amongst
the groups on the basis of the **d'Hondt system**. The Committees are as
follows:

1 Foreign Affairs and Security
  - subcommittee on security and disarmament
  - subcommittee on human rights
2 Agriculture and Rural Development
3 Budgets
4 Economic and Monetary Affairs and Industrial Policy
  - subcommittee on monetary affairs
5 Energy, Research and Technology
6 External Economic Relations
7 Legal Affairs and Citizens' Rights
8 Social Affairs, Employment and the Working Environment
9 Regional Policy, Regional Planning and Relations with Regional and Local Authorities
10 Transport and Tourism
11 Environment, Public Health and Consumer Protection
12 Culture, Youth, Education and the Media
13 Development and Cooperation
14 Civil Liberties
15 Budgetary Control
16 Institutional Affairs
17 Fisheries
18 Rules of Procedure, the Verification of Credentials and Immunities
19 Women's Rights
20 Petitions

Under Rule 136, the Parliament may also set up temporary *ad hoc* committees or Committees of Inquiry 'to investigate alleged contraventions of Community law or instances of maladministration in the implementation of Community law'. The right to set up such Committees of Inquiry is one of the powers granted to the Parliament in the **Maastricht Treaty** (Article 138c EEC).

The Parliament's standing committees meet at least once a month in Brussels for two days. As far as possible, committee meetings are not held at the same time as plenary sessions in Strasbourg. Once a year, each committee is allowed to hold a meeting elsewhere in the Union, but committees do not have their own budgets and any expenditure (such as that involved in the organization of 'hearings' with expert witnesses) must be approved by the Bureau. Most committee meetings are held in public, but committees are free to decide to hold them in private. Commission representatives attend and often take part in committee meetings, and at least once in each **presidency** the president of the relevant Council will attend a meeting of the appropriate parliamentary committee. Votes in committee are normally taken by a show of hands and only exceptionally by roll-call. Groups cannot, of course, exceed their quota of full members of the committee for voting. The quorum is one-quarter of the committee's members, or one-half of the members if so requested by one-sixth of the members before voting begins (Rule 150). At all meetings full interpretation is provided, documents are available in all official languages, and full minutes are kept. Contacts with other parliaments outside the Union are maintained through a system of delegations, each with its own officers. In the case of countries with which the Union has concluded **Association Agreements** or is negotiating treaties of **accession**, these delegations are known as joint parliamentary committees. Few of these delegations follow a regular pattern of meetings, but in most cases meetings are held alternately in the Union and in the country or countries concerned.

In addition to these delegations and joint parliamentary committees, there is the ACP-EU Joint Assembly, an organ of the **Lomé Convention**. Composed of a representative of each of the **ACP states** and an equal number of MEPs, the Joint Assembly has a general responsibility for overseeing the implementation of the Convention. It meets for a week-long session twice a year, once in the Union and once in one of the ACP states.

For most of the year the Parliament works in a monthly cycle: two weeks during which the Committee meetings take place, one week kept as far as possible free of committee meetings so that the political groups can meet; and a fourth week spent in Strasbourg. This cycle is suspended in August for the summer holiday and interrupted in autumn because there is usually a second part-session in October devoted to the Budget. Other meetings – of the Bureau, the Conference of Presidents, delegations, etc. – have to be fitted into this cycle, together with additional two-day plenary sessions held four or five times a year in Brussels. The need to secure premises and interpretation normally means that all meetings are fixed well in advance.

The Treaty of Rome (Article 139) requires the Parliament to hold an annual session, which begins on the second Tuesday in March. In a year in which European elections are held, the European Elections Act of 1976 (Article 10) specifies that the newly elected Parliament shall meet on the first Tuesday after one month has elapsed since the last day of polling (a Sunday). A Court of Justice ruling of 1964 established that the Parliament, whether or not it is actually sitting, is in continuous session: this ruling allows the regulation governing MEPs' immunities to apply throughout the year. Technically, therefore, the plenary sessions in Strasbourg and Brussels are part-sessions of an annual session, although they are normally referred to simply as plenary sessions.

The business of a plenary session consists for the most part of debates on reports adopted in committee and brought forward for adoption by the Parliament as a whole. The report is presented by the committee's **rapporteur**; the representatives of each of the political groups are given precedence in the debate that follows; the responsible Commissioner may intervene, especially if the Commission wants to comment on the proposals for amendment contained in the report; other MEPs may take part in the debate, within the limit of the speaking-time allocated to their political groups for the day; and once the debate is completed, the time at which the report is to be voted upon is announced from the chair. Provision exists for reports to be taken without debate. Other regular items on the plenary session agenda include question time to the Commission and the Council; statements by the Commission and/or the Council on major issues (sometimes followed by a debate); three hours set aside for debates on 'topical and urgent subjects of major importance' (up to a maximum of five), which enable the Parliament to discuss crises, disasters and infringements of human rights; a report by the Commission on action taken in response to the Parliament's **Opinions** and **Resolutions**; and at the beginning and end of every presidency, a report by the president-in-office of the Council or the European Council on the presidency's programme of work. Special events in the Parliament's annual calendar are the presentation by the president of the Commission of the Annual General Report; the presentation, also by the president, of the Commission's Annual Programme, to which is annexed an **annual legislative programme** agreed with the Conference of Presidents (see above); the adoption by the Parliament of the report on the Commission's farm price proposals; and the first and second readings of the Budget.

The Parliament's views on legislation are expressed in the form of reports embodying Opinions. Under Rule 44 these reports are composed of draft amendments (if any) to the proposal, a draft legislative resolution and an explanatory statement. A report may also contain Opinions drawn up by committees other than the one primarily responsible. Non-legislative reports contain only a draft resolution, an explanatory statement and the motion or motions to which the report refers. In neither case does the explanatory statement have any legal force. In line with Articles J7 and K6 of the Maastricht Treaty the Parliament may also address Recommendations to the Council on the **Common Foreign and Security Policy** (CFSP) and in the field of **Justice and Home Affairs** (JHA).

Voting in plenary sessions is normally by show of hands, but the numbers can be checked electronically by a system requiring MEPs to use voting cards. Exceptionally, and only by request, votes can be taken by electronic roll-call, and only in these cases will the record attached to the daily minutes show how individual MEPs voted. The quorum is a third of the Parliament's total membership, but votes are valid and voting may continue however few MEPs are present until the president, on request, formally establishes that the meeting is inquorate. A verbatim record (known as 'the Rainbow', from the variously coloured sheets upon which it was once typed) of speeches in the original language of delivery is published daily and in its final form translated into the official languages and annexed to the *Official Journal*.

Of all the institutions of the European Union, the Parliament is the one that has changed the most in point of its status, powers and composition. However, in respect of its internal organization, it has changed very little, except that the political groups now dominate the system even more than before. All major decisions are arrived at on the basis of deals between the leaders of the groups: for example, not since 1987 have the two largest groups, the Socialists and the European People's Party, contested the presidency. This is in contrast with the United States Congress, in which the committees play a much more influential role. The Parliament's efficiency is handicapped by not having a single place of work, but only a small minority of MEPs is seriously committed to resolving the problem.

The Parliament is very slowly securing more coverage (not all of it sympathetic) in the media. Again, some of the difficulties spring from not having a single place of work and from the fact that newspapers and broadcasting organizations find it troublesome and expensive to cover the proceedings of a Parliament that works in many languages, is seldom in one place for more than a few days, deals with some very abstruse subjects, has a power of final decision only in a few cases and is largely composed of people of whom the electorate has never heard. The Parliament does not make the job of the media any easier by voting at fixed times (sometimes the following day) to suit MEPs' convenience rather than at the end of each debate. This arrangement helps to address the problem of absenteeism, the subject of much media criticism of the Parliament. The Parliament is also widely criticized for voting itself substantial annual increases in its budget, which has grown from just over £300 million in 1990 to over £500 million in 1995 (these figures do not include MEPs' basic salaries, which are paid from national exchequers: see below).

The total membership of the Parliament is now 626 MEPs. If it is accepted that membership could never for practical reasons exceed 650–700, a European Union of 25 or more member states would entail a reduction in member states' current entitlement of MEPs. The larger states are already underrepresented by comparison with the smaller, even if Luxembourg, with six MEPs, is admitted to be a special case. Whatever solution is found, it is clear that a Parliament that is already administratively cumbersome cannot go on growing indefinitely.

Members

Although provision exists in Article 138.3 EEC for MEPs to be elected at some unspecified time in the future on the basis of a uniform electoral procedure, little progress has been made with this. At present, European elections are held on the basis of different national systems, all of them – with the exception of the single member, first-past-the-post system used in Great Britain – forms of proportional representation. The number of seats for each member state was laid down in the European Elections Act 1976, since modified by successive accession treaties, and by the decision taken by the European Council in December 1992. It can be altered only by unanimous agreement (see above).

The Act specifies that MEPs 'shall vote on an individual and personal basis. They shall not be bound by any instructions and shall not receive a binding mandate' (Article 4). Under the terms of an agreement reached between member states in 1978, MEPs' basic salaries are paid from national exchequers, and are subject to national tax at rates equivalent to those applied to national MPs. This means that there are wide discrepancies. However, there is a common system for expenses and allowances, which are paid from the European Parliament's budget and are calculated in ECUs. Within the Union MEPs are entitled to claim travel expenses for any official meeting calculated either from their home base or from another official meeting at a rate of about 57p per kilometre for the first 400 kilometres and about 29p per kilometre thereafter. Outside the Union, travel expenses are normally paid on a 'costs incurred' basis. For all official meetings within the Union MEPs are paid an attendance allowance, worth about £155 a day, as long as he or she has 'signed in' for the day in question. MEPs are also entitled to an office allowance, paid automatically, of about £2,131 a month, and a further £5,826 a month for the employment of staff, paid on the presentation of contracts of employment. MEPs can also claim travel costs, up to a maximum of about £2,340 a year, for attendance in an official capacity (i.e., on the basis of an official invitation) at meetings, conferences and so on anywhere in the world. MEPs have free office accommodation on the European Parliament's premises in Brussels and in the Palais de l'Europe in Strasbourg.

An MEP is normally a full member of one of the Parliament's 20 specialized committees and a substitute member of another. He or she may also be a full member of one of the Parliament's interparliamentary delegations. In an average month an MEP will spend three or four nights in Strasbourg at one of the Parliament's plenary sessions, and six or seven nights in Brussels at committee meetings, additional plenary sessions, delegation meetings, or meetings of his or her political group. MEPs who without good reason sign in for fewer than half the number of days set aside for plenary sessions in the year are liable to have their office allowances cut by half.

MEPs' immunities are set out in Articles 8–10 of the **protocol** on privileges and immunities of the European Communities annexed to the **Merger Treaty** of 1965. MEPs 'shall not be subject to any form of inquiry, detention or legal proceedings in respect of opinions expressed or votes cast by them in the performance of their duties' (Article 9). Within their own member states MEPs enjoy immunities from arrest and legal proceedings similar to those extended to national MPs; elsewhere in the Union, they enjoy 'immunity from any measure of detention and from legal proceedings' except when found *in flagrante delicto* (Article 10). Only the Parliament itself can waive the immunity of an MEP. This aspect of MEPs' lives was exhaustively studied in the report by the House of Lords Select Committee on the European Communities entitled *Privileges and Immunities of Members of the European Parliament* (1986).

MEPs are obliged to record their financial interests in a register kept for this purpose, and to declare such interests when taking part in a debate on a matter connected with them.

The European Parliament has an unusually high proportion of women MEPs (over a quarter of the total) compared with most national parliaments. The turnover of MEPs at European elections is also unusually high: of the 567 MEPs elected in 1994, less than half had sat in the previous parliament. However, there are substantial variations between national delegations, with the British delegation having the highest average length of service.

The background of MEPs also varies considerably from one country to another. About a quarter of MEPs have been members of their national parliaments, not including those currently exercising a dual mandate. The British are well below the average: not including the 3 MEPs from Northern Ireland, only 3 of the other 84 British MEPs have been MPs. Together with the Dutch and the Germans, the British are also well below average in terms of the number of MEPs who have held ministerial office in their home countries. A background in local or regional government is common amongst French, Italian and Spanish MEPs, less so amongst the British, the Danish and the Dutch. The list of well-known people who have been elected as MEPs since 1979 (including Willy Brandt, Jacques Chirac, Giulio Andreotti, Lord Plumb, Jacques Santer, Georges Marchais and Leo Tindemans) can be misleading. Many of them have simply headed their party lists for the elections and resigned from the Parliament at the earliest opportunity.

This cursory study of the background of MEPs (set out in much greater detail in Jacobs, Corbett and Shackleton, *The European Parliament*) illustrates the fact that in most countries there is a much less sharp distinction than there is in the United Kingdom between a national or local political career and a career in the European Parliament. The use of national or regional lists as the basis for European elections enables the transition from one sphere of political activity to another to be made much more easily. Although some British former MEPs have become MPs and gone on to be ministers, to date no British Commissioner has been an MEP: all have come from the House of Commons or, in one case, the House of Lords. The absence of a proper career structure in the European Parliament means that the more talented younger MEPs may become frustrated and take their abilities elsewhere.

Powers

The powers of the European Parliament fall under four main headings: powers relating to legislation, to the Budget, to the conclusion of international agreements, and general supervisory powers. The Parliament can scrutinize and amend all proposals for legislation under a variety of procedures (see below). It can, within a maximum rate of increase, make modifications to the proposals for expenditure in the Budget and, in certain circumstances, reject the Budget outright. The Parliament's assent must be obtained before agreements can be concluded with non-member countries or international organizations. The Parliament is consulted on appointments to the European Commission, which it can dismiss and whose activities are subject to the Parliament's overall supervision.

In the 44 years since it was founded (see above) the powers of the European Parliament have grown very substantially. The growth has occurred in four ways: as European integration has been extended into new areas (so-called 'horizontal' growth); as a result of formal agreements arrived at between the member states and normally embodied in treaty undertakings; on the basis of judgments of the Court of Justice (see **isoglucose case**); and in the form of **interinstitutional agreements**. Over this period the Parliament itself has consistently pressed for more powers, usually in the name of redressing the so-called **democratic deficit**, but to date there are no instances of the Parliament seizing power, as most national parliaments have done at some time in their history.

The basic outline of the Parliament's powers is discernible in the ECSC Treaty. The Common Assembly was entitled to discuss the annual report that the High Authority – the forerunner of the Commission – was required to lay before it by February at the latest of each year; by a two-thirds majority it could pass a motion of censure on the High Authority, thus forcing its members to resign 'as a body'; the High Authority was required to answer oral or written questions put to it by Members of the Assembly; and the Assembly was able to put forward proposals for amendments to the ECSC's budget. However, in spite of the 'supervisory' role that the Assembly was required by treaty to play, it was not the Assembly but the Consultative Committee attached to the High Authority – composed of between 30 and 51 people, involved in the coal and steel industries and appointed by the member states – which the High Authority was required to consult. Inevitably, the substance of the Assembly's work was technical rather than political (the only major exception being the Assembly's involvement in the debates on a **European Political Community** and a **European Defence Community** in the early 1950s).

With the establishment of the EEC and Euratom in 1958, the Assembly (known as the European Parliament from 1962) was given new powers. Its size was increased from 78 to 142 MEPs (see above). However, its role in legislation remained marginal: until the coming into force of the SEA in July 1987 the Parliament's powers were limited to the giving of Opinions and the submission of amendments on draft legislation, which the Council was obliged to refer to it. However, neither the Commission nor the Council was formally obliged to incorporate the Parliament's views and amendments in the legislation finally adopted. The Parliament's assent was required before the conclusion of new **Association Agreements** under Article 235 (now 238) EEC but, curiously, not for new Accession Treaties under Article 237 EEC (now Article O TEU).

As far as the Parliament's supervisory powers are concerned, the power to dismiss the Commission on the basis of a **motion of censure** carried by a two-thirds majority of votes cast representing more than half the total number of MEPs (Article 144 EEC; Rule 34 of the Parliament's Rules of Procedure) has never been used. It was attempted for the first time in June 1976, but the motion – tabled by Conservative MEPs on the Commission's chronic failure to deal with dairy surpluses – was overwhelmingly defeated. Since June 1976 motions of censure have been put to the vote on only four occasions.

There are several reasons why the Parliament has never used the most dramatic of its powers. In most areas the Parliament tends to regard the Commission as an ally, not an adversary, and there is little point in sacking Commissioners if the Parliament has no say (as was the case until recently) in who might replace them. Most Commissioners have sufficiently good party links to be able to appeal in the name of party loyalty to enough MEPs to make the two-thirds majority difficult to attain, and there are only very few issues for which enough cross-party support could be obtained to secure the majority necessary to pass a censure motion. The

Treaty requires a minimum of three days to elapse between the President's announcement of the receipt of a motion of censure and the vote, thus making it almost inevitable that a motion tabled during one part-session will not be voted on until the next, allowing ample time for MEPs to have second thoughts.

Under Article 175 EEC the Parliament is empowered, like other institutions of the Union and the governments of member states, to bring an action in the Court of Justice against the Commission or the Council for 'failure to act'. In September 1982 the Parliament decided to bring such an action for the first time against the Council, for the latter's persistent failure to adopt a **common transport policy** within the meaning of Article 74 EEC. Nearly three years later, after legal arguments on both the substance and admissibility of the Parliament's action, the Court delivered a judgment in the Parliament's favour (22 May 1985, Case 13/83).

As noted above, the ECSC Treaty (Article 23) required the High Authority to answer oral or written questions from Members of the Common Assembly. A similar provision was included with respect to the Commission in the EEC Treaty (Article 140), but it was not until 1973 that the Parliament made provision in its part-session agendas for a regular question time to the Commission. The Council, which is not under a similar Treaty obligation to answer MEPs' questions, agreed of its own volition in 1960 to reply to questions on matters that the Council had already considered, but again no regular question time was instituted until 1973. In 1975 it became possible to put questions to the foreign ministers meeting in **European Political Cooperation**. In 1983 the Council confirmed its willingness to answer written and oral questions in the **Stuttgart Declaration**.

No limit is placed upon the number of written questions that an MEP may ask (Rule 42). The questions are forwarded to the Commission or the Council through the president of the Parliament, and are supposed to be answered within six weeks and published in the *Official Journal*. 'Priority questions', limited to one per MEP per month, are defined as those requiring immediate answer but 'no detailed research'; for these the deadline is three weeks.

Oral questions for question time are limited to one per MEP to each of the institutions (Commission and Council; Rule 41). They are submitted through the President's office. Although guidelines annexed to the Rules of Procedure require questions and answers to be brief and question time to be briskly conducted, lacklustre chairing, long-winded participants and procedural disputes usually ensure that very few questions are fully dealt with. Question time, which since 1973 has been dominated by British MEPs, takes place late at night with barely a handful of MEPs present and neither press nor public. A representative of the presidency answers on behalf of the Council; members of the Commission are normally expected to answer questions in their own areas of responsibility, although technically answers are given on behalf of the Commission as a whole. A procedure was introduced in 1994 whereby questions can be put to the president of the Commission.

In addition to written questions and oral questions for question time, the Parliament may address to the Commission or the Council questions for oral answer in response to which a Resolution may be tabled and voted upon (Rule 40). Such questions may be tabled by a committee, a political group or a minimum of 23 MEPs. The decision whether or not to place such a question on the agenda rests with the Conference of Presidents (see above), which may decide to use a different procedure. This procedure allows the Parliament to explore issues in more depth than is possible in question time.

Although it was not recognized in the founding Treaties, every citizen of the Union has 'the right, individually or jointly with others, to address written requests or complaints (petitions) to the European Parliament' (Rule 156 of the Parliament's Rules of Procedure). This right, which dates from 1953, was given formal recognition in a 1989 Council–Commission–Parliament Joint Declaration and in the Maastricht Treaty (new Article 138d EEC). Since 1979 the number of petitions has risen from 57 to over 800, many of them mass petitions (of which one, on testing cosmetics on animals, was signed by more than 2.5 million people). Petitions have to relate to a matter in which there is some Union competence and are considered in the first instance by the Parliament's Petitions Committee. Once found admissible and duly considered, a petition may give rise to various forms of action: it may be referred to the appropriate parliamentary committee; it may be drawn to the attention of the Commission or the authorities in a member state; or the petitioner may draw upon the Parliament's support in resolving the problem at issue. The Petitions Committee submits an annual report to the Parliament.

Exceptionally, the Parliament may set up 'committees of inquiry to investigate alleged contraventions of Community law or instances of maladministration in the implementation of Community law' (Rule 136). Such committees may be composed of no more than 15 MEPs and must accomplish their work within nine months, reporting to the Parliament. Since 1979 subjects dealt with by committees of inquiry include: treatment and transport of toxic waste, the drugs problem, agricultural surpluses, and the rise of racism and fascism in Europe. The right to set up such committees was formally recognized in the Maastricht Treaty (new Article

138c EEC), with the proviso that matters which are *sub judice* cannot be investigated.

In the period leading up to the SEA (1987), the most significant increase in the Parliament's powers was in relation to the Budget. The switch from a system of contributions by member states to one that gave the Community its **own resources** under the Treaty of Luxembourg of 22 April 1970 was accompanied by measures to increase the Parliament's say in the allocation of expenditure (although not in revenue-raising). These measures were further strengthened in a second treaty signed in Brussels on 22 July 1975 (effective from 1 June 1977) based upon the proposals in the **Vedel Report** of 1972. The effect of these two treaties was to make the Parliament and the Council the joint budgetary authority. Basically, the Parliament was given the last word on non-compulsory expenditure, although its scope for increasing expenditure was limited by the maximum rate of increase fixed annually. This is calculated by the Commission, on the basis of economic growth, rates of inflation and levels of public expenditure in the member states. The Council retained the last word on **compulsory expenditure**, including, most notably, expenditure undertaken within the **Common Agricultural Policy** (CAP), which represents over 50 per cent of the overall Budget. The 1975 Treaty (Article 12, amending Article 203 EEC) allows the Parliament to reject the Budget as a whole 'if there are important reasons', and ask for a new draft to be submitted to it. The Parliament rejected the Budget for the first time in 1979 and again in 1984. The president of the Parliament is responsible for declaring the Budget adopted; his decision in December 1985 to declare the 1986 Budget adopted led to an action by the Council in the Court of Justice on the grounds that the maximum rate of increase had been exceeded. The Court found in favour of the Council (Case 34/86), but the new Budget agreed in July 1986 was broadly consistent with the Parliament's wishes.

The 1975 Treaty was supplemented by a Council–Commission–Parliament Joint Declaration of 4 March 1975 establishing a **conciliation** procedure. This was designed to forestall the possibility of the Parliament using its budgetary powers to impede legislation with 'appreciable financial implications' already agreed by the Council. The procedure may be triggered by either the Council or the Parliament, and allows representatives of the Parliament to meet face-to-face with the Council in order to reconcile differences. Seldom used at first, the conciliation procedure is now an established feature of the annual Council–Parliament discussions on the Budget, and – informally at least – its scope has been gradually widened. More recently, it has been subsumed in the **co-decision procedure** set out in the Maastricht Treaty (see below).

Although the Parliament's powers with respect to the Budget are substantial, they are circumscribed in several ways, and relations with the Council have often been bad as a consequence of disputes in the course of the budgetary procedure. First, because the Parliament has almost no say in revenue-raising, it is denied those opportunities (of which most national parliaments have at some time in their history taken advantage) of gaining power by withholding supply. Second, the classification of expenditure into compulsory and non-compulsory and the exclusion of certain types of expenditure (such as the **European Development Fund**) from the Budget have denied the Parliament an opportunity to examine and amend the Budget as a whole. Arguments over the classification of particular items in the Budget have frequently given rise to disputes between the Parliament and the Council. Third, as noted above, the rate of increase laid down by the Commission limits the scope for increasing non-compulsory expenditure: the rate can be changed only by agreement between the Council, acting by qualified majority (see **qualified majority voting**), and the Parliament, with the support of a majority of MEPs and three-fifths of the votes cast. On the other hand, the Parliament's position as part of the joint budgetary authority has been strengthened by its participation in the Council–Commission–Parliament 'interinstitutional agreement on budgetary discipline and the improvement of the budgetary procedure', first concluded in 1988. This agreement represented a move away from budgeting on a strictly annual basis and set a framework for Community expenditure over a four-year period.

In line with the Parliament's increased budgetary powers were extensions in its powers of budgetary control. Under the Treaty of 22 July 1975 (see above) the Parliament was given an exclusive right of **discharge** (Article 17; Article 206b EEC). The discharge to the Commission is granted on the basis of the accounts drawn up by the Commission on the implementation of the Budget in the preceding financial year, to which is attached a 'financial statement of the assets and liabilities of the Community' (Article 205a EEC). The Council is empowered, acting by a qualified majority, to make a Recommendation to the Parliament on the discharge, and both the Council and the Parliament are obliged when considering the discharge to take account of the annual report of the Court of Auditors.

As noted above, the original Treaties made only very modest provision for involving the Parliament in the negotiation and conclusion of international agreements. Negotiations are conducted by the Commission on the basis of a mandate laid down by the Council. In 1964 the Dutch Foreign Minister, Joseph Luns, then President-in-Office of the Council, wrote to the Parliament to express the Council's willingness to involve the Parliament in the discussions preceding the opening of negotiations for new Association Agreements and to keep Parliament informed of the progress of negotiations. This was known as the Luns Procedure. Nine years later, with the support of the Commission, this procedure was extended to all trade and commercial agreements under a procedure known as the **Luns–Westerterp procedure**. **Cooperation Agreements**, since they were not provided for in the Treaty, were concluded on the basis of **Article 235** EEC, under which consultation of the Parliament was anyway mandatory.

The communiqué issued after the meeting of the European Council in December 1974 said not only that direct elections to the European Parliament should be held as soon as possible, but that 'the competence of the European Assembly will be extended, in particular by granting it certain powers in the Communities' legislative process'. However, the first directly elected Parliament saw no immediate increase in its formal powers when it met for the first time in July 1979. Direct elections gave the Parliament greater legitimacy and hence more authority; more importantly, the elections created a Parliament largely composed of full-time MEPs, as opposed to the part-time MEPs in the Parliament that preceded it. It would clearly be more difficult for the Council and the Commission to ignore the Parliament's views, and MEPs would have the time, the tenacity and the expertise to enforce those views. The importance of the Parliament was dramatically underlined in the Court of Justice's 'isoglucose' ruling of 1980, which confirmed that a Council decision was void unless the opinion of Parliament had been not merely sought but actually obtained. In the Court's words, the procedures for the consultation of the Parliament were an 'essential factor in the institutional balance intended by the Treaty ... [which] reflects at Community level the fundamental principle that the people should take part in the exercise of power through the intermediary of a representative assembly' (Cases 138/79 and 139/79, judgment of 29 October 1980).

High on the new Parliament's list of priorities was the desire for greater formal powers in decision-making. The most ambitious of the Parliament's initiatives in this field was the Draft Treaty establishing the European Union (DTEU) adopted in February 1984. In 1980, **Altiero Spinelli** and others set up the **Crocodile Club** of Federalists and other enthusiasts for institutional reform. Two years later, in January 1982, the Parliament created a new Committee on Institutional Affairs whose central task would be the drawing up of a wholly new treaty. The theory was that the first directly elected Parliament would play the role of **constituent assembly**. The new treaty would be adopted and the Parliament would then – through the media, through political parties, through national parliaments, and through direct appeals to the public – set about securing support for its provisions. The DTEU would be the centrepiece of the 1984 European elections campaign: political parties would express support for it in their manifestos, and the election results would constitute a massive public endorsement of European union.

In the event, because of internal difficulties, the DTEU was not finally adopted until February 1984 by 237 votes to 31 with 43 abstentions (in a Parliament that by then contained 434 members). This meant that the DTEU was obviously too late to be included in party manifestos and that the process of winning support in national parliaments had to be abandoned. In no country except Italy did the DTEU feature prominently in the 1984 European elections campaign.

The DTEU did, however, win general support from the governments of Italy, the Netherlands, Belgium, West Germany and, most significantly (although somewhat ambiguously), France. In a speech to the European Parliament as President-in-Office of the European Council on 24 May 1984, President **François Mitterrand** said that France was willing 'to examine and defend your project, the inspiration behind which [France] approves. I therefore suggest that preparatory consultations leading up to a conference of the Member States concerned be started up.'

Such a conference – an **Intergovernmental Conference** (IGC) under Article 236 EEC – was precisely what Spinelli and his colleagues had hoped to avoid, since the treaty amendments that a conference would bring forward were subject to ratification (and, therefore, the possibility of a veto) in each member state. The Parliament under Spinelli's guidance had sought to get round this provision by claiming that the DTEU was not an amendment to the existing Treaties but a wholly new treaty, which would come into force *automatically* once a majority of member states, representing two-thirds of the Community's population, had ratified it. President Mitterrand's decision to press for an IGC meant that the governments had regained the initiative.

The Parliament was not the only institution concerned with institutional reform. At the governmental level the **Genscher–Colombo** plan of November 1981 proposed that a 'European Act' should be adopted by the member states 'as a further contribution to the establishment of the European Union'. In emasculated form the European Act was eventually promulgated as the Solemn Declaration on European Union made at the Stuttgart meeting of the European Council in June 1983 (see **Stuttgart Declaration**). As far as the Parliament was concerned, the Declaration provided for closer involvement in decision-making (including the conclusion of agreements with non-member countries) and a more substantial say in appointments to the Commission, but no new powers.

At the Fontainebleau meeting of the European Council in June 1984, the heads of government decided to set up a committee (variously known as the Ad Hoc Committee or the **Dooge Committee**, after its Irish chairman) composed of their personal representatives, some of whom were MEPs or former MEPs. The task of the Committee – modelled on the **Spaak Committee**, which had done much of the preliminary work on the Treaty of Rome – was to bring forward recommendations on institutional reform. In its report, submitted to the Milan meeting of the European Council in June 1985, the Committee recommended a new treaty, based on the *acquis communautaire* and the Stuttgart Declaration and 'guided by the spirit and the method' of the Parliament's DTEU. Three representatives – from Denmark, Greece and the United Kingdom – dissented from this view, in the belief that changes could simply be made to the existing Treaties. By a majority vote the Milan European Council decided to convene an IGC under Article 236 EEC.

The result of the IGC (the first of its kind in the history of the Community) was the SEA, which was signed in February 1986 and which came into force in July 1987. It introduced two new procedures, both of which significantly strengthened the Parliament's legislative role. Henceforth the normal procedure – under which the Parliament scrutinizes a proposal for legislation and adopts in plenary session an Opinion, which may embody amendments to the Commission's text – was to be known as the consultation procedure. The first new procedure, known as the **cooperation procedure**, allows the Parliament two readings, the second of them on the basis of the Council's preliminary conclusions, known as the **common position** (Article 189c EEC). At this point the Parliament can approve the text, propose amendments (which, if supported by the Commission, the Council can reject only by unanimity) or reject the text in its entirety (in the event of which the Council can adopt it only by unanimity with the agreement of the Commission). To amend or to reject, the Parliament must act by absolute majority of its members. Various deadlines and voting requirements are built into this procedure, which under the SEA was limited to legislation on the internal market, social policy, economic and social cohesion, and research and development. The second innovation in the SEA was the **assent procedure**, which gave the Parliament a right of assent over Association Agreements and Accession Treaties (including supplementary protocols to existing agreements).

The most recent additions to the Parliament's powers are those contained in the Maastricht Treaty, many of them as amendments or additions to the Treaty of Rome. Of these, the most important is the co-decision procedure (Article 189b EEC), which extends the cooperation procedure (see above) to allow the Parliament an opportunity to negotiate directly with the Council in a conciliation committee and a right of veto at the final stage if agreement cannot be reached. Also of importance are the Parliament's new powers with respect to the appointment of members of the European Commission (Article 158 EEC), the use of which in July 1994 almost resulted in the Parliament rejecting **Jacques Santer** as the successor to **Jacques Delors**. The Maastricht Treaty also gave the Parliament the right to be consulted on appointments to the Court of Auditors and to the presidency of the **European Central Bank** (ECB), formalized the Parliament's right to set up committees of inquiry (Article 138c EEC), empowered the Parliament to appoint an **Ombudsman** (Article 138e EEC) and came close to granting the Parliament a **right of initiative** (Article 138b EEC).

Less satisfactory to the Parliament was its only marginal involvement in the new '**pillars**' of the Maastricht Treaty, the **Common Foreign and Security Policy** (CFSP) and **Justice and Home Affairs** (JHA). The Parliament has the right to be consulted and kept informed in both areas and may make recommendations, ask questions and hold annual debates, but it has no right to examine and amend proposals in either field, still less to exercise a right of veto.

For the future, the Parliament's priorities with respect to its powers are to see co-decision extended into all areas where the Council takes decisions under qualified majority voting (QMV). The argument is that QMV allows individual ministers to be outvoted, with a consequent loss of the democratic control exercised by national parliaments, a loss that must be compensated for by a tightening of control at the level of the European Parliament if the democratic deficit is not to be widened. Many MEPs would also like to see the Parliament given the right to sack individual Commissioners, perhaps in exchange for the virtually unusable right to dismiss them as a body with a motion of censure (see above).

The powers of the European Parliament as laid down in the Treaties were directed primarily against the Commission, because it was assumed that the Commission would develop into a European government. The central fact with which the Parliament has had to come to terms is that the governments, through the Council and later the European Council and most recently the essentially intergovernmental 'pillars' of the Maastricht Treaty (see above), have remained the key element in the decision-making process. The principal tension within the system has not been between the Parliament and the Commission but between the Parliament and the Council. Indeed, the Parliament and the Commission are often on broadly the same side of the argument, but the Parliament has to vent its frustration against the Commission because its opportunities for doing so against the Council are so much more limited.

Some governments have more or less consistently supported the Parliament's ambitions for more powers. Italy, Germany and the **Benelux** countries have usually been on the Parliament's side, whereas France, the United Kingdom and Denmark have been ambivalent or openly hostile. On balance, a majority of the countries likely to join the Union over the next few years is sympathetic to the Parliament.

The most difficult area for the Parliament – because it led to direct rivalry with the Council – has been securing an increase in its legislative powers. With the exception of an extension of co-decision (see above), it is difficult to see how these powers could be taken further; but it may be asked whether legislation (in the sense of new legislative proposals) will ever again be as important in the life of the Union. In a larger, more heterogeneous Union the emphasis will be less on new legislation and more on enforcement. The Parliament's record on following up its own decisions is poor. This relates not so much to its formal powers but to its internal organization and the inclinations of its members, most of whom prefer the sensation and the glamour of being involved in great decisions to the more painstaking labour involved in ensuring that they are followed up, the law properly applied and money from the Budget spent effectively.

Within a national parliament a broad consensus exists on the role of a parliament and, by extension, on the role of an individual parliamentarian. Such a consensus is much less evident in the case of the European Parliament, which draws on two quite different traditions: the Latin tradition, in which parliament's role is to legitimize decisions of the executive; and the more adversarial Anglo-Saxon tradition, in which parliaments are deliberately set apart from executives (and their supporting bureaucracies) so that they may criticize them more effectively. The difference between the two traditions may be illustrated by MEPs' attitudes to question time (see above), which is almost wholly dominated by those coming from the latter tradition.

In common with most continental parliaments, the European Parliament is oriented towards consensus. This is made easier by the fact that it does not sustain a government and by the fact that a high proportion of its work is of a technical nature that does not lend itself to political divisions. Still in evidence too is the feeling, dating back to the Parliament's uncertain beginnings, that to have any influence within the system the Parliament's opinions have to command unanimous or near-unanimous support. The rapporteur system upon which the work of the committees is based is also oriented towards consensus. This feature of the Parliament's operational style was powerfully enhanced when the SEA came into effect in July 1987, since under the cooperation procedure (see above) the Parliament was required to act by an absolute majority of its members. The effect of this on the behaviour of the political groups is noted elsewhere. Cross-party consensus may indeed have served its principal purpose of getting **Single Market** legislation on to the statute-book in good time, but it lessened still further the scope for party-political debate and created habits of mind that serve to render issues over a wider field less clear-cut and therefore less arresting to the public. The price paid for this is the indifference of the media and a low turn-out in European elections. Unless the Parliament can establish itself as the forum in which competing views on the big issues affecting Europe's future are addressed and debated, rather than merely homogenized, it will fail to live up to its supporters' expectations. As **Winston Churchill** remarked, 'Building up a European Parliament must be gradual . . . It should roll forward on a tide of facts, events and impulses rather than by elaborate constitution-making' (speech in the Consultative Assembly of the Council of Europe, 11 August 1950).

European passport

The European passport was first discussed at the Paris **summit** of December 1974 and again in Rome the following year. The **Council of Ministers** adopted two **Resolutions** in June 1981 and June 1982 to settle the details, and the passport was gradually introduced from 1 January 1985. The long period of gestation was caused by disagreements between member states over the colour and format; the issue was further complicated by the wish on the part of some governments to introduce machine-readable pages, which in turn prompted arguments over what data should be included.

The European passport is in fact not a European passport at all, but a passport produced in a uniform format agreed amongst member states: smaller than the standard British passport, with a semi-soft red cover (variously described as 'Bordeaux' or 'Burgundy') bearing the words 'European Community' in the appropriate language as well as the name of the country of issue. The member states remain the issuing authorities.

The idea of a European passport is intended to have both symbolic and practical importance. The fact that all citizens of what is now the **European Union** have passports in a common format is meant to reinforce the notion of a **People's Europe** and to underline the idea of a common **citizenship**. At the practical level, a common-format European passport should help to ensure that all citizens of the European Union can instantly be recognized as such at the Union's internal and external frontiers and receive equal treatment at the hands of the authorities of non-member states.

European Patent Convention

Signed in 1977 by the **Benelux** countries, France, Germany, Switzerland and the United Kingdom, the European Patent Convention offers patent protection throughout the signatory states. It is the largest regional patent system in the world, and now covers all 15 member states of the European Union (except Finland), Liechtenstein, Monaco and Switzerland. By 1992 the European Patent Office in Munich had dealt with 500,000 patent applications and granted 200,000 patents. The Office is also important as a supplier of technical information, and is active internationally in the World Intellectual Property Organization and through bilateral contacts with national patent offices in central and eastern Europe.

European Political Community

In 1950 the proposal for a **European Defence Community** (EDC: see also **Pleven Plan**) gave rise to the suggestion that the federal army provided for in the EDC Treaty should be under the control of an elected supranational authority to be known as the EDC Assembly. Under Article 38 of the Treaty this proposal was to be worked out in detail by the Assembly of the **European Coal and Steel Community** (ECSC). On 10 September 1952 the foreign ministers of **the Six** set this work in hand: the ECSC Assembly (the forerunner of the **European Parliament**) was invited 'to draft a Treaty constituting a European Political Authority'. The proposals contained in this Treaty became known as the European Political Community (EPC).

That this task should be entrusted to the ECSC Assembly aroused the jealousy of the Consultative Assembly of the **Council of Europe**. This problem was solved by requiring the ECSC Assembly to be temporarily enlarged, drawing on members of the Consultative Assembly from the national parliaments of the Six. This enlarged ECSC Assembly, known as the Ad Hoc Assembly, met in **Strasbourg** under the presidency of **Paul-Henri Spaak**.

The draft Treaty was adopted by the Assembly on 10 March 1953. Under Article 1 it established 'a European Community of a supranational character . . . founded upon a union of peoples and States, upon respect for their personality and upon equal rights and duties for all'. The Community was to be equipped with a two-chamber Parliament, the first ('the People's Chamber') made up of 'deputies representing the peoples united in the Community', the second (the Senate) made up of 'senators representing the people of each State'. The former were to be directly elected every five years, the latter were to be elected by **national parliaments**. In principle, France, Germany and Italy each had 63 deputies and 21 senators; the first chamber had 268 members, the Senate 87. France was given seven extra deputies 'in order to take into account its overseas departments and territories'. The Parliament held two sessions every year.

The administration of the Community was in the hands of a European Executive Council. The president, elected by the Senate, appointed the other Council members, of whom not more than two could be of the same nationality. They were to be known as 'Ministers of the European Community'. The Council as a whole had to receive a vote of confidence from both chambers of the Parliament, either of which had the power to dismiss it. However, if the People's Chamber voted by a majority of less than three-fifths to dismiss the Council, the Council could then choose either to resign voluntarily or to dissolve the Chamber; the latter option could be overruled only by a vote of the Senate to dismiss the Council.

A Council of National Ministers was responsible for 'harmonizing the action of the European Executive Council with that of the Governments of Member States'. It was composed of one member from each government, with a rotating presidency.

The Court of Justice of the ECSC would act as the Court for the Community, which was also to be equipped with an Economic and Social Council 'in an advisory capacity'. Laws required the assent of both chambers. The Senate was empowered to request a second reading. The president of the European Executive Council was responsible for promulgating laws duly adopted, and the Council had the power to issue 'regulations to ensure the implementation of the laws of the Community'.

The Community would take over the powers and functions of the ECSC and the EDC, as well as pursue its own specific objectives. Prominent amongst these was the establishment of 'a common market among the Member States, based on the free movement of goods, capital and persons'. The Budget of the Community was made up of what would now be called **own resources** (which included taxes levied by the Community) and contributions from member states fixed by unanimous agreement in the Council of National Ministers.

Never formally rejected, the EPC Treaty was abandoned when on 30 August 1954 the French National Assembly voted against the EDC Treaty. As a project it was extremely ambitious, for although the basic institutional structure of the EPC reflected the quadripartite scheme already in place under the ECSC Treaty, there were many very striking differences in terms of the balance of power between the institutions. The extensive powers of the 'Ministers' in the European Executive Council were a substantial advance on those of the ECSC High Authority, and completely overshadowed those of the Council of National Ministers. The relation between the two bodies affords a very instructive comparison with the powers of the

Commission and the **Council of Ministers** as set out in the **Treaty of Rome** four years later. Similarly, to take only one example, the right of the European Executive Council to dissolve the Parliament was far in excess of anything contemplated before (or since) in the Commission–Parliament relationship as it has developed since 1958. Overall, much of the language of the EPC Treaty would be echoed in the Treaty of Rome. As **Jean Monnet** remarked of the EPC Treaty:

> Nothing that has been conscientiously made in this way is ever useless: for, by working together, everyone acquires a better knowledge of his partners and their problems, and he passes it on to others in his turn ... The constitution-makers were ... insufficiently [cautious] when they imagined that European unity would *begin* with the establishment of a federal political system ... It was a step in the right direction; but it proposed to go too fast, without waiting for the force of necessity to make it seem natural in the eyes of Europeans (*Memoirs*).

European Political Cooperation (EPC)

EPC refers to the procedures used from 1970 to allow member states of the European Community to discuss and coordinate their positions on foreign affairs and, where appropriate, act in concert. The principal decision-making body was the Conference of Foreign Ministers meeting in Political Cooperation. EPC procedures were replaced from November 1993 by those laid down in the **Common Foreign and Security Policy** (CFSP) provisions of the **Maastricht Treaty** (see also **political directors, COREUR**). The story of EPC up to that date is well told in Simon Nuttall, *European Political Cooperation* (1992).

European Regional Development Fund (ERDF)

Although the Preamble to the **Treaty of Rome** contains a commitment to 'reducing the differences between the various regions and the backwardness of the less-favoured regions', agreement was not reached on the establishment of the ERDF until 1972; it came into operation three years later. The creation of the ERDF was largely a British initiative, in the belief that receipts from the Fund would help compensate for the bias in the **Budget** towards agriculture. In the event, the ERDF began on a very small scale indeed and was initially shared between member states on the basis of fixed quotas.

The role of the ERDF was defined by the **Maastricht Treaty** in an amendment to the Treaty of Rome (Article 130c) as being 'to help to redress the main regional imbalances in the Community through participation in the development and structural adjustment of regions whose development is lagging behind and in the conversion of declining industrial regions'. In common with the other **structural funds** the ERDF is directed towards particular objectives, first drawn up in 1988 and revised in 1993. The ERDF is concerned mainly with Objectives 1 and 2: underdeveloped regions and those particularly affected by the decline of traditional industries such as coal, steel, shipbuilding and textiles. The problems of inner cities are also dealt with under Objective 2. Only projects in regions defined by the **European Commission** as qualifying for Objective 1 or Objective 2 assistance may receive ERDF aid under these headings. The ERDF also contributes to the development of rural areas under Objective 5b (see **European Agricultural Guidance and Guarantee Fund**).

Assistance from the ERDF is given in the form of grants within 'Community Support Frameworks' agreed with member states on the basis of development plans. Such assistance must complement, not substitute for, assistance from national sources (see **additionality**). In the Objective 1 regions ERDF assistance may not exceed 75 per cent of the total cost of a project and may not be less than 50 per cent of the total cost met from public funds. In Objective 2 regions these figures are reduced to 50 and 25 per cent respectively.

The ERDF, amounting to over 9 billion ECUs (about £7 billion) in 1994, is set to increase quite substantially between 1995 and the end of the decade (see **Edinburgh Growth Initiative**). This and the establishment of the **Committee of the Regions** further encourage the trend for local and regional authorities to establish their own direct links with the Commission instead of being obliged to operate through national government departments (see also **regionalism**).

European Social Charter

The original European Social Charter (not to be confused with the **Social Chapter** or with the European Community's 1989 Charter on the Fundamental Social Rights of Workers: see below) is the counterpart in respect of economic and social rights of the European Convention on Human Rights of 1950 (see **human rights**). Agreed in Turin in 1961 by the **Council of Europe**, the European Social Charter entered into force in 1965.

The Charter, composed of 38 Articles, an appendix, and 2 additional **protocols**, binds signatory states to accept at least 5 of a 'compulsory nucleus' of 7 basic rights, each in a separate Article. Overall, a signatory state must accept at least 10 of the Articles of the Convention. The basic rights are: the right to work (under which governments accept as 'one of their primary aims and responsibilities the achievement and maintenance of as high and stable a level of employment as possible, with a view to the attainment of full employment'), the right to organize, the right of collective bargaining, the right to social security, the right to social and medical assistance, the right to family benefits, and the right of migrant workers and their families to protection and assistance. Other rights are concerned with issues such as working conditions, special protection for young workers and vocational training – a total of 19 rights in all. Four further rights were set out in a 1988 protocol: equal opportunities and equal treatment, information and consultation, workers' involvement in questions of health and safety at the workplace, and special care for the elderly. Signatories to the protocol must agree to be bound by at least one of these.

Unlike the European Convention, the Charter is not backed up by judicial machinery for enforcement. Instead, observance is monitored by a Committee of Experts of not more than seven members appointed for a six-year term by the Committee of Ministers. It is the job of this Committee to examine the biennial reports submitted by the signatory states. Its conclusions and the reports are then forwarded to a subcommittee of the Council of Europe's Governmental Social Committee, which in turn forwards them to the Committee of Ministers. The Parliamentary Assembly may also submit its views on the conclusions of the Committee of Experts. In extreme cases the Committee of Ministers may decide, by a two-thirds majority, to make 'necessary recommendations' to a signatory state in default of its obligations under the Charter. The ambitious scope of the Charter is thus vitiated by the feebleness of the enforcement procedures, which are heavily weighted in favour of governments. The Charter illustrates very clearly the limitations of a system based upon voluntary compliance, by contrast with a system (such as prevails in the European Community) in which objectives are secured by means, ultimately, of binding legislation.

The European Community's Social Charter (formally, the Charter on the Fundamental Social Rights of Workers) was adopted in December 1989 by the **European Council** at its meeting in Strasbourg, with the participation of all member states except the United Kingdom. The Charter is backed up by a so-called 'Social Action Programme' of 47 proposals for legislation. The Social Chapter of the **Maastricht Treaty** – formally known as the Agreement on Social Policy or the Social Protocol – gives the Charter a legal basis and extends the scope of **qualified majority voting** (QMV) in the social field. The United Kingdom did not sign the 1989 Social Charter on the grounds that it was inconsistent with the three principles of the Community's involvement in the social field agreed at the European Council meeting in Madrid in June 1989: that the emphasis should be on job creation, that it should respect the doctrine of

subsidiarity, and that it should reflect the diversity of national practice and traditions. The United Kingdom has, however, chosen to implement most of the proposals brought forward under the Social Action Programme and to submit an annual report on the state of social and employment rights, in common with other member states.

The Charter requires the **Commission** to draw up an annual report on the application of the Charter. The scope of the Charter is very broad and includes living and working conditions, freedom of movement, social security, equal treatment for men and women, vocational training, health and safety, special measures for young people, the elderly, and the disabled, and the right to information, consultation, and participation. The various legislative measures brought forward to implement the Charter – of which between one-third and one-half have already been adopted – are supplemented by a number of research programmes.

European Social Fund (ESF)

The oldest of the European Union's **structural funds**, the ESF was established under Article 123 of the **Treaty of Rome**. This was done mainly at the instigation of Italy, the poorest country of **the Six**. Article 123 EEC, as revised by the **Maastricht Treaty**, states that the objective of the ESF is 'to render the employment of workers easier and to increase their geographical and occupational mobility within the Community, and to facilitate their adaptation to industrial changes and to changes in production systems, in particular through vocational training and retraining'. The ESF is administered by the **European Commission**, assisted by a committee of 'representatives of governments, trade unions and employers' organizations' (Article 124 EEC). The ESF amounted to about 6.5 billion ECUs (about £5 billion) in 1994.

The ESF is concerned mainly with combating long-term unemployment, with special measures to assist people under the age of 25, and with helping workers adapt to technological change (Objectives 3 and 4 of the structural funds). As with the other funds, ESF assistance is directed more towards programmes than towards individual projects. Only organizations financially supported by a public authority may apply for ESF aid, which is, in nearly all cases, intended to complement aid from national sources (see **additionality**). Particular attention is paid to people with special difficulties, such as migrant workers, women and the disabled. These last two categories also benefit from special programmes: NOW (New Opportunities for Women), which offers vocational training to women, and Horizon, which promotes the social and professional integration of the disabled (for details of both programmes, see the *Official Journal*, C327, 29 December 1990).

The **Council of Europe** also operates a Social Fund (correctly known as the Social Development Fund). This Fund makes loans worth some £875 million annually to projects in the fields of job creation, training, low-cost housing, and so on.

European Space Agency (ESA)

Established in 1975, the ESA brought together the European Space Research Organization (ESRO) and the European Organization for the Development and Construction of Space Vehicle Launchers (ELDO). ESA is not formally associated with the European Union. It has 15 member countries and its headquarters are in Paris. Most of ESA's work has been centred upon the launching from a site in French Guiana of satellites for communications, broadcasting, meteorology and space research, the underlying aim being to give Europe its own launching capability. The Ariane launcher was developed by ESA, as was the Giotto space laboratory, which studied Halley's Comet. Research continues into a staffed space laboratory (Spacelab), the Hermes space shuttle and, in collaboration with the United States, a manned space station. Most of the funding for ESA comes from participating states, although some revenue is earned from the launching of satellites on behalf of commercial interests. See Guy Collins, *Europe in Space* (1990).

European Space Research Organization

See **European Space Agency**.

European Trade Union Confederation (ETUC)

Founded as the European Secretariat within the International Confederation of Free Trade Unions in 1958, the ETUC dates in its present form from 1973. Its membership is made up of national trade union confederations in over 20 European countries, representing some 45 million trade unionists. The ETUC's main role is to seek to shape European legislation likely to affect the interests of trade unions and their members by lobbying the **Commission**, the **European Parliament** and especially the **Economic and Social Committee**. A conference is held every three years.

European Training Foundation (ETF)

The ETF was set up in May 1990 on the basis of a decision taken in December 1989 by the **European Council**. However, no agreement could be reached on where the ETF should be based (see **seat of the institutions**), and it was not until October 1993 that the decision was taken to locate it in Turin. Originally, the purpose of the ETF was to assist the countries in central and western Europe participating in the **PHARE** programme to retrain their workforce, with the aid of conferences, seminars, exchanges, joint ventures and so on, but in July 1994 it was decided to extend the scope of the ETF's activities to include Mongolia and the countries covered by the TACIS programme.

European Union

The phrase 'European Union' is not to be found in any of the basic **Treaties**. However, the preamble to the **Treaty of Rome** opens with the words 'Determined to lay the foundations of an ever closer union among the peoples of Europe . . .', a deliberate echo of the 'more perfect union' referred to in the Constitution of the United States. The commitment to a European Union was first formally made at the October 1972 Paris **summit**, at which the heads of government of the member states, the 'driving wheels of European construction', confirmed their intention of 'converting their entire relationship into a European Union before the end of this decade'. This was reaffirmed at the Copenhagen summit the following year (see also **European identity**). In fact, it was not until the 1991 **Maastricht Treaty**, the formal title of which is the Treaty on European Union, that a European Union was brought into existence.

'European Union' and similar phrases are to be found in many documents that mark the successive stages of the institutional development of the Union. Of the prewar proposals, the best known are the **Pan-Europa** of **Count Richard Coudenhove-Kalergi** and the plan for a European Federal Union put forward in 1929 by **Aristide Briand** in the **League of Nations**. The draft Treaty establishing the **European Political Community** of 1953 describes it as being 'founded upon a union of peoples and States'. The resolution adopted by the foreign ministers at the **Messina Conference** in 1955 refers to 'the setting up of a united Europe'. Even the 1962 **Fouchet Plan** (final version) spoke of 'a union of States and of European peoples, hereafter called "the European Union"'. The communiqué issued after the 1969 summit in The Hague referred to 'a United Europe capable of assuming its responsibilities in the world of tomorrow'.

Magniloquence apart, the first attempt to define what European Union might actually mean was made in the 1975 **Tindemans Report**. It identified the essential components of European Union as 'a united front to the outside world'; 'a common economic and monetary policy', backed by common policies for industry, agriculture, energy and research; and regional and social policies that would allow 'the solidarity of our peoples to be effective and adequate'. Above all, the European Union was to be founded upon 'institutions with the necessary powers to determine a common, coherent and all-inclusive political view, the efficiency needed for action, the legitimacy needed for democratic control'. Although little concrete action followed from the Tindemans Report, there was no dissent from its definition of European Union. Eight years later the member states reaffirmed the Paris summit commitment in the 1983 **Stuttgart Declaration** (formally known as the Solemn Declaration on European Union) in response to the proposals in the **Genscher–Colombo Plan**. The Declaration said that 'European Union is being achieved by deepening and broadening the scope of European activities so that they coherently cover ... a growing proportion of Member States' mutual relations and of their external relations'. The member states undertook to review progress within five years, and to 'decide whether the progress achieved should be incorporated in a Treaty on European Union'.

The most ambitious scheme of the early 1980s was the **Draft Treaty establishing the European Union** (DTEU) adopted by the **European Parliament** in February 1984 (see also **constituent assembly**). Unlike the Maastricht Treaty, the DTEU proposed a uniform structure rather than one based on so-called **pillars**. The European Union, which would have its own legal personality, would take over the whole of the *acquis communautaire* and its institutions would assume the functions presently carried out by the institutions of the Community.

In the preamble to the 1986 **Single European Act** (SEA) the member states once again reaffirmed their commitment to European Union as expressed at the Paris summit. The SEA envisaged a union based upon the European Communities on the one hand and a strengthened, formalized system of **European Political Cooperation** on the other. The latter had its own, essentially intergovernmental, decision-making procedures (see **intergovernmentalism**). This model, employing what would later become known as separate **pillars**, was refined and developed in the European Union established five years later under the Maastricht Treaty.

The word 'union' has always posed difficulties for the United Kingdom. Historically, the word arouses associations with the 1707 Act of Union, which brought about the near-total integration of England and Scotland. In the view of **Roy Jenkins**, 'union' is thought of on the Continent as an overall direction, in the United Kingdom as a destination, which serves to explain the peculiarly British interest in defining exactly what 'union' would entail. Some of the difficulties may be evaded by the judicious use of 'unity' or 'unification' in certain contexts. The latter in particular may be used to characterize the 'ever closer union' referred to in the Treaty of Rome as a *process* rather than as an *end-state* (see also **United States of Europe**). In an essay called 'Towards European Union' contributed to the July/August 1947 edition of the *Partisan Review*, George Orwell remarked that 'a Western European union is in itself a less improbable concatenation than the Soviet Union or the British Empire' (*Collected Essays, Journalism and Letters*, Vol. 4).

The report by the House of Lords Select Committee on the European Communities entitled *European Union* (23 July 1985) is a comprehensive study of the main issues raised by European Union and contains several of the basic texts. It also contains evidence from many expert witnesses (including that of Roy Jenkins noted above).

European Unit of Account

See **European Currency Unit**.

European University Institute (EUI)

Founded in 1976, the EUI is based in Fiesole near Florence, and offers postgraduate courses leading to a master's degree or a doctorate. There are four departments: history and civilization, economics, law, and political and social sciences. The EUI is also the repository of the historical archives of the **European Communities**. Although Article 9.2 of the **Euratom** Treaty specified that 'an institution of university status shall be established', the EUI is not a Union body and has its own legal personality independent of the **Treaties**. It is financed by direct contributions from member states. The President of the EUI heads a small administrative staff and a teaching staff largely composed of academics on three-year fellowships and Visiting Professors.

Europe des patries

Literally a 'Europe of nation-states' (*l'Europe des nations*), *Europe des patries* is a phrase associated with **Charles de Gaulle**. It encapsulates a model of European integration in which the states are the essential building blocks, and in which the decision-making procedures reflect the pre-eminence of the states within the system (see **intergovernmentalism**).

Europol

At the meeting of the **European Council** held in Luxembourg on 28–29 June 1991 it was decided on a proposal from the German government to establish a Community-wide organization, to be known as Europol, to facilitate cooperation between the police forces of member states. The decision was confirmed at a meeting of justice and home affairs ministers (the **Trevi Group**) in The Hague on 3 December 1991 and embodied in the **Maastricht Treaty** (Title VI, Article K1.9). The Treaty provides for 'police cooperation for the purposes of preventing and combating terrorism, unlawful drug trafficking and other serious forms of international crime, including if necessary certain aspects of customs cooperation, in connection with the organization of a Union-wide system for exchanging information within a European Police Office (Europol)'. A Declaration on Police Cooperation was annexed to the Maastricht Treaty, instructing the Trevi Group and the **Commission** to set up Europol 'at an early date'.

In the first phase Europol is planned as a system for the rapid and confidential exchange of information on issues such as drugs, suspected terrorists, arms shipments and asylum seekers. However, even this limited objective has met problems similar to those raised in the context of the **Schengen Agreement**, such as the individual's right to privacy, accountability for police action, different national laws (some of a constitutional nature) on such matters as extradition and public order and the role of the **Court of Justice**. All these issues were raised in the discussions between member states on the Europol Convention. Cooperation between police forces is made more difficult by the diversity of national police structures: the United Kingdom, for example, has 52 separate forces organized on a geographical basis, whereas the majority of other member states have at least one national force to supplement local forces. The first part of Europol to become operational was the Europol Drugs Unit in The Hague. The Europol Convention was not finally agreed until the Cannes meeting of the European Council in June 1995. The remit of Europol has been extended to cover illegal trade in nuclear materials. An annual report on Europol will be forwarded to the European Parliament.

Eurostat

Eurostat is the statistical office of the European Union. Based in Luxembourg, it is largely dependent on information supplied by member states, not all of it equally comprehensive and reliable and much of it posing problems of comparability. Eurostat publishes several series of statistics dealing with the economy, agriculture, trade and energy, and a periodic booklet entitled *Europe in Figures*. In most cases the tables incorporate comparisons between the Union's member states, other European countries, Japan and the United States. See also **Intrastat**.

Excessive Deficit Procedure

One of the **convergence** criteria under the provisions on **Economic and Monetary Union** (EMU) added to the **Treaty of Rome** by the **Maastricht Treaty** is the curbing of excessive deficits in levels of planned or actual public expenditure in relation to revenue (Article 104c EEC). The reference values set out in a **protocol** annexed to the Treaty of Rome allow the excess of expenditure over revenue (i.e., government borrowing at national, regional and local level) to be no more than 3 per cent of gross domestic product (GDP) in any year, and allow total government debt to be no more than 60 per cent of GDP. Under Article 3 of the protocol member states are required to 'report their planned and actual deficits and the levels of their debt promptly and regularly to the Commission', which in turn reports any cases of excessive deficit to the **Monetary Committee** and to the **Ecofin Council**. The Commission is allowed some latitude in the sense that countries in which the total public sector deficit, even if above 60 per cent, is obviously on a downward trend, may be said not to have an 'excessive' deficit.

The member states with the worst overall deficits are Belgium (134 per cent) and Italy (125 per cent). In September 1994 it was estimated that both countries would need 20 to 40 years of consistently rigorous public expenditure policies to reduce their levels of deficit to the 60 per cent target, disqualifying them from participating in EMU until 2015 at the earliest. Since Belgium is part of the **Belgo-Luxembourg Economic Union**, this poses a problem for Luxembourg, which has the lowest deficit of any member state.

A member state with a deficit found by the Ecofin Council to be excessive receives 'recommendations' from the Council. From the beginning of stage 3 of EMU these recommendations may, if persistently ignored, be followed up by other measures, such as a withdrawal of **European Investment Bank** (EIB) lending facilities, the obligation to make 'a non-interest-bearing deposit of an appropriate size' with the Community until the deficit is corrected, or fines.

Exchange-Rate Mechanism (ERM)

Introduced as part of the **European Monetary System** (EMS) in 1979, the ERM was devised as a means of minimizing currency fluctuations. Each participating currency has a central exchange rate against the ECU, which in turn allows a system of bilateral central rates to be calculated covering all the participating currencies. Each currency is allowed to fluctuate against the others by an agreed margin around these bilateral central rates: if it approaches its top or bottom limit a 'divergence indicator' is triggered, and at this point the national central banks intervene on exchange markets to bring the two currencies back into line (see **European Monetary Cooperation Fund**). Other measures, such as adjustments to interest rates, may also be taken. If a currency cannot be held within its agreed margins, a realignment may be negotiated in the **Monetary Committee**.

The ERM is the successor to a similar system for limiting currency fluctuations known as the '**Snake** in the tunnel' (see also **Werner Report**). When the ERM first came into operation in March 1979, eight currencies took part in the system: the Belgian and Luxembourg francs, the French franc, the Danish krone, the Deutsche Mark, the Dutch guilder, the Italian lira and the Irish pound. The pound sterling did not take part, nor did the Greek drachma when Greece joined the Community in 1981. The Spanish peseta joined the ERM in June 1989, the pound sterling in October 1990, and the Portuguese escudo in April 1992. All currencies were allowed to fluctuate within a margin of 2.25 per cent on either side of their bilateral central rates (the 'narrow band'), except the peseta, the lira, the escudo and the pound sterling, which were allowed a 'broad band' of 6 per cent.

Currency speculation on an unprecedented scale on 16 September 1992 ('Black Wednesday') caused the pound sterling and the lira to leave the ERM and the peseta to be devalued by 5 per cent. This speculation was prompted at least in part by the possibility of a 'No' vote in the French referendum on the **Maastricht Treaty** four days later. In the recriminations that followed, Germany was blamed for maintaining high interest rates (see **German reunification**). On 2 August 1993 further large-scale speculation all but destroyed the ERM. The wide band was increased to 15 per cent and extended to all currencies remaining within the system (although the Germans and the Dutch agreed bilaterally to retain the narrow band between their two currencies). Since then the majority of currencies remaining in the ERM have moved back to their pre-August 1993 alignments.

Previously, general realignments within the ERM took place only infrequently. Between April 1986 and September 1992 there were no realignments involving more than three currencies, and only eight such realignments over the whole period from 1979. With the new, very broad bands of 15 per cent (see above), further realignments are unlikely.

Before the introduction of broad bands in 1993 the ERM was widely credited with having achieved its primary goal of creating a zone of monetary stability amongst participating states, and in particular with having helped to shield their economies from the effects of the instability in international money markets caused by the rise and fall of the dollar. The ERM removed from member states the temptation to engage in competitive devaluations to secure short-term trading advantages. It also contributed to economic convergence by serving to lessen interest-rate differentials over the period and in general acted as an external discipline of which member states have taken advantage in the fight against inflation.

The ERM is part of the *acquis communautaire*, so all states acceding to the Union are required to be prepared to join it (although not necessarily immediately). Observance of the 'normal fluctuation margins' within the ERM for at least two years is also one of the **convergence criteria** that must be met by a member state wishing to proceed to stage 3 of **Economic and Monetary Union** (EMU).

External Frontiers Convention

The External Frontiers Convention, which remains unratified because of a dispute between Spain and the United Kingdom over its application to **Gibraltar**, deals with the treatment of nationals of non-member states at the external frontiers of the European Union. It provides for the issuing of visas by member states to be based on an agreed list of the countries whose nationals require visas and for there to be mutual recognition of visas for 'short stay' visits of up to three months. It allows member states to retain exclusive control over the admission of third-country nationals for stays longer than three months. It endorses the principle of 'carriers' liability', under which airlines and other commercial transport operators can be fined if their passengers are found on arrival not to have a right of entry. Common procedures are laid down for the removal of illegal immigrants and overstayers (see also **joint list**). In common with the **Dublin Asylum Convention**, the External Frontiers Convention was based on the commitment in Article 7a of the **Treaty of Rome** to create 'an area without internal frontiers in which the free movement of ... persons ... is ensured'.

In December 1993 the **Commission** brought forward proposals in the form of a revised draft Convention under Article K3 of the **Maastricht Treaty** and a **Regulation** containing a list of third countries whose nationals need a visa to enter the territory of the member states. Such a list is already provided for in the Convention (see above), but the Commission proposal was brought forward under Article 100c EEC as a separate measure with a view to speeding up the process of securing agreement amongst member states. Article 100c EEC, added by the Maastricht Treaty, provides for decisions on visas to be taken unanimously until 1 January 1996, after which **qualified majority voting** (QMV) will apply.

Work on all the matters covered by the two Conventions now proceeds within the framework laid down in the Maastricht Treaty for cooperation in the fields of **Justice and Home Affairs** (JHA; see also **free movement of persons**).

Factortame case

The Factortame case (*R* v *Secretary of State for Transport, ex parte Factortame Ltd*, Case C213/89) arose when a number of companies, largely Spanish-controlled, sought a judicial review of certain provisions of the British Merchant Shipping Act 1988, which were alleged to be discriminatory in respect of the rules for registering fishing vessels as British. The system of quotas and total allowable catches under the **Common Fisheries Policy** made it attractive to seek British registration, and until the 1988 Act the rules for such registration were relatively lax. The companies, which also claimed that their rights under Treaty provisions on **freedom of establishment** were being infringed, sought interim relief (i.e., that the relevant provisions of the Act should be waived) while the case was being decided, initially in the British courts.

Such relief was granted, but both the Court of Appeal and the House of Lords took the view that the Divisional Court in which the action was first brought had no power to order a waiver from the provisions of the Act. The **Court of Justice** ruled that unless such a power existed the effectiveness of Community law would be impaired. The Factortame case served to underline the **primacy** of Community law and the importance attached by the Court to the removal of any impediment to an individual's power to assert rights arising from Community law. It is discussed in more detail in Weatherill and Beaumont, *EC Law*.

Failure to act

Article 175 of the **Treaty of Rome**, as amended by the **Maastricht Treaty,** states: 'Should the **European Parliament**, the **Council** or the **Commission**, in infringement of this Treaty, fail to act, the Member States and the other institutions of the Community may bring an action before the **Court of Justice** to have the infringement established.' The institution concerned must first be 'called upon to act', and thereafter has two months within which to 'define its position'. If it does not, an action may be brought within a further two months. An institution that is found by the Court to have failed to act 'shall be required to take the necessary measures' (Article 176 EEC). It should be noted that the Court's power under Article 171 EEC (as revised by the Maastricht Treaty) to impose a 'lump sum or penalty payment' on a member state found to be in default of its Treaty obligations does not extend to the Council as the collective embodiment of the member states. Any individual or organization possessing legal personality may complain to the Court 'that an institution of the Community has failed to address to that person any act other than a Recommendation or an **Opinion**'.

Only a few actions have ever been brought under Article 175 EEC. The best-known example was a case brought by the European Parliament in 1983 against the Council for the latter's failure to enact a **common transport policy** as required under Articles 3e, 74 and 75 EEC (Case 13/83). The Court ruling of 22 May 1985 found partially in the Parliament's favour, and even though progress since that date in the field of transport has been well short of spectacular the case was a moral victory for the Parliament and helped to bring pressure to bear upon the Council.

Federalism
See **Federation**.

Federation

Federation is a form of political organization characterized by a division of responsibility between a central authority and component parts (usually states, regions or provinces) enjoying autonomy in certain fields. The distribution of powers between the centre and the component parts in any federal structure will vary from case to case and may vary over time (see also **confederation**), and is normally embodied in a constitution. Federation was defined by A. V. Dicey in *The Law of the Constitution* (1885) as 'a political contrivance intended to reconcile national unity and power with the maintenance of states' rights'.

Within Europe there are several types of federation, and several examples of federal structures that proved too fragile to contain ethnic differences or other causes of tension, such as Yugoslavia and Czechoslovakia. Federation may be adapted to the needs of a previously unitary state in which the component parts are seeking greater autonomy, as in Belgium; and to those of countries or states choosing to become integrated to a greater or lesser extent within a larger political unit, such as **Benelux**.

Amongst the areas usually reserved to the central federal authority are defence, foreign trade, external representation and the negotiation of treaties, immigration, the rights and duties flowing from citizenship, and the management of the currency. The tax structure and the system for raising and allocating revenue will normally reflect the extent to which the component parts of the federation have spending responsibilities, such as those in the field of health, education, housing, public works and the administration of justice. Most federations have a central bank, a supreme court and a two-chamber parliament in which the upper chamber is composed of representatives of the states, regions or provinces of which the federation is composed.

Federalist ideas were a powerful influence upon many of the pioneers of European integration, such as **Jean Monnet** and **Altiero Spinelli**, in the 1940s and early 1950s. The two world wars had done much to discredit **intergovernmentalism** and to call in question the nation-state as the basis for international relations. Federalist ideas, ambitions and assumptions are everywhere evident in the **Treaties** upon which the **European Communities** are based. Great importance is attached in the Treaties to supranational institutions of a federal type, and even though the **Commission** has not emerged as the real European government (with the **Council of Ministers** and the **European Parliament** as the upper and lower houses of a bicameral legislature) it is these institutions, together with the **Court of Justice**, that give the Community its distinctive quasi-federal structure. It was precisely the supranational and therefore federal character of the Community's main institutions that prompted the hostility of **Charles de Gaulle** and, later, **Margaret Thatcher**, both of whom interpreted the ambitions of Commission Presidents **Walter Hallstein** and **Jacques Delors** as a direct challenge to the integrity and authority of the nation-state and so of **sovereignty**. British reservations about 'federalism' were still sufficiently strong to secure the removal of the phrase 'of a federal type', to describe the European Union, from the final draft of the **Maastricht Treaty**. This was hailed, in the United Kingdom at least, as a triumph, in spite of the fact that the fundamentally federalist character of some of the Treaty's provisions (such as those empowering the Court of Justice to fine defaulting member states) not only remained intact but enjoyed vigorous British support. Another prominent feature of the Treaty, the doctrine of **subsidiarity**, is only meaningful in the context of a federal structure in which there is a balance of power between the Union institutions and national, regional or local authorities.

For some time yet federation and federalism are likely to remain poorly understood. On the one hand they are thought to be synonymous with the 'European superstate', with 'rule from Brussels' and the decline of nationhood. On the other, they are seen as safeguards against overweening central authority and the emergence of a Europe in which the hard-won rights of nations and communities to manage their own affairs are not only recognized but guaranteed.

FEOGA

See **European Agricultural Guidance and Guarantee Fund**.

Fiche d'impact

Appended to every important legislative proposal from the **Commission** is a (usually rather cursory) assessment of its impact, known as the *fiche d'impact*. Depending on the nature of the proposal, the *fiche d'impact* will normally deal with its impact on employment or the environment and will draw attention to any special problems likely to arise for small and medium-sized enterprises (SMEs). The impact of the proposal on the Union's **Budget** is the subject of a separate assessment known as a *fiche financière* (see also **budgetary discipline**).

Finalités politiques

This phrase is sometimes used to denote the ultimate goals of the European Union, forming part of the *acquis communautaire* but not necessarily (yet) to be found in the **Treaties**. An objective agreed at a meeting of the **European Council**, for example, may be regarded as amongst the *finalités politiques* even before it has been embodied in the Treaties or given rise to legislation.

Financial services

The 1985 **Cockfield White Paper** identified the opening up of the financial services market (mainly banking, mortgage lending and insurance) as an essential element in the **Single Market** programme. Progress in this sector had been slow, with several member states justifying their own national regulations on (sometimes spurious) consumer protection grounds. Although in theory financial services were covered by general Treaty provisions on **competition policy**, **freedom of establishment** and **freedom to provide services**, in fact, as Article 61.2 of the **Treaty of Rome** specified, liberalization was bound up with free movement of capital (see **capital movements**). Accordingly, it was not until the late 1980s that real progress was made, with Directives on credit institutions, funds, solvency ratios and the provision of financial services (the Second Banking Directive of 1989). Credit institutions may now establish branches freely in other member states and throughout the **European Economic Area** (EEA) while remaining subject to 'home country control', the conditions for which have been established on an agreed basis. To date, less progress has been made with opening up the insurance sector. This very complex field may be better understood with the aid of John A. Usher, *The Law of Money and Financial Services in the European Community* (Oxford, 1994).

Finland

Finland's proximity to the Soviet Union (in Tsarist times it was part of Russian territory as the Grand Duchy of Finland) meant that the country's approach to all alliances with the countries of the West was extremely cautious. Although a member of the **Council of Europe** and an active partner in the **Nordic Council**, Finland did not join the United Nations until 1955 and was at first only an associate member of the **European Free Trade Association** (EFTA) (full member from 1986). As an EFTA state, Finland signed the free trade agreement with the Community that came into effect in January 1973 and later the agreement establishing the **European Economic Area** (EEA). Finland applied for full membership of the Community on 18 March 1992. The motives were largely political in the sense that it was a means of emerging from the long shadow cast by the former USSR. Like Sweden, Finland has a long-standing *de facto* commitment to **neutrality**. However, since the **Maastricht Treaty** does not establish a military alliance and allows member states to continue with individual defence arrangements, Finland considers its provisions to be not incompatible with neutrality.

The Commission's **Opinion**, published later that year (*Bulletin of the European Communities*, supplement 6/92) noted that in a speech in Bruges (28 October 1992) President Koivisto accepted 'the *acquis communautaire*, the Maastricht Treaty and the *finalité politique* of the European Union'. The problems identified in the Commission's generally favourable Opinion included the need to make adjustments to the Finnish system of agricultural support and to the various state monopolies. Finnish industry and commerce were already adapting to the *acquis communautaire*, but certain anomalies remained in the fields of company taxation, direct taxation and social security. A peculiarity of the Finnish constitution is the autonomous status of the Swedish-speaking Åland Islands in the Gulf of Bothnia. This is of particular relevance to environmental legislation and to certain tax questions, for which the islands' Assembly has responsibility.

Negotiations with Finland were completed in March 1994, and resulted, *inter alia*, in a new Objective 6 category of region being created in relation to the **structural funds**. This allows aid to be given in recognition of under-population and the peculiarly harsh conditions affecting agriculture in Finland and Sweden. The **European Parliament** gave its assent to Finnish **accession** in May 1994. An advisory referendum was held on 16 October 1994, membership of the Union gaining the support of 56.9 per cent of the vote; the Åland Islands also voted in favour in a separate referendum. This was confirmed in the Finnish Parliament on 18 November

1994, and Finland became the fourteenth member of the Union on 1 January 1995.

The addition of Finnish to the list of official **languages** poses a particular problem since it is not related to any other language spoken in the Union.

Fontainebleau Agreement

The Fontainebleau Agreement of June 1984 marked the conclusion of the long-standing dispute over the United Kingdom's contribution to the **Budget** of the European Community (see **British Budget problem**). At Fontainebleau the **European Council** agreed to grant the United Kingdom an **abatement**, calculated annually, on the element of the British contribution based on value-added tax (VAT). The system has remained in force and was renewed until 1999 at the Edinburgh meeting of the European Council in December 1992.

Fortress Europe

'Fortress Europe' is a phrase used to embody the fears of the European Union's principal trading partners and supporters of free trade that the Union is becoming more protectionist. Such fears were prompted in the late 1980s by the moves to complete the 1992 **Single Market** programme, since it appeared that some member states were prepared to see the removal of barriers to trade within the Community only if it were accompanied by a strengthening of measures to control imports from non-member countries. It was thought that some member states would like to extend **Community preference** beyond agricultural trade to trade in manufactured goods and services. The lengthy dispute with the United States over agricultural export subsidies and the long-delayed **General Agreement on Tariffs and Trade** (GATT) settlement gave some substance to these fears, but on the whole, in spite of recession and high unemployment, the European Union has not resorted to protectionism.

'Fortress Europe' has a definite pejorative ring by virtue of its echo of Nazi Germany's *Festung Europa*, suggesting both impregnable defences and economic autarky.

Fouchet Plan

The Fouchet Plan of 1961–2 was a determined attempt by the French President, **Charles de Gaulle**, to alter the institutional balance of the European Community in favour of **intergovernmentalism** and in the process to establish a form of political cooperation that would secure Europe's independence from the Atlantic Alliance and the United States. Although unsuccessful, this initiative divided the advocates of closer European integration – with some, such as **Jean Monnet**, initially anxious to exploit de Gaulle's apparent preparedness to consolidate the political dimension of the Community – and provided a significant foretaste of the kind of intransigence which de Gaulle and his government were later to display on a number of European issues.

On 5 September 1960 de Gaulle unexpectedly stated at one of his regular press conferences in the Elysée Palace that 'ensuring regular cooperation in Western Europe is something which France considers desirable, possible and practicable in the political . . . and defence fields'. To promote this, he advocated 'regular organized concertation by the governments responsible', based on a new intergovernmental structure, answerable to an assembly of national parliamentarians and enjoying public endorsement by means of a 'vast European referendum'. The emphasis on strong ministerial or executive authority based on a direct mandate from the electorate – one of the most important features of Gaullism in France – was to be replicated at European level. Five months later, on 10 February 1961, the first-ever **summit** was hosted by de Gaulle in Paris. At this meeting he convinced the leaders of the five other member states to establish a special committee to consider possible amendments to the **Treaty of Rome** (although not formally constituted as an **Intergovernmental Conference** (IGC), this body served the same purpose). The intention was to add some form of political cooperation among the member states to the existing structure. The committee, chaired by Christian Fouchet, then a senior French diplomat and subsequently a minister under de Gaulle, met between March 1961 and April 1962. A second summit at Bad Godesberg in July 1961 reiterated political support for closer cooperation on foreign and security issues.

Instead of offering proposals likely to command consensus Fouchet attempted to redesign the Community's whole institutional structure, based on a stronger foreign policy component as a pretext for making the Community a looser, more intergovernmental organization.

The initial Fouchet proposals envisaged a 'union of states' to coexist with the existing Community in a number of new areas, most notably foreign policy, defence and culture. It would be governed by a political council of heads of government (or their foreign ministers) acting by **unanimity** and responsible to an assembly of national parliamentarians. The **Commission** would be bypassed by a new Paris-based 'political commission' of national civil servants (similar in format to the body now known as **COREPER**). The first draft of the Fouchet Plan, tabled in November 1961, aroused little enthusiasm, especially from the **Benelux** countries, which regarded the Commission as a safeguard for the interest of small countries and were opposed to any diminution of its authority. Germany, under **Konrad Adenauer**, held back from criticizing the texts in the hope of reaching an accommodation. However, a second draft, tabled in January 1962, envisaged crucial additional changes that accentuated still further the intergovernmental character of the proposed 'union', with a new network of ministerial committees to parallel the original **Council of Ministers**, and the economic aspects of the existing Community being potentially subsumed within the 'union', so undermining the existing institutions and the supranational character of **Community law**. The second draft also foresaw European foreign and defence cooperation taking place outside the framework of the Atlantic Alliance. The five other member states indicated that they could not accept a revised European Community along anything like these lines. The negotiations were suspended on 17 April 1962 and never resumed.

At a press conference on 15 May 1962 de Gaulle launched a dramatic verbal assault on the Community institutions, directed in particular against Commission President **Walter Hallstein**. He satirized its functionaries as 'stateless people' and its technocratic jargon as a 'Volapük' (an artificial international language akin to Esperanto). He declared that it was the United States, not the people of the Community, who would act as 'federator' of Europe, and that 'only the states are valid, legitimate and capable of achievement ... At present there is and can be no Europe other than a Europe of States – except of course a Europe of myths, fictions and pageants.' Exasperated by the growing bitterness and force of de Gaulle's attack on the Community, five pro-European ministers resigned from his government, including Maurice Schumann, a former foreign minister under the Fourth Republic, and Pierre Pflimlin, the penultimate Prime Minister of the Fourth Republic (in 1958) and subsequently a president of the **European Parliament** (1984–7). In addition, 296 French deputies signed a 'European Manifesto' protesting at the increasingly anti-European stance of the President.

The shock delivered to the Community by the Fouchet débâcle was severe. Although in Bad Godesberg they had expressed their intention to continue meeting regularly, the heads of government did not in fact reconvene for six years. A period of stagnation and crisis began, with de Gaulle announcing France's veto of the first British application to join the Community in January 1963, the Community becoming increasingly bogged down at French insistence in complex negotiations on the financing of the **Common Agricultural Policy** (CAP), France threatening to leave the Community in October 1964 unless agreement was reached on the CAP and, finally, in 1965 France boycotting the Council of Ministers in order to prevent the automatic introduction of **qualified majority voting** (QMV) planned for 1966 (the **empty chair crisis**). The consequent

Luxembourg Compromise, which allowed unanimity to prevail wherever important national interests were at stake, frustrated EC decision-making for the next 20 years.

'Fouchet Plan' is still used as a term of abuse amongst supporters of European integration. When in 1985 **Jacques Delors** heard of a Franco-German proposal to create a secretary-general who would direct the Community's foreign policy, he intervened with President **François Mitterrand** to denounce the idea as redolent of the Fouchet Plan. The proposal was withdrawn (Charles Grant, *Delors: The House that Jacques Built*).

Four freedoms

The 'four freedoms' that underpin the **Single Market** are, in the order in which they are listed in Article 3 of the **Treaty of Rome**, the **free movement of goods**, the **free movement of persons**, **freedom to provide services** and free movement of capital (see **capital movements**).

France

Of all the member states of the European Union, France is unquestionably the one with the best claim to have shaped its political development. France has provided both the impulses and the hesitations: the country of **Jean Monnet** and of the **Schuman Plan**, it is also the country that destroyed the **European Defence Community** and later instigated the **empty chair crisis**. All the enthusiasm and all the reticence that have shaped the European Union as it exists today may be found in France.

Amongst the central facts in the outlook of any French person in the early 1950s was the knowledge that three times in as many generations France had been attacked by Germany. The Schuman Plan was born not solely from a desire to put relations between states on an entirely new footing but from the idea of containment. If Germany could be placed within a supranational framework that allowed it to recover its prosperity and self-respect and yet required it to act responsibly, then France would benefit. France was confident of being able to exercise a controlling influence over the direction that the countries united within that framework would take. This had proved true in the **European Coal and Steel Community** (ECSC) and there was no reason why it should not continue to be true as **the Six** set themselves more ambitious goals within the **European Economic Community** (EEC).

Charles de Gaulle returned to power in 1958, the year in which the EEC came into operation. Whatever misgivings he had about its supranational character, he was sympathetic to its basic aim of containing

Germany. But he saw immediately that the admission of the United Kingdom would destroy the nicely calculated balance of power that allowed France to retain political hegemony. Primarily for this reason, but also because he shared neither British sympathy with the Americans nor their attachment to free trade, he vetoed British accession twice, in 1963 and in 1967. France was well aware that the other member states favoured British accession, but, as was also the case with the 1962 **Fouchet Plan** and later the so-called **Luxembourg Compromise** of 1966, it was perfectly content to be in a minority of one. At the same time de Gaulle established good relations with **Konrad Adenauer** and, with the 1963 Elysée Treaty, laid the foundations for **Franco-German cooperation**.

The resignation of de Gaulle in 1969 led to a marked change in French attitudes towards European integration. President Georges Pompidou allowed the United Kingdom, Denmark and Ireland to join the Community (endorsed by a **referendum** in France in April 1972). His successor, **Valéry Giscard d'Estaing**, was and remains a convinced pro-European, yet in his proposal to strengthen the intergovernmental component in Community decision-making by establishing a **European Council**, Giscard was giving expression to a traditionally French view of where ultimate power should lie. It was Giscard too who in 1977 was strongly opposed to **Roy Jenkins**, as President of the **Commission**, representing the Community as a whole at meetings of the **Group of Seven**.

Institutional questions aside, there are other areas of policy in which France has found itself in a minority. France has no record of enthusiasm for increasing the number of member states. This was understandable when Spanish accession was being negotiated, since Spain was thought to be a rival to French interests, especially in agriculture, but it is in fact part of a wider pattern of opposition to any diminution of French influence. In security issues France has chosen to remain outside the integrated military structure of the **North Atlantic Treaty Organization** (NATO) since 1966 and is jealous of its status as a nuclear power. In spite of Franco-German cooperation, France was most unwilling to allow the number of German seats in the **European Parliament** to be increased to take account of reunification, and threatened to block a settlement until **Strasbourg** was finally chosen as the seat of the Parliament (see **seat of the institutions**). It was France which, by raising last-minute objections to the Uruguay Round of the **General Agreement on Tariffs and Trade** (GATT) negotiations, almost blocked the agreement. And it is France which continually pushes Union rules on **state aids** to the limit.

Until recently it could have been said that support for European integration extended to all political parties in France with the exception of old-guard Communists and the far right. However, the debate on the

Maastricht Treaty, culminating in the extremely narrow 'Yes' vote in the referendum of September 1992, opened up clear divisions in the centre-right, where once again Gaullist ideas on the supremacy of the nation-state are in evidence. French Members of the European Parliament (MEPs) are scattered across more political groups than MEPs of any other nationality. However, since the 1980s France has drawn advantage from having, in **François Mitterrand** and **Jacques Delors**, two of the most influential personalities in European politics. Whatever disagreements there may be between and within the parties on European issues, France is absolutely determined not to be outstripped by Germany. It is this determination that underpins the so-called *Franc fort* policy of matching the pace set by the Deutsche Mark, even at the price of high unemployment. Above all, France wishes to remain, with Germany, in the position of leadership in Europe established over four decades, and to which the country feels entitled.

Franco-British union

In June 1940 the imminent surrender of France to Germany prompted **Jean Monnet**, then working in London as Chairman of the Anglo-French Coordinating Committee, to propose that the British and French governments should make a declaration proclaiming the 'indissoluble union' of the two countries. This union would entail common citizenship, a common currency, a customs union and joint armed forces. The principle was approved by **Winston Churchill** and by the Cabinet, and the proposal was communicated by **Charles de Gaulle** to the French Cabinet, which had left Paris and was meeting in Bordeaux. By 18 June, however, it was clear that with the resignation of Paul Reynaud, the French Prime Minister, the French surrender was complete and that a declaration of union would not help to keep France in the war. The episode forms the first chapter of Monnet's *Memoirs*.

Franco-German cooperation

The cornerstone of postwar cooperation between France and Germany is the Treaty of the Elysée, signed by **Charles de Gaulle** and **Konrad Adenauer** on 22 January 1963. The 1950s had been marked by a gradual convergence of French and German interests. Both countries were founder members of the **European Communities**, both were members of the **North Atlantic Treaty Organization** (NATO) (France 1949, West Germany 1955) and, most importantly, they had resolved their long-standing territorial dispute over the **Saarland**. Even though at the time the Treaty was signed France and Germany were divided over the question of the United Kingdom's application to join the Community, the Treaty was a very explicit statement, enjoying cross-party support, of the two countries' determination to pursue their interests in common.

The Treaty provides a framework for cooperation in three main areas. First, it provides for regular Franco-German summits and for meetings every three months between the ministers for foreign affairs. These meetings have not only been a useful forum for the discussion of general foreign policy questions, but they have also given rise to some of the most important initiatives in the field of European integration, such as direct elections to the **European Parliament** and the **European Monetary System** (EMS). They have also been supplemented by other forms of foreign affairs cooperation: for example, in May 1991 the French and German ambassadors accredited to the countries of central and eastern Europe met in Weimar to discuss political developments in the former Soviet bloc.

The second and most controversial area of Franco-German cooperation set out in the Treaty is defence and security. For many years the Treaty provisions remained a dead letter. This was, perhaps, hardly surprising in the light of the confusion and acrimony that followed the failure to establish the **European Defence Community** and the general willingness to rely on the Americans. Not until 1987 did French and German troops take part in joint manoeuvres. The same year, at a Franco-German summit in Karlsruhe, **François Mitterrand** and **Helmut Kohl** announced that a Franco-German Security Council would be set up: this was formalized the following year in a **protocol** signed in Bonn. The Bonn meeting also agreed on the joint development of a combat helicopter (Tiger) and a Franco-German brigade of 4,200 troops, operational since 1991. More recently, at the La Rochelle summit in May 1992, agreement was reached on a more ambitious Franco-German army corps (35,000 troops) with its headquarters in Strasbourg (see **Eurocorps**; see also **European Armaments Agency**).

The third area of Franco-German cooperation identified in the Treaty is education. At the first Franco-German summit, in Bonn in July 1963, the two governments agreed on a 'Youth Bureau' with its headquarters at Bad Honnef, near Bonn. Since its creation this Bureau has overseen some 5 million exchanges between French and German schoolchildren and some 3,000 twinnings between schools. Several thousand French students study in German universities, and vice versa. The work of the Bureau is supplemented by initiatives in the field of language teaching and cultural cooperation (agreed at the Frankfurt summit of 1986).

The Bonn summit of January 1988 established not only a Security Council (see above) but also an Economic and Financial Council under a separate protocol to the Treaty. This protocol enjoins the Council every year 'to examine the broad outlines of the national budgets before their adoption by the governments and the vote in the national parliaments' and in general terms to coordinate French and German economic policies as closely as possible.

Franco-German cooperation is overseen within each government by interministerial committees. In addition to the specific fields noted above cooperation between the two countries is extensive in other areas. Each is the other's most important trading partner, and each invests heavily in the other. The machinery for cooperation set out in the Elysée Treaty has underpinned the very good relations, political and personal, that have existed, regardless of party, between French and German leaders for more than three decades. And if some unresolved anxieties remain (over German interest rates, for example, or over what the Germans see as French laxity in environmental matters), Franco-German cooperation has not only brought benefits to the two countries concerned but also provided the Union as a whole with the stability that flows from a common sense of purpose between its two leading member states.

Francovich case

The Francovich case (*Francovich and others* v *Italy*, Cases C6/90 and C9/90) established the principle that the adoption of a Directive (see **legal instruments**) by the **Council of Ministers** confers rights on individuals, even in the event of a member state having failed to transpose the Directive into national law. An individual who suffers damages as a consequence of such a failure may have a claim for compensation against the authorities of that state.

Mr Francovich was an employee of an Italian firm that went bankrupt. A 1980 Directive on the protection of employees in such cases of insolvency had not been given effect in Italian law. The **Court of Justice** ruled that Mr Francovich could claim appropriate compensation from the Italian state.

The Francovich case reinforced the general obligation laid upon member states by the **Treaty of Rome** to 'take all appropriate measures . . . to ensure fulfilment of the obligations arising out of this Treaty or resulting from action taken by the institutions of the Community' (Article 5 EEC) and is of great importance as an example of how **Community law** serves to extend individual rights. It is discussed more fully in Weatherill and Beaumont, *EC Law*.

Fraud

The **Maastricht Treaty** added a new Article 209a to the **Treaty of Rome**:

Member States shall take the same measures to counter fraud affecting the financial interests of the Community as they take to counter
fraud affecting their own financial interests . . . [They] shall coordinate their action aimed at protecting the financial interests of the
Community against fraud . . . [and] shall organize, with the help of
the Commission, close and regular cooperation between the competent departments of their administrations.

Fraud, especially in respect of the **Common Agricultural Policy** (CAP),
is a problem of long standing. Estimates of its extent differ widely; what
seems certain is that reported fraud is only a small proportion of the
whole. In 1994, 4,264 cases of fraud or 'irregularity' were reported,
involving over 1 billion ECUs (less than 1.5 per cent of the **Budget**). Of
the sums lost through fraud, only a very small percentage is recovered. A
recent report by the House of Lords Select Committee on the European
Communities (*Financial Control and Fraud in the Community*, July 1994)
described such losses as a 'public scandal'.

The same report noted a 'worrying absence of indignation at the
amount of fraud and mismanagement' and 'a lack of political will . . . to
take remedial action', in spite of the fact that the **European Council** has
discussed fraud at three meetings (Edinburgh, December 1992; Copenhagen, June 1993; Essen, December 1994). Under the Maastricht Treaty the
Court of Auditors has been given new status and can now, if necessary,
bring actions in the **Court of Justice**. The **Commission** has put forward
a set of proposals for dealing with fraud and established a new unit
(known as UCLAF, *Unité coordinatrice pour la lutte anti-fraude*) reporting
directly to the secretary-general. In April 1994 the British government
proposed a **joint action** under the **Justice and Home Affairs** (JHA)
provisions of the Maastricht Treaty for measures that would, *inter alia*,
resolve some of the legal difficulties. Under this joint action, fraud would
become a criminal, extraditable offence in all member states, attracting
heavy penalties. An Advisory Committee for the Coordination of Fraud
Prevention has been set up, composed of 50 experts from all member
states, and a smaller group to expedite the recovery of misappropriated
funds. The Commission has also set up a 'fraud hotline' in each member
state, a telephone number that members of the public can ring free of
charge to report suspected fraud.

Although under Article 205 EEC the Commission is responsible for
implementing the Budget of the Union 'having regard to the principles
of sound financial management', in fact the disbursement of 80 per cent of
Union funds is in the hands of member states. It is sometimes suspected
that those states that are net beneficiaries of the Budget do not share the

keen interest in fraud taken by those that are net contributors. It may also be the case that some national authorities, upon whom the responsibility for reporting fraud rests, prefer not to take action that reflects discredit on their own citizens, and that may result in repayments having to be made to the Budget. Few states support an extension of the power of the Commission or the Court of Auditors to undertake investigations on national territory.

As with most wrong-doing, the best deterrent is the likelihood of detection and the prospect of heavy penalties. It is proposed that legislation and procedures with a bearing on the disbursement of funds should be made simpler, easier to interpret and easier to enforce, and so less vulnerable to fraud. Financial accountability should be more widely disseminated within the Commission, rather than concentrated, as at present, in the financial controller. Ministers in the Council and Members of the **European Parliament** (MEPs) should pay more attention to the recommendations of the Court of Auditors. The Parliament has set up a Committee of Inquiry (Article 138c EEC) to draw attention to the scale of fraud.

The best studies of fraud are the report by the House of Lords Select Committee noted above and an earlier report of February 1989, *Fraud against the Community*. Both contain testimony from expert witnesses and case-histories, which shed light not only on the kinds of fraud that are perpetrated but also on the relations between the institutions, national and European, concerned with the fight against fraud. The annual reports by the Court of Auditors are also useful; the report for 1993 is particularly critical of the Commission, especially in relation to the **European Agricultural Guidance and Guarantee Fund** (EAGGF). There is a useful and unbiased study of fraud in Dick Ruimschotel, 'The EC Budget: ten per cent fraud? A policy analysis approach', *Journal of Common Market Studies*, Vol. 32, no. 3, September 1994.

Free movement of goods

Perhaps the most fundamental of the '**four freedoms**', the free movement of goods within a **customs union** lies at the heart of the **Treaty of Rome**. By this means **the Six** sought, in the words of the preamble to the Treaty, to lay 'the foundations of an ever closer union among the peoples of Europe'.

Article 3 EEC refers to 'an **internal market** characterized by the abolition, as between Member States, of obstacles to the free movement of goods, persons, services and capital'. Article 7a EEC defines the internal market as 'an area without internal frontiers in which the free movement of goods, persons, services and capital is ensured'. The preamble to the Treaty places the free movement of goods not only within a broader political context but marks it out as a European contribution to the development of closer, mutually advantageous trading relations worldwide.

Article 9 EEC prohibits the imposition of 'customs duties on imports and exports and ... all charges having equivalent effect' between member states. Articles 30 and 34 EEC prohibit quantitative restrictions (i.e., quotas) in similar terms, although in fact there were few such quotas on trade between the Six when the Treaty came into force (1958). The Treaty laid down a 12-year transitional period during which the removal of customs duties and quotas was to be effected, but in the event the removal was accomplished 18 months ahead of schedule. This allowed the **Common External Tariff** to be applied from 1 July 1968.

The Treaty provisions left a number of instruments in the hands of national authorities wishing to favour or protect their domestic markets, of which the most important were tax measures (although Article 95 EEC prohibits discriminatory taxation) and product specifications. These led to a number of cases in the **Court of Justice**, many concerned with what the Treaty references to 'charges having equivalent effect' (see above) were intended to cover. Member states sought to justify product specifications on (sometimes dubious) health and safety, consumer protection or environmental grounds. It was the Commission's attempt to lay down Europe-wide specifications that would enable goods to circulate freely which became known as the **harmonization** programme (see also **Articles 100 and 100a**).

Eventually, it was the Court, in its 1979 judgment in the case known as '**Cassis de Dijon**', that laid down a new basis for ensuring the free movement of goods. Known as mutual recognition, it means essentially that goods in free and legal circulation in one member state cannot be excluded from others. Six years later, the 1985 **Cockfield White Paper** on the **Single Market** identified the remaining **non-tariff barriers** to the free movement of goods, dividing them into technical barriers (differing product specifications), physical barriers (frontier controls, customs formalities) and fiscal barriers (see **tax harmonization**). Many of them were simply bureaucratic: the **Kangaroo Group** published a list of the 46 documents needed by the driver of a semi-articulated lorry travelling from West Germany to Italy via Austria. The White Paper pointed out that one of the main reasons why the removal of these barriers was such a slow process was the requirement under Article 100 EEC that agreement in the **Council of Ministers** must be unanimous. This led to the introduction in the **Single European Act** (SEA) the following year of a new Article 100a EEC allowing for the extension of **qualified majority voting** (QMV) to this area. Other measures were also taken, such as the introduction of the so-called Single Administrative Document to ease the crossing of internal frontiers, the abolition of road haulage quotas (see **common transport policy**), the simplification of transit procedures, and the removal of animal and plant health controls from the point of entry to offices inside member states. Frontier controls affecting the free movement of goods were finally removed on 1 January 1993.

Community law relating to the free movement of goods is reviewed in detail in Weatherill and Beaumont, *EC Law*.

Free movement of persons

Four Articles of the **Treaty of Rome** have a direct bearing on free movement. Article 3 EEC refers to 'an **internal market** characterized by the abolition, as between Member States, of obstacles to the free movement of goods, persons, services and capital'. Article 8a EEC says that 'every citizen of the Union shall have the right to move and reside freely within the territory of the Member States' (see **citizenship**). Article 48 EEC lays down the principle of free movement for workers, 'subject to limitations justified on grounds of public policy, public security or public health', although employment in the public service is excluded from this provision (see **discrimination on grounds of nationality**).

Because an open labour market was an essential component of an internal market, legislation to give effect to these Treaty requirements concentrated initially on 'workers'. The right of workers to move and reside freely within the member states with a view to taking up or seeking employment was laid down in a Regulation and a Directive (see **legal instruments**) of 1968. With the aid of rulings from the **Court of Justice**, the definition of 'worker' was gradually extended (see also **Van Duyn case**). By the mid-1980s it was obvious that the drive to complete the **Single Market** should include the removal of frontier controls between member states, and that the Treaty requirement for the free movement of 'persons' would have to be given legislative form. The so-called Palma Document, discussed at the Madrid meeting of the **European Council** in June 1989, identified the priorities for action. In 1990 the **Council of Ministers** adopted three linked Directives on the right of residence for students, retired people and nationals of member states not covered by other provisions. Basically, any citizen of the Union may now reside anywhere in the Union as long as he or she is covered by sickness insurance and is in receipt of welfare benefits or other income sufficient 'to avoid becoming a burden on the social assistance system of the host Member State' (Article 1 of Directive 90/364). The **European passport** is supposed to make it quicker and easier to recognize citizens of the Union at frontiers.

However, the commitment in the Treaty is to free movement for 'persons', not solely for citizens of the Union. Relaxation or removal of controls at internal frontiers was linked to a strengthening of controls at external borders, and hence common agreement on immigration, visas, the right of asylum and other matters with a bearing on the treatment of nationals of non-member countries. Discussion of these points soon revealed profound differences of attitude amongst member states. In 1985 those who were willing to make rapid progress signed the **Schengen Agreement**. Limited progress was also made in 1991 with the **External Frontiers Convention** and the **Dublin Asylum Convention**; neither has yet been ratified by all member states (see also **joint list**).

Frontier controls, internal and external, are now dealt with under the **Justice and Home Affairs** (JHA) provisions of the **Maastricht Treaty**, which require them to be regarded 'as matters of common interest' (Article K1 TEU). The exception to this is visa policy, which is covered in a new Article 100c added to the Treaty of Rome. The positioning of this Article places it firmly within that portion of the Treaty dealing with the approximation of laws within the Single Market. This enjoins the Council, 'acting unanimously . . . [to] determine the third countries whose nationals must be in possession of a visa when crossing the external borders of the Member States'. However, from 1 January 1996 such decisions may be taken by **qualified majority voting** (QMV). A list of third countries was drawn up in this connection and was agreed in September 1995: part of the argument was concerned with the need to extend visa controls to nationals of certain Commonwealth countries who do not at present require visas to enter the United Kingdom.

As one of the '**four freedoms**', free movement of persons is not only one of the most basic goals of the Treaty, it is also of great symbolic importance as part of a **People's Europe**. The right of free movement now exists throughout the whole **European Economic Area** (EEA; the five **Nordic Council** countries already operate a passport union for their own nationals). However, at least until police cooperation (see **Europol**) is stepped up, controls are likely to be maintained at least at some internal frontiers as part of the fight against terrorism, organized crime and drug-trafficking. Equally, as long as there is an obligation to offer proof of identity when passing from one member state to another it will be argued that free movement has not yet been achieved. Free movement of persons raises, and will continue to raise, important and sensitive issues, such as the use of identity cards and the treatment of persons resident in a member state who are not citizens of the Union. There are also substantial costs involved in some of the proposals: for example, the redesigning of most major airports (which are both internal and external frontiers) to allow citizens of the Union and nationals of non-member states to be treated separately, depending on whether they are travelling within the Union, travelling to or from a destination outside the Union, or are in transit.

A comprehensive survey of the arguments and issues raised by free movement of persons may be found in a report by the House of Lords Select Committee on the European Communities, *Visas and Control of External Borders of the Member States* (July 1994). See also Weatherill and Beaumont, *EC Law*.

Free trade area

A free trade area exists when two or more states (normally but not necessarily contiguous) agree to remove all restrictions on trade between them, but continue to make individual arrangements for their trade with countries not party to the free trade agreement. A **customs union** denotes not only free trade between participating states, but also a common set of arrangements with respect to trade with other countries. A common market is a customs union within which the free movement of goods, services, capital and labour is guaranteed (see **Single Market**). These broad distinctions serve to explain the difference between, for example, the **European Free Trade Association** (EFTA) and the **European Economic Community** (EEC).

Freedom of establishment

Freedom of establishment – the right to practise a trade or profession – is guaranteed for the nationals of the member states throughout the European Union by Articles 52–54 of the **Treaty of Rome**, which cover both employed and self-employed persons. Article 55 EEC excludes 'activities . . . connected, even occasionally, with the exercise of official authority' (see **discrimination on the grounds of nationality**). Freedom of establishment, which is an essential component of the wider issue of **free movement of persons** in the **Single Market**, is facilitated by the **mutual recognition of qualifications** (see also **freedom to provide services**).

The basic legislation on freedom of establishment was agreed in the form of a 'General Programme' in 1962. On the basis of this programme proposals were brought forward by the **Commission** on particular sectors of economic activity, not including the professions, since progress first had to be made on the mutual recognition of qualifications. In the mid-1970s a number of judgments of the **Court of Justice** helped to accelerate the process of removing national restrictions on freedom of establishment: for example, doctors have been able to practise anywhere in the member states since 1976. With some exceptions, it is now the case that nationals of the member states are entitled to practise a trade or profession not only anywhere in the Union but throughout the **European Economic Area**. This very complex subject is fully covered in Chapter 19 of Weatherill and Beaumont, *EC Law*.

Freedom to provide services

Freedom to provide services is different from **freedom of establishment** in that it is concerned with performance of services anywhere within the Union without the provider of the service having his or her place of business established in the country where the service is performed. The **Single Market** is defined in Article 3 of the **Treaty of Rome** as being 'characterized by the abolition, as between Member States, of obstacles to the free movement of goods, persons, services and capital'.

Article 59 EEC requires member states to remove all restrictions on freedom to provide services with respect to citizens of the Union (see **citizenship**). The freedom may also be extended to nationals of non-member countries. Article 60 EEC makes it clear that the Treaty provisions on services are supplementary to those relating to goods, persons and capital, and identifies four types of service in particular: industrial, commercial, professional and craft industries. Special considerations apply to transport, banking and insurance under Article 61 EEC (see **common transport policy, financial services**). Member states are able to impose restrictions on public policy grounds and to exclude services involving the exercise of official authority.

A 'General Programme' adopted in 1962 identified the restrictions to be removed, such as those based on nationality, residence, qualifications and procedures for the cross-border transfer of funds to pay for the service. The General Programme was followed by legislation on particular professions, helped partly by rulings of the **Court of Justice**. However, it was not until the late 1980s, when substantial progress was finally made with the **mutual recognition of qualifications**, that freedom to provide services became more or less assured; it now applies throughout the **European Economic Area**. The services sector accounts for some 60 per cent of jobs and 65 per cent of gross domestic product (GDP) within the European Union but only 18 per cent of internal trade. Much more detail on the application of **Community law** to the services sector may be found in Weatherill and Beaumont, *EC Law*.

Functionalism

Functionalism is one of several theories of integration (see also **federation**,

intergovernmentalism). The term, which dates from the 1960s, denotes a form of integration between states that is based upon practical cooperation in well-defined areas with a minimum of institutional apparatus. By contrast with federalism, functionalism involves no institutional blueprint and is driven by economic, social and technical imperatives rather than by political forces. However, functionalists believe that as states acquire the habit of working together the number of areas in which they are willing to cooperate tends to be gradually extended (the concept of 'spillover'), a process that may lead eventually to demands for democratic control in these areas to be exercised by new supranational institutions. The term 'neofunctionalism' has been coined to denote the use of functionalist techniques to secure federalist objectives, of which the best example is the **European Coal and Steel Community** (ECSC; see also *engrenage*).

Applied to European integration, functionalism has always had an attraction for the British and the Scandinavians as being both more 'pragmatic' and less likely, at least in the short term, to raise sensitive issues of **sovereignty**. Attempts in the **Maastricht Treaty** and elsewhere to define more clearly the extent and nature of Community action – as opposed to action by national, regional, or local authorities – in the name of **subsidiarity** may be interpreted in functionalist terms as placing limits on the 'spillover' (see above).

Future financing

The debate over the future financing of the European Union (i.e., the overall size and structure of the Union's income and expenditure) spanned the period from 1986 until the Edinburgh meeting of the **European Council** in December 1992. It centred upon two 'packages' of proposals, known as Delors I and Delors II after **Jacques Delors**, the President of the **Commission**.

At the London meeting of the European Council in December 1986 Delors was invited to make a report on the finances of the Community. The accession of Portugal and Spain at the beginning of the year was placing new demands on the **structural funds**, and movements in world agricultural prices meant that once again expenditure under the **Common Agricultural Policy** (CAP) was threatening to run out of control. Delors's forecast was that the Community would run out of money in 1987, and the meeting invited him to make proposals to place the Community's finances on a firmer footing.

His package, entitled *Making a Success of the Single Act*, was drawn up two months later. By referring to the **Single European Act** (SEA) Delors hoped to get the member states to see his proposals in the context of the extra solidarity, or **cohesion**, that would be needed if the SEA were not simply to make the rich regions richer and the poor poorer. The SEA also envisaged more Community activity in areas such as **research** on a scale that would require extra resources in the **Budget**. In his proposals he suggested doubling the structural funds over five years, more spending on research, new measures to contain agricultural surpluses and a new system of agreeing the Budget based on a five-year framework covering the main items of expenditure (the 'financial perspective').

The reactions of the member states were mixed. The German government did not like the prospect of still higher net payments to the Budget arising from the increase in the structural funds, and the British government of **Margaret Thatcher** wanted tighter controls on CAP expenditure and stricter **budgetary discipline** overall. By the end of 1987 agreement had still not been reached, and a special meeting of the European Council in Brussels was called for February 1988.

In Brussels the European Council averted the crisis by agreeing on a doubling of the structural funds over six years, on a new **own resource** based on the gross national product (GNP) of member states, on a guideline limiting the growth of CAP expenditure, and a guarantee that by 1992 the Budget overall would represent no more than 1.2 per cent of Community gross domestic product (GDP; the 'own resources ceiling'). A further review of future financing was fixed for 1992.

Delors II, entitled *From the Single Act to Maastricht and Beyond: The Means to Match Our Ambitions*, was published in February 1992. The five-year (1992–7) financial perspective at the heart of the proposal indicated further substantial increases in the structural funds (now incorporating a **Cohesion Fund**) and in the very modest sum set aside for 'external actions', to allow the Community to respond to requests for financial assistance from central and eastern Europe. Overall, as a proportion of the Community's GNP, the Budget would rise from 1.2 to 1.37 per cent. In a revised financial perspective of November 1992 this was reduced to 1.32 per cent, and the system of own resources altered to the advantage of those countries with a GNP of less than 90 per cent of the Community average, with effect from 1995.

The Edinburgh meeting at which agreement was reached on the Delors II package took place against a background of severe public expenditure constraints in several member states, including most importantly Germany (as a result of **German reunification**). At the same time other member states and the Commission were seeking to develop new spending policies. In the event a seven-year (to 1999) financial perspective was drawn up, which allowed the own resources ceiling to remain fixed at 1.25 per cent of Community GNP until 1995, and thereafter to rise to 1.27 per cent by 1999. The own resources system was altered to lower the ceiling on contributions based on value-added tax (VAT), with other changes to benefit poorer countries by making the system less 'regressive' (i.e., weighing more heavily on poorer countries). The guideline for agricultural expenditure was reconfirmed, meaning that by 1999 CAP expenditure should be less than half the Budget. The structural funds were to be increased by about 60 per cent over the period, and spending on external actions by about 40 per cent (see **Edinburgh Growth Initiative**). The Commission was invited to make recommendations on a possible new own resource by 1999.

In sum, the Edinburgh agreement allowed for increases in the Budget less than half as large as those originally proposed in Delors II. It reconfirmed the agreement on the rebate for the United Kingdom (see **British Budget problem**). Overall, the six-year debate on future financing reflected the shifting balance between rich and poor member states brought about by the accession of Portugal and Spain, and, in particular, the concerns of poorer countries about the effects of the **Single Market** programme. It reflected too a number of external pressures, such as those from central and eastern Europe and, as far as CAP expenditure was concerned, from the United States and others in the context of the negotiations in the **General Agreement on Tariffs and Trade** (GATT).

General Agreement on Tariffs and Trade (GATT)

Based in Geneva, GATT was originally conceived as an independent agency of the United Nations, to be known as the International Trade Organization (ITO). The Agreement was negotiated in 1947 and came into effect with 23 signatories on 1 January 1948. However, difficulties arose with the ratification of the ITO Convention, and the project was abandoned. This left the Agreement as the only multilateral instrument for the orderly conduct of international trade, the lowering of tariffs, and the resolution of disputes. A small secretariat was established in Geneva, the number of officials slowly increasing to today's total of about 400 people. Signatory states of GATT are together responsible for about 90 per cent of world trade. Amongst the conclusions of the recent Uruguay Round was the decision to set up a World Trade Organization (WTO) in place of GATT. Geneva was preferred to Bonn as the seat of the WTO.

The GATT convention enjoins signatory states to reduce tariffs and not to engage in unilateral action likely to damage trade. It defines certain basic terms (such as 'dumping') used in international trade. It prohibits quantitative restrictions. It makes provision for retaliatory action and for the resolution of disputes, and is based upon non-discrimination (i.e., trading privileges granted to one state must be extended to all), although this does not apply to agriculture, to textiles (which are governed by the **Multi-Fibre Arrangement**), to 'regional trading arrangements' (see **customs union**) or, since 1971, to trading privileges granted to developing countries (see **Generalized System of Preferences**). Successive 'rounds' of negotiations have resulted in a general lowering of tariffs:

1947	Geneva
1949	Annecy
1951	Torquay
1955–6	Geneva
1959–62	Geneva ('Dillon')
1963–7	Geneva ('Kennedy')
1973–9	Geneva ('Tokyo')
1986–93	Geneva ('Uruguay')

All member states of the European Union belong to GATT, several of them as founder-members. Under Article 113 of the **Treaty of Rome** the **European Commission** represents the member states in international trade negotiations, and has done so in GATT since the Kennedy Round. The Commission operates on the basis of a mandate laid down by the **Council of Ministers** and in consultation with the **Article 113 Committee**. Under Article 229 EEC the Commission is responsible for maintaining 'appropriate relations' with the WTO.

The Uruguay Round of GATT negotiations, originally scheduled to end in December 1990, led to a dispute between the United States and the European Union over agricultural subsidies (see **Common Agricultural Policy**), and, at the last minute, between France and the United States over the audiovisual sector. The first was resolved on the basis of a bilateral compromise (the Blair House agreement), the second by the omission of this sector from the overall conclusions. The three main areas covered by the conclusions, which involved negotiators from 117 countries, were a further reduction by an overall average of 40 per cent in tariffs on manufactured goods; the extension of GATT rules to agriculture, public procurement and the services sector; and a new set of rules on intellectual property offering better world-wide protection for patents and stricter safeguards against pirated goods and infringements of copyright. The GATT conclusions were formally signed in Marrakesh in April 1994.

The GATT negotiations also led to disputes within the Council of Ministers and within the Commission. It opened up clear divisions between governments committed to trade liberalization – Denmark, Germany, the Netherlands, the United Kingdom – and those still attached to relatively high levels of agricultural protection. Such divisions were also reflected amongst members of the Commission, and led at one point to the resignation of the Commission's chief negotiator, Ray MacSharry, the Irish Commissioner responsible for agriculture. Attitudes on both sides of the Atlantic hardened as a consequence of electoral pressures, notably the American presidential elections of November 1992 and the French legislative elections of March 1993 (both of which resulted in changes of government). The eventual settlement entailed substantial cuts in export subsidies in agriculture and a lowering of tariffs on agricultural produce by an average of 36 per cent on the European side, and was widely regarded as a triumph for Sir Leon Brittan, the Commissioner responsible for external trade. Sir Leon's analysis of the Uruguay Round may be found in his introduction to a special edition of the *Common Market Law Review*, Volume 31/2, April 1994.

A further difficulty arose in 1994 in the form of a dispute between the member states and the Commission over the legal base for the agreements relating to the Uruguay Round and the responsibility for ratifying the

GATT settlements on behalf of the Union. The settlements covered both matters that are dealt with by the Union as a whole and others that are decided by the national authorities of member states. Although the dispute could probably have been settled by an agreed 'code of conduct', the Commission preferred to seek a ruling from the **Court of Justice** in order to clarify the Commission's future status when representing the Union within the WTO. In its judgment of 15 November 1994 the Court ruled that the Commission had exclusive competence with respect to trade matters, including action against counterfeit goods, and shared responsibility with the member states with respect to intellectual property rights and certain services.

Generalized System of Preferences (GSP)

The GSP scheme is a system of tariff preferences intended to benefit exports of manufactured goods and processed agricultural products from developing countries to the Union. It was introduced in 1971 in line with the recommendations of the United Nations Conference on Trade and Development (UNCTAD) meeting in New Delhi in 1968, and has been revised or renewed many times since then. About 150 countries are covered by the GSP scheme, with special advantages being given to the least-developed developing countries (LDCs). However, since customs duties have been progressively reduced as a result of negotiations in the **General Agreement on Tariffs and Trade** (GATT), the benefits offered under the GSP scheme have become less attractive. Efforts to make them more attractive result in an erosion of the privileged position that the countries covered by the **Lomé Convention** expect to enjoy. The GSP scheme has also been criticized for failing adequately to discriminate between the highly competitive newly industrialized countries (NICs), mainly in South-East Asia, and the desperately poor countries in the developing world.

The current GSP scheme, drawn up within a 10-year guideline covering the period 1995–2004, seeks to address these criticisms. Exports from LDCs are exempt from all duties, although in some cases the country concerned has to agree to take measures in the fight against drugs. Other 'encouragement clauses' have been introduced in favour of social and environmental measures.

Genscher, Hans-Dietrich (b. 1927)

Hans-Dietrich Genscher was leader of the German Free Democrats (Liberal) Party from 1974 to 1985 and German Foreign Minister from 1974 until 1992. Genscher was a key figure in all Community foreign policy developments over this long period. He was, with Emilio Colombo, then the Italian Foreign Minister, the architect of the so-called **Genscher–Colombo**

Plan of 1981. Having been born in what later became the German Democratic Republic, Genscher took a close personal interest in **German reunification** and in establishing better relations with the countries of central and eastern Europe after the collapse of Communism.

Genscher–Colombo Plan

The Genscher–Colombo Plan was a bilateral initiative taken in November 1981 by **Hans-Dietrich Genscher** and Emilio Colombo, the German and Italian Foreign Ministers, in which they proposed the adoption of a 'draft European Act' to supplement the **Treaty of Rome**. The Plan envisaged a 'common foreign policy' and 'coordination of security policy' based on the further development of **European Political Cooperation**. The **European Council** would become the 'organ of political guidance', with its president-in-office reporting every six months to the **European Parliament**. The latter body would be consulted before the appointment of the president of the **European Commission** and before further **enlargement** of the Community.

According to the Plan, the structure of the **Council of Ministers** would be extended to include regular meetings of Ministers of Justice and Culture, and potentially of ministers in any other policy areas not covered by the **Treaties**. 'Decisive importance' was attached to following the Council voting procedures set down in the Treaties (see **Luxembourg Compromise**), with an obligation on any member state to explain in writing why it might be attempting to block a decision requiring only a **qualified majority vote** (QMV). States would have the chance to defer a Council decision at two successive meetings. After that, by implication, a vote would be taken.

The reaction in the European Council to this proposal was somewhat ambiguous. France — which had yet to embark on the vigorously pro-European policy that would later characterize its new President, **François Mitterrand** — displayed little public enthusiasm either for the Bonn–Rome initiative, or for its clear exclusion from the exercise. The United Kingdom was fearful of the budgetary implications of an extension of Community activity into new areas and, with Denmark and Greece, concerned by any watering-down of the Luxembourg Compromise. The position in Bonn itself seemed uncertain as the commitment of Chancellor **Helmut Schmidt** to his Foreign Minister's proposals sometimes looked halfhearted.

In the event, the European Council, meeting in London on 26–27 November 1981, received the Genscher–Colombo text 'with satisfaction' and requested the foreign ministers to study it and report back in due course. During long negotiations in Brussels it was agreed to downgrade the document from a draft legislative text to a mere declaration without any binding effect. On this basis the Solemn Declaration on European Union was brought before the Stuttgart European Council 18 months later (see **Stuttgart Declaration**).

German reunification

The 1949 Constitution (*Grundgesetz*) of the Federal Republic of Germany (FRG) made provision for the eventual reunification of Germany without specifying in detail how it should be achieved. In the event, the FRG and the German Democratic Republic (GDR) agreed in 1990 that the individual *Länder* of the GDR (Brandenburg, Sachsen, Sachsen-Anhalt, Thüringen, Mecklenburg-Vorpommern and the city of East Berlin) would join the FRG under Article 23 of the Constitution, adding almost 17 million people to the population. However, this meant a *de facto* **enlargement** of the European Community of a kind not provided for in the **Treaty of Rome**. In April 1990 the **European Council** meeting in Dublin decided that the former GDR would be incorporated into the Community on reunification. The two Germanys consulted very closely with the Community institutions before reunification was finally and formally achieved under the Unification Treaty (*Einigungsvertrag*) on 3 October 1990.

Many of the most contentious issues were settled in the preparatory State Treaty (*Staatsvertrag*), which came into effect on 1 July 1990. In this Treaty the two Germanys agreed that **Community law** would apply in the former GDR with effect from reunification and that the GDR would progressively align its policies with Community practices and objectives. A **protocol** to the Treaty of Rome already allowed trade between the two Germanys to be regarded as 'internal trade' (i.e., not subject to the **Common External Tariff**) in line with the constitution of the FRG. Particular Articles of the State Treaty dealt with the application of the **Common Agricultural Policy** (CAP), monetary reform and, in general, the transition to a market economy.

On the Community side the reunification of Germany prompted a comprehensive review of the *acquis communautaire* and the identification of measures that would have to be modified to take account of the former GDR's special circumstances or applied only after a transitional period. A temporary committee of the **European Parliament** was set up for this purpose. An analysis was also made of the GDR's international obligations as set out in various treaties and agreements. In the institutional field the only major change consequent upon reunification was an increase in the number of German seats in the European Parliament. With effect from the date of reunification, 18 'observers' from the former GDR were added to the Parliament, with speaking rights in committees but without the right to vote. Initially, these observers were chosen by the GDR Parliament, the Volkskammer, but later by the Bundestag. In 1991 the Parliament voted by 241 votes to 62 (38 of whom were French) formally to increase the number of German members from 81 to 99, with effect from the 1994 European elections. This decision was controversial in some member states, and it was not endorsed until the European Council meeting in Edinburgh in December 1992. German representation in other institutions has not been increased, nor has the weighting attached to Germany's vote under the **qualified majority voting** (QMV) system.

The special status of Berlin, the presence of Russian troops in the GDR, the *de facto* incorporation of the former GDR into the **North Atlantic Treaty Organization** (NATO) and anxieties over a reunited Germany's eastern frontier with Poland gave rise to negotiations in July and August 1990 known as the 'Two plus Four' talks (i.e., the two Germanys plus France, the United Kingdom, the United States, and the USSR). Agreement was reached on the ending of the Allies' special status in Germany, on a new German–Polish Treaty, on the granting of full sovereignty to a reunited Germany, including the right to join NATO, and on the withdrawal of Soviet forces from German soil. The last of the 550,000 Russians (350,000 soldiers plus civilian employees and families) left Germany in mid-1994, at a cost to the German taxpayer of about DM13 billion.

Although the GDR was economically the most advanced of the **COMECON** states, it was very backward indeed by comparison with the FRG. This has meant that Germany now has both the richest and the poorest regions in the European Union. Levels of pollution in the GDR were particularly high, and the whole fabric of the country was in a poor state of repair. Dealing with these problems will demand huge resources for many years to come. However, the initial loss of population has been staunched and confidence is slowly returning, helped in part by the decision to make Berlin once more the capital.

A very important unforeseen side-effect of German reunification was the breakdown of the **Exchange–Rate Mechanism** (ERM) of the **European Monetary System** (EMS) in September 1992. The German authorities were determined to maintain international confidence in the Deutsche Mark and kept interest rates high. This in turn required other governments to keep their own interest rates high, so that their currencies could remain within the permitted narrow band of fluctuation against the Deutsche Mark. By September 1992 the strain was too much, and sterling and the Italian lira left the ERM. Germany was widely criticized for pursuing an essentially domestic interest-rate policy, with little or no regard for the wider European responsibilities that flowed from the Deutsche Mark's position in the ERM.

Politically, reunification was a substantial triumph for **Helmut Kohl**. The uncertainty that it engendered meant that his calmness and fixity of purpose suddenly became very attractive to the German electorate, and his party did well in the first all-German elections of December 1990, the European elections of June 1994 and the national elections four months later. In the longer term reunification is bound to strengthen Germany's position as the most influential member state of the Union.

For a detailed study of German reunification as it affected the Community see Barbara Lippert and Rosalind Stevens-Ströhmann, *German Unification and EC Integration* (1993).

Germany

Soon after the end of the Second World War it became clear in the light of the new threat from the East that the rehabilitation and reconstruction of Germany would have to be amongst the West's highest strategic priorities. The Federal Republic of Germany (FRG, or West Germany) was established in 1949 on the territory of the former American, British and French zones of occupation, with its capital in Bonn. Berlin remained divided into four sectors: from June 1948 until May 1949 the American, British and French sectors were blockaded by Soviet forces and supplied by the Berlin airlift. The first Chancellor of the FRG was **Konrad Adenauer**.

The FRG was admitted as a member of the **Council of Europe** in 1950 on the initiative of **Winston Churchill**. In the same year the **Schuman Plan** was launched, and in 1951 **the Six** signed the **Treaty of Paris** establishing the **European Coal and Steel Community** (ECSC). The Treaty was unanimously supported in the West German Bundestag by the Christian Democrats, but opposed by the Social Democrats on the grounds that it formalized the division of Germany. Two years later the Social Democrats raised similar objections to the **European Defence Community** Treaty. One consequence of the internationalization of the coal and steel industries within the ECSC was the resolution of the Saarland dispute with France in 1955, which led to the incorporation of the territory into the FRG. The FRG joined the **North Atlantic Treaty Organization** (NATO) the same year: the Soviet Union responded by setting up the **Warsaw Pact** and by recognizing the sovereignty of the German Democratic Republic (GDR, or East Germany), thus completing the division of Germany.

The 1950s and 1960s were the decades of the 'German economic miracle'. The FRG actively supported the proposal to set up what became the **European Economic Community** (EEC) at the 1955 **Messina Conference**, although in the argument that then ensued it was France rather than the FRG which vigorously opposed the alternative of a wider free trade area (see **Maudling Committee**). The bargain upon which the EEC was founded was a wider market for German manufactured goods in exchange for guaranteed markets for French agricultural produce, and a politico-institutional framework in which neither country could dominate the other. Outside that framework **Franco-German cooperation** led to the signing of a Treaty of Friendship (the Elysée Treaty) in 1963.

Unlike France, the FRG was not opposed to British accession to the EEC. Nor did the FRG share French misgivings about the supranational character of the EEC's institutions (especially the Commission under its German president **Walter Hallstein**), misgivings that led to the **empty chair crisis** of 1965. Within political circles the FRG's attitudes had little of the anti-American bias that characterized those of France until the resignation of **Charles de Gaulle** in 1969.

The election of Willy Brandt as Chancellor introduced the era of *Ostpolitik* – establishing better relations with the GDR within the framework of East–West detente. The policy was continued by his successor, Helmut Schmidt. However, this led to no slackening of interest in European integration: together with President **Valéry Giscard d'Estaing** of France, Schmidt played a key role in the establishment of the **European Monetary System** (EMS) in 1979.

Especially since **German reunification** Germany's economic ascendancy within the Union and the fact of its being by far the biggest net contributor to the **Budget** have meant that no major development can take place without German support. Such support was initially only grudgingly given to the reform of the **Common Agricultural Policy** (CAP), primarily because a succession of Bavarian ministers of agriculture were devoted above all to the interests of German farmers. Another area in which, for constitutional reasons, Germany found it difficult until recently to give wholehearted support was defence and security policy. Under the 1949 Constitution German forces could not be deployed outside Germany, and all-party agreement could not be reached on changing this provision. The problem was resolved by a ruling of the Constitutional Court in June 1994: German forces may now be deployed outside Germany, but only in operations backed by the United Nations. Some German forces have been committed to the **Eurocorps** since 1989.

In parallel with German reunification German policy is now strongly oriented towards enlarging the Union by admitting the countries of central and eastern Europe. Another very high priority is an orderly progression towards **Economic and Monetary Union** (EMU) especially since the future **European Central Bank** (ECB) is now located in Frankfurt. As the 1994 'Lamers paper' (see '**hard core**') makes clear, the German government sees EMU as the 'cornerstone' of the European political union to which it is committed. In the institutional field Germany is a supporter of more powers for the **European Parliament**, in which it has had an increase in its share of seats since June 1994 (although it has not sought an increase in its weighting within the **qualified majority voting** (QMV) system in the **Council of Ministers**). Even if Helmut Kohl had not been re-elected in November 1994 for a fourth term as Chancellor, these German priorities, which have cross-party support, would have remained the same.

The passage of the **Maastricht Treaty** required Germany to make some adjustments to its relations with the Union. The Treaty gave rise to fears on the part of the *Länder* authorities that the Federal Government was ceding to the Union powers that, under the Constitution, belonged to the *Länder*. Furthermore, the Treaty was challenged in the Constitutional Court by anti-Maastricht campaigners led by a former *chef de cabinet* to Martin Bangemann, the German Commissioner responsible for industry policy (see **Karlsruhe judgment**). The Constitution now requires any transfer of powers to the Union to be approved by a two-thirds majority in both the Bundestag (the lower house of the German Parliament) and the Bundesrat (the upper house, composed of representatives of the *Länder*). When required, ministers from *Länder* governments may represent the FRG in the Council of Ministers (see **regionalism**).

'A united Germany in a united Europe' is the phrase most commonly used to summarize how Germany sees the future. The policy of high interest rates, which led to the break-up and near collapse of the **Exchange-Rate Mechanism** (ERM) in September 1992, led many to suppose that, of the two, a united Germany was the higher priority. Since then, especially under the German **presidency** of the Council of Ministers in the latter half of 1994, Germany has been anxious to dispel the idea that it has lost interest in European integration. Germany is all too well aware of its responsibilities as the paymaster of the Union, its largest economy, its most successful exporter, and as the favoured European interlocutor of both the United States and Russia. European integration was attractive to Germany in the 1950s as an opportunity for a fresh start within a fair and equal partnership. A new generation of Germans now feels less need to expiate the guilt to which the Nazi era gave rise, but the European Union and 'the new Europe' remain attractive as a framework within which their formidable energies may be deployed in a common cause.

The most thoughtful as well as the most comprehensive politico-historical study of modern Germany is Timothy Garton Ash, *In Europe's Name* (1993).

Gibraltar

Gibraltar has been under British sovereignty since the Treaty of Utrecht in 1713. The colony occupies a narrow peninsula on Spain's southern Mediterranean coast, and was once of great strategic importance. It is five kilometres long and a little over one kilometre wide, with a total area of six kilometres. Its population is estimated to be around 30,000.

The political status of the peninsula has long been the source of dispute between the United Kingdom and Spain. The first people to settle on the Rock were the Moors in 711. Gibraltar was under Spanish rule from 1462 until 1704, when it was captured by the British. Under the terms of the 1713 Treaty the Spanish have a first right of refusal – before the Gibraltarians themselves – in the event of British sovereignty being relinquished. The airport is an additional complication, since it is built on reclaimed land not forming part of the original territory and therefore, in the Spanish view, not covered by the Treaty.

On 10 September 1967, following a United Nations resolution on the decolonization of Gibraltar, a referendum was held to determine whether the Gibraltarians wished to retain their links with the United Kingdom. The result was an almost unanimous vote in favour of remaining British: out of a total electorate of 12,762 people, only 44 voted for Spain.

Although Gibraltar as a European territory for whose external relations the United Kingdom is responsible is covered by the **Treaty of Rome** (Article 227.4 EEC), the people of Gibraltar are not represented in the **European Parliament**. The dispute over Gibraltar's status remains an irritant in Anglo-Spanish relations and has blocked the entry into force of the **External Frontiers Convention**. For a fuller treatment of the dispute, see D. S. Morris and R. H. Haigh, *Britain, Spain and Gibraltar 1945–90* (1992).

Gibraltar is self-governing in most domestic matters (the United Kingdom remains responsible for external affairs, defence and internal security), under a constitution that was introduced in 1969. Legislative power is vested in the House of Assembly, while executive authority is exercised by the governor, who is also commander-in-chief. The latter generally acts in concert with the Gibraltar Council.

Giscard d'Estaing, Valéry (b. 1926)

Valéry Giscard d'Estaing was elected to the Assemblée Nationale in 1956. By the 1960s he was leading his own party, the Républicains Indépendants, and serving under **Charles de Gaulle** as Finance Minister. He served President Georges Pompidou in the same capacity from 1969 until 1974, when he defeated **François Mitterrand** in the election for the presidency.

As President, he was responsible for the initiative that transformed the system of irregular European Community 'summits' into the **European Council**. He established good relations with Chancellor Helmut Schmidt of West Germany and throughout the 1970s Franco–German cooperation was the principal driving-force behind European integration. In particular, Giscard and Schmidt gave their strong personal support to **Economic and Monetary Union** (EMU) as relaunched by Commission President **Roy Jenkins** in 1977. In the same year Giscard first proposed the creation of an *espace judiciaire européen*.

Defeated by Mitterrand in the 1981 presidential election, Giscard partially withdrew from the European political scene. However, in 1989 he was elected to the **European Parliament**, where he became the leader of the Liberal Group (see **political groups**). At the end of 1991 he suddenly left the Liberals to join the Group of the European People's Party (Christian Democrats) and in 1993 left the Parliament altogether.

A convinced European, Giscard nevertheless evinces a characteristically French distaste for the supranational character of the European Union's institutions, notably the **European Commission**. This accounts for the entertaining but not wholly sympathetic portrait of Giscard in Roy Jenkins's *European Diary*. Giscard is the President of the **European Movement**.

Greece

Greece was the first country to conclude an **Association Agreement** with the Community (Treaty of Athens, 1961). At the time this was to **the Six** an important and welcome token of international recognition. The Agreement made explicit reference to full membership at a later date. During the period of military dictatorship (1967–74) the Agreement was suspended, and the 10-year transition to a **customs union** with the Community was interrupted. A year after the restoration of democratic rule Greece applied for membership of the Community, by then composed of nine members.

The **Opinion** delivered by the Commission was, in its original form, largely negative, on the grounds that neither Greece's economy nor its political and administrative system was yet ready for membership. This view was overturned by the **Council of Ministers**, who took the view that the overriding imperative was to consolidate Greek democracy. An **Accession** Treaty was signed in May 1979, and Greece became the tenth member of the Community in January 1981.

In October 1981 a Socialist government was elected on a platform openly critical of the accession terms negotiated by their political opponents. A renegotiation was demanded, similar to that which the 1974 Labour Government in the United Kingdom had secured (see **renegotia-**

tion). The Greek government's demands were made more urgent by the fact that two more southern European countries, Portugal and Spain, were by then negotiating for admission. Eventually, a solution was found for Greece, partly within the new framework of **Integrated Mediterranean Programmes**, but the Socialist government, which remained in power until 1990, was, at best, ambivalent about Greek membership of the Community. This was especially evident in Greece's refusal to share in common foreign policy stances and actions (such as sanctions against Iran) agreed as part of **European Political Cooperation**.

Together with Portugal, Greece is the poorest of the member states, and has a rate of inflation some four times greater than the average. It benefits substantially from the **structural funds** and takes only an occasional interest in other areas of policy. As might be expected, Greece is an implacable opponent of Turkish entry into the Union and takes a lively interest in the problem of **Cyprus**. After a brief period out of office, the Socialists returned to power and continued their independent and idiosyncratic foreign policy (for example, by imposing an embargo on trade with the former Yugoslav republic of Macedonia, which was said to have designs on the Greek region of the same name). Relations with the European Union continue to be a divisive issue in Greek politics (the Communist Party has pro-European and anti-European wings: see **Communism**) and Greece remains amongst the least enthusiastic supporters of further moves towards closer integration. However, rather surprisingly, Greece has chosen to become one of the countries committed to the removal of internal frontier controls under the **Schengen Agreement**.

Greenland

Greenland is an island of over 2 million square kilometres – an area larger than France, Germany, Italy, Spain and the United Kingdom put together – with a population of only 50,000 people. Until 1953 Greenland was a Danish colony. After that date it became an integral part of Denmark itself. In January 1973, as part of Denmark, Greenland joined the European Community. In May 1979 Greenland was granted a substantial measure of home rule within Denmark, including the right to hold a referendum on whether to remain inside the Community. The vote was held in February 1982, with a majority in favour of withdrawal. A treaty was accordingly signed in March 1984 'amending, with regard to Greenland, the Treaties establishing the European Communities', and Greenland's departure took effect in July 1986. Since then, it has been one of the **overseas countries and territories** (OCTs) of the Community. Unlike other OCTs, Greenland does not benefit from the **European Development Fund**, but instead receives an annual payment by way of compensation for access to its fishing grounds. Greenland also qualifies for assistance from the **structural funds**.

Group of Seven

The Western Economic Summits, better known as the Group of Seven or simply G–7 Summits, are regular meetings held since 1975 of the heads of government and finance ministers of the seven leading industrialized countries: the United States, Canada (since 1976), Japan, France, Germany, Italy and the United Kingdom. Since May 1977 the Group of Seven Summits have also been attended by the president of the **Commission** on behalf of the European Union as a whole (an account by **Roy Jenkins** of how he overcame French opposition to this during his **presidency** may be found in his *European Diary*).

The Group of Seven is to be distinguished from the Group of Twenty-four, the member countries of the **Organization for Economic Cooperation and Development**; and the Group of Ten, leading members of the International Monetary Fund: the Group of Seven plus Belgium, the Netherlands, Sweden and, since 1984, Switzerland, making, in fact, 11.

Gymnich meetings

Ministers of the European Union sometimes meet informally with only very few officials and interpreters to have discussions in a relaxed atmosphere without the need to reach formal decisions. These meetings are known as 'Gymnich meetings' after Schloss Gymnich near Bonn, where the first of such meetings was held in April 1974 (see **Council of Ministers**).

Hallstein, Walter (1901–82)

Walter Hallstein was the first President of the **European Commission**. Pursuing an academic career until becoming an adviser to **Konrad Adenauer** in 1950, he led the German delegation in the discussions on the **Schuman Plan** and in 1951 became Foreign Minister, in which capacity he developed the 'Hallstein doctrine': the refusal to have diplomatic relations with countries that recognized East Germany as a state. Hallstein represented West Germany at the **Messina Conference** and was active in the negotiations that led to the signing of the **Treaties** establishing the **European Economic Community** (EEC) and the **European Atomic Energy Community** (Euratom).

In 1958 Hallstein became President of the Commission and remained in that office for nine years. He built up the Commission (then employing about 3,000 officials) into the embryonic European government he thought it should be. Under his presidency it was agreed that the Commission in Brussels would serve all three European Communities (see **Merger Treaty**). His vigorous defence of the Commission's authority and independence brought him into conflict with national politicians such as **Charles de Gaulle** who were wary of the pretensions of supranational institutions (de Gaulle was particularly irritated by Hallstein's insistence on the Commission accepting the credentials of ambassadors accredited to the Community). The most serious conflict between Hallstein and de Gaulle was that of 1965 (the so-called **empty chair crisis**), eventually resolved by the **Luxembourg Compromise** of 1966. Hallstein resigned the following year and retired from public life in 1972.

Although sometimes dismissed as a determined technocrat, Hallstein never had any doubts about the fundamentally political nature of what the Community was trying to achieve. He emphasized this in his book *United Europe: Challenge and Opportunity* (1962), which was first delivered as lectures at Tufts University, Massachusetts. He reminded his American audience that 'the Iron Curtain is nearer to Brussels than Washington, D.C., is to Boston'. He said: 'The logic of economic integration not only leads on toward political unity by way of the fusion of interests; it also involves political action in itself.' Referring to the **Common Agricultural Policy** (CAP), member states' exchange-rate policies, and external trade issues, he added, 'Agreement on all these matters will require political courage certainly no less than that which was needed to sign the Community treaties in the first place. And that courage was considerable, for the treaties set in motion a process far more ambitious than the modest words "economic integration" would suggest.'

'Hard core'

A September 1994 paper entitled *Reflections on European Policy*, drawn up by Christian Democrats in the German Bundestag (and sometimes known as the 'Lamers paper' after one of its co-authors, Karl Lamers), drew attention to the existence of a 'hard core of [member states of the European Union] oriented to greater integration and closer cooperation' and called for it to be further strengthened in order 'to counteract the centrifugal forces generated by constant enlargement'. In the text that followed, it was made clear that the hard core was thought to be composed of Germany, France and the **Benelux** countries (i.e., the original **Six** with the exception of Italy).

Although the paper emphasized that the hard core 'must not be closed to other Member States . . . [but] be open to every Member State willing and able to meet its requirements', the use of the phrase caused widespread offence to member states that felt excluded (see Preface, page xi). The idea of a hard core was denounced by opponents of a **two-speed Europe**, which is effectively what the explicit recognition of such a core would entail. The paper also made clear that amongst the most precise and demanding 'requirements' for membership of the hard core were the **convergence criteria** for the third stage of **Economic and Monetary Union** (EMU), described as 'the cornerstone of political union'.

In a special reference to the United Kingdom, the paper said that the existence of a hard core and the intensification of **Franco-German cooperation** did not imply 'the abandoning of hopes that Great Britain will assume its role in the heart of Europe and thus in its core'. Rather, they were taken to be 'the best means of exerting a positive influence on the clarification of Great Britain's relationship with Europe and on its willingness to participate in further steps towards integration'. In response to this John Major, in a speech in Leiden on 7 September 1994, endorsed the idea of a non-exclusive hard core as part of the 'flexibility' he sought to encourage with respect to the pace and character of European integration.

In a speech to the Federal Trust in London on 17 November 1994 Lamers returned to the idea of a hard core, reiterating his 'firmly-held belief – a belief borne out by the entire course of European integration – that if a smaller group of countries presses ahead with particularly intensive and far-reaching economic and political integration, this group as core has a centripetal or magnetic effect on the other countries'.

Harmonization

The free circulation of goods within the **common market** was one of the fundamental objectives of the **Treaty of Rome**. However, differences between national product standards meant that free circulation was difficult to achieve, and such standards allowed member states too much scope for introducing or maintaining barriers to trade on (sometimes spurious) scientific or health and safety grounds. With the removal of tariffs and quotas on trade between member states under Articles 9 and 34 EEC, product standards became the key instrument for protectionism. Throughout the 1960s and 1970s the **Commission** sought to draw up common standards, a process usually known as harmonization but referred to in the Treaty as 'approximation'. Article 3 h EEC refers to the 'approximation of the laws of Member States to the extent required for the functioning of the common market' and the same expression is used in **Articles 100 and 100a**, which together constitute the legal base for harmonization.

Although harmonization was supported in principle by industry and commerce, progress was extremely slow. Before the **Single European Act** (SEA), agreement had to be unanimous in the **Council of Ministers**, and the extraordinarily detailed draft legislation to which harmonization gave rise prompted not only ridicule but hostility. For this and for other reasons, and encouraged by the judgments of the **Court of Justice** in the **Cassis de Dijon case** of 1980 (Case 120/78), the Commission adopted the so-called 'new approach' based on mutual recognition (see Council Resolution of 7 May 1985). It introduced the presumption that a product legally on sale in one member state may be sold in any other. The aim is now to set only minimum common standards on the basis of health and safety requirements, and to leave the technical details to be worked out by specialist bodies in consultation with manufacturers (see *Comité Européen de Normalisation*). Harmonization along these new lines is one of the essential foundations of the **Single Market** programme (see also **Cockfield White Paper**).

Heath, Edward (b. 1916)

Elected as a Conservative MP in 1950, Edward Heath made his maiden speech on the **Schuman Plan**. He was responsible as Lord Privy Seal for the negotiations that followed the United Kingdom's first attempt, in 1961, to join the European Community. The negotiations were brought to an abrupt conclusion by **Charles de Gaulle** in January 1963. Government documents suggest that Heath had been misled into thinking that the talks were going well, and that the ill-feeling caused by de Gaulle's veto was compounded by French accusations that the United Kingdom had signed 'secret agreements' with Washington (*The Times*, 1 January 1994).

In spite of this disappointment Heath continued to be involved with European issues as Secretary of State for Trade and Industry from 1963. After the Conservatives' 1964 election defeat he became the leader of the Conservative Party, which he led (rather unexpectedly) to victory in 1970. One of his Government's first acts was to complete the negotiations that had followed Britain's second application for Community membership, made by the Labour Government of Harold Wilson in 1967. Heath signed the **Treaty of Rome** on behalf of the United Kingdom in 1972. He was defeated in the elections held in February and October 1974, and in 1975 he lost the leadership of the Conservative Party to **Margaret Thatcher**.

Mrs Thatcher's policies towards Europe, especially after she became Prime Minister in 1979, provided Heath with many pretexts for criticizing the woman who had supplanted him. For this and for other reasons he became and remained a controversial figure within the Conservative Party. Nevertheless, his enthusiasm for Europe was genuine: in one of his best-remembered speeches, given in response to de Gaulle's 1963 veto, he declared 'We in Britain are not going to turn our backs on the mainland of Europe or on the countries of the Community. We are part of Europe by geography, tradition, history, culture and civilization. We shall continue to work with our friends in Europe for the true unity and strength of this continent.'

The phrase that gave Heath most trouble in the years preceding the **referendum of June 1975** was one he used in a speech to the British Chamber of Commerce in Paris on 5 May 1970. Speaking of the negotiations then in hand, he said that it would not be in the interests of the Community if it were to be enlarged without the 'full-hearted consent of the Parliaments and peoples of the new member countries'. The phrase was extensively used by opponents of British membership, Labour and Conservative, to strengthen the case for a referendum.

Heath has not written extensively on European questions, and for an understanding of his vision of Europe one must go back to his 1970 Godkin lectures delivered in the United States and published later that year as *Old World, New Horizons*. The fullest biography of Heath is by John Campbell (1994).

HELIOS

Adopted in 1988, the HELIOS (Handicapped people in Europe Living Independently in Open Society) programme groups together a number of initiatives on disabled people, including the promotion of cooperation between national bodies concerned with disablement. The Horizon programme draws from the **structural funds** to help the professional and social integration of disabled people.

Helsinki Final Act

Signed on 1 August 1975 by the 35 states that participated in the **Conference on Security and Cooperation in Europe** (CSCE) in Helsinki, the Final Act embodied the results of the Conference. Together with the **Charter of Paris** for a New Europe, signed on 21 November 1990, the Final Act is the legal basis for the CSCE system of cooperation, which now encompasses 53 states (all European states plus the United States, Canada and the central Asian republics of the former USSR).

Hierarchy of acts

A translation of the French *hierarchie des actes*, this is the name given to a body of ideas relating to the reordering of the different types of European Union legislation, modelled on the French constitutional reforms of 1958. At present, different types of **legal instrument** may be adopted under a variety of procedures, depending upon the legal base in the **Treaties** and in some cases upon the subject-matter. A 'hierarchy' would lay down different categories of legislation, ranging from the most important (e.g., Treaty amendments) to the most trivial, and specify the appropriate procedures. In so doing it would define the role of the various institutions, European and national, in the law-making process and establish a clear order of precedence. Ideas along these lines will figure in the **Intergovernmental Conference** (IGC) due to begin in 1996, a 'Declaration on the hierarchy of Community acts' having been annexed to the **Maastricht Treaty**.

High Authority

One of the four institutions of the **European Coal and Steel Community** (ECSC), the High Authority was the forerunner of the **European Commission**. Its first President (1952–4) was **Jean Monnet**. Under the 1965 **Merger Treaty** the High Authority was merged with the Commission with effect from July 1967.

Human rights

Amongst the first acts of the General Assembly of the United Nations was the adoption of the Universal Declaration of Human Rights (10 December 1948). This Declaration, although comprehensive, did not set out a means whereby respect for human rights could be enforced. When the **Council of Europe** was established the following year 'maintenance and further realisation of human rights and fundamental freedoms' was listed amongst its basic objectives. To this end a Convention for the Protection of Human Rights and Fundamental Freedoms was drawn up and signed in Rome on 4 November 1950. Less comprehensive than the Universal Declaration, the Convention was more ambitious in that it set up machinery for enforcement and required signatory states not only to accept certain duties of observance but also to recognize the fact of individuals having rights under international law. The Convention came into force on 3 September 1953.

Some states (not the United Kingdom) have chosen to incorporate the Convention into their domestic law. The Convention was never intended to supplant national measures for the protection of human rights, but to provide an additional guarantee at the international level. Exhaustion of national remedies is a precondition of bringing proceedings under the Convention.

The Convention has been amended several times since 1950 and several **protocols** have been added to it. It consists of 66 Articles. Amongst the rights guaranteed are: the right to life, liberty and security of person; the right to a fair trial, with the possibility of having the sentence reviewed by a higher tribunal; respect for privacy and family life; freedom of thought, conscience and religion; freedom of expression; freedom of the press; freedom of peaceful assembly and association; freedom from torture, inhuman or degrading treatment, slavery or forced labour; the prohibition of the death penalty; the right to leave or return to one's own country; and the elimination of discrimination in the enjoyment of rights and freedoms guaranteed under the Convention.

The institutions of the Convention are based in Strasbourg. The European Commission of Human Rights is composed of as many members as there are parties to the Convention, elected for a renewable six-year term by the Committee of Ministers from lists of names submitted by each state's delegation to the Parliamentary Assembly. Judges of the European Court of Human Rights are elected, one-third at a time, for a renewable nine-year term by the Parliamentary Assembly from lists of names, three for each vacancy, submitted by the signatory states. There are as many judges as there are members of the Council of Europe, but cases are normally heard by a panel of nine judges, of whom one will be a national of the state concerned in the case.

Complaints are directed in the first instance to the Commission. They may be brought by persons, groups or private organizations (if from a state that recognizes the right of individual petition) or by one state against another (interstate applications). The complainant must show that all domestic legal remedies have been exhausted and the complaint must be brought within six months of the final decision by the courts or authorities concerned. The first task of the Commission is to establish the admissibility of the complaint, sometimes with the help of further information or a preliminary hearing. Once declared admissible, the complaint is then examined in more depth. At this stage the Commission is required to establish the facts and to help the parties to the dispute reach an amicable settlement. If no settlement is reached, the Commission draws up a full report, which is voted upon by majority, and forwarded on a confidential basis to the state or states involved and to the Committee of Ministers; the report is not made available to the complainant.

At present, cases are forwarded to the Court only if within three months of the date of the report the Commission or one of the states concerned so decides; but when Protocol 9 to the Convention comes into force, individual complainants from states who have ratified the Protocol will also have this right. The defendant state must first have accepted the Court's jurisdiction. The Court hears the case in the light of the Commission's report and there is normally a public hearing with lawyers putting the various arguments. The Court's decision, which is final, is reached by majority, but since the Court has no powers of enforcement the responsibility for implementing the decision rests with the Committee of Ministers.

If the case is not referred to the Court, the Committee of Ministers itself makes the final decision by a two-thirds majority. When Protocol 10 to the Convention comes into force, a simple majority will be sufficient.

The Commission receives about 5,000 complaints every year. Of these, about 3,500 are eliminated as clearly inadmissible. Of those that receive further investigation, about 10 per cent are declared admissible. Only one interstate case has ever been referred to the Court: on methods used to interrogate terrorist suspects in Northern Ireland. The number of judgments delivered by the Court averaged only one a year during the Court's first 10 years, but the average is now more than 20. It can take up to six years for a case referred to the Court to be decided, and various measures have been taken or are in prospect to speed up the procedures. The most significant of these is the establishment of a single permanent court and the abandonment of the two-tier procedure. New facilities for the Commission and the Court are being built in Strasbourg.

The Council of Europe's human rights activities are increasing not only as a result of new accessions to the Council but also because the Convention itself has been supplemented by a **European Social Charter** (1965) and a European Convention for the Prevention of Torture and Inhuman or Degrading Treatment or Punishment (1989). New problems in the fields of biotechnology and the treatment of aliens are being addressed. Such activities (to which should be added the awarding of a Human Rights prize every two years) are the liveliest and most lasting of the Council of Europe's contributions to European integration.

By contrast, the **Treaty of Rome** establishing the European Economic Community (EEC) makes little mention of human rights. On 5 April 1977 the Presidents of the **Europe Parliament** and the **European Commission** and the President-in-Office of the **Council of Ministers** signed a Joint Declaration on Fundamental Rights, in which reference was made to the European Convention. The Declaration binds the three institutions 'in the exercise of their powers and in pursuance of the aims of the European Communities' to respect the fundamental rights derived from the Convention and from the constitutions of member states. This Declaration, reiterated in the preamble to the 1986 **Single European Act** (SEA), became part of the *acquis communautaire* and so something that all states wishing to join the Union are obliged to accept. More recently, Article F2 of the **Maastricht Treaty** requires the European Union to respect the rights set out in the Convention and in the constitutions of member states as 'general principles of **Community law**'.

Human rights considerations enter into all Commission **Opinions** on applications for membership, and have been used as an argument against Turkish membership. There is strong pressure from the European Parliament and elsewhere upon the Commission and the Council to insert human rights clauses into cooperation and **Association Agreements** with non-member countries, and the Parliament has used its powers under the **assent procedure** to block new financial **protocols** with Syria because of Syria's treatment of Jews. Similarly, the fourth **Lomé Convention** contains human rights provisions in accordance with the Parliament's wishes. A very wide range of cases of alleged abuses of human rights, both inside and outside the Union, are brought before the Parliament every month, and annual reports on human rights are drawn up. The Parliament has worked very closely through its Human Rights Unit with organizations such as Amnesty International and with internationally known human rights campaigners such as Andrei Sakharov (after whom the Parliament named its annual prize for Freedom of Thought). The Parliament's involvement in human rights is likely to increase as a result of the formalization in the Maastricht Treaty of the right to present petitions to the Parliament and the establishment of an **Ombudsman**.

One option, perhaps the neatest, would be for the Union itself to become a party to the European Convention on Human Rights. Both the European Commission and the European Parliament are in favour of this, which would not only bring together the two bodies with the greatest experience in this area but open up new opportunities for effective enforcement. The Council of Ministers has sought the opinion of the **Court of Justice** on this issue. For the role played by human rights in the jurisprudence of the Court, see Weatherill and Beaumont, *EC Law*.

Iceland

A Danish possession from 1380, Iceland became wholly independent in 1944. With a population of 264,000, the island has the lowest population density of any European country. About three-quarters of Iceland's export earnings are from fish products, for which the United Kingdom is by far the most important market. The Icelanders claim to have the oldest parliament in the world, the Althing.

In spite of its remoteness, Iceland has participated very extensively in European organizations as a member of the **Council of Europe**, the **North Atlantic Treaty Organization** (NATO), the **European Free Trade Association** (EFTA), and the **European Economic Area** (EEA) and as an associate member of the **Western European Union** (WEU). Iceland is also a member of the **Nordic Council**. Although there is some support in Iceland for membership of the European Union, no application is currently in prospect and none is likely to be forthcoming unless a means can be found of safeguarding the Icelandic fishing industry.

'Identikit Europe'

The phrase 'identikit Europe' is used pejoratively to denote those aspects of European integration that, if taken to their logical extreme, would result in the elimination of national or regional characteristics, and so of variety and diversity within the Union. It was used most effectively by **Margaret Thatcher** in her **Bruges speech** in September 1988, and is most often aimed at the effects of **harmonization** policies of various kinds. The inappropriateness of the phrase is worth noting in passing: an identikit is a police technique for building up, on the basis of eyewitness reports of specific characteristics, a picture that resembles as closely as possible that of a particular individual.

Implied competence

The **Treaties** establishing the **European Communities** give certain specific powers, or 'competences', to the Community institutions provided for in those Treaties. The doctrine of implied competence means that where Community institutions have the power to regulate a matter internally, they may also act externally. Furthermore, if the matter in question is the subject of formally established common rules, the Community's power to act externally becomes exclusive: individual member states may no longer act independently. Implied competence is of great importance in the field of external relations. See also **ERTA case**.

Independent European Programme Group (IEPG)

The IEPG, formed in 1976, was a forum within which European members of the **North Atlantic Treaty Organization** (NATO) discussed and coordinated their research and development programmes and equipment requirements in the defence field. Such coordination was intended to act as a counterpoise to the United States' overwhelming dominance in this area. The work of the IEPG is now carried out within the **Western European Union** (WEU) framework in the Armaments Group.

Industry policy

Although the European Union's origins are rooted in industry (see **European Coal and Steel Community**) and although many of its policies have a direct bearing on industry (see especially **competition policy**, **public purchasing**, **free movement of goods**, **Single Market**), there is no industry policy as such. Article 130 of the **Treaty of Rome**, added by the **Maastricht Treaty**, defines the aim as being solely to 'ensure that the conditions necessary for the competitiveness of the Community's industry exist' by means of measures to promote adaptation to structural change, the creation of an economic environment favourable to initiative and cross-frontier cooperation, and the application to industry of technological developments. The **Commission** may take 'any useful initiative'. The **Council of Ministers** may enact specific measures in support of action taken by member states, but only by unanimity. Industry may benefit from aid from the **structural funds** or from **European Investment Bank** (EIB) loans (see also **New Community Instrument**, **Edinburgh Growth Initiative**). Certain research programmes, such as ESPRIT, BRITE and RACE, also apply to industry. The first attempt at an industrial strategy dates from the Commission's 1990 study entitled *Industrial policy in an open and competitive environment*. Since then the Commission has drawn up an annual study entitled *Panorama of EC Industry*. Broadly speaking, Commission action has concentrated on the restructuring of older industries, such as steel, and on the attempt to place new industries on a Europe-wide footing to enable them to compete internationally.

Although the Commission has extensive powers in relation to the steel industry under the 1951 **Treaty of Paris**, the social and regional implications of restructuring (which means reductions in capacity, shared equitably amongst national steel industries) are so sensitive that the Commission prefers to draw up an agreed plan and then allow the steel industry itself to work out the details and monitor its enforcement. The problem is made more complex by the fact that national steel industries (such as the British) that have already on their own initiative applied a restructuring programme involving massive job losses expect to have this taken into account when an overall plan involving further cuts is being drawn up. Added to this is the political pressure to open up the market to imports of steel products from central and eastern Europe. Ultimately, the Commission has to rely on its powers of persuasion, backed by threats to withdraw financial support or bring actions in the **Court of Justice**. Problems analogous to those in the steel industry have also arisen with respect to textiles, coal and shipbuilding.

The Commission's main efforts in regard to new industries are directed towards information technology and telecommunications. In the Commission's view the fragmentation of the market in Europe means that no producer can take advantage of the economies of scale in investment, research and product development that the Single Market should, in theory, provide. However, to overcome this fragmentation the Commission tends to become involved in the invidious (and often unwelcome) business of 'picking winners', even if only in terms of common technical specifications to which all manufacturers can work. Until 1990 the telecommunications industry was amongst the sectors excluded from the Treaty rules on public purchasing.

Underlying industry policy are fundamental national differences on the role of the state and, by extension, the role of the Union institutions. For example, French governments of whatever party have tended always to support the idea of a centrally-planned industrial policy, whereas in several other countries (including, at least since 1979, the United Kingdom) the state's role is largely confined to creating and maintaining the economic circumstances in which industry can prosper. The minimalist requirements of Article 130 EEC represent a kind of compromise between these two positions, coloured by the fact that even the enthusiasts for industrial planning are unwilling to see a substantial measure of responsibility transferred to Brussels.

Integrated Mediterranean Programmes (IMPS)

The IMPS were established in response to a 1981 memorandum from the newly elected Socialist government of Greece, which had joined the Community at the beginning of that year. Basically, the memorandum expressed dissatisfaction with Greece's terms of **accession** and asserted that the country's special problems needed special help. A commitment to meet Greece's complaints was given by the **European Council** in March 1984.

The following year the European Council established the IMPs for seven years (1986–92) 'in favour of the southern regions of the present Community' (i.e., the whole of Greece, parts of southern France and most of southern Italy). The agreement was given special urgency by the fact of accession negotiations with Portugal and Spain having been largely completed, and the purpose of the IMPs was to enable the eligible regions 'to adjust under the best conditions possible to the new situation created by **enlargement**'. The IMPs were financed by a contribution from the **structural funds**, a special line in the **Budget** and a loan facility from the **European Investment Bank** (EIB). They have not been renewed, but Greece, Ireland, Portugal and Spain now benefit from the **Cohesion Fund**.

Intergovernmental Conference (IGC)

IGCs are special committees of representatives of the governments of the member states convened to consider amendments to the **Treaties**. They meet at the request of the **Council of Ministers**, in accordance with Article N of the **Maastricht Treaty**. Their conclusions must be reached 'by common accord' (that is, unanimously) and must then be submitted to **national parliaments** (and, in some cases, electorates) for **ratification** on the basis of domestic constitutional requirements.

Since the foundation of the Community there have been five significant revisions of the Treaties: the 1965 **Merger Treaty**, the 1970 and 1975 Treaties on the budgetary powers of the **European Parliament**, the 1986 **Single European Act** (SEA) and the 1992 Maastricht Treaty on European Union. All of these have formally required the convening of an IGC, but only the SEA and Maastricht Treaty negotiations became political events in their own right with real uncertainty about their outcomes.

IGCs are, in effect, the constitutional conventions of the European Union. From being purely procedural mechanisms for presenting treaty changes on which there is broad consensus among member states, they have emerged since 1985 as the key arenas in which competing visions of the structure and overall direction of the Union are articulated. The calling of an IGC sets up a clear presumption in favour of reform, putting the opponents of closer union on the defensive. Even if the conclusions of an IGC must be agreed unanimously and then ratified, the convening of an IGC requires only a simple majority of the member states, and once negotiations are under way there are strong pressures on member states to compromise. So far no IGC has failed to agree a text, although the 1961–2 intergovernmental negotiations on the **Fouchet Plan** (which were not, strictly speaking, an IGC under Article 236 EEC) broke down because of French intransigence.

Some advocates of closer European integration use IGCs as a means of moving towards federalism (see **federation**). For example, having failed in the Maastricht Treaty to secure as substantial a move towards political union as they wished, the immediate response of the German and **Benelux** governments was to obtain a commitment to convene another IGC in 1996 to review the Maastricht settlement (Article N2 TEU: see below). This will be convened in Turin in March 1996.

As the IGC has developed as the constitution-making forum within the Union, so criticism has grown about the secret intergovernmental negotiating process that is involved. It would be politically impossible to redesign the institutions of any member state on the basis of ministerial or official preferences alone, without any serious parliamentary participation or access by the people to the process. The 1985 SEA IGC was conducted very largely in secret, and initially the Maastricht Treaty negotiations followed the same course. During the course of 1991, however, the rigid application of official confidentiality began to break down as journalists became more ingenious in obtaining documents. This led to absurd situations like that of the British government refusing to make the June 1991 Luxembourg **presidency** draft treaty available to the House of Commons on the grounds that its publication would prejudice a diplomatic negotiation, even though the document was freely available to subscribers of a news service. During the second half of 1991, under the Dutch presidency, it became normal for major presidency proposals at least to be published, even if many other important papers remained undisclosed.

Much of the agenda of the 1996 IGC is already decided. The general review of the Maastricht Treaty arrangements will include in particular the role of the **Western European Union** (WEU), since the original 1948 **Treaty of Brussels** specified 1998 as the date when signatory states become free to withdraw from it. There is also a commitment to consider the possibility of introducing more specific provisions on civil protection, energy and tourism and of establishing a **hierarchy of acts**. Amongst the institutional issues on the agenda, the most important are a review of the **qualified majority voting** (QMV) system and of the **co-decision** procedure (Article 1896.8 EEC). Finally, the **interinstitutional agreement** on the **Budget** of October 1993 committed the IGC to a review of the procedure for adopting the Budget, including a review of the distinction between non-compulsory and **compulsory expenditure**. See Justus Lipsius, 'The 1996 Intergovernmental Conference', *European Law Review*, Vol. 20, no. 3, June 1995.

The unwillingness of the governments of some member states to see the benefits of open discussion in advance about proposals being considered within the IGC may help explain, for example, the striking lack of public interest or confidence in the Maastricht Treaty when it was finally agreed, and its subsequent repudiation by the Danish people in the June 1992 referendum. It may also explain how constitutional texts can continue to emerge that are to all intents and purposes incomprehensible to anyone other than lawyers, civil servants or academics.

IGCs are the point at which the historic instincts of the Council as an essentially diplomatic, and certainly intergovernmental, political organization intersect with the growing reality of the Union as a supranational political system in its own right. If the Union were simply an international organization like any other, it would be possible for governments to alter its founding Treaties at will behind closed doors. The fact that the Union has entered into the fabric of domestic political life makes this increasingly difficult.

Intergovernmentalism

Intergovernmentalism is both a theory of integration (see also **federation**, **functionalism**) and a term used to describe institutional arrangements and decision-making procedures that allow governments to cooperate in specific fields while retaining their **sovereignty**. The intergovernmental approach to European integration involves keeping supranational institutions to a minimum and is, accordingly, the opposite of federalism. The intergovernmental model is of a confederal Europe, sometimes known as a *Europe des patries*. The European Union of today has certain intergovernmental aspects, such as the so-called intergovernmental 'pillars' of the **Maastricht Treaty**. These represent an attempt on the part of the British government and others to keep certain sensitive areas, such as immigration and security, firmly within the ambit of the **Council of Ministers** and out of the hands of the other Union institutions; i.e., not subject to the right of legislative initiative enjoyed by the **Commission**, nor to the scrutiny of the **European Parliament**, nor to the arbitration in the event of a dispute that is the prerogative of the **Court of Justice**.

Examples of international organizations that are essentially intergovernmental include the **European Free Trade Association** (EFTA), the **Organization for Economic Cooperation and Development** and the **Council of Europe**. All three are equipped with central institutions and at least the nucleus of a permanent secretariat, but the real power rests with the governments of the countries that choose to participate, a power symbolized by the Committees of Ministers which take the final decisions.

Intergovernmentalism is attractive to defenders of both national and parliamentary sovereignty, although the extent to which individual **national parliaments** can in fact exercise control over governments acting in concert is very limited.

Interinstitutional agreements

Under Article N of the **Maastricht Treaty** major adjustments to the powers of and relations between the institutions of the European Union can formally be made only by Treaty amendment, requiring the unanimous consent of the member states and ratification by **national parliaments**. Minor adjustments are made under interinstitutional agreements, many of which are later embodied in Treaty amendments. There is a recent politico-legal study of such agreements in Joerg Monar, 'Inter-institutional agreements: the phenomenon and its new dynamics after Maastricht', *Common Market Law Review*, Vol. 31/4, August 1994.

Internal market

This phrase is used to distinguish economic activity within the member states of the European Union from external trade. Under Article 3c of the **Treaty of Rome** the internal market must allow the free movement of goods, persons, services and capital. See also **Single Market**.

Interpol

Interpol grew out of the International Criminal Police Commission (ICPC) founded in Vienna in 1923. By the end of the 1930s 34 countries were members of the ICPC, but after the Anschluss in 1938, the organization fell into the hands of the Nazis and was effectively disbanded. When the ICPC was refounded in 1946, its statute prevented it from becoming involved in cases of a political, religious, racial or military character (Article 3). It has been known as Interpol since 1956.

Interpol is primarily an organization for the gathering and exchange of information and a forum in which matters of common interest (police training, counter-terrorism, technical progress in communications) can be discussed. Its headquarters and general secretariat are in Lyons, and are supplemented by National Central Bureaux within the police forces of each participating state. It is wholly dependent upon the voluntary cooperation of its member states, of which there are about 170. The member states of the Union and other European countries are the most active members of Interpol and provide most of its budget. Interpol provides one obvious model for **Europol**.

Intervention

Intervention is one of the key features of the price support mechanism under the **Common Agricultural Policy** (CAP). If a product cannot be sold at an agreed price for that marketing year, it 'goes into intervention': it is bought and stored for future disposal. The cost is borne by the **Budget**. The responsibility for managing intervention rests with national authorities, the Intervention Boards in the case of the United Kingdom. Since the early 1980s efforts to reform the CAP have sought to limit the volume for surplus produce qualifying for intervention with the aid of 'stabilizers', of which the best-known are **quotas**. Not all products are covered by the price support mechanism.

Intra-Community trade

By establishing a **customs union** under the **Treaty of Rome**, **the Six** sought to stimulate trade amongst themselves. Over the period 1958–68, during which restrictions on trade were being dismantled, trade amongst the member states grew by an annual average of 28.4 per cent, although this was an acceleration of a trend that in fact began in the early 1950s as part of a general postwar recovery.

The table shows the percentage of total imports and exports for each member state of the Union represented by trade with the other member states, and the high percentage of Austrian, Finnish and Swedish trade which was already with the European Union two years before **accession**.

In some cases these figures represent the result of a substantial shift away from trade with non-member states. The most striking example is the United Kingdom, of whose exports in 1958 the other 11 member states were taking only 21.8 per cent. France, Portugal and Spain, three other

Intra-Community trade 1993

Member states	Imports	Exports
Belgo-Luxembourg Economic Union	71.4	73.6
Denmark	54.3	54.2
France	64.0	61.2
Germany	51.2	49.8
Greece	60.3	55.9
Ireland	69.5	69.1
Italy	55.4	53.3
Netherlands	66.1	73.9
Portugal	71.9	75.3
Spain	61.3	62.3
United Kingdom	48.9	52.5
Non-member states		
Austria	66.6	60.3
Finland	45.6	45.4
Sweden	55.0	53.0

Source: *Eurostat*

countries with well-established trading links outside Europe, have experienced a similar shift towards trade with other member states.

Intrastat

With the removal of frontier controls between member states under the **Single Market** programme, a new system, known as Intrastat, was devised to collect statistics on internal trade. Developed by the Statistical Office (see **Eurostat**) and operational from 1 January 1993, Intrastat involves collecting information directly from businesses and is closely linked to the system for assessing and collecting **value-added tax** (VAT). The administrative burden on small businesses has been eased by the application of a threshold, but in some member states problems of late or incomplete submissions are still being encountered.

Ireland

In the 1960s Ireland applied to join **the Six** in the wake of the United Kingdom, but was blocked by the vetoes on British **accession** exercised by **Charles de Gaulle**. Ireland eventually joined the Community, with Denmark and the United Kingdom, on 1 January 1973, a May 1972 referendum having resulted in 83.1 per cent of the votes being cast in favour of membership. The great attractions of membership were wider markets and massive support for Irish agriculture, and participation in an institutional framework that, in most respects, placed Ireland on an equal footing with the United Kingdom. Six years later, the entry into force of the **Exchange-Rate Mechanism** (ERM) was the occasion for the breaking of the link between the Irish pound and the pound sterling.

Only two anxieties have interrupted Ireland's state of contentment with Community membership. The first arose in the mid-1980s, when the member states started to move slowly but decisively towards closer involvement in defence and security issues. This was incompatible with Irish neutrality, and led to a last-minute challenge to the **Single European Act** (SEA) in the Irish Supreme Court and a referendum in May 1987. Ireland has remained outside all military alliances. The second arose as a consequence of the strengthened commitment to the free movement of persons in the **Maastricht Treaty**. **Protocols** were added both to the Treaty and the **Treaty of Rome** saying that this commitment did not 'affect the application' of Article 40.3.3 of the Irish Constitution, under which abortion is prohibited. In February 1992 a 14-year-old girl who had been raped was prevented from leaving Ireland in order to have an abortion in England. This action was challenged in the Irish Supreme Court, partly on the grounds that freedom of movement was guaranteed under the Treaty. The following month the Court ruled that since the girl's life was in danger, she was free to travel. In spite of a supplementary declaration agreed by the member states on 1 May 1992, the absolute right of Irish citizens to travel in order 'to obtain ... services lawfully available in Member States' remained unclear. This, however, did not prevent the Irish electorate from approving the Maastricht Treaty by a majority of two to one in a referendum on 18 June 1992.

Isle of Man

See **Channel Islands**.

Isoglucose case

The so-called 'isoglucose' case, the subject of a **Court of Justice** ruling in 1980, was of great importance in confirming the essential role played by the **European Parliament** in the legislative process. In fact, the case (*SA Roquette Frères* v *Council*, Case 138/79) was one of several concerned with isoglucose, a form of sugar extracted from cereals. The events may be summarized as follows. On 7 March 1979 the **European Commission** submitted to the **Council of Ministers** a proposal for a revised Regulation on isoglucose. The Council, as it was obliged to do under Article 143.2 EEC, sought the **Opinion** of the European Parliament and pointed out that, since the revised Regulation had to come into force on 1 July 1979, the Parliament would need to give its Opinion in April. In the event it was not until May that the Parliament considered the report drawn up by its Committee on Agriculture. The report was rejected and referred back to the Committee.

Because the first European elections were held in June 1979, the Parliament did not meet again in full session until 17 July 1979, by which time the Council had adopted the revised Regulation (25 June 1979) without any Opinion having been received. A firm affected by the production quota for isoglucose laid down by the Council therefore brought an action in the **Court of Justice** against the Council to have the revised Regulation declared void under Article 173 EEC on the grounds that an essential procedural requirement had been infringed.

In its judgment, the Court stated:

> The consultation provided for [in the **Treaty of Rome**] is the means which allows the Parliament to play an actual part in the legislative process of the Community. Such power represents an essential factor in the institutional balance intended by the Treaty. Although limited, it reflects at Community level the fundamental democratic principle that the peoples should take part in the exercise of power through the intermediary of a representative assembly.

Due consultation of the Parliament in the cases provided for by the Treaty therefore constitutes an essential formality, disregard of which means that the measure concerned is void.

The Court went on to say that the requirement of 'due consultation' cannot be satisfied 'by the Council's simply asking for [the Parliament's] opinion'.

Simple consultation of the type considered in the isoglucose case has largely been superseded by the **cooperation** and **co-decision procedures** introduced by the **Single European Act** (SEA) and extended by the **Maastricht Treaty**. Nevertheless, the isoglucose judgment, given so soon after the first European elections, was of lasting importance in terms of the Parliament's prestige and self-confidence. Together with the other cases concerned with isoglucose, it is conveniently summarized and analysed in Rudden, *Basic Community Cases*; see also Weatherill and Beaumont, *EC Law*.

Italy

The poorest of **the Six**, Italy was attracted to membership of the European Community as a means of re-establishing stability, credibility and respectability after a quarter-century of Fascist rule. **Alcide de Gasperi**, Italy's most noted statesman of the postwar decade, was determined that his country should play its full part in both European integration and, as a founder member of the **North Atlantic Treaty Organization** (NATO), the Atlantic Alliance.

There has always been a high level of support in Italy for European integration across all political parties and in every sector of society. This may be connected with a consistently low level of satisfaction with respect to the quality of national and local government in Italy and a corresponding readiness to see powers transferred to Brussels, and a pattern of personal loyalties in which the sense of nationhood does not loom very large. Italians are amongst the strongest supporters of federalism (see **Altiero Spinelli**): in 1984 the **European elections** in Italy were combined with a **referendum**, in which the Italian electorate enthusiastically endorsed the idea that the **European Parliament** should be a **constituent assembly** empowered to draw up a constitution for Europe.

Contrasting with this enthusiasm is a poor record with regard to the implementation and observance of Community law. In the great majority of cases this may be ascribed to the chaotic workings of Italian bureaucracy and to a somewhat freewheeling approach to law in general rather than to any deliberate act of defiance.

Italy has always been a strong supporter of the **structural funds** and a vigorous defender of the interests of Mediterranean agriculture, especially the wine and olive oil sectors. However, a lack of coherence and of strategic thinking in Italian governments and the inward-looking nature of Italian politics have resulted in there being few distinctively Italian policy stances and even fewer major Italian initiatives oriented towards Europe: with the partial exception of the 1981 **Genscher–Colombo Plan** there has been no such initiative at governmental level since the 1955 **Messina Conference**. The only Italian presidency of the **Commission** (Franco Maria Malfatti, 1970–72) was short and undistinguished: Malfatti resigned nine months before the end of his term in order to return to Italian politics. Italy can claim, however, to have invented Eurocommunism (see **Communism**). Upheavals in Italian politics in 1994 brought to power a new party, Forza Italia, which initially at least promised to take a more robust approach to European integration.

Jenkins, Roy (b. 1920)

Roy Jenkins was elected as a Labour MP in 1948. He rose rapidly within the Labour Party and in 1965 he was made Home Secretary in the first Government led by Harold Wilson. He was Chancellor of the Exchequer from 1967 until Wilson's defeat by **Edward Heath** in 1970. Jenkins was the leader of the 69 pro-European Labour MPs who defied the party whip in October 1971 when the United Kingdom's terms of **accession** to the European Community were finally agreed by the House of Commons (see **renegotiation**). He was also one of the leaders of the 'Britain in Europe' campaign in the **referendum of June 1975**. His outspoken support for Europe made him unpopular with many in the Labour Party and it came as no real surprise when he failed to secure the leadership after Wilson's resignation in 1976. That same year he was chosen to succeed François-Xavier Ortoli as President of the **European Commission**, and he remained in Brussels from 1977 until 1981, having resigned his House of Commons seat. Jenkins's presidency was marked by a steady growth in the Commission's standing and influence; against strong opposition from French President **Valéry Giscard d'Estaing**, Jenkins succeeded in ensuring that the President of the Commission attended the **Group of Seven** summits of the major industrialized nations, but his most enduring achievement was the relaunching of **Economic and Monetary Union** (EMU).

On his return to British politics Jenkins's commitment to Europe was once again evident in the importance attached to European questions by the new Social Democratic Party (SDP), which, as one of the 'Gang of Four', Jenkins helped to found in 1981 and which he led from 1981 until 1983. Re-elected to Parliament in 1982, he lost his seat five years later. Roy Jenkins was made a life peer in 1987 and was awarded the Order of Merit in 1993. He is Chancellor of Oxford University and leader of the Liberal Democrats in the House of Lords.

The author of many speeches and articles on European issues, Roy Jenkins has also published his *European Diary* covering his period in the Commission. Suavely written, this is uniquely fascinating as an insider's account of life at the top of the Community, with its extraordinary mixture of great issues and petty intrigue. Jenkins's character sketches of the politicians with whom he dealt, including his fellow Commissioners, are especially entertaining.

Joint action

The provisions in the **Maastricht Treaty** covering the new areas of Union competence, the **Common Foreign and Security Policy** (CFSP) and **Justice and Home Affairs** (JHA), do not allow for the use of the **legal instruments** specified in the **Treaty of Rome**. Instead, the **Council of Ministers** may adopt common (or joint) positions and take joint actions (Articles J1.3 and K3.2 TEU). In the case of the CFSP the **Council of Ministers** is empowered to decide, acting unanimously, on the basis of guidelines laid down by the **European Council**, 'that a matter should be the subject of joint action' (Article J3.1 TEU). In the case of JHA, any member state and, in certain fields, the **Commission** may propose a joint action (Article K3.2 TEU), which the Council may adopt by **unanimity**. The use of a joint action procedure under a unanimity rule guaranteeing a right of **veto** underlines the essentially intergovernmental nature (see **intergovernmentalism**) of these areas of Union activity and was an essential element in securing the acceptance of the Maastricht Treaty by member states. Once a joint action has been agreed, the Council may decide to make follow-up decisions by **qualified majority voting** (QMV).

Joint European Torus (JET)

The JET project, based at Culham, Oxfordshire, is the most ambitious **research** venture so far undertaken by the countries of the European Union. Switzerland also participates. One of only four large-scale projects in the world in the field of nuclear fusion, JET employs some 300 scientists. The long-term aim is to develop nuclear fusion as a cleaner, safer, more efficient source of nuclear energy than nuclear fission.

Culham was chosen as the site for JET in October 1977, after a long dispute in which Germany pushed very hard for an alternative site at Garching, near Munich. The issue was eventually settled in the course of a bilateral meeting between Prime Minister James Callaghan and Chancellor Helmut Schmidt. The incident was used to illustrate the absurdity of a decision-making system in which such issues were decided at so high a level, having become embroiled with other unrelated issues, such as agricultural reform and the **British Budget problem**. It was alleged that Europe's lead in this particular area of research was set back at least two years as a result of the dispute.

Joint List

The Joint List is a central feature of the **External Frontiers Convention**.

Article 7 of the Convention sets out a list of five requirements for any national of a non-member country wishing to enter the territory of the member states. The first four are basic: a passport, a visa where necessary, documentary evidence of the reason for entry (such as a job offer), and evidence of means of subsistence sufficient to cover the period of stay and the cost of a return journey to the country of origin or another country. The fifth requirement is more problematic: that the applicant for entry 'does not represent a threat to the public policy, national security, or international relations of Member States and, in particular, that his name does not appear on the joint list'. The Joint List is composed of names of persons considered as undesirable immigrants, and is based on information supplied by member states. The fact that the list is held on computer, is continuously updated and is based upon decisions by national authorities, against which there is in some cases no ready means of appeal, has given rise to anxieties amongst lawyers and experts on civil liberties.

Joint Research Centre (JRC)

Article 8 of the Treaty establishing the **European Atomic Energy Community** (Euratom) provided for the creation of a Joint Nuclear Research Centre. The centre, now officially known as the Joint Research Centre (JRC) since its work is no longer confined to nuclear research, is made up of nine separate institutes. Six of them are based at Ispra in northern Italy, the other three at Geel in Belgium, Karlsruhe in Germany, and Petten in the Netherlands. The JRC is the responsibility of the Research Directorate-General (D-G. XII) in the **European Commission**. The various institutes carry out research in the fields of nuclear safety, remote sensing by satellite, materials research, the environment, information technology and systems engineering (see also **Joint European Torus**). In April 1994 it was announced that an additional institute, to be known as the European Science and Technology Observatory, was to be set up in Seville. This observatory is intended to monitor all research, both within the Union and elsewhere, relevant to the policies and objectives of the Union. At the same meeting the **Council of Ministers** adopted new guidelines for the JRC, with effect from 1 January 1995. The JRC is now required to compete for research contracts, including those put out to tender by the Commission itself. It is also enabled to participate in 'research networks' with other public or private institutes situated in the member states (see also **research**, **Joint European Torus**, **European Space Agency**, **European Organization for Nuclear Research**).

Juste retour

The phrase '*juste retour*' became widely current in 1979–85, when the

British Budget problem was a regular item on the agenda of the **Council of Ministers**. It means that in broad terms and over a period a member state should receive from the **Budget** of the Union a 'fair return', i.e., sums roughly equivalent to those made over as a contribution. Strictly applied, the principle would, of course, reduce still further the redistributive effect of the Budget between member states. A looser definition of *juste retour* takes account not only of member states' contributions but also their relative prosperity and the extent to which they draw benefit from other policies. The phrase *juste retour* is now seldom used, having come to symbolize a narrow profit-and-loss approach to membership of the Union (see also **contributions and receipts**).

As Prime Minister in the 1970s, Harold Wilson once mildly rebuked those critics who demanded a *juste retour* from the Budget by quoting Wordsworth:

> . . . high Heaven rejects the lore
> Of nicely-calculated less or more.
> (Ecclesiastical Sonnets, no. 43)

Justice and Home Affairs (JHA)

In common with the other intergovernmental '**pillar**' of the **Maastricht Treaty**, the **Common Foreign and Security Policy** (CFSP), cooperation in the fields of Justice and Home Affairs has grown out of a variety of *ad hoc* procedures, some more formal than others, on specific subjects. The scope and forms of cooperation are set out in Title VI of the Treaty, which consists of a single Article K broken down into 10 subsidiary Articles. Article K1 specifies the subjects to be covered by JHA as 'matters of common interest': asylum policy, controls at the Union's external frontiers, immigration policy, drug addiction, international fraud, judicial cooperation in both civil and criminal matters, customs cooperation, and police cooperation in respect of 'terrorism, unlawful drug-trafficking and other serious forms of international crime . . . [and] the organization of a Union-wide system for exchanging information within a European Police Office (**Europol**)'.

Article K3 obliges member states to 'inform and consult one another' in these areas and provides for action under three headings: the adoption of joint positions, **joint action**, or the drawing up of conventions for adoption by member states. In respect of all but criminal matters, customs cooperation and police cooperation, member states and the **European Commission** have the right of initiative; only member states have this right in the exceptions noted above.

Article K4 sets up a coordinating committee of senior national officials (known as the K4 Committee) to assist the **Council of Ministers**, which can, in most areas, act only by unanimity. The Commission is 'fully associated' with JHA, but the involvement of the **European Parliament** is more ambiguous. Under Article K6 it must be kept informed and must be consulted on the 'principal aspects' of JHA; it is the responsibility of the Council **presidency** to ensure that the Parliament's views 'are duly taken into consideration'. Additionally, Members of the European Parliament (MEPs) may put questions to the Council, make Recommendations and hold an annual debate on JHA.

As with the CFSP, operational costs arising from JHA action may be borne either by the **Budget** of the Union or directly by member states 'in accordance with a scale to be decided'. Administrative expenditure is in all cases charged to the Budget.

Title VI contains what is commonly referred to as a *passerelle* (footbridge) clause, Article K9. This allows the Council, acting unanimously, to decide to deal with all matters in respect of which the Commission has a right of initiative (see above) under the new Article 100c EEC. This would bring them within the scope of European Community (as opposed to intergovernmental) action, involving, *inter alia*, consultation of the European Parliament, the adoption of Regulations and Directives (see **legal instruments**), and the possibility of recourse to the **Court of Justice**.

Article 100c was added to the **Treaty of Rome** by the Maastricht Treaty. It enjoins the Council, acting unanimously after consulting the European Parliament, to draw up a list of those countries 'whose nationals must be in possession of a visa when crossing the external borders of the Member States' (see **Joint List**). Provision is also made for a visa requirement to be imposed (by a **qualified majority vote** and for a maximum period of six months) on nationals of a country not included on the list if an emergency gives rise to a 'threat of a sudden inflow of nationals from that country'. Article 100c specifies that from 1 January 1996 all decisions relating to visa requirements shall be by qualified majority and that by that date there shall be an agreement on a common format for visas. The K4 Committee (see above) assists the Council in areas covered by Article 100c.

With some exceptions, the JHA provisions of the Maastricht Treaty were a consolidation and a rationalization of various intergovernmental arrangements that had grown up over the previous 20 years (the most significant of which is described under **Trevi Group**). However, the prolonged debate in 1992–3 over the Treaty brought these arrangements into the open. On the one hand the sensitivity of the issues dealt with was said to justify their being kept in governments' hands; on the other, many parliamentarians and journalists concerned with civil liberties have argued that intergovernmental arrangements mean too much power in the hands of officials not subject to adequate democratic scrutiny either at the national or at the European level. Even if the Council does decide under Article K9 (see above) to transfer many of the issues to the procedures laid down in Article 100c EEC, this will allow only simple consultation of the European Parliament: the Council will not be under any great pressure to act in accordance with the Parliament's wishes.

It was, of course, inevitable that the creation of a European Union within which citizens of the Union (see **citizenship**) have the right to move and reside freely under Article 8a EEC would make it necessary for member states to cooperate more closely on immigration, police matters and terrorism. The **Single Market** programme entailed the relaxation or removal of controls at internal frontiers and a shift of emphasis to the external frontiers (see **free movement of persons**). At the same time the member states are under greater pressure than ever before from immigration from the south and the east, and Germany in particular has been concerned to ensure that this pressure can be handled on a Union-wide basis. It is these three factors that have shaped JHA provisions as they now stand: whether or not the arrangements will work and how they will fit in with the more ambitious programme set out in the **Schengen Agreement** remain unclear. Certainly the European Parliament will press for closer involvement and there are several indications that **national parliaments** will do the same. The arguments are very clearly set out in a House of Lords report of November 1993 entitled *Scrutiny of the Intergovernmental Pillars of the European Union*; see also Joerg Monar and Roger Morgan (eds), *The Third Pillar of the European Union* (Brussels, 1994). There is a helpful analysis of the issues raised by JHA cooperation in John Benyon, 'Policing the European Union: the changing basis of cooperation on law enforcement', *International Affairs*, Vol. 70, no. 3, July 1994, and in U. Sieber, 'European unification and European criminal law', *European Journal of Crime, Criminal Law and Criminal Justice*, Vol. 2, no. 2, 1994.

Kaleidoscope 2000

Kaleidoscope 2000 is a programme under which assistance may be given from the **Budget** of the European Union to cultural activities. To qualify for assistance, an activity must involve participants from at least three member states (see **cultural policy**).

Kangaroo Group

Subtitled 'the movement for free movement', the Kangaroo Group was founded in the first directly elected **European Parliament** by members (MEPs) of all parties led by British Conservative Basil de Ferranti (1930–88). One of the most successful single-issue pressure groups ever established at Community level, the Group has campaigned for the removal of **non-tariff barriers** to trade between member states. It played a very important part in providing the rationale and political impetus for the 1985 **Single Market** programme (see also **Cockfield White Paper**). The Group attempts to influence governments and businesses through conferences and publications of various kinds, including the newspaper *Kangaroo News*.

Karlsruhe judgment

The Karlsruhe judgment, delivered by the German Federal Constitutional Court in Karlsruhe on 12 October 1993, arose from an action brought by campaigners opposed to the **Maastricht Treaty**, led by Manfred Brunner, formerly *chef de cabinet* to Martin Bangemann, the senior German member of the **Commission**. The action sought to challenge both the Treaty itself in terms of its compatibility with the Basic Law (*Grundgesetz*) of the Federal Republic and the amendments to the Basic Law that were consequent upon German ratification of the Treaty, in particular the new Article 23 on the transfer of powers to the European Union (in future, such transfers require a two-thirds majority in both the upper and lower chambers of the German Parliament). The Court rejected some of the specific complaints as inadmissible.

The judgment centred upon whether or not the provisions of the Treaty were consistent with Article 24 of the Basic Law, which permits 'sovereign powers' to be transferred to 'intergovernmental institutions', in the light of the fact that the Treaty sought to establish a Union that was more than merely intergovernmental. The Court ruled that since the **pillars** of the Union were essentially intergovernmental, it lacked certain attributes of statehood. The Treaty notwithstanding, it remained a *Staatenbund* (association of states) rather than a *Bundesstaat* (federal state). The second point of substance was whether the democratic guarantees in the Basic Law were compromised, particularly in the area of **Economic and Monetary Union** (EMU), by the transfer of powers from the national to the European level. The Court ruled that they were not, since the Treaty provisions allowed for adequate parliamentary supervision through the **European Parliament**.

The Karlsruhe judgment enabled Germany to ratify the Maastricht Treaty, the last member state to do so. Long extracts from the judgment are included in an article by Matthias Herdegen, 'Maastricht and the German Constitutional Court: constitutional restraints for an ever closer union', *Common Market Review*, Vol. 31/2, April 1994.

Kohl, Helmut (b. 1930)

Helmut Kohl entered politics at the *Land* level in his home state of Rhineland-Palatinate. In 1973 he became leader of the Christian Democratic Union (CDU), and was their unsuccessful candidate for Chancellor in 1976. He became Chancellor six years later, when the Free Democrats (Liberal) Party switched coalition partners from the Socialists to the CDU, thus bringing about a change of government. Since then, he has won four elections (1983, 1987, 1990 and 1994) as the leader of his party.

Kohl has always been a convinced pro-European in the tradition of **Konrad Adenauer**, and the size and strength of the German economy have enabled him to play a very influential role in Community affairs. He is also a staunch supporter of the Atlantic Alliance. He took a close personal interest, together with his Foreign Minister, **Hans-Dietrich Genscher**, in **German reunification**. The problems and uncertainties created by reunification gave rise to a political climate in which Kohl's virtues of dignity, sense of purpose and integrity were shown to particular advantage. He has continued his predecessors' policy of maintaining good relations with the President of France (see **Franco-German cooperation**).

Konver

Konver is a programme that draws on the **structural funds** to help regions heavily dependent on the defence sector cope with the economic and social consequences of cuts in defence budgets.

Languages

The rules governing the languages of the institutions of the Union are decided by the **Council of Ministers**, acting unanimously, under Article 217 of the **Treaty of Rome**. This was the legal base for Regulation 1 of 15 April 1958, which specified Dutch, French, German and Italian as 'the official languages and the working languages' in the institutions of **the Six** and gave them equal status. All official documents have to be available in all languages at meetings and full interpretation provided. With the accession of Denmark, Ireland and the United Kingdom in 1973 the number of working languages rose to six and the number of official languages to seven (although only a limited number of the documents, such as the **Treaties**, are available in Irish). Greek was added in 1981, Spanish and Portuguese in 1986, Finnish and Swedish in 1995.

Of the five main institutions of the European Union, only the **Court of Justice** is exempt from the requirement that all languages be accorded equal status. For each case before the Court, a procedural language or 'language of the case' is chosen, although full translation and interpretation are provided. In practice, English and French are the languages most widely used throughout the institutions for internal meetings and working-papers.

The problem of language is slightly eased by a rigorous system of colour-coding applied to the different language versions of all official documents: pink for Danish, yellow for German, light blue for Greek, lilac for English, red for Spanish, dark blue for French, light green for Italian, orange for Dutch, dark green for Portuguese, royal blue for Finnish and pale yellow for Swedish.

Eleven languages give rise to no fewer than 110 language combinations: the formula is $n^2 - n$, where n equals the number of languages in use. Each additional language adds a further $2(n - 1)$ combinations: for example, a twelfth language would bring the total of combinations up to 132. Overall, approximately one-third of the officials working in the Union's institutions are employed in connection with interpretation and translation. The **Commission** is one of the pioneers in the field of machine translation, using a system called Systran (originally developed in the United States for the rapid translation of transcripts of radio broadcasts from the Soviet Union). The Commission's translation service, which is based in Luxembourg, has an output of about 1 million pages a year. A new Translation Centre has been set up there to provide translations for the various new European Union bodies such as **Europol** and the **European Environment Agency**.

Interpreters work in teams of three per language at official meetings. For the more obscure combinations (Danish into Greek, for example) the interpretation is via a third language, a system known as 'relay'. A substantial number of interpreters are freelance and work for other international organizations. Their working conditions are strictly controlled, their discretion is absolute and their professional standards are very high indeed.

The **European Parliament** is the institution most seriously affected by the multiplicity of languages. In recent years, it has tried to cut down the number of languages used in meetings, particularly those held outside the member states. This can give rise to objections from Members (MEPs) representing minority languages, such as Danish, Greek or Portuguese, who are sensitive to any suggestion that some languages are less important than others. A high proportion of the Parliament's budget is spent on language-related work: every amendment tabled in plenary session generates an average of 1,000 pieces of paper per language, and reports that attract more than 50 amendments are not uncommon.

Although some MEPs are good linguists, the interpretation inevitably has a deadening effect on debates. Repartee, interruptions, most forms of humour (especially irony), quotations, literary or historical allusions and vivid metaphors all tend to get lost. And mistakes can be made: interpreting *une grande déception* ('a big disappointment') as 'a great deception' can cause resentment as well as confusion. Other traps abound: a *pavillon de complaisance* is not something you might expect to find in a rococo pleasure-garden but, more prosaically, a flag of convenience used in merchant shipping.

Approximately 27 languages are spoken within the European Union, not counting those spoken by immigrants, with English by far the most widely taught second language, and German the most widely spoken first language. That only 11 should be used as working languages within the institutions is progress of a kind, but with **enlargement** the situation is certain to get worse. A referendum on membership of the Union in an applicant state would certainly be lost if the electorate were to be informed that their national language was not to be used in the Union institutions. Some have argued for a more rigid distinction to be made between 'official' and 'working' languages or for a distinction between 'public' and 'internal' working languages, with a view to reducing the latter to three or four, but this would not help the European Parliament: diplomats and international civil servants may be expected to work in languages other than their own, but not elected politicians, least of all when considering texts that will have the force of law in their home countries. The United Nations uses six languages: English, French, Spanish, Russian, Arabic and Chinese. Even in the **Common Foreign and Security Policy** (CFSP), where a good practical case could be made for reducing the number of languages used to a bare minimum, Declaration 29 annexed to the **Maastricht Treaty** requires the normal rules to apply. There is a good survey of the problem of languages in Florian Coulnas (ed.), *A Language Policy for the European Community* (Berlin and New York, 1991).

League of Nations

The League of Nations was founded under a covenant of the Treaty of Versailles (1919) and came into existence on the date the Treaty came into effect (10 January 1920). The seat of the League was Geneva, Brussels having been rejected as too closely associated with the Great War. By the end of 1920 most European states had become members of the League, amongst them all the present member states of the European Union except Ireland (which joined as the Irish Free State in September 1923) and Germany (which joined in September 1926). By October 1935 the League had 58 members world-wide, half of them European states. However, the United States Congress had refused to ratify the Treaty of Versailles in 1920, so the United States was never a member of the League. Amongst League members were states as small as Panama and Honduras and as large as China and the USSR, but in terms of votes in the Council and the Assembly (see below) all were on an equal footing.

Under the terms of the Covenant members of the League committed themselves to 'the reduction of national armaments to the lowest point consistent with national safety' and to the exchange of 'full and frank information as to the scale of their armaments' (Article 8). The crucial Article 10 committed members of the League 'to respect and preserve as against external aggression the territorial integrity and existing political independence' of other members. Under Article 12 (as revised in 1924) members agreed to submit disputes to arbitration, judicial settlement or to an inquiry by the Council of the League and not to resort to war until at least three months after the adjudication was pronounced. A member that failed to respect this provision was 'deemed to have committed an act of war against all other Members of the League', which would then 'subject it to the severance of all trade or financial relations'; the nationals of the offending state would be denied contact with those of any other state, 'whether a Member of the League or not' (Article 16).

The permanent organs of the League were the Council, the Assembly, the Secretariat, and the International Court of Justice at The Hague. Like the Security Council of the United Nations, the Council was composed of permanent and non-permanent members, the latter elected by the Assembly. At first, there were four permanent members: the British Empire, France, Italy and Japan; a fifth, Germany, was added in 1926, the German government having insisted on permanent membership of the Council as a condition of Germany's membership of the League. The number of non-permanent members grew from 4 in 1920 to 11 in 1936. The Council was empowered to deal 'with any matter within the sphere of action of the League or affecting the peace of the world' (Article 4.4) and in practice met three times a year. Each member of the Council had one representative and one vote. A member state not represented in the Council was entitled to send a delegate to Council meetings at which matters affecting that state were discussed, and the delegate was entitled to vote.

The Assembly was composed of three representatives and three substitutes appointed by the governments of each member state. However, as in the Council, each member state had only one vote. Some representatives were parliamentarians, but many were not. The Assembly met in plenary session once a year in September in Geneva, but it was entitled to hold extraordinary sessions at other times and in other places. The Assembly's work was done in six (later seven) committees, to which each member had the right to appoint one representative: Legal Affairs, Disarmament, Budgetary Questions, and so on. More technical subjects, such as health and communications, were dealt with in committees of experts attached to the League, as were more recondite matters such as slavery, opium and European union (to consider the proposal for a European federation made in 1929 by **Aristide Briand**). The organs of the League were serviced by a small international secretariat headed by Sir Eric Drummond (Earl of Perth), later British Ambassador in Rome, and from 1933 by Joseph Avenol of France.

Although procedural matters could be settled by majority, substantive decisions of both the Council and the Assembly had to be unanimous (Article 5). Taken in conjunction with the absolute right of interested states to participate in Council deliberations (see above), this proved an insuperable obstacle to effective action. Although the League was responsible for several successful peacekeeping operations – such as the 1935 plebiscite in the **Saarland** – it failed totally to curb the aggressive policies of Hitler and Mussolini; indeed it was the failure to prevent Mussolini's invasion and annexation of Abyssinia (Ethiopia) that finally discredited the League and the ideals of interstate cooperation and collective security on which it was based. Both Germany and Italy were permanent members of the Council of the League until their withdrawal (1933 and 1937 respectively). With the outbreak of war in 1939 the League ceased to meet, but it was not formally dissolved until 1946, when it was succeeded by the United Nations.

The League was deliberately intended to mark a break with the 'old diplomacy', that is, with bilateral agreements (not all of them publicly acknowledged) between sovereign states, with the Great Powers playing the dominant role. Initially, it enjoyed widespread support, but, as Alfred Zimmern wrote in 1935,

> Statesmen have been as profuse in professions of loyalty to the League as they have been timid and vacillating in their handling of concrete issues of policy. Indeed, the existence of the League, with its multifarious armoury of diplomatic implements, by increasing the means at their disposal, has afforded them new and up-to-date pretexts for procrastination or evasion. (*The League of Nations and the Rule of Law, 1918–1935*, 2nd edn, 1939)

Few more recent studies of the League have found much to say in defence of the 'Geneva experiment', the importance of which today is as an idealistic model of international cooperation along intergovernmental lines (see **intergovernmentalism**) that was fatally compromised from the start by the frailty of the constraints it laid upon the **sovereignty** of the member states and by the absence of any effective means of enforcing its decisions. Many of the distinguishing features of the European Union – an independent **Commission**, a body of law taking precedence over national law, a directly elected **European Parliament** – can best be understood as springing from a determination on the part of **Jean Monnet** and others not to repeat the mistakes of the League (of which Monnet had been deputy secretary-general) and to move away from intergovernmental cooperation towards a system based upon supranational institutions.

Legal instruments

Article 189 of the **Treaty of Rome** lists five different types of legal instrument; the distinction between them is fundamental to an understanding of **Community law**.

A Regulation is of 'general application'. It is 'binding in its entirety and directly applicable in all Member States'. A Directive is 'binding, as to the result to be achieved, upon each Member State to which it is addressed', but leaves 'to the national authorities the choice of form and methods'. The expression 'framework Directive' is sometimes used to denote a Directive that identifies European Union objectives over a broad field and which in so doing prepares the way for legislative action on specific points. The essential difference between a Regulation and Directive is that whereas the latter must be transposed into national law (usually by a deadline) before entering into force, the former is directly applicable and therefore usually has **direct effect**.

A Decision is 'binding in its entirety upon those to whom it is addressed'. Recommendations and **Opinions** 'have no binding force': some authorities do not classify them as legal instruments. Article 191 EEC requires Regulations, Decisions and Directives addressed to all member states to be published in the *Official Journal*.

The choice of legal instrument in respect of particular actions is specified in the Treaty in some cases and in others left to the discretion of the **Commission**, as the institution that has the **right of initiative**.

The description of legal instruments set out in Article 189 EEC does not apply to measures undertaken in the fields of **Justice and Home Affairs** (JHA) and in the **Common Foreign and Security Policy** (CFSP): the relevant provisions of the **Maastricht Treaty** refer only to 'acts', 'decisions', '**joint actions**', and '**common positions**'. A **Declaration** annexed to the Treaty commits the 1996 **Intergovernmental Conference** (IGC) to reviewing all the different types of legal instrument with a view to establishing a **hierarchy of acts**.

For a fuller description of the different types of legal instrument, see Weatherill and Beaumont, *EC Law*, Chapter 5.

Leonardo

The Leonardo programme for 1995–9 is concerned with vocational and linguistic training as a contribution to the promotion of employment. It has replaced earlier programmes such as COMETT, **Lingua** and PETRA, and has an allocation of 620 million ECUs (about £480 million) from the **Budget** over its five-year span. Leonardo is open to participation from Cyprus, Malta and the countries of central and eastern Europe as well as from member states of the European Union.

Liberalism

In most member states of the European Union Liberal parties are descended from secular or dissenting parties with a strong base amongst the professional classes opposed to the influence of the Church, Conservatism and landed interests. Liberals were, broadly speaking, radical, progressive, republican, and often closely identified with agrarian reform. However, the introduction of universal suffrage and the rise of Socialist or Labour parties dislodged the Liberals from their traditional position. In some countries this pushed Liberals to the right, in others (including the United

Kingdom) to the left. This fundamental difference is still discernible amongst the parties now linked in the European Liberal, Democrat and Reform Party (ELDR; see **transnational political parties**).

At no time since the Second World War have the Liberals and their allies in Western Europe overall come close to rivalling the Socialists or the Christian Democrats in terms of electoral support. However, in several countries they have not infrequently held the balance of power in coalitions, allowing Liberals to hold major offices of state, including the presidency of France, in the person of **Valéry Giscard d'Estaing**, from 1974 to 1981. Liberals have twice held the presidency of the **Commission** (Jean Rey, 1967–70; Gaston Thorn, 1981–5). Other prominent Liberals include **Hans-Dietrich Genscher**, the German Foreign Minister from 1974 to 1992, and Simone Veil, the first President of the directly elected **European Parliament** (1979–82).

Liberals have a vigorous and long-standing tradition of support for European integration, having voted solidly in favour of the **Treaty of Paris** and, later, the **Treaty of Rome** in the 1950s. In the European Parliament the Liberals are the fourth largest of the **political groups** but are a long way behind the Socialist and European People's Party (Christian Democrats and Conservatives) Groups. One reason for this is the fact that the British Liberal Democrats, the largest Liberal party in Europe, are handicapped by the first-past-the-post electoral system: with 16.6 per cent of the vote nationally, they gained only two seats in June 1994, having had none at all since European elections were first held in 1979. The adoption of proportional representation in Great Britain is a high priority for the Liberals (see **uniform electoral procedure**).

In point of substance, the views of Liberals are, in most areas, indistinguishable from those of the Christian Democrats. There are, however, some differences of emphasis, Liberals tending to hold more progressive or libertarian views on moral issues and to be more outspoken in favour of free markets and free trade. On the great majority of institutional, foreign policy and security issues the Liberals vote with the Christian Democrats as committed federalists and supporters of the Atlantic Alliance.

The Liberals are not as well placed as their larger rivals to acquire new allies with **enlargement**. Even within the Union the Liberals are finding it increasingly difficult to establish and maintain a distinctive political profile and with it a secure share of the electoral middle ground. The German Liberals (the Free Democrats) disappeared from the European Parliament in June 1994, having failed to reach the 5 per cent national threshold. At the European level as well as at the national level, the Liberals' position between left and right is of little advantage to them as politics become less polarized. Their position serves also to draw attention to their own internal divisions, as they try to keep open the option of coalitions either to their right or to their left.

LIFE

The LIFE programme groups together several initiatives concerned with policies for the environment (see **environment policy**), including the protection of natural habitats, the promotion of new technologies and the provision of training and information.

Lingua

The Lingua programme, in operation since 1990, was designed to promote and improve the teaching of foreign languages within the Union, by means of student and teacher exchanges, in-service training for language teachers, and research into new methods and materials relevant to the study of languages. By 1994 it was helping over 10,000 students and over 6,000 teachers annually.

With effect from 1995, Lingua was merged into the **Socrates** and **Leonardo** programmes.

Linkage

'Linkage' denotes the practice, familiar in the European Union institutions and in all international bodies, of making agreement on one issue conditional upon the satisfactory resolution of another, there being no logical or material connection between the two. For example, the French government made their acceptance of additional seats for Germany and other member states in the **European Parliament** conditional upon an agreement to make Strasbourg the Parliament's official seat (see **seat of the institutions**). The scope for linkage is obviously greater when decisions can be taken only by **unanimity**, i.e., when individual member states have a right of **veto**. Linkage is an essential and an inescapable feature of the continuous, wide-ranging process of negotiation between member states and between institutions on which decisions in the European Union are based.

Lobbying

The fact that the decision-making procedures within the European institutions are little understood allied to the growing importance of the decisions taken (especially for industry and commerce) has provided fertile ground for Brussels-based lobbyists. Some, particularly trade associations, are well established, as are many single-issue lobbies in such fields as aid to the Third World, consumer protection, animal welfare and human rights. Many of the larger regions of the European Union, such as Catalonia,

Scotland and the German *Länder*, as well as several states of the United States, have representative offices in Brussels besides those of the **national representations**.

Since 1985 there has been a spectacular growth in professional lobbying, firms who will for a fee monitor developments in a particular subject-area, suggest contacts, arrange meetings and generally assist in the putting of a case. As the European institutions are relatively open by comparison with most national bureaucracies, so far lobbyists of all kinds have had little difficulty in gaining access to them. However, the growth in professional lobbying has led to calls for it to be regulated. The **Commission** has a list of several hundred bodies that it consults on technical aspects of legislation, with a bias towards bodies operating at European level, but neither the Commission nor the **European Parliament** has yet introduced a register of professional lobbyists.

A study edited by Sonia Maizey and Jeremy Richardson, *Lobbying in the European Community* (Oxford, 1993), is a good general survey of how lobbies operate and of their impact on decisions. There is a list of lobbyists and pressure-groups in *Directory of Pressure-Groups in the European Community* (Harlow, 1991) edited by Alan Butt Philip and some interesting case-studies in R. H. Pedler and M. P. C. M. Van Schendelen (eds), *Lobbying the European Union* (Aldershot, 1994).

Lomé Convention

The Lomé Convention, signed in Lomé, the capital of Togo, in 1975 is a comprehensive trade-and-aid agreement between the member states of the European Union and 70 developing countries in Africa, the Caribbean and the Pacific (the ACP **states**). Article 1 of the Convention states its purpose as being 'to promote and expedite the economic, cultural and social development of the ACP States and to consolidate and diversify their relations [with the Community and its member states] in a spirit of solidarity and mutual interest'. Of the 'fundamental principles' underlying the Convention, 'equality between partners, respect for their sovereignty, mutual interest and interdependence' are placed first (Article 2). The Convention has been reviewed at regular intervals: Lomé IV covers the period 1990–2000.

Based as it is on the idea of 'interdependence' with the ACP states, the Lomé Convention has its own institutions: the ACP–EU Council of Ministers; the ACP–EU Committee of Ambassadors; and the ACP–EU Joint Assembly, which is composed of a representative of each of the ACP states and an equal number of Members of the European Parliament (MEPs). The ACP countries have their own secretariat in Brussels, but most of the day-to-day administration of the Union's development policy is the responsibility of the Commission's Directorate-General VIII and the Union's representative offices in the countries concerned. The ACP–EU Council of Ministers is the principal decision-making body, with the Committee of Ambassadors acting as the equivalent of COREPER, and the Joint Assembly having a general power to oversee the application of the Convention. The work of the Assembly, which meets for a week-long session twice a year, is complemented by the European Parliament's Development and Cooperation Committee. For further details, see **development policy, European Development Fund**.

Luns–Westerterp Procedure

Originally, the **Treaty of Rome** required the **Council of Ministers** to consult the **European Parliament** only in respect of **Association Agreements** between the Community and non-member countries or international organizations. To strengthen this provision, a procedure was introduced informally in 1964 on the initiative of the Dutch Foreign Minister, Joseph Luns, whereby the Parliament became entitled to debate the matter before negotiations started, to be kept informed through the relevant committees of the progress of the negotiations, and to be told the substance of the outcome before the Association Treaty was formally signed. In 1973 this procedure, known as the Luns Procedure, was extended to trade agreements on the initiative of another Dutch minister, Tjerk Westerterp. Ten years later, in the **Stuttgart Declaration**, the **European Council** agreed to extend the Luns–Westerterp Procedure to 'all significant international agreements concluded by the Communities', upon which the Parliament now has the right to deliver a formal **Opinion**. These developments were incorporated into the Treaty as amendments to Articles 237 and 238 EEC by the 1986 **Single European Act** (SEA; see also **accession**). Since then, Article 237 EEC has been repealed by the **Maastricht Treaty**, and the procedure for the admission of new member states is now set out in Article O TEU.

Luxembourg Compromise

The Luxembourg Compromise was an informal arrangement, arrived at by **the Six** in January 1966, whereby decisions which the **Treaty of Rome** foresaw being taken by **majority voting** in the **Council of Ministers** could be postponed until unanimous agreement had been reached. Its effect was to create a national **veto** over all key decisions, and for at least 17 years it acted as a constraint in many important areas of policy. Although in some quarters it is believed that the Luxembourg Compromise still exists, it no longer has any discernible bearing on the way the Union functions. Majority voting now applies in all areas where it is provided for in the **Treaties**. A member state can veto a proposal only if **unanimity** is explicitly specified as the decision-making method.

The Luxembourg Compromise resolved an acute crisis in the Community's development, which had two linked but distinct components. The first was the rejection by France in June 1965 of a series of key proposals: on the financing of the new **Common Agricultural Policy** (CAP), the introduction of **own resources** and the widening of the budgetary powers of the **European Parliament**. The second was the outright refusal by France to accept that, when the so-called 'third stage' of the transitional phase of the Community's development came into effect in January 1966, majority voting should automatically be introduced on a significant range of issues in the Council.

So long as these important problems remained unresolved, the President of France, **Charles de Gaulle**, instructed his ministers to boycott all Council meetings during the second half of 1965 – a period that conveniently coincided with his re-election to office at home (for the first time by universal suffrage) at the end of the year. The **empty chair crisis**, as it became known, effectively immobilized Community decision-making and delivered a severe blow to the prospect of closer European integration.

Although the 1965 crisis was prompted by the CAP and own resources proposals, it escalated spectacularly in September of that year when de Gaulle chose to broaden the issues at stake to include the planned shift to majority voting in the Council, and, as a subsidiary question, the growing independence of the **European Commission** under its German President, **Walter Hallstein**. The French President had long been hostile towards what he considered the dangerously federal implications of majority voting, having asserted at the time of the 1961–2 **Fouchet Plan** that 'there is no way that a foreign majority can constrain recalcitrant nations' in the Community. Now he reiterated this position with growing precision, speaking of 'certain mistakes or ambiguities in the Treaties setting up the economic union of the Six. That is why the crisis was, sooner or later, inevitable.'

According to de Gaulle, the fact that the Treaty of Rome provided for the introduction of majority voting in 1966 was the result of its having been negotiated in 1957, during the Fourth Republic, when France had been weak and before 'we had decided to take our destiny into our own hands'. To accept majority voting now would leave France 'exposed to the possibility of being overruled in any economic matter whatsoever, and therefore in social and sometimes political matters' as well. De Gaulle also argued that majority voting would greatly strengthen the European Commission – 'this embryonic technocracy, for the most part foreign' – so long as amendments to a Commission proposal could still be made only unanimously (Article 149.1 EEC). There would be a presumption in favour of Commission's formulation, and a Commission veto over the changes by member states – 'unless by some extraordinary chance, the six states were unanimous in formulating an amendment'.

As the autumn proceeded it became clear that no agreement between de Gaulle and the other member states was likely at least until the December presidential election in France was out of the way. In the event, that contest proved a catalyst for compromise. De Gaulle failed to win an outright victory on the first ballot against two pro-European opponents, **François Mitterrand** and Jean Lecanuet, and the government's resolve on European affairs began to weaken. The Prime Minister, Georges Pompidou, predicted just before the second ballot that France might resume negotiations with its partners soon after the election.

De Gaulle having been re-elected, two special Council meetings were held in Luxembourg in January 1966, without the Commission being present. At the first, on 17–18 January, the five other member states held firm against French demands on majority voting, but progress was made towards a settlement on CAP financing, and agreement reached that the introduction of own resources should be postponed until 1970 and with it greater budgetary powers for the European Parliament. At the second meeting, on 28–29 January, the Council agreed, by a set of non-binding conclusions entered in its Minutes, on a formula in respect of majority voting. This was the essence of what became known as the Luxembourg Compromise.

The Council conclusions stated that if one member state considered that 'a very important national interest' was at stake (often referred to as a 'vital' national interest), then the Council would endeavour to reach, within a reasonable period, solutions that could be adopted unanimously. The French delegation considered that when very important interests were at issue, discussion 'must be continued' until unanimous agreement was reached. However, this more maximalist formulation – which is the one most widely associated with the Compromise – was not accepted by the other member states, and to describe it as a 'compromise' is misleading. It was simply noted that there was a difference of opinion on what precisely would happen when a complete resolution of a dispute within the Council was not achieved.

In the event, the Luxembourg Compromise created a firm presumption within the Council in favour of unanimous voting remaining the norm after 1966, even where majority voting was explicitly provided for in the Treaty and no 'very important national interest' had been identified. Since any country could invoke the Compromise at any time, there was little point in pressing a proposal if strong objections were raised by one of the member states. Discussion that failed to elicit the necessary degree of compromise in the Council was simply stalled, sometimes to the point where the Commission would withdraw the proposal in despair.

In a limited number of areas – such as certain technical decisions on the CAP and the adoption of the Community's **Budget** – majority voting was used after 1966. It was necessary to the continued operation of the Community and suited the interests of France. But the parameters of this shift were very clearly understood. The position was sufficiently clear for the 1971 White Paper on British **accession** to the Community to state: 'All the countries concerned recognize that an attempt to impose a majority view in a case where one or more members considered their vital interests to be at stake would imperil the very fabric of the Community ... [In such cases] it is Community practice to proceed only by unanimity.'

From time to time attempts were made to encourage the Council to return to majority voting, but always without success. The most notable followed the election to the French presidency of **Valéry Giscard d'Estaing** in May 1974. Anxious to move the Community forward from its institutional impasse, he secured an ostensibly radical commitment by the heads of government at the Paris **summit** in December 1974 'to renounce the practice which consists of making agreements on all questions conditional on the unanimous consent of the Member States'.

In practice, however, this declaration changed nothing. Matters blocked on routine policy grounds by one member state continued simply not to get adopted. It was not necessary for the Luxembourg Compromise to be invoked formally – recourse was had to it perhaps only 10 times in the 15 years after 1966 – for decision-making on literally hundreds of Commission proposals over these years to be stillborn. This pervasive immobilism within the Council prevailed until the early 1980s, when for a variety of reasons the Compromise began to fall into disuse. The crucial turning-point occurred in May 1982, when the United Kingdom invoked the Compromise on an agricultural issue on which, ironically, its position was pitted against the vested interests of France, once the arch-defender of the veto.

The British government, in pursuit of its claim for a reduction in its net contribution to the Budget, announced that it could not agree to the adoption of the annual agricultural prices settlement. The reaction to this move in the Council was almost uniformly hostile, with only Denmark and Greece supporting the previously accepted principle that it was entirely up to the member state in question to determine whether a 'very important national interest' might be at stake. All other member states indicated that the Compromise could be invoked only if the 'interest' at stake related directly to the substance of the proposal being considered. In this case, by definition, it was not. The prices package was adopted by majority voting in the Council against the British veto. In the minutes, five countries – all the original parties to the Luxembourg Compromise except France – indicated that their preference was henceforth that majority voting should be used wherever the Treaties so provided.

By the end of 1981 a new institutional reform agenda had started to emerge. The **Genscher–Colombo Plan** for a draft 'European Act' included proposals to limit the Luxembourg Compromise to genuine cases of 'vital' interest (Paragraph 8). The agricultural prices episode of May 1982 decisively hardened attitudes in favour of a substantial change in decision-making practice. This mood found a ready echo in the Commission and in the European Parliament. Guided by its specially formed Committee on Institutional Affairs (which began work in January 1982; see **Altiero Spinelli**), the Parliament became increasingly insistent on the need for the Council to follow strictly Treaty provisions on voting. It even launched a legal action in the **Court of Justice** against the Council for **failure to act** in respect of a **common transport policy**, for the establishment of which the Treaty of Rome had specified, in certain areas, recourse to majority voting. However, in the Parliament's 1984 **Draft Treaty establishing the European Union** (DTEU), the Luxembourg Compromise was to be maintained for a 10-year transitional period (Article 23.3).

In response to the Genscher–Colombo Plan, the **European Council** agreed a 'Solemn Declaration on European Union', in Stuttgart in June 1983, the so-called **Stuttgart Declaration**. On the question of voting, the document stated that the 'application of the decision-making procedures laid down in the Treaties is of vital importance' (Paragraph 2.2.2). It stopped short, however, of defining the limits of the Luxembourg Compromise – precisely because there was no agreement on what they were.

In the minutes of the Stuttgart meeting all governments entered statements about the Luxembourg Compromise, setting out their various interpretations. Belgium, Germany, Luxembourg, Italy and the Netherlands declared that 'the Presidency must have recourse to the vote where the Treaties allow for this'. France and Ireland declared that 'the President will have recourse to the vote where the Treaties allow for this, while accepting that the vote will be postponed if one or several Member States so request, in the name of defending a vital national interest of direct relevance to the subject under discussion, which they will confirm in writing'. Greece stated that 'discussion must continue until a unanimous decision has been reached where vital and essential national interests are at stake and written notification has been given to this effect'. The United

Kingdom and Denmark entered a maximalist formulation redolent of the French position in 1966, insisting that 'when a Member State considers its very important interests are at stake, the discussion should continue until unanimous agreement is reached'.

The French President, François Mitterrand, confirmed a further shift in his country's position on the Luxembourg Compromise in a speech to the European Parliament on 24 May 1984. He asked,

> How can the complex and diversified entity which the Community has become be governed by rules like those of the old Diet of the Kingdom of Poland, where every member could block decisions? It is time we returned to a more normal and promising way of doing things . . . The more frequent practice of voting on important questions heralds a return to the Treaties.

His remarks were greeted with sustained applause: France's break from the Gaullist conception of the Council was becoming more and more explicit. At the same time the prospect of **enlargement** to include Portugal and Spain was helping to secure general acceptance of the idea that the Community would not be able to make progress if individual member states were able to hold up decisions.

The institutional reform debate of the early 1980s culminated at the European Council meeting in Milan in June 1985 with a decision by the heads of government to convene an **Intergovernmental Conference** (IGC), under Article 236 EEC, to draft amendments to the Treaty of Rome. Against spirited opposition from the United Kingdom, Denmark and Greece, the Italian presidency decided to push the issue to the vote, arguing that only a simple majority was necessary to convene an IGC. Opposing governments suggested that unanimity should apply because vital national interests might be at stake. The presidency replied that they could not be since the calling of an IGC was in itself a purely procedural decision. Only the outcome of the IGC could raise such questions, and there the right of veto was safeguarded because agreement to Treaty amendments would require the approval of all governments and ratification by **national parliaments**. This interpretation prevailed.

The subsequent **Single European Act** (SEA), agreed by the Luxembourg IGC of 1985 and signed in 1986, sanctioned a substantial extension of majority voting with a view to completing the **Single Market**. At the time the implications of this change for the Luxembourg Compromise were unclear. Most commentators and official sources held that although majority voting would now certainly become the norm in any area where it was formally provided for, the residual right to invoke the Compromise would remain in any case where a vital national interest was legitimately threatened. It was thought that the SEA would make no particular difference to whether the Compromise survived.

In practice, however, and much to the surprise of many, the Luxembourg Compromise effectively died with the entry into force of the SEA in July 1987. The rules of procedure of the Council of Ministers were changed to enable a simple majority of member states to insist that a vote be taken whenever the Treaties so allowed. Since that date, there have been few attempts to use the Compromise. For example, in 1988 the Greek government objected to the size of the proposed devaluation of the green drachma (see **Common Agricultural Policy**) in an otherwise-agreed agricultural prices settlement, pleading a vital national interest. The United Kingdom, Denmark, France, Ireland and Portugal accepted that discussions should continue; other delegations objected. The Commission and the Greek government subsequently agreed a devaluation by bilateral negotiation, which was then accepted by the Council. However, when the Commission's interpretation of this agreement was disputed by Athens, which again threatened to use the veto, other member states refused to make any concessions, and the Greek government, completely isolated, had to give in. The following year, in similar circumstances, the Greeks chose not to press the point.

Throughout its life the Luxembourg Compromise was never accepted by either the Commission or the **Court of Justice**. The Commission used its exclusion from the January 1966 Council meeting to argue that it had never been a party to the agreement. It subsequently denounced the Compromise on many occasions. The Court, for its part, has frequently ruled that Resolutions or Declarations of political will by the Council or the member states collectively cannot prevail against the rules contained in the Treaties. In 1988 the Court held that 'a mere practice on the part of the Council cannot derogate from the rules laid down in the Treaty' (*United Kingdom* v *Council*, Case 68/86). This view is now, it would appear, accepted in the Council itself, and neither in the negotiations resulting in the **Maastricht Treaty** nor in any other forum has any member state suggested reviving the Luxembourg Compromise and giving it Treaty status.

Maastricht Treaty

Formally entitled the Treaty on European Union (TEU), the Maastricht Treaty was the outcome of two **Intergovernmental Conferences** (IGCs) and was agreed at a meeting of the **European Council** in Maastricht, the Netherlands, in December 1991. Formally signed in Maastricht on 7 February 1992, the Treaty entered into force in November 1993.

The two IGCs, one on **Economic and Monetary Union** (EMU) and one on European Political Union (EPU), were conducted in parallel. The EMU IGC was set in train by a decision of the European Council meeting in Madrid in June 1989, at which the **Delors Report** on EMU was discussed. The EPU IGC was based on an agreement reached a year later in Dublin, prompted by proposals on political union put forward by President **François Mitterrand**, Chancellor **Helmut Kohl** and the Belgian government the previous April. Both IGCs were to start in December 1990.

The EMU IGC, conducted by finance ministers, soon revealed disagreements about the pace of progress towards EMU and the institutions needed to manage it. A small minority of countries, the United Kingdom included, had deep reservations about the whole exercise. Germany too, obviously the most important participant in the discussions, had reservations of its own, based upon the German electorate's attachment to the Deutsche Mark and the suspicion that EMU would entail massive payments to the poorer or more profligate member states. The final compromise provided for an EMU in three stages (of which the first had already begun in 1990), set out in additions to the **Treaty of Rome** (Articles 109a–m); the British and Danish governments secured '**opt-outs**' allowing them to take separate decisions on the transition to a single currency controlled by a **European Central Bank** (ECB).

The EPU IGC, conducted by foreign ministers, was responsible for the basic structure of the Treaty itself. The first part proclaims the establishment of the European Union (Article A), sets out its aims (Article B), and requires the Union to 'respect the national identities of its Member States' (Article F). On British insistence, all references to **federalism** were removed. The second section contains amendments to the Treaty of Rome establishing the European Economic Community, henceforward to be called the European Community, and the third and fourth sections contain amendments to the **Treaty of Paris** and the **European Atomic Energy Community** Treaty. The fifth and sixth sections set up the so-called **pillars**, the **Common Foreign and Security Policy** (CFSP) and cooperation in the fields of **Justice and Home Affairs** (JHA). The seventh section contains general provisions, adapted from those formerly in the Treaty of Rome, on Treaty amendment (Article N), the procedure for **enlargement** (Article O) and **ratification** (Article R). The Maastricht Treaty was concluded for an unlimited period (Article Q).

Annexed to the Treaty are 17 **protocols**, all but the last of which relate to matters covered in the Treaty of Rome. They include an agreement on the non-retroactive applicability of the Barber judgment (see **equal treatment**), the Statutes of the **European Central Bank** (ECB) and the **European Monetary Institute** (EMI), details of the **excessive deficit procedure**, the British and Danish **opt-outs** on EMU (see above), the so-called Social Protocol (see **Social Chapter**), and a set of undertakings on cohesion (see **Cohesion Fund**) to benefit the poorer member states. Also annexed to the Treaty are 33 **Declarations** (see **protocols**), of which the most important are those on the role of **national parliaments**, the **hierarchy of acts**, on police cooperation (see **Justice and Home Affairs**) and on the future role of **Western European Union** (WEU).

The amendments to the Treaty of Rome contained in the Maastricht Treaty, as well as laying down the stages for progress towards EMU, made provision for a new **co-decision procedure**, an extension of the **assent procedure**, new powers to allow the **European Parliament** a decisive say in the appointment of the president and members of the **Commission**, and two new institutions, the **Committee of the Regions** and the **Ombudsman**. The **Court of Auditors** was given the full status of an institution and the **Court of Justice** the power to fine defaulting member states. The Treaty laid down the principle of **subsidiarity**, created **citizenship** of the Union and extended Community action in the fields of culture, education, vocational training, consumer protection, **trans-European networks** (TENs), industry policy, the environment and development policy.

The Maastricht Treaty ranged over a very wide field, but in spite of this evident attempt to satisfy all parties involved in the negotiations it was very nearly not ratified. It failed to secure the necessary five-sixths majority in the Danish Parliament, and in the referendum that followed (2 June 1992) it was defeated by 50.7 to 49.3 per cent of the vote. The following month the other governments decided to press ahead with ratification, even though technically the Treaty could not enter into force without having been ratified in all 12 member states. A referendum in Ireland followed on 18 June 1992, the Treaty securing a 67 per cent majority. In

July President Mitterrand announced that the Treaty would also be submitted to a referendum in France, even though there was no constitutional requirement to this effect. The referendum took place on 20 September, four days after the events of 'Black Wednesday' forced both the pound and the lira out of the **Exchange-Rate Mechanism** (ERM), and resulted in a tiny majority of only 51.05 per cent for the Treaty.

The Danish government was by now insisting on further opt-outs as the condition for holding a second referendum. These were specified in a paper of 30 October 1992 entitled *Denmark in Europe*. At the European Council meeting in Edinburgh in December Denmark was granted a permanent opt-out from stage three of EMU, and received the necessary clarifications on citizenship; Denmark's non-participation in 'decisions and actions of the Union which have defence implications' was formally recognized. A second Danish referendum was held on 18 May 1993, the Treaty securing a majority of 56.8 per cent.

It was in the United Kingdom that ratification posed the most serious problems. The result of the April 1992 general election gave John Major's Conservative Government a much smaller majority, giving the Conservative MPs most hostile to European integration in general and the Treaty in particular much greater influence. The Government promised that although the 'clause by clause, line by line' examination of the Maastricht Treaty Bill could be started, ratification would not be completed until the result of the second Danish referendum was known. The Labour Party, although not opposed to the Treaty, was fiercely critical of the opt-out from the Social Chapter, and understandably exulted in the Government's discomfiture. The passage of the Bill through the House of Commons was slow and acrimonious. The final vote, on 24 July 1993, was won by a very narrow majority, achieved only by means of a threat to dissolve Parliament and call an election (see David Baker, Andrew Gamble, Steve Ludlow, 'The parliamentary siege of Maastricht', *Political Affairs*, Vol. 47, no. 1, January 1994).

In fact, the last member state to ratify the Treaty was Germany, where anti-Maastricht campaigners had succeeded in referring the Treaty to the German Constitutional Court in Karlsruhe. The legal arguments were not resolved until a ruling in favour of ratification on 12 October 1993, allowing the Treaty to enter into force the following month (see **Karlsruhe judgment**).

However well-intentioned, a treaty covering so many heterogeneous issues, some very sensitive, negotiated largely in secret, and for the most part unintelligible to the general public, could hardly be expected to win friends. The period during which it was ratified coincided with a low point in the Community's fortunes: impotence in Yugoslavia, monetary instability, and rows over the Uruguay Round of the **General Agreement on Tariffs and Trade** (GATT) all contributed to a general impression of a Community that had lost its way. Against this background, the Treaty's grander aspirations seemed absurd, and the detailed provisions trivial. At the same time, in spite of its assurances on subsidiarity, by moving into areas such as citizenship, police cooperation and a common currency the Treaty seemed to portend the much-feared 'European superstate'.

MacDougall Report

In 1974 the **European Commission** invited an expert group of seven economists to prepare a report on the role of public finance in European integration. Their report, generally known as the MacDougall Report after the group's chairman, Sir Donald MacDougall, then Chief Economic Adviser to the Confederation of British Industry, was published in April 1977.

It studied the role of public finance both in unitary states (France, Italy and the United Kingdom) and in federations (Australia, Canada, Switzerland, the United States, the Federal Republic of Germany), with particular emphasis on its redistributive effects, the allocation of responsibility for revenue-raising and the scope for counter-cyclical measures in the interests of sustainable long-term growth. It assumed that the Community wanted to move towards economic integration, and applied the lessons learnt from the study of public finance in the national context to developments in the Community.

The report identified three distinct stages beyond the *status quo*: pre-federal integration, federation with a small Community-level public sector, and federation with a large Community-level public sector. When the report was written, total spending by the Community institutions was about 0.7 per cent of the Community's gross domestic product (GDP). 'Pre-federal integration' meant raising the latter figure to between 2 and 2.5 per cent. A 'small' Community public sector was reckoned to be from 5 to 7 per cent, and a 'large' something approaching 25 per cent of GDP. On this calculation, the European Union is still well short even of the 'pre-federal' stage: in 1994, total Union expenditure was estimated at less than 1.25 per cent of the Union's GDP.

The MacDougall Report was widely discussed, but, as the figures show, little concrete action flowed from it at the time, with the exception of the Commission's 1978 proposals on **own resources**. However, more recently, the growth in the **structural funds**, the **Cohesion Fund**, the extension of the Union's involvement in employment and training, and the emphasis on **convergence** are all in line with recommendations originally made in the report (see also **Padoa–Schioppa Report**).

Maghreb

The Maghreb countries (*maghreb* is Arabic for 'western') are Algeria, Morocco and Tunisia, with each of which the Community has concluded a **protocol** on financial and technical cooperation under Article 238 of the **Treaty of Rome** as part of its overall **Mediterranean policy** (see also **Mashreq**). These protocols are of five years' duration: the fourth in the series remains in force until 31 October 1996. Under the provisions governing the amount of aid to each country, such aid is in the form of both low-interest loans from the **European Investment Bank** (EIB) and grants from the **Budget** (some of which are contributions to risk-capital formation).

Majority voting

Within the **Council of Ministers** of the European Union, decisions may be taken either by unanimity or by majority voting, depending on which Treaty article has been used as the legal base for the proposal in question. The vote of each member state is given a 'weighting', ranging from 10 in the case of the larger states to 2 in the case of the smallest (Luxembourg). Majority voting may be simple majority (i.e., 8 member states out of 15 voting in favour) or, more usually, **qualified majority voting**. Article 148.1 of the **Treaty of Rome** lays down the general principle that 'the Council shall act by a majority of its members' (see also **veto**).

Malta

Malta was taken from Napoleon by the British in 1800 and in 1814 became a British dependency. In 1964 the country gained its independence under the British crown and 10 years later declared itself a republic. Malta's constitution, with its commitment to **neutrality** (see below), was last amended in 1987. The country remains a member of the Commonwealth, belongs to the United Nations and the **Council of Europe** and took part in the **Conference on Security and Cooperation in Europe** (CSCE).

Since 1970 Malta has had an **Association Agreement** with the Community, which was intended to lead in two five-year stages to Malta's becoming a part of the Community **customs union**. However, the Maltese Labour Party government that took office in 1971 was hostile to the idea of closer ties with the Community and the Association Agreement was effectively frozen at the conclusion of its first five-year stage. The pro-Community Nationalist Party took over the government in 1987, but instead of reactivating the Agreement decided to apply for full membership of the Community. The application was formally submitted on 16 July 1990.

The Commission's **Opinion** on the Maltese application identified three categories of problem: economic, institutional and political (*Bulletin of the European Communities*, supplement 4/93). Malta's economy is heavily protected, heavily subsidized and largely composed of very small firms. More than three-quarters of Maltese firms employ fewer than 5 people, and only 12 (out of 2,300 registered companies) more than 300. The public sector represents about 40 per cent of all employment. The structure of public revenue is such that about one-third of the government's total tax revenue is from customs and excise duties. The introduction of value-added tax (VAT), a *de facto* requirements of Community membership, has proved difficult.

The most important industries in terms of output and employment are textiles, clothing and footwear; electrical and electronic equipment; and shipbuilding and ship-repairing, a relic of Malta's importance as a base for the Royal Navy. However, levels of productivity are below average, and few industries could survive the exposure to competition and the removal of state subsidies that would result from Community membership. Such removal of trade restrictions as there has been under the Association Agreement has almost all been on the Community side, and very little progress has been made towards aligning Malta's customs tariffs and import levies (including the so-called 'local manufacturers' protection tax' introduced in 1989) with the Community's **Common External Tariff**.

On institutional questions, the Commission's **Opinion** notes that the fact of English being an official language in Malta might allow the Union to sidestep the problem of adding Maltese (of Semitic origin, and wholly unrelated to any other European language) to the list of official languages. More difficult is the fact of Malta having 'only a very few senior public officials with sufficient international experience to play a full part in the decision-making and operational processes of the Community institutions', most of whom will be kept fully occupied by the domestic reform process. Moreover, Malta has only about 15 embassies and consulates around the world. Against this background it is hard to imagine Malta assuming the responsibilities of the **presidency** of the Council.

The main political problem is that the Maltese Labour Party – which gained 46.5 per cent of the vote in the February 1992 elections – remains opposed to Maltese membership of the Union, and during its term of office pursued a policy of developing closer relations with Libya and certain Communist countries, notably China. In so polarized a political society, it seems unlikely that the kind of cross-party consensus that will be needed to underpin the reform process (uncomfortable for many sectors of the economy) and make a success of Union membership will be forthcoming.

Maltese **neutrality** is at the heart of the argument between the parties.

The Constitution declares that 'Malta is a neutral State actively pursuing peace . . . by adhering to a policy of non-alignment and refusing to participate in any military alliance'. Nevertheless, in the memorandum addressed to the Community by the Maltese government on 11 September 1992 it was said to be 'in Malta's interest to subscribe to the European Union's common foreign and security policy, including the eventual framing of a common defence policy'. Whether or not this can be done without amending the Constitution, which requires a two-thirds majority in the House of Assembly, is not clear.

Malta is unquestionably a European state. Its history is bound up with European history, from St Paul's shipwreck to the Second World War. Amongst the most handsome buildings in Valletta are the eight *auberges* of the various *langues* of the Knights of St John, who took up residence in Malta on being expelled from Rhodes at the time of the Crusades: Aragon, Auvergne, Castile, England, France, Germany, Italy and Provence. Three-quarters of the country's foreign trade is with the Union. The country's institutions are based on European models and the population is staunchly Roman Catholic. Although poor, with a per capita gross national product (GNP) only 40 per cent of the Union average, Malta is so small that the impact of its accession on the **Budget** would be negligible. However, its very smallness raises in the most acute form those institutional questions common to all **micro-states** wishing to join the Union, to which no one has yet found satisfactory answers. Taken in conjunction, these facts account for the very guarded nature of the conclusion to the Commission's Opinion:

> The Commission feels that it is important to send to the authorities and people of Malta a positive signal to encourage them to undertake vigorously the requisite reforms to transform Malta's economy into an open and competitive one . . . Such a signal could be given by announcing that the Community is willing to open accession negotiations with Malta as soon as conditions allow.

At their meeting in Corfu in June 1994, the **European Council** undertook to give priority to Malta and Cyprus in the next round of **enlargement**.

Management committee

Under the **Common Agricultural Policy** (CAP), since 1962 each commodity covered by the CAP has had its own management committee, composed of national civil servants, whose task it is to assist the **Commission** in the implementation of decisions taken by the **Council of Ministers**. Management committees have considerable power and this has given rise to concern over the extent to which they are sufficiently accountable (see **comitology**).

Mansholt Plan

The Mansholt Plan, named after Sicco Mansholt, then the Vice-President, and later the President, of the **Commission**, was the blueprint for the **Common Agricultural Policy** (CAP) adopted by the Community in 1972. Mansholt, who had been a Socialist minister of agriculture in the Netherlands from 1945 to 1958, produced the final version of his plan in 1968. He accepted that continental agriculture was badly in need of restructuring and that this would involve heavy job losses. The Plan allowed for generous compensation, to be paid for over the years by making agricultural production more cost-effective and so limiting the extent of price support through **intervention**. The Plan also laid emphasis on unified markets for each product, strict limits on national aids and a high degree of protection against imports. In spite of the balance it sought to strike between competing interests, the Plan was very controversial, and the CAP that eventually emerged was much less radical (see also **Stresa Conference**).

Marshall Plan

The Marshall Plan was the name given to the European Recovery Programme (ERP) under which the United States gave financial assistance totalling over $13 billion to promote the economic recovery of postwar Europe. Prompted by the realization that the countries of Western Europe, even the United Kingdom and France, were too enfeebled by war to resist Communist encroachment, the United States government under President Harry Truman resolved to make available American aid and to invite the European countries to draw up an agreed estimate of 'the requirements of the situation'. The offer was made by Secretary of State George C. Marshall in a Graduation Day speech at Harvard on 5 June 1947. No country was to be excluded, the only condition being that the proposal for an economic recovery programme should be 'a joint one, agreed to by a number of, if not all, European nations'.

As a result of pressure from the Soviet Union, the countries of eastern and central Europe (even those which, like Czechoslovakia, had at first responded favourably to the American offer) declined to attend the conference in Paris in July 1947 at which the ERP was to be worked out in detail. At the conference the Europeans were told that the aim of the ERP was 'the speediest possible reactivation of the European economic machine and . . . its restoration to a self-supporting basis'. Two conditions of great importance for the process of European unification were laid down: that the European countries needed to start dismantling barriers to trade amongst themselves, and that a European organization must be set up to oversee the process of economic recovery. This latter condition led to the establishment of the Organization for European Economic Cooperation (OEEC) in 1948, which was transformed into the **Organization for Economic Cooperation and Development** (OECD) in 1961.

Reactions to the American proposals were mixed. Particularly amongst the parties of the Left, the Marshall Plan was interpreted as US economic imperialism on the very boldest scale. All kinds of forebodings, resentment and anxieties about **sovereignty** were expressed, solicitously encouraged by Stalin's USSR. General Marshall himself was accorded a prominent place in Soviet demonology. Amongst the European nations who had experienced German occupation there was deep concern at the importance that the Americans clearly attached to putting the German economy back on its feet. Nor was the Plan uncontroversial in the United States: the prodigious efforts of the Administration to secure the approval of Congress are recounted in detail in Charles L. Mee's *The Marshall Plan: the launching of the Pax Americana*. Indeed, had it not been for the conviction and farsightedness of a handful of key figures in the Truman Administration (Marshall himself, George F. Kennan, Dean Acheson and William Clayton) and of Europeans like **Paul-Henri Spaak**, Georges Bidault and Ernest Bevin it is doubtful whether the Plan would have come to fruition. An interesting perspective on the Plan may be gained from Sallie Pisani, *The CIA and the Marshall Plan* (Edinburgh, 1991).

Mashreq

The Mashreq countries (*mashreq* is Arabic for 'eastern') are Egypt, Jordan, Lebanon and Syria, with each of which the Community has concluded a **protocol** on financial and technical cooperation under Article 238 of the **Treaty of Rome** as part of its overall **Mediterranean policy** (see also **Maghreb**). These protocols are of five years' duration: the fourth in the series remains in force until 31 October 1996. Under the provisions governing the amount of aid to each country, such aid is in the form of both low-interest loans from the **European Investment Bank** (EIB) and grants from the **Budget** (some of which are contributions to risk-capital formation).

Maudling Committee

By 1957 the British government had realized that **the Six** were in earnest in their desire to establish the **customs union** that was to be the basis of the **European Economic Community** (EEC; see also **Messina Conference**, **Spaak Committee**). Having failed to enlist American support in opposing the customs union idea, the government made a counter-proposal in the Organization for European Economic Cooperation (OEEC; see **Organization for Economic Cooperation and Development**): that a **free trade area** should be set up amongst all the European members of the OEEC, including the Six, but limited to trade in manufactured goods. In this way the British government hoped to avoid exclusion from continental markets while retaining Commonwealth preference for agricultural products. The OEEC appointed a committee under the chairmanship of Reginald Maudling, then President of the Board of Trade, to examine this proposal. Initially, it looked as though the West German government of **Konrad Adenauer** might support the British proposal, but by June 1958, with the return to power in France of **Charles de Gaulle**, it was clear that what the British called 'Plan G' was dead. Discussions in the OEEC were concluded later that year. The work of the Maudling Committee laid the foundations of the 1960 Stockholm Convention establishing the **European Free Trade Association** (EFTA). The whole episode is very fully described in Michael Charlton, *The Price of Victory*.

Mediterranean policy

Although for several decades the European Community had agreements of various types with the countries bordering the Mediterranean (see, for example, **Maghreb**, **Mashreq**), there had been no comprehensive policy covering the area. At the meeting of the **European Council** in Corfu in June 1994 it was decided to draw up a proposal for such a policy, partly as a means of redressing the balance in the Union's trade and aid relations with its near neighbours, which had, since 1991, shifted decisively in favour of the countries of central and eastern Europe. It was also believed that financial assistance and more political contacts would help to stabilize the region and relieve migratory pressures on the Union's southern frontiers.

An ambitious proposal for a 'Euro-Mediterranean partnership' was announced by the **Commission** on 18 October 1994. In the long term the aim is to establish by 2010 'the largest [industrial] free trade area in the world, covering the Union, the countries of Central and Eastern Europe . . . and also all the Mediterranean third countries' (i.e., some 40 countries with a population of about 700 million people). The Mediterranean countries would include the Maghreb and Mashreq states, Libya, Israel, **Cyprus**, **Malta**, **Turkey**, the Lebanon, Jordan, Syria, Albania and the former Yugoslavia. In June 1995 the European Council meeting in Cannes agreed to provide 4.7 billion ECUs (about £3.75 billion) worth of investment in the region. Amongst the specific measures proposed are scientific, technical and industrial cooperation, and joint action on the environment, illegal immigration and the fight against drugs, as well as financial assistance from the **European Investment Bank** (EIB). Political stability in the region will be promoted as part of the **Common Foreign and Security Policy** (CFSP). Both France and Spain see the development of a Mediterranean policy as a means of preventing the Union's centre of gravity from shifting too far to the north and east with **enlargement** and the opening up of central and eastern Europe. The European Union and eleven Mediterranean countries (and the PLO) signed a 'Barcelona Declaration' on 28 November 1995. There is a survey of relations with Mediterranean countries in Peter Ludlow, *Europe and the Mediterranean* (Brussels, 1994).

Merger controls

The idea of a monopoly or of a merger possibly prejudicial to competition is meaningful only with respect to a particular geographical market. With the establishment of the **Single Market** it became clear that national markets were no longer the appropriate dimension within which to consider monopolies and mergers, the vetting of which is now an important part of **competition policy**. Since 1989 the **Commission** has had sole authority to vet large-scale mergers, defined as those in which combined annual turnover world-wide of the concerns involved is greater than 5 billion ECUs (£4 billion), of which at least 250 million ECUs (£200 million) is generated by two or more concerns within the member states. However, if each of the concerns generates two-thirds of its Community-wide turnover in one member state, the proposed merger is vetted not by the Commission but by the relevant national authorities. The sensitivity of this issue may be inferred from the fact that it took the **Council of Ministers** 16 years to agree this **Regulation**, which has since been modified to take account of the establishment of the **European Economic Area** (EEA).

As the Continental Can case (*Europemballage Corporation and Continental Can Co. Inc.* v *Commission*, Case 6/72) established in 1975, a merger or acquisition may constitute an 'abuse of a dominant market position', which is prohibited under Article 86 of the **Treaty of Rome**. Such an 'abuse' may be proved even if the company cannot be shown actually to have exploited its market position to the detriment of competition.

Merger Treaty

The 1965 Merger Treaty, which entered into effect in July 1967, was the first amendment to the **Treaties** of Paris and Rome. The purpose was to create a common **Council of Ministers** and a common **Commission** serving all three **European Communities**. This move was seen as an important step towards the complete integration of the three Communities, and had been advocated by the **Action Committee for a United States of Europe** throughout the early 1960s. Article 32 of the Merger Treaty referred in passing to a 'Treaty establishing a Single European Community', something that was never drawn up.

Formally speaking, the new 'Council of the European Communities' (Article 1) replaced the Special Council of Ministers of the **European Coal and Steel Community** (ECSC), and the Councils of the **European Economic Community** (EEC) and the **European Atomic Energy Community** (Euratom). Similarly the new Commission of the European 'Communities' replaced the High Authority of the ECSC and the Commissions of the EEC and Euratom (Article 9). It was not necessary to provide for the amalgamation of the **European Parliament**, the **Court of Justice** and the **Economic and Social Committee** in the Merger Treaty, since the 1957 'Convention on Certain Institutions Common to the European Communities' – signed in parallel to the **Treaty of Rome** and having the same legal status – had already stipulated that one body in each case would exercise the functions set out in the original Treaties. The Merger Treaty provided for a common **Budget** of the Communities to replace the three separate budgets (Article 20). It also created a 'single administration' composed of the officials of the three original Communities (Article 24).

The Merger Treaty had the effect of consolidating the Communities' activities in Brussels. Under pressure from the Luxembourg government, the member states signed a separate agreement on the 'provisional location' of the institutions that required the secretariat of the European Parliament to remain in Luxembourg together with the Court of Justice and the **European Investment Bank** (EIB). The Council of Ministers was required to meet in Luxembourg in April, June and October (see **seat of the institutions**).

Messina Conference

On 20 August 1954 the French National Assembly rejected the Treaty that would have established the **European Defence Community**. This meant that progress could not be made with the **European Political Community** either, so **the Six**, anxious to reaffirm their commitment to European integration and to extend its scope beyond the relatively narrow base of the **European Coal and Steel Community** (ECSC, with which, in December 1954, the United Kingdom had signed an **Association Agreement**), decided to explore what could be done to establish free trade amongst themselves within a **customs union**. In June 1955 the foreign ministers of the Six met in Messina to consider memoranda on closer economic integration drawn up by the **Benelux** countries, Italy and West

Germany. A compromise agreement was reached and an intergovernmental committee was set up under **Paul-Henri Spaak**. The committee presented its report to the foreign ministers in Venice in May 1956, and this was used as the basis for negotiating two new Treaties, one establishing a **European Economic Community** (EEC) and the other a **European Atomic Energy Community** (Euratom). These Treaties were signed 10 months later and were ratified in time for them to come into effect on 1 January 1958.

The significance of the Messina Conference is that at a low point in the history of European integration there was still enough energy and enthusiasm amongst the Six to allow two very complex and far-reaching Treaties to be negotiated in a remarkably short time. The United Kingdom was invited to participate in the Conference and in the Spaak Committee but sent only an Under-Secretary of State from the Board of Trade (who subsequently withdrew: the story is told in full in Michael Charlton's *The Price of Victory*, 1983).

Micro-states

'Micro-states' is a term used by political scientists and students of international relations to denote very small sovereign states. There are five such states in western Europe, ranging from Andorra, with a population of about 54,000, to Vatican City, with a population of 802. Several micro-states are wholly within the territory of a member state of the European Union, but none is a member of the Union in its own right. In consequence, the Union has established particular relations with each of them (see also **Malta**).

Andorra

Until 14 May 1993, when the citizens of Andorra voted for a new republican constitution, the country was a 'co-principality' over which the Bishop of Urgell in Spain and the President of the French Republic (as heir to the rights and titles of the kings of France) exercised joint sovereignty. The official language is Catalan. The accession of Spain to the European Community in 1986 resulted in Andorra becoming part of the Community's **customs union** with effect from July 1991, but special arrangements apply to agricultural products. The customs agreement is managed by a joint committee. Andorra remains fiscally independent but does not issue its own currency. In 1993 Andorra was accepted as a member of the United Nations but has not sought to join the European Union or, as a neutral state (see **neutrality**), any defensive alliance. In 1994 Andorra joined the **Council of Europe**.

Liechtenstein

The principality of Liechtenstein has an area of 160 square kilometres and a population of about 30,000. Neutral in both world wars, it has had a customs union agreement with Switzerland since 1923 and the Swiss franc is used as the currency. As a member of the **European Free Trade Association** (EFTA), Liechtenstein took part in the negotiations for the creation of the **European Economic Area** (EEA) and its citizens confirmed their support for the EEA Agreement by referendum on 13 December 1992. However, a week earlier the Swiss had voted against EEA membership, and this necessitated certain adjustments to the Agreement. A second referendum was held on 9 April 1995, allowing Liechtenstein to join the EEA on 1 May 1995. This is a very radical step for Liechtenstein, since under the Agreement it is required not to discriminate against other EEA nationals in respect of the **free movement of persons**, capital and services, **freedom of establishment**, and the ownership of land. Liechtenstein has not applied for membership of the European Union, but has been a member of the Council of Europe since 1978 and of the United Nations since 1990. Liechtenstein has also taken part in the **Conference on Security and Cooperation in Europe** (CSCE) since 1972, but being a neutral state it has not joined any defensive alliances.

Monaco

The principality of Monaco also has a population of about 30,000 but a very much smaller land area – less than 2 square kilometres. Ruled by the Grimaldi family since the Middle Ages, Monaco (which until 1860 included the communes of Menton and Roquebrune) has at various times been under the protection of France, Spain and the Kingdom of Sardinia. The present treaty with France dates from July 1918 and the present constitution from 1962.

Monaco has had a customs union with France since 1865. Certain senior posts (including that of Prime Minister) in the Monégasque civil service are reserved for French nationals. In response to French pressure, Monaco's fiscal system was reformed in the 1960s so that companies and individuals operating in France could no longer take advantage of Monaco's very favourable tax regime. Revenue from turnover taxes, including value-added tax (VAT), is shared with France on the basis of a complicated formula. Monaco cannot be said to have a foreign policy distinguishable from that of France, and Monégasque laws on foreigners' rights of sojourn and of residence have to be compatible with those of France.

Monaco's customs union with France is governed by a convention dating from May 1963. Since this date the principality has had *ipso facto* a customs union with the European Community, but so far it has not sought to conclude an agreement in its own right to this effect. Monaco has not sought membership of the Council of Europe and has participated in the CSCE only since the adoption of the **Helsinki Final Act** in 1975. The principality was admitted to the United Nations in May 1993.

San Marino

With a population of about 26,000 and an area of 61 square kilometres, the Republic of San Marino has existed as a separate entity (although not always wholly independent) since the early Middle Ages. In 1862 a treaty was concluded that placed San Marino under the protection of the newly founded Kingdom of Italy. Under the current treaty, dating from 1939 and amended in 1971, San Marino established a customs union with Italy and *ipso facto* with the **European Economic Community** (EEC). Since 1862 the Italian lira has been legal tender in San Marino.

In 1983 San Marino began negotiations with the EEC on a customs union and cooperation agreement. The agreement was concluded in 1992, but because delays were expected in the ratification process an interim agreement was drawn up and entered into force in December 1992. The agreement, which is of indefinite duration, establishes free movement for most goods, industrial and agricultural, between San Marino and the EEC, enjoins the EEC to assist the San Marinese economy, provides for non-discrimination (but not the right of free movement) in respect of workers, and places relations between San Marino and the EEC in the hands of a Cooperation Committee.

San Marino has always participated in the activities of the CSCE. It has been a member of the Council of Europe since 1988 and of the United Nations since 1992.

Vatican City

The territory of the Holy See, fixed by the Lateran Treaty of 11 February 1929, extends to the Vatican Palace, St Peter's, the Lateran Palaces and the Papal villa of Castel Gandolfo. The smallest political entity in the world, the Vatican City is outside Italian customs territory, and goods entering the City are wholly exempt from Italian customs duties and other taxes. By the same token the Vatican City is outside the scope of the European Community treaties, and no special arrangements govern relations between the European Union and the Vatican City, which are conducted through the papal nuncio accredited to the **European Communities** in Brussels. The Holy See has had permanent observer status at the United Nations since 1964 and in the Council of Europe since 1970. It participates in some of the activities of the CSCE.

At different times international organizations have dealt with applications for membership from micro-states in different ways. The **League of Nations**, for example, opposed applications from San Marino and Liechtenstein mainly because of the problems that micro-states would pose within a decision-making system that allowed all members a veto and the same representation in the Assembly. Monaco's application was opposed on the grounds that Monégasque membership would in effect give France a second vote, although Andorra's application was opposed by France on the grounds that Andorra was not a sovereign state in international law. General misgivings were felt about the capacity of micro-states to meet the obligations set out in the Covenant of the League.

Since the end of the Second World War most international organizations have found ways to accommodate micro-states, many more of which came into being as a result of decolonization. The United Nations, for example, grew from 51 members in 1945 to 100 in 1960 and to 179 in 1992. As more micro-states were admitted, precedents were set and claims to sovereignty strengthened. Within Europe, both the Council of Europe and the CSCE showed greater willingness to admit micro-states, and the states themselves expressed greater determination to assert their individual identity on the international scene.

Micro-states – and for these purposes Cyprus, Iceland and Luxembourg must be included – continue to pose problems for the European Union. It is not merely that the range of obligations implicit in membership is much greater than is the case with other international organizations, but also the fact that the rights are so much more extensive: representation in the **Council of Ministers**, a **veto** in respect of many key decisions, a Commissioner, a judge in the **Court of Justice**, seats in the **European Parliament** and a turn at holding the **presidency**. The fact that a micro-state (Luxembourg) enjoys entrenched rights as one of the original **Six** makes the problem harder to resolve. Micro-states raise in the most acute form the conflict between **sovereignty** and effective collective action, between institutional efficiency and (in the words of the UN Charter) 'the equal rights . . . of nations large and small'.

Minorities

Minorities are normally considered under three distinct headings: ethnic minorities, religious minorities and linguistic minorities. Some minorities, such as the Lapps in the north of Finland, fall under all three headings, but most minorities in Western Europe (not including immigrant communities) under only one.

The redrawing of political frontiers after the First World War took account as far as possible of ethnic frontiers. However, the correspondence between the two was far from exact. The Covenant of the **League of Nations** was the first international agreement of its kind to grant special rights to minorities. These rights were granted to individuals as members of minority groups, not to minority groups as a whole: it was feared that the latter would encourage secessionist trends. Hitler's claim to be protecting the rights of the German minority first in the Sudetenland and later in Poland underlined the extent to which the League's provisions were open to abuse.

After the Second World War more ambitious goals were set with respect to the protection of **human rights** generally. The 1948 Universal Declaration of Human Rights makes no specific mention of minority rights, since it was felt that if the rights in the Declaration pertaining to individuals were fully respected, further action in respect of minorities was unnecessary. This was not the view taken by the **Council of Europe** when drawing up the European Convention on Human Rights (ECHR). Article 14 of the ECHR prohibits, *inter alia*, any discrimination on the basis of 'membership of a national minority' with respect to the rights and liberties recognized by the ECHR. In the view of the European Commission of Human Rights this provision, taken in conjunction with other Articles, lays an obligation on national authorities to create the conditions in which minorities can exercise to the full the rights and liberties laid down in the ECHR, i.e., to enact measures of positive discrimination in favour of minorities. This interpretation has given rise to three further Council of Europe agreements, the 1989 European Convention on the Protection of Minorities, the 1992 European Charter on Regional or Minority Languages, and the 1993 draft additional **protocol** to the ECHR. Minority rights issues were addressed at the Council of Europe's first-ever summit in Vienna in October 1993.

Neither the **Treaties** establishing the **European Communities** nor the **Maastricht Treaty** refer to minorities. The commitment of the Union's institutions to respect human rights generally is embodied in the tripartite declaration of 1977 (see **human rights**). The **citizenship** provisions of the **Treaty of Rome** apply equally to all nationals of the member states.

The rights of minorities have been studied and codified at length in the framework of the **Conference on Security and Cooperation in Europe** (CSCE). Initially, the provisions in the **Helsinki Final Act** of 1975 marked a return to the idea that machinery for the protection of individual rights would solve the problem of minorities, but in the Madrid and Vienna follow-up conferences, with strong backing from minority groups in central and eastern Europe, it was recognized that positive discrimination was needed. Furthermore, a monitoring mechanism was agreed, removing minority rights from the exclusive jurisdiction of national authorities.

The 1990 Copenhagen Conference on the human aspect of the CSCE took place at a time when the nations of central and eastern Europe were already beginning to reassert their identity. Partly for this reason, the document adopted at this conference was the most comprehensive statement to date on the rights of minorities. It obliged the signatory states to 'protect the ethnic, cultural, linguistic and religious identities of national minorities on their territory and ... create conditions suitable for encouraging the development of such identities'. The Copenhagen document was summarized in the relevant section of the 1990 **Charter of Paris**.

Minorities are protected under the constitutions of some member states of the European Union. In one case, Belgium, linguistic and cultural differences have resulted finally in the formation of a federal state under a new constitutional settlement, which also affords protection to the German-speaking minority in the east of the country. Denmark and Germany have reached bilateral agreement on the treatment of their linguistic minorities in the Schleswig-Holstein region. However, the treatment of minorities continues to cause tension between Austria and Italy in the South Tyrol, and, more seriously, in the Spanish Basque country and in Northern Ireland.

There is a summary of the minorities issue, with an account of work in the Council of Europe and the CSCE, in Hugh Miall (ed.), *Minority Rights in Europe* (1994).

Mitterrand, François (1916–96)

A deputy in the French parliament since 1946, by the 1950s François Mitterrand was already holding ministerial posts in successive Socialist administrations. In 1965 he stood unsuccessfully against **Charles de Gaulle** in an election for the presidency of France, attacking him not least for his idiosyncratic policies on European integration (see **empty chair crisis**). He became the leader of the Socialist Party in 1971, but three years later was defeated by **Valéry Giscard d'Estaing** in another attempt to secure the presidency. On his third attempt, in 1981, he was successful, and he was re-elected in 1988 for a second and final term.

Mitterrand's pro-European convictions were of long standing, and in spite of the electoral reverses suffered at various times by his own party he maintained them consistently. He benefited from his position as elder statesman at meetings of the **European Council**, deploying his long experience and political skills not only on behalf of French interests but also in the resolution of disputes; for example, it was under Mitterrand's presidency at Fontainebleau in 1984 that the **British Budget problem** was finally resolved (see also **Fontainebleau Agreement**).

Mitterrand's proposals on European Union, submitted jointly with **Helmut Kohl** to the Dublin meeting of the European Council in June 1990, led to the **Maastricht Treaty**. Later, on the domestic front, he made a rare error of judgement in holding a referendum in September 1992 on the Treaty to which approval was given by only a tiny majority. In common with his predecessors, Mitterrand attached great importance to **Franco-German cooperation** and lent his support to such proposals as the **Eurocorps**. On security issues generally, he was probably more of an Atlanticist by inclination than traditional French policy allowed him to be in fact.

Molitor Group

The Molitor Group, named after its German chairman, Bernhard Molitor, was a committee of national experts set up by the **Commission** in 1994. An initiative of the German government, the Group was concerned with the legislative and administrative simplification of **Community law** and related national law, with a view to job creation, competitiveness, respect for **subsidiarity** and its impact on small and medium-sized enterprises (SMEs). The Group's report was presented at the Cannes meeting of the **European Council** in June 1995.

Monetary Committee

The Monetary Committee was established under the **Treaty of Rome** (Article 109c EEC) as an official-level advisory body to the **Council of Ministers** in the economic and financial field. It is normally consulted on all major legislative or non-legislative issues before the Council of Economics and Finance Ministers (**Ecofin Council**) and its president often attends the meetings of the Ecofin Council to present its **Opinions**. The Monetary Committee plays an important role in the operation of the **European Monetary System** (EMS). It also coordinates the Union's positions in international financial institutions, most notably the International Monetary Fund.

The Committee, which has met more or less monthly since 1958, is composed of two officials from each member state – usually high-ranking officials from the national finance ministry and the central bank – as well as two from the **European Commission**. The president is elected for a period of two years. The Committee meets in secret and is serviced by the Commission. Its reports are not made public.

Although the members of the Monetary Committee are theoretically appointed in a 'personal capacity and shall, in the general interests of the

Community, be completely independent in the performance of their duties' (Statutes of the Committee, Article 5), in practice they are seen as the representatives of the governments, and their opinions are valued as such. A position agreed in the Committee is likely to provide the basis for an agreement in the Ecofin Council. However, the Committee only gives Opinions – it does not prepare the formal Decisions to be taken in the Ecofin Council (the responsibility of **COREPER**).

The original Treaty provides for the obligatory consultation of the Monetary Committee in respect of proposals on capital liberalization and emergency balance of payments loans or other assistance extended to individual member states. In addition, the 1974 Council decision on economic convergence requires the Committee to be consulted before any alteration in a currency's exchange-rate parity. When the EMS was created in 1979, this function was carried over into the new regime. The president of the Monetary Committee sits on the Committee of **Central Bank Governors** to help coordinate the work of the two bodies, especially in respect of exchange-rates.

The Monetary Committee now provides an official-level negotiating forum to help determine parities whenever currencies realign within the **Exchange-Rate Mechanism** (ERM) or new currencies join. When Portugal entered the ERM in 1992, for example, the Monetary Committee met in Brussels for nine hours to determine the escudo's cross-rates against other currencies. In this capacity, during the dramatic ERM crisis of September 1992, the Monetary Committee emerged for the first time as a major influence on events. On 13 September – only a week after finance ministers, meeting informally in Bath, had insisted that no realignment was desirable or necessary – the Committee suddenly issued a statement in Brussels devaluing the Italian lira by 7 per cent. In parallel, the British government (holding the **presidency** of the Council) indicated that German interest rates would be reduced the following day.

The realignment had been agreed by telephone between all the central banks and finance ministries, and, in conjunction with a German rate cut, was expected to be sufficient to relieve strains within the ERM. It was not. Three days later, in an emergency overnight session on 16–17 September 1992, the Committee convened for six hours, agreeing to suspend both the pound sterling and the lira from the ERM and to devalue the Spanish peseta by 5 per cent. The enormous publicity attending this meeting – at the height of the worst crisis in the ERM's history – greatly increased public awareness of the Monetary Committee's role and significance.

During stage 2 of **Economic and Monetary Union** (EMU) the Monetary Committee assists the Council in monitoring progress towards economic convergence by the member states, and provides advice on which countries have met the various **convergence criteria**, and which others might need **derogations** from stage 3. The reports that it provides to the Council on this matter are separate from those drawn up by the Commission and the **European Monetary Institute** (EMI).

The Monetary Committee will be replaced by a new Economic and Financial Committee at the beginning of stage 3 of EMU. This Committee will undertake the existing work of the Monetary Committee, together with a range of new tasks, and have its membership extended to include representatives of the **European Central Bank** (ECB).

Monnet, Jean (1888–1979)

Born in Cognac, Jean Monnet started his professional life as a salesman in his family's cognac business. During the First World War he worked in London in the field of economic cooperation amongst the Allies and in 1920 was appointed Deputy Secretary-General of the newly established **League of Nations**. He left the League in 1923 to return to his family business. For the next 15 years he was active in international finance before returning, this time in Washington, to planning economic cooperation between the United Kingdom, France and the United States. It was Monnet who, as France was in retreat before the German advance of June 1940, persuaded **Winston Churchill** to forward to Paul Reynaud, the French Prime Minister, a draft declaration proclaiming an 'indissoluble union' between France and the United Kingdom (see **Franco–British union**). He spent the remainder of the war in Washington as a British civil servant. After the war he was put in charge of the *Commissariat du Plan* responsible for the economic recovery of France. In 1950 he suggested to **Robert Schuman**, the French Foreign Minister, the idea of pooling French and German coal and steel production (see **Schuman Plan**). This led to the establishment of the **European Coal and Steel Community** (ECSC) with Monnet as the first President of the High Authority (the forerunner of the **European Commission**). However, his other great plan of this period, the **European Defence Community**, came to nothing, and in November 1954 he resigned from the High Authority to devote himself to freelance campaigning on behalf of European unification. At this time he created his **Action Committee for the United States of Europe**, with representatives of 20 political parties and 10 trade unions. The Committee was disbanded in 1975. Monnet died in 1979 and in November 1988 his body was transferred to the Panthéon.

Monnet's *Mémoires*, published in 1976, are an invaluable source-book for the history of European unification and the European Community in particular. Two principal ideas underpinned Monnet's tireless campaigning on behalf of Europe: that Europe would be built not on the basis of visions and generalities but on practical achievements (the *réalisations concrètes* of the speech setting out the Schuman Plan); and that common institutions, not intergovernmental cooperation, were the key to a durable European Community, since it is only through institutions, as repositories of experience and shared values, that human beings accumulate wisdom and transmit it to future generations.

Monnet was often in conflict with other political leaders in his own country, notably, of course, **Charles de Gaulle**, and was never a member of any political party. He appears to have had something of a technocrat's distaste for party politics and mistrust of politicians, especially of their inability to take a long-term view. He respected British pragmatism, and remained confident that the only way of convincing the United Kingdom to play a part in the unification of Europe was to create organizations that actually worked. There is a recent biography of Monnet by François Duchêne: *Jean Monnet: the first statesman of interdependence* (New York and London, 1994).

Morocco

The Kingdom of Morocco, one of the **Maghreb** states, applied for membership of the Community in 1987 on the basis of its European orientation and its democratic credentials. Later that year, the **Council of Ministers** rejected the application on the grounds that Morocco was not a European state, the only occasion on which it has been found necessary to invoke the requirement under Article 237 of the **Treaty of Rome** (now Article O of the **Maastricht Treaty**) that only European states are eligible for membership.

Multi-Fibre Arrangement (MFA)

The MFA is an agreement between industrialized countries and developing countries on trade in textiles. First negotiated in 1973 within the **General Agreement on Tariffs and Trade** (GATT) and revised several times since then, the MFA allows industrialized countries to maintain tariffs and quotas on textile imports as their own textile industries are phased out or restructured. The 1993 conclusions of the GATT Uruguay Round envisage the eventual abolition of the MFA.

Mutual recognition of qualifications

The mutual recognition of qualifications is an essential aspect of **freedom of establishment**, and thereby part of the wider issue of **free movement of persons** within the Union and an important component of the **Single Market**. Initially, the **Commission** sought to make progress by bringing forward draft Directives (see **legal instruments**) for each of the regulated professions. This proved very slow, primarily because not only the requirements but also the ways in which professions are regulated vary from one member state to another (in the United Kingdom, many professions are self-regulating). The notorious Architects' Directive was discussed for 15 years before it was adopted in 1985. This experience led the Commission, encouraged by rulings of the **Court of Justice**, to bring forward a proposal providing for the mutual recognition of all qualifications requiring at least three years of higher education and, where appropriate, the necessary professional training. This was agreed as a Directive of the **Council of Ministers** in December 1988 and covers both employed and self-employed persons. It was supplemented and amplified by a second Directive in 1992. Both now apply throughout the **European Economic Area** (EEA).

National parliaments

National parliaments have always been involved in the process of European integration if only by virtue of the fact that members of the Parliamentary Assembly of the **Council of Europe**, of the **North Atlantic Assembly**, and of the **Western European Union** (WEU) Assembly are drawn from national parliaments. Until 1979, when the first **European elections** were held, this was also true of the **European Parliament**, but now only a small minority of its Members (MEPs) are at the same time members of their national parliaments (see **dual mandate**). This has given rise to a sense of rivalry between MEPs and national parliamentarians, to overcome which various means have been devised, none of them wholly successful.

Dual membership aside, national parliaments are involved in European integration in other ways. First and most obviously, government ministers both in the **European Council** and the **Council of Ministers** of the European Union and in the Committee of Ministers of the Council of Europe remain responsible to national parliaments. This responsibility involves reporting back to the national parliament after meetings of ministers, answering questions and sometimes participating in a full debate. Second, the **Treaties** establishing the **European Communities** provide for the involvement of national parliaments in the ratification of agreements reached in certain areas (most notably, any new treaties embodying changes to the existing Treaties, changes to the system of **own resources** and **accession** agreements with non-member states). Third, the most commonly used instrument of **Community law**, the Directive, requires implementing legislation to be put before and passed by national parliaments (see **legal instruments**).

All national parliaments of the member states of the European Union have committees specializing in European affairs. In two cases (Ireland and Spain) these are joint committees of the upper and lower house. In some cases (Belgium and Germany, for example) specific provision is made for the involvement of MEPs in the work of the committee. Such committees are brought together with a group of MEPs every six months in a body known as COSAC (*Conférences des Organes Specialisés dans les Affaires Communautaires*) under the presidency of the parliament of whichever country is currently holding the **presidency** of the Council. This stems from an initiative of the French National Assembly in May 1989 at the Madrid Conference of Presidents of national parliaments and of the European Parliament (see below). COSAC meetings afford an opportunity to discuss, with the help of a report from the presidency, current major topics of European integration; a communiqué or report is normally drawn up by consensus.

Presidents of national parliaments (the British House of Commons is represented by the Speaker) and of European parliamentary assemblies meet regularly in two different bodies: the 'large' or 'full' conference, embracing representatives of the parliaments of the members of the Council of Europe, of the European Parliament and of the WEU Assembly; and the 'small' conference, confined to the member states of the European Union and the European Parliament. Supplementary to the latter are the **assizes**.

The European Parliament itself has regular formal contacts at parliamentary level through Joint Committees with the parliaments of those countries linked to the Union by **Association Agreements** (Malta, Cyprus and Turkey, for example) and through interparliamentary delegations with the parliaments of other countries. These afford an opportunity for parliamentarians to discuss anything affecting political or economic relations between the Union and its principal trading partners.

The extent to which the national parliaments of the member states of the Union can or should control or influence the overall direction of policy is much debated. At the time when all important decisions in the Council were in effect subject to the national veto under the terms of the **Luxembourg Compromise** national parliaments could be said – by virtue of the control they exercised over individual members of the Council – to control (at least in a negative sense) what the Council decided. The extension of **qualified majority voting** (QMV) since the **Single European Act** (SEA) has reduced the importance of this kind of control, which was, in any case, never more than a very blunt instrument, with a corresponding increase in fears about the so-called **democratic deficit**. The effectiveness of national parliaments' **scrutiny** procedures for the examination of law emanating from the Union varies enormously. In some countries scrutiny is at best rudimentary; in others, very rigorous. Of the latter, the most instructive example is perhaps Denmark's 'Market Committee', which can vote formally in such a fashion as to bind the Danish minister negotiating in the Council, and on occasion make it necessary for him or her to telephone Copenhagen for further instructions. Even this, however, is an essentially negative power. At almost the opposite extreme are the comprehensive, thoughtful reports by the House of Lords Select Committee on the European Communities, which are influential by virtue of their accuracy and fairmindedness, not by virtue of an implicit threat.

The psychology of relations between the European Parliament and national parliaments is affected by the electoral system. In those countries (the great majority) that use national or regional list systems for national and European elections, the ease with which parliamentarians can move from the European Parliament to the national parliament and vice versa is much greater, with the result that any sense of rivalry is less keenly felt. This, in turn, helps political parties, at a less formal level, to foster good (or at least constructive) relations between their national and European parliamentarians.

Those with misgivings – to put it no more strongly – about the European Union continue to attach importance to finding a more extensive and powerful European role for national parliaments as the embodiments of both national and popular **sovereignty**. At their most ambitious, their ideas have included establishing a 'European Senate', an upper house drawn from members of national parliaments with substantial powers of veto and amendment over all Community legislation. Unsurprisingly, the European Parliament is not enthusiastic about this idea, and it is unlikely to be endorsed by the 1996 **Intergovernmental Conference** (IGC) on institutional reform, if only because, with the establishment of the **Committee of the Regions**, a new layer of democratic control has only just been added.

Governments, amongst others, will nevertheless want to continue to press the claims of national parliaments for greater European involvement, or at least appear to do so. Of particular concern to national parliaments are the two additional '**pillars**' of the **Maastricht Treaty**, the one relating to **Justice and Home Affairs** (JHA), the other to **Common Foreign and Security Policy** (CFSP), and the transition to the third stage of **Economic and Monetary Union** (EMU; see **Karlsruhe judgment**). In December 1993 it was announced that the Dutch Parliament was planning to use the Danish Market Committee model (see above) as a means of exercising control over the Dutch minister in JHA. The French government has given an undertaking that it will not let a matter be decided by a vote in the Council of Ministers until the French Parliament has had an opportunity to express its views (see also **scrutiny**).

Two **Declarations** of relevance to national parliaments were appended to the Maastricht Treaty, the one enjoining the European Parliament and national parliaments to step up 'contacts . . . and the exchange of information', the other inviting governments to 'ensure . . . that national parliaments receive Commission proposals for legislation in good time' and supporting the idea of further assizes.

National representations

Each member state of the European Union maintains an embassy in Brussels, the purpose of which is to manage the country's dealings with the various institutions of the Union, most especially its direct involvement in the legislative process through the **Council of Ministers**. These bodies are unique in that they straddle both national governments and the Union structure, and as such they enjoy a unique vantage-point and considerable influence in decision-making, not only in Brussels but in national capitals. Their task is to represent and interpret the views of the member states within the Union institutions, while communicating back to national capitals accurate and complete information on developments in Brussels as the basis for domestic policy on European issues.

These embassies are officially known as permanent representations, and are more usually referred to as national representations. Only member states have representations to the Union; the embassies of other countries accredited to the Union are known as missions. The national representations to the Union are separate from the delegations to the **North Atlantic Treaty Organization** (NATO) or the embassies to Belgium also maintained by Union member states in Brussels. The British permanent representation is known as **UKREP**.

Each of the representations is headed by a permanent representative, or ambassador, who is normally a senior official of the country's foreign ministry. The ambassadors meet together regularly in **COREPER**, the powerful committee that prepares all Council meetings and operates as a central brokerage-point in the Union's legislative process. Ambassadors or their deputies sit beside ministers in meetings of the Council, and are second in importance only to heads of government and foreign ministers in their influence on European issues.

In addition to ambassadors and their deputies, national representations are composed of between 20 and 60 administrative-grade officials, drawn from both the country's foreign ministry and domestic government departments. The precise mix of career diplomats and domestic technicians varies from representation to representation. In general, the relationship is of the order of about six technicians to four diplomats, with diplomats heavily represented at the more senior levels. The overall complement of the representation depends on the size of the country, its physical proximity to Belgium and whether or not it is currently (or soon will be) occupying the **presidency** of the Council. During the six-month presidency all representations are larger than at other times.

While ambassadors and their deputies normally devote most of their time to meetings of COREPER and the full Council and to high-level communication with their foreign ministries, the day-to-day work of the national representations on most policy issues is conducted at the less senior level of counsellors and first secretaries. These mid-rank civil servants attend all working groups of the Council, reporting the details of the discussions to their domestic departments, and then trying to convert the instructions they receive back from their national capital into a series of workable negotiating positions. Their task is to identify and hold the line on the issues that matter so that they can be resolved at a higher, more political level – namely in COREPER or the full Council – and to settle purely technical questions.

There is a fundamental conflict of interest at the heart of the role that national representations play. On the one hand national representations are guided by an operational imperative within the Council to discharge its business efficiently and to resolve differences. The culture of the Council, especially since the extension of **majority voting** by the **Single European Act** (SEA) and the diminishing importance of the **Luxembourg Compromise**, is biased towards splitting differences and doing deals. This is compounded by the centripetal tendency of COREPER – whose members, unlike those in working groups or ministers in the Council, are not beholden to individual domestic departments – to find agreements wherever possible and avoid the need for issues to be settled at ministerial level. Here the bureaucratic instincts of foreign ministry officials operate in the service of a broader European interest.

On the other hand, however, national representations know that their very *raison d'être* is to defend and advance the particular position of the individual member states. Without the clear articulation of divergent national interests, the Council would lose its essentially intergovernmental character (see **intergovernmentalism**) and become little more than an adjunct to the **European Commission**. Member states guard that role in what they perceive as both their individual and collective interests, and are keen to ensure that decisions, so far as reasonably possible, should not offend particular national sensitivities, especially their own. Individual representations that fail to acknowledge this necessity would quickly lose the confidence of their national capitals and so forfeit the ability to speak authoritatively on behalf of their ministers.

Neutrality

A neutral state is one that adopts an attitude of impartiality between belligerents. The rights and duties of neutral states were laid down in 1907 in two conventions signed in The Hague. Briefly, a neutral state must neither assist nor hinder a belligerent; its territory (including its airspace and its territorial waters) is inviolable and must be defended; it must not allow recruiting activities on behalf of the belligerents on its territory, although it is under no obligation to prevent its nationals from volunteering to fight on one side or the other; it must not trade with a belligerent, although its nationals may do so as private individuals; and although the sick and wounded of a belligerent may transit the territory of a neutral state, any active members of a belligerent state's armed forces must be interned if they enter the territory of a neutral state (special provisions apply to warships undergoing essential maintenance, reprovisioning and so on in a neutral port). Some states are permanent neutrals in respect of all armed conflicts, other states declare themselves neutral in respect of particular conflicts (as Ireland did in the Second World War). Neutrality is to be distinguished from non-belligerency, which means favouring one side in a conflict without formally taking part in it.

Neutrality is an explicit provision of the constitutions of **Switzerland** (since 1815), Austria (since 1955) and **Malta** (since 1987). Other countries, such as Sweden and Finland, are effectively neutral by virtue of a long-standing policy. Neutrality poses a problem in the context of the **Maastricht Treaty**, which lays the foundations for collective action on the part of signatory states in the fields of foreign and security policy and which holds out the possibility of there being one day a 'common defence'. Clearly, neither common defence nor a collective action could be effective if a number of states chose not to take part on the grounds of their neutral status. With the ending of the Cold War, several countries – including those mentioned above – are redefining what 'neutrality' now means. For a recent study, see Sheila Harden (ed.), *Neutral States and the European Community* (1993).

New Community Instrument (NCI)

The NCI, sometimes known as the Ortoli Facility after François-Xavier Ortoli, President of the **Commission** 1973–7, was introduced in 1977 to supplement the **structural funds**. It enables the Commission on behalf of the European Community itself to contract loans from the **European Investment Bank** (EIB) in order to assist projects in less-developed member states in the fields of energy, transport and the environment, especially those involving small and medium-sized enterprises (SMEs). The EIB may give advice and may withhold a loan, but otherwise acts only as the Commission's agent in granting and administering loans under the NCI.

Noël, Emile (b. 1922)

Emile Noël began his career as a European civil servant in the **Council of Europe**, where he was involved in the drafting of the abortive **European Political Community** Treaty. From 1956 to 1958 he served in the office of the Prime Minister of France, whom he represented in the negotiations that led to the **European Economic Community** (EEC) and the **European Atomic Energy Community** (Euratom) in 1957. In 1958 he became Secretary-General of the EEC **Commission** under its President, **Walter Hallstein**. Nine years later, with the entry into force of the **Merger Treaty**, he became Secretary-General of the Commission serving all three Communities, a post he retained until his retirement in 1987. As Secretary-General, he was involved in the Commission's 1975 report on European Union and in the negotiations that led to the 1986 **Single European Act** (SEA). From 1987 until 1994 Noël was Principal of the **European University Institute**.

'Non-Europe'

A term made current by the 1988 **Cecchini Report** on the **Single Market**, 'non-Europe' means the fragmentation of the market in such areas as public procurement, telecommunications, building materials and product standards. The fragmentation, it was believed, could be costed ('the cost of non-Europe'), and to this end the Commission published a series of 13 sector-by-sector reports carried out by independent consultants. These reports provided the intellectual underpinning of the Single Market programme.

Non-paper

A non-paper is a discussion document on a matter of current controversy, put forward by a member state or an institution of the European Union but not embodying the formal position of that state or institution on the matter. Normally, the purpose of a non-paper is to test the reaction of other parties. Non-papers, circulated informally, may often serve, especially at the level of the **national representations**, to resolve issues that by virtue of their complexity or sensitivity cannot easily be settled in the more open and formal context of meetings of the **Council of Ministers** or the **European Council**.

Non-Proliferation Treaty

At the Corfu meeting of the **European Council** on 24–25 June 1994 the member states agreed that preparations for the 1995 review conference on the Treaty on the Non-Proliferation of Nuclear Weapons (NPT) should be a **joint action** under the **Common Foreign and Security Policy** (CFSP). Their agreed joint aims are to secure indefinite, unconditional acceptance of the NPT from as many countries as possible.

Non-tariff barriers

A non-tariff barrier is an obstacle to trade arising not from the imposition of tariffs, levies or quantitative restrictions (quotas) but from different product specifications, discriminatory public purchasing policies, restrictive pricing or distribution agreements, patent or copyright difficulties, major discrepancies in the tax structure and so on (see Swann, *The Economics of the Common Market*, Chapter 5). The establishment of the **customs union** in 1968 effectively removed tariffs, levies and quotas from **intra-Community trade**, and the need to remove non-tariff barriers was the prime purpose of the **Single Market** programme (1992). Non-tariff barriers afford many means of resorting to covert protectionism and their removal is also a priority for other bodies committed to free trade, such as the **General Agreement on Tariffs and Trade** (GATT) and its successor, the World Trade Organization (WTO).

Nordic Council

The five countries that participate in the Nordic Council – Denmark, Finland, Iceland, Norway and Sweden – have a long history of contact of various kinds: as colonies or possessions of each other, as unions brought about by conquest or intermarriage and as trading partners. Norway, a Danish possession until 1814, gained its independence from Sweden in 1905; Finland, formerly Swedish, was a Grand Duchy within the Russian Empire and became independent in 1917; Iceland secured dominion status under the Danish Crown in 1918 and independence in 1944. Denmark, Norway and Sweden established the Nordic Interparliamentary Union in 1907, and in 1919 the Norden Association, a private body, was set up to promote cultural contacts. In 1938 the Danish Foreign Minister proposed the creation of a Nordic Council but the idea was not taken up until after the Second World War. In the late 1940s unsuccessful attempts were made to establish both a Nordic Customs Union and a Nordic Defence Union; progress was made with a Passport Union (completed in 1958). In 1951, at the suggestion of the Danish Prime Minister, the Nordic Interparliamentary Union endorsed the idea of a Nordic Council, and by the end of 1952 the parliaments of Denmark, Iceland, Norway and Sweden had approved an agreement establishing the institutions of the Council and defining the scope of cooperation between the signatory states; because of Soviet hostility Finland did not join until 1955.

The Nordic Council consists of 87 parliamentary representatives: 20 chosen by each of the national parliaments of Denmark, Finland, Norway and Sweden, and 7 from Iceland. They are joined by an unspecified number of ministerial representatives, who have no voting rights. Special provision is made within the Danish delegation for representatives of the autonomous communities of Greenland and the Faeroe Islands and within the Finnish delegation for the Åland Islands. The Council has six standing committees, but meets in plenary session only twice a year, the signatory states taking turns to host the meetings and act as president. Votes are taken by simple majority, but on measures affecting particular states only the representatives from those states may vote. Decisions, in the form of Recommendations, are communicated to the governments.

In 1962 the Nordic Council was given more formal status with the signing of a treaty in Helsinki. The areas for cooperation were defined but not extended: juridical matters, cultural contacts, social security and communications (including passport union). With the revision of the Helsinki Treaty in 1971 came the establishment of a Nordic Council of Ministers, with a secretariat in Copenhagen, and a small permanent secretariat in Stockholm for the Nordic Council itself. The revised Treaty specified once again the areas in which the signatory states would cooperate: communications and transport, cultural matters, economic policy, juridical and social affairs; the protection of the environment was added three years later.

Since 1974 all five governments have had ministers specifically responsible for coordination through the Nordic Council of Ministers and who attend the meetings. Regular contact is maintained between government departments at official level in 14 specialist committees. The Nordic Council of Ministers oversees the work of the Nordic Investment Bank, the Nordic Fund for Technology and Industrial Development, the Nordic Cultural Fund and a number of joint development projects in the Third World. It provides the forum through which the five governments can coordinate their positions in other international bodies.

In recent years, the Nordic Council has established links with all the states bordering the Baltic Sea and has encouraged the **Baltic states** to set up their own machinery for cooperation. North of the Arctic Circle in the Barents Sea formal contacts have also been established at the regional level with Russia.

Although well established and with substantial achievements to its credit, the machinery of Nordic cooperation has proved inadequate in certain respects. Determined efforts to establish a Nordic Economic Union came to nothing: a customs union was achieved only within the **European Free Trade Association** (EFTA) in 1960; security coordination has been limited to discussion of a Nordic 'nuclear-free zone'; and the attempt to address the cultural, legal and technical challenges of satellite broadcasting failed almost entirely. Nordic cooperation is sometimes put forward as a model for wider European cooperation as an alternative to the more ambitious, supranational, legislation-based model followed by the European Community. Its limitations, however, are clear, in spite of the advantages the Nordic countries enjoy by virtue of a substantial degree of cultural, linguistic and economic homogeneity. It is these limitations that prompted Denmark, Finland, Norway and Sweden to seek membership of the Community (see **enlargement**).

North Atlantic Assembly

Founded in July 1955 as the Conference of Members of Parliament from the member countries of the **North Atlantic Treaty Organization** (NATO), the North Atlantic Assembly took its present name in 1966. The Assembly is composed of 188 parliamentarians (ministers are not eligible) from the 16 NATO countries, appointed by **national parliaments**. Associate membership has been extended to parliamentarians from the 11 countries that are not members of NATO but which belong to the **North Atlantic Cooperation Council** (NACC).

The role of the North Atlantic Assembly, which was not provided for in the 1949 Treaty of Washington and which remains independent of NATO, is to provide a parliamentary forum for the discussion of defence and security issues, to promote mutual understanding and to strengthen parliamentary links with the countries of central and eastern Europe. The Assembly meets in plenary session twice a year in different NATO countries, its committees and subcommittees more frequently. Its opinions are expressed in the form of Recommendations and Resolutions. It has a small international secretariat at its headquarters in Brussels.

North Atlantic Cooperation Council (NACC)

At a **summit** meeting of the **North Atlantic Treaty Organization** (NATO) in Rome in November 1991 agreement was reached on the establishment of the NACC. The purpose was to create a forum in which the member states of NATO could discuss and coordinate their positions on security issues with the countries of central and eastern Europe and the **Baltic states** without giving them membership of NATO and the security guarantees that flow from membership. An inaugural meeting of the NACC was held the following month in Brussels. In March 1992 the 11 republics that form the Commonwealth of Independent States (CIS) also joined the NACC, raising the number of members to 37 countries (16 NATO members, Bulgaria, the Czech Republic, Hungary, Poland, Romania, Slovakia, the 3 Baltic states, 11 CIS states, and Georgia). Full meetings of the NACC are normally held as an adjunct to the autumn meeting of NATO ministers (i.e., the North Atlantic Council). On 9 May 1994 the Council of Ministers of the **Western European Union** (WEU) agreed to extend 'Associate status' to the same six countries of central and eastern Europe and to the three Baltic states.

North Atlantic Treaty Organization (NATO)

On 17 March 1948 Belgium, France, Luxembourg, the Netherlands and the United Kingdom signed a 50-year agreement on economic, social and cultural collaboration and collective self-defence known as the **Treaty of Brussels**. Three months later the beginning of the Berlin blockade marked a further deterioration in relations between the United States and the Soviet Union, and on 6 July 1948 talks began in Washington between the United States, Canada and the Brussels Treaty powers on a new collective security alliance to be known as the North Atlantic Treaty Organization (NATO) and covering the whole of the North Atlantic area. Formal negotiations began on 10 December 1948 and the draft Treaty was published three months later. Five more countries (Denmark, Iceland, Italy, Norway and Portugal) were invited to sign the Treaty, and – in spite of opposition from the Soviet Union, which claimed that the Treaty was contrary to the United Nations Charter – the signing ceremony took place on 4 April 1949. The Treaty entered into force on 24 August 1949. Greece and Turkey joined NATO in 1952, West Germany in 1955 and Spain in 1982 (confirmed by referendum on 12 March 1986). The headquarters of NATO and its various organs were initially in France, but with the withdrawal of France from NATO's integrated military structure in 1966 the headquarters were transferred to Brussels and the NATO Defence College was moved to Rome. The Spanish referendum on NATO membership of 1986 resulted in Spain also withdrawing from the integrated military structure.

The NATO Treaty contains only 14 articles. The commitment to collective security is in Article 5:

> The Parties agree that an armed attack against one or more of them in Europe or North America shall be considered an attack against them all, and consequently they agree that, if such an armed attack occurs, each of them, in exercise of the right of individual or collective self-defence recognized by Article 51 of the Charter of the United Nations, will assist the Party or Parties so attacked by taking forthwith, individually, and in concert with the other Parties, such action as it deems necessary, including the use of armed force, to restore and maintain the security of the North Atlantic area.

Article 6 defines the 'NATO area' as the territory of any of the signatory states in Europe or North America, the territory of Turkey and 'the islands under the jurisdiction [of any of the signatory states] in the North Atlantic area north of the Tropic of Cancer'.

The principal civilian decision-making bodies are the North Atlantic

Council (foreign ministers), the Defence Planning Committee (defence ministers) and the Nuclear Planning Group (defence ministers). All three bodies meet regularly at permanent representative (ambassador) level. The Military Committee, the highest military authority in the alliance, is composed for the most part of Chiefs of Staff. In addition, NATO has a staff of international civil servants headed by a secretary-general, and an international military staff (see also **Supreme Headquarters Allied Powers Europe**). A measure of democratic supervision is provided by the **North Atlantic Assembly** which was founded in 1955 and meets in plenary session twice a year. It is composed of 188 members of **national parliaments** sitting in national delegations.

Various means were established within NATO to allow the European members to work together on specifically European security issues. The **Eurogroup**, never formally part of NATO, was an association of European defence ministers (except those of France and Iceland) holding regular meetings alongside full meetings of the alliance. Similarly, the **Independent European Programme Group** was a forum designed to promote all forms of cooperation amongst European NATO members in the field of the design, manufacture and supply of military equipment. The work of both groups has now been largely taken over by the **Western European Union** (WEU) as the body responsible for providing the organizational and operational nucleus for the European Union's growing involvement in security issues under the **Maastricht Treaty** (see **Common Foreign and Security Policy**).

The end of the Cold War has prompted a reappraisal of NATO's role and structure, accompanied by cuts in national defence budgets. Since the NATO summit in Rome in November 1991 the organization has concentrated upon developing relations with the countries of central and eastern Europe, including the former Soviet Union (see **North Atlantic Cooperation Council**, **Partnership for Peace**), and defining for itself a broader peacekeeping and humanitarian role with the aid of an **Allied Rapid Reaction Corps**. Legal difficulties remain, however, in the way of deploying NATO forces 'out of area' (see above) even in defence of NATO countries' extra-territorial interests.

The NATO summit of January 1994 confirmed that membership of the alliance remained open in principle to other European countries, and endorsed the concept of Combined Joint Task Forces (CJTFs). The CJTFs would operate broadly within the NATO framework, but the possibility of involving forces from non-NATO countries would be left open. Also noteworthy was President Clinton's assurance that 100,000 American troops would be stationed in Europe for the foreseeable future. The following month, at 17.45 on 28 February 1994, NATO forces fired their first-ever shots in anger while enforcing the no-fly zone over Serbia imposed by the UN Security Council.

Norway

Norway was a founder member of the **North Atlantic Treaty Organization** (NATO) in 1949 and of the **European Free Trade Association** (EFTA) in 1960, and has been a member of the **Council of Europe** since 1950. In 1962 and again in 1967 Norway applied for membership of the European Community and in response to the second application a draft Treaty of Accession was successfully negotiated. However, in September 1972 53.6 per cent of the population voted against entry in a referendum.

In common with other EFTA states, Norway has had a free trade agreement with the Community since 1973 and in May 1992 became a signatory to the agreement establishing a **European Economic Area** (EEA). In spite of this high level of economic integration with the Community the Labour Government of Mrs Gro Harlem Brundtland took the view – prompted by the fact that Austria, Sweden and Finland had already applied for membership – that once again Norway should seek to join the Community. The application was forwarded to the Council on 25 November 1992 and the Commission's generally favourable **Opinion** was given the following year (*Bulletin of the European Communities*, supplement 2/93). The Commission noted the extent to which Norway had already adapted to the *acquis communautaire* in several fields and the contribution that Norway could make by virtue of its healthy economic performance and record of achievement in environmental protection and Third World development. The Union accounts for 50 per cent of Norwegian imports and 66 per cent of exports, with energy exports assuming great importance. Norway, with one of the largest merchant fleets in the world, is particularly interested in the development of a maritime policy. Negotiations with Norway were completed in March 1994.

Membership of the Union proved to be still controversial in Norway, especially in rural areas. Emotionally, the people remain attached to independence (gained from Sweden in 1905) and to Nordic cooperation (Norway has always been active in the **Nordic Council**), and to many Norwegians most countries of the Union seem very remote. Church groups campaigned against the Union on the grounds that the breaking of the state monopoly on alcoholic drinks would lead to alcoholism and other social evils. Although the two main parties were officially in favour of membership, the Norwegian people rejected membership of the Union by 52.5 per cent to 47.5 per cent in a **referendum** held on 28 November 1994.

'Nouvelles Frontières' case

The 'Nouvelles Frontières' case (*Ministre Public* v *Asjes*, Cases 209–13/84) resulted from a challenge to the French Civil Aviation Code by a French travel agency, which queried the compatibility of the price-fixing arrangements in the Code with the **competition policy** provisions of the **Treaty of Rome**. In April 1986 the **Court of Justice** ruled that the competition provisions did apply and clarified the powers of the **Commission** to enforce them. The case was an important step in the attempts to extend competition rules to air transport (see **common transport policy**). There is an account of this and other relevant cases in Mark A. Johnson, 'Removing barriers to market entry in the air transport industry: the application of European Community competition rules', *Legal Issues of European Integration*, no. 2, 1993.

'Occupied field'

An 'occupied field' is an area of policy in which the European Union is capable, under the **Treaties**, of taking legislative action. It may not have taken action, but the fact that it could may inhibit national authorities from acting independently, since Community law enjoys **primacy** over national law in member states.

An example of this occurred in relation to seat-belts in motor coaches. Two serious accidents in the United Kingdom involving coaches led to calls for all passenger-seats to be equipped with seat belts. This matter, in common with other technical specifications for coaches, is part of the broader issue of transport safety and as such is covered by Article 75.1 of the **Treaty of Rome**. It also relates to the **Single Market** requirement for common rules in respect of type-approval for motor vehicles, and is therefore also covered by **Article 100a** EEC. At the time of the accidents no action on seat-belts in coaches had been taken at Community level, but the **Commission** was known to have considered the question and was quite clearly empowered under the Treaty to make a proposal. The British government therefore had to choose between taking unilateral action in advance of a Union-wide agreement, thereby running the risk of involving coach manufacturers and coach operators in two sets of costly changes, and awaiting such an agreement. Given the length of time it can take to reach agreement, one consequence of the 'occupied field' can be that years pass before any action is taken at all.

Official Journal

The *Official Journal of the European Communities*, normally referred to as the OJ, is published almost daily throughout most of the year in three distinct series and in all official languages. The 'L' (Legislation) series contains the texts of all legislative acts of the Communities, including **Decisions** taken by representatives of the governments of member states. The 'C' series (Communications) contains a wide range of other material, including the texts of legislative proposals from the **Commission, Opinions** thereon delivered by other institutions, lists of cases brought before the **Court of Justice**, key extracts from judgments of the Court, the daily value of the ECU expressed in the currencies of the member states, and appointments to Union bodies. The minutes of sittings of the **European Parliament** are also published in the 'C' series, the verbatim report of proceedings in an Annex. Since 1978 there has also been an OJ 'S' (supplement) series, concerned mainly with invitations to tender for public works contracts (see **public purchasing**) both within the **European Economic Area** and in countries eligible for aid from the **European Development Fund**. Also available is a two-part monthly index to the OJ and an annual cumulative index. The OJ is published by the Office for Official Publications in Luxembourg and is available in the United Kingdom through HMSO.

Publication of legislative acts in the OJ is an essential procedural requirement. Article 191 EEC specifically provides for Regulations and Directives (see **legal instruments**) addressed to all member states to be published in the OJ and for them to enter into force 'on the date specified in them or . . . on the twentieth day following their publication'. Care is taken to ensure that the date of publication of each issue of the OJ is, in fact, the date upon which the issue is actually available in all the official languages from the Office for Official Publications.

Ombudsman

The institution generally known as the Ombudsman is of Scandinavian origin (the first Ombudsman was appointed in Sweden in 1809). The Ombudsman acts as an intermediary between the citizen and the public authorities, local or national. Only a minority of European countries have an ombudsman, and the exact title is subject to many variations: in the United Kingdom, the Ombudsman is known as the Parliamentary Commissioner for Administration, in France, simply as the *Médiateur*. The precise duties of the Ombudsman also vary, but broadly speaking they are directed towards the investigation of complaints brought by individuals against the authorities. The Ombudsman is required to be both impartial and independent of government.

The idea that there might be a European Community Ombudsman was first put forward in the 1970s, but it was not until the 1991 **Maastricht Treaty** that the matter was finally agreed. The Maastricht Treaty introduced a new Article 138e into the **Treaty of Rome**, requiring the **European Parliament** to 'appoint an Ombudsman empowered to receive complaints from any citizen of the Union or any natural or legal person residing or having its registered office in a Member State concerning instances of maladministration in the activities of the Community institutions or bodies, with the exception of the **Court of Justice** and the Court of First Instance acting in their judicial role'. The use of the word 'maladministration' to describe the subject of the Ombudsman's investigations means that within the Community institutions the remit is similar to that of the Ombudsman in the United Kingdom. 'Maladministration' covers both incompetence (undue delay, failure to follow agreed procedures, etc.) and deliberate wrong-doing.

The Ombudsman may make investigations either on his own initiative or on the basis of complaints brought to his attention, either directly or through a Member of the European Parliament (MEP), except in relation to matters that are or have been the subject of legal proceedings. The Ombudsman has no powers of sanction. The results of his investigations are forwarded to the European Parliament and the institution concerned. His five-year term of office coincides with that of the European Parliament and he may be dismissed only by the Court of Justice at the request of the Parliament. He is required to submit to the Parliament an annual report 'on the outcome of his inquiries'. A Finn, Jacob Söderman, was elected as Ombudsman on 12 July 1995.

Opinion

In the context of the European Union, 'Opinion' (the French word *avis* is sometimes used) has several distinct meanings:

1 The procedures in the **Treaty of Rome** for consulting the **European Parliament** empower it to give Opinions on the draft legislation referred to it. The Opinion is not only the resolution adopted in plenary session but also the suggested amendments to the draft in question. The expression *avis conforme* is used to denote one of that special category of Opinions given under the **assent procedure** that the Parliament must adopt by an absolute majority of its members: for example, on draft Treaties of **Accession** (see **enlargement**). The indispensability of the Parliament's Opinions in the Union's legislative process was established by the **isoglucose case**.

2 Within the Parliament, if a committee other than the one primarily responsible for preparing a report on a piece of draft legislation wants to contribute to the Parliament's consideration of the matter, it does this in the form of an Opinion.

3 Both the **Economic and Social Committee** and the **Committee of the Regions** are also entitled to give Opinions on draft legislation referred to them.

4 Under Article 189 EEC Opinions are listed as one of the types of legislative act that may be delivered by the **Council of Ministers** or the **European Commission** (see **legal instruments**). However, unlike Regulations, Directives or Decisions, neither Recommendations nor Opinions are binding.

5 More importantly, under Article O of the **Maastricht Treaty** the Commission is required to give its Opinion before negotiations on accession can proceed with an applicant state (see **enlargement**).

6 In the **Court of Justice** the function of an **advocate-general** is to give an Opinion upon the basis of which the Court reaches its final judgment. Less commonly used is the procedure under Article 228 EEC, which allows the Council, the Commission or a member state to seek the Opinion of the Court on the compatibility between the Treaty and an agreement that the Union proposes to conclude with a non-member state or an international organization. Such Opinions are binding (see **European Economic Area** for a recent example).

7 Under Article 206a EEC the **Court of Auditors** may also deliver Opinions at the request of one of the other institutions.

8 Both the **European Monetary Institute** (EMI) and its successor, the **European Central Bank** (ECB), may deliver Opinions (Articles 109f and 108a EEC), as may the **Monetary Committee** (Article 109a EEC).

Opt-out

A member state of the European Union that chooses not to participate in a Union activity covered by Treaty provisions is said to have an 'opt-out'. The best-known is the British opt-out from the **Social Chapter**. An opt-out is formalized in a **protocol** to the treaty in question. A Union characterized by member states opting out from particular activities would be one of **variable geometry** or **Europe à la carte**.

Organization for Economic Cooperation and Development (OECD)

The OECD is a Paris-based intergovernmental organization (see **intergovernmentalism**) established to promote economic cooperation between industrialized states, to coordinate development assistance to the Third World and to provide a forum for the resolution of problems affecting world trade and economic growth. The OECD was founded as the Organization for European Economic Cooperation (OEEC) in 1948 to oversee the implementation of the European Recovery Programme established under the **Marshall Plan**. The founding members were Austria, Belgium, Denmark, France, Greece, Iceland, Ireland, Italy, Luxembourg, the Netherlands, Norway, Portugal, Sweden, Turkey, the United Kingdom, and the British, French and American zones of occupied Germany. The Federal Republic of Germany joined the OEEC in 1949, and the United States and Canada became associate members in 1950. Spain joined the OEEC in 1959. The OEEC had a small international secretariat but was intergovernmental in character: all important decisions were taken by a Council, which could act only by unanimity (abstentions not counted), each member state having one vote.

Amongst the first achievements of the OEEC was a European Payments Union, which allowed member states to settle their bilateral trading accounts on a multilateral basis through the **Bank for International Settlements** and was able to extend credit to economies in temporary difficulties. The OEEC was the forum in which **the Six** began the discussions that led to the **Messina Conference** and the **Treaty of Rome**. At the same time the United Kingdom sought to establish a **free trade area** amongst the OEEC states, but once the Six had established the more ambitious **European Economic Community** (EEC) the United Kingdom and its partners had to be content with a rival organization, the **European Free Trade Association** (EFTA), composed of Austria, Denmark, Norway, Portugal, Sweden, Switzerland and the United Kingdom.

The EEC/EFTA division effectively split the OEEC and in 1960 it was refounded under its new title with the United States and Canada as full members. At the same time the scope of the organization was widened to include relations with developing countries, but its intergovernmental character remained unchanged. The OECD retains its importance in the field of international economic cooperation, and its reports on member countries' economic performance are authoritative and influential. Japan joined the OECD in 1964, Finland in 1969, Australia in 1971 and New Zealand in 1973. The OECD has also fostered the setting up of other organizations, such as the International Energy Agency and the **Group of Seven** (G7) leading industrialized economies. The OECD works very closely wherever necessary with the **European Commission**, for example, on development issues through the Development Assistance Committee. It was OECD member states (meeting as the Group of 24) that founded the **European Bank for Reconstruction and Development** in May 1990. Mexico, the Czech Republic and Hungary are now also members.

The OECD Council, like its OEEC predecessor (see above), can take decisions that are binding on member states and can make recommendations. The OECD can enter into agreements with non-member states and international organizations. However, unlike the European Union, the OECD has no supranational machinery for the resolution of disputes or the enforcement of decisions, nor do its workings create a body of law enjoying **primacy** over national law. It also lacks a parliamentary body responsible for general supervision of its activities.

There is an account of the political and economic background to the founding of OEEC in Milward, *The Reconstruction of Western Europe 1945–1951* and an up-to-date description of OECD in Archer, *Organizing Europe*. The OECD itself publishes many reports and studies.

Organization for European Economic Cooperation

The forerunner of the **Organization for Economic Cooperation and Development**.

Organization for Security and Cooperation in Europe

See **Conference on Security and Cooperation in Europe**.

Overseas countries and territories (OCTs)

The OCTs are the scattered remains, most of them very small islands, of the British, French and Dutch overseas possessions. Part IV of the **Treaty of Rome** sets out the legal framework for the association of the OCTs with the European Community, the purpose of which is 'to promote the economic and social development of the countries and territories and to establish close economic relations between them and the Community as a whole' (Article 131 EEC). **Greenland** is now also counted amongst the OCTs.

The OCTs may be listed in four groups:

1 *British* OCTs In the Caribbean: Anguilla, Antigua, the British Virgin Islands, the Cayman Islands, Montserrat, the Turks and Caicos Islands; in the south Atlantic: the Falkland Islands, Saint Helena and its dependencies, South Georgia and the South Sandwich Islands; in the Pacific: Pitcairn; British Antarctic Territory; British Indian Ocean Territory.
2 *French* OCTs In the Pacific: French Polynesia, New Caledonia and its dependencies, Wallis and Futuna Islands; French Southern and Antarctic Territories. French OCTs also include the 'territorial collectivities' of Mayotte off the coast of Madagascar, and St Pierre and Miquelon (Newfoundland). The French overseas departments (Réunion, Guadeloupe, Guiana and Martinique) are an integral part of France and so of the European Union. They benefit from various forms of special assistance under Article 227.2 EEC.
3 *Dutch* OCTs In the Caribbean: Aruba, the Netherlands Antilles.
4 *Danish* OCTs Greenland.

Not only are the OCTs extremely diverse in respect of geography, resources, climate, population, population density and prosperity, but the provisions governing their status in relation to the European Union (and hence the applicability of **Community law**) also vary from one OCT to another, even amongst those historically associated with the same member state. In general terms Community law is applicable only to member states' European territory, not to their OCTs. However, member states apply to their trade with the OCTs the same treatment as they apply to each other, and the OCTs apply to every member state the treatment applied to the state with which they have special relations. Moreover, since citizens of the Danish, Dutch and French OCTs (and of the Falkland Islands amongst British OCTs) are nationals of the parent country, they are also citizens of the European Union (see **citizenship**).

Two problems in particular are of concern to the OCTs: **right of establishment** and **free movement of persons**. With respect to the first, Article 176 of Council Decision 86/223 (30 June 1986) enjoins the OCTs not to discriminate on the basis of nationality between Community firms or individuals wishing to invest or become established in an OCT. With respect to the second, Article 135 EEC provides for freedom of movement between the OCTs and the member states to be the subject of a decision requiring unanimous agreement. No such decision has so far been reached, nor any measure been taken to clarify the legal situation in the member states of workers from an OCT, or in the OCTs of workers from a member state.

Underlying many of these legal and commercial issues is the broader question of whether or not the OCTs, with their historic and constitutional links with one or other member state, should enjoy a privileged relationship with the Union over and above that which ACP **states** enjoy under the **Lomé Convention**. At the very least, it would be illogical were their position to be less advantageous than that of ACP countries, the great majority of which are former colonies that have opted for independence. Accordingly, the Union takes care to ensure that the periodic renegotiations of the Lomé Convention do not result in the OCTs being left behind, and as far as possible the OCTs' interests are taken into account in decisions on the **Common Commercial Policy**, often on the basis of direct consultations with OCT authorities. In the **European Development Fund** (1990–5) the OCTs were allocated 140 million ECUs in grants and a further 25 million ECUs in loans from the **European Investment Bank** (EIB).

'Own resources'

The revenue of the European Union, as defined by the Council of Ministers in Decisions of 21 April 1970 and 24 June 1988 (see below), is known as 'own resources' to distinguish it from the contributions made by member states to finance the **Budget** before the 1970 Decision, and to underline the fact that under the terms of this Decision certain revenues accrue to the Union as of right.

Article 201 (since revised) of the **Treaty of Rome** made provision for the contributions of member states to be replaced by a system of 'own resources'. The 1970 Decision established three sources of revenue: agricultural levies, customs duties and up to 1 per cent of national revenue from

value-added tax (VAT) applied to a uniform base. The Budget was to be financed from these sources of revenue with effect from 1 January 1975, but delays in the adoption and implementation of measures necessary to establish the uniform VAT base (the Sixth VAT Directive) meant that the new system was not introduced until the 1980 financial year. In a Council Decision of 7 May 1985 the VAT limit was raised from 1 per cent to 1.4 per cent. By 1987, however, it was clear that revenue was inadequate to finance existing policies and new policies laid down in the **Single European Act** (SEA) of 1986, not least because of the 'shrinkage' in the revenue drawn from customs duties and agricultural levies as a consequence of tariff cuts and of concessionary trade agreements. Accordingly, the **Commission** submitted a set of proposals (the 'Delors package') that, *inter alia*, provided for a fourth 'own resource'. These proposals were discussed at meetings of the **European Council** in Brussels in June 1987 and February 1988. The new system of own resources was set out in a Council Decision of 24 June 1988, which came into force on 1 February 1989 with retroactive effect from 1 January 1988 (see **future financing**). A major British preoccupation in the negotiations leading up to the June 1988 Decision was, of course, the maintenance of the special arrangements for the United Kingdom contained in the **Fontainebleau Agreement**.

The Decision of 24 June 1988 set out four types of revenue:

1 **Common External Tariff** (CET) duties and duties on products covered by the **European Coal and Steel Community** (ECSC) Treaty;
2 agricultural levies on trade with non-member countries, together with duties on sugar and isoglucose produced in the member states;
3 1.4 per cent of each member state's VAT revenue as applied to an assessment base 'determined in a uniform manner according to Community rules';
4 a contribution from each member state related to its gross national product (GNP) at a rate to be determined annually in the light of the overall budgetary situation.

With respect to resources 1 and 2, member states are allowed to retain 10 per cent of the revenue to cover the costs of collection. With respect to resource 3, the Decision specifies that the uniform base for the assessment of VAT may not exceed 55 per cent of any member state's GNP. This safeguards the interests of poorer countries, since revenue from VAT, as a turnover tax, is not an accurate indicator of relative wealth.

For the first time, the system embodied in the Own Resources Decision provided for an overall limit on own resources, expressed as a percentage (currently 1.2 per cent) of the Union's total GNP (see **budgetary discipline**). By introducing a fourth GNP-related resource to compensate for any shortfall in revenue from the other three resources, the new system places the Budget on a reasonably secure footing, at least for the next few years. But as the Union assumes new responsibilities – especially in eastern Europe – it is difficult to see how the question of new own resources can be left unresolved. Various proposals have been made, including one for a tax on hydrocarbons (which would, of course, tie in with the Union's policies for the environment), and at least in some quarters it has been suggested that eventually the Union should receive some of its revenue directly from the taxpayer. In this context it is worth noting the conclusion of the 1977 **MacDougall Report**, which said that if the Budget were to have any substantial redistributive effect, it would need to rise to between 5 and 7 per cent of the gross domestic product (GDP).

The system of own resources sets the European Union apart from other international organizations and is an important symbol of its independence from member states. Because of its sensitivity, it is an area in which decisions at the level of the Council of Ministers must be unanimous and are subject to ratification by all **national parliaments**. It is also an area in which the **European Parliament** enjoys only a right of consultation (Article 201 EEC), by contrast with its very much more extensive powers on the expenditure side of the Budget. There is much useful background material in Michael Shackleton's short study *Financing the European Community* (1990).

Pact on Stability in Europe

A proposal originating with French Prime Minister Edouard Balladur, the idea of a pact was endorsed at an inaugural conference held in Paris on 26–27 May 1994. It provides a new set of undertakings and a new framework within which signatory states (the list is broadly the same as the list of states which participated in the **Conference on Security and Cooperation in Europe** (CSCE)) can 'create a climate of confidence which will be favourable to the strengthening of democracy, to respect for human rights and to economic progress and peace, while at the same time respecting the identities of peoples' (paragraph 1.3 of the Paris document). Great emphasis is laid on neighbouring signatory states resolving disputes bilaterally and exploring new forms of cooperation. The Paris document set up two 'regional round tables', one for the **Baltic states** and the other for the countries of central and eastern Europe. The Pact was formally signed on 21 March 1995, thus establishing 'an area of lasting good-neighbourliness and cooperation in Europe'. It is not proposed to set up new institutions, but to entrust to the CSCE's successor, the OSCE, responsibility for monitoring the implementation of the Pact and for putting in hand any follow-up activities.

Balladur made his proposal for a pact within the European Union framework, and so the initiative is one of the first **joint actions** taken under the **Common Foreign and Security Policy** (CFSP). The Union has offered its services as a 'moderator', if so desired, in the case of problems that prove difficult to resolve bilaterally. The Pact was welcomed by Russia as a continuation of work already undertaken in the CSCE context (see also **Charter of Paris**, **Partnership for Peace**).

Padoa-Schioppa Report

In April 1986 a group of independent experts led by Tommaso Padoa-Schioppa was asked by the **Commission** to prepare a report on the economic consequences of two key decisions taken the previous year: to admit Spain and Portugal to the European Community and to create a **Single Market** by the end of 1992. Their report, entitled *Efficiency, Stability and Equity*, was published in April 1987, and in book form, with a preface by **Jacques Delors**, later in the same year.

The report reviewed progress to date towards economic integration in the Community: the removal of exchange controls, the elimination of barriers to trade, the **harmonization** of **state aids**, the attempt to improve the mobility of the labour market, the **European Monetary System** (EMS), and the **structural funds**. Overall, progress was mixed, both between sectors and between member states, with potential damage to longer-term objectives. For the first time since the 1977 **MacDougall Report**, the redistributive effects and potential of the Community Budget were re-examined. The report favoured an increase in the structural funds, with priority being given to peripheral regions and to those dependent on outdated industries, and a system of **contributions and receipts** amongst member states that took account of their relative prosperity. With respect to the institutions, the report concluded that in three areas the Community's powers needed to be strengthened: monetary policy, regional policy and measures to improve the competitiveness of Community industry. By contrast, and in line with the principle of **subsidiarity**, there was scope for reducing the Community's role in social and employment questions, and for decentralizing the application and enforcement of Community policy, in the field of harmonization, for example, or in connection with rates of indirect taxes.

Pan-Europa

One of several 'macro-nationalisms' (Pan-Slavism, Pan-Africanism, etc.), Pan-Europa is an idea most closely associated with the name of **Count Richard Coudenhove-Kalergi** and is noteworthy as a forerunner of the idea of a United Europe (see **European Union**) in the interwar years. Under Coudenhove-Kalergi's scheme, the best prospect for world peace lay in the emergence of very large units encompassing, in most cases, many independent states or nations. The idea of Pan-Europa was linked to the widely held belief that, if it were to succeed, the **League of Nations** would have to be underpinned by strong regional groupings. There were to be six of these: the British Empire, Pan-Europa, Pan-America, the Soviet Union, China and Japan. This scheme clearly cut across several contemporary macro-nationalisms organized on straightforwardly ethnic lines (notably the Pan-Germanism developed under the Second Reich and taken to catastrophic extremes under the Third). Pan-Europa gave its name to Coudenhove-Kalergi's Pan-European Union and was the title of his best-known book (1927). The Pan-European Union is still in existence.

Paris, Treaty of

Signed in April 1951, the Treaty of Paris established the **European Coal and Steel Community** (ECSC) amongst **the Six**. The ECSC, which owed its origins to the 1950 **Schuman Plan**, was the model for the other **European Communities**. See also **Treaties**.

Partnership Agreement

Partnership Agreements were devised to suit the particular circumstances of the countries of the former Soviet Union. Like **Cooperation Agreements**, Partnership Agreements are drawn up under Articles 113 and 235 of the **Treaty of Rome**, but are more ambitious in respect of the provisions for political contacts at ministerial and parliamentary level, and are concluded for 10 years (with tacit prolongation) rather than 5. In fact, Partnership Agreements closely resemble **Europe Agreements**, the main difference being that they make no provision for eventual membership of the Union; however, in each case the preamble makes reference to the creation of a **free trade area**.

Partnership for Peace

The Partnership for Peace is an initiative of the **North Atlantic Treaty Organization** (NATO), intended, in the words of the document issued at the conclusion of the meeting of the North Atlantic Council that endorsed the initiative (10–11 January 1994), to 'forge new security relationships between the North Atlantic Alliance and its Partners for Peace'. Aimed principally at the countries of central and eastern Europe and the **Baltic states**, the Partnership for Peace framework document invites participating states to forward to NATO a document 'identifying the steps they will take to achieve the political goals of the Partnership and the military and other assets that might be used for Partnership activities ... Each subscribing state will develop with NATO an individual Partnership Programme.' Amongst the 'political goals' is 'ensuring democratic control for defence forces' in Partner states.

The Partnership for Peace initiative is a military complement to the **North Atlantic Cooperation Council** (NACC). It allows Partner states to establish liaison offices with NATO headquarters and with the 'Partnership Coordination Cell' at the **Supreme Headquarters Allied Powers Europe** (SHAPE), to participate (at their own expense) in planning and military exercises and in NATO peacekeeping, humanitarian, and search and rescue missions, and to share 'in a reciprocal exchange of information on defence planning and budgeting'. The NATO countries undertake to 'consult with any active participant in the Partnership if that Partner perceives a direct threat to its territorial integrity, political independence, or security' (paragraph 8).

This last undertaking falls some way short of the security guarantees enjoyed by full NATO members, but the Partnership for Peace initiative has been welcomed by the countries of central and eastern Europe. Most importantly, Russia indicated in May 1994 its willingness to enter into a partnership with NATO, on the basis of a programme that took account of Russia's status as a nuclear power (see also **Pact on Stability in Europe**).

People's Europe

At various times and for various reasons, measures have been proposed to bring Europe, in the words of the 1975 **Tindemans Report**, 'close to the citizens'. The most ambitious proposals to date were those made by the Committee for a People's Europe, set up by the **European Council** meeting in Fontainebleau in June 1984 and sometimes known as the Adonnino Committee, after its Italian chairman. The Committee drew up two reports, the first submitted to the European Council meeting in Brussels in March 1985 and the second, longer report to the European Council meeting in Milan the following June ('A people's Europe', *Bulletin of the EC*, Supplement 7, 1985).

Many of the Committee's proposals were enacted in the **Maastricht Treaty**, such as the provisions on **citizenship**, now incorporated in the **Treaty of Rome** (Articles 8–8e EEC), and the proposal for an **Ombudsman** (Article 138e EEC). Other proposals, such as those for a **European passport** and a **European flag**, were already well advanced by the time the Committee submitted its reports. A third category of proposals have been enacted in the context of the **Single Market** programme, including the easing of frontier controls (see **free movement of persons**), the **mutual recognition of qualifications**, and the **freedom of establishment**.

Amongst the proposals not so far enacted are those for a **uniform electoral procedure** for European elections, the introduction of common postage stamps and the establishment of a Europe-wide lottery.

Outside the immediate context of the Committee, the phrase 'People's Europe' is used in connection with measures that have an immediate and beneficial effect on the lives of individuals (as opposed to those relevant primarily to states, public bodies and commercial enterprises) and that serve to promote a sense of **European identity**.

PETRA

The Partnership between Education and Training was an action programme for the vocational training of young people and their preparation for adult and working life, operational from 1989. It provided financial assistance from the **Budget** for schemes that allowed young people to supplement their schooling with vocational training and work experience, sometimes in another member state. Since 1995 it has been absorbed into the **Leonardo** programme.

PHARE

The PHARE programme (*Pologne, Hongrie, Assistance à la Réstructuration Economique*) was set up by a decision of the **Group of Seven** in July 1989 as the means whereby aid of all kinds from the industrialized world would be channelled to Poland and Hungary. It was agreed that PHARE would be administered by the **Commission** and would come into operation in June 1990. PHARE was soon extended to Bulgaria, the former East Germany and the former Czechoslovakia, and now also covers Albania, Romania, Slovenia and the Baltic states (see also TACIS). Aid from the European Union is given in the framework of the **Europe Agreements**.

The five areas upon which the PHARE programme concentrates are the restructuring and privatization of state-owned enterprises; aid to the private sector, especially small and medium-sized enterprises (SMEs); the services sector, especially tourism; the modernization of financial systems (tax, banking, insurance); and welfare systems (see also **European Training Foundation**). PHARE is also engaged in projects to consolidate democratic decision-making, by encouraging the growth of professional associations, trade unions and the media. PHARE works closely with other agencies active in this field (see **European Bank for Reconstruction and Development**) and with the Aid Coordination Authority in each beneficiary state. Together, the PHARE and TACIS programmes amount to almost £1.3 billion, about a third of the sums allocated to 'external actions' in the **Budget** for 1995.

'Pillars'

The expression 'pillars' springs from a metaphor commonly used to describe the structure of the European Union established by the **Maastricht Treaty**. The Union is said to resemble the pediment of a temple and to rest upon three pillars (Article A TEU): the **European Communities**, the **Common Foreign and Security Policy** (CFSP), and cooperation in the fields of **Justice and Home Affairs** (JHA). In some versions of this model the first pillar is composed solely of the European Community, formerly the European Economic Community. Essentially, the difference between the first pillar and the other two is that only the first makes use of the **legal instruments** and procedures set out in the **Treaty of Rome**. The CFSP and JHA pillars are dominated by the **European Council** and the **Council of Ministers**, with the **Commission** and the **European Parliament** playing subordinate roles; the **Court of Justice** is wholly absent. In other words, the CFSP and JHA pillars are essentially intergovernmental in character (see **intergovernmentalism**).

Pleven Plan

The Pleven Plan, named after the French Prime Minister René Pleven, was a proposal for a **European Defence Community** (EDC) amongst **the Six**. Put forward in the French National Assembly on 24 October 1950, it was approved by 343 votes to 225. The Plan was controversial principally because it provided for a rearmed Germany to contribute units to a defence force under a unified supranational command. The vote in the Assembly was in marked contrast to the vote against the EDC Treaty four years later. Pleven claimed that the inspiration for his Plan was drawn from **Winston Churchill**'s call in August 1950 for the creation of a **European army**.

Political directors

The political directors are very senior officials in the Foreign Offices of the member states of the European Union who in 1970 were entrusted with general supervision of the system of foreign policy coordination known as **European Political Cooperation**. Meeting approximately once a month under the chairmanship of whichever country occupied the **presidency** of the **Council of Ministers**, the political directors discussed foreign policy issues and prepared meetings of the Foreign Affairs Council.

Under the **Common Foreign and Security Policy** (CFSP) provisions of the **Maastricht Treaty** the system of political directors has been maintained and their role more clearly defined. Article J8.5 TEU refers to 'a Political Committee consisting of Political Directors' whose task is to 'monitor the international situation' in areas covered by the CFSP, 'contribute to the definition of policies . . . [and] monitor the implementation of agreed policies' (see also **COREUR**).

Political groups

Members of the **European Parliament** (MEPs) sit neither in national delegations nor in alphabetical order but in groups formed on the basis of party political affiliation. The existence of such groups dates back to the very beginnings of the Parliament, since they were also a feature of the Common Assembly of the **European Coal and Steel Community** (ECSC). MEPs have sat in the political groups to which they belong since March 1958 and this practice sets the Parliament apart from all other international parliamentary bodies.

The rules governing the formation of political groups and their status within the European Parliament have, of course, changed over time, but certain constant features may be discerned. For the formation of a political group, Rule 29 of the Parliament's rules of procedure requires a minimum number of members: 29 members if all of the same nationality, 23 members if of two nationalities, 18 members if of three nationalities, or 14 if of four or more nationalities. Once formed, a group is required to deposit its name, the signatures of its members and the names of its officers with the president of the Parliament. Once formally recognized, the group is automatically entitled to its own funds from the Parliament's budget and to employ a secretariat composed of people recruited by the group but paid by the Parliament (technically known as *agents temporaires*). The size of the funds and the number of people in the secretariat are related primarily to the size of the group and are recalculated after every European election. Each group is also entitled to a proportionate share of the various posts in the Parliament (vice-presidencies, committee and delegation officers, etc.) and, within each committee, of the **rapporteurs** appointed to prepare the reports on matters coming before the committee. This apportionment is done in accordance with a mathematical formula known as the **d'Hondt system**. Speaking time in plenary session debates is shared out amongst the groups in proportion to the number of members, and a member called to speak on behalf of his or her group will normally be amongst the first speakers in a particular debate.

This summary of the advantages enjoyed by political groups explains why, in a Parliament of 626 MEPs, in which about 100 political parties are represented, only very few MEPs are genuine independents (known as '*non-inscrits*' or non-attached MEPs). However, even they have their own budget, their own secretariat and their own share of speaking time.

Over the years the size and composition of the various political groups have been constantly changing (see **European elections**). Groups have been formed only to disappear, or to reappear under a different name. MEPs have switched from one group to another. MEPs elected under proportional representation on a single list have joined different groups on taking their seats in the Parliament. And some groups are in the process of becoming **transnational political parties**.

In the Common Assembly of the ECSC only the three established political 'families' of continental Europe – Socialists, Christian Democrats and Liberals – were represented as political groups. The period of the indirectly elected Parliament of **the Six** (1958–72) saw the emergence of a European Democratic Union (Gaullist) Group composed exclusively of French MEPs who had left the Liberal Group: the rules were changed to allow this to happen.

With the first enlargement of 1973 an Anglo-Danish European Conservative Group and a Franco-Italian Communist Group were formed, bringing the total number of groups to 6 in a Parliament of 198. With direct elections in 1979 and the increase in the number of MEPs to 410, the opportunity could have been taken to increase substantially the number of members (originally 17 but reduced in 1965 to 14) necessary to form a group, but a vigorous rearguard action by MEPs from very small political parties prevented this. The period since 1979 has seen the establishment of some groups whose members have only the very loosest political affinity and even of groups that specifically disclaim any such affinity. Groups in the latter category usually have the formula 'technical coordination' somewhere in their official title: in other words, they are taking entirely cynical advantage of the substantial political and material benefits of forming a group. Of the groups formed during this period the Greens still survive, but the others have radically changed. In 1989 the Communist Group finally abandoned the long struggle to keep its Stalinist and Eurocommunist elements together and split into two groups, one known as the Group for the European Unitarian Left (most of whom joined the Party of European Socialists Group in January 1993) and the other, confusingly, as Left Unity. In May 1992 MEPs belonging to the Conservative Group (officially the European Democratic Group since 1979) joined the Group of the European People's Party (Christian Democrats) as allied members.

The particular position of political group leaders should be noted. All are elected by their colleagues in the group, but their powers of patronage – and so, ultimately, their ability to enforce discipline – are shared with the leaders of the national sections of which the group is composed. Their patronage is also limited by the absence of a coherent career structure within the Parliament, by the need to take nationality as well as ability into account and by the operation of the d'Hondt system. The leaders of the national sections – but not necessarily the group leaders – can play a decisive role in deciding the order of the names when parties draw up their lists, regional or national, for European elections.

The present composition of the Parliament is as follows:

Group of the Party of European Socialists (PES Group, 221 members). MEPs from all the Socialist, Social Democratic and Labour parties in the member states.

Group of the European People's Party (EPP Group, 172 members). MEPs from all the Christian Democratic parties in the member states, together with MEPs from New Democracy (Greece), the Partido Popular (Spain), and the Danish, Swedish, and Finnish Conservatives and Moderates. The British Conservative MEPs, an Ulster Unionist and a number of French MEPs sit as allied members of the EPP Group.

Union for Europe (54 members). Mainly French Gaullist (RPR), Italian Forza Italia, Irish Fianna Fail and Portuguese Centre Democrat MEPs.

European Liberal, Democrat and Reformist Group (ELDR Group, 52 members). MEPs from all the Liberal parties in the member states (except the German Free Democrats, who failed to reach the 5 per cent threshold in the June 1994 European elections) together with the Portuguese Social Democrats and the Italian Northern League.

Group of the European Unitarian Left/Nordic Green Left (GUE Group, 31 members). Communist MEPs from Italy, Greece and France and MEPs from various left-wing parties in Scandinavia.

The Green Group (25 members). MEPs from various Green and Ecology parties.

European Radical Alliance (ARE Group, 19 members). Composed mainly of MEPs from regional parties (including two Scottish Nationalists) and French MEPs elected on the Energie Radicale list.

Europe of the Nations (EN Group, 19 members). Composed largely of French and Danish anti-Maastricht MEPs.

Independents (31 members). Belgian (Francophone and Flemish), French, Austrian and Italian nationalist MEPs and Dr Ian Paisley from Northern Ireland.

This summary of the present composition of the political groups in the European Parliament illustrates the fact that the Parliament has developed into a two-party system in which the two big groups command almost two-thirds of the votes. This trend is likely to be confirmed as more parties become represented in the Parliament with **enlargement**, since the great majority of parties in the applicant states already have close links with either the Socialists or the Christian Democrats. It should be noted that the relative strength of the ELDR Group has been significantly diminished, and the overall balance between left and right seriously affected, by the use of the first-past-the-post electoral system in Great Britain. Under this system, the Liberal Democrats – the largest Liberal Party in Europe – failed to win any seats in European elections until June 1994, while the wild swings to which the system is prone resulted in Conservative MEPs dropping from 60 (1979) to 18 (1994) and Labour MEPs increasing from 17 (1979) to 62 (1994). The existence of two very large groups and the extent of the collusion between them have made it easier for the Parliament to organize its business and to muster the votes necessary for it to play its part in the **cooperation, co-decision** and **assent procedures**. The leaders of the political groups, together with the president, act as business managers (the 'usual channels' in a Westminster-type system) and are involved, through the Conference of Presidents, in all decisions affecting the day-to-day running of the Parliament: its budget, senior staff appointments, the composition of its committees, and so on. Although the interests of the small groups are to a certain extent protected by the widespread use of the d'Hondt system, the two big groups can, if they reach an agreement, dominate every aspect of the Parliament's workings, including most obviously the election of its president. More generally, it is open to question whether or not the representativeness and, therefore, the credibility and authority of the Parliament in the eyes of the European electorate are best served by the emergence of a two-party system based upon a 'left versus right' model of doubtful relevance to many of the issues laid before the Parliament.

Political groups also exist in the Parliamentary Assembly of the **Council of Europe**, although its members and substitutes appointed by **national parliaments** in the 38 member states sit in alphabetical order. Under Rule 41 of the Assembly's rules of procedure at least 15 members or substitutes of at least 3 nationalities are needed to form a group (a requirement more exacting than the equivalent provision in the rules of the European Parliament). At present there are five political groups:

Socialist Group (148 members). Socialists from nearly all the member states.
Group of the European People's Party (127 members). Christian Democrats from most of the member states and representatives of the True Path Party from Turkey.
Liberal, Democratic and Reformers Group (92 members). Liberals and Republicans from most of the member states and Irish Fianna Fail members.
European Democratic Group (82 members). Conservatives from the United Kingdom, Denmark, Sweden and Norway, French Gaullists, members of the Turkish Motherland Party, Progressives from Iceland, and other representatives from Hungary, the Czech Republic, Poland, Finland and Italy.
Group of the Unified European Left (15 members). Left-wing Socialists and Communists, six from Romania and the remainder from seven other countries. This group's continued existence is under threat, its membership having fallen to the minimum required.

There are 21 independent members and vacancies in several delegations.

Pompidou Group

Set up in 1971 on the initiative of French President Georges Pompidou, the Pompidou Group is concerned with cooperation between national authorities in the fight against drugs. Initially composed of representatives of **the Six** and the United Kingdom, the Group now involves most

European countries. It has met within the framework of the **Council of Europe** since 1980.

Portugal

A founder member of both the **European Free Trade Association** (EFTA) and the **North Atlantic Treaty Organization** (NATO), Portugal was initially barred from membership of the European Community because of the non-democratic nature of the Portuguese government under the premiership of Antonio Salazar (1932–68) and Marcelo Caetano (1968–74). The Armed Forces Movement seized power in April 1974 and democracy was finally re-established in 1976. By then, Portugal, together with other EFTA states, was benefiting from special trading arrangements with the Community, but for political reasons – mainly bound up with the consolidation of democracy and the personal commitment of the Prime Minister, Mario Soares – an application for full membership was made on 28 March 1977. A favourable **Opinion** from the **Commission** was published the following year, and Portugal joined the Community on 1 January 1986. Like Spain, Portugal was attracted to membership of the Community as a means of modernizing its economy and society and of re-emerging on the European stage. Community membership stood for prosperity, stability and self-respect.

Portugal remains, with Greece, the poorest of the member states, and has taken a keen interest in the **structural funds**. Portugal also has substantial fishing and agricultural interests, and, with many Portuguese working in other member states (especially France, Belgium and Luxembourg), the Portuguese government has done its best to facilitate **free movement of persons**. On the whole, the Portuguese negotiating style is to allow larger, more vociferous southern European states like Spain and Italy take the lead and then to insist upon Portugal's share of the proceeds. The only opposition to European integration in Portugal is from the Communist Party.

Positive and negative integration

These terms were first used by the British political scientist John Pinder in an article in *The World Today* (January 1968) to describe two broad categories of integration between member states. In a later work Pinder summarized the distinction as follows: 'The removal of barriers to free trade needs to be accompanied by the integration of policies beyond trade liberalization . . . with the removal of barriers termed negative integration and the making of common policies beyond that termed positive integration' (*European Community: The Building of a Union* (1991)). Whether or not it is accepted that they must accompany one another (for example, the removal of barriers to trade under the **Single Market** programme needs to be complemented by a 'social Europe'), the distinction between these two basic types of integration remains useful.

Preliminary ruling

Article 177 of the **Treaty of Rome** allows national courts and tribunals to refer to the **Court of Justice** requests for rulings on points of **Community law**. Such references are mandatory in the case of courts against whose judgments there is no possibility of appeal in national law (in the United Kingdom, this definition would include the House of Lords). The national court must propose precisely which point of Community law should be the subject of the Court's ruling, and it must be a point directly relevant to the outcome of the case. The Court is careful in its preliminary rulings to address only the points specifically raised, which are normally on the substance or the applicability of Community law, and to deal only with the facts of the case as established by the national court.

Under Article 107 of the 1992 Agreement establishing the **European Economic Area** (EEA), the right to seek a preliminary ruling is extended to the courts of **European Free Trade Association** (EFTA) states. The procedure is set out in Protocol 34 of the Agreement. Preliminary rulings are considered in detail in Weatherill and Beaumont, *EC Law*, Chapter 9.

Presidency

The presidency of the **Council of Ministers** and the **European Council** rotates amongst the member states of the European Union every six months. The president of any individual Council – whether of Agriculture or Finance or Industry Ministers – will be styled President-in-Office of that Council, but as the senior national representative in the Council of Ministers, it is always the foreign minister of the member state concerned who is President-in-Office of the Council of Ministers as a whole. The head of government of the same member state is termed President-in-Office of the European Council. The member state holding the presidency occupies two seats in the Council, one as president, one as a national delegation. The positions adopted by the same country in these two guises need not be identical.

Until January 1993 the presidency was held by the member states in alphabetical order, each state's position in the order being determined by the country's name in the language of that country. This had one disadvantage: it tended always to be the same states holding the 'shorter' presidency in the second half of the year, which coincides with the summer and Christmas holiday periods. Agreement was reached to reverse each annual pair of presidencies, so that Danmark would precede Belgique, Ellas

(Greece) would precede Deutschland, and so on. This cycle is due to continue until 1998. In the context of the **enlargement** negotiations, a different cycle has been laid down, which will provide for each **troika** of presidencies to include one large member state (see below).

The presidency is responsible for managing the business of the Council during its six-month term. It convenes meetings, establishes the agenda, drafts compromise texts from the chair, and calls votes where **majority voting** applies. The presidency represents the Council and the member states in dealings with third countries and speaks for the Council before the **European Parliament**, the **Economic and Social Committee** and other bodies. It replies on behalf of the Council to oral and written questions posed in the European Parliament, and both presents its prospectus to the Parliament at the beginning of each term and reports back to it at the end of each term. Although the foreign minister normally speaks for the presidency in the Parliament, heads of government have taken to delivering the six-monthly report-back in person. A decision of principle was taken by the heads of government in June 1981 to institute this process, and it fell to **Margaret Thatcher** to inaugurate it at the end of the British presidency in December 1981. The rationale for the arrangement was that, since the six-monthly European Council normally rounds off each presidency, it makes sense for the head of government who hosted that meeting to present its conclusions to the Parliament. The new practice was confirmed in the **Stuttgart Declaration** of June 1983 and has been consistently followed since then.

Each presidency usually tries to secure agreement on as many issues as possible on the Council agenda. During the passage of the **Single Market** programme (1985–92) it became common to assess presidencies very largely on the basis of their legislative output. This pressure to deliver results, facilitated by the extension of majority voting under the 1986 **Single European Act** (SEA), has combined with the growing importance of the European Council to revitalize the Council of Ministers as a decision-taking body. In particular, successive presidencies try to ensure that the meetings of the European Council that they chair reach agreement on major issues.

The five large member states tend to have clear ambitions for their presidencies. The smaller countries usually prefer to concentrate on simply being 'good presidents'. Sometimes, especially for a large member state, the competing pressures of advocacy and neutrality can collide, but usually the presidency will sacrifice its particular objectives for wider agreement. Paradoxically, it is often thought to be advantageous for the Council to be chaired by a sceptical member state when a controversial issue is discussed. It can neutralize the objections of the country concerned and convert it into a cautious advocate of reform.

The presidency of the Council has acquired increasing public prominence as a result of the growing importance of the Union's role in world affairs. Speaking for the Union in multilateral fora such as the United Nations General Assembly and in meetings with third countries, the president-in-office can easily gain a world prominence that his or her own national activities might rarely merit. The most telling recent example of this was in the first half of 1991 when, in an unlikely turn of events, it fell to the little-known Luxembourg Foreign Minister, Jacques Poos, to speak on behalf of the member states during the Gulf War. This kind of exposure is likely to increase as progress is made with the **Common Foreign and Security Policy** (CFSP) introduced under the **Maastricht Treaty**.

Over the period 1996–2002, the presidency will be held by the member states as follows:

1996	Italy
	Ireland
1997	Netherlands
	Luxembourg
1998	United Kingdom
	Austria
1999	Germany
	Finland
2000	Portugal
	France
2001	Sweden
	Belgium
2002	Spain
	Denmark

Primacy

The primacy of **Community law** over national law was established by the judgment of the **Court of Justice** in the *Costa* v *ENEL* case (Case 6/64). The Court ruled that:

> the law stemming from the Treaty ... [cannot] be overridden by domestic legal provisions ... The transfer by the States from their domestic legal systems to the Community legal system of the rights and obligations arising under the Treaty carries with it a permanent limitation of their sovereign rights against which a subsequent unilateral act incompatible with the concept of the Community cannot prevail.

The primacy of Community law over constitutional law was established in the Internationale Handelsgesellschaft case (Case 11/70). Together with **direct effect**, primacy is one of the fundamental principles of Community law (see Weatherill and Beaumont, *EC Law*, and Rudden, *Basic Community Cases*; see also **occupied field**).

Proportionality

Like **subsidiarity**, proportionality is a principle devised with a view to restraining what is thought to be the excessive enthusiasm of the **European Commission** for detailed regulation. Proportionality requires the legislative means to be no more than the strict minimum required to achieve a particular end. In fact, there is plenty of evidence (particularly in the United Kingdom) to suggest that overzealous enforcement on the part of local or national authorities is the main cause of excessively detailed legislation, coupled with the willingness of national civil servants to add extra requirements to European Directives when they are passed into national law (a practice sometimes referred to as 'gold-plating'). The **Treaty of Rome**, as revised by the **Maastricht Treaty**, refers to proportionality in Article 3b EEC (the subsidiarity Article), which says: 'Any action by the Community shall not go beyond what is necessary to achieve the objectives of this Treaty.' In fact, the jurisprudence of the **Court of Justice** had already developed proportionality as a general principle of **Community law** (see Weatherill and Beaumont, *EC Law*).

Protocol

Most treaties have annexed to them protocols and **Declarations**. A protocol has legal force, and usually embodies detailed provision on matters touched on in the treaty to which it is attached. For example, the Statute of the **Court of Justice** is annexed as a protocol to the **Treaty of Rome**. An **opt-out** from a treaty undertaking (as in the case of the British opt-out from the **Social Chapter**) is formalized in a protocol, thus providing scope for **variable geometry** or **Europe à la carte**. A Declaration has no legal force, but is intended to have political force, and may touch on matters not otherwise dealt with: for example, a Declaration on animal welfare was annexed to the **Maastricht Treaty** at the behest of the British government. Declarations may also take the form of an undertaking to examine or re-examine an issue at some future date, or of an agreed interpretation of some provision in the treaty, and recourse is often had to such Declarations as a way of resolving disagreements that proved insoluble in the course of negotiations. Some Declarations are made in the name of only certain parties to the treaty, and often result from the desire of particular governments to make formal statements for domestic particular reasons.

Public health

Article 3 of the **Treaty of Rome**, as amended by the **Maastricht Treaty**, refers to 'a high level of health protection', but makes it clear that Union action in this field is complementary to that of member states. Some degree of coordination between national authorities responsible for public health is necessary in relation to the free movement of persons and goods: **Article 100a** EEC repeats the requirement that a high level of protection must be the basis for legislation arising from such coordination.

The framework for action in the public health field was set out in a **Council of Ministers** Resolution of 2 June 1994. The highest priority is to be given to cancer research, drug dependence, AIDS and other communicable diseases, the collection of comparable data on health issues, and measures in respect of health promotion, education and training. The Council also emphasized the need for closer coordination between Union institutions, national authorities and the relevant international organizations. The Commission was invited to bring forward specific proposals on all these issues, with the aid of a new 'consultative body'.

Public purchasing

The annual value of contracts placed by national, regional and local public authorities in the European Union has been estimated at about 10 per cent of gross domestic product (GDP). If contracts by publicly owned enterprises are also included, the figure is around 20 per cent. For this reason the opening up of public purchasing has long been a Community objective, with a direct bearing both on **competition policy** and the **Single Market**.

Two Directives of 1971 and 1977 established the ground-rules for public purchasing. The distinction was drawn between public supply (or procurement) and public works. Public supply contracts of a value above 200,000 ECUs (about £150,000) and all public works contracts above 5 million ECUs (about £4 million) had to be advertised in the *Official Journal* and tendering procedures were harmonized. However, certain key sectors (telecommunications, energy, transport, water, military equipment) were excluded.

A review of public purchasing in 1984 revealed that public authorities were still finding ways of favouring local suppliers: for example, by subdividing contracts so that they fell below the threshold requiring them to be advertised in the *Official Journal*, or by inserting skilfully drafted special requirements into the specifications, or by abusing 'fast track' procedures for awarding contracts. Accordingly, as part of the Single Market programme, the Directives were revised: public supply is now governed by a 1988 Directive, public works by a Directive adopted the following year. A Directive establishing an appeals procedure for suppliers alleging unfair treatment was also adopted in 1989. The so-called 'excluded sectors' (see above) were brought within the scope of the system in 1990. This was an important step, since these sectors represent some 80 per cent of all contracts, the percentage of high technology contracts being even higher. The public purchasing system now applies not only within the Union, but to the **European Economic Area** (EEA) and to very many countries associated with the Union (such as those covered by **Europe Agreements** and by the **Lomé Convention**). However, at a time of high unemployment it remains very vulnerable to domestic political pressures, and although in 1993 there were some 67,000 invitations to tender in the *Official Journal* (compared with 19,000 in 1988), the **Commission** is still not satisfied that the system is working properly.

Qualified Majority Voting (QMV)

The most widely used method of voting in the **Council of Ministers**, QMV entails giving the vote of each member state a 'weighting', which very broadly reflects its population. These weightings are specified in the **Treaty of Rome** (Article 148), as is the total number of assenting votes (the threshold) necessary for a measure to be adopted under QMV. At present, the weightings are as follows:

France	10
Germany	10
Italy	10
United Kingdom	10
Spain	8
Belgium	5
Greece	5
Netherlands	5
Portugal	5
Austria	4
Sweden	4
Denmark	3
Finland	3
Ireland	3
Luxembourg	2
Total	87

The total number of votes necessary for a measure to be adopted on a proposal from the **Commission** is 62 (an abstention is equivalent to a vote against). A very small number of Treaty articles allow the Council to take a decision by QMV without a Commission proposal: in such cases the 62 votes must be cast by at least 10 member states.

QMV applies to the first stage – the Council's 'common position' – of any measure brought forward under the **co-decision procedure** (Article 189b EEC) or the **cooperation procedure** (Article 189c EEC) and may apply at various stages thereafter. It also applies to most stages of the **Budget** procedure.

The subject areas covered by QMV, already numerous in the Treaty of

Rome, were greatly extended by the 1986 **Single European Act** (SEA) and again by the 1991 **Maastricht Treaty**. The SEA extended QMV mainly into areas connected with the **Single Market** programme, including many previously subject to **unanimity**. The Maastricht Treaty did not substitute QMV for unanimity in any area, but provided for QMV in most of the areas that were either wholly new (such as **trans-European networks** (TENs), education and **public health**) or subject to more extensive provisions (such as the environment and economic and monetary policy). In relation to the **excessive deficit procedure** (Article 104c EEC), QMV operates on the basis of a two-thirds majority of votes weighted in the normal way, not counting the votes of the member state allegedly guilty of the deficit.

Additionally, the Maastricht Treaty allows QMV to be used in both the **Common Foreign and Security Policy** (CFSP) and in the field of **Justice and Home Affairs** (JHA). In both cases the Council must, as a general rule, act by unanimity, but may decide, also by unanimity, that implementing measures in an area already agreed as subject to '**joint action**' may be decided by QMV (Articles J3 and K3 TEU).

The QMV system arose as a direct consequence of the enormous disparity between the original **Six** in terms of the size of their populations. Then as now, Luxembourg was much the smallest country, with barely a third of a million inhabitants, while at the other end of the scale France, Italy and West Germany each had a population of over 50 million. Giving each member state one vote was clearly not an option, but the smaller states needed some safeguards against the larger. Accordingly, a system of weightings was devised, and so framed as to favour the smaller states:

France	4
Italy	4
West Germany	4
Belgium	2
Netherlands	2
Luxembourg	1

For a measure to be adopted, 12 assenting votes were necessary, cast by 4 member states in the absence of a Commission proposal.

QMV was introduced gradually. Initially (1958–65), most votes were taken by unanimity. The prospect of changing to QMV was one of the causes of the **empty chair crisis**, which led ultimately to the **Luxembourg Compromise**.

The system needs to be adjusted for each **enlargement**. The first enlargement (Denmark, Ireland, the United Kingdom) in 1973 resulted in the following weightings:

France	10
Italy	10
United Kingdom	10
West Germany	10
Belgium	5
Netherlands	5
Denmark	3
Ireland	3
Luxembourg	2

Assent required 41 votes, cast by at least 6 member states in the absence of a Commission proposal. In 1981 Greece was given a weighting of 5, and 45 became the minimum for assent. With the **accession** of Portugal and Spain in 1986 the minimum was raised to 54 out of 76 votes.

Certain features of QMV have remained constant. The system continues to favour small states (Belgium, for example, has a population roughly one-eighth the size of Germany's, yet a weighting under QMV of 5 compared with Germany's 10). A blocking minority has remained more or less constant at approximately a third of available votes (35.3 per cent until 1973; 31 per cent 1973–80; 30.2 per cent 1981–5; 30.3 per cent 1986–94; 29.9 per cent since 1995). The position of large states has become weaker: before 1973, the three large states could, theoretically, force through a Commission proposal opposed by the others; since 1973, the large states have not had enough votes to do this, and even with the addition of Spain from 1986 the large states, which represent almost 80 per cent of the Union's total population, need at least two allies to secure the enactment of a measure by QMV. However, the extent to which decisions are still taken on the basis of consensus is illustrated by the fact that of the 272 legislative acts adopted between December 1993 and February 1995, only 38 were adopted with abstentions or votes against.

Various factors have drawn attention to the anomalies in QMV and prompted a debate on possible adjustments to it. First, in 1987 the SEA introduced an extension of QMV in association with the Single Market programme. This was accompanied by the greatly diminished role of the right of veto embodied in the Luxembourg Compromise. Second, the reunification of Germany increased the discrepancy between the largest member state and the smallest (although the German government has been careful at no time to suggest an addition to Germany's QMV weighting). Third, the emergence of North versus South rivalry in budgetary and agricultural issues has created alliances that transcend the differences between large states and small, which QMV was designed to resolve. And fourth, the prospect of membership being extended to four small, prosperous, northern countries has prompted a reconsideration of the balance between large countries and small, especially in the light of the fact that two very small countries, Malta and Cyprus, have also submitted applications for membership.

In the final stages of the enlargement negotiations with Austria, Finland, Norway and Sweden, it was the British government that was most concerned about adjustments to QMV. The argument, which in March 1994 looked almost as if it could disrupt the negotiations completely, centred not upon the weightings to be given to the new members (Austria 4, Sweden 4, Finland 3, Norway 3) but on the size of the blocking minority. The Greek **presidency** proposed an increase in the threshold from 54 votes out of 76 to 64 votes out of the new total of 90 (this assumed that all four countries would join the Union at the same time). Although this proposal kept the percentage of votes necessary to block an agreement more or less the same, it meant that the blocking minority was 27 votes rather than 23. This represented, in the British government's view, a further weakening of the position of larger states such as the United Kingdom, and made the system still less 'democratic' in terms of the correlation between population and voting strength. The British government proposed to leave the blocking minority at 23; their only ally, the Spanish government, supported this proposal on the grounds that it made it easier for southern member states to thwart measures put forward by the northern majority, which enlargement was set to strengthen. The British government also argued that a blocking minority of 27 out of 90 would mean, for example, that a combination of countries such as Germany, the Netherlands and the United Kingdom, representing 154 million people, would be less able to defend their interests than a group of small states representing about 45 million people. Put another way, it would mean that a combination representing over 40 per cent of the Union's population could be outvoted. It would also mean that the larger states, which at present represent 86.5 per cent of the population but have only 63 per cent of the votes, would see their position still further weakened to 53 per cent of the votes and 80 per cent of the population.

The dispute was settled at a meeting of foreign ministers in Ioannina, northern Greece, at the end of March 1994 in the form of a *Beschluss* annexed to the minutes. The foreign ministers agreed that the whole system of QMV (i.e., not just the weightings but the threshold too) would be examined in the course of the **Intergovernmental Conference** (IGC) in 1996, and that the qualified majority would be fixed at 64 out of 90 votes. The British objection was met by a commitment binding the Council to do 'all in its power to reach, within a reasonable time . . . a satisfactory solution' were a proposal to be confronted by a blocking minority commanding 23 to 26 votes. This compromise, which, like the presidency proposal, was posited on the assumption that all four applicant states would accede to the Union at the same time, will remain in force until the Treaty provisions on QMV are formally amended in line with the decision of the IGC. The applicant states expressed their agreement with this arrangement. With effect from 1 January 1995, the qualified majority was changed to 62 votes and the blocking minority to 23–5 votes to take account of Norway's decision not to join the Union.

The argument over QMV in an enlarged European Union reopened some of the most fundamental questions of democracy, efficiency, member states' rights and the protection of minority interests. The **European Parliament** saw the dispute and the compromise that resolved it as an unwelcome reassertion of national interests in contradistinction to those of the Union. However, it is clear that had the matter not been raised in the enlargement negotiations in 1993/4 it would most certainly have been raised in the context of the second round of enlargement later in the decade – by which time precedents thought to be prejudicial to the interests of larger states would have been set.

The dispute illustrated a number of characteristic national attitudes. Neither France nor Germany took much part in it, probably by virtue of that lively sense of their own indispensability in the integration process that allows them to be less dependent on procedural means of safeguarding their interests. Italy, as a large Mediterranean state, could appreciate both the British and the Spanish arguments, but eventually sided with the majority. The smaller states, understandably, were perfectly content with a system that serves them well.

In fact, QMV is part of a broader strategy in accordance with which smaller states are overrepresented in the institutions of the Union. Each German Member of the European Parliament (MEP) represents over 800,000 people: each Luxembourg MEP 66,667. The average is about 590,000 people for each MEP, but the figures for all the smaller states are well below that.

Had the Six adopted the model of Congress embodied in the United States Constitution – equal representation for all states, regardless of population, in the upper house (the Council) and population-related representation in the lower (the European Parliament) – QMV would, of course, never have existed, but it is highly unlikely that such a system could ever have worked. In the twenty-second of the Federalist Papers (14 December 1787), James Madison reviewed the arguments for and against allowing states of unequal size equal representation:

> Sophistry may reply, that sovereigns are equal, and that a majority
> of votes of the States will be a majority of federated America. But

this kind of logical legerdemain will never counteract the plain suggestions of justice and common-sense. It may happen that this majority of States is a small minority of the people of America; and two-thirds of the people of America could not long be persuaded, upon the credit of artificial distinction and syllogistic subtleties, to submit their interests to the management and disposal of one third. The larger States would after a while revolt from the idea of receiving the law from the smaller.

(See also paper no. 62 on 'a compound republic, partaking both of the national and federal character ... founded on a mixture of the principles of proportional and equal representation'.)

Another comparison is to be found in the **League of Nations**, which allowed each member state, regardless of size, one vote in the Council and one vote in the Assembly, and like its successor, the United Nations, favoured certain large states only by granting them permanent membership of the Council. This solution was clearly inapplicable to an integration process that sought to move beyond an intergovernmental model.

The most widely canvassed reform of QMV involves a 'double majority', meaning a majority of member states (four-fifths, for example) representing a similar majority of the Union's population: weightings would be abandoned. Such a double majority might be introduced for measures currently requiring unanimity, such as a change to the Treaties. The idea of a double majority, which allows for many different permutations, has a precedent in Article 28 of the **Treaty of Paris** establishing the **European Coal and Steel Community** (ECSC). This Article allows the ECSC Council to adopt a measure by 'an absolute majority of the representatives of the Member States, including the votes of the representatives of two Member States which each produce one ninth of the total coal and steel output of the Community'. Similarly, when the 15 finance ministers are acting as the Board of Governors of the **European Investment Bank** (EIB), they use QMV with the additional refinement that the 54 assenting votes must be cast by countries representing 50 per cent of the Bank's subscribed capital (Article 10 of the Statute of the European Investment Bank). For each member state's vote to be weighted not solely in accordance with population but also with economic performance or economic weight would be the most radical reform of all.

Quotas

Under the **Common Agricultural Policy** (CAP) quotas were introduced into the dairy sector in 1984 as 'stabilizers' to limit the quantity of milk qualifying for **intervention** under the price-support system. This was as a consequence of the failure of an earlier scheme, the co-responsibility levy, to bring spending on the dairy sector under control. Sometimes known as maximum guaranteed quantities (MGQs), quotas have since been extended to other products, in spite of the many legal, technical and administrative problems involved. Quotas are applied at the level of individual holdings, within a framework of production quotas for each member state.

In trade policy generally, quotas are a form of quantitative restriction, and are prohibited as far as trade between member states is concerned under Article 30 of the **Treaty of Rome**.

The programme for Research and Development in Advanced Communications Technology for Europe is concerned with research into broadband communications for image and data transmission, mobile and personal telecommunications equipment, network compatibility, and other aspects of the telecommunications industry.

Racism and xenophobia

In Strasbourg on 11 June 1986 the presidents of the **European Parliament** and of the **European Commission** and the president-in-office of the **Council of Ministers** signed a 'Joint Declaration against Racism and Xenophobia'. This Declaration, which was largely an initiative of the European Commission, condemned 'all forms of intolerance, hostility and use of force ... on the grounds of racial, religious, cultural, social or national differences' and committed the three institutions 'to protect the individuality and dignity of every member of society and to reject any form of segregation of foreigners'. The Declaration, like the Joint Declaration on Fundamental Rights of 1977 (see **human rights**), has no legal force but remains part of the *acquis communautaire* and usefully supplements the **Treaties** in an area in which they are otherwise silent. Earlier in the same year (16 January 1986) the European Parliament had adopted a comprehensive report by an all-party Committee of Inquiry into 'the rise of racism and fascism in Europe'.

A series of incidents involving racially motivated violence, prompted in part by an increase in the number of immigrants from central and eastern Europe, led the **European Council** at a meeting in Corfu in June 1994 to set up a Consultative Commission of 'eminent personalities' to advise the institutions of the Union on action against racism. The Commission's report was discussed at the Cannes meeting of the European Council in June 1995.

The background is well set out in Geoffrey Harris, *The Dark Side of Europe* (2nd edn, Edinburgh, 1993) and in Roger Eatwell, 'The Fascist and Racist Revival in western Europe', *Political Quarterly*, Vol. 65, no. 3, July–September 1994.

Railways

The development of the railway network in Europe affords one of the earliest examples of cross-frontier cooperation between public and private bodies. Prompted by practical needs rather than by a broader political vision, it has both successes and failures to its credit.

At an early stage of the great period of railway building (1830–80) the track gauge was standardized for nearly all main lines at 4 feet 8½ inches (1.435 metres). The only exceptions to this were on the periphery of Europe: in Ireland, Northern Ireland, Russia and other parts of the former Russian Empire (including Finland), Portugal and Spain, all of which used a broader gauge (although in the case of Spain the new high-speed line from Madrid to Seville, the AVE, is built to standard gauge). The loading-gauge (the height and width of the rolling-stock) is also standardized to what is known as the Berne Gauge, except in the British Isles. This is why special rolling-stock has to be used for the **Channel Tunnel**, British bridges and tunnels being built to smaller dimensions. However, there was no agreement on left-hand versus right-hand running, and to this day, although right-hand running is the general rule, left-hand running is retained on many lines (such as those in Belgium and the northern region of France) originally built under British influence as well as on those in the British Isles.

More seriously, when electrification was introduced, although the overhead catenary system became universal (except on Southern Region in England, once again posing problems for the Channel Tunnel) there was no agreement on the type of current or the voltage. This still hampers through running on many international lines.

The railway companies have a long history of cooperation at the administrative level, with respect to such matters as tickets and timetables. In the last century the railways were one of the most powerful influences in favour of the adoption of standard time zones. Cross-frontier cooperation was further developed with the extension of sleeping-car and boat-train services and, later, of long-distance freight. However, patterns of ownership and of state involvement varied widely, as did levels and types of subsidy, and these were to pose a problem later in the framework of the **common transport policy** provided for in the **Treaty of Rome**.

After several decades of declining market shares for both passengers and freight, railways are now entering a period of expansion. Helped in part by their relatively modest impact on the environment and their economic use of energy, railways are in a better position to compete in particular sectors, such as bulk freight and suburban passenger services in large conurbations. At present, emphasis is on the development of high-speed services, but the two main competing systems, the French TGV and the German ICE, are incompatible. Unless such differences can be resolved, the longer-term position of high-speed railways within the **trans-European networks** (TENs) may be compromised.

Railway companies in over 60 countries cooperate internationally through the International Union of Railways (founded in 1922), in which their votes are weighted in accordance with the number of kilometres operated. Railways within the European Union plus Switzerland work together in the Community of European Railways, which, through its headquarters in Brussels, is the main point of contact between the railways and the institutions of the Union. The **Commission**'s proposals for the European rail network of the future may be found in the *Official Journal*, C220, 8 April 1994.

Rapporteur

A feature of many continental parliamentary systems, a rapporteur is the member of a committee who is responsible for drawing up a report on a matter referred to that committee or examined by that committee acting on its own initiative. Once the report is adopted in the committee, the rapporteur will be responsible for presenting the report on the committee's behalf to the full parliament and for advising members on the amendments tabled to it. The job of being a rapporteur is obviously attractive when the subject of the report is important or politically sensitive, and rapporteur-ships are normally allocated amongst members by agreement amongst the political parties or groups represented in the committee. Although there is scope for the rapporteur to inject his or her personal bias into the report, the need to represent the views of the committee as a whole and to gain the support of a majority both in committee and in the full parliament imposes a constraint. The system of rapporteurs is used in the **European Parliament**.

Ratification

In international law ratification is the confirmation of an international agreement. Originally, this entailed formal approval by the sovereign of an agreement entered into on his or her behalf by an agent; in those rare instances of agreements concluded between sovereigns on the basis of direct negotiations (such as the 'Holy Alliance' of 1815 between Russia, Prussia and Austria) ratification was not necessary. Although in some countries, including the United Kingdom, ratification remains a prerogative of the head of state, the term is now most frequently used to denote parliamentary approval of an international agreement.

Most major agreements contain a ratification clause. This may specify that the agreement will not enter into force until all signatories have ratified it, or allow for entry into force as soon as a certain number of signatories have ratified. All the major treaties and agreements on which the European Union is based are of the former type, and the same provisions apply to any amendments to them. The **Treaty of Rome** (Article 247), for example, says: 'This Treaty shall be ratified by the High Contracting Parties in accordance with their respective constitutional requirements . . . This Treaty shall enter into force on the first day of the month following the deposit of the instrument of ratification by the last signatory state to take this step.'

The *de facto* 'constitutional requirements' of most member states involve parliamentary approval. In some cases approval is by popular **referendum** (whether or not 'advisory' in character). For example, had approval of the **Maastricht Treaty** secured a five-sixths majority in the Danish parliament, the narrowly lost Danish referendum of June 1992 would not have been necessary. The French referendum of September 1992 was a political option, not a constitutional requirement. The Irish referendum of June 1992 was based on a constitutional requirement: in Ireland, as in several other countries, an agreement involving a change to the constitution must be put to a referendum.

In proposals to amend the **Treaties**, use is sometimes made of a ratification formula that allows the new draft to enter into force as soon as some of the contracting parties have ratified. This is an attempt to force or at least encourage the laggards to move with the majority and is usually denounced as an attempt to create a **two-speed Europe** (see **Draft Treaty establishing the European Union**).

The role of the **European Parliament** in the approval of treaties and international agreements is set out under **assent procedure**. It has no formal role in approving amendments to the Maastricht Treaty or the other Treaties upon which the European Union is founded.

RECHAR

Operational since 1989, the RECHAR programme draws on the **structural funds** to help coalmining regions cope with the social and economic problems of industrial decline. Similar programmes exist for steel (RE-SIDER), textiles (RETEX), and shipbuilding (RENAVAL).

Reconsultation

If a legislative proposal is amended in a way substantially at variance with the **European Parliament**'s amendments after the Parliament has delivered its formal **Opinion**, or if the facts of the matter with which the proposal is concerned substantially change, then the Parliament may require the **Council of Ministers** to reconsult it. This right dates back to an **interinstitutional agreement** between the Parliament, the Council and the **European Commission** in 1973 and has been recognized by the **Court of Justice** (Cases C65/90 and C388/92).

Referendum

In many member states of the European Union any change to the constitution must be put to the people in a referendum. Accordingly, a change to the **Treaties** with a bearing on the constitution can be ratified only by means of a referendum. As well as being a constitutional requirement, a referendum may also be a political option, held to resolve an issue that has proved intractable or for some other reason. Some referendum results are constitutionally binding, others (in theory) only advisory. The following table sets out some notable referendum results.

Country	Issue	Date	Result %	
			Yes	No
France	EC enlargement	21 April 1972	67.7	32.3
Ireland	EC membership	10 May 1972	83.0	17.0
Norway	EC membership	25 September 1972	46.5	53.5
Denmark	EC membership	3 October 1972	63.3	36.7
United Kingdom	Staying in EC	5 June 1975	67.2	32.8
Greenland	Staying in EC	23 February 1982	48.0	52.0
Denmark	Single European Act	27 February 1986	56.2	43.8
Ireland	Single European Act	26 May 1987	70.0	30.0
Denmark	Maastricht Treaty	2 June 1992	49.3	50.7
Ireland	Maastricht Treaty	18 June 1992	67.0	33.0
France	Maastricht Treaty	20 September 1992	51.0	49.0
Denmark	Maastricht Treaty	18 May 1993	56.8	43.2
Austria	EU membership	19 June 1994	66.4	33.6
Finland	EU membership	16 October 1994	56.9	43.1
Sweden	EU membership	13 November 1994	52.2	46.9
Norway	EU membership	28 November 1994	47.5	52.5

Referendum of June 1975

Until it became part of Labour's policy of **renegotiation**, no political party in the United Kingdom had been in favour of a referendum on British membership of the Community. On 10 December 1969 a backbench motion calling for a referendum was defeated in the House of Commons, having been opposed by leading members of all parties whether or not they were in favour of membership of the Community.

The Referendum Bill was passed by the House of Commons on 10 April 1975. Since the issue crossed the normal divisions between the parties, the campaign was fought by all-party organizations: 'Britain in Europe' in favour of the Community and the 'National Referendum Campaign' against it. Each organization prepared a booklet that was widely circulated with the aid of public funds. In addition the Government circulated its own booklet, *Britain's New Deal in Europe*, in which it summarized the results of the renegotiation and committed itself to abide by the decision of the electorate. A Referendum Information Unit was set up in the Cabinet Office to prepare factual briefing.

In the referendum, which was held on 5 June 1975, 64.5 per cent of the electorate voted. In response to the proposition 'Do you think that the United Kingdom should stay in the European Community (the Common Market)?' 17,378,581 votes (67.2 per cent) were cast in favour and 8,470,073 (32.8 per cent) against. Results were counted on a county basis (except in Northern Ireland) and all counties of the United Kingdom except the Shetlands and the Western Isles pronounced themselves in favour of continued membership.

Published accounts revealed gross disparities between the two sides' expenditure. Each was given £125,000 from public funds. 'Britain in Europe' claimed to have spent £1,481,583 on the campaign, their opponents less than one-tenth of that sum (£131,354).

It cannot be said that the June 1975 referendum, the only national plebiscite of its kind in British history, resolved the question of Community membership once and for all. It did not even resolve the differences within the Labour Party, which by 1983 was once again formally opposed to membership. These two facts have been used as arguments against the more recent calls for referenda on other issues, such as the **Maastricht Treaty**, although the main arguments remain the extent to which a referendum is a negation of that parliamentary sovereignty that many opponents of the Community are passionately concerned to defend and the difficulty of requiring yes or no answers to complex questions. Almost the only benefit of the 1975 referendum was that it resulted in a better-informed electorate, at least as far as the facts were concerned; and in May/June 1975 no fewer than 41 per cent of respondents in the United Kingdom replied to a standard **Eurobarometer** question that they would be 'very sorry' were they to be told that the United Kingdom was leaving the Common Market, the highest level ever recorded. The referendum campaign and its immediate political repercussions are described in David Butler and Uwe Kitzinger, *The 1975 Referendum* (1976). In retrospect it is clear that the arguments of the 'Britain in Europe' campaign resulted in the dynamic effects of Community membership being 'oversold' to the electorate at precisely the moment when the Community economy was moving into a period of low or negative growth. It is also clear that the pro-Community campaigners were less than wholly honest in the emphasis they laid on the **veto** as the permanent and ultimate safeguard of the national interest. The great attraction of this argument in the context of a referendum was, of course, its intelligibility, in return for which the risk of oversimplification seemed a price worth paying.

Reflection Group

The **European Council** meeting in Corfu on 24–25 June 1994 set up a Reflection Group over the period June–December 1995 to prepare the 1996 **Intergovernmental Conference**. Composed mainly of representatives of the foreign ministers, the Group met under a Spanish chairman, and involved two members of the **European Parliament**. It was specifically mandated to solicit the views of other institutions on progress towards **European Union** and possible amendments to the **Maastricht Treaty**.

Regionalism

The idea that European integration along supranational lines would provide an overarching framework for the re-emergence of the regions of Europe can be traced back at least as far as the immediate postwar years. Several bodies providing for direct cooperation between regions were founded in the 1950s (see below). Some, but not all, regions have an ethnic or linguistic dimension (Flanders, the Val d'Aosta, Catalonia) and considerations of national unity, notably in France, the United Kingdom and Franco's Spain, led many countries to resist the emergence of powerful regional entities within their borders (see also **minorities**). The original **Treaty of Rome** made no explicit provision for regional representation in decision-making. However, under the **Maastricht Treaty** Article 146 EEC was amended to allow for representatives of regional governments occasionally to take the place of national ministers in the **Council of Ministers** and a **Committee of the Regions** was set up.

The position of subnational levels of government varies widely within the member states. Some states, such as Portugal and France, are unitary states, while others, such as Germany and Belgium, have an explicitly federal structure. Both Spain and Italy have regions with a special constitutional status, as does the United Kingdom in respect of Scotland. Supporters of devolution have been quick to point out that the **subsidiarity** principle may be applied to the division of responsibility between national and regional government as well as to that between member states and the institutions of the Union. Some, but not all, of the responsibilities that regional governments exercise or are seeking have a European dimension in the sense that they are covered by the **Treaties**. One of the reasons why the Maastricht Treaty was challenged in the German Constitutional Court (see **Karlsruhe judgment**) was that amongst many of the *Länder* it was felt that the federal government was ceding to the Union powers that under the Constitution belonged wholly or partly to them.

A quite different type of regional activity has emerged in areas possessing a common economic interest. For example, in the Franco–German–Swiss region between the Vosges, the Black Forest and the Jura and centred upon the international Basle–Mulhouse–Freiburg airport a number of bodies have been set up for regular consultations on issues affecting the area. This and many similar regions are members of the Association of European Border Regions founded in 1971. An association of a similar type is the Conference of Peripheral Maritime Regions in the European Community, set up in 1973 with its headquarters in Rennes. The Conference aims to represent the common interest of coastal regions from the Western Isles to the Aegean and from the Baltic to the Azores in fishing, tourism, the environment and the coastal economy.

The **Council of Europe** has a long-standing involvement in regional government. Initially through the Standing Conference of Local and Regional Authorities of Europe and since January 1994 through the Congress, the Council seeks to engage local and regional authorities in all aspects of its work. The composition of the Congress replicates that of the Council's Parliamentary Assembly. However, unlike the Committee of the Regions, the Congress is bicameral, with one chamber for regional authorities and a second for local authorities. A standing committee allows the Congress's work to be continued between the annual sessions, the first of which was held from 31 May to 3 June 1994.

A quite separate body, the Council of European Municipalities (CEM) and Regions, was founded in 1951. It seeks to enlist the support of its membership of some 100,000 local and regional authorities in 20 countries for a 'united and democratic Europe', and in recent years has been engaged in re-establishing effective local government in central and eastern Europe. The CEM, which has its headquarters in Paris, is responsible for the 'town-twinning' programme (involving bizarre conjunctions such as that between Mainz, Valencia, Zagreb, Dijon and Watford) and helps local authorities with applications for aid from the European Union's **structural funds**.

A third body, the Assembly of European Regions (AER), was founded as the Council of European Regions in 1985. It has its headquarters in Strasbourg and a representative office in Brussels. The main aim of the AER is 'to promote regionalism and federalism in Europe' and 'to reinforce regional representation within the European institutions'. Like the CEM, the AER is extending its membership to central and eastern Europe.

RENAVAL
See **RECHAR**.

Renegotiation

In June 1971 the Conservative Government of **Edward Heath** completed the negotiations on British entry into the European Community. The conclusions were set out in a White Paper and laid before the House of Commons. The Labour Party was seriously split on the issue, and the best formula the Labour leader, Harold Wilson, could devise was for the party to remain in favour of the principle of membership but to oppose the so-called 'Tory terms'. Accordingly, on 28 October 1971 a majority of Labour MPs voted against British membership. In April 1972 the Labour Party came out in favour of a referendum on the issue and in July 1972 Labour's strategy of 'renegotiation' was set out in *Labour's Programme for Britain*. The United Kingdom joined the Community on 1 January 1973.

By a narrow margin, the Labour Party won the February 1974 election. The manifesto contained a commitment to 'renegotiate' Britain's terms of entry and to submit the results to the British people in order to allow the renegotiated terms to be endorsed 'through a General Election or a Consultative Referendum'. In January 1975 Harold Wilson confirmed that a referendum would be held.

The renegotiation centred on the United Kingdom's contributions to the Community **Budget**, reform of the **Common Agricultural Policy** (CAP), control over capital movements, the possible extension of value-added tax (VAT), **Economic and Monetary Union** (EMU), development policy and the powers of Parliament to decide on regional and fiscal policies. The renegotiation was completed at the Dublin meeting of the **European Council** on 10–11 March 1975. A week later the Cabinet voted by 16 votes to 7 in favour of recommending a 'Yes' vote in the referendum. This was endorsed by a majority of 226 in the House of Commons on 9 April 1975.

The 'renegotiation' exercise was a disastrous start to the United Kingdom's membership of the Community. It remains the only example of a member state having renegotiated its terms of entry and held a referendum *after* accession; and although the result (see **referendum of June 1975**) was a triumph for those in favour of membership, the uncertainty it engendered meant that for two and a half years British business was slow to concentrate its energies on Europe. Little of substance was achieved in the negotiations, and nothing that could not have been, in Mr Whitelaw's words, 'obtained in the course of the Community's normal development and without the whole business of renegotiation under threat of withdrawal' (*Hansard*, 7 April 1975). Nor in the event did the renegotiation resolve the divisions within the Labour Party. A special conference on 26 April 1975 condemned the renegotiated terms, and by 1983 the Party was once again formally opposed to British membership of the Community. Moreover, by 1977 it was clear that the 'corrective mechanism' agreed in Dublin to prevent the United Kingdom's net contribution to the Community Budget from becoming disproportionately large was not working (see **British Budget problem**). Worst of all, the renegotiation exercise confirmed other member states' fears about the halfhearted and self-interested nature of British commitment to the Community, symbolized by the fact that from January 1973 until July 1975 the Labour Party sent no representatives to the **European Parliament**.

Research

Initially, various legal bases for research policy in the European Community were to be found in all three of the founding **Treaties**. A **Resolution** adopted by the **Council of Ministers** on 14 January 1974 was the first attempt to introduce a coherent overall strategy, based primarily on the coordination of national policies and the identification of projects of Community interest. This provided the basis for provisions introduced into the **Treaty of Rome** by the **Single European Act** (SEA) and further amended by the **Maastricht Treaty**.

Article 130f EEC defines the objective of research policy as 'strengthening the scientific and technological bases of Community industry and encouraging it to become more competitive at international level'. Under Article 130g EEC four activities were specified: promoting cooperation with and between undertakings, research centres and universities (see **Joint Research Centre**); promoting cooperation with non-member countries and international organizations; dissemination of research findings; and improving the training and mobility of researchers in the member states. Article 130h EEC empowers the member states and the Community to coordinate their research activities. Articles 130i–m EEC provide for research to be undertaken within a multi-annual framework programme (see below), drawn up by the Council of Ministers and the **European Parliament** under the **co-decision procedure**; unusually, however, at every stage in the procedure the Council must act unanimously.

The fourth framework programme (1995–8) was adopted on 22 March 1994. It incorporates the main priorities of earlier programmes (information and telecommunications technology, environmental research (including the use of 'cleaner' technologies in industry), biotechnology and health research, energy) and adds transport technology (e.g., new traffic guidance systems) and research into the impact of technology on society (see also

Joint European Torus, European Organization for Nuclear Research, European Space Agency, BRITE-EURAM, COMETT, COST, EUREKA, LIFE, RACE).

The sums available from the **Budget** are small by comparison with overall research expenditure, representing some 4 per cent of publicly funded research in the member states (2 per cent of public and private expenditure on research). Unlike the **structural funds**, resources in the Budget for research are not subject to national quotas: project sponsors apply direct to the **Commission**. As a general rule, only projects at the 'pre-competitive' stage are eligible for financial assistance (i.e., projects sufficiently far advanced to be close to competing in the open market are not normally supported) and all projects must involve cooperation between partners from at least two member states.

Public expenditure on research in the member states is low by comparison with that in Japan or the United States, whether measured as a percentage of gross domestic product (GDP) or of public expenditure overall. In GDP terms, the average is about 1 per cent (civil and military expenditure) and in terms of public expenditure overall, 3.26 per cent. If private expenditure is taken into account, research expenditure represents about 2 per cent of GDP in the member states, by comparison with 2.8 per cent in the United States and 3.1 per cent in Japan.

RESIDER

See **RECHAR**.

Resolution

A Resolution by the **Council of Ministers** or the **European Council** is a type of Decision not recognized in the **Treaties**. It is used to embody a firm political consensus, yet in a strict sense has no legal force. For example, the original 1978 agreement in the European Council establishing the **European Monetary System** (EMS) was in the form of a Resolution, as was the 1981 decision by member states' representatives on the **European passport**.

Resolutions are also used by the **European Parliament** to express its views and form part of the Parliament's **Opinions**. The expression 'legislative resolution' denotes Opinions given under the **consultation, cooperation, co-decision** and **assent procedures** to distinguish them from Resolutions delivered on the Parliament's own initiative.

RETEX

See **RECHAR**.

Right of initiative

The expression 'right of initiative' denotes one of the essential prerogatives of the **European Commission**, its responsibility for drafting proposals for legislation under the **Treaties**. Although the object, character and timing of the draft legislation may spring from a decision of the **European Council**, the **Council of Ministers** or the **European Parliament** (see below), the draft itself is the work of the Commission and it remains the Commission's proposal throughout the legislative process in the sense that the Commission may withdraw or modify it at any time. In fact, it is estimated that 90 per cent of these proposals owe their origin to organizations other than the Commission, including member states, trade associations and pressure groups. The right of initiative is the most jealously guarded token of the Commission's independence.

Article 155 of the **Treaty of Rome** empowers the Commission to 'participate in the shaping of measures taken by the Council and by the European Parliament in the manner provided for in this Treaty'. Before formally submitting a draft proposal, the Commission will take soundings amongst interested parties and may issue a consultation document (for which the English expression 'green paper' is normally used). The proposal will also figure in the **annual legislative programme** submitted to the European Parliament, and the Parliament's comments at this stage may well be reflected in the final draft. Increasingly, the Commission has to give careful thought not only to the detail of the draft but also to its legal base in the Treaties, since this will dictate the voting procedures used at the various stages of the legislative process and may materially affect its chance of being adopted. All but the simplest proposals are discussed collectively by the Commissioners at one of their weekly meetings. Once adopted by the Commission, draft proposals are published in the *Official Journal*.

The right of initiative enjoyed by the Commission applies also to the **Budget** and to the negotiation of external agreements. In the former case the Commission forwards to the Council and to the European Parliament a preliminary draft budget based on its own expenditure estimates and on those drawn up by other institutions. In the latter case the Commission submits to the Council 'recommendations' (Article 228 EEC), which form the basis of the Commission's negotiating mandate.

In recent years several proposals have sought either to remove the Commission's right of initiative or to allow the right to be shared with other institutions and with member states. The **Maastricht Treaty** came close to granting the European Parliament a right of initiative in Article 138b EEC, under which it may, 'acting by a majority of its Members, request the Commission to submit any appropriate proposal on matters on which it considers that a Community act is required for the purpose of implementing this Treaty'. In the **Common Foreign and Security Policy** (CFSP) provisions of the Maastricht Treaty the Commission and member states may 'submit proposals' to the Council (Article J8 TEU). A similar provision applies to **Justice and Home Affairs** (JHA), except that member states alone may take the initiative in matters relating to criminal law, police cooperation and customs matters (Article K1 TEU).

In a wider sense the Commission has a power of initiative outside the legislative process. Spectacular examples of this include the 1977 speech by **Roy Jenkins**, as President of the Commission, in which he relaunched the idea of **Economic and Monetary Union** (EMU); the **Cockfield White Paper** of 1985; and the 1987 proposals on the **future financing** of the Community put forward by **Jacques Delors**.

The right of initiative is one of the features of the Commission's powers that distinguish it from other international bureaucracies. It affords a direct link with the idea espoused by **Jean Monnet** and others that the Commission should be an embryonic European government (see **High Authority**), and this in turn has made the right of initiative an obvious target for opponents of **federalism**. Nevertheless, it is hard to see how the European Community could work on any basis other than that of draft legislation being brought forward and steered through the legislative process by a body that is independent of member states; and the more member states there are, the more essential such an independent body will be.

Rome, Treaty of

Signed by **the Six** in March 1957, the Treaty of Rome established the **European Economic Community** (EEC). The Treaty establishing the **European Atomic Energy Community** (EAEC or Euratom) was signed at the same time. The main features of the Treaty of Rome are described in separate entries: the institutions and procedures laid down in the Treaty were modelled largely on those already operational in the **European Coal and Steel Community** (ECSC). See also **Treaties**, **Messina Conference**, **Spaak Committee**.

Saarland

The economic importance of the Saarland, one of the smallest of the German *Länder*, resides in the richness of its coalfields, which lie along the frontier of Lorraine in north-eastern France and upon which the steelworks of that region largely depend. For this reason the French government insisted at the end of the First World War that the coalmines be given to France as compensation for the loss of those in northern France and that the territory be governed for 15 years by an international commission under the auspices of the **League of Nations**. Under this arrangement a plebiscite was to be held: in 1935 the local population – who had retained their German nationality – voted in favour of the Saarland being restored to Germany.

At the end of the Second World War the Saarland lay within the French zone of occupied Germany. A customs barrier was created in 1947 between the Saarland and the rest of the zone, and with the support of 83 per cent of the population a statute of independence was drawn up. In 1950 the Saarland became an associate member of the **Council of Europe**. More importantly, as a territory economically integrated into France, the Saarland became part of the **European Coal and Steel Community** (ECSC) in 1951 (Saarbrücken, the capital of the Saarland, was proposed by **Robert Schuman** as the **seat of the institutions** of the ECSC, but this was opposed by the German government). By this time, support for the reintegration of the Saarland was growing in the newly established Federal Republic of Germany. In 1955 the people of the Saarland rejected a French proposal to give the territory a special autonomous status (see **Western European Union**). Negotiations then began for the reincorporation of the Saarland into West Germany, a process that was completed in July 1959.

The dispute over the Saarland, one of the longest-running territorial disputes in European history, was an irritant in Franco–German relations throughout the formative years of the European Community. The absence of a formal peace treaty concluding the Second World War and establishing postwar frontiers meant that France and West Germany were obliged to resolve the matter on a bilateral basis. The amicable settlement finally reached was an important token of **Franco-German cooperation**, made possible by the fact that the original cause of the dispute – the coalfields – had been effectively internationalized by the establishment of the ECSC.

Santer, Jacques (b. 1937)

Jacques Santer was Prime Minister of Luxembourg from 1984 until January 1995, when he succeeded **Jacques Delors** as President of the **European Commission**.

At the Corfu meeting of the **European Council** in June 1994 John Major, the Prime Minister of the United Kingdom, blocked the candidacy of Jean-Luc Dehaene, the Prime Minister of Belgium, to succeed Delors, in spite of his having the support of a clear majority of the other governments. Major's official candidate for the **presidency** was Sir Leon Brittan, who withdrew his name having received only British support. Ruud Lubbers, the long-serving Prime Minister of the Netherlands, was also a candidate but was known to be strongly opposed by his fellow Christian Democrat, **Helmut Kohl**. He too withdrew from the contest. Since the **Treaty of Rome** (Article 158.2) requires the governments to act 'by common accord' in choosing their nominee, Major's veto resulted in no decision being taken.

In his official statement Major spoke of the need 'to make sure that we have the best candidate for this vitally important job'. His objection to Dehaene was that he came from 'a tradition of big government and of intervention . . . not quite in touch with the direction in which Europe is now moving'.

Jacques Santer, like Dehaene and Lubbers a Christian Democrat from a **Benelux** country, emerged as a compromise choice. However, primarily because of the behind-the-scenes wrangling amongst the member states between the Corfu meeting and the special meeting of the European Council in Brussels (15 July 1994), the **European Parliament**, using its new power under the **Maastricht Treaty** to approve the appointment, very nearly failed to endorse Jacques Santer at its July 1994 session (Santer was approved by 260 votes to 238, with 23 abstentions). Santer's speech to the Parliament on that occasion confirmed what had been widely suspected at the time of the European Council meeting in Corfu: that his attachment to what he referred to as 'the Community model' of European integration was no different from Dehaene's.

Schengen Agreement

Schengen is a village in Luxembourg, where on 14 June 1985 the three **Benelux** countries, France and the Federal Republic of Germany signed an agreement 'on the gradual abolition of controls at the common frontiers'. The 33 articles of the Agreement are divided into short-term measures (abolition of systematic checks, easing of formalities, approximation of visa regulations, closer cooperation between border police, etc.) and long-term measures (strengthening the external frontiers, harmonization of value-added tax (VAT), excise duties, duty-free allowances, etc.). The Agreement was followed by a 'Convention on the application of the Agreement', signed in Schengen on 19 June 1990. The Convention, composed of 142 articles, sets out in detail exactly how the Agreement should be applied, how disputes should be resolved, and a series of provisions on complex and sensitive questions, such as extradition, the transmission of personal data, control of drugs and firearms, and asylum. The Schengen Agreement and the Convention were widely regarded as models of how frontier controls could be eased or abolished as part of creating the **Single Market** (they do not apply to the **overseas countries and territories** (OCTs) of France and the Netherlands). At the same time they were criticized for their essentially intergovernmental character (the Community institutions were not involved in the negotiations) and by upholders of civil liberties for the fact that so many questions with a direct bearing on the rights of the individual had been agreed between governments without any parliamentary approval or consultation. After many delays, the Schengen Convention entered into force in March 1995 in the original five signatory states, together with Portugal and Spain. Italy and Greece are due to follow suit, and Austria has also ratified the Convention. Denmark, Finland, and Sweden are likely to join the Schengen group in 1996: the three countries are already linked to Iceland and Norway in a passport union (see **Nordic Council**). There is a good study of the difficulties in Alexis Pauly (ed.), *Schengen en panne* (Maastricht, 1994). See also **free movement of persons**, **Justice and Home Affairs**.

Schuman, Robert (1886–1963)

Although he was born in Luxembourg, Robert Schuman made his political career in France. A member of the Mouvement Républicain Populaire (MRP), the closest French equivalent to Christian Democracy, he rose to be Prime Minister (1947–8) and Foreign Minister (1948–53). His claim to be regarded as one of the founding fathers of the European Union rests upon the **Schuman Plan**. The anniversary of the day upon which Schuman announced his proposal for the pooling of French and German coal and steel production, 9 May 1950, is still celebrated within the Union institutions as a holiday. According to **Jean Monnet**, the originator of Schuman's proposals, Schuman 'didn't really understand the treaty which bore his name' (i.e., the **Treaty of Paris** of 1951), a remark recorded by

Roy Jenkins after a conversation with Monnet on 20 February 1978 (Jenkins, *European Diary*, p.220). Schuman's name is also given to medals awarded annually by the Schuman Foundation to persons who have given distinguished service to the cause of European unity. In his speech announcing the Schuman Plan, Schuman said 'Europe will not be built at a stroke, nor constructed in accordance with some overall plan: it will be built upon concrete achievements [*réalisations concrètes*] which first create a *de facto* solidarity.'

Schuman Plan

On 9 May 1950 **Robert Schuman**, the French Foreign Minister, proposed that French and German coal and steel production should be 'pooled' and placed under a common supranational authority. This proposal was the basis for the first of the three **European Communities**, the **European Coal and Steel Community** (ECSC), and was largely the work of **Jean Monnet**. The Plan was and remains amongst the most powerful symbols of Franco-German postwar reconciliation.

Three months later Schuman presented his proposal to the Consultative Assembly of the **Council of Europe**. Referring to what became the High Authority of the ECSC (the forerunner of the **European Commission**) he said: 'The signatories of the treaty will, with certain guarantees, submit to the authority that they will have set up . . . The Authority . . . will be the first example of an independent supranational institution.' Amongst the contributors to the debate was Harold Macmillan MP. He said: 'To the great majority of Europeans, by far the most significant aspect of M. Schuman's initiative is the political. It is not, in its essentials, a purely economic or industrial conception; it is a grand design for a new Europe; it is not just a piece of convenient machinery; it is a revolutionary, almost mystical, conception.' It was precisely the supranational element in the Schuman Plan that led both the Labour Government in 1950 and the Conservative Government that came into office the following year to reject the idea of participation. As Macmillan put it, 'We will not hand over to any supranational Authority the right to close down our pits or our steelworks . . . No Government could do it; no party could stand for it' (see also **Konrad Adenauer, Winston Churchill**).

Scrutiny

'Scrutiny' is the word used to denote the various procedures whereby **national parliaments** monitor and seek to influence legislation emanating from the European Union. In the United Kingdom, for example, the procedure is centred upon the 'scrutiny reserve', under which no British minister in the **Council of Ministers** may give his or her agreement to any legislative proposal until the House of Commons Select Committee on European Legislation (the 'Scrutiny Committee') has completed its examination of the proposal or until the House, on the recommendation of the Committee, has come to a resolution on the matter (Resolution of the House of 24 October 1990).

Seat of the institutions

The long-running dispute over where the main European institutions should be located, one of the most arid and unedifying in the Union's history, was resolved, in the view of the member states, at the Edinburgh meeting of the **European Council** in December 1992 (*Official Journal*, C341, 23 December 1992). The **Council of Ministers** now has its 'seat' in **Brussels**, but continues to hold its April, June and October meetings in Luxembourg. The **Commission** has its seat in Brussels, certain departments remaining in Luxembourg. The **Economic and Social Committee** is also located in Brussels, together with the **Committee of the Regions**. Luxembourg is the seat of the **Court of Justice**, the **Court of First Instance**, the **Court of Auditors** and the **European Investment Bank** (EIB).

The decision on the seat of the **European Parliament** was more complicated and more controversial. Its seat was designated as **Strasbourg**, 'where the twelve periods of monthly plenary sessions . . . shall be held . . . Additional plenary sessions shall be held in Brussels. The Committees of the European Parliament shall meet in Brussels. The General Secretariat of the European Parliament and its departments shall remain in Luxembourg' (Article 1a). The Parliament views this decision as inconsistent with the provisions of the **Treaties** (see below).

The dispute over the seat of the institutions has legal, linguistic and political dimensions. Article 77 of the 1951 **European Coal and Steel Community** (ECSC) Treaty says: 'The seat of the institutions of the Community shall be determined by common accord of the Governments of the Member States.' Identical provisions are to be found in Article 216 of the **Treaty of Rome** and Article 189 of the Treaty establishing the **European Atomic Energy Community** (Euratom). Two points should be noted. First, the fact that the word 'seat' is in the singular implies, but does not conclusively prove, that the intention was to have all the institutions − Council, Commission, Parliament, Court − in one place. Second, the expression 'by common accord of the Governments of the Member States' means that a decision on the seat must be taken by the governments meeting *as governments*, not as the Council or the European Council, and that it must be unanimous.

The High Authority of the ECSC was located in Luxembourg on a provisional basis. Both the Council and the Court were also established there, but Luxembourg could not offer facilities for the Common Assembly (the forerunner of the European Parliament). Accordingly, the Assembly borrowed the building in Strasbourg used by the Consultative Assembly of the **Council of Europe** for its plenary sessions, although its staff were based in Luxembourg. Six years later the **European Economic Community** (EEC) and Euratom were established. Until the 1965 **Merger Treaty** (see below) the three Communities had separate Councils of Ministers and separate Commissions (that of the ECSC continuing to be known as the High Authority), but from 1958 the Court of Justice and the European Assembly (as the ECSC Common Assembly was now called) served all three Communities. The EEC Commission and the Euratom Commission were based in Brussels. The three Councils met in Brussels. The committees of the European Assembly were by now meeting in Brussels, but the staff of the Assembly remained in Luxembourg and plenary sessions continued to be held in Strasbourg.

This situation, based on a series of 'provisional' decisions, was brought to a head by the Merger Treaty. Under this Treaty the institutions of the three Communities were to be merged; and the Luxembourgers, fearing that they would lose everything to Brussels, insisted that Luxembourg retain a share of the institutions. Strasbourg too wanted to keep the plenary sessions of the Assembly. The result was the 'Decision . . . on the provisional location of certain institutions and departments of the Communities' annexed to the Merger Treaty (8 April 1965). In this Decision the governments decided that 'Luxembourg, Brussels and Strasbourg shall remain the provisional places of work of the institutions of the Communities' (Article 1). In April, June and October the Council would meet in Luxembourg (Article 2). The Court would remain in Luxembourg (Article 3), as would the staff of the European Parliament, as the Assembly was now called (Article 4). The EIB would be based in Luxembourg (Article 5), as would certain Commission departments (Article 4). No specific mention was made of the committees and plenary sessions of the European Parliament.

The effect of this Decision, which was 'without prejudice' to the eventual application of those Treaty articles empowering the governments to take a final decision on the seat of the institutions, was to confirm the *status quo* and to strengthen the position of Luxembourg. It also introduced a new juridical concept: instead of 'seat' the Decision spoke of 'places of work'. From 1967 the Parliament began of its own volition to hold some of its monthly part-sessions in Luxembourg; this practice continued throughout the 1970s against the opposition of the French.

The position of Luxembourg was seriously weakened in 1979 by the fact that there was nowhere in Luxembourg for the new 434-member directly elected Parliament to meet. Members of the European Parliament (MEPs) accordingly got used to the idea of holding part-sessions exclusively in Strasbourg; and on 7 July 1981, not long after a newly built chamber became available to the Parliament in Luxembourg, they voted to hold all part-sessions in Strasbourg and all committee meetings in Brussels. Luxembourg challenged the legality of this decision in the Court of Justice, since at the Maastricht meeting of the European Council in March 1981 the governments had confirmed the *status quo* as set out in the 1965 Decision. The Court, however, ruled that the Parliament's decision was legal, since it had the right under the Treaties 'to adopt appropriate measures to ensure the due functioning and conduct of its proceedings' and that since the Parliament had held part-sessions in Luxembourg since 1967 of its own volition, it was free to abandon the practice at any time (Case 230/81, 10 February 1983). The governments' right under the Treaties to determine the seat of the institutions was confirmed, the Court merely observing that it was a duty as well as a right. The Court's decision also allowed the Parliament to transfer small numbers of staff to Brussels in the interests of 'due functioning', but the great majority were obliged to remain in Luxembourg.

Many attempts have been made to resolve the question of the seat. As early as June 1958 the European Parliament – the institution most seriously affected by the absence of a single seat – voted in favour of a 'European district' in which all the institutions would be located. In the first vote on the choice of city Strasbourg emerged, by one vote, as the favourite over Brussels, followed by Nice, Milan, Luxembourg, Paris, Stresa, Turin, Monza and Oise. In the second and final vote Brussels was nine votes ahead of Strasbourg, followed by Milan, Nice and Luxembourg. Subsequent votes in the Parliament on where its working place should be have consistently given Brussels a lead over Strasbourg, but Strasbourg is still strongly supported by the French, some German MEPs and a substantial proportion of MEPs from southern Europe.

The Parliament is affected in five ways. First, certain basic facilities (such as the main library and the offices of the committee secretariats) remain in Luxembourg, where few MEPs ever go. Second, the Parliament is physically remote from the two institutions, the Commission and the Council, over which it is supposed to exercise a measure of democratic control. Third, the dispersal of its activities over two cities means that the Parliament has to organize its work on the basis of a monthly cycle, which is both inefficient and exhausting. It is also expensive: the cost to the Parliament of not being in one place has been estimated to be at least 10 per cent of its annual budget. Fourth, the willingness of the media to cover the proceedings of the Parliament is greatly reduced by the cost and inconvenience of having to send correspondents to Strasbourg. And finally, the Parliament is denied the symbolic advantage of a building clearly associated in the public mind with the idea of democratic control exercised at European level.

The Parliament has made only halfhearted attempts to resolve the question of its place of work. In 1982 a special part-session was held for the first time in Brussels, but it was devoted to one issue (unemployment) and was not a typical part-session in respect of the practical requirements (staff, printing facilities, electronic voting, etc.). On 24 October 1985 the Parliament adopted a resolution by 132 votes to 113, with 13 abstentions, calling for the construction of a new 600-seat building, that would enable part-sessions to be held in Brussels. This was promptly challenged in the Court of Justice by the French and Luxembourg governments, and the Court eventually ruled against the Parliament. In January 1989 the Parliament adopted by 222 votes to 176, with 4 abstentions, a report that called for the transfer of staff from Luxembourg to reflect Parliament's operational needs and reasserted the right to hold occasional part-sessions outside Strasbourg. Even this very modest proposal, in a report that specifically confirmed the historic and political importance of Strasbourg, was carried by a surprisingly small majority and was challenged, once again, by both the Luxembourg and the French governments. The President of the Parliament made no mention of the seat issue in his address to the Edinburgh meeting of the European Council.

The French government has never been anything other than nakedly opportunistic in any matter affecting the future of Strasbourg. In 1991 it threatened to block all decisions on the siting of new institutions (such as the **European Environment Agency**) unless the governments finally declared Strasbourg to be the seat of the European Parliament. This was opposed by the Belgians and the Luxembourgers. It was **German reunification** that gave the French government the weapon it needed to secure the decision it wanted. The French, both in the government and in the Assemblée Nationale, made it clear that they would block the agreement giving Germany (and certain other member states) extra seats in the Parliament from June 1994 unless Strasbourg was made the seat of the Parliament and the Parliament's authorities bound themselves to lease the new premises being built in Strasbourg for the 12 plenary sessions specified in the Edinburgh decision. In March 1994 the Parliament agreed to the French demand.

The Parliament cannot challenge the Edinburgh decision in the Court of Justice because it has no power to bring actions against the governments *acting as governments* (and not as the Council). It could, if it chose, act deliberately in defiance of the decision, in the near-certainty that one or more member states would take the matter to the Court. Ironically, the weakest part of the decision is the requirement that the Parliament's committees should meet in Brussels (since this is a matter of its internal organization), but this is the one part of the decision with which pro-Brussels MEPs are content. Formally, the Parliament remains of the view that the governments have not exercised their powers under Article 216 EEC.

Whatever arguments there may be in favour of not having all the main institutions of the European Union in one place, there can be no argument in favour of having the Parliament's activities spread over two locations while its secretariat remains in a third. However, by the time the Edinburgh decision was taken the *status quo* had been in effect for so long that a substantial physical and commercial infrastructure had built up around the Parliament in Brussels, Luxembourg and Strasbourg, involving several massive new buildings and annual rents in all three cities (the Parliament owns hardly any of the buildings it uses). The extent of this infrastructure and its commercial importance to the cities involved made the issue of the seat more difficult to resolve.

The Belgian government was never willing to press as hard as some MEPs wished to have the Parliament located in Brussels. Many of the Flemish-speaking majority in Belgium view the presence of international institutions as strengthening the hand of the Francophones, and many Bruxellois regard the European institutions as responsible for high prices, ugly buildings and urban congestion. This ambivalence on the part of the Belgian government further enhanced the position of Strasbourg.

The Edinburgh decision was sufficiently satisfactory to the French to enable the member states meeting as the European Council in Brussels in October 1993 to take decisions on the location of other bodies (*Official Journal*, C323, 30 November 1993). Of these, the most important were the **European Monetary Institute** and the **European Central Bank** (Frankfurt), **Europol** and the Europol Drugs Unit (The Hague) and the **European Environment Agency** (Copenhagen). Other new bodies were to be located in London (the **European Medicines Evaluation Agency**), Turin, Lisbon, Ireland and Spain. In a declaration annexed to the decision, it was agreed to move the **European Centre for the Development of Vocational Training** from Berlin to Thessaloniki.

It is now highly unlikely that there will ever be a major change in the location of the institutions. No member state and no institution except the Parliament has an interest in raising the issue. The Edinburgh decision contained a commitment to give priority in the siting of new bodies to member states other than Belgium, France and Luxembourg (see above), thus giving every one an interest in maintaining the *status quo*. The various schemes put forward in the past for a European capital territory (along the lines of Canberra, Washington DC, or Brasilia) will never be revived. For the Parliament, the implications are profound, since it is condemned for the foreseeable future to the expensive, inefficient and discreditable monthly cycle of activity summed up in the phrase 'a travelling circus'. The possibility that this is precisely what the governments of the member states had in mind cannot be wholly ruled out. **Jean Monnet** relates in his *Memoirs* how, with only weeks to go before the ECSC was due to come into operation in 1952, Luxembourg was put forward as the compromise choice between the competing claims of Liège, Turin and The Hague. 'That night', Monnet wrote, 'gave us the final proof . . . that a Europe of sovereign States was incapable, despite its leaders' goodwill, of reaching the sensible decisions that were needed for the common good.'

'Set-aside'

Introduced in 1988 as a means of limiting overproduction under the **Common Agricultural Policy** (CAP), 'set-aside' allows farmers to be paid compensation for taking at least one-fifth of their land out of production for at least five years. To qualify for compensation, 'set-aside' land must be kept in environmentally sound condition.

Single European Act (SEA)

The 1986 SEA, which came into force in July 1987, was the first substantial revision of the **Treaties**. The first part of the SEA contained a small number of common provisions, of which the most important gave the first formal Treaty recognition to the **European Council** (Article 2 SEA). The second part set out additions and amendments to the Treaties. The third part was a new, separate Treaty text formalizing the procedures known as **European Political Cooperation** (EPC). The document was called the *single* European Act (*Acte Unique*) to underline the fact that it was to be regarded as a coherent whole, an agreement amongst member states that might fall to pieces if picked apart when submitted for **ratification**.

The SEA was the member states' response to the demands for institutional reform that emerged in the early 1980s. Of these, the most important were the 1981 **Genscher–Colombo** proposals, which resulted in the **Stuttgart Declaration**, pressure from the **European Parliament** (see **Draft Treaty establishing the European Union**) and the realization in the **Commission** and elsewhere that the prospect of further **enlargement** to include Portugal and Spain made institutional reform necessary and urgent. By

1985 it was clear too that if the ambitious legislative programme set out in the **Cockfield White Paper** for the completion of the **Single Market** were to be accomplished, decision-making procedures would have to be accelerated.

The Milan meeting of the European Council in June 1985, which endorsed the Cockfield White Paper, also considered the final report of the **Dooge Committee**, which had been set up the previous year. Amongst the Committee's recommendations was that an **Intergovernmental Conference** (IGC) should be convened to consider amendments to the Treaties. Against British, Danish and Greek opposition, this was agreed.

The first meeting of the IGC took place the following September. At the Luxembourg meeting of the European Council in December political agreement was reached on all but a few points: these were left to be resolved by the Foreign Affairs Council later in the month. By January 1986 the draft, now known as the Single European Act, was ready for signature. In all but two countries this gave rise to no difficulty. The Italian government made its acceptance conditional upon the European Parliament's approval, and the Danish parliament voted to reject the SEA on the grounds that it gave too many new powers to the European Parliament. The member states were not prepared to reopen the negotiations, so 9 of the 12 (i.e, all except Denmark, Greece and Italy) signed the SEA in Luxembourg in February 1986. In a referendum on 27 February the Danish people voted in favour of the SEA, and the following day a second and final signing ceremony took place in The Hague. However, the SEA was not ratified in all the member states in time for it to enter into force by the target date of January 1987. The last member state to ratify was Ireland, where a referendum was held on 26 May 1987 because of a High Court ruling that the SEA entailed a change to the Irish constitution. The SEA came into force five weeks later.

The main changes to the Treaties introduced by the SEA were the extension of **qualified majority voting** (QMV); the **cooperation procedure**; the **assent procedure**; the **Court of First Instance**; the 31 December 1992 deadline for the completion of the Single Market; and new Treaty Articles on **cohesion**, research and technology, and **environment policy**. Many of these changes have since been modified, superseded or supplemented by the **Maastricht Treaty**, as has the third section on European political cooperation (see **Common Foreign and Security Policy**).

The SEA fell far short of the European Parliament's hopes and was widely regarded as being only of technical interest as an exercise in tidying up the Treaties. In fact, the provisions on QMV and the cooperation procedure proved to be of great importance, far beyond anything that could have been achieved on the basis of the 'gentlemen's agreement' that the British government originally favoured as an alternative to changing the Treaties.

The most comprehensive collection of texts on the IGC and the SEA is *Towards European Union II*, edited by Marina Gazzo and published by Agence Europe in Brussels (1986).

Single Market

Sometimes known as the 'internal market' to distinguish it from the European Community's external trade, the Single Market is the totality of economic activity within the member states, with particular emphasis on cross-frontier trade. The phrase used in the Treaties is 'common market', meaning a unitary market governed by a single set of rules. Article 2 of the **Treaty of Rome**, before it was amended by the **Maastricht Treaty**, said:

> The Community shall have as its task, by establishing a common market and progressively approximating the economic policies of the Member States, to promote throughout the Community a harmonious development of economic activities, a continuous and balanced expansion, an increase in stability, an accelerated raising of the standard of living and closer relations between the States belonging to it.

The Article is quoted at length to demonstrate how high the expectations were of the benefits that would flow from the achievement of this, the most basic of the Community's objectives.

In the years immediately after the Second World War the idea that the economic recovery of Western Europe would be accelerated if countries refrained from re-erecting barriers against each other's goods found many supporters. It was fundamental to American policy and to the thinking behind the **Marshall Plan**. Paul Hoffman, the head of the American Economic Cooperation Administration, which supervised the disbursement of Marshall Aid, called for the creation of a 'single large market' in Western Europe in a speech in Paris on 31 October 1949. In this respect, the newly founded **Organization for European Economic Cooperation** was a disappointment to the Americans and others who hoped that it might lead to the creation of federal institutions capable of reorganizing the economy and the commerce of Western Europe on a continental scale.

Against this background the decision, announced in the **Schuman Plan** of 9 May 1950, to create a single market for coal and steel seems relatively modest. But by the end of the decade **the Six** had agreed to form a

customs union and to embark upon a programme for 'the approximation of the laws of the Member States to the extent required for the proper functioning of the common market' (Article 3 EEC).

The customs union was completed by 1 July 1968, but the Single Market had to wait rather longer. According to the account in Nicholas Colchester and David Buchan, *Europe Relaunched* (1990), several tributaries flowed into the stream that became the 1992 programme. First was the impact of the 1979 **'Cassis de Dijon'** judgment by the **Court of Justice**. Second was the **Kangaroo Group** in the European Parliament and the report they commissioned, *Towards European Economic Recovery in the 1980s* (known as the **Albert–Ball Report**). Third was the feeling amongst leading European industrialists that the fragmentation of the Community market was hampering the ability of European firms to compete internationally. And fourth were the two leading figures in the drive to complete the Single Market, **Jacques Delors** and Lord Cockfield. Delors, who in 1984 was appointed as the next President of the Commission, believed that the Community was badly in need of a bold, imaginative idea upon which to focus its energies. The idea that seemed to command most support in national capitals was the completion of the Single Market. The following year the **Cockfield White Paper** started the process by identifying the legislative measures that would need to be taken. The deadline of 1992 was chosen as the lifespan of two Commissions.

In parallel with the moves towards completing the Single Market were the negotiations that led to the **Single European Act** (SEA). It was generally recognized that the ambitious legislative programme set out in the Cockfield White Paper could not be completed unless decision-making was speeded up by the use of **qualified majority voting** (QMV) in the **Council of Ministers**. Accordingly, a new **Article 100a** was added to the **Treaty of Rome** to allow Single Market measures to be agreed not by **unanimity** (as under the original **Article 100**) but by qualified majority, the only exceptions being 'fiscal provisions, . . . the free movement of persons [and] the rights and interests of employed persons' (Article 100a.2). Another new Article gave the 31 December 1992 deadline formal status, and defined the internal market as 'an area without internal frontiers in which the free movement of goods, persons, services and capital is ensured in accordance with the provisions of this Treaty' (Article 8a). The SEA came into force on 1 July 1987.

The publicity surrounding the Single Market programme aroused great interest amongst businessmen. Governments of member states mounted 'awareness' programmes to ensure that their own businessmen were prepared for the more intense competition likely to flow from it. The date '1992' achieved an extraordinarily high level of recognition even amongst the general public and, as **Eurobarometer** showed, those who thought it would be 'a good thing' outnumbered those who thought the opposite by three to one. Perhaps most beneficial of all, successive presidencies of the Council competed with each other to see how many items of Single Market legislation could be agreed within each six-month period.

By December 1992 some 260 out of the original list of 282 legislative measures had been agreed, although a number of these had not yet been implemented in national law and many had not yet entered into force. Nevertheless, the Single Market was firmly in place, and on 31 December 1992 members of the Kangaroo Group hired a cross-Channel ferry to celebrate the ease with which goods could now be carried across frontiers.

Goods

In 1988 the introduction of the Single Administrative Document (SAD) simplified frontier formalities for goods in transit from one member state to another. Formalities were removed altogether from 1 January 1993.

Tax

Differing rates of value-added tax (VAT) were responsible for many of the delays at frontiers. New procedures agreed in the Council in 1991 allowed tax controls to be removed from the frontiers, and tax matters are now dealt with at points within member states. **Tax harmonization** measures agreed in 1991 introduced a minimum standard rate of VAT of 15 per cent, with exceptions for certain essentials. According to experts, tax differences have an impact on cross-border shopping only if they exceed 6 per cent, so standard rates can be fixed at up to 21 per cent. The minimum standard rate is subject to periodic review. The member states are also committed to making VAT payable in the country of origin rather than (as now) in the country in which the goods are finally sold.

Tax-free goods

The logic behind tax-free goods disappears once consumers are free to buy goods anywhere in the Union wherever they are cheapest and bring them home without paying duty. However, under pressure from airports and others it was agreed that tax-free sales would be maintained even for intra-Union travellers at least until 1999.

Tax-paid goods

From 1 January 1993 there was a substantial rise in the quantities of alcoholic drinks and tobacco products that travellers can freely convey across the Union's internal frontiers, as long as both tax and duty have been paid in the country of purchase.

Barriers to trade

Although the principle of mutual recognition established in the 'Cassis de Dijon' case removed many of the obstacles to trade caused by different product standards, some harmonization remains necessary in the fields of public health, product safety and consumer protection. Purely technical harmonization is left to the relevant industries to sort out themselves, along broad guidelines laid down by public authorities, and in many cases no longer involves legislation.

With effect from 1 January 1994, most Single Market legislation applies throughout the **European Economic Area**.

The Six

'The Six' refers to the six countries – Belgium, France, Italy, Luxembourg, the Netherlands and West Germany – that formed the **European Coal and Steel Community** (ECSC) in 1951 under the **Treaty of Paris** and went on to form the **European Economic Community** (EEC) and the **European Atomic Energy Community** (Euratom) under two Treaties signed in Rome in 1957. With the accession of Denmark, Ireland and the United Kingdom, the Six became the Nine in 1973, the Ten in 1981 with the accession of Greece, the Twelve in 1986 with the accession of Portugal and Spain, and the Fifteen in 1995 with the accession of Austria, Finland and Sweden. In the pre-1973 literature on the European Community 'the Six' is often used to distinguish the member states of the Community from 'the Seven', the members of the **European Free Trade Association** (EFTA).

'Snake in the tunnel'

The 'Snake in the tunnel' was the popular name for a 1972 agreement to allow the currencies of member states only a narrow margin of fluctuation against the dollar (1.125 per cent on either side) and so against each other (see **Werner Report**). Developed from an earlier, simpler 'snake', the 'Snake in the tunnel' was a form of **Exchange-Rate Mechanism** (ERM), but by 1976 it had been abandoned by all participants except West Germany and the **Benelux** countries. The 'Snake' was the fluctuating line created as currencies rose and fell, the 'tunnel' was the 1.125 per cent limit above and below the dollar.

Soames affair

On 4 February 1969, President **Charles de Gaulle** invited Sir Christopher Soames, the British Ambassador to France, to a private meeting at which he outlined his concerns about the integrationist direction in which **the Six** seemed to be moving. He indicated that France might after all prefer to be part of a **free trade area** including the United Kingdom, Ireland and Scandinavia, to be run largely by the four big countries, France, Italy, the United Kingdom and West Germany. What he was looking for was an indication that this might be acceptable to the British, whose application to join the Six he had twice vetoed (in 1963 and 1967).

These revelations posed a problem for the British government, which did not want to be a party to a French plot against the Community. Accordingly, the West German government was informed, together with the United States and the other members of the **Western European Union** (WEU). Inevitably, the story found its way into the French newspapers. The French government reacted by accusing the British of betraying diplomatic confidences. Two months later de Gaulle resigned, and in December the French veto on the British application was formally lifted by the new President, Georges Pompidou.

Social Chapter

Not to be confused with the **European Social Charter**, the Social Chapter, as its name implies, was originally intended to form part of that section of the **Maastricht Treaty** containing additions to the **Treaty of Rome** (which already contained a Title or 'chapter' on social policy). At the Maastricht meeting of the **European Council** in December 1991 John Major refused to accept amendments to the Social Chapter, with the result that they were taken out of the draft Treaty and signed by the other 11 member states as an agreement in a separate Social **Protocol** (the so-called 'British **opt-out**').

Article 1 of the Agreement committed the 11 member states to 'the promotion of employment, improved living and working conditions, proper social protection, dialogue between management and labour, the development of human resources with a view to lasting high employment and the combating of exclusion'. It required account to be taken 'of the diverse forms of national practices ... and the need to maintain the competitiveness of the Community economy'.

Under the Agreement, the **Council of Ministers** adopts legislation under the **cooperation procedure**, with the system of **qualified majority voting** (QMV) adjusted to take account of the non-participation of the United Kingdom. However, certain measures (social security, dismissals, representation of workers' and employers' interests, the employment rights of nationals of non-member countries, the financing of schemes to promote employment) are subject to unanimity under the **consultation procedure**. Exceptionally, Article 2.4 of the Agreement allows management and labour (that is, the **social partners**) to be responsible, 'at their joint request', for measures to implement Directives adopted under the Agreement.

In September 1994 the British opt-out was exercised for the first time in relation to draft Directives on works councils and parental leave brought forward under normal Treaty Articles. The exercise of the opt-out meant that the proposals were withdrawn and resubmitted under the Social Protocol. In this form, they were adopted.

All of the countries that joined the European Union in 1995 accepted the Social Protocol. The British Labour Party is committed to signing the Social Protocol in the event of becoming the party of government in the United Kingdom.

'Social dumping'

'Social dumping' occurs when one member state, by virtue of less restrictive labour laws or lower labour costs, succeeds in attracting or retaining job-creating investment in competition with other member states. The state thereby 'exports' unemployment to other states. The accusation of 'social dumping' is frequently made when a multinational company cuts production and jobs in one country and moves them to another within the Union, as happened in February 1993 when Hoover switched production from Dijon in France to Cambuslang near Glasgow. The United Kingdom's **opt-out** from the **Social Chapter** is widely believed in other member states to confer an advantage on British industry and commerce by opening up opportunities for 'social dumping'.

Social partners

By origin a French expression (*partenaires sociaux*), 'social partners' denotes what in English are better known as 'the two sides of industry', i.e., employers and employees. Within the European Union the **Economic and Social Committee** (ESC) is the institutional expression of the corporatism implicit in the idea of 'social partners'.

Social policy

'Social policy' is the expression normally used to denote labour law, the promotion of employment, working conditions and certain aspects of vocational training. Within the European Union it is governed by Articles 117–27 of the **Treaty of Rome**. The first of these Articles is unusually worded in that it merely records the fact that 'Member States agree upon the need to promote improved working conditions and an improved standard of living for workers' and that they 'believe' that this will be brought about by the functioning of the common market and by legislative action. The role of the **Commission** is to promote 'close cooperation between Member States in the social field' with respect to employment, labour law and working conditions, vocational training, social security, health and safety at work, and the rights of employees. The Commission, having consulted the **Economic and Social Committee** (ESC), is empowered to deliver **Opinions** in this field, to make studies and to arrange consultations. Article 118b EEC requires the Commission to 'endeavour to develop the dialogue between management and labour at European level' (see **social partners**). Other Articles deal with **equal treatment** of men and women and the **European Social Fund** (see also **education policy, European Centre for the Development of Vocational Training, European Foundation for the Improvement of Living and Working Conditions**). All these measures are intended to secure what Article 2 EEC describes as 'a high level of employment and of social protection, the raising of the standard of living and greater quality of life, and economic and social cohesion and solidarity among Member States'.

This apparently straightforward legal base in the Treaty has been made more complicated by the so-called 'British **opt-out**' from the **Social Chapter** in 1991, foreshadowed by the earlier refusal to sign the 1989 **European Social Charter**. The Commission may now bring forward legislative proposals in the normal way on the basis of the Treaty, and in the event of objections from the United Kingdom, resubmit them under the Social Chapter (officially, the 'Agreement on Social Policy' or Social Protocol). Disputes have also arisen over the legal base for social policy legislation: for example, in March 1994 the British government brought an action in the **Court of Justice** seeking to challenge the legal base upon which in November 1993 the **Council of Ministers** had adopted a Directive on working time. This had been proposed as a health and safety measure under Article 118a EEC, which allowed it to be adopted by **qualified majority**. The British government argued that the substance of the measure had little or no connection with health and safety, and that either **Article 100** or **Article 235** EEC – both of which require unanimous agreement – should have been chosen as the legal base.

In 1993 the Commission drew up a White Paper entitled *Growth, Competitiveness and Employment: the challenges and ways forward into the 21st century*. This was discussed at the Brussels meeting of the **European Council** on 10–11 December 1993 and accepted as 'a reference point for future work'. The White Paper showed how unemployment in the Union had risen during the late 1980s, and that by comparison with the United States and Japan, the Union had a far higher proportion of long-term unemployment (more than 40 per cent of the total had been unemployed for over a year) and a preponderance of young people. Unemployment might be cyclical in that it was related directly to changes in the level of economic activity, structural in so far as it related to underlying changes in the factors of production, or technological in the sense that it might originate from a failure to keep pace with technological advances. The Commission set a target of 15 million new jobs by the year 2000, an ambitious total given the failure of member states to create more than about 3 million jobs since 1974 (compared with almost 30 million in the United States). The Commission identified the main causes of unemployment as low rates of growth and of investment, declining international competitiveness, relatively high labour costs (wage and non-wage), failure to take advantage of new technology, 'inflexible' labour markets in the sense of low geographical and sectoral mobility, and an ageing population. The European Council accepted this analysis. On 22 December 1993 the Council of Ministers adopted a 'Recommendation on the broad guidelines of the economic policies of the Member States and of the Community', including exploiting the full potential of the **Single Market**, speeding up the completion of **trans-European networks** (TENs), reducing the indirect cost of labour, increasing expenditure on **research** and, most of all, securing 'non-inflationary, strong and employment-creating growth, lasting over many years and respecting the environment'. The Council also made some suggestions to member states as to how access to training and the mobility of labour might be improved.

The Commission followed up this Recommendation with the July 1994 White Paper on *European Social Policy: A way forward for the Union*. This refers to 'the European social model', defined as a 'unique blend of economic well-being, social cohesiveness and high overall quality of life'. At the same time it accepts the importance of maintaining Europe's international competitiveness as the key to job creation, which it identifies as the main priority against a background of high unemployment (estimated at 18 million people, some 11.6 per cent of the work force, in 1995). The White Paper recognizes the absence of consensus among member states on the role of European legislation in creating high labour standards and on the balance to be struck between such standards and a flexible, competitive labour market. Partly for this reason, the White Paper does not lay the groundwork for major new initiatives in social policy, preferring instead to consolidate progress so far achieved and to continue to press for solutions to problems already raised (such as the treatment of immigrant workers, improvements to the quality and availability of vocational training, and the need for further action on the **free movement of persons**).

It points out that 52 million people in the Union live below the 'poverty line', i.e., in households in which the expenditure is less than half the national average, and that demographic changes are steadily reducing the number of persons of working age as a proportion of the population as a whole (see **demography**).

Currently, social policy is one of the few areas of Union activity in which there are political as well as national differences of real substance permeating the debate. As President of the Commission, **Jacques Delors** sought to present social policy as the essential complement of the Single Market, the means whereby greater economic prosperity would be equitably shared. Delors was responsible for the moral urgency evident in many of the Commission's proposals. The next major step is likely to be an attempt to entrench social rights in the Treaty of Rome itself, on the basis of amendments agreed in the 1996 **Intergovernmental Conference** (IGC). Social policy has moved a long way from its modest beginnings as a means of ensuring that European-wide labour standards contributed to equal conditions of competition (see **social dumping**), and although the accusation of 'social engineering' is still sometimes heard, there is now widespread acceptance of the idea that something that is called a Community must have a social dimension.

Socialism

Socialist and Social Democratic parties are the largest political family in Europe. The Group of the Party of European Socialists (PES; see **transnational political parties**) is the largest of the **political groups** in the **European Parliament**. Amongst the newly emergent parties in central and eastern Europe, there are many that call themselves Social or Social Democrat, although several are largely made up of former Communists.

Historically, by comparison with Christian Democrats or Liberals, the Socialists have been less committed to European integration. In Italy and West Germany the Socialists voted against the **Treaty of Paris** when it was laid before **national parliaments** for their approval; in Belgium they abstained. French and Italian Socialists abstained when the **Treaty of Rome** was put to the vote, and in West Germany the Socialists expressed strong reservations. By far the most prominent Socialist pro-Europeans of the early years were the Belgian **Paul-Henri Spaak** and the Dutchman Sicco Mansholt (see **Mansholt Plan**). Well into the 1980s the British Labour Party, amongst the largest Socialist parties in Europe, was formally opposed to membership of the Community (the Party boycotted the European Parliament for the first two and a half years of British membership).

In recent years the Socialists, although not opposed in principle to the

Single Market programme, have none the less demanded a price for their support in the form of measures in the social and employment field. For example, in the European Parliament the PES Group effectively blocked measures to open up the insurance market until progress was made with the 1989 **Social Charter**. In this area, they have worked in collaboration with **Jacques Delors**. The Socialists have also tended to be more critical than other groups of the **Common Agricultural Policy** (CAP) and have been very active on environmental and consumer protection issues and in relation to the rights of minorities. With some exceptions, notably amongst British Labour Members, the Socialists have supported the Parliament's institutional initiatives such as the **Draft Treaty establishing the European Union** (DTEU). In foreign and security policy a strong anti-American feeling is still very much a factor, particularly amongst British, French and Spanish Socialists, some of whom have called for the **North Atlantic Treaty Organization** (NATO) to be wound up.

In spite of some reverses in national elections the Socialists seem certain to remain the most influential political force in Europe. **Enlargement** will bring into the Union many well-established Socialist parties already closely involved with the PES. By comparison with most other parties, the Socialists have a longer and livelier tradition of cross-frontier cooperation between parties, not least because the notion that class interests cut across those of the nation still informs much Socialist thinking.

There is a very extensive literature on Socialism, although much of the research is based on individual Socialist parties in particular countries. For Socialists' attitudes to European integration, see Kevin Featherstone, *Socialist Parties and European Integration: a comparative history* (Manchester, 1988).

Socrates

The Socrates programme of 1995–9 replaced the earlier ERASMUS and **Lingua** programmes in the field of student and teacher exchanges, language teaching and other activities concerned with the European dimension in education (see **education policy**).

Sovereignty

If sovereignty in relation to states is defined as an exclusive and comprehensive right of independent action, then it must follow that the member states of the European Union remain sovereign only in the sense that they could secede from the Union if they so wished. First under the **Treaty of Paris** and later under the **Treaty of Rome**, the signatory states committed themselves to creating, in the words of the preamble to the Treaty of Rome, an 'ever closer union among the peoples of Europe', and established independent supranational institutions enjoying their own exclusive jurisdiction. These institutions were endowed by Treaty with a capacity for making laws possessing both **primacy** and **direct effect** in the signatory states. The Treaty of Rome (unlike the Treaty of Paris) was concluded for an indefinite period and contained no provisions under which a signatory state could withdraw from the **European Economic Community** (EEC) thereby created.

It is sometimes said that in signing the **Treaties** the member states 'pooled' or 'merged' their sovereignty in the sense that they thereby committed themselves to exercising their sovereignty in common in certain specified areas. This idea is not consistent with the definition of sovereignty given above, under which the joint exercise of sovereignty is a contradiction in terms. It is more helpful to regard member states as having delegated their powers within certain well-defined limits to the institutions of what is now the European Union, albeit for an indefinite period. Such a delegation has occurred with respect to both internal and external actions. Member states have also chosen in those areas in which the European Union acts on an intergovernmental basis to exercise their powers in cooperation with one another (see **intergovernmentalism**).

In many contexts the word 'sovereignty' refers in fact to what is more accurately described as 'parliamentary sovereignty'. This may be defined as the exclusive and comprehensive right of a **national parliament** to make laws within the national constitutional framework. However, there now exists a Union-wide constitutional framework (see **Community law**) and as a consequence of this, national parliaments have lost their exclusive right to make laws that are binding upon their citizens. Until the **European Parliament** was directly elected in 1979, it could have been said that national parliaments had 'pooled' their sovereignty by appointing the Members of the European Parliament (MEPs), but now that direct elections have given the MEPs their own democratic legitimacy such authority as the Parliament enjoys is no longer dependent on the pooling of national parliamentary sovereignty.

That membership of the European Community or *a fortiori* of the European Union entails 'loss of sovereignty' is amongst the most basic of all the arguments deployed by anti-Europeans, especially in the context of **federalism**. It is usually countered by the assertion that the only sovereignty that counts is the ability of a state to defend or promote its own interests, and that to this end there may be some marginal sacrifice of the trappings of sovereignty in order to retain the substance. This counterargument misunderstands the nature of sovereignty and, in so doing, denies it the absolute value which those concerned with sovereignty believe it to possess.

Most treaties curtail the freedom of action of the signatory states in certain specific areas. To take only the most obvious example, the treaty establishing the **North Atlantic Treaty Organization** (NATO) obliges the signatory states to come to the aid of any NATO member threatened by aggression, and if necessary to go to war. In some sense therefore all treaties embodying obligations entail a loss of sovereignty; however, in international law a capacity freely to enter into obligations laid down by treaty is part of the definition of a sovereign state. What makes the Treaty of Rome and its successor Treaties qualitatively different from other treaties is the fact that the supranational institutions they create are able to draw up and adopt laws that are binding upon the signatory states. Moreover, the range of subjects goes well beyond those external actions with which most international treaties are concerned.

There is an extensive theoretical literature on sovereignty. Both provocative and accessible is Noel Malcolm, *Sense on Sovereignty* (1991), which is also useful for its references to other treatments of the subject. Still well worth reading is Stanley Hoffmann, 'Reflections on the Nation-State in Europe today', *Journal of Common Market Studies*, Vol. 21, nos 1 and 2 (1982), reprinted in *The European Sisyphus* (Boulder, Colorado, 1995).

Spaak, Paul-Henri (1899–1972)

Paul-Henri Spaak was a prominent figure in Belgian politics before the Second World War, holding ministerial office (including that of Foreign Minister) in various Socialist administrations. During the war he was a member of the Belgian government-in-exile in London. Much of his postwar career was in international or European politics. He was the first President of the General Assembly of the United Nations in 1946 and of the Consultative Assembly of the **Council of Europe** (1949–51, a post he resigned in protest against the United Kingdom's rejection of the **Schuman Plan**). A leading figure in negotiations amongst **the Six**, he chaired the committee (see **Spaak Committee**) set up after the **Messina Conference** to do the detailed preparatory work for the **European Economic Community**. From 1957 until 1961, he was Secretary-General of the **North Atlantic Treaty Organization** (NATO), before returning to Belgian politics as Foreign Minister.

Spaak was amongst the best-known advocates of European integration. At the same time, he was a strong Atlanticist and a keen supporter of British membership of the Community.

Spaak Committee

One of the decisions of the 1955 **Messina Conference** was to set up 'a Committee of government delegates' chaired by **Paul-Henri Spaak** to make proposals for closer economic integration amongst **the Six**. The Spaak Committee met for the first time in September 1955 and again in February 1956. Its final report was presented to the foreign ministers of the Six in Venice in May 1956.

The report, which was the basis for the two Treaties establishing the **European Economic Community** (EEC) and the **European Atomic Energy Community** (Euratom), was in three parts: the common market, nuclear energy, and the priority sectors requiring urgent action (including non-nuclear energy, transport and telecommunications). The foreign ministers accepted the report after only a brief discussion, the single proviso being that the **overseas countries and territories** (OCTs) of the signatory states should be included in any new economic unit (a concession to France). The report dealt only cursorily with institutional questions, proposing an institutional model broadly similar to that already established for the **European Coal and Steel Community** (ECSC): a Council of national ministers, an independent Commission, a Parliament, and a Court of Justice.

The United Kingdom government had sent an observer to the Messina Conference but, although invited, took no part in the work of the Spaak Committee. Officially, its position was that the **customs union** towards which the Six were obviously moving was incompatible with British preferential trading arrangements with the Commonwealth. However, against the background of the Suez Crisis and the abortive Hungarian uprising, the Six were determined to move ahead as rapidly as possible. Ten months after the Venice meeting the EEC and Euratom Treaties were signed in Rome (see also **Pierre Uri**).

The Spaak Committee is often referred to as a turning-point in the prehistory of European Union. Its success was in part attributed to the fact that it was composed not of officials but of people who by virtue of their experience and seniority enjoyed the confidence of the leaders of the various governments. For this reason the 1984 **Dooge Committee** was deliberately modelled on the Spaak Committee.

Spain

Spain originally applied to join **the Six** in 1962, but the application was blocked on the grounds that the regime of General Francisco Franco was undemocratic. After Franco's death in 1975, Spain applied again (28 July 1977), three months after Portugal. A favourable Commission **Opinion** was published the following year and Spain joined the Community on 1 January 1986.

Like Portugal, Spain was attracted to Community membership as a means of re-entering the European political and economic mainstream after more than a generation of near-total isolation. However, unlike Portugal, Spain was a formidable commercial, industrial and agricultural rival to the Community's member states, especially France and Italy. **Accession** negotiations were long and difficult, not least because adaptation to Community disciplines required Spain to dismantle much of the protectionist, corporatist apparatus that was part of the Francoist legacy. Community membership was particularly attractive to many of the larger Spanish regions, such as the Basque provinces and Catalonia, as providing an alternative institutional framework to the one offered by the Spanish state. The **structural funds**, for example, from which Spain has drawn substantial benefits, were interesting to the regions as a pretext for direct contacts with Brussels: and in the **Maastricht Treaty** negotiations Spain was a strong supporter of the proposal for a **Committee of the Regions**. In the same negotiations Spain put forward the proposals on **citizenship**.

Internationally, Spanish accession resulted in a reorientation of the Community's trade and development policies towards Latin America, although perhaps not on the scale that the Spanish would have liked. **Gibraltar** remains an irritant in relations with the United Kingdom. Spain has an enormous fishing fleet, and full integration into the **Common Fisheries Policy** has always been a high Spanish priority.

Latent anti-American feeling led to a divisive referendum in 1986 on Spain's continued membership of the **North Atlantic Treaty Organization** (NATO), which the country had joined in 1982. More recently, Spain has decided to commit forces to the **Eurocorps**.

There is no significant opposition to European integration in Spain. Europe remains identified with liberty, modernization, prosperity and the energetic pursuit of Spanish interests.

Spinelli, Altiero (1907–86)

Born in Rome, Altiero Spinelli was a lifelong advocate of **federalism**. A journalist and a vigorous opponent of fascism, he was arrested in 1927 and spent 10 years in prison and a further 6 in 'confinement'. During the Second World War he was interned on the island of Ventotene in the Gulf of Gaeta along with some 800 others hostile to Mussolini's regime.

In June 1941 Spinelli and a small group of federalists completed a 'manifesto', the final version of which was written on cigarette papers and concealed in the false bottom of a tin box. It was circulated clandestinely within the Resistance and adopted as the programme of the Movimento Federalista Europeo, which Spinelli founded in August 1943. It has been published both in Italian and in translation many times since.

The manifesto began with a critique of the totalitarian state, which had developed from the 'ideology of national independence' and 'the seeds of capitalist imperialism'. However, the defeat of Germany would merely allow the British and the Americans to restore the nation-states in their old form, in a pattern consistent with their economic and geopolitical interests. This must be resisted at all costs: federalists must seize the opportunity presented by the turmoil and uncertainty that would accompany the end of the war to establish a 'European Federation . . . a free and united Europe'. Chief amongst the tasks of such a federation must be social reconstruction, ending the pre-eminence of the Catholic Church, and the abandonment of corporatism. In short, the federalists should prepare a set of new institutions as the moulds into which the 'incandescent lava' of popular feeling could be allowed to pour, there to cool and settle.

After the war Spinelli resumed his career as a journalist. He was the founder of the Istituto per Affari Internazionali in 1967 and in 1970 became a member of the **European Commission**, with responsibility for industrial policy. He resigned towards the end of 1976 in order to stand for election to the Camera dei Deputati, where he served on the Foreign Affairs Committee and became chairman of his parliamentary group. At the same time he was nominated as a Member of the **European Parliament** (MEP).

In 1979 he was elected to the European Parliament as an Independent of the Left (Indipendente di Sinistra) in the first direct elections, and joined the Communist Group. Although a man of the Left (he joined the Italian Communist Party in 1924 but resigned in 1937), Spinelli was too independent to fit at all easily into any particular party. A powerful rather than subtle orator, his ability to persuade people rested upon his force of personality and the tenacity with which he pursued an argument.

Until his death in 1986, Spinelli campaigned vigorously for wide-ranging reforms to the Community institutions. He did this first through a series of informal meetings known as the **Crocodile Club** (after the Strasbourg restaurant in which the Group was founded in July 1980) and from January 1981 in the newly established Committee on Institutional Affairs. The European Parliament's **Draft Treaty establishing the European Union** (DTEU), which was adopted in February 1984, was the principal monument to the final period of Spinelli's life.

In his autobiography, *Come ho tentato di diventare saggio* (How I Sought To Become Wise), Spinelli outlined the intellectual basis of his passionate attachment to federalism and to European unity. Ironically, in the light of the very cool reception his ideas received in the United Kingdom, he always claimed that his principal source of inspiration were the federalist ideas of British and American theorists such as Lothian and Madison. Although his DTEU did not in the end command widespread support outside the Parliament, there were many who argued (amongst them

Jacques Delors) that without it the **Single European Act** (SEA) could never have been brought into being.

State aids

State aids – financial assistance from public funds to commercial enterprises, public or private – that distort conditions of competition within the Union are subject to strict rules laid down in Articles 92–4 of the **Treaty of Rome** as part of **competition policy**. Such aids must in all circumstances be notified to the **Commission**, which can block them or, in the case of state aids already granted, insist upon repayment. To be approved, state aids must be of a specified amount and time-limited, and in the case of an enterprise in difficulties may be given only in conjunction with a restructuring programme. They may also be approved if it can be shown that they are consistent with broader regional policy aims, likely to create new investment, given in response to emergency needs, linked to 'an important project of common European interest' or designed to 'remedy a serious disturbance in the economy of a Member State'. The **Court of Justice** is the ultimate arbiter of the lawfulness of state aids.

Some decisions on state aids can be controversial, as in the case of the approval given by the Commission to the operating subsidies granted to Air France and other airlines in June 1994. The long list in the Treaty of circumstances in which state aids may be granted provides plenty of scope for ingenious economic arguments driven by essentially political motives. Under the **European Economic Area** (EEA) Treaty the rules on state aids now apply throughout the EEA.

Strasbourg

The capital of Alsace, Strasbourg is an ancient cathedral city of about 500,000 inhabitants on the French side of the Rhine. In common with the rest of Alsace, Strasbourg has changed hands several times between France and Germany over the centuries and its inhabitants speak both French and a German dialect known as *Elsässisch*. For this reason the city has been regarded as a symbol of Franco-German reconciliation since the Second World War.

In 1949, on a proposal from the British Foreign Secretary Ernest Bevin, Strasbourg was chosen as the seat of the **Council of Europe**. A Palais de l'Europe was built, which by 1952 was serving not only as the headquarters of the Council of Europe but also as the place in which meetings of the Common Assembly of the **European Coal and Steel Community** (ECSC) were held (see **seat of the institutions**). Since 1958 the **European Parliament**, the successor to the Common Assembly, has held most of its monthly part-sessions in Strasbourg. A larger Palais was built in 1977 to accommodate the directly elected European Parliament, but by the late 1990s this too will have been outgrown and a third, even larger Palais is now being built.

Strasbourg's status as the self-styled 'parliamentary capital of Europe' is under threat from moves to concentrate the main institutions of the European Union in **Brussels**. Although the Council of Europe, the European Court of Human Rights and, since 1991, the **Eurocorps** would in any case remain in Strasbourg, the city is determined to retain the part-sessions of the European Parliament. This position has always been defended with peculiar tenacity by French governments of whatever political complexion, to the point of Strasbourg's status being non-negotiable. By showing themselves prepared to block other decisions on the siting of newly created European institutions, the French finally secured agreement at the Edinburgh meeting of the European Council in December 1992 that Strasbourg should be the 'seat' of the European Parliament and that its normal monthly part-sessions should continue to be held there. Since this decision did not curb the desire of many Members of the European Parliament (MEPs) to move to Brussels, where an even larger building programme is under way, the French National Assembly, backed by the French government, took the further step in 1994 of blocking the agreement to increase the number of MEPs in time for the June 1994 European elections until 'precise and written' assurances were given on the holding of 12 part-sessions a year in Strasbourg and the lease on the new premises was signed.

Although the behaviour of the French on the subject of Strasbourg may be thought unreasonable, they are not alone in their attachment to the city as a symbol of Franco-German reconciliation. Many Germans feel the same way: as Helmut Schmidt once replied when asked whether he favoured Brussels or Strasbourg, 'My head is in Brussels but my heart is in Strasbourg.' Although the city, the *département* and the French state have all invested very heavily in keeping the Parliament in Strasbourg, the city is handicapped by poor air services to the rest of Europe. By car or by train Strasbourg is over four hours away from Brussels. In 1993 a general sense of outrage greeted the French railways' proposal to bypass Strasbourg on the TGV-Est route from Paris to (ultimately) Munich. The proposal was altered accordingly.

In addition to the revenue generated for the city's hotels and restaurants by the regular presence of several thousand MEPs, officials and journalists, the European Parliament paid rent amounting to over £10 million in 1993 for the buildings (debating chamber, MEPs' offices, offices for officials) used in Strasbourg for a maximum of 60 days in the year (*Hansard*, WA Col. 82, 18 October 1993).

Stresa Conference

In July 1958, soon after the **Treaty of Rome** came into force, Sicco Mansholt (see **Mansholt Plan**), the Dutch Vice-President of the **Commission** and responsible for the **Common Agricultural Policy** (CAP), convened a conference of Commission officials, national experts and representatives of farmers' organizations to decide how to accomplish the objectives of the CAP as set out in Article 39 EEC. The conference was held at Stresa on Lake Maggiore. Perhaps its most far-reaching decision was to support agriculture through a system of guaranteed prices rather than direct income aids (see **intervention**).

Structural funds

The term 'structural funds' is used to denote the **European Social Fund** (ESF), the **European Regional Development Fund** (ERDF), the 'guidance' section of the **European Agricultural Guidance and Guarantee Fund** (EAGGF) and the Fisheries Guidance Instrument (FGI). They are the principal means whereby aid is directed towards the less-developed regions of the European Union. In total, the structural funds amounted to almost £16 billion in 1994, and by 2000 will represent about one-third of the Union's **Budget**. Building on the reform of the structural funds that came into effect in 1989, five basic objectives were identified:

Objective 1 assisting underdeveloped regions;
Objective 2 assisting regions affected by the decline of traditional industries;
Objective 3 combating long-term unemployment (defined as more than 12 months) and the integration of young people (under-25s) into the labour market;
Objective 4 helping workers adapt to technological change;
Objective 5 (a) structural reform of agriculture and (b) helping rural areas.

Of these, Objective 1 is by far the most important, absorbing some 70 per cent of total funds. The **enlargement** negotiations with Austria, Finland, Norway and Sweden resulted in the creation of an Objective 6 category, designed primarily to allow assistance to be given to the Arctic regions. To qualify for Objective 6 assistance an area must have a population density of fewer than eight people per square kilometre and a below-average per capita gross domestic product (GDP).

The ERDF is concerned primarily with Objectives 1 and 2, the ESF with Objectives 3 and 4, and the EAGGF with Objective 5 (although all three funds may contribute towards Objective 5b). Objectives 1, 2 and 5b require maps to be drawn, and periodically redrawn, to define which areas qualify for assistance. This is done by the **European Commission** in consultation with member states. Objective 1 regions cover approximately 27 per cent of the Union's total population. In all cases financial assistance from the structural funds, which is always given in the form of grants, is intended to complement assistance given at the national level (see **addition- ality**). In certain cases assistance may also be given in the form of loans by the **European Investment Bank** (EIB).

The first stage, known as the planning stage, requires member states, in consultation with regional or local authorities, to prepare development plans that set out how structural fund assistance will be used and, where relevant, the environmental impact of the projects envisaged. On the basis of these, the Commission draws up 'Community Support Frameworks'. The operational stage is the responsibility of national, regional or local authorities. The final stage allows the programmes and projects to be monitored and evaluated and, if necessary, adjusted in the light of experi- ence. Some 9 per cent of structural fund aid is reserved for initiatives devised and administered directly by the Commission.

The accession of Greece in 1981 and of Portugal and Spain in 1986 posed a challenge to the commitment in the Preamble to the **Treaty of Rome** to 'reduce the differences existing between the various regions and the backwardness of the less-favoured regions'. It was also argued that the programme for the completion of the **Single Market** would increase still further the advantages enjoyed by the core regions over those on the periphery. **Integrated Mediterranean Programmes** (IMPs) were set up to give special help to Greece and the Mediterranean regions of France and Italy, and between 1987 and 1993 the structural funds were doubled in size. At the Edinburgh meeting of the **European Council** in December 1992 it was agreed to double the funds again over the period 1994–9 (see **Edinburgh Growth Initiative**). The **Maastricht Treaty** set out the role of the structural funds in amendments to the Treaty of Rome (Articles 130a–e) under the title 'Economic and social cohesion' and required a **Cohesion Fund** to be set up before 31 December 1993.

Although they have grown substantially since their inception, in 1993 the structural funds amounted to barely a third of 1 per cent of the member states' combined GDP. As the **MacDougall Report** demonstrated in 1977, this is well short of the sums required for a significant redistributive effect. However, in the main beneficiary countries (Ireland, Greece and Portugal) receipts from the structural funds amount to some 5 per cent of GDP. In other countries too, notably Italy, Spain and the United Kingdom, the structural funds have had an impact on particular regions. Although regional disparities lessened slightly in the 1970s, they widened again in the 1980s. With **German reunification** they have widened further: Germany now has both the richest (Hamburg) and the poorest (Thüringen) regions in the Union. The difficulty of calculating the overall economic impact of the structural funds is compounded by what is known as 'leakage': the fact that a beneficiary region will increase its imports from other parts of the Union as a result of new investment, thus benefiting other more prosperous regions. The methodological problems and some tentative conclusions are clearly set out in a European Parliament study of December 1993 entitled *The efficiency of regional policy in the European Union*.

Stuttgart Declaration

The Stuttgart Declaration, formally known as the Solemn Declaration on European Union, was a wide-ranging statement concerning the institutions and policies of the European Community issued by the **European Council** meeting in Stuttgart on 17–19 June 1983. It represented the first serious attempt by the European Council to address the question of institutional reform and to push forward the 1972 objective of converting the Community into some form of **European Union**. In terms deliberately reminiscent of the Paris summit, the heads of government restated their determination to 'transform the whole complex of relations between their states into a European Union', envisaging for the first time the future adoption of a Treaty on European Union. It also attempted to codify the evolving role of the European Council in decision-making, and suggested that the position of the **European Parliament** should be significantly enhanced and the scope of Community activity further broadened.

The Stuttgart Declaration was the governments' response to the **Genscher–Colombo Plan**, the text of which it echoed in a number of respects. It stressed the importance of developing **European Political Cooperation** and of common action in respect of 'the political and economic aspects of security', although it fell short of proposing a 'common foreign policy'. It explained the European Council's role in promoting closer integration, declaring that henceforth the European Council would be able to act 'in its capacity as the Council [of Ministers]' in any area of Community responsibility (which was, in fact, legally invalid, since action still required the latter's separate and subsequent endorsement). It confirmed that the President-in-Office of the European Council would report to the European Parliament at least once every six months.

The Stuttgart Declaration did not attempt to subvert the **Luxembourg Compromise**, but it did assert that 'the application of the decision-making procedures laid down in the Treaties is of vital importance in order to improve the EC's capacity to act' (Paragraph 2.2.2). Even this statement was sufficiently controversial to generate statements in the Minutes from all 10 member states, setting out their various views on the Luxembourg Compromise. The Declaration did not endorse the proposal in the Genscher–Colombo Plan to establish new councils for policy areas not provided for in the **Treaties**.

The Declaration was generous in its acknowledgement of the growing role of the European Parliament. It took up the proposal in the Genscher–Colombo Plan to engage in non-binding consultation with the Parliament before the President of the **Commission** was appointed and before new member states were admitted to the Community. Consultation was extended to include all 'significant' international agreements (see **assent procedure**).

The Declaration sought to extend Community activity across a broad range of pressing issues. In this it reflected the growing interest of the French government in using the European Community to counteract the effects of recession. It spoke of an 'overall economic strategy' to combat unemployment and inflation, and to promote convergence among national economies. It proposed a strengthening of the **European Monetary System** (EMS), including the development of a European Monetary Fund. It identified the 'completion of the internal market' – one of the first official statements to use this phrase – and the 'development of an industrial strategy' as key Community objectives. It asserted that European Union was being achieved 'by deepening and broadening the scope of European activities so that they coherently cover . . . a growing proportion of Member States' mutual relations', a process it evidently welcomed.

The fact that the Stuttgart Declaration was a statement of political will, not a Treaty, rendered its conclusions ultimately unenforceable. However, the striking fact is that many of them were given legal force three years later in the **Single European Act** (SEA). The two exercises were linked by the commitment at the end of the Declaration to decide within five years on 'whether the progress achieved [in the interim] should be incorporated in a Treaty on European Union'.

The Stuttgart Declaration was widely criticized in the European Parliament and elsewhere for the non-binding nature of its commitments (the Parliament's much more ambitious **Draft Treaty establishing the European Union** (DTEU) was adopted the following year). The Declaration did, however, mark a decisive shift in favour of closer integration, especially on the part of the French government. It was under a French **presidency** that the Versailles European Council set up both the **Dooge Committee** and the Adonnino Committee on a **People's Europe** in June 1984.

Subsidiarity

Subsidiarity is the principle that decisions should be taken at the lowest level consistent with effective action within a political system. Held to be a guiding principle of federalism (see **federation**), it has also been widely invoked in recent years as a means of limiting the European Union's competence. The **Maastricht Treaty** introduced a subsidiarity clause into the **Treaty of Rome**: 'In areas which do not fall within its exclusive competence, the Community shall take action, in accordance with the principle of subsidiarity, only if and in so far as the objectives of the proposed action cannot be sufficiently achieved by the Member States and can therefore, by reason of the scale or effects of the proposed action, be better achieved by the Community' (Article 3b EEC; see also **proportionality**). Although the principle now enjoys Treaty status, most commentators are uncertain about its long-term significance in the integration process. In particular, many lawyers doubt that the principle is 'justiciable', that is, sufficiently precise in point of substance and intent to be capable of being enforced.

The principle of subsidiarity finds a parallel in the Tenth Amendment to the United States Constitution and in Article 30 of the German Constitution, both of which reserve to the states or *Länder* powers not specifically allocated to the federal government. The principle is also to be found in Pope Pius XI's encyclical '*Quadragesimo Anno*' of 1931, in which it was invoked as a means of maintaining the authority of the Church against the ever-encroaching power of the state.

In the context of European integration, subsidiarity was referred to for the first time in the **European Commission**'s submission to the **Tindemans Report** on European Union in June 1975. Paragraph 12 states: 'No more than the existing Communities have done so, European Union is not to give birth to a centralizing superstate. Consequently, and in accordance with the *principe de subsidiarité*, the Union will be given responsibility only for those matters which the Member States are no longer capable of dealing with efficiently.' The Commission's motive for invoking subsidiarity was to reassure those who feared that conversion of the Community into a European Union would substantially erode the powers of national governments and parliaments. The Tindemans Report itself went less far than the Commission would have liked in proposing immediate steps towards Union, and perhaps for that reason did not include the subsidiarity principle among its recommendations. Little more was heard of the idea, outside academic circles, for several years.

Subsidiarity was revived in February 1984 when the **European Parlia-**

ment adopted its ambitious and highly integrationist **Draft Treaty establishing the European Union** (DTEU). Like the Commission in 1975, the Parliament sought to invoke subsidiarity as a means of forestalling concern within national political circles that closer European integration must necessarily involve an open-ended transfer of powers to centralized bodies at European level. The Parliament's text sought to entrench subsidiarity as a central principle of further unification by writing it into the Draft Treaty – the proposed successor document to the Treaty of Rome – in two ways: first, by a general reference in the Preamble, and second, in a more specific Article defining the relationship between the new Union and the member states in areas where they shared competence.

In the Preamble, Parliament's aim was 'to entrust common institutions ... only with those powers required to complete successfully the tasks they may carry out more satisfactorily than the states acting independently'. The more detailed formula later in the text asserted that 'the Union shall only act to carry out those tasks which may be undertaken more effectively in common than by the Member States acting separately, in particular those whose execution requires action by the Union because their dimensions or effects extend beyond national frontiers' (Article 12(2)).

Although several member states sympathized with the Parliament's objectives, discussion of the principle was surprisingly muted during the subsequent **Intergovernmental Conference** leading to the 1986 **Single European Act** (SEA). The final text eschewed any general reference to subsidiarity, but did embody the principle indirectly in one policy area – environmental affairs. It inserted a new article into the Treaty of Rome, which stated: 'The Community shall take action relating to the environment to the extent to which [objectives] can be attained better at the Community level than at the level of individual Member States' (Article 130r.4, since repealed).

Although not yet of general application, the principle of subsidiarity was invoked from the mid-1980s by national governments intent upon keeping the Commission in check. This was especially true of the British government, which in 1989 cited subsidiarity as one of the reasons for not signing the **Social Charter**. By the time the Maastricht Treaty was finally agreed in December 1991, subsidiarity had also become important to the German government, which was seeking to address the problems of **German reunification** while maintaining its strongly pro-integration stance in European affairs. Defeats in *Länder* elections had resulted in a loss of control of the Bundesrat (composed of representatives of the *Länder*) and the government turned to the subsidiarity principle as a means of affirming its attachment both to the rights of the *Länder* and to strong European institutions. The wording of the subsidiarity clause in the Treaty of Rome (see above) was a compromise between the British and German positions. The Maastricht Treaty itself described the new European Union as one 'in which decisions are taken as closely as possible to the citizen' (Article A).

The 'no' vote in the Danish referendum of June 1992 made it clear that the Maastricht Treaty wording on subsidiarity was inadequate. Accordingly, a fuller definition was drawn up at the Birmingham meeting of the **European Council** in October 1992: 'Decisions must be taken as closely as possible to the citizen. Greater unity can be achieved without excessive centralization. It is for each Member State to decide how its powers should be exercised domestically ... Action at the Community level should happen only when proper and necessary.'

The incorporation of subsidiarity into the Treaty of Rome prompted **Jacques Delors** to suggest that animal welfare might be an area in which the Commission should cease to be involved – an area that he knew to be of great interest to the British. A more considered Commission response, even before the Maastricht Treaty finally entered into force in November 1993, was to review all current and draft European Union legislation with a view to identifying matters on which it was no longer appropriate for action to be taken at European level. Since the Brussels meeting of the European Council in December 1993 the Commission has been required to produce an annual report on the application of the subsidiarity principle.

As the wording of Article 3b EEC makes clear, subsidiarity applies only to areas that do not fall within the 'exclusive competence' of the Community. This means that however effective the subsidiarity principle may prove to be as a way of preventing the Union institutions from moving into new areas, it is of only very limited use to those who would like to see the institutions returning powers to national or local authorities in areas already covered by the **Treaties**. The wording gives no guidance with regard to how an assessment could be made of whether an objective might be 'better achieved by the Community', and it is this reliance on essentially subjective judgments that is at the root of the legal difficulties posed by the subsidiarity clause.

The long-term importance of subsidiarity will depend on how and if the **Court of Justice** chooses to interpret and apply the principle. The Court may either find the subsidiarity clause to be too general to use in specific rulings, or choose to interpret its ambiguous provisions in a consistently pro-integrationist direction, so defeating the purpose for which it was intended. Some experts fear that it will introduce a new legal principle that cuts across the whole basis of existing jurisprudence in an unpredictable and confusing way, further politicizing the Court and prejudicing its authority. The **Council of Ministers** has denied that subsidiarity has any bearing on the allocation of powers within member states. Moreover, the European Council has stated that the subsidiarity principle does not have **direct effect** (see Joint Answer to Written Questions by Mr Arbeloa Muru, *Official Journal*, C102, 11 April 1994).

Subsidiarity is perhaps best seen as a political, not a judicial, principle. Once legislation has been passed, the Court's responsibility should extend not to whether any law was actually necessary or desirable, but only to whether its adoption was procedurally correct and consistent with the established limits of Union competence. It is not the function of the Court to make essentially political judgments about effectiveness and the sufficiency of the powers of member states by comparison with those of the institutions of the Union.

In the short term subsidiarity has already made a substantial impact. Few speeches are made on the development of the Union without some reference to subsidiarity. Easy to enunciate but difficult to apply, the principle will serve a useful purpose if it prompts clear thinking on the role and efficiency of national and European institutions within a larger, more diverse European Union.

Subsidiarity already has a literature of its own, much of it in learned periodicals. See especially Andrew Adonis and Andrew Tyrie, *Subsidiarity, as History and Policy* (1990); *Subsidiarity: the challenge of change* (proceedings of the Jacques Delors colloquium at the European Institute of Public Administration, Maastricht, 1991); Andrew Adonis and Andrew Tyrie, *Subsidiarity: No Panacea* (1992); Akos Toth, 'Is subsidiarity justiciable?', *European Law Review*, Vol. 19, no. 3, June 1994; John Peterson, 'Subsidiarity: a definition to suit any vision', *Political Affairs*, Vol. 47, no. 1, January 1994; Centre for Economic Policy Research, *Making Sense of Subsidiarity* (1993); Anthony L. Teasdale, 'Subsidiarity in Post-Maastricht Europe', *Political Quarterly*, Vol. 64, no. 2, April–June 1993.

Summer time

Summer time begins on the same day throughout the European Union and ends on the fourth Sunday in September in all countries except Ireland and the United Kingdom. In those two countries summer time ends four weeks later, resulting in additional costs for transport operators and confusion for travellers. It is proposed that from 1997 summer time should begin on the fourth Sunday in March and end on the fourth Sunday in October throughout the **European Economic Area** (EEA). It is not proposed to make the EEA a single time zone. The sun rises in the most easterly part of Finland some two and a half hours earlier than in the west of Ireland.

Summit

Meetings of heads of government are often referred to as summits. The first summit involving heads of government of the member states of the European Community (then **the Six**) was held in February 1961 (see **Fouchet Plan**). Formalized since 1975, such summits are now known as meetings of the **European Council**.

Supreme Headquarters Allied Powers Europe (SHAPE)

In December 1950 a Supreme Allied Commander Europe (SACEUR) was appointed within the framework of the **North Atlantic Treaty Organization** (NATO). SACEUR's headquarters, known as Supreme Headquarters Allied Powers Europe (SHAPE), were set up the following year in Rocquencourt, near Paris. In 1967, when France withdrew from NATO's integrated military command structure, SHAPE was moved to its present site outside Mons, Belgium. Over 1,000 officers and 2,000 other service personnel (plus 1,500 civilians) make up the SHAPE staff, including the national military representatives accredited to SACEUR. Under the **Partnership for Peace** initiative, Partner states are entitled to establish liaison offices at SHAPE.

Sweden

Although Sweden, a neutral country in both World Wars, has consistently followed a policy of not joining military alliances, it was nevertheless a founder member of the **Organization for Economic Cooperation and Development** (OECD), the **Council of Europe** and the **European Free Trade Association** (EFTA). Sweden has also played a very active role in the **Nordic Council**. Like Austria, Sweden sought at an early stage to establish closer economic ties with the Community, but the negotiations of the 1960s and 1970s resulted only in the free trade arrangement extended to all EFTA countries with effect from January 1973 and, later, in Sweden's membership of the **European Economic Area** (EEA). The question of full membership of the Community remained an issue in Swedish politics and eventually an application for membership was deposited by the Socialist Government of Ingvar Carlsson on 1 July 1991. On the conclusion of the **Maastricht Treaty** in December 1991 Carlsson's successor, the Conservative Carl Bildt, reaffirmed his government's commitment to the aims of the European Union established by the Treaty, including its provisions for a **Common Foreign and Security Policy** (CFSP): this was particularly significant in the light of Sweden's long-standing unilateral commitment to **neutrality**. In 1991 the decision was taken to link the Swedish krona to the ECU.

In point of performance the economy of Sweden – one of the most prosperous countries in the world – poses few problems. However, as the Commission's generally favourable **Opinion** pointed out, the structure of the economy, and notably the numerous state monopolies, cartels and the absence of competition generally, will require some adjustment if it is to conform with the **Treaty of Rome** (*Bulletin of the European Communities*, supplement 5/92). Much of this adjustment has been undertaken in the context of the EEA Treaty, and Sweden already applies most of the **Single Market** legislation. Unlike Austria's, Sweden's commitment to neutrality is not enshrined in the constitution, but is none the less well established over a long period. The decline in East–West tension prompted a debate within Sweden on what 'neutrality' now means in practice, and it is now believed to be compatible with the European Union's aspirations towards a common security policy and with the concrete actions arising from it.

The negotiations with Sweden were completed in March 1994. Two months later the **European Parliament** gave its assent to membership. The public debate that preceded the **referendum** of 13 November 1994 (in which membership was supported by 52.2 per cent of the vote) centred upon the future of Swedish agriculture and the impact on the 'Swedish model' of society. The Union is likely to benefit from Sweden's prosperity, stability and high standards in such areas as education, the environment and respect for women's rights. Sweden will also bring into the Union a strong tradition of openness (see **transparency**) in public affairs. Equally, Sweden may hope to gain from exposure to more vigorous competition and the challenge of having to play a role on a wider political stage. Sweden became the fifteenth member of the European Union on 1 January 1995. In the September 1995 European elections, 11 of Sweden's 22 MEPs were elected from anti-European parties.

Switzerland

Switzerland's well-established policy of not joining the international organizations to which most other Western countries belong began to change in the 1990s. Switzerland became a member of the International Monetary Fund and the World Bank in 1992, but in the same year membership of the **European Economic Area** (EEA) was rejected in a **referendum**. Although a member of the **Council of Europe** since 1963 and a founder member of the **European Free Trade Association** (EFTA), Switzerland remains only an observer member of the United Nations, having rejected full membership in a 1986 referendum. In June 1992 the Swiss government applied for membership of the Union; the rejection of the EEA Agreement resulted in the application being left in abeyance. In common with other EFTA states, Switzerland already had free trade arrangements for manufactured goods with the European Community, but the establishment of the **Single Market** and the relaxation of East–West tension led to a reappraisal of Swiss interests and of the country's long tradition of **neutrality**. Bilateral agreements between Switzerland and the European Union are being negotiated in the following areas: **free movement of persons**, **research** and technology, agriculture, mutual recognition of product standards and **public purchasing**.

Intra-Community commercial traffic through Switzerland has long been governed by a series of transit agreements. In February 1994 the Swiss voted in a referendum effectively to ban all commercial road traffic through their country with effect from 2004. This decision is being followed up in a number of very ambitious projects involving new railway tunnels through the Alps (notably the St Gotthard route) and the further development of combined road–rail transport.

Switzerland is a confederation, with four official languages, in which a very strong sense of local identity co-exists with an equally strong sense of national identity. For this reason Switzerland has occasionally been held up as a model of how a united Europe could work. In fact, the Swiss nation was built up gradually over some 700 years on the basis of a very particular combination of geographic, political, religious and historical circumstances. The country is governed at the federal, cantonal and communal level, at each of which recourse may be had to a referendum under constitutional provisions introduced in 1874 as a means of limiting the power of central government. Amongst the most prosperous countries in the world, Switzerland could easily meet the economic obligations of membership of the Union. What is less certain is whether the Swiss, with their lively attachment to direct democracy, neutrality and separate identity, are yet prepared to adapt to a system in which supranational institutions play a pre-eminent role and which would require them to open both their frontiers and their economy to other Europeans.

TACIS

The TACIS programme (Technical Assistance to the Commonwealth of Independent States, CIS) dates from a December 1990 decision by the **European Council** meeting in Rome. Its main objective is to help the so-called Newly Independent States (NIS; the 10 members of the CIS plus Azerbaijan and Georgia) make the transition to a market economy and a democratic society. TACIS, which is administered by the **Commission**, became operational in 1991. Assistance of the type given by TACIS has been extended to Mongolia (see also **PHARE**).

Five priority sectors were identified in 1991: training (see also **European Training Foundation**), energy (including, most importantly, nuclear safety), transport, support for industrial and commercial enterprises, food production and distribution. TACIS aid is given in the form of grants, on the basis of indicative programmes drawn up in consultation with the beneficiary states. The TACIS authorities also work closely with other countries and international agencies in this field, a process that began with the Coordinating Conference on Assistance to the NIS held in Washington, Lisbon and Tokyo in 1992. At the time of this conference it was estimated that the European Community and its member states were responsible for about three-quarters of the aid being given to the NIS. A Central Consultancy Register of firms within the Union interested in participating in TACIS projects is held by the Commission. Together, the TACIS and PHARE programmes amount to almost £1.3 billion, about a third of the sums allocated to 'external actions' in the **Budget** for 1995.

Tax harmonization

Tax harmonization has always been subsidiary to other Treaty objectives, never an area of Community action in its own right, and is almost wholly limited to indirect taxation. Articles 95–8 of the **Treaty of Rome** require member states not to apply discriminatory taxes in order to favour domestically produced goods. Article 99 EEC empowers the **Council of Ministers** to 'adopt provisions for the harmonization of legislation concerning turnover taxes, excise duties and other forms of indirect taxation to the extent that such harmonization is necessary to ensure the establishment and the functioning of the internal market'. Tax measures may also be taken under Article 100 EEC (see **Articles 100 and 100a**). An indication of the sensitivity of the subject is the fact that, as an exception to what is now the general rule where **Single Market** measures are concerned, **unanimity** is required for all Council measures on tax (see also **value-added tax**). Some proposals on direct taxation of companies were first put forward as long ago as 1969.

The 1985 **Cockfield White Paper** identified the fiscal barriers to trade within the Single Market. Amongst these were different rates and systems of excise duties. Minimum rates of duty for alcohol, tobacco, cigarettes and mineral oil were agreed in 1992. However, as part of the removal of frontier controls, the point at which goods are taxed is being moved from the country of destination to the country of origin: this means that whatever differences there may be in national tax systems and tax rates, adjustments to the amounts of tax paid no longer have to be made at borders between member states. The full system, based on the origin principle, is due to come into effect by the end of 1996.

The harmonization of indirect tax rates within the Single Market combined with the removal of frontier controls pointed to the termination of 'duty-free' sales. Under a special arrangement, these will be continued until 1999, accompanied by very substantial increases in the quantities of dutiable tax-paid goods that travellers within the Union may now convey without formalities across internal frontiers.

The background to tax harmonization is set out very clearly in Dennis Swann, *The Economics of the Common Market*.

Thatcher, Margaret (b. 1925)

Margaret Thatcher defeated **Edward Heath** in the contest for the leadership of the Conservative Party (then in opposition) in February 1975. Four years later, in May 1979, the Conservative Party was returned to power under her leadership and the following month, the Conservatives won 60 out of the 78 seats in Great Britain in the first **European elections**.

In the **referendum of June 1975** Mrs Thatcher campaigned conscientiously but not especially enthusiastically in favour of the United Kingdom remaining a member of the Community. Her first quarrel with the Community began in November 1979 over the level of the British net contribution to the Budget (see **British Budget problem**). The dilatory manner in which this problem was addressed (it remained unresolved until the **Fontainebleau Agreement** of June 1984) did little to inspire confidence and respect on Mrs Thatcher's part for the institutions and procedures of the Community. She was frustrated too in her efforts to reform the **Common Agricultural Policy** (CAP). However, in the **Single Market** programme, launched the year after the Fontainebleau settlement, Mrs Thatcher found a Community objective to which she could give whole-hearted support. In 1986 she endorsed the **Single European Act** (SEA), primarily as a means of speeding up decision-making on Single Market legislation. She was later to argue that at the time she was not made fully aware of the implications of the SEA for the balance of power between the Community institutions and, in particular, for member states' rights of veto (see **qualified majority voting**).

Mrs Thatcher's view of how European integration should move forward was broadly similar to that of **Charles de Gaulle**: she shared his hostility to the supranational character of the **European Commission** and the **European Parliament** and his belief in the pre-eminence of the nation-states. The fullest expression of her views was in the **Bruges speech** of September 1988.

In June 1989 Mrs Thatcher was eventually persuaded to agree at the Madrid meeting of the **European Council** to British participation in the first stage of **Economic and Monetary Union** (EMU). Both her Chancellor of the Exchequer, Nigel Lawson, and her Foreign Secretary, Sir Geoffrey Howe, had threatened to resign if she continued to block progress towards EMU. At the Strasbourg meeting of the European Council in December 1989 she refused to sign the **Social Charter**.

By 1990 Mrs Thatcher's increasingly strident opposition to the European Community was giving rise to concern amongst Conservative MPS and amongst her Cabinet colleagues. In November 1990 Sir Geoffrey Howe's resignation from the Cabinet prompted a leadership election from which Mrs Thatcher withdrew after the first ballot, having failed to secure the necessary majority for an outright win over Michael Heseltine. After a second ballot John Major became leader of the Conservative Party and Prime Minister. Mrs Thatcher did not stand in the 1992 General Election, retiring instead to the House of Lords as Baroness Thatcher.

Mrs Thatcher's adversarial style of politics was particularly ill-adapted to the conventions and procedures of a consensus-oriented decision-making system. In her autobiography *The Downing Street Years* (1993) she expressed no regrets with respect to her robust stance on European issues. She blamed the Conservatives' very poor results in the 1989 European elections on the unwillingness of candidates to follow her lead. She justified her defence of nation-states by describing them as 'functioning democracies' and as 'intractable political realities which it would be folly to seek to override or suppress in favour of a wider but as yet theoretical European nationhood'.

'Three Wise Men'

The **European Council** meeting in Brussels in December 1978 decided to appoint three 'eminent persons' to report on ways of making the Community institutions more effective and on progress towards **European Union**. They were required to work within the provisions and procedures of the **Treaties** and in the light of the probable **enlargement** of the Community from 9 to 12 members. The 'Three Wise Men', as they were called, were Barend Biesheuvel, a former Prime Minister of the Netherlands; Edmund Dell, who had just resigned as Secretary of State for Trade in the Labour Government in the United Kingdom; and Robert Marjolin, a French economist and former Vice-President of the **Commission**. Their *Report on European Institutions*, published in October 1979, contained both general reflections, most of them well founded, on the overall health of the institutions and many practical proposals on how procedures could be improved. The Report was studied in detail by the foreign ministers and featured briefly on the agenda of European Council meetings in Dublin (November 1979) and Luxembourg (April and December 1980), but very few of its recommendations were put into effect.

Tindemans Report

Published in 1975, the Tindemans Report, drawn up at the request of the **European Council** by Leo Tindemans, then Prime Minister of Belgium, was a wide-ranging study of **European Union** and of the steps that might be taken to achieve a more integrated Europe closer to the citizen (see **People's Europe**). The contribution by the **European Commission** to the Tindemans Report was noteworthy for having contained the first reference to **subsidiarity** in the Community context (see also **two-speed Europe**).

Trans-European networks (TENs)

Article 129b of the **Treaty of Rome** provides for 'the establishment and development of trans-European networks in the areas of transport, telecommunications and energy infrastructures'. The second part of the Article refers to 'the interaction and interoperability of national networks' and to 'the need to link island, landlocked and peripheral regions with the central regions of the Community'. This and the two following Articles (129c–d) were added to the Treaty of Rome by the **Maastricht Treaty**.

TENs are intended to complement the **Single Market** by allowing transport, telecommunications and energy grids (electricity supplies, oil and gas pipelines) to be planned on a Union-wide basis, sometimes with a contribution from the **Budget**. Funds were allocated to TENs as part of the **Edinburgh Growth Initiative** (see also **cohesion**). TENs are also intended to help the Union's regional policy by enabling outlying regions to be more efficiently linked with the centre. Detailed planning remains the responsibility of member states; the **Commission** is entitled to 'take any useful initiative', such as the identification of transport bottlenecks and the provision of technical assistance. The guidelines for TENs, decided under the **co-decision procedure**, are intended to identify 'projects of common interest'.

Amongst the TENs being built in the energy field are links between the electricity grids of Greece and Italy, and between those of Ireland and the United Kingdom. In the transport field the high-speed rail network (incorporating the **Channel Tunnel**) between London, Paris, Brussels, Cologne and Amsterdam is amongst the most ambitious TENs. Other TENs in this field include improvements to the railway–ferry connections between Great Britain and Ireland and to the 'Nordic triangle' of rail connections between Copenhagen, Oslo and Stockholm. In the telecommunications field progress is being made with new digital exchanges, cross-border electronic clearing systems for banks and credit card operations, data transmission and mobile telephone networks.

Some TENs link the Union with countries outside its borders. Examples include natural gas pipelines between Tunisia and Italy, and between Morocco and Spain. In the planning of future TENs much emphasis is being laid on developing better links between the Union and the countries of central and eastern Europe.

Transitional period

The phrase 'transitional period' normally refers to the period of grace during which new member states may be allowed progressively to introduce and apply Union rules, the immediate adoption of which would cause difficulties. Agreement as to the length of any transitional periods and their field of application is reached in the course of the **enlargement** negotiations and laid down in the Act of **Accession**.

'Transitional period' has a secondary meaning with reference to the history of the Community. Article 8 of the original **Treaty of Rome** required **the Six** to establish the **Common Market** 'during a transitional period of twelve years, . . . divided into three stages of four years each'. Article 14 EEC specified in detail the stages by which tariffs, customs duties and quantitative restrictions on trade between the Six were to be removed, starting on 1 January 1958. In the event, the process was completed ahead of schedule, on 1 July 1968. The Treaty commitment to more **majority voting** at the beginning of the third stage of the transitional period on 1 January 1966 was one of the causes of the **empty chair crisis**.

Transnational political parties

The establishment over the past 50 years of parliamentary institutions operating at European level has encouraged the growth of transnational party federations. Further impetus was given by the first **European elections** to the **European Parliament** in 1979, and more recently all four of the party federations have been transformed into political parties. This development was recognized in the **Maastricht Treaty** in an additional Article 138a inserted into the **Treaty of Rome**: 'Political parties at European level are important as a factor for integration within the Union. They contribute to forming a European awareness and to expressing the political will of the citizens of the Union.'

Party of European Socialists (PES)

A confederation of Socialist parties in the European Community was formed in 1974 within the Socialist International. This replaced the Liaison Bureau amongst the Socialist parties of **the Six**, which had been in operation since 1957. The confederation became the Party of European Socialists (PES) in November 1992. It has a total of 20 member parties and a further 8 associates and observers. MEPs belonging to PES member parties make up the PES Group in the European Parliament, the largest of the **political groups**. The leader of the PES Group is an ex-officio member of the PES Party Leaders' Conference. Socialist members of the **Commission**, the President-in-office of the **Council of Ministers** and the President of the European Parliament (when Socialists), and the leader of the PES Group in the Parliamentary Assembly of the **Council of Europe** all have consultative status in the Bureau of the PES, which meets at least four times a year. Socialist party leaders, in and out of government, meet under PES auspices before every meeting of the **European Council** to coordinate their positions, together with Socialist members of the European Commission.

The Congress is the 'supreme organ' of the PES. Held every two years and at least six months before every round of European elections, the Congress elects the officers of the PES, passes resolutions on the activities of the PES and of the PES Group in the European Parliament, and adopts the PES manifesto for European elections.

Article 9.3 of the PES Statutes says that 'political decisions shall in principle be taken on the basis of consensus'. However, decisions that may be taken by majority in the Council of Ministers may be taken by **qualified majority voting** (QMV) in the PES. Decisions on administrative and organizational matters may be taken by simple majority in the Bureau of the PES.

European People's Party (Christian Democrats)
Twenty-nine Christian Democrat (CD; see **Christian Democracy**) parties
are linked in the European Union of Christian Democrats (EUCD), founded
in 1965, with its headquarters and a small secretariat in Brussels. Another
14 parties have observer status. In 1976 CD parties in the member states of
the Community formed a federation of their own within the EUCD,
known as the European People's Party (EPP), as part of their preparations
for the first direct elections to the European Parliament. The EPP shares a
common secretariat with the EUCD. Within the Parliament, the MEPs
belonging to EPP member parties, together with a number of allies (of
which the most numerous are British Conservative MEPs), form the Group
of the European People's Party, the second largest of the political groups
in the Parliament. The EPP is the only transnational political party to make
provision for individual membership (Article 6 of the Statutes adopted in
1990).

A congress of EPP member parties is held every two years. Most
decisions require an absolute majority of those present and entitled to
vote. Day-to-day decisions are in the hands of the leader, the
deputy leaders (the leaders of member parties), and various office-holders.
There is also a 'political bureau'. The EPP has a number of sections: a
women's section, a trade union section, a young people's section, etc. It is
funded (on a modest scale) mainly by subscriptions from member parties
and from the EPP Group in the European Parliament. The EPP maintains
close and regular contacts with members of the European Commission.
More importantly, it is the forum in which leaders of Christian Democrat
parties, in and out of government, meet before meetings of the European
Council.

European Liberal, Democrat and Reform Party
A federation of European Liberal parties was formed in 1976 as part of the
Liberals' preparations for direct elections to the European Parliament. The
European Liberal, Democrat and Reform Party (ELDR) was founded in
December 1993. Its aims are similar to those of the PES and EPP: preparation
of a common programme, mutual assistance and support, and discussion of
problems of common interest. At present it has 32 members and
'affiliates'. MEPs from ELDR member parties form the European Liberal,
Democrat and Reform Group, the fourth largest political group in the
European Parliament.

A congress is held annually. Most decisions are taken (by majority) in
the Council, composed of representatives of member parties, members
directly elected by the congress, Liberal members of the European Commission, the leader of the ELDR Group in the European Parliament, and a

representative of the Liberals' European youth movement. The Party is funded by member parties and by the ELDR Group. Its very small secretariat is based in Brussels.

European Federation of Green Parties

In March 1984 the Green parties of Europe established a coordinating body at a conference in Liège, Belgium. This developed into a European Federation of Green Parties (EFGP) under a set of statutes and a statement of 'guiding principles' adopted at a conference in Masala, Finland, in June 1993. The EFGP has 28 member parties from all over Europe. Its headquarters are in Vienna.

According to its statutes, the EFGP is founded upon 'the common wish to establish a European House built on ecological, democratic, social and pacifist principles'. The statement of guiding principles is binding upon member parties at the European level, but at the national and regional level the parties 'maintain their name, identity and autonomy'. The EFGP is represented in the European Parliament by the Green Group (see **political groups**). The organs of the EFGP are a congress (meeting every three years), a governing council and an administrative committee. Representation of member parties in these bodies is based upon complicated formulae involving numbers of members and votes obtained in national and European elections. Most decisions are taken by a two-thirds majority.

The guiding principles commit the Green parties to 'ecodevelopment', equity and social justice, 'planetary solidarity', women's rights, an increased role for the United Nations, a Europe of the Regions, an end to nuclear energy, disarmament and 'a pan-European security system' based upon the **Conference on Security and Cooperation in Europe**.

Free European Alliance

A new transnational party, composed of French, Italian, Spanish, British and Belgian regionalist parties, was founded in October 1995.

If the test of a genuinely transnational political party is a single leader, common policies, provision for individual membership, a common system for the adoption of candidates and a unified budget, none of the parties listed above would qualify. Even the most ambitious of them are in fact little more than fora for the exchange of ideas, for the drawing up of common programmes for European elections and for various kinds of mutual support of a practical nature.

In recent years all the transnational parties have been anxious to make contacts with newly founded parties in European countries outside the European Union, especially those that have applied for membership. In central and eastern European countries the transnational parties have given material and moral support to many parties engaged, perhaps for the first time, in free elections and provided a means by which parties outside the Union can be kept informed of political developments. However, it has not always been easy for the transnational parties to identify reliable, respectable allies outside the Union, such is the pace and unpredictability of political change.

The transnational party manifestos for European elections, although produced with immense care and trouble, have not so far proved to be of more than marginal interest except to political scientists and, occasionally, to journalists. In all cases such manifestos are necessarily pitched at a level of generality that obscures substantial points of difference between the parties, and are expressed in language so abstract as to be almost unreadably bland. Most national parties continue to produce their own manifestos, so that at this stage all the transnational manifestos can provide is an over-arching framework.

There are immense problems in the way of the transnational parties developing any further. First, their constitutional and legal status is uncertain. This, in turn, affects their financial status with respect, for example, to their liability for value-added tax (VAT) in different member states, and inhibits their cross-frontier political activities in other ways. The fact that such parties are now recognized in the Treaty (see above) may be the first step towards giving them an official status at the European constitutional level. Second, the transnational parties are almost wholly dependent for staff and income on their member parties and the political groups in the European Parliament, and all are kept on very tight budgets. Third, until such time as party political activity at the European level becomes more important than that at the national level, with Union-wide issues separating the parties and Union-wide media in which such issues can be debated, the natural focus for politicians' energies and the electorate's attention is national politics. The transnational parties can offer no independent career structure to the aspiring politician, since nearly all key posts are held either *ex officio* or by virtue of behind-the-scenes agreements between national parties. Fourth, progress towards a **uniform electoral procedure** for European elections has been very slow; were such a procedure to be adopted, it would open up new opportunities for parties to cooperate and compete freely across frontiers. Fifth, political parties as they exist at national level have many diverse origins – political, social, ethnic and historical – and, by and large, the transnational parties represent an attempt to transpose the established political 'families' to the European level. Whether such a transposition can be achieved as an act of will, or whether it should happen naturally if at all, are the central questions facing transnational parties.

Transparency

A term frequently encountered in recent years in discussion within or about the European Union and its institutions, 'transparency' relates not only to the clarity of the decision-making procedures used therein but also to the extent to which the public has access to them. 'Openness' is sometimes used instead of 'transparency'.

In common with other bureaucracies, especially those which take decisions that directly affect people's lives and livelihoods, the institutions of the European Union have frequently been criticized as remote, secretive and subject to all kinds of hidden influences. Whether or not it was the spate of legislation necessary for the completion of the **Single Market** that brought matters to a head, the need for greater transparency was a theme that ran through the negotiations that led to the 1991 **Maastricht Treaty**. At the Maastricht meeting of the **European Council** in December 1991 a Declaration was adopted on the right of access to information. 'Transparency of the decision-making process', it said, 'strengthens the democratic nature of the institutions and the public's confidence in the administration', and the Commission was invited to submit proposals. The following year allegations about the secretiveness of the Brussels bureaucracy played a part in delivering the Danish 'no' vote to the Maastricht Treaty in the June 1992 **referendum**, and the European Council meeting in Birmingham returned to the theme of transparency, in conjunction with its declaration on **subsidiarity**, in October 1992. The idea was further developed at the Edinburgh and Copenhagen meetings of the European Council in December 1992 and June 1993.

Well before the **Commission** published its proposals in a communication entitled *Public Access to the Institutions' Documents* (May 1993), it had already taken steps to reform its own practices. These reforms included more extensive use of green papers to promote discussion on legislative proposals, earlier publication of its **annual legislative programme** and better public distribution of key documents. The Commission's communication put forward some general guidelines and hinted very strongly that these should also be followed by the other institutions and by the member states. It thus laid the foundations for a tripartite Council–Commission–Parliament 'declaration on democracy, transparency and subsidiarity' agreed in Luxembourg on 25 October 1993. In the **Declaration** the institutions reaffirmed 'their attachment to the implementation of transparency', and each set out the steps it proposed to take or was already taking towards this end.

Transparency affects the different institutions in different ways. As far as the **European Parliament**'s formal business is concerned, either in committee or in plenary session, transparency is not a problem, since most meetings are open to the public. Indeed, the Parliament goes to great lengths – not very successfully – to interest the electorate in its affairs. Transparency is of more concern to the Parliament as a guarantee that *other* institutions should be under an obligation to provide information to the Parliament in its capacity as the guardian of the public interest (see below).

The problem for the Commission is rather different. The Commission receives a very great deal of information and documentation from public authorities, interest groups, international bodies, governments of non-member states, companies and individuals, some of it furnished on a confidential basis. This confidentiality may impose a constraint on the Commission when it is pressed for information or when invited to say how and why it reached a particular conclusion. For this reason the Commission has not yet given a general undertaking to divulge information in its possession; it has, however, undertaken to consult more widely and more systematically before finalizing its legislative proposals, to make documents available more promptly, and to improve its contacts with the general public. When its annual legislative programme is published in October, and after the Parliament has formally expressed its view on the programme, the **Council of Ministers** will do the same, indicating the areas to which it attaches priority.

The Council of Ministers is the least transparent of the institutions and likely to remain so. The reasons are clear: ministers in the Council are engaged in a process designed to reach consensus if at all possible, for the attainment of which a willingness to compromise is an absolute precondition. Compromise may well entail the surrendering of a position previously taken up, and this is something more easily done in private. Once compromise is reached, the surrender can be justified to press and public on the basis of some greater benefit obtained in exchange. Amongst Council papers are also 'interpretative statements' on legal texts. If these were made public, they could give rise to confusion, since only the **Court of Justice** has the formal power to make such interpretations.

Attempts to open up the proceedings of the Council have been made for many years. The Council, it was pointed out, was the only legislative body in the Western world to legislate in secret. Its rules of procedure were not published in the *Official Journal* until July 1979. Information about Council proceedings was available only in the form of leaks or anodyne press releases, and answers given in response to Members of the European Parliament (MEPs) were bland or evasive, or both. The principal object of the first attempts to open up the Council was to prevent member states from invoking the **Luxembourg Compromise** for trivial reasons: the member state was to be named and its reasons for invoking the Luxembourg Compromise given in the minutes. The force of this argument was largely lost with the virtual abandonment of the Luxembourg Compromise after the entry into force of the **Single European Act** (SEA) in 1987. However, an important distinction had been established between the 'deliberative' (i.e., negotiating) function of the Council and the 'legislative' function (both may, of course, be combined in a single Council meeting). The former would remain confidential, but the latter would be fully minuted and the minutes would be published. Most important of all, votes would be recorded.

After some embarrassing false starts in 1993 (the Council opened its meetings but few journalists and no members of the public bothered to attend), the Council is now slightly more open. Under the tripartite declaration of October 1993 the Council undertook to open some of its meetings to the public on a regular basis, publish records of voting, publish its common positions (see **cooperation procedure**) and improve the provision of information to the press and public.

At a Council meeting on 6–7 December 1993 the Council and the Commission agreed on a 'Code of conduct concerning public access to Council and Commission documents'. The Code laid down the general principle that 'the public will have the widest possible access' to such documents, but applications for access to documents not originating with either institution are referred to the original authors. General exceptions allowing applications to be refused include the protection of the public interest, the individual right of privacy, commercial and industrial secrecy, and the Union's financial interests. Most importantly, either Council or Commission may 'refuse access in order to protect the institution's interest in the confidentiality of its proceedings'. At the same meeting the Council amended, by simple majority, its own Rules of Procedure in order to meet its obligations under the tripartite declaration of October 1993 (see above). Henceforth, votes in the Council will be made public 'systematically . . . whenever the Council acts as legislator' unless by simple majority it is decided otherwise. Other votes may be published if it is so decided, by simple majority, at the request of a member state. However, when the Council is acting under the procedures laid down in Titles V and VI of the Maastricht Treaty (the **Common Foreign and Security Policy** or cooperation in the fields of **Justice and Home Affairs**) a decision to publish the voting record must be unanimous. If the record is made public, explanations of vote are automatically made public too. The Dutch and Danish foreign ministers voted against these new procedures on the grounds that they did not go far enough; the Greek foreign minister opposed them because they went too far. Further refinements were made by the Council at a meeting on 20 December 1993.

The Council's willingness to open its proceedings was soon put to the test by the *Guardian*. The newspaper requested a copy of the record of votes taken in the Council of Justice Ministers. At first, the information was supplied, but a second, supplementary request was met with a refusal and a statement to the effect that 'an error' had been made in meeting the first request. The *Guardian* persisted, and the *Financial Times* joined the campaign with a request for a record of all votes taken by qualified majority since 1989. Such a record, the newspaper was told, 'did not exist' (in fact, votes are recorded in the minutes of Council sessions, but had never been brought together in a summary document). On 16 May 1994 the Foreign Affairs Council discussed the matter and instructed officials to bring forward further proposals. By this stage the United Kingdom had pronounced itself in favour of greater openness, and ministers were well aware that all three Scandinavian applicant states had well-established traditions allowing public access to official documents. On 5 July 1994 it was agreed that in future the Council's Legal Service should keep and publish a register of votes on legislation. Having still not had a satisfactory reply to its original request, the *Guardian* brought an action against the Council in the **Court of First Instance**. Judgment in the *Guardian*'s favour was given on 19 October 1995.

Of all the problems associated with transparency, amongst the most sensitive are those associated with the **Ombudsman** and with the European Parliament's Committees of Inquiry. Clearly, if the Ombudsman is successfully to investigate allegations of 'maladministration' on the part of the Union institutions, he or she must have very extensive access to institutions' files. Member states are, however, reluctant to allow the Ombudsman free access to documents that they may have communicated to Union institutions. A compromise was reached at the same meeting that agreed the October 1993 tripartite declaration (see above): the Ombudsman will have access to all files held by Union institutions except on 'duly substantiated grounds of secrecy'. Access to màterial 'originating in a Member State' and classified as secret will be given only with the permission of that member state; access to non-secret material may be given if the relevant member state is so informed. Member states are laid under a general obligation to provide, through their **national representations**, any information that may help to clarify instances of maladministration by Union institutions or bodies unless such information is secret. The Ombudsman and his staff are, in turn, laid under an obligation not to divulge any information secured in the performance of their duties. A similar compromise has been reached with respect to the European Parliament's Committees of Inquiry.

Many of the arguments bearing upon transparency are long familiar from the national political histories of member states, most obviously the need for a balance between the operational requirements of any complex system of government and the public's right to know what is done or decided in its name. Other arguments are given a new dimension by the federal or semi-federal nature of the institutions and by the peculiar character of the tension between them. The compromises reached are new and untried and it is unlikely that all parties are equally committed to making them work. Amongst the few conclusions that can be drawn with certainty is that until the various commitments are put to the test in specific cases it will be difficult to judge their efficacy: only time – and the Court of First Instance – will tell.

Juliet Lodge, 'Transparency and democratic legitimacy', *Journal of Common Market Studies*, Vol. 32, no. 3, September 1994, contains a clear and balanced analysis of the main issues.

Treaties

The European Union is based upon and governed in accordance with a number of Treaties between the member states. These Treaties are the most fundamental part of the *acquis communautaire* and in every case have been the subject of (sometimes prolonged) negotiations leading to unanimous agreement amongst governments and **ratification** by **national parliaments** and, in some cases, by **referendum** too. The Treaties not only serve as the Union's constitution but are also prescriptive in that several of them set objectives for the future, usually accompanied by a deadline and sometimes by a precise timetable. Most of the Treaties contain provisions for their own amendment (see **Intergovernmental Conference**) and, with one exception, were concluded for an unlimited period. In common with the rest of the *acquis communautaire*, the Treaties must be accepted in their entirety by states wishing to join the Union.

The table opposite lists the main Treaties and Acts in chronological order, together with the date of entry into force and a brief summary, where relevant, of how each relates to the others. The first three Treaties, establishing three legally distinct Communities, are sometimes referred to as the 'founding Treaties'. Most are the subject of separate entries.

Trevi Group

At the **European Council** meeting in Rome in December 1975 it was agreed on the basis of a British proposal that 'Community Ministers for the Interior (or Ministers with similar responsibilities) should meet to discuss matters coming within their competence, in particular with regard to law and order'. The following year, in the wake of several cases of terrorism and hostage-taking, it was decided to invite ministers of justice to participate in this work. The first meeting of what became known as

Treaty	In force	Summary
European Coal and Steel Community (ECSC) Treaty (Treaty of Paris, 1951)	1952	Concluded for 50 years amongst **the Six** on the basis of the **Schuman Plan**
European Economic Community (EEC) Treaty (Treaty of Rome, 1957)	1958	Concluded on the model of the ECSC Treaty but with a much broader range of objectives; the most important of the Treaties
European Atomic Energy Community (EAEC or Euratom) Treaty (also signed in Rome, 1957)	1958	A sector-specific Treaty of limited application
Treaty establishing a Single Council and a Single Commission of the European Communities (Merger Treaty, 1965)	July 1967	Amended the ECSC, EEC and Euratom Treaties to create a Council and a Commission serving all three Communities
Treaty amending certain Budgetary Provisions of the Treaties establishing the European Communities (and of the Merger Treaty) (Treaty of Luxembourg, 1970)	1971	Laid down a new procedure for settling the **Budget** and introduced the system of '**own resources**'
Treaty amending certain Financial Provisions of the Treaties establishing the European Communities (and of the Merger Treaty) (1975)	1978	Refined the budgetary procedure to give the **European Parliament** more power and set up the **Court of Auditors**
Act concerning the election of the representatives of the European Parliament by direct universal suffrage (European Elections Act, 1976)	1978	The basis for the first (1979) and subsequent **European elections**
Single European Act (1986)	July 1987	Amended and expanded the EEC Treaty (most importantly, by extending the scope of **qualified majority voting**) and laid down new procedures for foreign policy cooperation
Treaty on European Union (Maastricht Treaty, 1992)	November 1993	Established the European Union; amended and expanded the EEC Treaty; created the **co-decision procedure**; created '**pillars**' of **Common Foreign and Security Policy** (CFSP) and Cooperation in the Fields of **Justice and Home Affairs** (JHA)

the Trevi Group was held in Luxembourg on 29 June 1976. The origin of the name 'Trevi' is disputed. It may have been a pun on the name of Mr Fonteijn, the Director-General in the Dutch Ministry of Justice, who was one of the initiators of the Group, or a reference to the Trevi Fountain in Rome, where the decision to establish the Group was first taken. 'Trevi' was subsequently turned into an acronym for '*terrorisme, radicalisme, extrémisme, et violence internationale*'. Since 1993 the work of the Trevi Group has been incorporated into the **Justice and Home Affairs** (JHA) provisions of the **Maastricht Treaty** (Article K).

The Trevi Group was an informal body for cooperation in the field of law and order. Most of the subjects with which it dealt were outside the scope of the Treaty, and the **Commission** was not associated with the work of the Group. Ministerial-level meetings, chaired by the country holding the **presidency**, were held in June and December. These meetings were prepared by meetings of senior civil servants, including police officers, who met in May and November. From 1989 both sets of meetings were serviced by a '*piatnika*' (a five-person version of a **troika**), composed of the president-in-office, two predecessors and two successors. There was no permanent secretariat, but meetings of 'experts' took place under Trevi auspices in various working-parties. Both the ministerial meetings and the working-parties had regular contacts with countries known as the 'friends of Trevi': Austria, Morocco, Norway, Sweden, Switzerland, the United States and Canada.

Since the Trevi Group was not an official Community body, ministers were not obliged to answer questions about their Trevi activities from Members of the **European Parliament** (MEPs). However, ministers remained accountable to their **national parliaments**; and once in every presidency, the minister currently chairing meetings of the Trevi Group reported to the European Parliament's Committee on Civil Liberties and Internal Affairs.

Troika

'Troika' is a Russian word meaning a sledge drawn by three horses. It was first introduced into politics in the early 1960s, when the Soviet Union suggested that the Secretary-General of the United Nations should be replaced by a troika composed of representatives of the Eastern bloc, the Western alliance and the non-aligned states. In the European Union it means a three-member group composed of the current president of the **Council of Ministers** together with his or her immediate predecessor and successor. Such groups are most commonly used in the foreign affairs field to ensure a measure of continuity from one **presidency** to another, and were first introduced in 1977 as an operational necessity in the field of

European Political Cooperation. At the European Council meeting in Brussels in December 1993 it was agreed to introduce with effect from 1996 a system for the rotation of the presidency of the Council which would ensure that in every troika there is a minister from one of the large member states.

Truman Doctrine

In a message to the United States Congress on 12 March 1947 President Harry Truman pledged the United States 'to support free peoples who are resisting attempted subjugation by armed minorities or by outside pressures'. This was a reference to the state of civil war in Greece as Communist guerrillas attempted to take over the country. Congress adopted what became known as the Truman Doctrine on 22 April 1947, and this is generally regarded as the formal assumption by the United States of its postwar role as a world power. Its counterpart was the **Brezhnev Doctrine** of 1968.

Turkey

Turkey first concluded an **Association Agreement** with the Community in 1963, the second country to do so. The Agreement was 'frozen' during periods of military rule in Turkey, but it provides for Turkey eventually to become part of a **customs union** with the member states. In March 1995 the Association Council agreed on a customs union with effect from January 1996.

On 14 April 1987 the Turkish government applied for full membership of the Community. The Commission's **Opinion**, delivered in December 1989, was unfavourable. The Commission took the view that 'any decision to open negotiations ... must be based on a strong conviction that a positive conclusion is possible, indeed probable, within a reasonable period'. In the case of Turkey there was no such conviction, the difficulties being compounded by the country's high birth-rate and relative poverty: the Turkish population is projected to reach 68 million by 2000, while its per capita gross domestic product (GDP) is less than a third that of Greece, the poorest of the member states. The Commission also expressed doubts about whether the country's **human rights** record was consistent with Community standards, and whether Turkish membership might have 'negative effects' on the Greek–Turkish dispute over **Cyprus**. The conclusion was that 'it would not be useful to open accession negotiations with Turkey'. Instead, the Commission proposed an intensification of political, commercial and economic relations with Turkey within the framework of the Association Agreement. These conclusions were broadly endorsed by the member states.

Turkey, by virtue of its membership of the **Council of Europe** and the **North Atlantic Treaty Organization** (NATO), is normally considered a European state, even though 96 per cent of its territory is geographically in Asia (see also **Morocco**). Turkey also took part in the **Conference on Security and Cooperation in Europe** (CSCE).

Two-speed Europe

Sometimes known as a 'two-tier Europe', the idea of a two-speed Europe (*Europe à deux vitesses*) was first set out in the **Tindemans Report** of 1975. This report sought to recognize the fact that not all member states were willing and able to proceed towards integration at the same pace, and that some means should be found of allowing the more enthusiastic to make progress without being held back by the others. Which countries proceeded at which speed would vary from case to case, and those opting for the slower speed would do so on the basis of reasons recognized as valid by the **Council of Ministers** on a proposal from the **Commission**. The Report also enjoined those countries proceeding at the faster pace to lend as much assistance as possible to the others.

Like much else in the Report, the idea of a two-speed Europe did not find favour with the governments of the member states, especially those which feared that they would find themselves on most issues in the second rank. A two-speed Europe would, it was argued, have damaging consequences for the uniform application of the *acquis communautaire*, for Community solidarity (especially in external relations) and for the Community **Budget**. It would also call into question the rights of member states to an equal share in decision-making. However, although formally rejected, something very close to a two-speed Europe was given *de facto* recognition in 1979 with the setting up of the **Exchange-Rate Mechanism** (ERM) of the **European Monetary System** (EMS); and with a larger and more heterogeneous Union in prospect as a consequence of **enlargement**, the idea is by no means dead (see also **concentric circles**, 'hard core').

UKREP

UKREP is the acronym for the United Kingdom Permanent Representation to the European Union. Each of the member states maintains a **national representation** or 'embassy' in Brussels to manage its dealings with the various Union institutions, most especially its direct involvement in the legislative process in the **Council of Ministers**. UKREP is one of the largest of the representations and is sometimes considered the most professional. It is composed of about 50 administrative-grade officials, and is divided into 6 policy-area groupings. All officials dealing with institutional and foreign policy issues normally come from the Foreign and Commonwealth Office (FCO), including the permanent representative or ambassador. The deputy permanent representative and a number (but far from all) of the officials dealing with technical matters – such as transport, environment or energy – are seconded from Whitehall departments. It is usual for the officials dealing with financial and agricultural matters to be on loan from the Treasury and the Ministry of Agriculture. All officials, regardless of their department of origin, are responsible, through UKREP, to the FCO in London.

UKREP officials spend a large amount of time in meetings of COREPER and working groups within the Council structure. Every meeting is followed by a 'reporting telegram' for the FCO's attention in London. Similar telegrams describe new **Commission** initiatives, events in the **European Parliament** and other political developments of potential significance to London. The telegrams are circulated in Whitehall and form the basis of the government's collective intelligence on European affairs. UKREP also monitors the position of British officials in the Brussels institutions.

Unanimity

Decisions in the **Council of Ministers** of the European Union may be taken either by unanimity or on the basis of **majority voting**. Only in respect of the former do individual member states enjoy a right of **veto** under the **Treaties**.

Uniform electoral procedure

The idea that the **European Parliament** should be elected on the basis of a uniform electoral procedure (UEP) used throughout the member states is to be found in the 1951 **Treaty of Paris** establishing the **European Coal and Steel Community** (ECSC). It was repeated in the **Treaty of Rome**: Article 138.3 says: 'The European Parliament shall draw up proposals for elections by direct universal suffrage in accordance with a uniform procedure in all Member States.' It was repeated again in Article 7 of the 1976 European Elections Act (see below), but in spite of several efforts to establish such a procedure **European elections** are still held on the basis of different national systems and arrangements for these elections remain in the hands of national authorities. The drawing up of proposals for a UEP is the one area in which the European Parliament, not the **Commission**, specifically enjoys the **right of initiative**. Once adopted, the proposals are forwarded to the **Council of Ministers**. The Council, acting unanimously, must 'lay down the appropriate provisions' with the approval of a majority of the Parliament's members (Article 138.3 EEC), and these provisions must then be ratified by all member states. There is no deadline by which a UEP must be in place.

Under the Treaties of Paris and Rome, the European Parliament was composed of members (MEPs) nominated by and from the **national parliaments** of member states, pending the introduction of direct elections on the basis of a UEP. In 1960 the Parliament made the first of several unsuccessful attempts to draw up proposals for a UEP, and met with no response from the Council. However, in December 1974 the heads of state and of government at the Paris **summit** agreed that direct elections 'should take place in or after 1978'. A political decision was taken to regard secret and direct elections based on universal suffrage and held on the same date as sufficiently 'uniform' to satisfy the Treaty criteria, and the choice of electoral system was left to member states. The Parliament drew up new proposals (the Patijn Report of 1975) dealing with the number of seats, the allocations of seats amongst the member states, the date, the length of the mandate, the list of offices incompatible with membership of the Parliament, and the verification of Members' credentials. Only some of the Parliament's views were embodied in the European Elections Act of 20 September 1976, on the basis of which the first direct elections were held in 1979 (the original 1978 target date was missed because of the British Labour Government's abortive attempt to get the House of Commons to accept the regional list system upon which the Liberals were then insisting). In 1979 and in all subsequent European elections proportional representation (PR) in various forms was used throughout the member states except in Great Britain (then as now, Northern Ireland was treated as a single three-member constituency in which the single transferable vote (STV) system of PR was used). It soon became apparent that in the Parliament's view the criterion of 'uniformity' would be satisfied if PR in some form were used in all member states, and this was the main purpose behind the 1982 Seitlinger Report. No action followed in the Council. A second report of 1988 ran into so many difficulties within the Parliament that it was never adopted. In 1991 the Liberal Democrats in the United Kingdom brought an action in the **Court of Justice** against the European Parliament for **failure to act**, but before the case was settled the Parliament had adopted another set of proposals for a UEP (the De Gucht Report of June 1992).

The difficulties in the way of establishing a UEP are threefold: procedural, political and legal. The Treaty (see above) requires proposals from the European Parliament, unanimity in the Council, an absolute majority in the Parliament for the Council's conclusions, and ratification in the member states. Each of these four stages is problematic, and taken together they constitute a process that could not be accomplished within one of the Parliament's five-year mandates. The Treaty does not allow for a UEP to be established in stages.

The political difficulty springs from the word 'uniform'. It is not enough for all member states to use PR, it must be the *same* form. Member states such as France and Spain are as attached to the national list system of PR as Belgium and Italy are to the regional list. Experience has shown that to secure the necessary majority in the Parliament, a proposal has to be so hedged about with compromises, qualifications and special cases as to be no longer consistent with what the Treaty clearly means by uniformity. Electoral systems in the member states are founded upon historical and political processes and assumptions that cannot easily be gainsaid. Inevitably, every political party, every government and every individual MEP approaches UEP in terms of party political advantage, and the notional Treaty commitment to uniformity is simply not strong enough to overcome this.

The legal difficulties spring from the word 'procedure'. An electoral procedure is not just a voting system or a formula for translating votes into seats. Its scope is much wider: it embraces, for example, the question of the voting age, the right to stand for election, the electoral threshold, disqualifications, the rules governing independent candidates, and so on. Many of these are sensitive issues in their own right. The Parliament has implicitly acknowledged this by dealing with such matters in its own proposals and it was confirmed in the Court of Justice's judgment of 1985 in the case of *Les Verts* v *the European Parliament* (Case 294/83). The Court ruled, in effect, that all provisions governed by law with a bearing on the equality of candidates' chances were covered by the notion of a 'procedure'. The Council is of the view that the Parliament's June 1992 report (see above) 'contains only general principles' and that 'much more specific provisions' will be required (Answer to Written Question by Mr Vertemati, *Official Journal*, C333, 8 December 1993).

Another problem with UEP is that it raises the question of the number of seats allocated to each member state in the European Parliament. Under the present arrangements the smaller member states are over-represented in terms of electors per seat, and the changes agreed at the Edinburgh European Council in December 1992 (see **European Parliament**: history, composition and procedure) make only a modest difference. This highly political question, made more complex by **enlargement**, could never be settled at anything other than **European Council** level.

In its provisions on **citizenship** the Maastricht Treaty gave every citizen of the European Union the right to vote and stand in European elections wherever resident in the Union under the same conditions as nationals of the state in which he or she resides (Article 8b.2 EEC). However, even this right is subject to '**derogations** where warranted by problems specific to a Member State' (a reference to the large number of Portuguese resident in Luxembourg).

If progress is ever to be made towards a UEP, it can only be made on the basis of an agreement between the institutions to proceed in stages. The least contentious questions (such as the voting age) would be addressed in the first stage and only at the end of this process would the most difficult issues (such as the system whereby votes are translated into seats) be raised. Meanwhile, there is nothing to prevent member states from agreeing outside the Treaty framework on a UEP that happens to suit them and enacting it individually but in concert. No member state and very few political parties show any interest in moving towards a UEP, not least because changes agreed at European level would have an impact on national electoral law. Whether the present diversity of procedures seriously affects the standing of the European Parliament in the eyes of the electorate is an open question.

Union of Industrial and Employers' Confederations of Europe (UNICE)

UNICE was founded in 1958 as the Union of Industries of the European Community. Composed of 32 organizations in 22 countries, UNICE is the principal European-level lobbying organization for industry and commerce, and is an important channel of communication between the European institutions (notably the **European Parliament**, the **Commission**, and especially the **Economic and Social Committee**) and business interests.

United Kingdom

To the disappointment of **the Six**, the United Kingdom chose not to take part in the negotiations in 1950 that followed the **Schuman Plan** and led a year later to the establishment of the **European Coal and Steel Community** (ECSC). Similarly, five years later the British government sent only a middle-ranking official from the Board of Trade as an observer to the 1955 **Messina Conference** at which the outline of the **European Economic Community** (EEC) was first discussed. In both cases the main obstacle was the supranational character of the institutions upon which the Communities were to be founded and the conviction, shared by **Winston Churchill** and others, that the country's destiny lay with a wider English-speaking fraternity of nations centred upon the countries of the British Empire. By contrast, the United Kingdom played an active part in all the other European organizations – the **Council of Europe**, the Brussels Treaty Organization (from 1954 known as the **Western European Union**), the Organization for European Economic Cooperation (see **Organization for Economic Cooperation and Development**), and the **European Free Trade Association** (EFTA) – established in the postwar period.

In 1961 the Conservative Government of Harold Macmillan decided, with cross-party support, to make an application to join the European Community. This was prompted by the realization that the Six had established a working arrangement that was bringing benefits in terms of stability, prosperity and global influence from which the United Kingdom did not wish to be excluded. At the same time it was becoming clear that the Commonwealth was in the longer term no longer an adequate basis for British political and economic interests. As for the 'special relationship' with the **United States of America**, the Americans had long been in favour of a United Europe that included the United Kingdom.

Macmillan's application and the Labour Government's application of 1967 were both effectively vetoed by **Charles de Gaulle**, primarily because he (with some justice) took the United Kingdom's traditionally pro-American, pro-free-trade stance to be inconsistent with French interests. Moreover, he realized that the United Kingdom would certainly compete with France for the political leadership of the Community, although, ironically, de Gaulle's essentially intergovernmental model of the Community, as typified in the **Fouchet Plan**, could certainly have won British support. Even though British membership of the Community was strongly and consistently supported by the other member states, it was not until de Gaulle was succeeded as President of France in 1969 by Georges Pompidou that the French veto was lifted and negotiations with the United Kingdom, Denmark, Ireland and Norway were begun in earnest.

In 1971 the Conservative Government of **Edward Heath** brought the negotiations to a successful conclusion. Later that year the House of Commons approved the European Communities Act. However, by this time elements in the Labour Party were opposed to membership in principle and the Party as a whole was officially opposed to the so-called 'Tory terms'. In 1974, the year after British **accession**, the Labour Party won the February and October elections with a commitment to 'renegoti-ate' the terms, and the following year the **referendum of June 1975** was held, endorsing British membership of the Community by a majority of two to one. The whole episode had nevertheless been a disastrous start to the United Kingdom's relations with its new partners, and in particular allowed the British commitment to the underlying purposes of the Commu-nity to be called into question.

Soon after the Conservative Government of **Margaret Thatcher** came to power in 1979 another source of tension arose in the form of the **British Budget problem**, which remained unresolved until 1984. It was hardly to be expected that a prime minister who scorned consensus and was committed to a reduction in the role of the state and a raising of national self-confidence would resist the temptation to be outspokenly critical of 'Brussels'. Not until the 1986 **Single European Act** (SEA) could it be said that the British had contributed positively to the Commu-nity's development, with the **Single Market** programme and the exten-sion of **European Political Cooperation** (unless one counts the **Euro-pean Regional Development Fund**, operational from 1975, and the inclusion of many Commonwealth countries in the first **Lomé Conven-tion**, also dating from 1975). Since 1986 the British have been amongst the most enthusiastic supporters of **enlargement**, tempered only by a reticence with regard to the institutional reforms that, in the view of many, must accompany it (see **wider versus deeper**, **qualified majority voting**).

Amongst other areas upon which United Kingdom policy has concen-trated are reform of the **Common Agricultural Policy** (CAP), **budget-ary discipline** and **competition policy**. The United Kingdom has always supported the rigorous and equal enforcement of Community law, although the preoccupation with **sovereignty** has so far prevented this support from being expressed in terms of wanting inspectorates responsible to the Union rather than to member states individually.

The acrimonious debate in the House of Commons on the **Maastricht Treaty** brought out two key themes that are likely to feature in the British approach to the 1996 **Intergovernmental Conference** (IGC). One is the continuing importance of **subsidiarity** in the division of responsibility between the institutions of the Union and those of member states. The other is a preference for intergovernmental procedures (as typified in the additional '**pillars**' introduced by the Maastricht Treaty). Characteristic, too, of British attitudes is sympathy for a **Europe à la carte** involving '**opt-outs**' similar to those which the United Kingdom secured on the **Social Chapter** and the third stage of **Economic and Monetary Union** (EMU).

Perhaps in no area is a certain British ambivalence towards the Union more consistently evident than in relation to the powers of the **European Parliament**. Before the United Kingdom joined the Community in 1973, one of the arguments most commonly heard in favour of British membership was that the United Kingdom's long and unbroken tradition of parliamentary democracy would serve to make Community decision-making more democratic; or, as the argument is now expressed, that the **democratic deficit** would be reduced. In fact, from January 1973 to July 1975 the Labour Party refused to take up its entitlement of seats in the European Parliament; and the first **European elections** were held a year after the original 1978 target date because of difficulties in getting the necessary legislation through the House of Commons. The United Kingdom has had by far the lowest average turnout in the four European elections held so far. British support for additional powers for the European Parliament has been extremely grudging, and in no member state is there a keener sense of rivalry between the **national parliament** and the European Parliament.

Neither defeated nor occupied in the course of the Second World War, the United Kingdom did not share the desire of the Six to place political and economic relations between Western European states on a radically new footing. Nor had confidence in British institutions been shaken to the extent of the United Kingdom being prepared to countenance new supra-national institutions that cut across traditional notions of sovereignty. To this extent, in the crucial postwar years the United Kingdom was set apart from those impulses that led to the foundation of the Community. The afterglow of victory cast quite a different light on what seemed the obvious way forward to **Jean Monnet** and others.

The European Union is the only major organization to which the United Kingdom belongs of which it is not a founder member. A great deal of British energy has gone into reforming policies that, had the United Kingdom joined with the Six, could have been shaped from the beginning in a fashion more consistent with British interests and preferences. Few of the arguments have been won as quickly and as convincingly as the United Kingdom would have wished. The British Budget problem in particular soured relations with other member states across the whole field. More importantly, it reduced public support for British membership to dangerously low levels, which in turn limited the scope for political initiatives designed to restore the country's European credentials and capture the imagination of the electorate.

Of the national political parties, only the Liberal Democrats can claim to have been consistently and wholeheartedly in favour of membership of the Community. In 1983, 10 years after British accession, the Labour Party fought the General Election on a commitment to withdraw from the Community. And within the Conservative Party, the self-styled 'party of Europe', divisions on European issues remain both very public and very deep.

The decision-making system within the European Union is oriented towards consensus, whereas the British political system is essentially adversarial. The British system delivers winners and losers, majorities and minorities, and governments accustomed to being able to carry out their legislative programmes with a minimum of compromise. This affects the way political issues are reported and understood, and, as far as European issues are concerned, it serves to distort the nature of the negotiating process in Brussels. A British minister putting a case to his or her colleagues in the Council of Ministers is said to have 'clashed' with them; making any concession in the course of negotiation is 'giving way'; a final decision not on all points consistent with the original British position is a 'defeat'; and a discussion that breaks up without a decision is a 'row'. The use of such language, day after day, can only confirm in the public mind the impression that the Union is either incapable of taking action or acts regularly in a fashion hostile to British interests. Added to this is the willingness of the Opposition to draw attention to any aspect of a decision reached in Brussels that can be laid as a 'failure' at the Government's door.

When in 1930 **Aristide Briand** presented his plan for a European Federal Union to the **League of Nations**, the Foreign Office advised that the Government's attitude 'should be one of caution, though cordial caution' (internal memorandum, quoted in James Joll (ed.), *Britain and Europe*). The memorandum went on to speak of the need for 'a discriminating sympathy for all such re-organization of Europe as is not in unjustified contravention of British rights and interests'. More than two generations later the caution still outweighs the cordiality, and the sympathy is as discriminating as ever.

United Nations (UN)

Since the 1960s and the beginnings of **European Political Cooperation** (see **Common Foreign and Security Policy**) the member states of the Community have sought, on the whole successfully, to act as one within the United Nations (UN). This is done on the basis of regular coordination at official level and amongst foreign ministers and is symbolized by the fact that the president-in-office of the Council (see **presidency**) addresses the UN General Assembly every year on behalf of the Union.

Two member states, France and the United Kingdom, are permanent members of the UN Security Council, together with China, Russia and the United States. It has been suggested that membership should be extended to the Union as a whole, with France and the United Kingdom ceasing to be members in their own right. This view is not held by either the French or the British government, which point out that this would involve the 'European' voice in the Security Council being reduced by half (although as a result of elections in the General Assembly in October 1994 both Germany and Italy will serve as members of the Security Council in 1995–6). Meanwhile, under Article J5.4 of the **Maastricht Treaty**, France and the United Kingdom are responsible for keeping the other member states 'fully informed' and ensuring 'the defence of the positions and the interests of the Union' in the Security Council.

United States of America

The United States of America has always been broadly sympathetic to the idea of European unification. It was the **Marshall Plan** in the immediate postwar period that led to the founding of the Organization for European Economic Cooperation (see **Organization for Economic Cooperation and Development**). One of the first public utterances in favour of Western Europe becoming a 'single large market' was made by an American in 1949 (see **Single Market**). The American perception that in the Cold War the front line was on the Rhine led to the formation of the **North Atlantic Treaty Organization** (NATO) under a treaty signed in Washington in 1949, and as recently as January 1994 President Bill Clinton confirmed that 100,000 American troops would remain stationed in Europe for the foreseeable future. In the debate between **the Six** and the supporters (including the United Kingdom) of a **free trade area** (see **Maudling Plan**), American support was decisively on the side of the Six. Successive American presidents, beginning with John Kennedy in Philadelphia on 4 July 1962, have made speeches supporting European integration, which was described by Bill Clinton on 9 January 1994 as, together with the fall of the Soviet Empire, one of 'the two greatest advances for peace in the last half of the twentieth century'. Secretary of State Henry Kissinger declared 1973 to be the 'Year of Europe', and a similar focusing of attention on Europe took place in July 1994 with the second of what are now biannual **summits** between the president of the United States, the president-in-office of the **European Council** and the president of the **Commission**. The month before, President Clinton had become the first US president since Woodrow Wilson in 1919 to address the French National Assembly. The Transatlantic Declaration of November 1990 and the New Transatlantic Agenda of December 1995 lay down a framework for regular consultations between the European Union's foreign ministers and the US secretary of state, and between the Commission and the US government. The background to postwar American attitudes may be found in John Lamberton Harper, *American Visions of Europe* (Cambridge, 1994).

The idea of a **United States of Europe** has been a source of inspiration to advocates of European unity from Victor Hugo to **Winston Churchill** (see **Zürich speech**), and the United States Constitution served as an indirect model for several key phrases and concepts in the **Treaties**. From the very beginning, American officials and scholars, brought up on the history of their own constitution, showed an informed understanding of the problems of integration. Two of the earliest and best studies of the nascent European Community are by Americans (see Haas, *The Uniting of Europe*, and Lindberg, *The Political Dynamics of European Economic Integration*).

On most issues Americans and Europeans have cooperated regularly and successfully in international institutions. Disagreements have arisen with respect to trade issues, such as **Airbus**, and agriculture (especially export subsidies). However, these commercial differences, although occasionally dramatic, are relatively minor by comparison with the extent of overall cooperation.

More serious have been disagreements over security policy. At least from the early 1980s the argument that the Europeans were wealthy enough to assume a larger share of the overall burden of security within the Atlantic Alliance steadily gained ground amongst American politicians and the American public. On the European side, there were those who argued that if the Europeans did more, the Americans would seize the opportunity of doing less, and that this was a risk Europe could not take. Equally, there were others who argued that *unless* the Europeans did more, the Americans, under pressure to cut defence spending, would lose patience. The two points of view remained unresolved, although some progress was made in the early 1980s with developing a 'European pillar' within the Alliance. Against this background the meeting between President Ronald Reagan and Mikhail Gorbachev of the Soviet Union in

Reykjavik in 1986 came as a shock: contrary to what he knew to be the views of his NATO allies, the American President arrived at an agreement that, on one interpretation, exposed Europe to the risk of conventional war against vastly superior **Warsaw Pact** forces, under what later became known as the INF (intermediate-range nuclear forces) Treaty.

In the 1960s the United States supported the United Kingdom's attempts to join the Six, in the belief that British influence could help to steer the **European Economic Community** (EEC) away from protectionism. However, since British links with the United States were one of the reasons why **Charles de Gaulle** was opposed to British entry, American support had to be expressed very carefully. Described by one Congressman as 'the most ungrateful man since Judas Iscariot', de Gaulle was especially opposed to American involvement in security issues through its command-ing position in NATO – which is why France left NATO's integrated military structure in 1966. By the late 1960s the Vietnam war had resulted in widespread anti-American feeling in Western Europe, especially in the universities, a feeling that was still evident in the debate over the siting of Cruise missiles on European soil in 1983–4.

It was Henry Kissinger who wrote in 1969 that 'American policy has been extremely ambivalent: it has urged European unity while recoiling before its probable consequences'. The end of the Cold War has resulted in this ambivalence becoming less marked. Nevertheless the experience of the Gulf Crisis and Yugoslavia has underlined how far the European Union has to go before becoming the self-reliant, stable, prosperous and depend-able partner that the United States would like it to be.

United States of Europe

Although the best-known use of this phrase is a passage in **Winston Churchill**'s 1946 **Zürich speech**, the origin of the idea of a United States of Europe is much earlier. In 1849 Victor Hugo told a conference in Paris:

> There will come a day when all of you, France, Russia, Italy, Britain, Germany, all you nations of this continent, without losing your distinctive qualities or your glorious individuality, will merge closely into a higher unity and will form the fraternity of Europe, just as Normandy, Brittany, Burgundy, Lorraine, Alsace, all our provinces, have merged to become France ... Two huge groups will be seen, the United States of America and the United States of Europe, holding out their hands to one another across the ocean ... (quoted in Denis de Rougemont, *The Meaning of Europe*)

In fact, the period that followed this speech was marked by the apogee of nationalism and national rivalries in Europe and by the channelling of

Europe's energies into the acquisition of colonies overseas. The idea of a United States of Europe continued to be put forward as a way of resolving these rivalries; for example, the anthropologist J. G. Frazer in an essay of 1906 entitled 'Pax Occidentis: A League of the West' called for

> a federation . . . among the European powers [which] beginning as a League of Peace and Defence between two or three states . . . might in time expand into a federation of the whole of Europe: the United States of Europe might stand beside the United States of America as friendly rivals in the promotion of civilization and peace. (*The Gorgon's Head and other literary pieces*)

The idea of a United States of Europe retains a certain resonance but the phrase is now seldom used. This stems partly from the realization that the **European Union** created by the **Maastricht Treaty** is *sui generis* and partly from the desire to avoid misleading parallels between two quite different processes of integration: the one between relatively small, newly founded states enjoying a high degree of cultural and political homogeneity, the other between much larger, more complex and long-established entities, each with its own distinctive history and traditions. The first citation in the *Oxford English Dictionary* for 'United States of Europe' dates from 1869. (See also **Pan-Europa**.)

Uri, Pierre (1911–92)

The French economist Pierre Uri was the most important colleague of **Jean Monnet**. Having helped to draft the **Schuman Plan**, he went on to draft the **European Coal and Steel Community** (ECSC) Treaty of 1951. Five years later he was invited to draft the two Treaties establishing the **European Economic Community** (EEC) and the **European Atomic Energy Community** (EAEC or Euratom) on the basis of the recommendations of the **Spaak Committee**, in whose work he had been involved. In the 1960s and 1970s he wrote a large number of books and, as a Socialist, became a close associate of **François Mitterrand**, although he never held any government office. According to his obituary in *The Independent* (24 July 1992), Uri was 'a man without a trace of self-doubt and . . . an admired if formidable academic and negotiating figure' (see also *The Times* of 24 July 1992). In his *Memoirs* Jean Monnet wrote of Uri's 'exceptional ability to think out new and rigorous solutions to the most complex problems . . . [He] gets to the heart of them, where everything is simple; but this can only be done after going through the maze of details in which very intelligent people seem almost to enjoy losing their way.'

Value-added tax

In 1967 **the Six** agreed two Directives that required all member states to adopt a system of value-added tax (VAT), and since that date VAT has been a *de facto* requirement of membership of the European Community. VAT-based revenue is an important part of the Union's **own resources** (just over 50 per cent in 1994): each member state pays a contribution to the **Budget** of up to 1.4 per cent, not of VAT actually collected, but of the VAT that would have been collected had VAT been applied at common rates to an agreed range of goods and services. In fact, initially, rates differed widely, as did the 'base' to which VAT is applied across the member states. Because these differences affected patterns of trade (and therefore competition) and made fiscal controls necessary at the Community's internal frontiers, the Commission's 1985 White Paper on the completion of the **Single Market** proposed an approximation of VAT rates. This was followed up in a 1987 proposal for a 'standard' rate and a 'reduced' rate, each represented by a band of a few percentage points. Little progress having been made, a second proposal was made in 1989 for a minimum 'standard' rate of 15 per cent. At a meeting of the **Ecofin Council** on 19 October 1992 agreement was reached on this proposal. The minimum 'standard' rate of 15 per cent applies until 31 December 1996, at which time it may be renewed by unanimous agreement. Member states may also apply 'reduced' rates to a specific list of goods and services, and existing zero-rates (a particular feature of the British system) may be maintained but not extended.

A common system of VAT on second-hand goods and works of art is in force under the so-called Seventh VAT Directive. Sales between private individuals are exempt. VAT is levied at the standard rate on the seller's margin for professional sales on the origin principle (see **tax harmonization**). Special rules apply to works of art. To be classified as 'second-hand' a car must have been in use for six months and clocked up at least 6,000 kilometres.

It is clear that a single market can exist without VAT rates and the VAT base being exactly the same throughout that market. Economists differ on the degree of variation that may be permitted without significantly distorting competition, and arguments on this aspect will, no doubt, be a feature of the 1996 review. VAT approximation is sensitive not only because very large amounts of revenue are at stake at a time when member states are trying to reduce their budget deficits, but also because the right to fix tax rates is, in many people's view, an essential component of national and parliamentary **sovereignty**. Since the removal of fiscal frontiers between member states on the completion of the Single Market, VAT returns are now the basis of statistics on trade within the Union (see **Intrastat**).

Van Duyn case

The van Duyn case (*Yvonne van Duyn* v *Home Office*, Case 41/74) concerned a Dutch Scientologist who in 1973 was refused entry into the United Kingdom to take up employment at the Hubbard College of Scientology in East Grinstead. The British authorities justified their refusal on the grounds that it was 'undesirable' to admit persons intending to work for a cult they regarded as 'socially harmful'. In this they relied upon the 'public policy' exceptions to the right of **free movements of persons** set out in Article 48 of the **Treaty of Rome** (although there was no prohibition on British nationals working for the College of Scientology). Miss van Duyn argued that these exceptions, which had been defined more fully in a 1964 Directive, could be applied only in relation to her personal conduct. The case was referred to the **Court of Justice**.

In its ruling the following year the Court held that Article 48 conferred a right of free movement directly on individuals (see **direct effect**) without any need for implementing measures at the national level, a right that must be upheld by national courts.

'Variable geometry'

This phrase denotes a model of European integration in which member states decide whether or not to participate in a particular activity, although there will normally be a number of 'core activities' in which all states take part (see **concentric circles**). If it were always the same states that chose not to take part in new activities, then this could lead to a **two-speed Europe**. For this reason, with a few notable exceptions (such as the British 'opt-out' from the **Social Chapter** of the **Maastricht Treaty**), the European Union has chosen to venture into new areas of activity only if all member states are willing to become involved. The legal, political, procedural and budgetary complexities of a Union in which member states are active only in areas of direct benefit to them are obvious. Nevertheless, with the prospect of a larger, more heterogeneous Union the 'variable geometry' model is sure to find some supporters on the grounds that it offers greater flexibility and corresponds more closely to political reality. See also **Europe** *à la carte*, '**hard core**'.

Vedel Report

In March 1972 a working-party of independent experts chaired by the French political scientist Professor Georges Vedel published a report requested by the **Commission**, which was intended to take account of the new system of **own resources** and the new arrangements for the Community **Budget** laid down in the 1970 Treaty of Luxembourg. In fact, the report dealt at some length with the legislative powers of the **European Parliament**, and recommended that these be increased in two stages: first, by granting it a right of co-decision, a right of consultation and a suspensory veto; and second, by extending co-decision to cover more or less the whole field of Community legislation (see **co-decision procedure**). The report also recommended that the Parliament should be involved in the appointment of the president of the Commission.

The Vedel Report was the most ambitious attempt since the **Fouchet Plan** to effect a radical adjustment in the balance of power between the institutions. Indeed, it is doubtful whether the full range of responsibilities assigned to the Parliament in the report's recommendations could have been discharged by what was then only a part-time Parliament composed of Members (MEPs) appointed by and from **national parliaments**. In the event, only the recommendations on the Parliament's budgetary powers were followed up, and formed the basis of the new procedures adopted in 1975. The recommendations on co-decision and on involving the Parliament in the appointment of the president of the Commission were taken up 19 years later in the **Maastricht Treaty**.

Veto

The mechanism known as the 'veto' allows any member state, however small, to block a decision, both in the **Council of Ministers** and when representatives of the member states are meeting outside the Council framework (see below). Formally, the right of veto exists in all Treaty articles that require the Council to take decisions by **unanimity**. The number of such articles has declined over the years (see especially **Single European Act**), but many key areas – such as **own resources**, **free movement of persons**, amendments to the **Treaties**, and the **accession** of new member states – are still included. Unanimity in the Council is also required at various stages of the **cooperation** and **co-decision procedures**. In some areas the Treaty provides for decisions to be taken by representatives of the governments of member states acting 'by common accord', and this too allows for a right of veto: examples include appointments to the **Commission** and decisions on the **seat of the institutions**.

The Council is under a general obligation to act by unanimity in respect of the **Common Foreign and Security Policy** (CFSP) and **Justice and Home Affairs** (JHA) provisions of the **Maastricht Treaty** (Articles J8.2 and K4.3 TEU), but may decide that measures to implement **joint actions** be agreed by **qualified majority voting** (QMV).

Outside the Treaty, a right of veto existed for many years by virtue of the so-called **Luxembourg Compromise** of 1966. Briefly, this allowed any member state that considered a 'very important' national interest to be at stake to insist in the Council that discussion be continued until a satisfactory consensus was found, even in matters that could under the Treaty be decided by QMV. The veto was, in fact, rarely used under this procedure, since normally the mere threat of invoking the Luxembourg Compromise was enough.

The right of veto raises in the most acute and intelligible form all the most sensitive questions of **sovereignty**. It also has a direct bearing on the role of **national parliaments** in European integration: in so far as individual ministers in the Council are responsible to their national parliaments and enjoy a right of veto, national parliaments can exercise control (at least in a negative sense) over developments in the Council. On the one hand, the veto is seen by some as an essential safeguard against coercion; on the other, as a bar to collective action and a means by which a minority can frustrate the will of the majority.

On the whole, the compromise laid down in the Treaties (a right of veto in certain key areas, decisions by majority, simple or qualified, in all other fields) has worked well. Clearly, the European Community could not have worked on the same basis as the **League of Nations**, in which every state, however small, had a right of veto over all but procedural decisions. Nor could the Community have adopted a two-tier system like that of the **United Nations**, with the larger member states enjoying a right of veto by virtue of permanent membership of the Security Council. By comparison with those in other international decision-making systems, the rights of veto enjoyed by individual member states in the European Union are very limited, and with the **enlargement** of the Union this trend seems bound to continue. In this perspective, the **opt-out** (and the **variable geometry** to which it gives rise) may replace the veto as member states' weapon of last resort.

Visegrad states

The 'Visegrad states' are the Czech Republic, Hungary, Poland and Slovakia. In February 1991 at Visegrad, in Hungary, the leaders of Hungary, Poland and what was then Czechoslovakia met to discuss their approach to European integration. Since 1989 the three countries had been cooperating within the **Warsaw Pact**. They confirmed their wish for 'total integration into the European political, economic, security and legislative order' and agreed to cooperate in their progressive achievement of such integration. As a first step, all four countries have concluded **Europe Agreements** with the European Union, and are members of the **North Atlantic Cooperation Council** and of the **Council of Europe**. For most purposes, Bulgaria and Romania are now included with the Visegrad states.

Warsaw Pact

On 7 May 1955 the USSR formally annulled the wartime alliances concluded with the United Kingdom (1942) and France (1944). A week later in Warsaw, the USSR, Albania, Bulgaria, Czechoslovakia, Hungary, Poland and Romania signed a mutual defence treaty. The treaty required signatory states to assist each other in the case of 'armed aggression in Europe' (Article 4) and provided for 'a joint command of their armed forces' (Article 5). East Germany became a member in 1956, and Albania withdrew in 1968. East Germany withdrew on being reunited with West Germany in 1990 (see **German reunification**), one year before the Pact was formally dissolved. The Warsaw Pact enabled the USSR to station forces in the states of the Eastern Bloc on a 'friendly' basis (as many as 20 Soviet divisions were based in East Germany), thus facilitating the application of the **Brezhnev Doctrine**. The USSR provided about three-quarters of the Warsaw Pact forces, as well as successive commanders-in-chief. The Warsaw Pact – signed in the same month in which the Western Allies recognized the independence of West Germany and admitted it to the **North Atlantic Treaty Organization** (NATO) – marked the end of Soviet ambitions to 'neutralize' Germany and a new hardening of attitudes in the Cold War.

Werner Report

The Werner Report of 1970 was an early blueprint for the achievement of **Economic and Monetary Union** (EMU) amongst **the Six**. It inspired a number of important initiatives, including the 1971 European currency management system known as the '**Snake**' and a commitment by heads of government in 1972 to move to a single currency by 1980. The EMU process embarked upon was, however, unexpectedly disrupted by the successive effects of dollar instability in 1971 and the worldwide recession begun by the first oil crisis of 1973–4. By the mid-1970s there was little to show for this ambitious project.

Soon after the election in 1969 of Georges Pompidou as President of France and Willy Brandt as Chancellor of West Germany political momentum began to emerge for renewed progress towards closer European integration. At more or less the same time, both the French and German currencies suffered substantial turbulence on the foreign-exchange markets, proving unable to remain within the 1.5 per cent fluctuation margins around the US dollar prescribed by agreements within the International Monetary Fund (IMF). In August 1969 the French franc was devalued by 11 per cent; in September the Deutsche Mark was floated, and finally revalued by 9 per cent the following month.

In December 1969 the heads of government, meeting in The Hague, decided that EMU should be a long-term Community objective. At the same **summit** – the only such meeting to be held between 1967 and 1972 – Pompidou announced the lifting of France's veto on British membership of the Community, and the member states decided to move from the third stage of the 'transitional' phase of the Community's development (which had begun in 1966; see **transitional period**) to the final phase, starting in 1973.

The **European Commission** saw in the economic and political changes of 1969 an opportunity to make EMU a major Community priority, something it did with surprising success. Raymond Barre, the Commissioner responsible for economic and financial affairs, brought forward specific plans to realize an objective that had neither featured in the **Treaty of Rome** nor been agreed by the member states at any point since 1958. In the so-called Barre Report of 1969 the Commission proposed that to counter currency instability, macro-economic coordination should be improved, and that the fluctuation margins around the currencies of the Six should be eliminated as the first step towards fusing them into a single unit. This proposal was especially appealing to the new government in Paris, which was anxious to use the EMU goal as a means of bolstering its currency on world markets and defending parities within the **Common Agricultural Policy** (CAP). It also appealed to all those who wanted to see Europe's economic dependence on the United States reduced at a time of growing economic strain across the Atlantic.

Work was put in hand within the **Ecofin Council** on devising transitional arrangements on the road to full EMU. The latter goal was agreed in February 1970 to be the adoption of a single currency. Early differences of opinion emerged, however, about the best way forward. France (backed by Barre in Brussels) favoured the rapid freezing of exchange rates as an interim measure, and argued that such a move would of itself promote the degree of **convergence** between member states' economies necessary before the adoption of a single currency. Germany argued the opposite case, proposing convergence as a precondition to a later locking of exchange rates, for fear that premature moves might generate serious inflationary side-effects.

Germany also argued that, to provide a political foundation for EMU,

majority voting should apply in the Ecofin Council on monetary matters, and that the **European Parliament** should be more closely associated with EMU decisions. The otherwise sympathetic French Finance Minister, **Valéry Giscard d'Estaing**, indicated that his government would have difficulty in accepting any institutional formula that made explicit the transfer of monetary **sovereignty** from national to European level. Its preference was to leave institutional consolidation until later.

In March 1970 the Ecofin Council established a special study group under Pierre Werner, the Prime Minister and Finance Minister of Luxembourg, to review the EMU dossier in greater detail and propose a concrete plan for moving ahead. Werner was a well-known advocate of closer monetary integration, and had floated some ideas of his own as early as September 1968 in what was known at the time as the 'Werner Plan'. The study group, which included the chairman of the Committee of **Central Bank Governors** of the Six and the chairman of the **Monetary Committee**, completed its work very quickly. An interim report was presented to the Ecofin Council in June 1970, and the final report was delivered in October. The latter immediately became the baseline for all discussion of the issue.

The Werner Report trod a careful path between the competing French and German preferences on EMU. It proposed a three-stage move to full EMU, lasting from 1971 to 1980. The first stage would be directed at getting the economic underpinnings right and preparing the ground for any institutional development. The second stage would consolidate the economic and institutional progress of the first, leading in the third stage to the irrevocable fixing of exchange rates and finally the adoption of a single currency. The single currency was deemed to be desirable, but not strictly necessary, to the project. During the first two stages, the domestic economic policies of member states would be increasingly closely coordinated at European level to promote convergence. In parallel, there would be a progressive narrowing of currency fluctuation bands, starting as soon as possible.

Institutional innovation would be kept to a minimum. There would be no need for a **European Central Bank** (ECB). Instead, a new **European Monetary Cooperation Fund** (EMCF) would be created in the second stage to manage an increasing proportion of the reserves of member states and provide any short-term balance of payments support needed by weaker economies. The EMCF would be responsible to the existing Committee of Central Bank Governors – to be reconstituted as a 'Community system of central banks' – charged with coordinating monetary and exchange-rate policy. Macro-economic policy would need to be coordinated by 'an economic centre of decision' responsible to the European

Parliament. There seemed no reason why this could not be accomplished by the existing Ecofin Council in revised form. The report stated delphically that 'a deeper study of institutions' was not within its remit, leaving open the precise content of any amendments to be made later to the Treaty of Rome.

Gaullist opposition to the Werner Report proved more intense than even Giscard had foreseen, and he was forced to indicate to the Ecofin Council in November 1970 that only a modest first stage would be acceptable to Paris. France could certainly agree to a managed currency arrangement, but institutional consolidation would have to be evolutionary and cautious. Although the other member states were sceptical of managing rates outside a binding framework, it seemed inconceivable that any progress could be made except on French terms. Anxious not to let the political initiative slip, Germany appeared willing to experiment in this way against its earlier better judgement.

In March 1971 the Ecofin Council duly agreed a lengthy resolution on attaining EMU 'during the coming decade' by stages, only the first of which (1971–4) was elaborated. The resolution identified a series of future Council Decisions needed to bolster macro-economic coordination over the medium term. Mechanisms for closer cooperation between central banks were agreed. Most importantly, the member states committed themselves 'from the beginning of the first stage and on an experimental basis' to intervene to ensure that their currencies fluctuated against each other by less than the existing fluctuation margin allowed by the IMF against the US dollar: a 1.2 per cent band within a 1.5 per cent one. Germany insisted, successfully, that unless agreement was reached on the second and more substantive stage of EMU by January 1976, the monetary cooperation measures begun during the first stage would be discontinued.

The new exchange-rate arrangement – which was quickly dubbed the 'Snake' because the currencies of the Six were now tied to one another, rather than simply to the dollar, but on a flexible basis – had been agreed at what was to prove an extraordinarily unpropitious moment. In May 1971 the Deutsche Mark had to be revalued again unilaterally when strong upward pressure on the German currency followed a flight from the dollar, by now beset by serious balance-of-payments problems. The Snake's formal entry into effect in mid-June had to be postponed as dollar instability returned on an even greater scale. In August the dollar itself became a freely floating currency, and the whole Bretton Woods system of cross-rate parities against the dollar effectively collapsed. The anchor of the world monetary order was broken, and the EMU initiative looked stillborn.

In the course of 1972 efforts were made to salvage the project. The

Snake was relaunched in April as the so-called 'Snake in the tunnel': now applied to the Nine (see **the Six**), currencies were allowed to fluctuate within a 2.25 per cent band against the dollar, as opposed to the 4.5 per cent band laid down by the IMF. (The Smithsonian Agreement of December 1971 had devised the 4.5 per cent band as the basis for returning the dollar to 'fixed' exchange rates, although on a new, 'more realistic', set of parities.) Within a year the currencies of four countries (the United Kingdom, Ireland, Denmark and Italy) had withdrawn from the system. Nevertheless, the meeting of heads of government in Paris in October 1972 – in which the United Kingdom took part for the first time – strongly reaffirmed the Community's EMU objective, formally committing member states to its full realization by 1980. In the interim 'fixed but adjustable parities' would be pursued. Already, however, the credibility of the whole exercise had been fatally prejudiced. When the European Commission duly proposed in April 1973 that the Community move to the second stage of EMU on schedule in 1974, there was no agreement in the Ecofin Council.

By the time the heads of government met again in Paris two years later, they could note only that 'internal and international difficulties have prevented in 1973 and 1974 the accomplishment of expected progress on the road to EMU'. Their assertion that 'their will has not weakened and that their objective has not changed since the [last] Paris Conference' had a ritualistic air. The first, uncompleted stage of EMU was by now clearly in serious trouble. After the December 1974 declaration, nothing happened. Work on the Werner project was left in abeyance, and the 1980 EMU objective was quickly forgotten.

The only concrete achievements of the Werner Report and its follow-up by the Ecofin Council were, in addition to the March 1971 decision on strengthening cooperation among central banks, the creation of the EMCF in April 1973 along broadly the lines foreseen in the Report (and in advance of the latter's timetable), and the February 1974 Council Decision 'on the attainment of a high degree of convergence of the economic policies of the Member States'. The latter requires the Council to examine the economic situation in the Community at least three times a year, to adopt an annual economic report drafted by the European Commission and to establish annual economic guidelines to be followed by the Community and member states. The Council may adopt such legislation as it deems necessary to enforce these guidelines.

Several important lessons had been learnt about the economic and political difficulties of moving towards EMU. A sustained record of stable currency management was an indispensable precondition for any serious attempt to adopt a single currency. The absence of stable currencies would render the goal of a single currency meaningless, and governments needed to undertake legally binding commitments, confirmed in the Treaty, if the objective were to stand much chance of being realized. Vague commitments in principle, without a firm timetable fixed in advance, were no good. No lasting progress towards EMU could be achieved without appropriate institutional reforms guaranteeing a transfer of responsibility in the macro-economic field from national to European level. Otherwise, old habits would reassert themselves, governed by domestic imperatives, allowing little by way of a concerted reaction to international economic circumstances.

It is perhaps for these reasons that the 1989 **Delors Report** recommended a series of moves towards EMU on a much firmer legal base and in accordance with a stricter timetable than those proposed in the Werner Report or subsequently adopted by the Council. It could only do so credibly because the undoubted success of the **European Monetary System** (EMS) meant that much of the Community was already operating on the foundation of quasi-fixed exchange rates. The Werner Report rehearsed many of the arguments that arose again 20 years later, especially those relating to the interaction between convergence and fixed exchange rates, but economic and political circumstances eventually exposed the essential frailty of its recommendations.

Western European Union (WEU)

After the rejection by the French Assemblée Nationale of plans for a **European Defence Community** in August 1954, Anthony Eden, then Foreign Secretary, convened a meeting of the **Brussels Treaty** powers (the United Kingdom, France and the **Benelux** countries) together with West Germany, Italy, Canada and the United States to discuss ways of strengthening collective defence and extending cooperation into other areas. A ministerial conference was held in Paris in October 1954, and agreement was reached on modifications to the Brussels Treaty. Italy and West Germany were to be invited to become signatories to the Treaty. West Germany was allowed to rearm and was admitted to the **North Atlantic Treaty Organization** (NATO), and the last vestiges of the Allied occupation were to be removed from the Federal Republic. A condition of German rearmament was a prohibition on the possession of atomic, biological and chemical weapons. The United Kingdom agreed to maintain a certain level of forces on mainland Europe. With the ratification of these modifications, the WEU was established on 6 May 1955, with its headquarters in London.

The seven original members of the WEU have since been joined by Portugal, Spain and Greece. Denmark and Ireland are observer members, together with (since 1995) Austria, Finland and Sweden. Associate status has been extended to the other European members of NATO (Iceland, Norway and Turkey). Nine central and eastern European countries are 'associate partners'.

The Council of WEU is composed of the foreign ministers and defence ministers of the member countries. The Council meets twice a year at ministerial level and more frequently (normally twice a month) at ambassadorial level. The secretariat of WEU is headed by a secretary-general. The WEU Assembly is a parliamentary body, based in Paris, the members of which are drawn from each country's representatives to the Parliamentary Assembly of the **Council of Europe**: it meets twice a year, and draws up and debates reports on security issues. The WEU has three specialized agencies and (since 1990) an Institute for Security Studies, all of them based in Paris. It also operates its own Satellite Centre in Torrejòn, Spain. WEU has no independent military capability, being wholly dependent on forces assigned to it by member states. However, unlike NATO, it can act 'out of area', as it did by undertaking minesweeping in the Gulf during the Iran–Iraq war.

WEU got off to an inauspicious start. Its proposals to resolve the question of the **Saarland** were rejected by referendum in 1955. Its new powers, under the modified Brussels Treaty, for cooperation in the field of social and cultural affairs were transferred to the Council of Europe in 1960. WEU's importance in the 1960s stemmed primarily from the fact that it was the only European organization in which **the Six** and the United Kingdom – whose application to join the Six had been blocked by **Charles de Gaulle** – were able to meet regularly. However, in October 1984 a WEU Council meeting in Rome decided to reactivate WEU as a forum for the discussion of specifically European security questions. This was followed up three years later in The Hague with the adoption of the 'Platform on European Security Interests', which contained the commitment to develop a 'more cohesive European defence identity'. In 1990 the military response on the part of West European countries to the Gulf crisis was coordinated through WEU. At the **European Council** meeting in Maastricht in December 1991 the member states of WEU agreed to transfer the headquarters of WEU from London to Brussels. In their 'Petersberg Declaration' of June 1992 the WEU Foreign Ministers widened the organization's remit to include peace-keeping, humanitarian and rescue tasks.

In the words of the decision reached in The Hague, WEU is to be built up in stages 'as the defence component of the European Union', with meetings of WEU Chiefs of Defence Staff and 'military units answerable to WEU'. This decision was annexed to the **Maastricht Treaty** in a Declaration. The Treaty describes WEU as 'an integral part of the development of the

Union', and invites it 'to elaborate and implement decisions and actions of the Union which have defence implications' (Article J4 TEU; see **Common Foreign and Security Policy**). The Declaration sets out the 'gradual process' by which the role of WEU and its relations with the European Union and the Atlantic Alliance are to be strengthened. As part of a general tidying-up of European security structures, WEU has already assumed responsibility for most of the work formerly done by the **Euro-group** and the **Independent European Programme Group**. WEU is developing relations with the countries of central and eastern Europe.

A review of the role and structure of WEU will be one of the main features of the **Intergovernmental Conference** (IGC) due to be convened in 1996. This arises from an undertaking in Article J4.6 of the Maastricht Treaty, which in turn springs from the fact that the original Brussels Treaty of 1948 was concluded for an initial period of 50 years (some authorities, however, calculate this period from the modified Brussels Treaty of 1954: see above).

Wider versus deeper

An argument that arises frequently in the context of the **enlargement** of the European Union, 'wider versus deeper' is concerned with two contrary propositions. On the one hand there are those who believe that enlarging the Union is a political imperative and that 'deepening' it – that is, extending the range of the Union's activities and strengthening the Union's institutions – would make enlargement more difficult, given the obligation laid upon all new member states to accept the *acquis communautaire*. On the other hand there are those who emphasize the fact that enlargement will make the Union more heterogeneous and institutionally more un-wieldy, and that if progress towards the 'ever closer union' called for in the **Treaty of Rome** is to be maintained, deepening must accompany, or even precede, widening.

Much can be read between these lines. The prospect of enlargement and its alleged consequences are used to strengthen the case, on the one hand, for slowing down the integration process and, on the other, for speeding it up. A third position, held by those governments that support the fundamen-tally intergovernmental character of much of the **Maastricht Treaty**, points to **intergovernmentalism** as the key to the problem: it allows for further '**pillars**' to be added within a Union structure, yet in a way more likely to be palatable to new member states concerned about possible loss of **sovereignty** and more flexible in terms of the degree of active involvement.

The Commission's reflections, entitled 'Europe and the challenge of enlargement' (*Bulletin of the European Communities*, supplement 3/92), were submitted to the Lisbon meeting of the **European Council** in June 1992, and were unequivocal. The Commission concluded that 'the accession of new members will increase the [European Union's] diversity and heterogeneity. But widening must not be at the expense of deepening. Enlargement must not be a dilution of the Community's achievements.' The European Council itself concluded that 'if the challenges of a European Union composed of a larger number of Member States are to be met successfully, parallel progress is needed as regards the internal development of the Union'.

Yaoundé Convention

The Yaoundé Convention was a trade and aid agreement between **the Six** and the 18-member Associated African States and Madagascar (AASM), signed in Yaoundé, Cameroon, in 1963. Most of the AASM states were former French or Belgian colonies. The Convention entered into force in June 1964, was renegotiated in 1969, and was superseded by the **Lomé Convention** of 1975.

Youth for Europe

Established in 1988 and renewed for the period 1995–9, Youth for Europe is a European Union scheme that allows financial assistance to be given from the **Budget** for a wide range of projects relevant to young people, especially in the fields of education, **equal treatment**, and **citizenship**.

Zürich speech

In March 1946 **Winston Churchill** made his famous 'Iron Curtain' speech in Fulton, Missouri, in which he drew attention to the threat posed by the USSR to world peace. Four months later, at a meeting of foreign ministers in Paris, relations between the United States and the USSR took a decisive turn for the worse, and it became clear that the idea of a lasting peace underwritten by the Great Powers was not likely to be realized. Churchill therefore returned to a theme that he had touched on in a speech to both houses of the Belgian parliament on 16 November 1945, the idea of a **'United States of Europe**, which will unify this Continent in a manner never known since the fall of the Roman Empire'.

Churchill's prime concern was to set out what Europe could do to contain the Soviet threat. In a speech in Zürich on 19 September 1946 he painted a characteristically broad and vivid picture of postwar devastation in Europe: 'Over wide areas a vast quivering mass of tormented, hungry, care-worn and bewildered human beings gape at the ruins of their cities and homes, and scan the dark horizons for the approach of some new peril, tyranny or terror.' But, he said, there was a 'sovereign remedy . . . to re-create the European family, or as much of it as we can, and provide it with a structure under which it can dwell in peace, in safety, and in freedom. We must build a kind of United States of Europe.'

Churchill went on to make it clear that the United States of Europe would be a regional organization within the United Nations that 'could give a sense of enlarged patriotism and common citizenship to the distracted peoples of this turbulent and mighty continent'. From this passage and from others in the same speech it is evident that Churchill did not see the United Kingdom as part of the United States of Europe but as its 'friend and sponsor': the primary British obligation was to another 'natural grouping', the Commonwealth.

Then followed the passage that, as Churchill was well aware, was the most striking of the whole speech:

> I am now going to say something that will astonish you. The first step in the re-creation of the European family must be a partnership between France and Germany. In this way only can France recover

the moral leadership of Europe. There can be no revival of Europe without a spiritually great France and a spiritually great Germany. The structure of the United States of Europe, if well and truly built, will be such as to make the material strength of a single state less important. Small nations will count as much as large ones and gain their honour by their contribution to the common cause.

(Robert Rhodes James (ed.), *Winston S. Churchill: His complete speeches, 1897–1963*, Vol. VII)

The speech concluded with a practical suggestion: 'The first step is to form a **Council of Europe**. If at first all the states of Europe are not willing or able to join the Union, we must nevertheless proceed to assemble and combine those who will and those who can.'

The impact of this speech was enormous. The fact that a statesman of Churchill's standing had taken up the European cause gave it fresh impetus, and made Churchill the obvious choice as the man to preside over the **Congress of Europe** two years later. At the same time, the speech gave a misleading impression of the extent to which the United Kingdom or, more especially, the Conservative Party (of which Churchill, although no longer Prime Minister, was then still leader) was prepared to become involved in European integration.

Bibliography

There is a vast and steadily expanding literature on the subject of European integration, and even a list of those books and articles currently available in English would be well beyond the scope of this *Companion*. However, the radical changes brought about by the Single European Act, the collapse of the Soviet Union, the Maastricht Treaty and the prospect of further enlargement have meant that many works are neither sufficiently up-to-date to be useful nor old enough to be historically interesting.

Some of the more specialized bibliographical references are to be found in the entries that form the main part of this book. In the bibliography that follows, which is limited, with few exceptions, to works in English, I have listed a broad selection of books both old and new, most of which contain bibliographies of their own. For reasons of space, I have had to omit all references to periodicals (the main ones are listed in Section 10). With very few exceptions, I have also omitted references to biographies and autobiographies of postwar politicians (such as Harold Macmillan, Konrad Adenauer or Georges Pompidou), even though many of these contain information or insights with a bearing on European integration, and to books aimed primarily at specific professional groups (such as businessmen or lawyers wanting to know more about the Single Market).

The most up-to-date bibliography of material in English on the European Communities is by John Paxton in the International Organizations series of 'selective, critical, annotated bibliographies' (Clio Press, Oxford, 1992). This work, with 682 entries, contains only a small selection of references to periodical literature. Some idea of the quantity of pre-1977 material may be gained from Karl Kujath's *Bibliographie zur Europäischen Integration* (in German, French and English: Bonn, 1977), which runs to 732 pages.

The flow of information from European institutions is so enormous that some special guidance is necessary. As far as the institutions and ancillary bodies of the European Union are concerned, Ian Thomson's *The Documentation of the European Communities* (1989) is indispensable. Thomson is also the editor of *European Access*, published every two months, which includes bibliographical references and brief reviews of all new material, including newspaper articles, as it is published. *EUR-OP News*, published quarterly by the Office for Official Publications of the European Communities in Luxembourg, also lists and describes new publications.

A comprehensive range of materials may be found in the Commission's library in Brussels or in the European Parliament's main library in Luxembourg (there is a subsidiary reference collection in Brussels): both grant access to *bona fide* researchers, but neither lends material nor supplies documentation. The historical archives of the European Communities are kept at the European University Institute at Fiesole, near Florence.

The Information Offices of the European Commission in most major national capitals worldwide and of the European Parliament in the capitals of the member states may also be helpful; some have libraries open to the public. The United Kingdom now has an extensive network of European Information Centres (EICs) and European Documentation Centres (EDCs), details of which are obtainable from the Information Offices. Much material is, of course, obtainable on various databases, in particular, the CELEX database operated by the Commission, which contains full texts of all legislation and other official documents, and which may be accessed from any EIC or EDC. The *Annual General Report* and the monthly *Bulletin of the European Union* are comprehensive guides to the activities of all the institutions, and contain references to official documents. Some of the main official documents are available as supplements to the *Bulletin*. The sales agent for all publications of the European Union in the United Kingdom is Her Majesty's Stationery Office, from whom catalogues may be obtained.

Most of the other major European organizations – such as the Council of Europe and the Western European Union – put out regular publications, either free or on subscription. The titles of these publications may be obtained either from the organization direct or from the appropriate entry in, for example, the *Yearbook of International Organizations*. Many of these organizations also have libraries open to the public or a press and information service.

Except where stated otherwise, the place of publication for all books listed below is London.

1 General reference

Boudant, Joel, and Gounelle, Max, *Les grandes dates de l'Europe communautaire* (Paris, 1989).
A comprehensive and well-arranged chronology, the fullest of its kind.

Cook, Chris, and Paxton, John, *European Political Facts 1918–1990* (rev. ed. 1994).
The standard reference-book in English, although the emphasis is on the European states rather than on European integration.

Cook, Chris, and Stevenson, John, *The Longman Handbook of Modern European History, 1763–1991* (1992).
Concise, reliable reference book.

Drost, Harry, *What's What and Who's Who in Europe* (1995).
Uniquely comprehensive 'fact book' on current affairs.

The Economist Pocket Europe (2nd edn, 1994).
The most accessible one-volume collection of facts about the European states and international institutions.

European Communities Encyclopaedia and Directory 1992 (1991).
Expensive and cumbersome, but the encyclopaedia, by Derek Urwin, is excellent.

Europe: A Thematic Atlas (1992).
Published by *The Economist*, the atlas is a clear and comprehensive, if in places idiosyncratic, presentation of a wide range of data.

Fernandez-Armesto, Felipe (ed.), *The Peoples of Europe* (1994).
Very useful socio-ethnographic handbook to all the national groupings in Europe, large and small.

Gondrand, François, *Eurospeak: A User's Guide* (trs. Peter Bowen, 1992).
The fullest and most entertaining guide to the acronyms and argot of the Brussels institutions.

Joyaux, François, *Encyclopédie de l'Europe* (Paris, 1993).
An excellent one-volume encyclopaedia, with a full description of international institutions and concise histories of individual states.

Keegan, Victor, and Kettle, Martin, *The New Europe* (1993).
Lively and informative survey by a team of writers from the *Guardian*.

Leonard, Dick, *The Economist Guide to the European Union* (4th edn, 1994).
The best general handbook.

The Times Guide to the European Parliament (1979, 1984, 1989 and 1994 edns).
Short biographies and photographs of all MEPs, with useful data on the results, the issues, the campaigns, etc., in all the member states.

Weidenfeld, Werner, and Wessels, Wolfgang (eds), *Europa von A–Z* 3rd edn, Bonn, 1994).
Reliable one-volume encyclopaedia.

Young, John W., *The Longman Companion to Cold War and Detente 1941–91* (1993).
Very useful factual guide to the politico-military background to European unification.

2 History

Barker, Sir Ernest, Clark, Sir George, and Vaucher, P. (eds.), *The European Inheritance* (3 vols, Oxford, 1954).
A survey by an international team of scholars, from the Bronze Age to 1950.

Beloff, Max, *The United States and the Unity of Europe* (1963).
Classic study, now partially superseded by Duignan and Gann (see below).

Brugmans, Hendrik (ed.), *Europe: Dream, Adventure, Reality* (Brussels, n.d.).
A valuable collection of essays, many of them by pioneers of integration, prepared for the thirtieth anniversary of the Treaty of Rome.

Delouche, Frédéric (ed.), *Illustrated History of Europe* (1993).
Wide-ranging, well-balanced narrative by an international team.

Duignan, Peter, and Gann, L. H., *The United States and the New Europe, 1945–1993* (Oxford, 1994).
The fullest and most recent account of US–Europe relations.

Duroselle, Jean-Baptiste, *Europe: A History of its Peoples* (trs. Richard Mayne, 1990).
A succinct history of Europe from a 'European' point of view.

European Movement, *The European Movement and the Council of Europe* (n.d.).
Of great interest for its account of the 1948 Congress of Europe in The Hague.

Fursdon, Edward, *The European Defence Community: A History* (1980).
A very clear background to European states' postwar collaboration in the defence field; the standard work in English.

Haas, Ernst B., *The Uniting of Europe: Political, Social and Economic Forces, 1950–1957* (Stanford, 1958).
Pioneering and sympathetic study by an American scholar.

Hay, Denys, *Europe: the Emergence of an Idea* (rev. edn, Edinburgh, 1968).
A pioneering study, still the only one of its kind in English.

Hogan, Michael, *The Marshall Plan: America, Britain, and the Reconstruction of Western Europe, 1947–1952* (Cambridge, 1987).
Not as readable as Mee (see below), but more detailed.

Joll, James, *Europe since 1870* (3rd edn, Harmondsworth, 1983).
Reliable and well-written concise history.

Laqueur, Walter, *Europe in Our Time* (Harmondsworth, 1993).
A handy supplement to Joll (see above) covering the postwar period.

Lindberg, Leon L., *The Political Dynamics of European Economic Integration* (Stanford, 1963).
Perceptive study within a conceptual framework still widely used; particularly strong on the customs union versus free trade area debate.

Lipgens, Walter, *A History of European Integration*, Vol. 1, 1945–1947 (only volume published: Oxford, 1982).
Immensely detailed; the standard work in English.

Lipgens, Walter (ed.), *Documents on the History of European Integration* (Berlin/New York): Vol. 1, *Continental Plans for European Union, 1939–1945* (1985); Vol. 2, *Plans for European Union in Great Britain and in Exile, 1939–1945* (1986); Vol. 3, *The Struggle for European Union by Political Parties and Pressure Groups in Western European Countries, 1945–1950* (1988).
Voluminous and authoritative collection of documents, with commentary; the only work of its kind.

Mayne, Richard, *The Community of Europe* (1962); *The Recovery of Europe* (1970); *Postwar: The Dawn of Today's Europe* (1983).
Although these three books overlap, they are all worth reading as lucid, well-informed accounts of European integration written from the inside.

Mayne, Richard, and Pinder, John, *Federal Union: The Pioneers* (1990).
The only comprehensive study of the contribution made by British federalists to European integration, but too partisan for the non-specialist.

Mee, Charles L., *The Marshall Plan: the launching of the Pax Americana* (New York, 1984).
Stronger on the politics than the economics, but a readable account of a decisive episode (see also Hogan above).

Milward, Alan, *The Reconstruction of Western Europe 1945–1951* (1984).
The most authoritative account in English of the early years of European integration.

Milward, Alan, *The European Rescue of the Nation-State* (1992).
Very detailed and independent-minded study of the birth of the European institutions; the basic thesis is implicit in the title.

Pinder, John, *The European Community and Eastern Europe* (1991).
Out of date in the details, but useful for the historical background.

Scott, George, *The Rise and Fall of the League of Nations* (1973).
Clearly written non-specialist study of the League, offering some instructive parallels with postwar European institutions.

Temperley, A. C., *The Whispering Gallery of Europe* (1938).
An inside account of the League of Nations by the man who acted as military adviser to successive British delegations.

Urwin, Derek, *The Community of Europe: A History of European Integration since 1945* (2nd edn, 1995).
Serviceable and reliable history.

Wallace, William, *The Transformation of Western Europe* (1990).
Good analysis, but written at a time of rapid change.

Weigall, David, and Stirk, Peter (eds), *The Origins and Development of the European Community* (Leicester, 1992).
Digs deeper and more widely than most comparable studies, to good effect.

Western European Union, *Ten Years of Seven-Power Europe* (Paris, 1964).
Concentrates on security issues, but contains a very good essay by Peter Kirk MP, the first Conservative leader in the European Parliament, on 'The British Question-mark to Europe'.

White, Theodore H., *Fire in the Ashes: Europe in Mid-Century* (1954).
Stimulating survey of postwar Europe by a distinguished American historian.

Young, John W., *Britain, France and the Unity of Europe 1945–51* (Leicester, 1984).
Standard history of Franco-British relations in the immediate postwar years: particularly valuable for its account of the origins of the Council of Europe and the British reaction to the Schuman Plan.

3 The United Kingdom and Europe

Black, Jeremy, *Convergence or Divergence? Britain and the Continent* (1994).
Comprehensive survey of relations between the United Kingdom and the Continent since the time of the Romans.

Brivati, Brian, and Jones, Harriet (eds), *From Reconstruction to Integration: Britain and Europe Since 1945* (Leicester, 1993).
The most comprehensive politico-historical survey.

Bullen, Roger, and Pelly, M. E. (eds), *Documents on British Policy Overseas*, Series II, Vol. I (1986).
Documents from official archives on the Schuman Plan and the Council of Europe, 1950–52, with introduction, detailed chronology and explanatory notes.

Bulmer, Simon, George, Stephen, and Scott, Andrew (eds), *The United Kingdom and EC Membership Evaluated* (1992).
One of a useful series of comprehensive country-by-country studies.

Charlton, Michael, *The Price of Victory* (1983).
Uniquely interesting and valuable account of the United Kingdom's attitude to European integration, much of it based on interviews with those politicians and civil servants directly involved.

George, Stephen, *An Awkward Partner: Britain in the EC* (Oxford, 1990).
Balanced general survey.

George, Stephen, *Britain and European Integration since 1945* (2nd edn, Oxford, 1994).
Similar in scope to Young (see below), and reaches broadly the same conclusions.

Joll, James (ed.), *Britain and Europe: Pitt to Churchill, 1793–1940* (1950).
Selected texts with a commentary.

Kitzinger, Uwe, *Diplomacy and Persuasion: How Britain joined the Common Market* (1973).
The standard history.

Nutting, Anthony, *Europe Will Not Wait* (1960).
Widely read in its day, a plea by a former minister of the Foreign and Commonwealth Office, who resigned over Suez, for Britain to get more involved in European integration.

Radice, Giles, *Offshore* (1992).
Penetrating politico-psychological study by a pro-European Labour MP.

Seton-Watson, R. W., *Britain in Europe 1789–1914* (Cambridge, 1937).
The historical background to British attitudes to Europe, diplomatic and political.

Skidelsky, Robert, 'Britain and Europe' in *Interests and Obsessions* (1993).
Thoughtful and suggestive essay.

Young, John W., *Britain and European Unity, 1945–1992* (1993).
Up-to-date study of the European argument in the United Kingdom, from Clement Attlee to John Major.

4 The Institutions of the European Union

Abeles, Marc, *La vie quotidienne au Parlement Européen* (Paris, 1992).
Lively 'anthropological' study of the Parliament and its inhabitants, their rituals, social organization and belief-systems.

Archer, Clive, *Organizing Europe: the Institutions of Integration* (2nd edn, 1994).
A very clear, non-specialist account of the institutions and the relations between them.

Archer, Clive, and Butler, Fiona, *The European Community: Structure and Process* (1992).
A good general handbook.

Bulmer, Simon, and Wessels, Wolfgang, *The European Council* (1987).
No longer up to date, but useful as background.

de La Guerivière, Jean, *Voyage à l'intérieur de l'Eurocratie* (new edn, Paris, 1993).
Entomological study of the Eurocrat.

Edwards, Geoffrey, and Spence, David (eds), *The European Commission* (Harlow, 1995).
The fullest and clearest description of the Commission in English.

Heertje, Arnold (ed.), *Investing in Europe's Future* (1983).
Description and analysis of the European Investment Bank.

Jacobs, Francis, Corbett, Richard, and Shackleton, Michael, *The European Parliament* (3rd edn, 1995).
Authoritative and comprehensive study by a team of insiders.

King, Preston, and Bosco, Andrea (eds), *A Constitution for Europe* (1991).
Study by a team of federalists, with much recondite historical information.

Lasok, K. P. E., *The European Court of Justice: Practice and Procedure* (1984).
The standard description of the Court of Justice.

Laursen, Finn, and Vanhoonecker, Sophie (eds), *The Intergovernmental Conference on Political Union* (The Hague, 1992).
The institutional and political background to the Maastricht Treaty; for specialists only.

Lodge, Juliet, and Herman, Valentine, *Direct Elections to the European Parliament* (1992).
Lodge, Juliet (ed.), *Direct Elections to the European Parliament 1984* (1986).
The first of these books sets out the political and legislative background to the first (1979) European elections, the second is a survey of the 1984 European elections campaign throughout the member states.

Marquand, David, *Parliament for Europe* (1979).
A suggestive and stimulating study, written at the time of the first European elections.

Middlemas, Keith, *Orchestrating Europe* (1995).
Based on 'elite oral history', a stimulating but not always accurate study of 'informal politics'.

Spierenburg, Dirk, and Poidevin, Raymond, *The History of the High Authority of the European Coal and Steel Community* (1994).
Comprehensive and specialized; the standard work.

Wallace, H. and W., and Webb, Carole, *Policy-Making in the European Community* (2nd edn, Chichester, 1983).
Predates the latest Treaty changes, but still valuable as general background to how policy is made in different areas.

Westlake, Martin, *The Commission and the Parliament* (1994).
Careful, slightly clinical study of the Commission–Parliament relationship, with many incidental insights.

Westlake, Martin, *Britain's Emerging Euro-Elite? The British in the European Parliament, 1979–1992* (Aldershot, 1994).
The impact of British MEPs in the Parliament since the first European elections.

Westlake, Martin, *The Council of the European Union* (1995).
The only up-to-date study of the Council.

Westlake, Martin, *A Modern Guide to the European Parliament* (1994).
The best book on the Parliament.

5 Law

Arnull, Anthony, *The General Principles of EEC Law and the Individual* (Leicester, 1990).
Predates the Maastricht Treaty provisions on citizenship but useful none the less.

Benyon, John *et al.* (eds), *Police Co-operation in Europe: an investigation* (Leicester, 1993).
The fullest study to date, by a team from Leicester University's Centre for the Study of Public Order.

Church, Clive H., and Phinnemore, David, *European Union and European Community* (1994).
Very useful and accessible politico-legal commentary on the Treaties by a team from the University of Kent.

Corbett, Richard, *The Treaty of Maastricht* (1993).
Text with politico-legal commentary.

Green, Nicholas, Hartley, Trevor C., and Usher, John A., *The Legal Foundations of the Single European Market* (Oxford, 1992).
The best work in its field.

Harding, Christopher, *European Community Investigations and Sanctions* (Leicester, 1993).
Concentrates on how Treaty provisions with a bearing on industry and commerce are enforced.

Hartley, Trevor C., *The Foundations of European Community Law* (3rd edn, Oxford, 1994).
Excellent general background.

Lasok, D., and Bridge, J. W., *Law and Institutions of the European Community* (6th edn, 1994).
A standard work, many times revised.

Markesinis, Basil (ed.), *The Gradual Convergence* (Oxford, 1994).
How the different legal systems in Europe are learning from each other.

Oppenheimer, Andrew (ed.), *The Relationship Between European Community Law and National Law: The Cases* (Cambridge, 1994).
Clear account of a key aspect of Community law.

Paterson, Gerald, *The European Patent System* (1992).
Authoritative account of an increasingly important area of law in the European Union.

Pauly, Alexis (ed.), *Les accords de Schengen* (Maastricht, 1993).
The Schengen Agreement from every possible angle (the proceedings of a 1992 conference).

Rudden, Bernard, *Basic Community Cases* (Oxford, 1987).
A selection of the key cases that bring out fundamental principles of Community law.

Rudden, Bernard, and Wyatt, Derrick, *Basic Community Laws* (5th edn, Oxford, 1994).
Key passages from the Treaties, with commentary.

Toth, A. G., *The Oxford Encyclopaedia of European Community Law*; Vol. 1, *Institutional Law* (Oxford, 1990).
The first volume of what promises to be the standard work in English.

Usher, John A., *Cases and Materials on the Law of the European Communities* (3rd edn, 1993).
Assembles for each main area of activity the relevant Treaty passages plus key legislation and Court of Justice rulings: an extremely useful book.

Weatherill, Stephen, and Beaumont, Paul, *EC Law* (2nd edn, Harmondsworth, 1995).
A clear, comprehensive and accessible handbook to every aspect of Community law.

Wyatt, Derrick, and Dashwood, Alan, *European Community Law* (3rd edn, 1993).
Latest edition of a standard work: more emphasis on legal concepts than Lasok and Bridge (see above).

6 Economics and the Single Market

Bulmer, Simon, and Scott, Andrew (eds), *Economic and Political Integration in Europe* (Oxford, 1994).
Essays on various aspects of integration, most of a high standard.

Colchester, Nicholas, and Buchan, David, *Europe Relaunched: Truths and Illusions on the Way to 1992* (1990).
Lively and well-informed account of the personal and political background to the Single Market programme.

de Grauwe, Paul, and Papademos, Lucas (eds), *The European Monetary System in the 1990s* (1990).
Although they predate the partial collapse of the ERM in September 1992, these essays are still useful as general background.

El-Agraa, Ali M., *The Economics of the European Community* (4th edn, 1994).
Well-established standard textbook.

Emerson, Michael, *et al.*, *One Market, One Money* (Oxford, 1992).
Excellent collection of essays by an expert team.

Ernst and Young/NIESR, *A Strategy for the ECU* (1990).
Specialized survey of how the ECU works and how it might work in the future.

Goodman, S. F., *The European Community* (2nd edn, 1993).
Good standard textbook.

Johnson, Christopher, and Collingnon, Stefan (eds), *The Monetary Economics of Europe* (1994).
Good collection of essays from a broadly pro-EMU standpoint.

Ludlow, Peter, *The Making of the European Monetary System* (1982).
The standard work in English.

Manser, William A. P., *Control from Brussels* (1993).
Survey of all business activities subject to Community law.

Padoa-Schioppa, Tommaso, *Efficiency, Stability, and Equity* (Oxford, 1987).
The Commission's study of the effects of the Single Market programme.

Padoa-Schioppa, Tommaso, *The Road to Monetary Union in Europe: the Emperor, the Kings, and the Genies* (Oxford, 1994).
Narrative and analytical account of EMU: accessible and up to date.

Steinherr, Alfred (ed.), *Thirty Years of European Monetary Integration* (1994).
Good non-specialist general survey; contains essay by Valéry Giscard d'Estaing on the year 2000, 'The European currency's first birthday'.

Swann, Dennis, *The Economics of the Common Market* (8th edn, Harmondsworth, 1995).
The standard textbook, many times revised.

Swann, Dennis (ed.), *The Single European Market and Beyond* (1992).
Good combination of analysis and informed speculation.

Tsoukalis, Loukas, *The New European Economy* (2nd edn, Oxford, 1993).
Lively but authoritative study, especially good on trade policy.

7 Politics and political parties

Butler, David, and Jowett, Paul, *Party Strategies in Britain* (1985).
Appraises the campaign and the results in the 1984 European elections.

Butler, David, and Marquand, David, *European Elections and British Politics* (1981).
Examines the 1979 European elections as a phenomenon in British politics.

Featherstone, Kevin, *Socialist Parties and European Integration* (Manchester, 1988).
Especially useful for the historical background to Socialist attitudes.

Hanley, David (ed.), *Christian Democracy in Europe: a comparative perspective* (1994).
The only recent major study in English on an important topic.

Irving, R. E. M., *The Christian Democratic Parties of Western Europe* (1979).
Out of date, but useful as background reading.

Jacobs, Francis (ed.), *Western European Political Parties* (Harlow, 1989).
An essential reference work, the only one of its kind in English.

Morgan, Roger, *West European Politics since 1945: the Shaping of the European Community* (1972).
Lucid and balanced account, from the postwar years to the first enlargement of the Community.

Reif, Karlheinz, *Ten European Elections* (1985).
Underlines the separateness of national campaigns in the 1984 European elections.

Smith, Gordon, *Politics in Western Europe* (5th edn, Aldershot, 1989).
The standard handbook: the basic typology classifying the various political 'families' is widely used. See especially Michael Smart's research note on party strengths, 1946–88.

Urwin, Derek, and Paterson, William (eds), *Politics in Western Europe Today* (1990).
Good collection of essays.

8 Memoirs and biographies

Brinkley, Douglas, and Hackett, Clifford (eds), *Jean Monnet: The Path to European Unity* (New York, 1991).
Essays on Monnet, many by people who knew him personally.

Duchêne, François, *Jean Monnet: The First Statesman of Interdependence* (New York and London, 1994).
A very full and readable biography, by one of Monnet's associates.

Grant, Charles, *Delors: The House that Jacques Built* (1994).
Excellent biography of Jacques Delors, with much incidental detail on the workings of the Commission.

Jenkins, Roy, *European Diary, 1977–1981* (1989).
Lively and informative account of the author's presidency of the Commission.

Marjolin, Robert, *Architect of European Unity: Memoirs 1911–1986* (1989).
The author, a distinguished economist, was a member of the Commission from 1958 to 1967 and later one of the 'Three Wise Men'.

Monnet, Jean, *Memoirs* (trs. Richard Mayne, 1978).
Essential reading, especially valuable for his account of the Schuman Plan and the Treaty of Paris.

Ross, George, *Jacques Delors and European Integration* (Cambridge, 1995).
Close-up study by an American political scientist, based on extensive contacts with the Delors *cabinet*.

Spaak, Paul-Henri, *The Continuing Battle* (1971).
Autobiography by the Belgian statesman, a key figure in European integration during the postwar period.

Spender, Stephen, *European Witness* (1946).
Illuminating account of a visit to occupied Germany in 1945, to report back on what remained of German intellectual life.

9 General studies

Arter, David, *The Politics of European Integration* (1994).
Ingenious and original account of the external and internal forces that shaped the integration process.

Baldassarri, Mario, and Mundell, Robert (eds), *Building the New Europe* (2 vols, 1993).
Bulky, expensive and specialized, with a bias towards economics, but with some good essays.

Beloff, Max, *Europe and the Europeans* (1957).
Ambitious report from a Council of Europe study group.

Blacksell, Mark, and Williams, Alan M. (eds), *The European Challenge* (Oxford, 1994).
Assorted essays, mainly from a politico-geographical point of view.

Brittan, Sir Leon, *The Europe We Need* (1994).
How Europe should develop, by the senior British Commissioner.

Browning, Alison, *L'Europe et les intellectuels* (Paris, 1984).
Intelligent interviews with leading European intellectuals.

Brugmans, Henri, *L'idée européenne* (Bruges, 1965).
Historical analysis of the 'European idea' since 1918.

Buchan, David, *Europe: the Strange Superpower* (Aldershot, 1993).
Stimulating appraisal by a *Financial Times* journalist of Europe's performance as an actor on the world's stage (see also Ginsberg below).

Bulmer, Simon, and Scott, Andrew (eds), *Economic and Political Integration in Europe* (Oxford, 1994).
Valuable general survey: particularly good essays on the reform of the European Monetary System and developments in the Court of Justice.

Burgess, Michael (ed.), *Federalism and Federation in Western Europe* (1986).
Collection of essays on the federalist contribution to European integration and on federal systems in Europe.

Burgess, Michael, *Federalism and European Union* (1989).
How federalist ideas have influenced European integration since 1972.

Butler, Michael, *Europe: More than a Continent* (1986).
General survey by the former British Permanent Representative in Brussels, with lucid account of the British Budget dispute.

Cafruny, Alan W., and Rosenthal, Glenda W. (eds), *The State of the European Community* (Harlow, 1993).
The second in a biennial series: good essay on the Maastricht ratification debate in the United Kingdom.

Cole, G. D. H., and Cole, Margaret, *The Intelligent Man's Review of Europe Today* (1933).
Pioneering prewar survey.

Cole, John, and Cole, Francis, *The Geography of the European Community* (1993).
Integration from a geographical point of view, with many revealing insights into regional policy, transport, energy, etc.

Collett, Peter, *Foreign Bodies* (1993).
Entertaining and revealing account of how manners and mannerisms vary across Europe.

Curry, George (ed.), *Tomorrows in Europe* (Columbia, South Carolina, 1973).
Three excellent studies, originally delivered as lectures: by Hugh Seton-Watson on nationalism in central Europe, by Roy Jenkins on EC–US relations, and by Robert Rhodes James on Churchill.

Dahrendorf, Ralf, *Reflections on the Revolution in Europe* (1990).
Consciously modelled on Burke, a stimulating essay on the collapse of Soviet hegemony in eastern Europe.

Dawson, Andrew H., *A Geography of European Integration* (1993).
Refreshing alternative to political, economic, or institutional studies.

Delors, Jacques, *Our Europe* (trs. Brian Pearce, 1992; originally published as *La France par l'Europe*, Paris, 1988).
Authoritative but slightly bland: Charles Grant's biography (see Section 8) is more revealing.

de Rougemont, Denis, *28 siècles d'Europe* (1961, rep. Brussels, 1990).
The 'European idea' from its origins to modern times.

de Rougemont, Denis, *The Meaning of Europe* (trs. Alan Braley, 1965).
Wide-ranging, ruminative essay by a once-influential Swiss writer.

Duff, Andrew, Pinder, John, and Pryce, Roy, *Maastricht and Beyond* (1994).
Polemical and speculative essay by a team of committed federalists.

Duursma, Jorri, *Self-determination, Statehood and International Relations of Micro-States* (doctoral thesis, University of Leyden, 1994).
A comprehensive and interesting survey of how micro-states (Andorra, Liechtenstein, Monaco, San Marino and the Vatican City) survive and prosper.

Elazar, Daniel J. (ed.), *Federal Systems of the World: A Handbook of Federal, Confederal and Autonomy Arrangements* (1991).
The only survey of its kind; underlines the diversity of federal systems.

Emerson, Michael, *What Moves for Europe?* (Cambridge, Mass., 1988).
Well-informed speculation by one of the architects of EMU.

Franklin, Michael, *Britain's Future in Europe* (1990).
Intelligent essay by a committed and experienced pro-European.

Ginsberg, Roy H., *Foreign Policy Actions of the European Community* (Boulder, Colorado, 1989).

Thoroughgoing analysis of the EC's performance in foreign affairs, with complete list of 'foreign policy actions' 1958–85.

Giordan, Henri (ed.), *Les minorités en Europe* (Paris, 1992).
Wide-ranging, scholarly survey of how minorities are treated in Europe.

Gunther, John, *Inside Europe* (rev. illustrated edn, November 1938); *Inside Europe Today* (1961).
These two books by John Gunther, the best-known American journalist of his day, are lively, well-informed, occasionally cynical reviews of the state of Europe, with many entertaining biographical sketches.

Hallstein, Walter, *United Europe: Challenge and Opportunity* (1962).
Originally delivered as lectures in the US, these are forceful and well-argued reflections by the first President of the Commission

Hallstein, Walter, *Europe in the Making* (1972).
An English translation of Hallstein's *Der Unvollendete Bundesstaat* (1969), this is more wide-ranging and more polemical than *United Europe*.

Hinsley, F. H., *Sovereignty* (2nd edn, Cambridge, 1986).
Short, authoritative study from the viewpoint of international relations.

Hodges, Michael (ed.), *European Integration* (Harmondsworth, 1972).
Pioneering collection of academic texts.

Hoffmann, Stanley, *The European Sisyphus* (Boulder, Colorado, 1995).
Thoughtful essays 1964–94 by a distinguished American scholar.

Holland, Martin, *European Integration* (1994).
Good chapters on the United States of Europe and the enlargement of the Union.

Jacquemin, Alexis, and Wright, David (eds), *The European Challenges post-1992* (1993).
Good collection of essays, with a bias towards trade and economics.

Keohane, Robert, and Hoffmann, Stanley (eds), *The New European Community* (1991).
Six excellent essays: those on the Commission (by Peter Ludlow) and a European constitution (by G. F. Mancini) are outstanding.

King, Russell (ed.), *The New Geography of European Migrations* (1993).
Interesting study of post-Cold War population shifts and political pressures.

Kramer, Jane, *Unsettling Europe* (New York, 1980); *Europeans* (New York, 1988).
Two extremely well-written and sympathetic accounts of the lives of ordinary Europeans, by a *New Yorker* journalist.

Lodge, Juliet (ed.), *The European Community and the Challenge of the Future* (2nd edn, 1993).
Wide-ranging essays, including an excellent one on referendums.

Lodge, Juliet (ed.), *European Union* (1986).
No longer up to date, but contains good essays on the Crocodile initiative and on Altiero Spinelli.

Lubbers, Ruud, *Europe: A Continent of Traditions* (Cambridge, 1993).
The text of a lecture delivered in Cambridge by the Dutch Prime Minister (1982–94) and convinced European.

Miall, Hugh (ed.), *Redefining Europe* (1994).
Short study of the new relations with central and eastern Europe.

Milward, Alan, *et al., The Frontiers of National Sovereignty* (1993).
Case histories by an international team of the postwar tension between interdependence and integration in Europe.

Nicoll, William, and Salmon, Trevor C., *Understanding the New European Community* (1994).
Good general introduction.

Nugent, Neil, *Government and Politics in the European Community* (3rd edn, Oxford, 1994).
Clear, solid guide to how the institutions work.

Oakeshott, Michael, *The Social and Political Doctrines of Contemporary Europe* (1939).
Key texts, with interlinking essays.

Pinder, John, *European Community: The Building of a Union* (2nd edn, Oxford, 1995).
Lucid, non-specialist account of European integration past and present.

Pryce, Roy (ed.), *The Dynamics of European Union* (1987).
High points and low points in postwar European integration: the study by Otto Schmuck on the Draft Treaty establishing the European Union is particularly interesting.

Rundle, Stanley, *Language as a Social and Political Factor in Europe* (1946).
Quirky but intelligent survey of the language issue.

Shonfield, Andrew, *Europe: Journey to an Unknown Destination* (Harmondsworth, 1973).
The Reith lectures, in the year of the UK's accession to the EC.

Siedentopf, Heinrich, and Ziller, Jacques (eds), *Making European Policies Work* (2 vols, Brussels, 1988).
A unique survey, built around case-histories, of how policies agreed at European level are put into practice in the member states.

Smith, Anthony D., *National Identity* (Harmondsworth, 1991).
Very informative and clearly written account of how national identity is shaped and expressed.

Smith, M. L., and Stirk, P. M. R. (eds), *Making the New Europe* (1990).
Variable collection of essays, but valuable for Michael Burgess's essay 'Political Catholicism, European unity and the rise of Christian Democracy'.

Story, Jonathan (ed.), *The New Europe: Politics, Government and Economy since 1945* (Oxford, 1993).
Wide-ranging and suggestive collection of essays by an international team.

Thomas, Hugh, *Europe: the Radical Challenge* (1973); *Ever Closer Union* (1991).

Two stimulating essays by a distinguished historian 'in private practice' and unconventional European.

Tugendhat, Christopher, *Making Sense of Europe* (Harmondsworth, 1986).
Thoughtful analysis by long-serving British Commissioner, with entertaining brief survey of national attitudes.

Wallace, Helen (ed.), *The Wider Western Europe: Reshaping the EC/EFTA Relationship* (1991).
Predates the EEA Treaty, but useful general background.

Wallace, William (ed.), *The Dynamics of European Integration* (1990).
Excellent collection of essays by distinguished international team of scholars; see especially P. de Schoutheete, 'The European Community and its sub-systems'.

Wistrich, Ernest, *After 1992* (rev. edn, 1991); *The United States of Europe* (1994).
Two lively exercises in informed speculation by a pro-European of long standing.

10 Periodicals

The best-known periodicals on European integration are:

Common Market Law Review
Journal of Common Market Studies
Journal of European Public Policy
West European Politics

However, other periodicals concerned with politics and current affairs (such as *The World Today* and *Government and Opposition*) also quite frequently include items or book reviews on various aspects of European integration.

Europe, published six days a week throughout the year by Agence Europe in Brussels, covers every single development in European institutions and European politics and carries full texts of key documents. Widely read by professionals, it is available only on subscription. Slightly less comprehensive but still useful is the twice-weekly *European Report*. More specialized publications of a similar character cover developments in agriculture, energy, the environment, the Third World, etc.

Synoptic Index

The following broad subject-headings are intended to help the reader find the main entries relevant to particular aspects of European Union.

Economic integration and the Single Market

History

Law

Models of integration

Chamber of States
Concentric circles
Confederation
Europe *à la carte*
European Union
Federation
Fouchet Plan
Functionalism
Hard core
Intergovernmentalism
Pillars
Positive and negative integration
Two-speed Europe
Variable geometry
Wider and deeper

Procedures

Assent procedure
Co-decision procedure
Cooperation procedure
Majority voting
Right of initiative
Scrutiny
Veto

Security and defence

Brezhnev Doctrine
Brussels, Treaty of
Common Foreign and Security Policy
Conference on Security and Cooperation in Europe
Dunkirk, Treaty of
Eurocorps
European army
European Defence Community
North Atlantic Treaty Organization
Truman Doctrine
Warsaw Pact
Western European Union

READ MORE IN PENGUIN

In every corner of the world, on every subject under the sun, Penguin represents quality and variety – the very best in publishing today.

For complete information about books available from Penguin – including Puffins, Penguin Classics and Arkana – and how to order them, write to us at the appropriate address below. Please note that for copyright reasons the selection of books varies from country to country.

In the United Kingdom: Please write to *Dept. EP, Penguin Books Ltd, Bath Road, Harmondsworth, West Drayton, Middlesex UB7 ODA*

In the United States: Please write to *Consumer Sales, Penguin USA, P.O. Box 999, Dept. 17109, Bergenfield, New Jersey 07621-0120.* VISA and MasterCard holders call 1-800-253-6476 to order Penguin titles

In Canada: Please write to *Penguin Books Canada Ltd, 10 Alcorn Avenue, Suite 300, Toronto, Ontario M4V 3B2*

In Australia: Please write to *Penguin Books Australia Ltd, P.O. Box 257, Ringwood, Victoria 3134*

In New Zealand: Please write to *Penguin Books (NZ) Ltd, Private Bag 102902, North Shore Mail Centre, Auckland 10*

In India: Please write to *Penguin Books India Pvt Ltd, 706 Eros Apartments, 56 Nehru Place, New Delhi 110 019*

In the Netherlands: Please write to *Penguin Books Netherlands bv, Postbus 3507, NL-1001 AH Amsterdam*

In Germany: Please write to *Penguin Books Deutschland GmbH, Metzlerstrasse 26, 60594 Frankfurt am Main*

In Spain: Please write to *Penguin Books S. A., Bravo Murillo 19, 1° B, 28015 Madrid*

In Italy: Please write to *Penguin Italia s.r.l., Via Felice Casati 20, I–20124 Milano*

In France: Please write to *Penguin France S. A., 17 rue Lejeune, F–31000 Toulouse*

In Japan: Please write to *Penguin Books Japan, Ishikiribashi Building, 2–5–4, Suido, Bunkyo-ku, Tokyo 112*

In South Africa: Please write to *Longman Penguin Southern Africa (Pty) Ltd, Private Bag X08, Bertsham 2013*

READ MORE IN PENGUIN

BUSINESS AND ECONOMICS

North and South   David Smith

'This authoritative study ... gives a very effective account of the incredible centralization of decision-making in London, not just in government and administration, but in the press, communications and the management of every major company' – *New Statesman & Society*

I am Right – You are Wrong   Edward de Bono

Edward de Bono expects his ideas to outrage conventional thinkers, yet time has been on his side, and the ideas that he first put forward twenty years ago are now accepted mainstream thinking. Here, in this brilliantly argued assault on outmoded thought patterns, he calls for nothing less than a New Renaissance.

Lloyds Bank Small Business Guide   Sara Williams

This long-running guide to making a success of your small business deals with real issues in a practical way. 'As comprehensive an introduction to setting up a business as anyone could need' – *Daily Telegraph*

The *Economist* Economics   Rupert Pennant-Rea and Clive Crook

Based on a series of 'briefs' published in the *Economist*, this is a clear and accessible guide to the key issues of today's economics for the general reader.

The Rise and Fall of Monetarism   David Smith

Now that even Conservatives have consigned monetarism to the scrap heap of history, David Smith draws out the unhappy lessons of a fundamentally flawed economic experiment, driven by a doctrine that for years had been regarded as outmoded and irrelevant.

Understanding Organizations   Charles B. Handy

Of practical as well as theoretical interest, this book shows how general concepts can help solve specific organizational problems.

READ MORE IN PENGUIN

BUSINESS AND ECONOMICS

The Affluent Society   John Kenneth Galbraith

Classical economics was born in a harsh world of mass poverty, and it has left us with a set of preoccupations hard to adapt to the realities of our own richer age. Our unfamiliar problems need a new approach, and the reception given to this famous book has shown the value of its fresh, lively ideas.

Lloyds Bank Tax Guide   Sara Williams and John Willman

An average employee tax bill is over £4,000 a year. But how much time do you spend checking it? Four out of ten never check the bill – and most spend less than an hour. Mistakes happen. This guide can save YOU money. 'An unstuffy read, packed with sound information' – *Observer*

Trouble Shooter II   John Harvey-Jones

The former chairman of ICI and Britain's best-known businessman resumes his role as consultant to six British companies facing a variety of problems – and sharing a new one: the recession.

Managing on the Edge   Richard Pascale

Nothing fails like success: companies flourish, then lose their edge through a process that is both relentless and largely invisible. 'Pascale's analysis and prescription for "managing on the edge" are unusually subtle for such a readable business book' – *Financial Times*

The Money Machine: How the City Works   Philip Coggan

How are the big deals made? Which are the institutions that really matter? What causes the pound to rise or interest rates to fall? This book provides clear and concise answers to a huge variety of money-related questions.

READ MORE IN PENGUIN

POLITICS AND SOCIAL SCIENCES

National Identity Anthony D. Smith

In this stimulating new book, Anthony D. Smith asks why the first modern nation states developed in the West. He considers how ethnic origins, religion, language and shared symbols can provide a sense of nation and illuminates his argument with a wealth of detailed examples.

The Feminine Mystique Betty Friedan

'A brilliantly researched, passionately argued book – a time-bomb flung into the Mom-and-Apple-Pie image . . . Out of the debris of that shattered ideal, the Women's Liberation Movement was born' – Ann Leslie

Faith and Credit Susan George and Fabrizio Sabelli

In its fifty years of existence, the World Bank has influenced more lives in the Third World than any other institution yet remains largely unknown, even enigmatic. This richly illuminating and lively overview examines the policies of the Bank, its internal culture and the interests it serves.

Political Ideas Edited by David Thomson

From Machiavelli to Marx – a stimulating and informative introduction to the last 500 years of European political thinkers and political thought.

Structural Anthropology Volumes 1–2 Claude Lévi-Strauss

'That the complex ensemble of Lévi-Strauss's achievement . . . is one of the most original and intellectually exciting of the present age seems undeniable. No one seriously interested in language or literature, in sociology or psychology, can afford to ignore it' – George Steiner

Invitation to Sociology Peter L. Berger

Sociology is defined as 'the science of the development and nature and laws of human society'. But what is its purpose? Without belittling its scientific procedures Professor Berger stresses the humanistic affinity of sociology with history and philosophy. It is a discipline which encourages a fuller awareness of the human world . . . with the purpose of bettering it.

READ MORE IN PENGUIN

POLITICS AND SOCIAL SCIENCES

Conservatism   Ted Honderich

'It offers a powerful critique of the major beliefs of modern conservatism, and shows how much a rigorous philosopher can contribute to
understanding the fashionable but deeply ruinous absurdities of his times'
– *New Statesman & Society*

The Battle for Scotland   Andrew Marr

A nation without a parliament of its own, Scotland has been wrestling with
its identity and status for a century. In this excellent and up-to-date account
of the distinctive history of Scottish politics, Andrew Marr uses party and
individual records, pamphlets, learned works, interviews and literature to
tell a colourful and often surprising account.

Bricks of Shame: Britain's Prisons   Vivien Stern

'Her well-researched book presents a chillingly realistic picture of the
British sytstem and lucid argument for changes which could and should be
made before a degrading and explosive situation deteriorates still further'
– *Sunday Times*

Inside the Third World   Paul Harrison

This comprehensive book brings home a wealth of facts and analysis on
the often tragic realities of life for the poor people and communities of
Asia, Africa and Latin America.

'Just like a Girl'   Sue Sharpe
How Girls Learn to be Women

Sue Sharpe's unprecedented research and analysis of the attitudes and
hopes of teenage girls from four London schools has become a classic of
its kind. This new edition focuses on girls in the nineties – some of whom
could even be the daughters of the teenagers she interviewed in the
seventies – and represents their views and ideas on education, work,
marriage, gender roles, feminism and women's rights.

READ MORE IN PENGUIN

HISTORY

The Making of Europe Robert Bartlett

'Bartlett does more than anyone before him to bring out the way in which medieval Europe was shaped by [a] great wave of internal conquest, colonization and evangelization. He also stresses its consequences for the future history of the world' – *Guardian*

The Somme Battlefields Martin and Mary Middlebrook

This evocative, original book provides a definitive guide to the cemeteries, memorials and battlefields from the age of Crécy and Agincourt to the great Allied sweep which drove the Germans back in 1944, concentrating above all on the scenes of ferocious fighting in 1916 and 1918.

Ancient Slavery and Modern Ideology M. I. Finley

Few topics in the study of classical civilization could be more central – and more controversial – than slavery. In this magnificent book, M. I. Finley cuts through the thickets of modern ideology to get at the essential facts. 'A major creative achievement in historical interpretation' – *The Times Higher Education Supplement*

The Penguin History of Greece A. R. Burn

Readable, erudite, enthusiastic and balanced, this one-volume history of Hellas sweeps the reader along from the days of Mycenae and the splendours of Athens to the conquests of Alexander and the final dark decades.

The Laurel and the Ivy Robert Kee

'Parnell continues to haunt the Irish historical imagination a century after his death ... Robert Kee's patient and delicate probing enables him to reconstruct the workings of that elusive mind as persuasively, or at least as plausibly, as seems possible ... This splendid biography, which is as readable as it is rigorous, greatly enhances our understanding of both Parnell, and of the Ireland of his time' – *The Times Literary Supplement*

READ MORE IN PENGUIN

HISTORY

A History of Wales   John Davies

'Outstanding ... Dr Davies casts a coolly appraising eye upon myths, false premises and silver linings ... He is impartial. He grasps the story of his country with immense confidence and tells it in vigorous and lucid prose ... Its scope is unique. It is the history Wales needed' – *Daily Telegraph*

Daily Life in Ancient Rome   Jerome Carcopino

This classic study, which includes a bibliography and notes by Professor Rowell, describes the streets, houses and multi-storeyed apartments of the city of over a million inhabitants, the social classes from senators to slaves, and the Roman family and the position of women, causing *The Times Literary Supplement* to hail it as a 'thorough, lively and readable book'.

The Anglo-Saxons   Edited by James Campbell

'For anyone who wishes to understand the broad sweep of English history, Anglo-Saxon society is an important and fascinating subject. And Campbell's is an important and fascinating book. It is also a finely produced and, at times, a very beautiful book' – *London Review of Books*

Customs in Common   E. P. Thompson

Eighteenth-century Britain saw a profound distancing between the culture of the patricians and the plebs. E. P. Thompson explains why in this series of brilliant essays on the customs of the working people, which, he argues, emerged as a culture of resistance towards an innovative market economy. 'One of the most eloquent, powerful and independent voices of our time' – *Observer*

The Habsburg Monarchy 1809–1918   A J P Taylor

Dissolved in 1918, the Habsburg Empire 'had a unique character, out of time and out of place'. Scholarly and vividly accessible, this 'very good book indeed' (*Spectator*) elucidates the problems always inherent in the attempt to give peace, stability and a common loyalty to a heterogeneous population.

READ MORE IN PENGUIN

HISTORY

Citizens Simon Schama

The award-winning chronicle of the French Revolution. 'The most marvellous book I have read about the French Revolution in the last fifty years' – Richard Cobb in *The Times*

To the Finland Station Edmund Wilson

In this authoritative work Edmund Wilson, considered by many to be America's greatest twentieth-century critic, turns his attention to Europe's revolutionary traditions, tracing the roots of nationalism, socialism and Marxism as these movements spread across the Continent creating unrest, revolt and widespread social change.

The Tyranny of History W. J. F. Jenner

A fifth of the world's population lives within the boundaries of China, a vast empire barely under the control of the repressive ruling Communist regime. Beneath the economic boom China is in a state of crisis that goes far deeper than the problems of its current leaders to a value system that is rooted in the autocratic traditions of China's past.

The English Bible and the Seventeenth-Century Revolution
Christopher Hill

'What caused the English civil war? What brought Charles I to the scaffold?' Answer to both questions: the Bible. To sustain this provocative thesis, Christopher Hill's new book maps English intellectual history from the Reformation to 1660, showing how scripture dominated every department of thought from sexual relations to political theory . . . 'His erudition is staggering' – *Sunday Times*

Private Lives, Public Spirit: Britain 1870–1914 Jose Harris

'Provides the most convincing – and demanding – synthesis yet available of these crowded and tumultuous years' – *Observer* Books of the Year. 'Remarkable . . . it locates the origins of far-reaching social change as far back as the 1880s [and] goes on to challenge most of the popular assumptions made about the Victorian and Edwardian periods' – *Literary Review*